THE INSURER'S DUTY TO DEFEND

Issues and Analysis

DOUGLAS R. RICHMOND AND SAMUEL J. ARENA, JR.
EDITORS

AMERICAN BAR ASSOCIATION
Tort Trial and Insurance Practice Section

Cover design by Elizabeth Kulak/ABA Design

Printed in the United States of America.

28 27 26 25 24 5 4 3 2 1

A catalog record for this book is available from the Library of Congress.

Contents

About the Editors and Authors

Editors

Douglas R. Richmond is a senior vice president with the Lockton Companies. Before joining Lockton, he spent 20 years as a senior leader of Aon's Professional Services Practice. Doug previously was a partner with Armstrong Teasdale LLP in Kansas City, Missouri (1989–2004), where he had a broad civil trial and appellate practice. He tried numerous major cases as "first chair." In 1998, he was named the nation's top defense lawyer in an insurance industry poll as reported in the publications *Inside Litigation* and *Of Counsel*. He has served on the ABA's Standing Committee on Lawyers' Professional Liability (2020–23) and the ABA's Standing Committee on Ethics & Professional Responsibility (2016–19). He is a Fellow in the American College of Coverage Counsel (Hon.) and a member of the American Bar Foundation, American Board of Trial Advocates, Federation of Defense and Corporate Counsel, and International Association Defense Counsel, and was named by the Euromoney Legal Media Group as one of the World's Leading Insurance and Reinsurance Lawyers. As an elected member of the American Law Institute, he served as an adviser for the *Restatement of the Law of Liability Insurance*. Doug is the lead author of the book *Professional Responsibility in Litigation* (3d ed. 2021), and co-author of an insurance law treatise, *Understanding Insurance Law* (6th ed. 2018), and an insurance law casebook, *Cases and Materials on Insurance Law* (9th ed. 2021). He has published more than 90 articles in university law reviews, and many more articles in other scholarly and professional journals. Doug teaches legal ethics at the Northwestern University School of Law; insurance law and seminars on legal malpractice law and liability insurance law at the University of Florida College of Law; and legal malpractice law at the Texas A&M University School of Law. He previously taught trial advocacy and insurance law at the University of Kansas School of Law, and insurance law at the University of Missouri School of Law.

Samuel J. Arena, Jr. serves as senior counsel in the Philadelphia office of Stradley, Ronon, Stevens & Young, LLP, having concentrated his practice on insurance law and fidelity and surety law during his 40-plus year career with the firm. A leader in Stradley Ronon's Insurance Practice Group, he has represented insurance companies nationally in all phases of complex insurance coverage, extra-contractual liability, and fidelity and surety matters. He is a Fellow of the American College of Coverage Counsel and an adjunct professor of law at Villanova University School of Law, where he teaches Advanced Insurance Law: Coverage Disputes and serves as a guest lecturer for, and has taught, the law school's principles of insurance law course, Insurance Law and Policy. Sam remains abreast of developments in insurance law and the insurance industry through his academic service at Villanova University School of Law; his active participation in a number of American Bar Association and insurance industry organizations; and as a frequent speaker, author, panelist, and panel moderator. He graduated *magna cum laude* from Ursinus College and *cum laude* from Villanova University School of Law. In law school, Sam served as an associate editor of the *Villanova Law Review*, was a member of the Order of the Coif, and received the Dr. Arthur Clement Pulling Award for his contributions to the *Villanova Law Review* and the Hyman-Goodman Award for his contributions to the School of Law through his academic and extracurricular achievements. He has been recognized by *The Best Lawyers in America*; *Pennsylvania Super Lawyers*; Martindale-Hubbell (AV Preeminent Rating); and the American Bar Association as a recipient of the ABA's Martin J. Andrew Award for Lifetime Achievement in Fidelity and Surety Law.

Authors

Maida Chinosi is a partner in the New Jersey office of Hinshaw & Culbertson, LLP. Maida concentrates her practice on complex insurance coverage litigation and insurance defense. She counsels clients on first-party property and third-party liability claims and handles matters involving high potential exposure and allegations of bad faith. Maida's practice also includes counseling and representing corporate clients and domestic and international insurers on risk management, claims handling, and general business matters. In addition, she has extensive experience handling complex civil litigation and defending individuals and businesses in New Jersey state and federal courts. Maida earned her JD from Seton Hall University School of Law and her BA from Rutgers, The State University of New Jersey. Prior to becoming an attorney, Maida worked on Wall Street and in the pharmaceutical industry for more than seven years. Maida is the current New Jersey State Bar Association, Insurance Law Section, CLE Chair, 2023–2024. She is also a member of the New Jersey State Bar Association's Minorities in the Profession Section, New Jersey Hispanic Bar Association, New Jersey Women's Lawyers Association, and National Hispanic Bar Association.

Madeline R. Cook is an associate in the Washington, DC, office of Hinshaw & Culbertson LLP. She graduated from Seattle University and from The George Washington University Law School. During law school, Madeline was a member of the International Law in Domestic Courts Journal, and she was awarded Law School and University Gold Recognition for pro bono service. Madeline's practice focuses on complex coverage disputes and bad faith litigation.

Stephanie V. Corrao is a counsel in Crowell & Moring LLP's Insurance/Reinsurance Group, where she represents insurers and reinsurers on a range of matters, from providing pre-dispute advice and legal analysis of specific contract provisions and coverage issues to resolving complex disputes before courts and arbitrators. Stephanie's practice centers on difficult coverage issues such as allocation of liability, cyber risk, trigger of coverage, and issues pertaining to excess insurance such as horizontal versus vertical exhaustion. In addition, Stephanie supports the firm's amicus work for insurer trade association clients. Before shifting to insurance practice in 2002, Stephanie worked in-house with Sun Microsystems Federal, Inc. for several years, where she managed all litigation involving Sun Federal. Stephanie is committed to pro bono work and, in 2012, she received the Harry L. Carrico Pro Bono Award presented by Legal Services of Northern Virginia.

Laura Foggan is a partner in the Washington, DC, office of Crowell & Morning LLP. She is a leading trial lawyer in high-stakes coverage matters and a preeminent appellate advocate. Laura litigates complex, high-value claims in trial and appellate courts, and counsels clients on pivotal emerging issues. Repeatedly named to Benchmark Litigation's Top 250 Women Litigators list, she has participated in many of the largest insurance matters on record, such as the World Trade Center litigation, Hurricane Katrina-related disputes, the Merck NotPetya case, Covid-related insurance MDL claims, and suits involving alleged loss of or damage to aviation assets remaining in Russia after the invasion of Ukraine. At the same time, Laura is nationally known for her high-profile appellate work in federal and state courts. She has represented insurers and trade group amici in more than 300 significant appeals across the country. Laura was the American Property Casualty Insurance Association's liaison for the American Law Institute's *Restatement of the Law of Liability Insurance* and the *Restatement of the Law (Third) Torts: Miscellaneous Provisions*. Laura has been an adjunct professor at the University of Connecticut School of Law's Insurance Law Center since 2017, and is a past chair of the ABA Section of Litigation's Insurance Coverage Litigation Committee and member of the TIPS Insurance Coverage Litigation and Appellate Advocacy Committees. A fellow in the American College of Coverage Counsel, Laura holds a long list of honors, including being named by Best Lawyers in America as Lawyer of the Year, Washington, D.C. Litigation—Insurance five times. She has been named as Who's Who Legal: Insurance and Reinsurance Lawyer of the Year, and included in Chambers USA and DC for insurance litigation; Euromoney: Best of the Best Global Expert Guide; Business Today: Top 10 Most Influential Insurance Lawyers in the District of Columbia; Super Lawyers: DC's Top 100 Lawyers, Top 10 Lawyers, and Top 50 Women Lawyers; Who's Who Legal: Global Elite Thought Leader for Insurance & Reinsurance; Insurance Business America: Elite Women; ALM: Women Leaders in the Law; and The American Registry: America's Leading Lawyers for Business Nationwide.

Rachel E. Hudgins is counsel in the Atlanta office of Hunton Andrews Kurth LLP. Rachel began her career representing insurers, primarily in the Lloyd's of London market. Her practice now focuses on advising and representing policyholders in multiple sectors, including logistics, healthcare, real estate, construction, manufacturing, and the arts. Rachel graduated from Emory University and the University of Georgia School of Law. She writes and speaks extensively on insurance coverage issues, particularly in the area of bad faith.

Robert H. Jerry, II is the Floyd R. Gibson Missouri Endowed Professor-Emeritus at the University of Missouri School of Law. He is also Dean-Emeritus and Levin, Mabie and Levin Professor-Emeritus at the University of Florida Levin College of Law. A leading insurance law scholar, and he is the author of numerous books, book chapters, articles, and essays in the field, including the treatise *Understanding Insurance Law* (6th ed. 2018) (with Doug Richmond) and the book *Advanced Introduction to Insurance Law* (2023). He has also written, presented, or taught in the fields of healthcare ethics, healthcare finance and access, alternative dispute resolution, negotiation, and leadership studies. He is an elected member of the American Law Institute, a Fellow of the American Bar Foundation, and past chair of the Insurance Law Section of the Association of American Law Schools. In 2020, he received the Robert B. McKay Law Professor Award, which is awarded annually by the ABA's Tort, Trial & Insurance Practice Section. He received his BS from Indiana State University and his JD from the University of Michigan. Following law school, he clerked for Judge George MacKinnon in the U.S. Circuit Court of Appeals for the District of Columbia Circuit, practiced law in Indianapolis, and then held academic appointments for nearly 40 years at the University of Missouri (1998–2003, 2015–2019), the University of Florida (2003–2015), the University of Kansas (1981–1994), and the University of Memphis (1994–1998).

Patrick J. Kenny is a partner with Armstrong Teasdale LLP in St. Louis, Missouri. For more than 30 years Patrick has concentrated his trial and appellate work on insurance coverage and bad faith litigation. He presents and publishes frequently on an array of issues related to insurance coverage and bad faith. Patrick is a Fellow in the American College of Coverage Counsel, a former chair of the Lex Mundi Insurance and Reinsurance Practice Group, and has long been active in DRI, previously serving as editor-in-chief of *Daubert Online* and holding various positions on the Commercial Litigation Committee and the Life, Health and Disability Committee. He was named the Best Lawyers 2016 Insurance Law "Lawyer of the Year" in St. Louis and has received numerous other recognitions in connection with his insurance and commercial litigation practices. Those include long-term listings in Best Lawyers in America for Insurance Law, as a Top Rated Lawyer in Commercial Litigation by Martindale-Hubbell and American Lawyer Media, as a "Super Lawyer" by Missouri/Kansas Super Lawyers/Super Lawyers Business Edition, and inclusion in Chambers USA's Missouri insurance lawyers listing and in America's Leading Lawyers for Business. Before joining Armstrong Teasdale in 1993, Patrick served as a judicial clerk for Judge Pasco Bowman of the U.S. Court of Appeals for the Eighth Circuit.

Seth Lamden is a partner in the Chicago office of Blank Rome LLP. Since 2000, his practice has focused exclusively on helping policyholders understand and enforce their rights to insurance coverage. Through litigation and negotiation, Seth has helped policyholders recover hundreds of millions of dollars from their insurers under nearly all types of commercial insurance policies. Seth is a Fellow of the American College of Coverage Counsel and is widely recognized for his work, including by Chambers USA, which noted that Seth "has an encyclopedic knowledge of insurance law, is a creative strategist and an excellent writer." The American Lawyer magazine named Seth a "Midwest Trailblazer" and he was profiled as one of "40 Illinois Attorneys Under Forty to Watch" by the Chicago Daily Law Bulletin. Seth maintains an AV Preeminent® Peer Review Rating (5.0) from Martindale-Hubbell® and is listed in The Legal 500, Best Lawyers in America, and Illinois Super Lawyers.

Lorelie S. Masters is a partner with Hunton Andrew Kurth LLP in Washington, DC. She is a veteran insurance coverage litigator and is regarded as a "much-admired practitioner, with an impressive expertise in the London market and Bermuda Form arbitrations" according to Chambers USA, which ranks her in the upper echelons of insurance practitioners nationwide. She has helped recover billions of dollars of insurance coverage for clients for products, environmental, employment, directors and officers, cyber, and other liabilities and losses. She co-authors *Insurance Coverage Litigation* (Wolters Kluwer) and *Liability Insurance in International Arbitration: The Bermuda Form* (Bloomsbury Publishing), which the English Court of Appeal called "the standard work on the topic." Lorie is a founding member of the American College of Coverage

Counsel, and has served on the ABA Board of Governors, as an officer of ABA Section of Litigation, and as National Policyholder Chair of the Section of Litigation's Insurance Coverage Litigation Committee. She is co-chair of the Section's 2024 annual conference and a member of its Federal Practice Task Force. The American Law Institute appointed her as an Adviser to its *Restatement of Law of Liability Insurance*, a role in which she served from 2010 to 2019. Lorie writes and speaks extensively on insurance coverage, technology, and litigation, as well as on diversity and inclusion. She has represented many individuals and groups pro bono, including policyholders denied healthcare coverage and victims of human trafficking. She also has extensive experience with voting rights and District of Columbia democracy issues.

Douglas R. Richmond is a senior vice president with the Lockton Companies. Before joining Lockton, he spent 20 years as a senior leader of Aon's Professional Services Practice. Previously, Doug was a partner with Armstrong Teasdale LLP in Kansas City, Missouri (1989–2004), where he had a broad civil trial and appellate practice. He tried numerous major cases as "first chair." In 1998, he was named the nation's top defense lawyer in an insurance industry poll as reported in the publications *Inside Litigation* and *Of Counsel*. He has served on the ABA's Standing Committee on Lawyers' Professional Liability (2020–23) and the ABA's Standing Committee on Ethics & Professional Responsibility (2016–19). He is a Fellow in the American College of Coverage Counsel (Hon.) and a member of the American Bar Foundation, American Board of Trial Advocates, Federation of Defense and Corporate Counsel, and International Association Defense Counsel, and was named by the Euromoney Legal Media Group as one of the World's Leading Insurance and Reinsurance Lawyers. As an elected member of the American Law Institute, he served as an adviser for the *Restatement of the Law of Liability Insurance*. Doug is the lead author of the book *Professional Responsibility in Litigation* (3d ed. 2021), and co-author of an insurance law treatise, *Understanding Insurance Law* (6th ed. 2018), and an insurance law casebook, *Cases and Materials on Insurance Law* (9th ed. 2021). He has published more than 90 articles in university law reviews, and many more articles in other scholarly and professional journals. Doug teaches legal ethics at the Northwestern University School of Law; insurance law and seminars on legal malpractice law and liability insurance law at the University of Florida College of Law; and legal malpractice law at the Texas A&M University School of Law. He previously taught trial advocacy and insurance law at the University of Kansas School of Law, and insurance law at the University of Missouri School of Law.

Scott M. Seaman is a partner at Hinshaw & Culbertson, LLP, where he co-chairs the firm's global Insurance Services Practice Group and serves as Insurance Industry Group Leader. For more than 36 years, Scott has represented insurers and reinsurers before trial courts, appellate courts, and arbitration panels across the country in a variety of coverage, reinsurance, and extra-contractual cases and arbitrations. He also has handled international, professional liability, tort and product liability, director and officer liability, health/life sciences, and business matters. Scott provides advice to companies on cyber and privacy, social inflation, ESG, M&A coverages, social change, and other emerging issues. He is a prolific author and speaker on insurance, reinsurance, and litigation topics. His treatise, *Allocation of Losses in Complex Insurance Coverage Claims* (11th ed. 2023), addresses many important issues in contemporary insurance and reinsurance disputes. Among other honors, he is named in Chambers USA, America's Leading Lawyers for Business (Band 1), The Best Lawyers in America, Illinois Super Lawyers, Leading Lawyers, International Who's Who of Insurance and Reinsurance Lawyers, and Euromoney Legal Media Group World's Leading Insurance and Reinsurance Lawyers. He is a founding fellow of the American College of Coverage Counsel and a fellow of the American Bar Foundation and the Litigation Counsel of America. He was one of 50 lawyers named to The American Lawyer magazine's inaugural list of Midwest Trailblazers for his representation of clients in high-profile, complex insurance coverage cases nationwide, which resulted in precedent setting rulings that have altered insurance law.

CHAPTER 1
The Duty to Defend Framework

Douglas R. Richmond

I. Introduction

Insurance policies are contracts. Standard liability insurance policies expressly obligate the insurance company to defend the insured against lawsuits seeking covered damages. For example, a standard commercial general liability (CGL) policy states that the insurer "will pay those sums that the insured becomes legally obligated to pay as damages because of 'bodily injury' or 'property damage' to which [the policy] applies" and that the insurer "will have the right and duty to defend the insured against any 'suit' seeking those damages."[1] A standard personal auto policy provides that the insurance company "will settle or defend, as [it] consider[s] appropriate, any claim or suit asking for [covered] damages."[2] The most popular form of homeowners insurance policy states that if a claim is made or suit is brought against an insured seeking damages because of bodily injury or property damage caused by an "occurrence," the insurer will provide a defense at its expense by counsel of its choice, "even if the suit is groundless, false or fraudulent."[3]

Liability insurance policies that businesses and individuals typically purchase provide that the insurance company will pay the cost of the insured's defense in addition to the policy's liability limits. This is a valuable benefit to the insured because defense costs may, and often do, exceed any settlement or judgment ultimately paid. An insurer's duty to defend also incorporates

1. Ins. Servs. Off., Inc., Commercial General Liability Coverage Form (CG 00 01 04 13), at 1 (2012).

2. Ins. Servs. Off., Inc., Personal Auto Policy (PP 00 01 09 18), at 2 (2017).

3. Ins. Servs. Off., Inc., Homeowners 3 – Special Form (HO 00 03 05 11), at 17 (2010).

a duty to hire competent defense counsel for the insured.[4] For most individual insureds and many commercial policyholders, the insurer's appointment of capable defense counsel relieves them of a major burden. More generally, insurers have significant litigation expertise that most insureds lack. Liability insurers are in the business of managing lawsuits; they are professional defenders of litigation.

In summary, the duty to defend is a critical aspect of the liability insurance bargain.[5] Indeed, the duty to defend is so vital to the insurer-insured relationship that courts often describe liability insurance as "litigation insurance."[6]

II. To Whom Is the Duty to Defend Owed?

A. The Duty to Defend Is Owed Only to Insureds

Analyzing the duty to defend begins with a deceptively simple question: To whom is the duty to defend owed? The short answer is the named insured and any other insureds, regardless of whether they are omnibus insureds because they fall within the policy definition of "Who Is an Insured" or because they have been made additional insureds to the policy by endorsement.[7]

Finding the answer becomes complicated where a party claims to be an insured and thus asserts that it is owed a defense, but the facts suggest that the party is not an insured under the policy in question. Generally, if a party claims incorrectly that it is an insured—perhaps because it mistakenly believes that it is as an additional insured under a policy issued to a co-defendant or erroneously believes that it qualifies as an omnibus insured under another party's policy—the insurer need not provide a defense if it can establish through evidence extrinsic to the plaintiff's complaint or petition that the party is not an insured.[8] The same rule holds true where one co-defendant claims that it is an

4. Compulink Mgmt. Ctr., Inc. v. St. Paul Fire & Marine Ins. Co., 87 Cal. Rptr. 3d 72, 75 (Ct. App. 2008).

5. *See* Campbell v. Super. Ct., 52 Cal. Rptr. 2d 385, 392–93 (Ct. App. 1996) ("[O]ne of the primary benefits of an insurance policy is that the insured can expect the insurer to defend against third-party claims."); Pine Oak Builders, Inc. v. Great Am. Lloyds Ins. Co., 279 S.W.3d 650, 655 (Tex. 2009) ("A defense of third-party claims provided by the insurer is a valuable benefit granted to the insured by the policy, separate from the duty to indemnify."); Woo v. Fireman's Fund Ins. Co., 164 P.3d 454, 459–60 (Wash. 2007) ("The duty to defend is a valuable service paid for by the insured and one of the principal benefits of the liability insurance policy.").

6. *See, e.g.*, Stoncor Grp., Inc. v. Peerless Ins. Co., No. 16-cv-4574 (LAK), 2022 WL 3701640, at *4 (S.D.N.Y. Aug. 26, 2022); Ill. Tool Works, Inc. v. Travelers Cas. & Sur. Co., 26 N.E.3d 421, 431 (Ill. App. Ct. 2015).

7. Robert H. Jerry, II & Douglas R. Richmond, Understanding Insurance Law 695 (6th ed. 2018).

8. *See* Navajo Freight Lines, Inc. v. Liberty Mut. Ins. Co., 471 P.2d 309, 315 (Ariz. Ct. App. 1970) ("A [s]ine qua non to the existence of any obligation to defend, or pay, whether the suit be groundless

insured under another co-defendant's policy based on the allegations in the plaintiff's complaint or petition.[9] As a practical matter, this means that until the insurer establishes that the defendant is not an insured, it may find itself defending a stranger to its policy. Alternatively, the insurer might negotiate an arrangement with the alleged insured whereby the alleged insured pays for its own defense until its status is determined, at which time the insurer will either reimburse the insured for its defense costs and assume the defense going forward, or, if it turns out that the party is not an insured, the party will continue with its own defense. Finally, the insurer may decline to defend the alleged insured and thereafter litigate coverage in a declaratory judgment action or equitable garnishment proceeding. Depending on the facts, this last option carries with it the risk that the supposed insured will default, defend ineffectively, or enter into a consent judgment with the plaintiff and the insurer, if it was wrong about the party's status as an insured, will owe an amount greater than it might have had to pay had it defended the party and later settled the case or litigated it to conclusion.

B. Illustrative Cases

As noted, a defendant may contend that it is an insured under a co-defendant's policy based on allegations in the plaintiff's complaint or petition, as oil industry giant Texaco did in *Texaco, Inc. v. Hartford Accident & Indemnity*.[10] That declaratory judgment action arose out of an Oklahoma state court case in which A. P. Vaughn and his wife sued Texaco, Crowl Oil, Inc., and James L. Crowl (collectively Crowl). Hartford Accident & Indemnity (Hartford) insured Crowl. The Vaughns alleged in their petition that while delivering gasoline to their service station and store, Crowl employee Roy Jameson started a ruinous fire that injured Mr. Vaughn. They further alleged that Crowl was acting

---

or otherwise, is the pre-existing relationship of insurer-insured. The creation of this basic relationship cannot be left to the imagination of the drafter of a complaint."); Nateman v. Hartford Cas. Ins. Co., 544 So. 2d 1026, 1027 (Fla. Dist. Ct. App. 1989) (citation omitted) ("While, as a general rule, the obligation to defend an insured . . . must be measured and determined by the allegations of the petition . . . , an obvious exception must be made . . . where, notwithstanding allegations in the petition to the contrary, the insurer successfully urges the alleged insured is not in fact an insured under the policy. . . . The insurer is not obligated to provide a defense for a stranger merely because the plaintiff alleges that the defendant is an insured or alleges facts which, if true, would make the defendant an insured. The mere allegations of the plaintiff's petition may not create an obligation on the part of the insurer to defend where no such obligation previously existed."); Restatement of the L. of Liab. Ins. § 13(3)(a) (Am. L. Inst. 2019) (stating that an insurer may rely on extrinsic evidence to show that a defendant is not an insured under the insurance policy pursuant to which the duty to defend is asserted).

9. *See, e.g.*, Weingarten Realty Mgmt. Co. v. Liberty Mut. Ins. Co., 343 S.W.3d 859, 865–69 (Tex. App. 2011) (recognizing a narrow exception to the eight corners rule for this purpose).

10. 453 F. Supp. 1109 (E.D. Okla. 1978).

as Texaco's agent and that Texaco negligently mislocated the gasoline storage tank for the service station.

Texaco denied an agency relationship with Crowl. In the declaratory judgment action, Texaco and Hartford stipulated that (1) there was no agency relationship between Texaco and Crowl; (2) Texaco did not own or lease Crowl's gasoline truck; (3) Texaco did not employ Crowl; and (4) Texaco had nothing to do with the placement of the Vaughns' gasoline tank.[11]

Texaco and Hartford filed cross-motions for summary judgment on Hartford's duty to defend Texaco in the Vaughns' lawsuit. The key issue was whether Texaco was an insured under Crowl's policy with Hartford. The Hartford policy contained the following "Persons Insured" section:

> Each of the following is an insured under the insurance to the extent set forth below:
>
> (a) the named insured;
>
> (b) any partner or executive officer thereof, but with respect to a temporary substitute automobile only while such automobile is being used in the business of the named insured;
>
> (c) any other person while using an owned automobile or a temporary substitute automobile with the permission of the named insured, provided his actual operation or (if he is not operating) his other actual use thereof is within the scope of such permission, but with respect to bodily injury or property damage arising out of the loading or unloading thereof, such other person shall be an insured only if he is:
>
> (1) a lessee or borrower of the automobile, or
>
> (2) an employee of the named insured or of such lessee or borrower;
>
> (d) any other person or organization but only with respect to his or its liability because of acts or omissions of an insured under (a), (b) or (c) above.[12]

Texaco asserted that it qualified as an insured under paragraph (d) because the Vaughns had alleged in their petition that the named insured, Crowl, acted negligently through Jameson, and that they both were Texaco's agents. Texaco based its argument on "the general rule" that a liability insurer's duty to defend an insured "'is to be determined by the allegations of the complaint or petition . . . even if they are groundless or false.'"[13]

11. *Id.* at 1110.
12. *Id.* at 1111.
13. *Id.* (quoting 44 AM. JUR. 2D *Insurance* § 1539 (1969)).

Hartford countered that Texaco could not be exposed to liability based on Crowl's or Jameson's conduct because Texaco had stipulated in the declaratory judgment action that there was no agency relationship between it on the one hand and Crowl and Jameson on the other, so there was no basis for imputing Crowl's or Jameson's negligence, if any, to Texaco.[14] The court agreed with Hartford.[15] The court further noted Hartford's and Texaco's stipulation that Texaco had nothing to do with the placement of the gasoline tank involved in the accident. The *Texaco* court also explained that Hartford had no duty to defend Texaco because, even though an insurer's duty to defend generally pivots on the allegations in the plaintiff's complaint or petition, it is also a general rule that an insurer's duty to defend "'is determined by the actual facts brought to the attention of the company rather than pertinent allegations contained in the complaint or petition . . . which are not true.'"[16]

The *Texaco* court granted Hartford's summary judgment motion and denied Texaco's motion. In doing so, the court declared that Hartford had no duty to defend Texaco in the Vaughn's state court action.[17]

Beattie v. Home Indemnity Insurance Co.[18] is another case in which a defendant's status as insured and thus competing insurers' responsibility for the defense became an issue because of allegations in the plaintiff's complaint. *Beattie* stemmed from a crash between a Buick, owned and driven by Nicholas Kolovas, and another car driven by James McCarthy. A passenger in McCarthy's car, Brian Sosnowski, was killed in the wreck. Kolovas, who was insured by Home Indemnity Insurance Co. (Home), had purchased the Buick from Linda Beattie about three weeks before the accident. When Beattie owned the Buick, she was insured by Nationwide Insurance Co. (Nationwide).

Sosnowski's estate (the Estate) filed a lawsuit in which its complaint mistakenly stated that Beattie owned the Buick and that Kolovas was driving it with her permission. Beattie asked Home to defend her in the lawsuit. Home refused because she was not an insured under Kolovas's policy. Beattie's former insurer, Nationwide, then defended her in the Estate's lawsuit. It was eventually revealed that Beattie did not own the Buick when the accident happened.[19]

Nationwide and Beattie subsequently sued Home. They asserted that Home had a duty to defend Beattie in the Estate's lawsuit based on the allegations in the Estate's complaint and that Home was thus required to reimburse

14. *Id.*
15. *Id.* at 1112.
16. *Id.* (quoting Am. Motorists Ins. Co. v. Sw. Greyhound Lines, Inc., 283 F.2d 648, 649 (10th Cir. 1960)).
17. *Id.* at 1116.
18. 566 N.Y.S.2d 335 (App. Div. 1991).
19. *Id.*

Nationwide for its defense expenses. The trial court agreed. The trial court concluded that the allegations in the complaint concerning Beattie's ownership of the Buick and Kolovas's permissive use of the car obligated Home to defend Beattie.[20] Home appealed.

The *Beattie* court began its analysis by noting the breadth of an insurer's duty to defend and by acknowledging that under New York law, the duty to defend is generally determined by comparing the allegations in the plaintiff's complaint to the terms of the policy at issue.[21] Furthermore, when deciding whether an insurer owes a duty to defend, a court must liberally construe the facts alleged in favor of the insured. But even given that generally pro-insured approach, the trial court erred when it determined that Home had a duty to defend Beattie.[22] Beattie was neither a named insured under Home's policy nor was she someone to whom the policy's definition of an "insured" applied.[23] To require Home to defend Beattie—a complete stranger to its policy—would be to create a duty to defend where there was no possible factual or legal basis on which Home could ever be obligated to indemnify her.[24] The *Beattie* court accordingly reversed the trial court and held that Home had no duty to defend Beattie.

C. Summary

As *Texaco* and *Beattie* make clear, an insurer's duty to defend runs only to its insureds.[25] A stranger to the insurance policy paid no premiums for coverage and thus should not be owed a defense, even if the plaintiff alleges in its complaint or petition that the stranger is an insured under the policy at issue. A court should allow an insurer to rely on extrinsic evidence to establish that a party who claims to be an insured or who is alleged to be one does not, in fact, so qualify.[26]

20. *Id.* at 336.
21. *Id.*
22. *Id.*
23. *Id.*
24. *Id.* at 336–37 (quoting Servidone Constr. Corp. v. Sec. Ins. Co. of Hartford, 477 N.E.2d 441, 444 (N.Y. 1985)).
25. *See also* Emps. Mut. Cas. Co. v. Est. of Buckles, 443 P.3d 534, 538 (Mont. 2019) ("[B]efore a duty to defend can arise . . . the party seeking insurance coverage must be an insured under the policy."); McCarty v. Parks, 564 P.2d 1122, 1124 (Utah 1977) (stating that an insurer's duty to defend "only runs to those insured under the policy").
26. Restatement of the L. of Liab. Ins. § 13(3)(a) (Am. L. Inst. 2019).

III. The Requirement of a "Suit" Seeking "Damages"

A. Overview

Liability insurance policies typically provide that the insurer will defend any "suit" seeking covered "damages." To use a common example, a standard CGL policy states that the insurer "will pay those sums that the insured becomes legally obligated to pay as damages because of 'bodily injury' or 'property damage' to which [the policy] applies" and that the insurer "will have the right and duty to defend the insured against any 'suit' seeking those damages."[27] The term "suit" is generally understood to refer to a lawsuit filed in a court.[28] The meaning of "suit" may further be controlled by the terms of the insurance policy under which a defense is sought. A standard CGL policy defines a "suit" as follows:

> "Suit" means a civil proceeding in which damages because of "bodily injury", "property damage" or "personal and advertising injury" to which this insurance applies are alleged. "Suit" includes:
>
> a. An arbitration proceeding in which such damages are claimed and to which the insured must submit or does submit with our consent; or
>
> b. Any other alternative dispute resolution proceeding in which such damages are claimed and to which the insured submits with our consent.[29]

Because a standard CGL policy defines the term "suit," a court interpreting the policy must apply that definition.[30] The court cannot disregard the policy's definition of a "suit" in favor of a definition it prefers. Reliance on defined

27. Ins. Servs. Off., Inc., Commercial General Liability Coverage Form (CG 00 01 04 13), at 1 (2012).

28. *See, e.g.*, Trident Fasteners, Inc. v. Selective Ins. Co. of S.C., 533 F. Supp. 3d 560, 565 (W.D. Mich. 2021) (stating that under Michigan law, the duty to defend "does not arise until a lawsuit is actually filed"); Aztec Abstract & Title Ins., Inc. v. Maxum Specialty Corp., 302 F. Supp. 3d 1274, 1281 (D.N.M. 2018) ("New Mexico caselaw indicates that a lawsuit must be filed in a court before a duty to defend arises."); Ill. Tool Works, Inc. v. Ace Specialty Ins. Co., 142 N.E.3d 227 (Ill. App. Ct. 2019) (stating that it is "well settled that the term 'suit' in an insurance policy is unambiguous, and 'requires the commencement of some action in a court of law'" to trigger an insurer's duty to defend (quoting Lapham-Hickey Steel Corp. v. Prot. Mut. Ins. Co., 655 N.E.2d 842, 847 (Ill. 1995))).

29. Ins. Servs. Off., Inc., Commercial General Liability Coverage Form (CG 00 01 04 13), at 16 (2012).

30. St. Paul Fire & Marine Ins. Co. v. Christiansen Marine, Inc., 893 So. 2d 1124, 1136 (Ala. 2004); Farmers Ins. Exch. v. Bradford, 460 S.W.3d 810, 813 (Ark. Ct. App. 2015); Maxie v. Bates, 338 So. 3d 564, 570 (La. Ct. App. 2022); M.P. *ex rel.* Zipfel v. Trexis One Ins. Corp., 652 S.W.3d 685, 689 (Mo. Ct. App. 2022); Harleysville Mut. Ins. Co. v. Buzz Off Insect Shield, L.L.C., 692 S.E.2d 605, 612 (N.C. 2010); Twigg v. Admiral Ins. Co., 525 P.3d 478, 484 (Or. Ct. App. 2023); Evanston Ins. Co. v. Legacy of Life, Inc., 370 S.W.3d 377, 381 (Tex. 2012).

terms in an insurance policy is necessary to ascertain the parties' intent and is essential to the application of basic principles of contract interpretation to the policy.[31] As will be discussed later, however, courts have been willing to deem some actions to be the functional equivalent of a "suit" sufficient to create a duty to defend.

The term "damages" describes a monetary award to compensate a plaintiff for harm caused by an insured.[32] Standard CGL, homeowners, and auto insurance policies do not define "damages."[33]

If an insured is involved in a controversy where either or both of these contractual terms are not satisfied, the insurer should not owe a duty to defend.[34] Thus, insurers generally have no duty to defend their insureds in criminal cases,[35] declaratory judgment actions,[36] a declaratory judgment action filed by the insurer to determine the insurer's obligations under the policy issued

31. Provident Life & Accident Ins. Co. v. Knott, 128 S.W.3d 211, 219 (Tex. 2003).

32. *See* Glob. Modular, Inc. v. Kadena Pac., Inc., 222 Cal. Rptr. 3d 819, 833 (Ct. App. 2017) ("The policy does not define damages, but courts generally interpret the term to mean payments made to compensate a party for direct and consequential injuries caused by the acts of another."); City of Maple Lake v. Am. States Ins. Co., 509 N.W.2d 399, 404 (Minn. Ct. App. 1993) ("The term 'damages' refers to compensation for an injury caused by a violation of a legal right."); Farm Bureau Ins. Co. v. Witte, 594 N.W.2d 574, 582 (Neb. 1999) (describing "damages" as sums the insured "becomes legally obligated to pay because of injury caused to a third party by acts of the insured").

33. In contrast, professional liability insurance policies often define "damages." *See, e.g.*, Marcus v. Allied World Ins. Co., 384 F. Supp. 3d 115, 119 (D. Me. 2019) (involving a lawyers' professional liability policy).

34. *See, e.g.*, Modular Steel Sys. Inc. v. Westfield Ins., No. 21-1766, 2022 WL 832048, at *3 (3d Cir. Mar. 21, 2022) (finding no "suit" or "damages" where the insured voluntarily fixed damage caused by construction defects even though the project's owner never pursued related legal action); Allegheny Design Mgmt., Inc. v. Travelers Indem. Co. of Am., 572 F. App'x 98, 101–02 (3d Cir. 2014) (holding that an informal assertion by the claimant's legal department that the insured was responsible for property damage did not trigger the insurer's duty to defend); W. Nat'l Mut. Ins. Co. v. Speedway, Inc., 507 F. Supp. 3d 1071, 1075–76 (D. Minn. 2020) (explaining that a pedestrian's notice to the insured of her injury from falling on the insured's property was not a "suit" that triggered the insurer's duty to defend); Glob. Caravan Techs., Inc. v. Cincinnati Ins. Co., 135 N.E.3d 584, 593 (Ind. Ct. App. 2019) (concluding that the insured's voluntary intervention in a case where there was never a claim for damages made against it was not a "suit" that implicated the insurer's duty to defend).

35. *See, e.g.*, Perzik v. St. Paul Fire & Marine Ins. Co., 279 Cal. Rptr. 498, 500–01 (Ct. App. 1991) (explaining that federal criminal proceedings were not a suit for damages); Hoyle v. Utica Mut. Ins. Co., 48 P.3d 1256, 1263 (Idaho 2002) (reasoning that any restitution the state might seek did not constitute damages, so the criminal case against the insured was not a suit for damages); Derdarian v. Essex Ins. Co., 44 A.3d 122, 129 (R.I. 2012) (concluding that criminal indictments neither initiated a civil proceeding nor alleged damages).

36. *See* Prince George Parish of Prince George Winyah v. GuideOne Mut. Ins. Co., 839 F. App'x 779, 780 (4th Cir. 2020) (applying South Carolina law); Moore v. State Farm Mut. Auto. Ins. Co., 304 F. App'x 329, 331 (5th Cir. 2008) (stating that claims seeking declaratory relief were not covered because they did not seek monetary damages); Fin. Res. Network, Inc. v. Brown & Brown, Inc., 754 F. Supp. 2d 128, 144 (D. Mass. 2010) ("A declaratory judgment is not a claim for monetary damages. It is a claim for non-pecuniary relief in the form of a declaration.").

to the insured,[37] guardianship proceedings,[38] juvenile cases,[39] mandamus actions,[40] actions to approve settlements,[41] cases seeking only restitution or disgorgement of funds improperly obtained,[42] actions seeking solely injunctive relief,[43] cases where fines or civil penalties are assessed rather than damages being awarded,[44] in mediations or settlement negotiations preceding litigation

37. *See, e.g.*, Boatright v. Old Dominion Ins. Co., 695 S.E.2d 408, 413 (Ga. Ct. App. 2010) ("A liability policy that . . . obligates an insurer to defend an insured against actions arising from bodily injury does not obligate the insurer also to defend the insured in a declaratory judgment action seeking to determine the insurer's liabilities and obligations under the policy.").

38. *See, e.g.*, Felice v. St. Paul Fire & Marine Ins. Co., 711 P.2d 1066, 1069–70 (Wash. Ct. App. 1985) ("The petition did not contain allegations concerning . . . damages nor a prayer for monetary relief. . . . It sought [Felice's] removal as guardian and repayment of [his] attorney fees. Hence, we hold the policy language at issue here was not intended to cover situations where third parties seek to discharge an attorney as guardian.").

39. *See, e.g.*, United Pac. Ins. Co. v. Hall, 245 Cal. Rptr. 99, 102 (Ct. App. 1988) (stating that because the juvenile proceeding sought no damages, the insurer had no duty to provide a defense).

40. *See, e.g.*, City of Maple Lake v. Am. States Ins. Co., 509 N.W.2d 399, 403 (Minn. Ct. App. 1993) ("An action for mandamus is not a suit 'seeking damages' as required in a liability insurance policy.").

41. *See, e.g.*, NL Corp. v. Seneca Specialty Ins. Co., No. 28927, 2021 WL 1828100, at *5 (Ohio Ct. App. May 7, 2021) ("The probate case in Missouri was a 'civil proceeding,' but it did not seek damages, being merely a proceeding to approve the settlement. Therefore, Seneca was not obligated to appoint counsel for NL.").

42. *See, e.g.*, Prince George Parish of Prince George Winyah v. GuideOne Mut. Ins. Co., 839 F. App'x 779, 780 (4th Cir. 2020) (applying South Carolina law); Allstate Ins. Co. v. Rosfeld as Trs. of the Rosfeld Living Tr. Dated Oct. 29, 2003, 619 F. Supp. 3d 1050, 1063 (D. Haw. 2022) (applying Hawaii law); Bank of the W. v. Super. Ct., 833 P.2d 545, 546 (Cal. 1992) ("[O]ne may not insure against the risk of being ordered to return money or property that has been wrongfully acquired. Such orders do not award 'damages' as that term is used in insurance policies."); Vigilant Ins. Co. v. Credit Suisse First Boston Corp., 782 N.Y.S.2d 19, 20 (App. Div. 2004) ("Restitution of ill-gotten funds does not constitute 'damages' or a 'loss' as those terms are used in insurance policies[.]"). *But see* Wayne Mut. Ins. Co. v. McNabb, 45 N.E.3d 1081, 1089 (Ohio Ct. App. 2016) (reasoning that the term "damages" is broad enough to include sums ordered to be paid as restitution).

43. *See, e.g.*, Nat'l Union Fire Ins. Co. v. Dish Network, L.L.C., 17 F.4th 22, 32 (10th Cir. 2021) (applying Colorado law); Moore v. State Farm Mut. Auto. Ins. Co., 304 F. App'x 329, 331 (5th Cir. 2008) (stating that injunctive relief claims were not covered because they did not seek monetary damages); MJCM, Inc. v. Hartford Cas. Ins. Co., No. 8:09-CV-2275-T-17TBM, 2010 WL 1949585, at *7 (M.D. Fla. May 14, 2010) (stating that a lawsuit seeking only injunctive relief is not a "suit" under a liability insurance policy); One Gateway Assocs. v. Westfield Ins. Co., 184 F. Supp. 2d 527, 533 (S.D. W. Va. 2002) (determining that the insurer owed no duty to defend because only injunctive relief was sought); Bloomfield Rd., LLC v. DeMichele, No. 2007AP2396, 2008 WL 4923582, at *1–2 (Wis. Ct. App. Nov. 19, 2008) (holding that the insurer had no duty to defend where the plaintiff sought declaratory and injunctive relief to force adjacent lakefront property owners to reposition their docks, meaning the insured would not have to pay monetary damages). In some jurisdictions, however, an insured's costs in complying with an injunction may constitute damages for purposes of the insurer's duty to indemnify. *See, e.g.*, *In re* Certification of Question of Law from United States Dist. Ct., 960 N.W.2d 829, 836 (S.D. 2021). Also, if the insured pleads its entitlement to "other relief deemed appropriate" or something similar in addition to seeking injunctive relief, the request for such other relief likely qualifies as a request for damages sufficient to trigger the insurer's duty to defend. *See, e.g.*, Country Mut. Ins. Co. v. Bible Pork, Inc., 42 N.E.3d 958, 964 (Ill. App. Ct. 2015).

44. *See, e.g.*, Bullock v. Md. Cas. Co., 102 Cal. Rptr. 2d 804, 813 (Ct. App. 2001) (finding no duty to defend where both an ordinance and the city's complaint described the sums to be paid as

or unrelated to pending litigation,[45] when presented with a cease and desist letter,[46] or when objecting to proofs of claim in bankruptcy cases.[47] But there are other types of actions or proceedings that implicate an insurer's duty to defend.

B. The Duty to Defend in Arbitration

An insured may be named as a defendant or respondent in an arbitration proceeding. This may come about one of three ways. First, the insured may be sued in court and thereafter successfully move to compel arbitration based on a provision in a contract with the plaintiff. Second, the party aggrieved by the insured's alleged misconduct may initiate arbitration with the insured by filing a demand for arbitration with an alternative dispute resolution provider, such as the American Arbitration Association, rather than suing the insured in a court. Third, the insured and the other party may voluntarily agree to arbitrate their dispute rather than vindicating their rights in court.

Regardless of how the parties end up in arbitration, it generally should be clear that the insurer has a duty to defend the insured in that proceeding just as it would if the dispute were instead in court. Arbitration is a substitute for litigation. Indeed, arbitration *is* litigation, just in a different forum. An arbitration demand or notice of claim is analogous to a complaint or petition in a civil case in court.[48] Both lay and expert witnesses testify in arbitrations and

"penalties"); A.Y. McDonald Indus., Inc. v. Ins. Co. of N. Am., 475 N.W.2d 607, 626 (Iowa 1991) (holding that civil penalties imposed for violating RCRA were not "damages"); State Farm Fire & Cas. Co. v. Martinez, 995 P.2d 890, 896 (Kan. Ct. App. 2000) (concluding that public policy prevents a wrongdoer from insuring against civil penalties imposed for violating the Kansas Consumer Protection Act).

45. *See, e.g.*, Sanders v. Phoenix Ins. Co., 843 F.3d 37, 45–46 (1st Cir. 2016) (rejecting the insured's claim that a voluntary mediation was the functional equivalent of a "suit"); Meyers Warehouse, Inc. v. Canal Indem. Co., 614 F. App'x 719, 722 (5th Cir. 2015) (referring to an informal settlement negotiation that precedes the commencement of any civil action); Hurricane Elec., LLC v. Nat'l Fire Ins. Co. of Hartford, No. 20-cv-05840-CRB, 2020 WL 6743926, at *5–6 (N.D. Cal. Nov. 17, 2020) (highlighting the insured's failure to obtain the insurer's consent to the mediation); Recall Total Info. Mgmt., Inc. v. Fed. Ins. Co., 83 A.3d 664, 671 (Conn. App. Ct. 2014) ("[W]e cannot conclude that the term 'suit' or phrase 'other dispute resolution proceeding' was meant to encompass the mere negotiations that took place in this case. . . . [T]o construe 'suit' to include mere negotiations following a demand, would obliterate the distinction between 'suit' and 'claim.' This construction must be rejected."); Ill. Tool Works, Inc. v. Ace Am. Ins. Co., 142 N.E.3d 227, 233 (Ill. App. Ct. 2019) (explaining that the mediation was neither a "suit" nor a continuation of another lawsuit).

46. *See, e.g.*, *Hurricane Elec.*, 2020 WL 6743926, at *4 (stating that a cease and desist letter was not a "suit" and was at most a "claim," so it did not trigger the insurer's duty to defend).

47. *See, e.g.*, USA Gymnastics v. Ace Am. Ins. Co. (*In re* USA Gymnastics), 624 B.R. 443, 451–53 (Bankr. S.D. Ind. 2021) (explaining why a bankruptcy case is not a "suit" under a CGL policy).

48. *See, e.g.*, DeWitt Constr. Inc. v. Charter Oak Fire Ins. Co., 307 F.3d 1127, 1137 (9th Cir. 2002) (stating that the insurer's duty to defend was triggered by the filing of the arbitration demand); Century Sur. Co. v. S & R Dev., Inc., 483 F. Supp. 3d 400, 405 (S.D. Miss. 2020) (treating the arbitration

the parties offer evidence for the arbitrators to consider. Parties seek monetary damages in arbitrations. In short, when evaluating the duty to defend, there is no principled basis to distinguish an arbitration proceeding in which the insured is aligned as a defendant and a lawsuit against the insured. For that matter, insurers do not draw such lines; they regularly defend their insureds in arbitrations without questioning the forum's or process's effect on their duty to defend.

Under a standard CGL policy, the insurer's definition of "suit" generally compels it to defend the insured in arbitration. If the insured is not required to submit to arbitration, the insured must obtain the insurer's consent to arbitration. An insurer may waive an insured's failure to obtain consent to arbitration as a defense to coverage just as it may waive other coverage defenses based on an insured's noncompliance with policy terms.[49]

C. The Duty to Defend Environmental Enforcement Proceedings

1. *Introduction*

An insurer's duty to defend under a CGL policy has often been litigated in relation to enforcement actions under the Comprehensive Environmental Response, Compensation, and Liability Act of 1980 (CERCLA). Briefly, CERCLA establishes financial responsibility for cleaning up hazardous waste sites. The U.S. Environmental Protection Agency (EPA) is authorized to clean up hazardous waste sites. To enable EPA to fulfill this responsibility, CERCLA created the Hazardous Substances Trust Fund, better known as "Superfund," to pay for remediation efforts. CERCLA empowers EPA to recover "all costs of removal or remedial action" it incurs in remediating a Superfund site from potentially responsible parties, or PRPs.[50] Ominously, CERCLA imposes strict liability for response costs.[51] In addition to cleanup costs, PRPs may be strictly liable for damages for injury to, destruction of, or loss of natural resources resulting from the release of hazardous substances.[52] Beyond CERCLA, some states have adopted their own statutory regimes for remediating hazardous waste sites.

---

demand and supplemental arbitration demand as the "operative complaint" in determining the insurer's duty to defend); Wm. C. Vick Constr. Co. v. Pa. Nat'l Mut. Cas. Ins. Co., 52 F. Supp. 2d 569, 578–79 (E.D.N.C. 1999) (using the "comparison test" used to determine an insurer's duty to defend a lawsuit in connection with an arbitration proceeding).

49. *See* Auto-Owners Ins. Co. v. High Country Coatings, Inc., 388 F. Supp. 3d 1328, 1334–35 (D. Colo. 2019) (applying Colorado law).

50. 42 U.S.C. § 9607(a)(4)(A) (2018).

51. *Id.*

52. *Id.* § 9607(a)(4)(C).

2. *PRP Letters and Related Administrative Proceedings as "Suits"*

An insured often learns of its potential Superfund liability through a general "Notice of Liability" letter from EPA, commonly described as a "PRP letter." A PRP letter informs the recipient that it has been identified as a PRP at a Superfund site and that it may be liable for cleanup costs at the site, and explains the process for negotiating a related settlement with EPA. The letter also includes information on the Superfund program and the specific site and may request information from the insured.

The issue then becomes whether the PRP letter (or a similar notice from a state agency) qualifies as a "suit" within the meaning of the party's CGL policy for purposes of the insurer's duty to defend. More particularly, must the insurer defend the insured in the administrative proceedings that follow the PRP letter? The great majority of courts that have considered the issue have held that a PRP letter is the first step in an adversarial administrative process that is functionally equivalent to a lawsuit, and that EPA's threatened use of legal process to coerce conduct or payment by the insured is sufficient to trigger the duty to defend.[53] The same result generally follows where a state

53. *See, e.g.*, Ash Grove Cement Co. v. Liberty Mut. Ins. Co., 649 F. App'x 585, 587–88 (9th Cir. 2016) (stating that a PRP letter is a coercive information demand that is an attempt to gain an end through legal process and is thus a "suit" under Oregon law (quoting Anderson Bros., Inc. v. St. Paul Fire & Marine Ins. Co., 729 F.3d 923, 932–33, 935 (9th Cir. 2013))); Land O' Lakes, Inc. v. Emps. Ins. of Wausau, 728 F.3d 822, 827–29 (8th Cir. 2013) (interpreting Minnesota and Oklahoma law); Century Indem. Co. v. Marine Grp., LLC, 648 F. Supp. 2d 1238, 1255–56 (D. Or. 2012) ("Here, administrative communications, including the 104(e) letter and notifications of PRP status, provided clear notice of the need to affirmatively defend allegations of liability for environmental contamination and were sufficient to trigger Defendants' duty to defend. Accordingly, the court finds that, at least as early as the 104(e) notices, the agency actions and communications gave rise to a 'suit' as a matter of law."); Travelers Cas. & Sur. Co. v. Ala. Gas Corp., 117 So. 3d 695, 708 (Ala. 2012) ("The authority given the EPA in regard to determining liability on the part of PRPs, while not absolute, is very nearly so. Given the severe penalties for failure to cooperate and other enforcement tools available to the EPA, a decision by the EPA to designate an insured as a PRP cannot on any practical level be understood as anything less that the initiation of a 'legal action' constituting a 'suit'. . . ."); Compass Ins. Co. v. City of Littleton, 984 P.2d 606, 622 (Colo. 1999) ("We find that the term 'suit' is ambiguous, and we hold that an EPA action under CERCLA is sufficiently coercive to constitute a 'suit' as that term is used in the insurance policies."); R.T. Vanderbilt Co. v. Cont'l Cas. Co., 870 A.2d 1048, 1060 (Conn. 2005) (citation omitted) (concluding that "because a PRP letter is an 'attempt to recover a right or claim through legal action' . . . under CERCLA's statutory scheme, it constitutes a suit within the meaning of a [CGL] insurance policy"); A.Y. McDonald Indus., Inc. v. Ins. Co. of N. Am., 475 N.W.2d 607, 628–29 (Iowa 1991) (concluding that the EPA administrative process gave rise to a duty to defend and stating that a "suit" includes "any attempt to gain an end by legal process"); Hartford Accident & Indem. Co. v. Dana Corp., 690 N.E.2d 285, 296–97 (Ind. Ct. App. 1997) ("[W]e hold that § 104 requests coupled with a specific allegation of liability, § 106 orders, § 107 demands, and § 122(e) offers, as well as analogous proceedings by state and local agencies, are 'suits,'. . . . Less coercive actions, however, do not rise to the level of 'suit.' These would include mere notification or investigation when no enforcement action is contemplated."); Aetna Cas. & Sur. Co. v. Commonwealth, 179 S.W.3d 830, 837–38 (Ky. 2005) (refusing to let the insurance company "cling[] to an archaic definition of 'suit'"); Hazen Paper Co. v. U.S. Fid. & Guar. Co., 555 N.E.2d 576, 580 (Mass. 1990) ("We conclude that the litigation defense protection that Hazen purchased from USF&G would be substantially compromised if USF&G had no obligation to defend Hazen's interests in response to the

agency, rather than EPA, notifies an insured of its potential environmental liability.[54]

McGinnes Industrial Maintenance Corp. v. Phoenix Insurance Co.[55] reflects the majority rule. In the 1960s, McGinnes Industrial Maintenance Corp. (McGinnes) dumped paper mill waste into disposal pits in Pasadena, Texas. In 2005, the EPA began investigating environmental contamination at the site. In November 2007, EPA sent a PRP letter to McGinnes's parent company and invited it to enter into negotiations over cleaning up the site and reimbursing EPA's costs. In December 2008, EPA sent a similar letter to McGinnes. The PRP letter to McGinnes contained burdensome requests for information regarding McGinnes's role at the site. The letter also noted that a failure to respond could result in daily penalties of up to $32,500.[56]

In July 2009, EPA sent McGinnes a special notice letter in which it announced that it had determined that McGinnes was responsible for cleaning up the site and demanded that McGinnes pay nearly $379,000 in costs.[57] The

EPA letter."); Dutton-Lainson Co. v. Cont'l Cas. Co., 778 N.W.2d 433, 449 (Neb. 2010) ("The term 'suit' can be readily understood to apply to actions that are the functional equivalent of a suit filed in a court of law. The PRP letter advised Dutton that it was immediately at risk. If Dutton declined the necessary response, its substantive rights and ultimate liability were affected from the receipt of the PRP letter. . . . [A]n ordinary person would believe that the receipt of a PRP letter was in effect the commencement of a suit. . . .") (citations omitted); Coakley v. Me. Bonding & Cas. Co., 618 A.2d 777, 786–87 (N.H. 1992) ("While it is true that the PRP notice does not purport to establish the Coakleys' liability . . . , CERCLA liability is strict. . . . The predominant question . . . is not whether a PRP is liable, but rather *for how much*. . . . One would not expect a traditional tort defendant to concede the 'damages' portion of a case, and it likewise would be myopic to conclude that the Coakleys' rights are not substantially determined by the administrative process described in the PRP notice. . . . We therefore find that the EPA's action fits the . . . definition of [a] 'suit'. . . .") (citations omitted); McGinnes Indus. Maint. Corp. v. Phoenix Ins. Co., 477 S.W.3d 786, 787 (Tex. 2015) (agreeing with most courts that Superfund cleanup proceedings are a "suit"); Johnson Controls, Inc. v. Emps. Ins. of Wausau, 665 N.W.2d 257, 285 (Wis. 2003) (concluding an insurer has a duty to defend an insured who receives a PRP letter seeking remediation or remediation costs).

54. *See, e.g.*, Pac. Hide & Fur Depot v. Great Am. Ins. Co., 23 F. Supp. 3d 1208, 1213–18 (D. Mont. 2014) (finding a duty to defend under Montana's analog to CERCLA); Nucor Corp. v. Emps. Ins. of Wausau, 296 P.3d 74, 83 (Ariz. Ct. App. 2012) (concluding that a letter from the Arizona Department of Environmental Quality triggered the insurer's duty to defend); SCSC Corp. v. Allied Mut. Ins. Co., 536 N.W.2d 305, 315 (Minn. 1995) (concluding that a "Request for Information" from the Minnesota Pollution Control Agency qualified as a "suit" for purposes of the duty to defend), *overruled on other grounds by* Bahr v. Boise Cascade Corp., 766 N.W.2d 910, 919 (Minn. 2009); C.D. Spangler Constr. Co. v. Indus. Crankshaft & Eng'g Co., 388 S.E.2d 557, 570 (N.C. 1990) ("Because this Court must give effect to reasonable interpretations which favor the policyholder, we conclude that the term 'suit' as used in the policies covers the [state] compliance orders.") (citations omitted); Certain Underwriters at Lloyd's London v. Mass. Bonding & Ins. Co., 230 P.3d 103, 120–21 (Or. Ct. App. 2010) (involving a letter from the Oregon Department of Environmental Quality about cleaning up a site); Pa. Mfrs.' Ass'n Ins. Co. v. Johnson Matthey, Inc., 243 A.3d 298, 310 (Pa. Commw. Ct. 2020) (concluding that a PRP letter issued by the Pennsylvania Department of Environmental Protection triggered the insurer's duty to defend); State v. CNA Ins. Cos., 779 A.2d 662, 667 (Vt. 2001) (stating that because of the "coercive adversarial nature" of a state agency's requests for information, the following administrative proceedings were a "suit").

55. 477 S.W.3d 786 (Tex. 2015).

56. *Id.* at 790.

57. *Id.*

letter further required McGinnes to make a good faith settlement offer within 60 days. When McGinnes did not comply, EPA issued an administrative order directing McGinnes to conduct a remedial investigation and feasibility study. The letter warned McGinnes that its willful failure to do so would subject it to daily civil penalties of $37,500, as well as punitive damages.[58]

In May 2008, McGinnes asked its CGL insurers from the 1960s, Phoenix Insurance Co. and Travelers Indemnity Co., to defend it in the EPA proceedings. The insurers refused on the basis that there was no "suit" under their policies.[59] McGinnes then sued them in a Texas federal court. The district court awarded the insurers partial summary judgment, holding that they had no duty to defend McGinnes, but certified its order for interlocutory appeal. On appeal, the U.S. Court of Appeals for the Fifth Circuit certified the following question to the Texas Supreme Court: "Whether the EPA's PRP letters and/or unilateral administrative order, issued pursuant to CERCLA, constitute a 'suit' within the meaning of the CGL policies, triggering the duty to defend."[60]

The Texas Supreme Court agreed with the insurers that the term "suit" generally refers to a court proceeding.[61] But the court further reasoned that "suit" as used in a CGL policy must include CERCLA enforcement proceedings:

> When the policies at issue were written, the main avenue of redress for pollution was by suing in court on common law or statutory claims. One effect of CERCLA was to authorize the EPA to conduct on its own what otherwise would have amounted to pretrial proceedings, but without having to initiate a court action until the end of the process. The PRP notice letters serve as pleadings. The EPA obtains discovery through requests for information, indistinguishable from interrogatories under the rules of civil procedure. It engages in mediation through its invitations to settle. A unilateral administrative order resembles summary judgment. The fines and penalties for willful non-cooperation in the process are like sanctions in a court proceeding, only prescribed by statute. And part of the judicial function is ceded to the EPA by limiting a PRP's opportunity for review until the end of the process, and then limiting that review to an abuse of discretion by the EPA, based on its own record.
>
> McGinnes argues that EPA proceedings are the functional equivalent of a suit, but in actuality, they are the suit itself, only conducted outside a courtroom. Had the EPA wanted to force McGinnes to clean up the Site before 1980, it would have been required to sue first, and the CGL policies would have obligated the Insurers to defend . . . all without fear of being sanctioned

58. *Id.*
59. *Id.*
60. *Id.* (footnote omitted).
61. *Id.* at 791.

> at the very end for not having cooperated with the opponent. CERCLA effectively redefined a "suit" on cleanup claims to mean proceedings conducted by one of the parties, the EPA, followed by an enforcement action in court, if necessary. McGinnes's rights under its policies should not be emasculated by the enactment of a statute intended not to affect insurance, but to streamline the EPA's ability to clean up pollution.[62]

The insurers argued that to hold that their duty to defend applied to EPA enforcement proceedings would extend their duty to every demand letter.[63] The court disagreed. According to the *McGinnes* court, a demand letter foreshadowing a lawsuit is nothing like a PRP letter or unilateral administrative order, which mandate compliance.[64] The court also rejected the insurers' argument that a PRP letter or unilateral administrative order is merely a claim rather than a suit because EPA's demands and directives, which are backed by threatened penalties, resemble interlocutory rulings more than they do claims.[65] The insurers' contention that EPA proceedings are really pre-suit settlement mechanisms rather than suits failed because before CERCLA was enacted, EPA's only course lay in judicial proceedings.[66]

Retreating, the insurers contended that if the term "suit" encompassed CERCLA proceedings, it necessarily subsumed all administrative proceedings.[67] The court again disagreed. In comparison to most administrative actions, "EPA enforcement proceedings are unusual: not only are they like judicial proceedings, they were judicial proceedings before CERCLA was enacted."[68]

Finally, the *McGinnes* court observed that 13 of the 16 state supreme courts that had considered the insurers' urged interpretation of "suit" in this context had rejected it.[69] Stressing the importance of uniformity when identical insurance policy terms will be interpreted in various jurisdictions, the court concluded that Texas insureds should not be deprived of the coverage enjoyed by insureds in 13 other states.[70] The court therefore answered the Fifth Circuit's certified question "yes."[71]

In contrast, a handful of courts have concluded that a PRP letter and state analogs do not introduce a "suit" and, consequently, do not trigger an insurer's

62. *Id.* (footnote omitted).
63. *Id.* at 792.
64. *Id.*
65. *Id.*
66. *Id.*
67. *Id.*
68. *Id.*
69. *Id.* at 793.
70. *Id.* at 794.
71. *Id.*

duty to defend.[72] *Professional Rental, Inc. v. Shelby Insurance Co.*[73] is instructive. There, an Ohio court reasoned that it was necessary to elevate substance over form in deciding whether Professional Rental, Inc. (Professional) was subjected to a "suit" or its functional equivalent.[74] The court concluded that the term "suit" includes "substantial efforts which force the insured to take action or suffer serious consequences if the insured fails to cooperate."[75] With that in mind, the court determined that the PRP letters Professional received from EPA did not constitute a "suit" for purposes of a liability insurance policy.

> If the PRP chooses not to respond to the initial PRP letter, the EPA will take one of several steps: (1) seek an injunction in district court forcing the PRP to act; (2) issue a Section 104(e) or 106(a) administrative order either demanding information or forcing PRP cleanup; or (3) send additional notice letters, known colloquially as "drop dead" letters, informing the PRP's that they must follow the EPA's suggested cleanup "voluntarily"—otherwise, the government will expurgate the pollution itself, and thereafter demand reimbursement through a CERCLA Section 107 cost recovery action.
>
> The EPA's strategy is confrontational, and seemingly coercive, as identified PRPs must either abide by what the EPA desires or the agency may clean up the pollution itself, typically at a higher cost. By sending a PRP notification, "the agency in effect has issued an ultimatum of 'settle on the government's terms or litigate and lose.'"
>
> Nevertheless, receiving a PRP notification, by itself, does not impose liability. Moreover, failing to respond to a PRP notification does not, *by itself*, authorize the EPA to assess fines or provide a basis for punitive damages. Rather, it is necessary for the EPA to do "something more" in order to *force or compel* the insured to take action or suffer serious consequences. The "something more" is present when the EPA issues an *administrative order*, pursuant to CERCLA Sections 106(a) or 104(e), making the PRP susceptible to stiff fines or punitive damages for failure to abide by the terms of the order.

72. *See, e.g.*, Liberty Mut. Ins. Co. v. FAG Bearings Corp., 335 F.3d 752, 765–66 (8th Cir. 2003) (applying Missouri law); Foster-Gardner, Inc. v. Nat'l Union Fire Ins. Co., 959 P.2d 265, 279 (Cal. 1998) ("The insurers assert that the word 'suit' . . . means a civil action commenced by filing a complaint. Anything short of this is a 'claim.' . . . We agree with the insurers."); Lapham-Hickey Steel Corp. v. Prot. Mut. Ins. Co., 655 N.E.2d 842, 848 (Ill. 1995) ("Neither the initial letter from the EPA, the draft consent order nor the 'no-action' letter initiated a suit. None was filed in a court of law and none accomplished service of process. . . . Rather, the draft consent order and ultimately the 'no-action' letter were mechanisms used to encourage Lapham-Hickey to voluntarily investigate the contamination at the facility. Though the tone . . . may have been confrontational, these documents . . . are not complaints and do not impose liability."); Patrons Oxford Mut. Ins. Co. v. Marois, 573 A.2d 16, 20 (Me. 1990) (finding that a state administrative proceeding was not a "suit" seeking damages).

73. 599 N.E.2d 423 (Ohio Ct. App. 1991).

74. *Id.* at 427–28.

75. *Id.* at 428.

> Moreover, the same degree of compulsion is present when the EPA seeks an injunctive order in federal district court under CERCLA Section 106(a), or institutes a cost recovery action under CERCLA Section 107.[76]

The *Professional Rental* court calculated that despite EPA's confrontational posture, Professional was not faced with the functional equivalent of a lawsuit.[77] The PRP letters were in essence "claims" of liability and demands for restitution, coupled with threats of unilateral action if Professional failed to join in remedial action. EPA's threats, demands, and warnings did not force Professional to settle or suffer severe financial repercussions.[78]

The court acknowledged that because CERCLA liability is strict, a party's receipt of a PRP letter may be perceived as an apocalyptic event; however, the severity of the claim does not transform a PRP letter into a "suit."[79] When EPA enforces CERCLA's strict liability against the insured, however, the situation changes. EPA has then signaled "that the *force* of its powers under CERCLA" is being asserted in a fashion that "threatens the insured with probable and imminent financial consequences."[80] The *Professional Rental* court accordingly held that a "suit" is initiated for purposes of an insurer's duty to defend when EPA "issues an administrative order which the PRP is legally obligated to obey, or otherwise attempts to enforce liability through an injunctive action or cost recovery action filed in a court of law."[81]

Given CERCLA's peculiar regulatory scheme and the liabilities the statute creates for PRPs, courts that recognize a duty to defend upon an insured's receipt of a PRP letter have a solid rationale for reaching that result, but a notice of potential liability is still not a suit. The *Professional Rental* court's approach to the duty to defend is a logical compromise.

3. *Response Costs as "Damages"*

Under the CGL policy's insuring agreement, the insurer promises to pay those sums the insured becomes legally obligated to pay "as damages" because of "bodily injury" or "property damage" to which the policy applies.[82] Because standard CGL policies do not define "damages," this issue has been repeatedly litigated. Most courts have concluded that amounts an insured must pay "as

---

76. *Id.* at 429–30 (footnotes omitted).
77. *Id.* at 430.
78. *Id.*
79. *Id.*
80. *Id.*
81. *Id.*
82. Ins. Servs. Off., Inc., Commercial General Liability Coverage Form (CG 00 01 04 13), at 1 (2012).

damages" include government-mandated response costs under CERCLA.[83] As Maryland's highest court explained in reaching this conclusion:

> "Damages" in common usage means the reparation in money for a detriment or injury sustained. The reasonably prudent layperson does not cut nice distinctions between the remedies offered at law and in equity. Absent an express provision in the document itself, insurance policy-holders surely do not anticipate that coverage will depend on the mode of relief, i.e. a cash payment rather than an injunction, sought by an injured party. Policy-holders will, instead, reasonably infer that the insurer's pledge to pay damages will apply generally to compensatory outlays of various kinds, including expenditures made to comply with administrative orders or formal injunctions. The ordinary person understands "damages" as meaning money paid to make good an insured loss. In this context, environmental response costs fall within that definition.[84]

83. *See, e.g.*, Anderson Dev. Co. v. Travelers Indem. Co., 49 F.3d 1128, 1133 (6th Cir. 1995) (applying Michigan law); Olin Corp. v. Landmark Ins. Co., 517 F. Supp. 3d 161, 180 (S.D.N.Y. 2021) (applying New York law); Teck Metals, Ltd. v. Certain Underwriters at Lloyd's, London, 735 F. Supp. 2d 1260, 1268 (E.D. Wash. 2010) (finding that under Washington law, the response costs the insured incurred pursuant to its settlement agreement with the EPA fell within the meaning of "damages"); A.Y. McDonald Indus., Inc. v. Ins. Co. of N. Am., 475 N.W.2d 607, 624 (Iowa 1991) ("We hold that any injury to the environment resulting from contamination by hazardous waste constitutes 'property damage' within the meaning of the CGL policies. We further hold that any injury to the environment resulting from contamination is incurred 'because of property damage' and represents the measure of damages to the property."); Hartford Accident & Indem. Co. v. Dana Corp., 690 N.E.2d 285, 298 (Ind. Ct. App. 1997) (holding that "the ordinary meaning of the term 'damages' in a CGL policy includes EPA or state-mandated cleanup and response costs"); Aetna Cas. & Sur. Co. v. Commonwealth, 179 S.W.3d 830, 838–39 (Ky. 2005) ("We agree with the majority of state appellate courts that hold the ordinary meaning of 'damages' is broad enough to, and does include, government mandated response or cleanup costs under CERCLA and similar state environmental protection statutes: as long as the purpose is to rectify, correct, control, lessen or stop ongoing injury of the premises."); Bausch & Lomb Inc. v. Utica Mut. Ins. Co., 625 A.2d 1021, 1033 (Md. 1993) (footnote omitted) ("The ordinary person understands 'damages' as meaning money paid to make good an insured loss. In this context, environmental response costs fall within that definition."); Hazen Paper Co. v. U.S. Fid. & Guar. Co., 555 N.E.2d 576, 583 (Mass. 1990) (holding that cleanup costs were covered "damages" and reasoning that an insured "would fairly expect that the policy covered amounts he must spend to correct pollution damage for which the law holds him responsible"); Farmland Indus., Inc. v. Republic Ins. Co., 941 S.W.2d 505, 512 (Mo. 1997) (holding that environmental response costs incurred under CERCLA and similar state laws are "damages"); Coakley v. Me. Bonding & Cas. Co., 618 A.2d 777, 785 (N.H. 1992) (concluding that "cleanup costs and reimbursement for related investigatory costs satisfy the plain and ordinary definition of 'damages'"); C.D. Spangler Constr. Co. v. Indus. Crankshaft & Eng'g Co., 388 S.E.2d 557, 565, 568 (N.C. 1990) (holding that the insured's costs of complying with state orders were "damages"; the term was "not being used in its legal and technical sense" in the insured's policies and encompassed response costs); Helena Chem. Co. v. Allianz Underwriters Ins. Co., 594 S.E.2d 455, 458–60 (S.C. 2004) (aligning with the majority of jurisdictions); Johnson Controls, Inc. v. Emps. Ins. of Wausau, 665 N.W.2d 257, 263–64 (Wis. 2003) ("[A]n insured's costs of restoring and remediating damaged property, whether the costs are based on remediation efforts by a third party (including the government) or are incurred directly by the insured, are covered damages under applicable CGL policies, provided that other policy exclusions do not apply."). *But see* Certain Underwriters at Lloyd's of London v. Super. Ct., 16 P.3d 94, 106 (Cal. 2001) (stating that an insurer's duty to indemnify is limited to money that a court orders to be paid).

84. *Bausch & Lomb*, 625 A.2d at 1032–33 (footnote omitted).

Related to the "as damages" issue is another question: If the insured in anticipation of governmental or private action against it voluntarily cleans up a toxic waste site, is the liability insurer responsible for the associated costs on the basis that they constitute "damages"?[85] If the insured had not cleaned up the site and EPA or another party did, with EPA or the other party thereafter suing the insured for the expense of the cleanup, in many states the liability insurer would be required to defend and indemnify the insured. It therefore makes sense that if the insured voluntarily incurs remediation expenses, particularly if the voluntary action mitigates future damage, the liability insurer should indemnify the insured for those costs. Again, the weight of authority holds that voluntary cleanup expenses are covered by a standard CGL policy.[86]

But whether voluntary cleanup expenses are "damages" does not alone determine the insurer's duty to defend where the insured voluntarily remediates a hazardous waste site. A "suit" or the functional equivalent is still required for the insurer to have a duty to defend, as the court in *Gull Industries, Inc. v. State Farm Fire & Casualty Co.*[87] explained.

Gull Industries, Inc. (Gull) owned a gas station in Washington state. Gull had liability coverage with Transamerica Insurance Group (TIG). Gull leased the station to Hayes and Mary Johnson from 1972 to 1982. The Johnsons were insured by State Farm Fire & Casualty Co. (State Farm). Gull was an additional insured under the Johnsons' State Farm policy. In 1984, Gull investigated the underground storage tanks at the station and discovered that they had leaked fuel continuously while the Johnsons leased the station. Gull voluntarily cleaned up the contaminated soil and groundwater.

In 2005, Gull notified the Washington Department of Environment (DOE) of the leaks. DOE responded with a letter in which it acknowledged receipt of Gull's notice that the property was contaminated, and that Gull intended to pursue a voluntary cleanup. DOE notified Gull that the contaminated soil and groundwater were above the Model Toxic Controls Act's (MTCA) "Method A Cleanup levels" and that DOE had listed the property as awaiting cleanup. The letter also advised Gull to "'be aware that there are requirements in state law which must be adhered to'" but did not identify any consequences that

85. There is a colorable argument that an insured who cleans up a toxic waste site rather than facing an EPA or state agency action and incurring strict liability under CERCLA or an equivalent state statute is not truly acting "voluntarily." *See* Cent. Ill. Light Co. v. Home Ins. Co., 821 N.E.2d 206, 219, 223–24 (Ill. 2004).

86. *See, e.g.*, *Cent. Ill. Light Co.*, 821 N.E.2d at 224 (responding to a regulatory notice to avoid strict liability is not truly voluntary); *Bausch & Lomb*, 625 A.2d at 1026–27, 1032–33 (holding that the insured's voluntary cleanup costs were covered); *Helena Chem. Co.*, 594 S.E.2d at 458–60 (following *Bausch & Lomb*); Weyerhaeuser Co. v. Aetna Cas. & Sur. Co., 874 P.2d 142, 145 (Wash. 1994) (stating that CGL policies may provide coverage when an insured cleans up pollution damages in cooperation with an environmental agency).

87. 326 P.3d 782 (Wash. Ct. App. 2015).

might attach to the failure to meet those requirements.[88] The letter stated that DOE had not determined that Gull was a Potentially Liable Party (PLP) under the MTCA and was silent as to whether DOE approved of Gull's remedial action. Finally, the letter explained that Gull could seek state assistance with the cleanup. The DOE letter never expressly or impliedly threatened immediate and severe consequences because of the contamination.[89]

In 2009, Gull tendered its claims for defense and indemnification for the costs of the cleanup to TIG and State Farm. Both insurers denied coverage. Gull then sued TIG, State Farm, and several other insurers on several theories. State Farm and TIG moved for partial summary judgment on the basis that they had no duty to defend Gull. In opposing the motion, Gull argued that the insurers' duty to defend was triggered because it faced strict liability for environmental cleanup costs under the MTCA.[90] The trial court granted the insurers' motion and Gull appealed to the Washington Court of Appeals.

The *Gull* court noted that under Washington precedent, voluntary cleanup costs were "damages" for purposes of an insurer's duty to indemnify.[91] But an insurer's duty to defend is distinct from its duty to indemnify and must be analyzed separately.[92] Here, the insurance policies did not define the term "suit." The court concluded that the term was ambiguous in the environmental liability context and could include administrative actions that were the functional equivalent of a lawsuit.[93] Unfortunately for Gull, the court's conclusion that the term "suit" included functionally equivalent actions was not enough to support a duty to defend. Because the DOE letter did not expressly or impliedly threaten immediate and severe consequences due to the contamination, it was not the functional equivalent of a "suit" that would trigger the insurers' duty to defend.[94]

Invoking public policy, Gull urged that interpreting "suit" to exclude voluntary remediation by an insured who was liable under the MTCA but not yet subject to a formal enforcement action by DOE would discourage property owners from voluntarily cleaning up toxic waste sites. The *Gull* court explained that such public policy concerns carry little weight when analyzing the duty to defend. Under the language of the insurance policies at issue, "the public policy of promoting voluntary cleanups alone does not compel an automatic duty to defend; the duty to defend is triggered by the functional equivalent of a lawsuit."[95]

88. *Id.* at 790 (quoting the DOE letter).
89. *Id.*
90. *Id.* at 786.
91. *Id.* at 787–88.
92. *Id.* at 786.
93. *Id.* at 790.
94. *See id.*
95. *Id.* at 790–91.

Gull also contended that the court should find a duty to defend because insureds need insurance proceeds to help pay for investigating the need to clean up a site. The court rejected this argument because insurance policy construction does not turn on the insured's needs.[96]

Finally, Gull argued that "suit" should not be given a technical or lawyerly definition and that a typical policyholder does not distinguish between having to pay legal and other defense costs because of actual coercive action from a government agency, as opposed to the implicit threat of such action. But, the *Gull* court responded, the duty to defend implies the need "to 'defend' against something."[97] In the absence of any adversarial or coercive action, an average policyholder would not likely believe that its insurer owed it a duty to defend.[98]

In conclusion, because the DOE letter neither explicitly nor implicitly threatened Gull with immediate and severe consequences arising from the contamination at its property, Gull was not faced with the functional equivalent of a "suit," and TIG and State Farm had no duty to defend it. The *Gull* court therefore affirmed the insurers' trial court win.

D. The Duty to Defend under Right to Repair Statutes

1. *Background*

Some states have enacted "right to repair" statutes that come into play in construction defect cases.[99] These statutes typically require a claimant to notify a contractor of alleged deficiencies and satisfy specified procedural requirements before suing the contractor. The contractor is afforded the opportunity to respond to the notice and repair the defect or settle the claim. A failure to respond to a notice may have various consequences for the contractor.

2. *Approaches to the Duty to Defend under Right to Repair Statutes*

In some states, the effect of a claimant's notice of defect for duty to defend purposes is statutorily prescribed.[100] In California, for example, a homeowner's

96. *Id.* at 791.
97. *Id.*
98. *Id.*
99. *See, e.g.*, Alaska Stat. §§ 09.45.881–09.45.899 (2022) ("Action for Dwelling Design, Construction, or Remodeling Claims"); Ariz. Rev. Stat. §§ 12-1361 to -1366 (2023) ("Purchaser Dwelling Actions"); Cal. Civ. Code §§ 895–945.5 (2023) ("Requirements for Actions for Construction Defects"); Colo. Rev. Stat. §§ 13-20-801 to -808 (2022) ("Construction Defect Action Reform Act"); Fla. Stat. §§ 558.001–558.005 (2022) ("Construction Defects"); Nev. Rev. Stat. §§ 40.600–40.695 (2022) ("Actions Resulting from Construction Defect"); Tex. Prop. Code Ann. §§ 27.001–27.007 (2021) ("Residential Construction Liability").
100. *See, e.g.*, Colo. Rev. Stat. § 13-20-808(7)(a) (2022) ("An insurer's duty to defend a construction professional or other insured under a liability insurance policy issued to a construction

notice to a builder has "the same force and effect as a notice of commencement of a legal proceeding."[101] In Nevada, if a contractor, subcontractor, supplier, or design professional receives written notice of a construction defect, it may present the claim to its liability insurer, which "(a) [m]ust treat the claim as if a civil action has been brought against the [insured]; and (b) [m]ust provide coverage to the extent available under [its] policy . . . as if a civil action has been brought against the contractor, subcontractor, supplier or design professional."[102]

In other states, whether a statutory notice triggers the duty to defend is a question for the courts. If there is any judicial consensus on this issue, it is that right to repair notices are not lawsuits but may qualify as "suits" under some policies on the basis that they are alternative dispute resolution proceedings.[103] *Altman Contractors, Inc. v. Crum & Forster Specialty Insurance Co.*[104] and *Cincinnati Insurance Co. v. AMSCO Windows*[105] exemplify courts' reasoning.

In *Altman*, Altman Contractors, Inc. (Altman) was the general contractor for the construction of the high-rise Sapphire Condominium (Sapphire) on Florida's east coast. Altman was insured under several consecutive CGL policies issued by Crum & Forster Specialty Insurance Co. (C & F). In 2012, Sapphire served Altman with several chapter 558 notices of claim, which cumulatively asserted hundreds of construction defects.[106] In early 2013, Altman notified C & F of Sapphire's claims and demanded that C & F defend and indemnify it. C & F denied that Sapphire's notices of claim invoked its duty to defend because they were not a "suit."[107] Altman ultimately settled Sapphire's claims on its own.

Altman Sued C & F in a Florida federal court seeking a declaration that C & F owed a duty to defend and indemnify it against Sapphire's construction defect claims. Altman lost at summary judgment. Altman then appealed to

professional shall be triggered by a potentially covered liability described in: (I) A notice of claim made pursuant to section 13-20-803.5. . . .").

101. Cal. Civ. Code § 910(a) (2023).

102. Nev. Rev. Stat. § 40.649 (2022).

103. *See, e.g.*, Hardesty Builders, Inc. v. Mid-Continent Cas. Co., No. C-10-142, 2010 WL 5146597, at *7–8 (S.D. Tex. Dec. 13, 2010) (applying Texas law); Melssen v. Auto-Owners Ins. Co., 285 P.3d 328, 334–35 (Colo. App. 2012).

104. 232 So. 3d 273 (Fla. 2017).

105. 593 F. App'x 802 (10th Cir. 2014) (applying Utah law).

106. A "558 notice" is sent to satisfy chapter 558 of the Florida statutes, which concerns construction defects. *See* Fla. Stat. § 558.003 (2022) ("A claimant may not file an action subject to this chapter without first complying with the requirements of this chapter. . . ."); § 558.004(1)(a) ("In actions brought alleging a construction defect, the claimant shall, at least 60 days before filing any action . . . serve written notice of claim on the contractor, subcontractor, supplier, or design professional, as applicable. . . ."); § 558.004(1)(b) ("The notice of claim must describe in reasonable detail the nature of each alleged construction defect and, if known, the damage or loss resulting from the defect.").

107. *Altman*, 232 So. 3d at 275.

the U.S. Court of Appeals for the Eleventh Circuit, which certified the following question to the Florida Supreme Court: "Is the notice and repair process set forth in chapter 558, Florida Statutes, a 'suit' within the meaning of the commercial general liability policy issued by C & F to Altman?"[108] The Florida Supreme Court answered affirmatively on the basis that the chapter 558 pre-litigation process is an "alternative dispute resolution proceeding" under a CGL policy's definition of a "suit."[109]

The court began its analysis by outlining the chapter 558 process that a claimant must follow before suing a contractor for an alleged construction defect:

> Specifically, a claimant must "serve written notice of claim on the contractor, subcontractor, supplier, or design professional, as applicable" before the claimant may file an action for a construction defect. . . .
>
> Upon receipt of a chapter 558 notice of claim, the recipient "must serve a written response to the claimant" within the statutorily specified time-period, providing either an offer "to remedy the alleged construction defect at no cost to the claimant," "to compromise and settle the claim by monetary payment," "to compromise and settle the claim by a combination of repairs and monetary payment," a statement disputing the claim, or a statement that any monetary payment will be determined by the recipient's insurer. . . . Once the claimant "receives a timely settlement offer," the claimant "must accept or reject the offer" in writing. . . .
>
> "[T]he claimant may, without further notice, proceed with an action" against the recipient if the parties either agree to "a partial settlement or compromise of the claim," the recipient "disputes the claim and will neither remedy the defect nor compromise and settle the claim," or the claimant does not receive a response "within the time provided." . . . If the offeror satisfies the parties' agreement within a reasonable period of time, "the claimant is barred from proceeding with an action for the claim described in the notice of claim or as otherwise provided in the accepted settlement offer." . . . "[A]ny offer or failure to offer . . . to remedy an alleged construction defect or to compromise and settle the claim by monetary payment does not constitute an admission of liability with respect to the defect and is not admissible" in a subsequent lawsuit. . . . "If a claimant initiates an action without first accepting or rejecting the offer, the court shall stay the action upon timely motion until the claimant complies with this subsection."[110]

With that background, the court next quoted the definition of "suit" in Altman's CGL policies with C & F:

108. *Id.* at 274.
109. *Id.*
110. *Id.* at 276–77 (citations to statutes and footnotes omitted).

> "Suit" means a civil proceeding in which damages because of "bodily injury," "property damage" or "personal and advertising injury" to which this insurance applies are alleged. "Suit" includes:
>
> a. An arbitration proceeding in which such damages are claimed and to which the insured must submit or does submit with our consent; or
>
> b. Any other alternative dispute resolution proceeding in which such damages are claimed and to which the insured submits with our consent.[111]

The *Altman* court concluded that the chapter 558 process could not be considered a "civil proceeding" because the recipient's participation in the chapter 558 settlement process is not mandatory or adjudicative.[112] The recipient of a notice of a claim may choose to not respond and thereby force the claimant to sue to recover for the alleged deficiency. Chapter 558 does not obligate the insured to participate in the process. The chapter 558 framework is merely a voluntary dispute resolution process despite its mandate that the claimant serve the insured with a notice before suing. Moreover, the chapter 558 process does not take place in court or before an adjudicatory body, nor does it produce legally binding results. Rather, chapter 558 provides a structure for parties to resolve a claim through a negotiated settlement or voluntary repairs short of litigation. The court thus concluded that the chapter 558 process is not a "civil proceeding" within the policy definition of "suit."[113]

The determination that the chapter 558 process did not constitute a "suit" did not end the inquiry, however, because the C & F policies defined "suit" to include "'[a]ny other alternative dispute resolution proceeding in which such damages are claimed and to which the insured submits with [C&F's] consent.'"[114] The court interpreted "alternative dispute resolution" to mean "[a] procedure for settling a dispute by means other than litigation."[115] The court reasoned that chapter 558 fell within this definition as a statutorily required pre-suit process intended to encourage the claimant and insured to settle short of litigation. Indeed, the Florida legislature had explicitly described chapter 558 as "'[a]n effective alternative dispute resolution mechanism,' intended to be beneficial for reducing construction defect litigation."[116] The court therefore concluded that the chapter 558 process was an alternative dispute resolution proceeding under the policies, just as mediation would be.[117]

111. *Id.* at 277 (quoting the C & F policies).
112. *Id.* (citing FLA. STAT. § 558.004(5)–(6) (2012)).
113. *Id.* at 278.
114. *Id.* (quoting the C & F policies).
115. *Id.* (quoting BLACK'S LAW DICTIONARY 91 (9th ed. 2009)).
116. *Id.* (quoting FLA. STAT. § 558.001 (2012)) (internal quotation marks omitted).
117. *Id.*

The policies' definition of "suit" also required that covered damages be claimed in the alternative dispute resolution proceeding for C & F to owe a duty to defend. This requirement was easily satisfied because chapter 558 explicitly allows claimants to seek damages and provides for "monetary payment" as a means of resolving a claim.[118]

Finally, the *Altman* court noted that the policies required C & F's consent to Altman's submission to an alternative dispute resolution proceeding to trigger C & F's duty to defend. There was no need for the court to address whether C & F consented to Altman's participation in the chapter 558 process, however, because it was beyond the scope of the certified question and because it was a disputed issue of fact in the case.[119]

In *Cincinnati Insurance Co. v. AMSCO Windows*,[120] the insured, AMSCO Windows (AMSCO), manufactured windows. One of its dealers, J & L, sold its windows for installation in homes in Nevada. Some Nevada homeowners sued the contractors who built their homes and alleged that defective windows and their improper installation damaged their homes. The contractors then sued J & L and others, who, in turn, asserted claims against AMSCO.

Some of the homeowners' claims arose under "Chapter 40," a Nevada statute that governs residential construction defect claims.[121] Under Chapter 40, before suing over construction defects, a claimant must provide written notice to the contractor, stating in detail the alleged defects and the nature and extent of the resulting damage. The claimant must then give the contractor a reasonable opportunity to inspect the home and repair any damage. The contractor must forward the claimant's notice to each supplier or subcontractor that the contractor reasonably believes is responsible for a given defect. At the conclusion of this process, any unresolved claims may be litigated in a Nevada state court.

AMSCO tendered its defense of the Nevada homeowners' claims to its CGL insurer, Cincinnati Insurance Co. (Cincinnati), which refused to defend AMSCO. Instead, Cincinnati filed a declaratory judgment action in a Utah federal court seeking a determination that it had no duty to defend or indemnify AMSCO against the Nevada homeowners' claims under Utah law, which governed the interpretation of its policies.[122] Applying Utah law, the district court ruled that Cincinnati had no duty to defend AMSCO in any Chapter 40 proceedings because they were not "suits." AMSCO appealed the district court's decision to the Tenth Circuit.

118. *Id.*
119. *Id.*
120. 593 F. App'x 802 (10th Cir. 2014).
121. *Id.* at 804.
122. *Id.* at 805. Cincinnati insured AMSCO for a five-year period through a series of one-year renewable CGL policies. *Id.* at 804.

The *AMSCO Windows* court began its analysis by observing that Cincinnati's duty to defend extended only to "suits," which the policy defined as "civil proceedings," including certain arbitrations and alternative dispute resolution proceedings.[123] AMSCO argued that "civil proceedings" encompassed the Chapter 40 process because Chapter 40 proceedings (1) are not "criminal," so they must be "civil"; (2) relate to private rights and remedies; (3) involve formal statutory requirements; and (4) involve special masters, mediators, and potentially judges.[124] The Tenth Circuit, however, pointed out that AMSCO had overlooked the key difference between civil proceedings and the Chapter 40 process: while Chapter 40 ostensibly mandates participation by contractors, subcontractors, and suppliers, their failure to join in does not result in any adverse judgment or obligation; rather, it imposes limited consequences in any later litigation.[125] As the court further explained:

> Chapter 40 uses language traditionally interpreted as mandatory—specifically, the terms "must" and "shall"—to require contractors or suppliers to take certain actions in response to homeowner construction defect claims. . . .
>
> However, parties who fail to comply with Chapter 40 face only limited consequences when a claimant's action eventually proceeds to state court. For example, under § 40.650, if a contractor or supplier fails to send a written response to a claimant—responding to each alleged construction defect and stating whether he has elected to repair the defect, offer monetary compensation, or disclaim liability for the defect—then Chapter 40's limitations on damages and defenses to liability in subsequent lawsuits are nullified. *Id.* § 40.650. If a contractor or supplier fails to appear in mediation or refuses to mediate in "good faith," the mediator may choose to issue a report that is admissible in subsequent litigation. *Id.* § 40.680(8).
>
> These results, although serious, are not parallel to the often case-determinative consequences of noncompliance in the context of lawsuits or mandatory arbitrations. Indeed, there are instances when a cost-benefit analysis would lead a contractor to "opt[ ] not to exercise its opportunity to repair" and encourage the claimant to commence litigation.[126]

AMSCO also argued that Cincinnati's provision of coverage in Nevada required it to comply with Nevada law, including a Chapter 40 section stating that an insurer must treat a Chapter 40 claim like a civil action.[127] The district court had rejected this argument on the basis that the parties' agreement that Utah law governed the construction of the Cincinnati policies neutered "Nevada's attempt to dictate the meaning of insurance policy language 'by leg-

123. *Id.* at 809.
124. *Id.*
125. *Id.*
126. *Id.* at 809–10 (footnote omitted).
127. *Id.* at 810.

islative fiat.'"[128] The *AMSCO Windows* court agreed with the district court.[129] Utah law governed the interpretation of the policies. A rule of construction imposed by a Nevada statute did not bind the court even though that rule related to the disputed policy provision.[130] Nor did the Nevada legislature's policy decisions about how to encourage compliance with its pre-litigation procedures apply in Utah. This was especially true given other courts' conclusions that similar proceedings were not "suits" as defined in standard CGL policies.[131]

Finally, even if the court were to conclude that the Chapter 40 process was a "civil proceeding," it would be an "alternative dispute resolution proceeding" as defined in the Cincinnati policies.[132] That determination would not benefit AMSCO, however, because the policies obligated Cincinnati to defend AMSCO in such proceedings only if Cincinnati had consented to AMSCO's participation, which was not the situation here.[133]

In the end, the *AMSCO Windows* court affirmed the district court. The court declined AMSCO's request to certify the issues raised in the appeal to the Utah Supreme Court.

3. Summary

Evaluating an insurer's duty to defend in connection with a notice sent under a right to repair statute starts with the statutory language. In *AMSCO Windows*, for example, the result would have been quite different had Nevada law rather than Utah law controlled the dispute. Absent contrary statutory language, however, a notice under a right to repair statute is not analogous to a lawsuit because such notices are not coercive like a complaint or petition, nor is the related procedure as consequential as litigation.

If the right to repair process can be said to fall within the CGL definition of a "suit," in can only be as an "alternative dispute resolution proceeding" in which the claimant seeks damages because of "property damage." In that instance, the insurer still must consent to the insured's participation in the process for there to be a duty to defend. Whether an insured should participate in the process, whether the insured should seek the insurer's consent to its participation to obtain a defense, and whether the insurer should consent to the insured's participation and furnish a defense, are case- and fact-specific inquiries.

---

128. *Id.* (quoting the district court).
129. *Id.*
130. *Id.*
131. *Id.* (citing Hardesty Builders, Inc. v. Mid-Continent Cas. Co., No. C-10-142, 2010 WL 5146597, at *7–9 (S.D. Tex. Dec. 13, 2010)).
132. *Id.* at 811.
133. *Id.*

E. Other Administrative Actions or Proceedings

Insureds may be named as respondents or defendants in a wide range of administrative proceedings. Whether an insurer must defend its insured in any administrative proceeding requires case-by-case analysis. Courts frequently hold that an insurer owes no duty to defend based on a straightforward reading of policy language.[134]

In *Maine State Academy of Hair Design, Inc. v. Commercial Union Insurance Co.*,[135] Amber Martin complained that she was sexually harassed and discriminated against while employed by the Maine State Academy of Hair Design (the Academy) and was fired when she told a supervisor that she was contemplating a lawsuit over her unlawful treatment. She later filed a complaint with the Maine Human Rights Commission (MHRC). The Academy was insured under a CGL policy issued by Commercial Union Insurance Co. (Commercial Union). The Academy asked that Commercial Union defend it in the MHRC proceeding but Commercial Union refused. The Academy consequently sued Commercial Union in state court but lost at summary judgment. The Academy then appealed to the Maine Supreme Court.

On appeal, the Academy argued that Commercial Union's duty to defend was limited only by the policy's definition of "suit."[136] The Academy further argued that Commercial Union had a duty to defend because the MHRC proceeding was a civil proceeding in which damages were alleged.[137] The Academy was twice wrong.

First, the Commercial Union policy—like any standard CGL policy—clearly stated that the insurer's duty to defend was limited to suits seeking damages covered by the policy, and not just any "suit" included within the policy definition.[138] An MHRC proceeding does not lead to a damage award; rather, the claimant may seek damages only in a subsequent action in a state trial court.[139] Second, an MHRC proceeding is not a prerequisite to a lawsuit based on the same conduct. Instead, filing an MHRC complaint is merely a

134. *See, e.g.*, Dupuis v. Utica Mut. Ins. Co., No. 250766, 2006 WL 1084336, at *5–6 (Mich. Ct. App. Apr. 25, 2006) (concluding that a license revocation proceeding before the insurance commissioner was neither a "suit" nor a "claim," and the proceeding sought a penalty rather than damages); Campbell Soup Co. v. Liberty Mut. Ins. Co., 571 A.2d 1013, 1021 (N.J. Super. Ct. Ch. Div. 1988) ("Campbell Soup Co. . . . is in the conciliation phase of the EEOC process. No suit has been instituted against it by the EEOC. No adjudicatory proceeding has been held. . . . Campbell need not participate in that process if it does not voluntarily agree to so do. It is only after a suit is brought in the federal district court by the EEOC, or the aggrieved employee or prospective employee, that an adjudicatory process commences. It is then, for the first time, that the obligation of the insurer to defend should properly be raised."), *aff'd*, 571 A.2d 969 (N.J. Super. Ct. App. Div. 1990).

135. 699 A.2d 1153 (Me. 1997).

136. *Id.* at 1159.

137. *Id.*

138. *Id.* at 1160.

139. *Id.*

prerequisite to obtaining attorney fees and civil penal damages in a subsequent lawsuit.[140] Commercial Union thus had no duty to defend the Academy in Martin's MHRC proceeding.[141]

Broughton v. Ohio Casualty Insurance Co.[142] arose out of a dispute before the Trademark Trial and Appeal Board (TTAB). A furniture company, Fyrn, and its chief product designer, Roskear Broughton, asserted that Fyrn's CGL insurer, Ohio Casualty, wrongfully refused to defend Broughton in a TTAB proceeding brought by a competing furniture company, FSL, to cancel Broughton's registration of the FYRN trademark. A key issue was whether Ohio Casualty owed a defense under Coverage B in its policy, which provided that it would "pay those sums that the insured becomes legally obligated to pay as damages because of 'personal and advertising injury' to which this insurance applies" and stated that it would "have the right and duty to defend the insured against any 'suit seeking those damages.'"[143]

In alleging that Ohio Casualty breached its duty to defend, Fyrn and Broughton focused on the policy's definition of "suit," which meant "a 'civil proceeding in which damages because of bodily injury, property damage, or personal and advertising injury to which this insurance applies are alleged.'"[144] They maintained that this language required only that damages be alleged in the underlying "suit," and that the TTAB proceeding satisfied this definition because FSL claimed that it was damaged by the FYRN trademark.[145] Fyrn and Broughton also contended that any ambiguity regarding whether Coverage B required that damages must be sought or merely alleged should be resolved in their favor.[146] The *Broughton* court flatly rejected their arguments.

The *Broughton* court succinctly explained that the Ohio Casualty policy clearly and explicitly required a "suit" seeking "those damages," meaning damages because of personal and advertising injury.[147] Although FSL claimed that it was damaged by Fyrn's trademark infringement, it did not seek damages in the TTAB proceeding, and controlling Ninth Circuit authority established that the TTAB had no power to award damages.[148] Accordingly, the TTAB proceeding was not a "suit" seeking covered damages and Ohio Casualty had no duty under Coverage B to defend Broughton or Fyrn in the TTAB proceeding.[149]

140. *Id.*
141. *Id.*
142. 533 F. Supp. 3d 838 (N.D. Cal. 2021).
143. *Id.* at 841–42 (quoting the Ohio Casualty policy).
144. *Id.* at 845 (quoting the Ohio Casualty policy).
145. *Id.*
146. *Id.*
147. *Id.*
148. *Id.* (first citing Rhoades v. Avon Prods., Inc., 504 F.3d 1151, 1158 (9th Cir. 2007); then citing V.V.V. & Sons Edible Oils Ltd. v. Meenakshi Overseas, L.L.C., 946 F.3d 542, 546 (9th Cir. 2019)).
149. *Id.* at 846.

In *Ameron International Corp. v. Insurance Co. of the State of Pennsylvania*,[150] on the other hand, the California Supreme Court held that a proceeding before an administrative law judge of the former U.S. Department of Interior Board of Contract Appeals (IBCA), which involved a multiday trial, witness testimony, the introduction of evidence, and a determination of the insured's monetary liability was "a 'suit' as a reasonable insured would understand the term."[151] As a result, the insurers had a duty to defend the insured, Ameron International Corp. (Ameron), in the IBCA proceeding.[152] The IBCA proceeding was a result of Ameron appealing a decision by a contracting officer of the Department of the Interior's Bureau of Land Reclamation (the Bureau) that concrete siphons Ameron made were flawed and that Ameron and its indemnitee consequently owed $40 million in damages to the government.

In concluding that the IBCA proceeding was a "suit," the court compared the IBCA's complaint requirements to those found in the California Code of Civil Procedure. The court also examined Congress's intent in establishing the IBCA, and considered the structure of the IBCA proceedings themselves.

The IBCA was created under the federal Contract Disputes Act of 1978, with statutory authority to conduct trials, determine liability, and award money damages. Congress intended the IBCA to serve as a vehicle for resolving contract disputes quickly, informally, and inexpensively. Congress created concurrent jurisdiction in the U.S. Court of Claims (now the U.S. Court of Federal Claims) and the IBCA to hear appeals from federal contracting officers' decisions. Ameron thus had a choice of forums in which to appeal the decision of the Bureau's contracting officer, and it selected the IBCA.[153]

IBCA procedures required a contractor appealing a Bureau contracting officer's decision "to file a complaint, 'setting forth simple, concise, and direct statements of each claim, alleging the basis with appropriate reference to contract provisions for each claim, and the dollar amount claimed.'"[154] An IBCA complaint must "fulfill the generally recognized requirements of a complaint."[155] Although the contractor initiates an IBCA proceeding, the purpose of the proceeding is to resolve the claim against the contractor, who is thus cast as a defendant.[156] Moreover, the Code of Federal Regulations (C.F.R.) labels the required IBCA pleading a "complaint" and the requirements for that complaint serve the same notice purpose as California's civil complaint requirement.[157]

---

150. 242 P.3d 1020 (Cal. 2010).
151. *Id.* at 1022.
152. *Id.* at 1030. The CGL policies at issue in *Ameron* did not define the term "suit." *Id.* at 1022.
153. *Id.* at 1028.
154. *Id.* (quoting 43 C.F.R. § 4.107(a) (2009)).
155. *Id.* (quoting 43 C.F.R. § 4.107(a) (2009)).
156. *Id.* at 1028–29.
157. *Id.* at 1029.

It was clear to the court that the IBCA pleading requirements met the standards for a complaint under the California Code of Civil Procedure.[158] The specificity required of an IBCA complaint afforded an insurer as much, if not more, notice regarding claims against an insured than did the specificity mandated by the California Code of Civil Procedure.[159] If there were any doubt whether Congress intended an IBCA complaint to serve the same purpose as a complaint in a court of law, the C.F.R. dispelled it: "This pleading shall fulfill the generally recognized requirements of a complaint."[160] Long story short, it would exalt form over substance to find that an IBCA complaint did not qualify as a "suit" simply because the IBCA was not a court of law, especially where, as here, the insurers argued that they rely on the substantive contents of a complaint to make coverage decisions.[161]

Finally, the *Ameron* court considered Ameron's reasonable expectations in concluding that the IBCA proceeding was a "suit." To start, relevant sections of the United States Code used the term "suit" to describe the IBCA complaint process. Based on those references, the court explained, a reasonable policyholder would believe that an insurance policy providing coverage for a "suit" would cover an IBCA proceeding.[162] In addition, an IBCA proceeding affords a contractor its "day in court."[163] Ameron's IBCA hearing spanned 22 days, during which witnesses testified and evidence was introduced. The parties then mediated their dispute and reached a settlement in which Ameron agreed to pay the government $10 million. Certainly, a reasonable policyholder would recognize such proceedings as a suit and would expect to be defended and, if necessary, indemnified by its insurer.[164]

F. Pre-Suit Demand Letters

We have discussed PRP letters and similar notices from government agencies, but those are not "demand letters" as that term is commonly understood in litigation.[165] Potential plaintiffs often send demand letters to insureds before fil-

158. *Id.*
159. *Id.*
160. *Id.* (quoting 43 C.F.R. § 4.107(a) (2009)).
161. *Id.*
162. *Id.* at 1030.
163. *Id.* (internal quotation marks omitted).
164. *Id.*
165. Courts distinguish PRP letters and analogous letters from state agencies from demand letters sent in other contexts (sometimes described as "conventional," "garden variety," or "simple" demand letters), thereby clearly implying—if not outright stating—that a letter in the latter category is not a "suit." *See, e.g.*, N. Sec. Ins. Co. v. Mitec Telecom, Inc., 38 F. Supp. 2d 345, 348 (D. Vt. 1999) (distinguishing a "conventional demand letter" from a PRP letter); A.Y. McDonald Indus., Inc. v. Ins. Co. of N. Am., 475 N.W.2d 607, 628 (Iowa 1991) (stating that an EPA demand letter "is not the same as a conventional demand letter based on a personal injury claim"); Hazen Paper Co. v. U.S. Fid. & Guar. Co., 555 N.E.2d 576, 581 (Mass. 1990) ("The EPA letter was not the equivalent of a conventional

ing suit. A demand letter usually seeks a monetary payment to compensate the putative plaintiff for claimed harm attributable to the insured's alleged misconduct and threatens litigation if the parties cannot resolve the matter informally. Courts generally do not treat such demand letters as a "suit" that triggers an insurer's duty to defend.[166] That is the correct approach. Although an insured may need to inform its insurer that it received a demand letter to comply with the notice requirement in its policy, the insured's rights or liability generally will not be affected by a failure to respond to the demand letter. For that matter, a party's decision to ignore a demand letter that threatens litigation will not necessarily result in litigation. A demand letter is simply not sufficiently coercive or consequential to count as the functional equivalent of a lawsuit. In addition, a demand letter is neither an alternative dispute resolution proceeding in and of itself nor does it represent the initiation of one, even if it invites the insured to negotiate a settlement.

Sanders v. Phoenix Insurance Co.[167] is generally considered the leading case on demand letters in connection with the duty to defend. In *Sanders*, a lawyer described only as John Doe had a sexual relationship with a client, Nancy Andersen, who he knew suffered from severe depression and anxiety. When Doe's ardor cooled and he did not meet Andersen at her apartment as he had promised, Andersen became distraught and drank herself to death. The executor of Andersen's estate, Harry Sanders, sent Doe a demand letter pursuant to a Massachusetts statute commonly known as Chapter 93A.[168] A party who fails to respond to a Chapter 93A demand letter or make a reasonable

---

demand letter based on a personal injury claim."); McGinnes Indus. Maint. Corp. v. Phoenix Ins. Co., 477 S.W.3d 786, 792 (Tex. 2015) (footnote omitted) ("[A] simple demand letter threatening or prefacing a lawsuit is nothing like a PRP letter or unilateral administrative order, which, to use the United States Supreme Court's choice of words, 'command' compliance.").

166. *See, e.g.*, Houston Cas. Co. v. Swinerton Builders, No. 20-cv-03558-NYW, 2022 WL 523434, at *13–16 (D. Colo. Feb. 22, 2022) (applying Colorado law and concluding that a demand letter is neither a "suit" nor an "alternative dispute resolution proceeding"); Nat'l Mech. Servs., Inc. v. Kinsale Ins. Co., 634 F. Supp. 3d 907, 909 (S.D. Cal. 2022) (applying California law); Crescent City Baptist Church v. Church Mut. Ins. Co., No. CIV.A. 05-2200, 2006 WL 508060, at *5 (E.D. La. Feb. 22, 2006) ("Under the unambiguous terms of the . . . policy, a demand letter is not a 'suit.' 'Suit' requires the existence of a civil proceeding, a forced or consented to arbitration, or a consented to alternative dispute resolution proceeding. A demand letter does not remotely constitute any of these. As a result, even if the . . . demand letter asserted demand for monetary relief, it still would not trigger the duty to defend . . . because it is not a 'suit.'"); Monarch Greenback, LLC v. Monticello Ins. Co., 118 F. Supp. 2d 1068, 1075 (D. Idaho 1999) ("[A] demand letter from a private corporation does not fall into the policy's definition of 'suit.' Even using the most liberal construction of a 'civil proceeding' favoring [the insured], a demand letter from a private organization does not meet the requirements of a civil proceeding. A demand letter does not qualify as a proceeding in front of a court, agency, tribunal, bureau, or someone authorized by the court to do so. . . ."); Samson v. Allstate Ins. Co., 949 F. Supp. 748, 752–53 (N.D. Cal. 1996) (explaining that a "garden variety" demand letter was not a "suit" that triggered the insurer's duty to defend); Zecco, Inc. v. Travelers, Inc., 938 F. Supp. 65, 68–69 (D. Mass. 1996) (applying Massachusetts law and explaining why the demand letter was not a "suit").

167. 843 F.3d 37 (1st Cir. 2016).

168. *Id.* at 41.

settlement offer in certain kinds of cases may be exposed to double or treble damages, attorney fees, and costs.[169]

Because some of his romantic interludes with Andersen occurred at his home, Doe notified his homeowner's insurer, Phoenix Insurance Co. (Phoenix), about Sanders's letter. Phoenix denied coverage. Eventually, Doe agreed that his liability to Sanders amounted to $500,000 and assigned to Sanders all his rights under his policy with Phoenix as a result of its alleged failure to defend or indemnify him.[170] Sanders then sued Phoenix in a Massachusetts state court. Phoenix removed the suit to federal court and successfully moved to dismiss the case. Sanders promptly appealed to the First Circuit.

On appeal, Sanders argued that Phoenix owed Doe a defense on the theory that a Chapter 93A letter is akin to a PRP letter because the failure to respond to a Chapter 93A letter or to make a reasonable settlement offer can expose an insured to multiple damages, attorney fees, and costs.[171] The First Circuit, however, reasoned that a Chapter 93A demand letter is more like a demand letter in a personal injury case, which does not trigger an insurer's duty to defend.[172] An insured's failure to participate in the administrative process a PRP letter launches would eviscerate its case. Ignoring a Chapter 93A demand letter, on the other hand, will not substantially impair the insured's position; a failure to respond has much lesser consequences than stiff-arming EPA.[173] Notably, Doe's liability could not have been affected by the Chapter 93A letter and his exposure to statutory damages, attorney fees, and costs would only come to pass if a court found him liable for Andersen's death.[174]

In the end, the *Sanders* court equated Chapter 93A demand letters "to demand letters sent in anticipation of garden-variety personal injury litigation."[175] After addressing some other issues, the First Circuit affirmed the district court's judgment for Phoenix.

Sanders is noteworthy because the court adhered to "the general rule that there is no duty to defend before the filing of a suit"[176] even though Doe's failure to respond to Sanders's Chapter 93A demand letter had greater potential ramifications than would ignoring any other pre-suit demand letter outside the

169. Mass. Gen. Laws ch. 93A, § 9(3)–(4) (2022).

170. Sanders also demanded a settlement from Doe's law firm. The firm agreed to pay Sanders $500,000 to settle the estate's claims against the firm. That still left Doe personally liable, however, hence his admission of liability in the amount of the Phoenix policy limits and his assignment of rights. *See Sanders*, 843 F.3d at 43.

171. *Id.* at 44.

172. *Id.* (quoting Hazen Paper Co. v. U.S. Fid. & Guar. Co., 555 N.E.2d 576, 581 (Mass. 1990)).

173. *Id.* (quoting *Hazen Paper*, 555 N.E.2d at 580).

174. *Id.*

175. *Id.* at 45.

176. *Id.* at 43.

environmental liability context.[177] Again, typical demand letters simply are not so coercive nor are the consequences of ignoring them so immediate or severe that they can be equated with a lawsuit. That is true even where the would-be defendant's failure to respond to the demand letter may expose it to liability for prejudgment interest, attorney fees, or enhanced damages if it loses a subsequent lawsuit.

G. Summary

An insurer's duty to defend generally does not arise until the insured is sued.[178] This result frequently is dictated by the policy's definition of "suit," although even in the absence of a definition, "suit" as used in a liability policy is generally understood to describe a lawsuit filed in a court. In comparison, under an "occurrence" policy, an insurer has no duty to defend a "claim" against an insured. Rather, the insurer enjoys the discretion to investigate and settle a claim against the insured.[179] As the standard CGL policy states: "We may, at our discretion, investigate any 'occurrence' and settle any claim or 'suit' that may result."[180] Clearly, "claim" and "suit" are not synonymous.[181] Were it otherwise, one of those terms would be rendered superfluous, which would violate basic rules of contract interpretation. In sum, the term "suit" generally refers to a proceeding filed in a court, while a "claim" may be any number of actions, events, or things that do not rise to the formal level of a lawsuit.[182] These might include a demand letter, a document a party must file as a prerequisite to suing a governmental entity or agency, or documents used to initiate various administrative proceedings.[183]

There are a few recurring exceptions to the general rule that the term "suit" confines an insurer's duty to defend to a lawsuit against an insured filed in a court: (1) obviously, any other actions or proceedings explicitly provided for in a policy; (2) PRP letters sent by EPA and state agencies; and (3) if characterized

177. *But see* Cytosol Labs., Inc. v. Fed. Ins. Co., 536 F. Supp. 2d 80, 87 (D. Mass. 2008) (stating that a Chapter 93A demand letter triggered the insurer's duty to defend).

178. Ayers v. State Farm Mut. Auto. Ins. Co., 316 F. Supp. 3d 1324, 1328–30 (M.D. Fla. 2018); Santa Clara Valley Water Dist. v. Century Indem. Co., 306 Cal. Rptr. 3d 724, 753 (Ct. App. 2023); Phila. Indem. Ins. Co. v. Pace Suburban Bus Serv., 67 N.E.3d 556, 568 (Ill. App. Ct. 2016); Mahan v. Am. Std. Ins. Co., 862 N.E.2d 669, 676 (Ind. Ct. App. 2007); Tenneco Inc. v. Amerisure Mut. Ins. Co., 761 N.W.2d 846, 861 (Mich. Ct. App. 2008); Chief Indus., Inc. v. Great N. Ins. Co., 683 N.W.2d 374, 382 (Neb. 2004); NL Corp. v. Seneca Specialty Ins. Co., No. 28927, 2021 WL 1828100, at *5 (Ohio Ct. App. May 7, 2021); Black v. Allstate Ins. Co., 100 P.3d 1163, 1170 (Utah 2004).

179. San Diego Hous. Comm'n v. Indus. Indem. Co., 80 Cal. Rptr. 2d 393, 400 (Ct. App. 1998).

180. Ins. Servs. Off., Inc., Commercial General Liability Coverage Form (CG 00 01 04 13), at 1 (2012).

181. Lapham-Hickey Steel Corp. v. Prot. Mut. Ins. Co., 655 N.E.2d 842, 847–48 (Ill. 1995).

182. Fireman's Fund. Ins. Co. v. Super. Ct., 78 Cal. Rptr. 2d 418, 425 (Ct. App. 1997).

183. *Id.*

as alternative dispute resolution proceedings, notices under right to repair statutes. Of course, apart from those expressly provided for in a policy, not all courts recognize all these exceptions. More broadly, whether an administrative proceeding constitutes a "suit" or is the functional equivalent of one depends on the nature of the proceeding. The more the proceeding resembles a lawsuit in a court of law, the more likely it is that it will be deemed a "suit" for duty to defend purposes. *Ameron* richly illustrates this last point.

Additionally, for the insurer to have a duty to defend, any "suit" must seek damages covered by the policy. Unless a policy defines the term differently, "damages" describes a monetary award to compensate a plaintiff for harm caused by an insured. Standard CGL, auto liability, and homeowners policies do not define "damages," but professional liability policies and other forms of liability insurance may define the term.

Finally, an insurer may choose to assume an insured's defense before a suit is filed. In some situations, that may be a wise strategic choice. In other instances, an insurer may opt to defend an insured in an action in which damages are not sought. An insurer's voluntary assumption of an insured's defense in the absence of a "suit," however, should not be mistaken for a duty to do so in that case or any other. The same is true where an insurer makes a business or strategic decision to defend an insured in a proceeding in which the adversary does not seek damages.

IV. Triggering the Duty to Defend

A. Actual Notice of the Suit versus Tender of the Defense

Courts often say that an insurer's duty to defend requires it to act "immediately" when a suit against an insured alleges facts that are potentially within the coverage afforded by the applicable insurance policy.[184] An insurer obviously can have no duty to defend a suit of which it is unaware.[185] But assuming that the insurer receives notice of the lawsuit from the insured or even from another party, is such notice sufficient to trigger the insurer's duty to defend or must the insured formally "tender" its defense to the insurer?

184. *See, e.g.*, L.A. Terminals, Inc. v. United Nat'l Ins. Co., 608 F. Supp. 3d 968, 982 (C.D. Cal. 2022) ("To defend meaningfully, an insurer must defend immediately and entirely."); State Farm Mut. Auto. Ins. Co. v. Freyer, 312 P.3d 403, 415 (Mont. 2013) ("The . . . duty to defend requires an insurer to act immediately to defend the insured from a claim.").

185. Dreaded, Inc. v. St. Paul Guardian Ins. Co., 904 N.E.2d 1267, 1273 (Ind. 2009); Rent-A-Roofer, Inc. v. Farm Bureau Prop. & Cas. Ins. Co., 869 N.W.2d 99, 107 (Neb. 2015).

1. *Actual Notice of the Suit against the Insured Triggers the Insurer's Duty to Defend*

Because the essence of the duty to defend is providing the insured with a defense in litigation in which the insured's potential liability is at issue, many courts hold that the duty to defend arises when the insurer has actual notice of the litigation.[186] "Actual notice" requires that the insurer (1) know of the lawsuit and (2) know that the complaint alleges facts that are at least potentially within coverage.[187] Both prongs of the test must be met for the insurer to have actual notice of a lawsuit against the insured and thus a duty to defend.[188] Under the actual notice approach, the insured is not required to expressly request a defense to trigger the insurer's duty to defend.[189] In fact, notice sufficient to trigger the insurer's duty to defend may come from someone other than the insured.[190] For example, a plaintiff's lawyer who knows the identity of a defendant's insurer might send the insurer a copy of the complaint that the lawyer has filed and, by doing so, trigger the insurer's duty to defend the lawsuit. The key is that the insurer receives sufficient information to locate and defend the case.

The actual notice approach to triggering the duty to defend does not automatically require the insurer to involve itself in the litigation against the insured. In the commercial context, for example, the insured may not want the insurer to defend it where the insured is an additional insured under another entity's policy or where the insured is owed a defense and indemnity under a contract with another party. In those situations, the insured may want to avoid any negative loss history with respect to its own policy, which it can do by relying on a defense and indemnity from another party's insurer or from another party rather than requesting a defense from its insurer. In any event, an insurer that learns of a lawsuit against its insured should inquire whether the insured

186. *See, e.g.*, Ash Grove Cement Co. v. Liberty Mut. Ins. Co., 649 F. App'x 585, 588 (9th Cir. 2016) (discussing Oregon law); Am. Serv. Ins. Co. v. China Ocean Shipping Co. (Americas) Inc., 932 N.E.2d 8, 19 (Ill. App. Ct. 2010); Vaughn v. Franklin, 785 So. 2d 79, 87 (La. Ct. App. 2001); Baker Donelson Bearman & Caldwell, P.C. v. Muirhead, 920 So. 2d 440, 451 (Miss. 2006); White Mountain Cable Constr. Co. v. Transamerica Ins. Co., 631 A.2d 907, 910 (N.H. 1993); Garcia v. Underwriters at Lloyd's, London, 182 P.3d 113, 118–19 (N.M. 2007); Kubit v. MAG Mut. Ins. Co., 708 S.E.2d 138, 154 (N.C. Ct. App. 2011); Johnson Controls, Inc. v. Emps. Ins. of Wausau, 665 N.W.2d 257, 283 (Wis. 2003).

187. Cincinnati Cos. v. W. Am. Ins Co., 701 N.E.2d 499, 505 (Ill. 1998); *Baker Donelson*, 920 So. 2d at 451.

188. Home Ins. Co. v. U.S. Fid. & Guar. Ins. Co., 755 N.E.2d 122, 132 (Ill. App. Ct. 2001).

189. Harriman v. Associated Indus. Ins. Co., 544 F. Supp. 3d 605, 614 (D.S.C. 2021) (applying South Carolina law); Travelers Indem. Co. of Ill. v. United Food & Com. Workers Int'l Union, 770 A.2d 978, 991 (D.C. 2001); Progressive Ins. Co. v. Universal Cas. Co., 807 N.E.2d 577, 587 (Ill. App. Ct. 2004); Murphy-Brown, LLC v. ACE Am. Ins. Co., No. 19 CVS 02793, 2020 WL 7711360, at *17 (N.C. Bus. Ct. Dec. 22, 2020).

190. Ins. Co. of Ill. v. Fed. Kemper Ins. Co., 683 N.E.2d 947, 950 (Ill. App. Ct. 1997); Nat'l Indem. Co. v. State, 499 P.3d 516, 528 (Mont. 2021); *Garcia*, 182 P.3d at 120.

wants a defense. If the insured declines a defense, or is unresponsive or uncooperative, the insurer's duty to defend will be excused.[191] If, on the other hand, the insured requests a defense—which seems more likely—the insurer's duty to defend continues.[192]

It is possible that in a case with multiple defendants, more than one of them may be insured by the same insurance company. If one of the insured defendants gives the insurer notice of the lawsuit, that notice triggers the insurer's duty to defend only with respect to that insured defendant; it does not suffice as notice for any other insured defendant. Moreover, the insurer does not need to scour its records to determine whether it insures any of the other defendants in the case.[193]

Courts offer three reasons for preferring actual notice as the duty to defend trigger over a specific request for a defense by the insured. First, the insurer is normally in a better position than even a sophisticated insured to know the scope of the coverage its policy provides and its duties under the policy.[194] Given this general disparity in information and knowledge of insurance law, it makes little practical sense to interpret an insured's silence as a statement of intent to forgo its insurer's assistance in litigation, especially since an insured usually does, in fact, want the insurer to defend it.[195] In addition, requiring the insurer to simply inquire of the insured whether it wants a defense—a requirement that the insurer can satisfy through a letter or telephone call to the insured—places no burden to speak of on the insurer.[196] Second, allowing actual notice of a suit to trigger the duty to defend best ensures that the insured receives the benefits of the insurance contract.[197] The insurer, having collected a premium for the policy and knowing about the lawsuit against the insured, should not be allowed to evade its contractual obligations through the insured's lack of awareness.[198] Third, the state has an interest in having an

---

191. *Cincinnati Cos.*, 701 N.E.2d at 504.

192. *Id.*

193. Town of Mount Pleasant v. Hartford Accident & Indem. Co., 625 N.W.2d 317, 321 (Wis. Ct. App. 2001).

194. *Cincinnati Cos.*, 701 N.E.2d at 504–05.

195. *Id.* at 505.

196. *Id.*; *see also* Garcia v. Underwriters at Lloyd's, London, 182 P.3d 113, 118 (N.M. 2007) ("Given that the entire purpose of the contract between the parties is for the insurer to defend and cover the liabilities incurred by its insured, it makes sense for the insurer to assume that the insured desires a defense and to seek clarification if any notice it receives is unclear on that point."); Towne Realty, Inc. v. Zurich Ins. Co., 548 N.W.2d 64, 67 (Wis. 1996) ("[I]f it is unclear or ambiguous whether the insured wishes the insurer to defend the suit, it becomes the responsibility of the insurer to communicate with the insured before the insurer unilaterally forgoes the defense. . . . Despite Zurich's protestations, this holding should not create an onerous duty for insurers: a simple letter requesting clarification of the insured's position should suffice.") (citation and footnotes omitted).

197. *Cincinnati Cos.*, 701 N.E.2d at 505.

198. *Id.* (citing Federated Mut. Ins. Co. v. State Farm Mut. Auto. Ins. Co., 668 N.E.2d 627, 633 (Ill. App. Ct. 1996)).

insured adequately represented in litigation against it.[199] A rule that requires only actual notice rather than a formal tender to trigger the duty to defend protects the state's interest.[200]

2. *Tender of the Defense Is Required to Trigger the Duty to Defend*

In contrast to the actual notice approach, some courts take a narrower view and hold that an insurer's duty arises upon the insured's tender of its defense.[201] Tendering a defense distills to the insured's request that the insurer defend the insured in a lawsuit.[202] Until the insured requests a defense, the insurer is under no duty to provide one, even if the insurer is aware of the litigation against the insured.[203]

The insured generally tenders its defense simply by notifying the insurer of the lawsuit.[204] Although some courts require that the insured specifically request a defense at the time it notifies the insurer of the suit,[205] most courts consider the mere act of sending the suit papers to the insurer sufficient for tender. By sending the suit papers to the insurer, the insured gives the insurer notice of the lawsuit and the opportunity to defend it, which is the essence of tender.[206] Otherwise, the term "tender" does not connote any unique requirements.[207] There are no magic words that an insured must recite to validly

199. *Id.*

200. *Id.* (citing *Federated Mut.*, 668 N.E.2d at 633).

201. *See, e.g.*, Santa Clara Valley Water Dist. v. Century Indem. Co., 306 Cal. Rptr. 3d 724, 748 (Ct. App. 2023) (quoting Foster-Gardner, Inc. v. Nat'l Union Fire Ins. Co., 959 P.2d 265, 285 (Cal. 1998)); Remodeling Dimensions, Inc. v. Integrity Mut. Ins. Co., 819 N.W.2d 602, 616 (Minn. 2012); Allstate Ins. Co. v. Miller, 212 P.3d 318, 325 (Nev. 2009); Summerhaze Co., L.C. v. Fed. Deposit Ins. Corp., 332 P.3d 908, 920–21 (Utah 2014); Mut. of Enumclaw Ins. Co. v. USF Ins. Co., 191 P.3d 866, 873 (Wash. 2008).

202. Crawford v. Belhaven Realty LLC, 109 N.E.3d 763, 772–73 (Ill. App. Ct. 2018).

203. Moreno v. Sentinel Ins. Co., Ltd., 35 F.4th 965, 975 (5th Cir. 2022) (applying Texas law); Gen. Refractories Co. v. First State Ins. Co., 94 F. Supp. 3d 649, 663 (E.D. Pa. 2015) (applying Pennsylvania law); Detroit Auto. Inter-Ins. Exch. v. Higginbotham, 290 N.W.2d 414, 417 (Mich. Ct. App. 1980); First Bank of Turley v. Fid. & Deposit Ins. Co. of Md., 928 P.2d 298, 304 (Okla. 1996).

204. *See* Travelers Indem. Co. of Ill. v. United Food & Com. Workers Int'l Union, 770 A.2d 978, 991 (D.C. 2001) (quoting 14 Couch on Insurance 3d § 200:35 (1999)); White Mountain Cable Constr. Co. v. Transamerica Ins. Co., 631 A.2d 907, 910 (N.H. 1993) ("[I]n order for an insured to tender the defense to the insurer, it need only put the insurer on notice of the claim."); Johnson Controls, Inc. v. Emps. Ins. of Wausau, 665 N.W.2d 257, 283 (Wis. 2003) ("A tender of defense occurs when the insurer has notice that there is a claim against the insured."); *see also* Cherry v. Am. Country Ins. Co., 449 F. Supp. 3d 701, 712 (E.D. Mich. 2020) (providing the insurer with "adequate information" about the lawsuit suffices for tender).

205. *See, e.g.*, Nat'l Union Fire Ins. Co. v. Crocker, 246 S.W.3d 603, 608 (Tex. 2008).

206. *See* Home Ins. Co. v. Nat'l Union Fire Ins. Co., 658 N.W.2d 522, 532 (Minn. 2003); Summerhaze Co., L.C. v. Fed. Deposit Ins. Corp., 332 P.3d 908, 920 (Utah 2014).

207. Jerry & Richmond, *supra* note 7, at 711; *see* Snohomish Cnty. v. Allied World Nat'l Assur. Co., 276 F. Supp. 3d 1046, 1054 (W.D. Wash. 2017) ("The concept of 'tender' merely connotes a certain form of notice from an insured to its insurer, communicating its belief that the insurer's obligations of coverage and defense have been triggered by an event or series of events and inviting the insurer's participation. The mechanism by which that is accomplished need not be complicated nor [sic] overly formal.").

tender its defense.[208] In fact, insureds usually request a defense simply by providing the suit papers to their insurance agent or broker, who, in turn, forwards them to the insurer. In other instances, the insurance policy may specify how the insured is to give the insurer notice of a suit, as where a policy provides a claims department telephone number for the insured to call, an email address to enable the insured to report a claim or suit electronically, or a fax number to send suit papers by facsimile.

B. Targeted Tender of the Defense

An insured may be insured under more than one liability insurance policy that applies to a lawsuit. For instance, a landowner may be named as an additional insured on a general contractor's CGL policy. To use another example, a doctor may be covered for alleged malpractice under a personal professional liability policy and under a hospital's policy. In any event, an insured may prefer to be indemnified under one policy and not the other because of differing liability limits, deductibles, or retentions, or because by obtaining coverage under another party's policy, the insured can avoid any negative effects on its own loss history, such as increased future premiums or even cancellation of the policy. These situations implicate the "targeted tender" doctrine, also called the "selective tender" doctrine.[209]

The targeted tender doctrine allows an insured covered by multiple concurrent primary policies to pick which insurer will defend and indemnify it in connection with a lawsuit.[210] The targeted tender doctrine does not apply to consecutive policies.[211] The targeted tender doctrine does not apply to auto policies either because doing so would contravene the public policy contained in statutes mandating insurance coverage.[212]

Courts often describe concurrent insurers from which the insured does not request a defense as having been "deselected." The targeted tender doctrine is based on the principle that an insured has a "paramount right" to choose or knowingly forgo an insurer's assistance in its defense.[213] The targeted tender doctrine further permits an insured to "deactivate" coverage with an insurer

208. Osborne Constr. Co. v. Zurich Am. Ins. Co., 356 F. Supp. 3d 1085, 1094 (W.D. Wash. 2018).

209. *See* Nat'l Union Fire Ins. Co. v. Am. Motorists Ins. Co., 707 F.3d 797, 802 (7th Cir. 2013) ("The 'targeted tender' doctrine of insurance law allows an insured with multiple insurers to pick one to seek indemnity from and thus leave the others in peace. . . . Commonly . . . the 'targeted' insurer is not the insured's principal insurer, as the insured would especially not want *that* insurer to raise its premiums to punish the insured for having submitted a big claim.") (citations omitted).

210. Kajima Constr. Servs., Inc. v. St. Paul Fire & Marine Ins. Co., 879 N.E.2d 305, 309 (Ill. 2007).

211. Greenwich Ins. Co. v. John Sexton Sand & Gravel Corp., No. 1-15-1606, 2016 WL 4035709, at *14 (Ill. App. Ct. June 24, 2016); Ill. Sch. Dist. Agency v. St. Charles Cmty. Unit Sch. Dist. 303, 971 N.E.2d 1099, 1109–10 (Ill. App. Ct. 2012).

212. Statewide Ins. Co. v. Houston Gen. Ins. Co., 920 N.E.2d 611, 627 (Ill. App. Ct. 2009).

213. AMCO Ins. Co. v. Cincinnati Ins. Co., 10 N.E.3d 374, 378 (Ill. App. Ct. 2014).

that is defending it and tender its defense to another concurrent insurer.[214] Although relieved from any immediate obligation to the insured, the deactivated insurer or a deselected insurer must be prepared to step in and defend the insured should the targeted insurer decline to provide a defense.[215]

When an insured selects one insurer to defend and indemnify it and knowingly forgoes coverage afforded by another carrier, the targeted insurer becomes solely responsible for defending and indemnifying the insured up to its policy limits and it cannot seek equitable contribution from a deselected insurer.[216] The presence of an "other insurance" clause in the targeted insurer's policy does not alter this rule.[217] Consistent with the doctrine of horizontal exhaustion, however, where defense or indemnity costs exceed the targeted primary insurer's policy limits, the deselected insurer's primary policy must pay before the insured can seek coverage under the targeted insurer's excess or umbrella policy.[218] In a capsule, the targeted tender doctrine permits an insured to tender its defense to any of its primary insurers, even though those insurers have "other insurance" clauses in their policies, but it does not permit the insured to force an excess insurer to accept a tender of primary coverage.[219]

For an insured to have a paramount right to select which of several insurers will defend it under the targeted tender doctrine, the insured must have paid a premium for the targeted policy or have bargained for coverage under it.[220] Being a named insured or an additional insured on a policy, or otherwise being provided with coverage under another person's or entity's policy by agreement, is significant for targeted tender purposes because:

> [T]he rationale for allowing an insured to deselect coverage is that it vests the named insured with the right to choose between two policies for which the named insured has either paid the premium or negotiated for the right to be on the policy. In contrast, when a party has only contracted with, and paid the premium for, one policy and attempts to deselect its policy in favor of a policy

---

214. *Id.*; Chi. Hosp. Risk Pooling Prog. v. Ill. State Med. Inter-Ins. Exch., 925 N.E.2d 1216, 1234–35 (Ill. App. Ct. 2010); Legion Ins. Co. v. Empire Fire & Marine Ins. Co., 822 N.E.2d 1, 5 (Ill. App. Ct. 2004).

215. *See Chi. Hosp. Risk Pooling Prog.*, 925 N.E.2d at 1235 (citation omitted) ("A target tender is not negated merely by an expressed desire to keep the deactivated insurer on notice as standby coverage in the event that the selected insurer refuses the tender. . . ."); *Legion Ins. Co.*, 822 N.E.2d at 7 (referring to the deselected insurer's obligation as being limited to providing "standby coverage").

216. Cincinnati Cos. v. W. Am. Ins. Co., 701 N.E.2d 499, 503 (Ill. 1998); Mut. of Enumclaw Ins. Co. v. USF Ins. Co., 191 P.3d 866, 878 (Wash. 2008).

217. John Burns Constr. Co. v. Ind. Ins. Co., 727 N.E.2d 211, 217 (Ill. 2000); Capitol Constr. Sols., Inc. v. Selective Ins. Co. of S.C., No. 1-20-0808, 2022 WL 3088415, at *4 (Ill. App. Ct. Aug. 3, 2022); United Nat'l Ins. Co. v. 200 N. Dearborn P'ship, 979 N.E.2d 920, 929 (Ill. App. Ct. 2012).

218. Kajima Constr. Servs., Inc. v. St. Paul Fire & Marine Ins. Co., 879 N.E.2d 305, 314 (Ill. 2007); Am. Guarantee & Liab. Ins. Co. v. EXP US Servs., No. 1-21-0821, 2023 WL 1881939, at *7 (Ill. App. Ct. Feb. 10, 2023).

219. *Capitol Constr. Sols.*, 2022 WL 3088415, at *5.

220. Vedder v. Cont'l W. Ins. Co., 978 N.E.2d 1111, 1117 (Ill. App. Ct. 2012).

> on which it has not paid the premium or negotiated to be the named insured, this rationale is inapplicable.[221]

An insured's coverage under a policy as an omnibus insured, standing alone, will not support targeted tender.[222]

The targeted tender doctrine has not been widely adopted outside of Illinois. Indeed, only two other states currently appear to follow the doctrine: Montana and Washington.[223] For that matter, few courts outside of Illinois have even considered the doctrine.[224] In *Insurance Co. of the State of Pennsylvania v. Great Northern Insurance Co.*,[225] the Massachusetts Supreme Judicial Court explained that selective tender conflicted with Massachusetts law governing late notice of a suit.[226] The court also reasoned that the doctrine violated Massachusetts public policy where liability insurance is concerned:[227]

> Its adoption would also be contrary to sound public policy because it would reward insurers that try to ignore their coverage obligations at the expense of those that conscientiously honor them. Under the selective tender [doctrine], an insured that has two insurers of the same risk might choose to tender the claim to the insurance company that will promptly honor and pay the claim with minimum inconvenience and paperwork, and avoid tendering the claim to the insurance company that would delay payment of the claim and maximize the inconvenience and paperwork involved in obtaining payment. Selective tender would prevent the conscientious insurer from seeking equitable contribution from its less conscientious coinsurer. It would reward the "bad" insurer, who would be spared paying its fair share of the claim, and punish the "good" insurer, who would be required to pay the entirety of the claim alone.

221. *Id.*; *see also* State Auto Prop. & Cas. Ins. Co., 916 N.E.2d 157, 161 (Ill. App. Ct. 2009) (providing this rationale).

222. *See, e.g.*, *Vedder*, 978 N.E.2d at 1117; Pekin Ins. Co. v. Fid. & Guar. Ins. Co., 830 N.E.2d 10, 19 (Ill. App. Ct. 2005).

223. *See* XL Specialty Ins. Co. v. Progressive Cas. Ins. Co., 411 F. App'x 78, 81 (9th Cir. 2011) (first citing Cas. Indem. Exch. Ins. Co. v. Liberty Nat'l Fire Ins. Co., 902 F. Supp. 1235, 1238 (D. Mont. 1995); then citing Mut. of Enumclaw Ins. Co. v. USF Ins. Co., 191 P.3d 866, 873 (Wash. 2008)).

224. *See, e.g.*, Am. States Ins. Co. v. Nat'l Fire Ins. Co. of Hartford, 135 Cal. Rptr. 3d 177, 187 n.8 (Ct. App. 2011) (observing that the selective tender rule appeared to be inconsistent with California law); *see also* Workers Comp. Fund v. Utah Bus. Ins. Co., 296 P.3d 734, 739 (Utah 2013) (concluding that Utah's statutory scheme prevented the court from adopting the targeted tender doctrine in the workers compensation context).

225. 45 N.E.3d 1283 (Mass. 2016).

226. *See id.* at 1289 ("[I]n Massachusetts, an insured's failure to tender a claim by giving timely notice does not protect the insurance company from liability on the claim, even if the failure were intentional, unless the insurance company was prejudiced. . . . Because the premise of the selective tender doctrine is that an insurer is not liable on a claim where the insured fails to give timely notice, adoption of the selective tender exception would be in conflict with our . . . law governing liability insurance.").

227. *Insurance Co. of the State of Pennsylvania* was principally concerned with the application of the selective tender doctrine to equitable contribution claims in workers compensation insurance. *See id.* at 1287–89. The court concluded that the selective tender doctrine did not apply in that context. *Id.* at 1288–89.

> Insurers should be encouraged to promptly accept their coverage obligations and begin defending claims; they should not be rewarded for failing to do.[228]

The *Insurance Co. of the State of Pennsylvania* court's public policy rationale is suspect. Insureds typically tender their defense to one insurer over another for reasons having nothing to do with the insurers' relative claims-handling practices. Moreover, potential liability for bad faith provides a powerful disincentive for an insurance company to deliberately delay paying a claim or frustrate the insured's attempt to obtain indemnification. Rejecting the targeted tender doctrine to permit equitable contribution between insurers may represent desirable public policy but that choice should rest on a rationale different from that offered by the Massachusetts Supreme Judicial Court.

C. Insurers' Potential Liability for Pre-Tender Defense Costs

An insured that has been sued may not promptly notify its insurer of the lawsuit despite its contractual obligation to do so. For instance, an insured might defend the lawsuit itself rather than looking to its insurer where it is not aware that it has coverage for the suit, or where it initially believes that the suit can be resolved within its self-insured retention. If the insured later requests a defense from its insurer, and the insurer agrees to defend the insured, the question then becomes whether the insurer must pay the insured's defense costs incurred before the insured requested a defense. In other words, is the insurer liable for the insured's "pre-tender" defense costs? Courts answer this question several ways.

1. *The Insurer Is Not Obligated to Pay Pre-Tender Defense Costs*

An insurer that acknowledges its duty to defend an insured generally is not responsible for paying the insured's pre-tender defense costs.[229] There are three principal reasons that an insurer may not owe pre-tender defense costs.

228. *Id.* at 1289–90.

229. In contrast, if the insurer breaches the duty to defend, it ordinarily becomes liable for all the insured's defense costs, including those incurred pre-tender. TPLC, Inc. v. United Nat'l Ins. Co., 44 F.3d 1484, 1493 (10th Cir. 1995) (applying Pennsylvania law); Sherwood Brands, Inc. v. Hartford Accident & Indem. Co., 698 A.2d 1078, 1086–87 (Md. 1997); 1 Allan D. Windt, Insurance Claims and Disputes § 4:44, at 4-334 (6th ed. 2013 & Supp. 2023). *But see* Sprint Lumber, Inc. v. Union Ins. Co., 627 S.W.3d 96, 123 (Mo. Ct. App. 2021) (citations omitted) ("Where an insurance company refuses to defend an insured who is in fact covered, it is liable to the limits of its policy plus attorney fees, expenses, and other damages incurred in defending the underlying action. . . . An insurer, however, has no duty to pay for fees incurred prior to the insured's demand for coverage."). This rule at least initially seems like a dubious proposition. After all, an insurer cannot breach the duty to defend if it does not know of the lawsuit supposedly to be defended. Rent-A-Roofer, Inc. v. Farm Bureau Prop. & Cas. Ins. Co., 869 N.W.2d 99, 107 (Neb. 2015); Nat'l Sur. Corp. v. Immunex Corp., 297 P.3d 688, 696 (Wash. 2013) (quoting Griffin v. Allstate Ins. Co., 29 P.3d 777, 782 (Wash. Ct. App. 2001 And, if there can be no breach of the duty to defend before the insurer receives actual notice of the lawsuit

First, liability insurance policies generally state that an insured may not, except at its own cost, voluntarily make a payment or incur any expense without the insurer's consent.[230] Where the insured initially failed to request a defense, the insurer has no duty to pay pre-tender defense costs that were voluntarily incurred without its consent.[231] The fact that the insurer was not prejudiced by the insured's delay in seeking a defense does not obligate it to pay pre-tender defense costs;[232] prejudice generally is required only where the insurer refuses to defend or indemnify the insured based on late notice of the suit. This result is consistent with the language of a standard voluntary payments provision, which, unlike the notice provisions in some policies, does not indicate that the insured's failure to comply with it may work a forfeiture of coverage.[233] All that said, some courts hold that an insurer may refuse to pay pre-tender defense costs only where it was prejudiced by the insured's delay in requesting a defense.[234] These courts often reach this result by evaluating the

or tender of the defense (depending on how the court describes the duty to defend trigger), there can be no damages in the absence of breach. In any event, the insurer's breach cannot have caused the insured damages in the form of its pre-tender expenses. But as the *Sherwood Brands* court reasoned, if the insurer "would have declined the defense in any event based on its mistaken conclusion that there was no potential coverage," it "should not later be allowed to use the delay as a bar to reimbursing the insured for the reasonable expenses incurred in defending the covered claim." *Sherwood Brands*, 698 A.2d at 1086–87 (footnote omitted).

230. Ins. Servs. Off., Inc., Commercial General Liability Coverage Form (CG 00 01 04 13), at 11 (2012) ("No insured will, except at that insured's own cost, voluntarily make a payment, assume any obligation, or incur any expense, other than for first aid, without our consent."); Ins. Servs. Off., Inc., Homeowners 3 – Special Form (HO 00 03 05 11), at 22 (2010) ("No 'insured' shall, except at such 'insured's' own cost, voluntarily make payment, assume obligation or incur expense other than for first aid to others at the time of the 'bodily injury.'").

231. Kmart Corp. v. Footstar, Inc., 777 F.3d 923, 932 (7th Cir. 2015) (applying New Jersey law); Rsch. Corp. v. Westport Ins. Corp., 289 F. App'x 989, 994 (9th Cir. 2008) (applying Arizona law); Faust v. The Travelers, 55 F.3d 471, 473 (9th Cir. 1995) (applying California law); Abrams v. RSUI Indem. Co., 272 F. Supp. 3d 676, 640–43 (S.D.N.Y. 2017) (interpreting Delaware law); Scottsdale Ins. Co. v. Am. Empire Surplus Lines Ins. Co., 791 F. Supp. 1079, 1085 (D. Md. 1992) (applying Maryland law); Tradewinds Escrow, Inc. v. Truck Ins. Exch., 118 Cal. Rptr. 2d 561, 565 (Ct. App. 2002); Interface Flooring Sys., Inc. v. Aetna Cas. & Sur. Co., 804 A.2d 201, 208–11 (Conn. 2002) (applying Georgia law); Rass Corp. v. Travelers Cos., 63 N.E.3d 40, 47 (Mass. App. Ct. 2016); Domtar, Inc. v. Niagara Fire Ins. Co., 563 N.W.2d 724, 739 (Minn. 1997); E & L Chipping Co. v. Hanover Ins. Co., 962 S.W.2d 272, 278 (Tex. App. 1998); Nagel v. Ky. Cent. Ins. Co., 894 S.W.2d 19, 21–22 (Tex. App. 1994) (rejecting the insureds' quantum meruit argument); *see also* L'Atrium on the Creek I, L.P. v. Nat'l Union Fire Ins. Co., 326 F. Supp. 2d 787, 792–93 (N.D. Tex. 2004) (holding that while an insurer's notice of a suit can come from any source, including the plaintiff, the insurer was not liable for pre-tender defense costs between the time it received notice of the suit from the plaintiff and the insureds tendered their defense and explaining the reason for its holding); Wm. C. Vick Constr. Co. v. Pa. Nat'l Mut. Cas. Ins. Co., 52 F. Supp. 2d 569, 596 (E.D.N.C. 1999) (relying on the notice provisions in the insurance policy rather than the voluntary payments provision).

232. Legacy Partners, Inc. v. Travelers Indem. Co. of Ill., 83 F. App'x 183, 189 (9th Cir. 2003) (applying Texas law); *Abrams*, 272 F. Supp. 3d at 642–43; *Tradewinds Escrow*, 118 Cal. Rptr. 2d at 566; Gully & Assocs. v. Wausau Ins. Cos., 536 So. 2d 816, 818 (La. Ct. App. 1988).

233. *See Faust*, 55 F.3d at 472–73.

234. *See, e.g.*, Cincinnati Ins. Co. v. Jacob Rieger & Co., LLC, 58 F.4th 386, 390 (8th Cir. 2023) (applying Missouri law); Pekin Ins. Co. v. XData Sols., Inc., 958 N.E.2d 397, 404 (Ill. App. Ct. 2011); *Sherwood Brands*, 698 A.2d at 1086; *Rent-A-Roofer*, 869 N.W.2d at 106–07.

insurer's liability for pre-tender defense costs through the lens of late notice.[235] That approach is a mistake:

> The "no pre-notice defense costs" rule does not conflict with the "notice-prejudice" rule. For one thing, the two are contingent on separate acts. In deciding whether there is a duty to defend, the court must inquire into whether the insured tendered the defense to the insurer. . . . It often happens that the insured tenders the defense when it provides notice of the claim. However, courts recognize that the two are not identical. . . . On the other hand, in deciding whether late notice has absolved an insurer of its duty to reimburse for defense costs, the court must evaluate if—considering when the insured gave notice of the occurrence or claim—the insurer was prejudiced. The lines of inquiry are separate.
>
> Moreover, the policies that prompted courts to graft the prejudice requirement onto the notice requirement have little bearing on the question of pre-tender defense costs. The prejudice requirement was adopted to prevent complete forfeiture based upon technical failure of the insured to provide timely notice. In contrast, enforcement of the rule that pre-tender defense costs are not recoverable does not result in complete forfeiture of an insured's right to recover fees. Rather, the rule gives the insured the choice of defending some or all of a claim on its own. There are tactical reasons why an insured may want to withhold the defense from an insurer that clearly covers a risk. For example, especially in a high-profile case, an insured may not want to lose control of events to the insurer. "An insured can waive some past defense cost coverage without waiving future coverage." . . . Because the policies justifying the prejudice requirement do not apply to the tender requirement, . . . the "no pre-tender defense costs" rule remains viable even in jurisdictions that have adopted the "notice-prejudice" rule.[236]

Where prejudice is mistakenly required to excuse an insurer's obligation to pay pre-tender defense costs, it certainly seems that an insurer is prejudiced by an insured's delayed request for a defense where the insurer is denied the opportunity to appoint counsel and is thus presented with unreasonable attorney fees.[237] In that situation, however, any prejudice presumably may be eliminated

235. *See, e.g.*, *Jacob Rieger & Co.*, 58 F.4th at 390 ("We first consider whether Cincinnati was required to reimburse Rieger for pre-notice fees. . . . Missouri law requires us to consider whether the insurer was prejudiced by the insured's untimely notice."); *Sherwood Brands*, 698 A.2d at 1086 (referring to notice requirements); *Rent-A-Roofer*, 869 N.W.2d at 106 ("Given the similarity in purpose between notice provisions and voluntary payments provisions, we find that it is proper to maintain the prejudice requirement when an insurer seeks to avoid the policy for breach of a voluntary payments provision."). Not all courts do so; some have simply grafted a prejudice requirement onto liability for breach of a voluntary payments provision. *See, e.g.*, *Pekins Ins. Co.*, 958 N.E.2d at 404.

236. Am. Mut. Liab. Ins. Co. v. Beatrice Cos., 924 F. Supp. 861, 873–74 (N.D. Ill. 1996) (footnote and citations omitted).

237. Rsch. Corp. v. Westport Ins. Corp., 289 F. App'x 989, 994 (9th Cir. 2008) (applying Arizona law).

or mitigated by limiting the insurer's obligation to pay the insured's attorney fees to those fees the insurer would normally pay counsel of its choice.[238]

An obvious issue where the policy bars coverage for voluntary payments made without the insurer's consent is what sort of pre-tender defense costs qualify as *involuntary*, such that the insurer may have to pay them. Payments may be declared involuntary if they were made because of circumstances that were beyond the insured's control.[239] This could be the case where the insured does not know the identity of the insurer or is unaware of the terms of the applicable insurance policy.[240] Pre-tender payments of defense costs may also qualify as involuntary where the insured must act urgently to protect its legal interests, as where the insured must respond immediately to avoid a default.[241] Similarly, a payment may be deemed involuntary if time pressures force the insured to spend money pre-tender "under duress."[242] Whether an insured acted urgently to protect its legal interests or was under duress sufficient to render its pre-tender defense payments involuntary are case-specific determinations.

Second, some courts hold that regardless of whether a policy contains a voluntary payments provision, an insurer has no duty to pay pre-tender defense costs because (1) there is no duty to defend until the insurer receives actual notice of the lawsuit against the insured and (2) defense costs are not payable until the policy is triggered.[243] Courts taking this approach sometimes further hold that the insurer has no duty to pay defense costs until the insured requests a defense.[244]

---

238. *See generally Sherwood Brands*, 698 A.2d at 1086 n.7 ("The fact that an expense incurred by the insured was, itself, reasonable in amount does not necessarily resolve the question of prejudice. The insurer may, for example, have an arrangement with competent defense counsel . . . to provide service at a negotiated rate. If the insured, in derogation of its contractual duty not to do so, employs counsel . . . at rates that, though not facially unreasonable, are nonetheless substantially in excess of those that would have otherwise been paid by the insurer had it been notified and undertaken the defense earlier, the insurer may have some basis for claiming prejudice, at least to the extent of the difference.").

239. Jamestown Builders, Inc. v. Gen. Star Indem. Co., 91 Cal. Rptr. 2d 514, 518 (Ct. App. 1999).

240. *Id.* (citing Shell Oil Co. v. Nat'l Union Fire Ins. Co., 52 Cal. Rptr. 2d 580, 589 (Ct. App. 1996)).

241. *Id.* (citing Fiorito v. Super. Ct., 277 Cal. Rptr. 27, 30–31 (Ct. App. 1990)).

242. Zurich Am. Ins. Co. v. N.Y. Marine & Gen. Ins. Co., No. N19C-09-288 PRW CCLD, 2021 WL 424007, at *5 (Del. Super. Ct. Feb. 8, 2021) (applying California law).

243. *See, e.g.*, Henderson v. Bismark Constr. Co., No. FBTCV176062488S, 2019 WL 3546481, at *7 (Conn. Super. Ct. July 10, 2019); Dreaded, Inc. v. St. Paul Guardian Ins. Co., 904 N.E.2d 1267, 1273 (Ind. 2009); Kubit v. MAG Mut. Ins. Co., 708 S.E.2d 138, 153–54 (N.C. Ct. App. 2011).

244. *See, e.g.*, C.J. Duffey Paper Co. v. Liberty Mut. Ins. Co., 76 F.3d 177, 178 (8th Cir. 1996) (applying Minnesota law); Century Indem. Co. v. Aero-Motive Co., 318 F. Supp. 2d 530, 544 (W.D. Mich. 2003) (Although . . . the duty to defend arises when the underlying suit is initiated against the insured, the Court rejects Aero's argument that an insurer is liable for pretender defense costs, at least where the insured fails to allege that the insurer created a conflict of interest. . . . A contrary result would essentially turn an insurer's defense obligation into a duty to reimburse, without affording the insurer the opportunity to control the defense and settlement of the underlying obligation. . . ."); Sprint Lumber, Inc. v. Union Ins. Co., 627 S.W.3d 96, 123 (Mo. Ct. App. 2021) (stating that an insurer

Third, courts occasionally hold that an insurer does not owe pre-tender defense costs as a result of the insured's waiver.[245] That is, by voluntarily incurring defense costs rather than requesting a defense by its insurer, the insured waives the right to recover those costs from the insurer. In *Great American Insurance Co. v. Aetna Casualty & Surety Co.*,[246] for example, the court held that "[c]onsidering the totality of the circumstances," the insured, Mitsui & Co., waived its right to recover its pre-tender defense costs because "it presumably knew by its records" that Great American insured it at relevant times but it "voluntarily chose to retain its own counsel until it tendered its defense to Great American . . . after incurring approximately $77,500 in legal fees."[247]

Waiver was a viable theory in *Great American* because of Mitsui & Co.'s knowledge of its insurance coverage. Waiver will not apply where pre-tender defense costs are claimed if the insured was unaware that it had coverage for the suit when it incurred those costs because, in that case, the insured did not voluntarily relinquish a known right. Here, as elsewhere, a party's negligence or mistake should not support a finding of waiver.

2. *The Insurer Is Presumptively Liable for Pre-Tender Defense Costs*

A few courts hold that an insurer is presumptively liable for an insured's pre-tender defense costs.[248] The reasoning goes something like this: the duty to defend attaches when a suit is filed against the insured that alleges a potentially covered claim. An insurer's payment of defense costs for suits that are potentially covered is part of the bargained-for exchange between the insurer and the insured. Thus, even if an insurance policy requires notice of the suit as a condition precedent to the duty to defend, an insurer is liable for an insured's pre-tender defense costs unless the insurer can show that it was prejudiced by the insured's delayed tender.[249] This approach is not materially different from the one taken by courts that require an insurer to prove prejudice to avoid liability for pre-tender defense costs based on an insured's breach of a voluntary payments provision.

has no duty to pay fees incurred prior to the insured's request for coverage); Dhein v. Frankenmuth Mut. Ins. Co., 950 N.W.2d 861, 876 n.15 (Wis. Ct. App. 2020).

245. *See, e.g.*, Fireman's Fund Ins. Cos. v. Ex-Cell-O Corp., 790 F. Supp. 1318, 1330–33 (E.D. Mich. 1992) (applying Michigan law).

246. 876 P.2d 1314 (Haw. 1994).

247. *Id.* at 1320.

248. *See, e.g.*, Truck Ins. Exch. v. Vanport Homes, Inc., 58 P.3d 276, 281 n.5 (Wash. 2002); Griffin v. Allstate Ins. Co., 29 P.3d 777, 779 (Wash. Ct. App. 2001) ("Subject to policy based defenses, an insurer is liable for fees and costs incurred before the insured tenders defense of a covered claim.").

249. *See* Nat'l Sur. Corp. v. Immunex Corp., 297 P.3d 688, 696 (Wash. 2013).

V. Key Contours of the Duty to Defend

A. Comparing the Duty to Defend and the Duty to Indemnify

In addition to owing an insured a contractual duty to defend, a liability insurer owes the insured a contractual duty to indemnify. As between the duty to defend and the duty to indemnify, courts often assert that the duty to defend is broader.[250] This observation is predicated on the fact that an insurer is contractually obligated to defend even meritless suits that potentially fall within coverage.[251] Presumably, the insured defendant will prevail in a meritless suit and the insurer will incur no indemnity obligation. Until the merits are resolved in the insured's favor, however, the insurer must defend the insured at the insurer's expense.[252] In effect, the insured receives "coverage" for the defense, even though no duty to indemnify will exist in that situation. None of this means, however, that any given policy's coverage is broader with respect to the duty to defend than the duty to indemnify; indeed, both duties are defined by the insuring agreement.[253] "The duty to defend does not attach where, as a matter of law, there is no basis on which the insurer may be held liable for indemnification."[254] Stated more simply, an insurer owes no duty to defend where there is no possibility of coverage.[255]

---

250. *See, e.g.*, Westfield Nat'l Ins. Co. v. Quest Pharms., Inc., 57 F.4th 558, 562 (6th Cir. 2023) (applying Kentucky law); Hartford Cas. Ins. Co. v. Swift Distrib., Inc., 326 P.3d 253, 258 (Cal. 2014); Lift-Up, Inc. v. Colony Ins. Co., 261 A.3d 825, 833 (Conn. App. Ct. 2021); W. Bend Mut. Ins. Co. v. Cmty. Unit Sch. Dist. 300, 193 N.E.3d 266, 273 (Ill. App. Ct. 2021); Ebert v. Ill. Cas. Co., 188 N.E.3d 858, 865 (Ind. 2022); Brilliant Nat'l Servs., Inc. v. Travelers Indem. Co., 349 So. 3d 581, 585 (La. Ct. App. 2022); John Moriarty & Assocs., Inc. v. Zurich Am. Ins. Co., 207 N.E.3d 542, 548 (Mass. App. Ct. 2023); Sturkin v. Miss. Ass'n of Supervisors, Inc., 315 So. 3d 521, 537 (Miss. Ct. App. 2020); Sprint Lumber, Inc. v. Union Ins. Co., 627 S.W.3d 96, 106 (Mo. Ct. App. 2021); Gateway Hospitality Grp., Inc. v. Phila. Indem. Ins. Co., 464 P.3d 44, 54 (Mont. 2020); Merrick v. Fischer, Rounds & Assocs., Inc., 939 N.W.2d 795, 807 (Neb. 2020); Am. W. Home Ins. Co. v. Gjonaj Realty & Mgmt. Co., 138 N.Y.S.3d 626, 631 (App. Div. 2020); Acuity v. Masters Pharm., Inc., 205 N.E.3d 460, 465 (Ohio 2022); Robbins v. Mason Cnty. Title Ins. Co., 462 P.3d 430, 435 (Wash. 2020).

251. *See* Carolina Cas. Ins. Co. v. Burlington Ins. Co., 951 F.3d 1199, 1210 (10th Cir. 2020) ("The duty to defend is broader than the duty to indemnify, because the duty to defend is not based on ultimate liability or the merits of the underlying lawsuit."); Jerry's Sport Ctr., Inc. v. Am. & Foreign Ins. Co., 2 A.3d 526, 541 (Pa. 2010) ("[T]he duty to defend is not limited to meritorious actions; it even extends to actions that are 'groundless, false, or fraudulent' as long as there exists the possibility that the allegations implicate coverage.").

252. *See* Anderson v. Kayser Ford, Inc., 925 N.W.2d 547, 554 (Wis. Ct. App. 2019) ("[A]n insurer has a duty to defend as long as it has an 'arguable' obligation to indemnify its insured if the plaintiff prevails on the merits.").

253. *See* Wear v. Selective Ins. Co., 190 A.3d 519, 528–29 (N.J. Super. Ct. App. Div. 2018) ("Neither the duty to defend nor the duty to indemnify 'exists except with respect to occurrences for which the policy provides coverage.'" (quoting Hartford Accident & Indem. Co. v. Aetna Life & Cas. Ins. Co., 483 A.2d 402, 405 (N.J. 1984))).

254. Zurich Am. Ins. Co. v. Ace Am. Ins. Co., 86 N.Y.S.3d 468, 469 (App. Div. 2018).

255. 24th & Hoffman Inv., LLC v. Northfield Ins. Co., 298 Cal. Rptr. 3d 816, 822 (Ct. App. 2022); Spencer v. Hartford Cas., 556 S.W.3d 679, 683 (Mo. Ct. App. 2018); *Merrick*, 939 N.W.2d at 807;

Contract law, and within it the law of conditions, provide a helpful framework for understanding the difference in breadth between the duty to defend and the duty to indemnify. Contract law certainly is a natural place to seek guidance because, after all, insurance policies are contracts.

Under contract law, a condition is an event that must occur before a contractual duty subject to that condition becomes due—that is, before the duty must be performed.[256] Both the duty to defend and the duty to indemnify are conditional, but the conditioning events are different. The duty to indemnify exists as soon as the contract is formed, but the duty is not due and owing until the insured's liability is established.[257] The duty to defend is not similarly conditioned. The duty to defend also exists as soon as the contract is formed, but it is activated when the insured is sued on a claim that is potentially within coverage, regardless of whether the law would impose liability on those facts.[258] Because the duty to indemnify is conditioned on the insured's liability and the duty to defend is not subject to the same condition, the duty to defend is triggered in more situations. This difference does not, however, alter the essential relationship between the duty to defend and the existence of coverage.[259]

Because the duty to defend attaches where there is merely the potential for coverage, an insurer may have a duty to defend an insured even though it ultimately has no duty to indemnify the insured.[260] Relatedly, because the duty to defend requires only the potential for coverage while the duty to indemnify

---

Zurich Am. Ins. Co. v. Ironshore Specialty Ins. Co., 497 P.3d 625, 629 (Nev. 2021) (quoting United Nat'l Ins. Co. v. Frontier Ins. Co., 99 P.3d 1153, 1158 (Nev. 2004)).

256. Jerry & Richmond, *supra* note 7, at 693.

257. *See* First Mercury Ins. Co. v. Nationwide Sec. Servs., Inc., 54 N.E.3d 323, 330 (Ill. App. Ct. 2016) ("The duty to indemnify arises only when the insured becomes legally obligated to pay damages in the underlying action that gives rise to a claim under the policy."); Wilkinson v. Citation Ins. Co., 856 N.E.2d 829, 836 (Mass. 2006) (stating that the insurer's duty to indemnify "arises only after the insured's liability has been established"); Belsito v. State Farm Mut. Ins. Co., 811 N.Y.S.2d 762, 763 (App. Div. 2006) ("The duty to indemnify on the part of an insurer requires a determination that the insured is liable for a loss that is covered by the policy. . . ."); McCruter v. Travelers Home & Marine Ins. Co., 168 N.E.3d 1, 19 (Ohio Ct. App. 2021) ("[T]he duty to indemnify arises from the conclusive facts and resulting judgment."); Bighorn Logging Corp. v. Truck Ins. Exch., 437 P.3d 287, 293 (Or. Ct. App. 2019) ("An insurer's duty to indemnify is determined by whether the insured is found to be liable for harm or injury that is covered by the insurance policy.").

258. *See* Dua v. Stillwater Ins. Co., 308 Cal. Rptr. 3d 110, 119 (Ct. App. 2023) (explaining how the insurer had conflated the duty to defend with the possibility of the insured's liability); Jones v. Fla. Ins. Guar. Ass'n, Inc., 908 So. 2d 435, 443 (Fla. 2005) (explaining that "the insurer must defend even if the allegations in the complaint are factually incorrect or meritless"); Abouzaid v. Mansard Gardens Assocs., LLC, 23 A.3d 338, 347 (N.J. 2011) (stating that when evaluating an insurer's duty to defend, "the potential merit of the claim is immaterial"); Great Lakes Beverages, LLC v. Wochinski, 892 N.W.2d 333, 338 (Wis. Ct. App. 2017) ("The duty to defend hinges on the nature, not the merits, of the plaintiff's claim.").

259. Jerry & Richmond, *supra* note 7, at 693.

260. Greene v. Westfield Ins. Co., 963 F.3d 619, 628 (7th Cir. 2020) (applying Indiana law); U-Haul Co. of Mo. v. Carter, 567 S.W.3d 680, 685 (Mo. Ct. App. 2019) (quoting Arch Ins. Co. v. Sunset Fin. Servs., Inc., 475 S.W.3d 730, 733 (Mo. Ct. App. 2015)); Zurich Am. Ins. Co. v. Nokia, Inc., 268 S.W.3d 487, 490–91 (Tex. 2008); Fire Ins. Exch. v. Est. of Therkelsen, 27 P.3d 555, 560 (Utah 2001).

requires actual coverage,[261] an insurer that does not owe a duty to defend can almost never owe a duty to indemnify.[262] The "almost never" qualification is necessary here because of the rare case where a policy is written in a way that could cause the court to conclude that the insurer owes a duty to indemnify the insured without also owing a duty to defend,[263] or the equally rare case where facts adduced at the trial of the third-party action trigger the duty to indemnify even though the facts were never pleaded sufficiently to trigger the duty to defend.[264]

B. Determining the Duty to Defend

When it comes to determining an insurer's duty to defend, courts take two approaches. First, there is the four corners rule or eight corners rule, also known as the comparison test, the complaint allegation rule, or the exclusive pleading rule. Second, there is the extrinsic evidence approach. The existence of a duty to defend is a question of law.[265]

1. *The Eight Corners Rule*

Under what we will call the eight corners rule, the factual allegations in the plaintiff's complaint or petition are compared with the policy, and the insurer owes a defense only if those allegations potentially implicate the insurer's duty to indemnify the insured.[266] As the explanation of the rule indicates, the "eight

---

261. Keystone Consol. Indus., Inc. v. Emps. Ins. of Wausau, 456 F.3d 758, 762 (7th Cir. 2006) (stating that the duty to defend "arises in cases of arguable or potential coverage" while the duty to indemnify "arises only in circumstances of *actual* coverage"); *see* Carolina Cas. Ins. Co. v. Burlington Ins. Co., 951 F.3d 1199, 1213 (10th Cir. 2020) ("The duty to defend applies even when an insured has a mere potential for policy coverage, but the duty to indemnify applies only when an insurer is responsible to cover its insured's liability."); Selective Way Ins. Co. v. Fireman's Fund Ins. Co., 289 A.3d 719, 748 (Md. App. Ct. 2023) ("Under the typical liability insurance policy, the insurer is obligated to indemnify the insured for covered claims and to defend the insured against claims potentially covered by the policy.").

262. Westfield Nat'l Ins. Co. v. Quest Pharms., Inc., 57 F.4th 558, 562 (6th Cir. 2023) (applying Kentucky law); Warzecha v. USAA Cas. Ins. Co., 259 A.3d 1251, 1254 (Conn. App. Ct. 2021); Ebert v. Ill. Cas. Co., 188 N.E.3d 858, 865 (Ind. 2022); OTARMA v. Miami Twp., 210 N.E.3d 665, 668 (Ohio Ct. App. 2023).

263. *See, e.g.*, *Keystone*, 456 F.3d at 761–65 (focusing on policy language that stated that the insurer "shall not be obligated to pay any claim or judgment *or* to defend any suit after the applicable limit of the company's liability has been exhausted by payment of judgments or settlements" (emphasis added), and reasoning that the disjunctive reference to claims or judgments indicated that a lawsuit was not necessary to trigger the duty to indemnify).

264. *See, e.g.*, Gilbane Bldg. Co. v. Admiral Ins. Co., 664 F.3d 589, 601 & n.4 (5th Cir. 2011) (applying Texas law).

265. Lyda Swinerton Builders, Inc. v. Okla. Sur. Co., 903 F.3d 435, 445 (5th Cir. 2018) (applying Texas law); Marco v. Starr Indem. & Liab. Co., 256 A.3d 184, 193 (Conn. App. Ct. 2021); Harlor v. Amica Mut. Ins. Co., 150 A.3d 793, 797 (Me. 2016); Wosinski v. Advance Cast Stone Co., 901 N.W.2d 797, 829 (Wis. Ct. App. 2017) (referring specifically to the four corners rule).

266. DeWall v. Med. Prot. Co., 59 F.4th 364, 368 (8th Cir. 2023) (quoting Emps. Mut. Cas. Co. v. Cedar Rapids TV Co., 552 N.W.2d 639, 641 (Iowa 1996)); Banner Bank v. First Am. Title Ins. Co.,

corners" describe the four corners of the complaint or petition combined with the four corners of the insurance policy.[267] A court performing this analysis concentrates on the *facts* alleged in the plaintiff's pleading when comparing it to the coverage provided by the policy.[268] An insurer evaluating its duty to defend should do likewise.

A court analyzing an insurer's duty to defend under the eight corners rule uses a three-step process.[269] First, the court determines whether the policy initially grants coverage for the allegations stated in the complaint or petition. If the allegations set forth in the pleading do not fall within the scope of the policy's insuring agreement, the inquiry ends. Second, if the allegations do fall within the insuring agreement, the court next considers whether any policy exclusions apply. Third, if an exclusion applies, the court next considers whether an exception to the exclusion restores coverage. If coverage is not restored by an exception to an exclusion, then there is no duty to defend. A claims professional evaluating an insurer's duty to defend ordinarily takes the same approach that courts employ.

No matter who is applying the eight corners rule, the labels a plaintiff assigns to claims or causes of action do not control the determination of the duty to defend; again, it is the facts alleged in the plaintiff's pleading that matter.[270] More specifically, it is only the facts that are *actually alleged* that dictate the insurer's duty to defend.[271] "An insurer's duty to defend is not triggered by the insured's speculation about facts or claims that a plaintiff might plead,"[272]

916 F.3d 1323, 1326–27 (10th Cir. 2019) (discussing Utah law); Lupu v. Loan City, LLC, 903 F.3d 382, 389–92 (3d Cir. 2018) (applying Pennsylvania law); Bighorn Logging Corp. v. Truck Ins. Exch., 437 P.3d 287, 293 (Or. Ct. App. 2019).

267. Richards v. State Farm Lloyds, 597 S.W.3d 492, 494–95 (Tex. 2020); AES Corp. v. Steadfast Ins. Co., 725 S.E.2d 532, 535 (Va. 2012).

268. Valley Forge Ins. Co. v. Swiderski Elecs., Inc., 860 N.E.2d 307, 314 (Ill. 2006); Brilliant Nat'l Servs., Inc. v. Travelers Indem. Co., 349 So. 3d 606, 619 (La. Ct. App. 2022); N.C. Farm Bureau Mut. Ins. Co. v. Carpenter, 879 S.E.2d 313, 319 (N.C. Ct. App. 2022); Pharr-San Juan-Alamo Indep. Sch. Dist. v. Tex. Pol. Subdivs. Prop./Cas. Self Ins. Fund, 642 S.W.3d 466, 472 (Tex. 2022).

269. Water Wells Sols. Serv. Grp., Inc. v. Consol. Ins. Co., 881 N.W.2d 285, 291–92 (Wis. 2016).

270. *See* Peerless Indem. Ins. Co. v. Cremation Servs., Inc., No. 1-21-1634, 2023 WL 2961388, at *7 (Ill. App. Ct. Apr. 14, 2023); City of Hartsville v. S.C. Mun. Ins. & Risk Fin. Fund, 677 S.E.2d 574, 579 (S.C. 2009); Integrated Techs., Inc. v. Crum & Forster Specialty Ins. Co., 217 A.3d 528, 535 (Vt. 2019) (quoting cases); *see, e.g.*, Gold Coast Commodities, Inc. v. Crum & Forster Specialty Ins. Co., 68 F.4th 963, 968 (5th Cir. 2023) (stating that when evaluating the duty to defend, "labels aren't binding"); Matlack v. Mountain W. Farm Bureau Mut. Ins. Co., 44 P.3d 73, 80 (Wyo. 2002) ("All the causes of action rely upon the same facts: the intentional trespass. Simply because Ms. Matlack sought to denominate causes of action as 'negligence' or 'negligent infliction of emotional distress,' the facts cannot be magically transformed and thereby create a duty to defend.").

271. *See* Amerisure Mut. Ins. Co. v. Microplastics, Inc., 622 F.3d 806, 812 (7th Cir. 2010) (stating that the duty to defend "applies only to facts that are explicitly alleged").

272. Allstate Ins. Co. v. Naai, 684 F. Supp. 2d 1220, 1226 (D. Haw. 2010); *see also* Shanahan v. State Farm Gen. Ins. Co., 122 Cal. Rptr. 3d 572, 577 (Ct. App. 2011) (stating that an insured may not speculate about unpled claims to manufacture coverage (quoting Michaelian v. State Comp. Ins. Fund, 58 Cal. Rptr. 2d 133, 141 (Ct. App. 1996))); Gunderson v. Fire Ins. Exch., 44 Cal. Rptr. 2d 272,

nor will a court supply facts to create a duty to defend.[273] An insurer evaluating its duty to defend need only consider the complaint or petition before it—not some hypothetical version.[274]

Under the eight corners rule, facts outside the pleadings are not material to the determination of the insurer's duty to defend.[275] If a pleading does not allege facts stating a potentially covered claim, the insurer does not owe a duty to defend.[276] That said, if a pleading does not allege facts potentially implicating coverage but the plaintiff files an amending pleading that does, the amended pleading may trigger coverage where the original pleading did not.[277] There must, however, be an actual amended pleading that alleges facts sufficient to trigger coverage for the duty to defend to be reconsidered or revived; mere speculation about the prospect of such an amendment is insufficient.[278] Furthermore, the insured must inform the insurer of the new allegations for the insurer to then have a duty to defend.[279] Once it properly denies coverage, the

277 (Ct. App. 1995) ("An insured may not trigger the duty to defend by speculating about extraneous 'facts' regarding potential liability or ways in which the third party claimant might amend its complaint at some future date. This approach misconstrues the principle of 'potential liability' under an insurance policy."); Lopez *ex rel.* Lopez v. Am. Fam. Mut. Ins. Co., 148 P.3d 438, 440 (Colo. App. 2006) (stating that a court "may not read hypothetical facts into the pleadings"); Bernie's Bar & Grill, Inc. v. U.S. Liab. Ins. Co., 152 A.3d 613, 615 (Me. 2016) (stating that courts are not obliged "to conjure the duty to defend from speculation or supposition"); Farmers Ins. Exch. v. Minemyer, 532 P.3d 837, 846 (Mont. 2023) ("Liberal construction of a complaint in favor of the insured does not require a court to insert facts that have not been alleged in order to find coverage."); Fire Ins. Exch. v. Weitzel, 371 P.3d 457, 463 (Mont. 2016) ("We have never held that an insurer's duty to defend may be triggered by speculating about extrinsic facts and unpled claims regarding potential liability. Nor have we ever held that an insurer's duty to defend is triggered where the potential for liability is tenuous and far removed from the actual facts pled."); State Farm Fire & Cas. Co. v. Easy PC Sols., LLC, 874 N.W.2d 585, 588 (Wis. Ct. App. 2015) ("We do not require an insurer to speculate beyond the written words of the complaint in order to imagine a claim that a plaintiff might be making or to determine all the potential issues that could be sought when the insurer is evaluating its duty to defend.").

273. *Easy PC Sols.*, 874 N.W.2d at 587.

274. *Amerisure*, 622 F.3d at 812 (quoting Del Monte Fresh Produce N.A., Inc. v. Transportation Ins. Co., 500 F.3d 640, 643 (7th Cir. 2007)).

275. Chavez v. Ariz. Auto. Ins. Co., 947 F.3d 642, 646 (10th Cir. 2020) (applying Colorado law); Kiely v. Phila. Contributionship Ins. Co., 206 A.3d 1140, 1146 (Pa. Super. Ct. 2019); Water Well Sols. Serv. Grp., Inc. v. Consol. Ins. Co., 881 N.W.2d 285, 294–97 (Wis. 2016).

276. *See* Choinsky v. Emps. Ins. of Wausau, 938 N.W.2d 548, 555 (Wis. 2020).

277. Blackburn v. Fid. & Deposit Co. of Md., 667 So. 2d 661, 670 (Ala. 1995); SM Brickell Ltd. P'ship v. St. Paul Fire & Marine Ins. Co., 786 So. 2d 1204, 1206 (Fla. Dist. Ct. App. 2001); Farmers Union Mut. Ins. Co. v. Decker, 704 N.W.2d 857, 863 (N.D. 2005).

278. Garamendi v. Golden Eagle Ins. Co., 25 Cal. Rptr. 3d 642, 648 (Ct. App. 2005).

279. *See* COMSAT Corp. v. St. Paul Fire & Marine Ins. Co., 246 F.3d 1101, 1107 (8th Cir. 2001) (applying Minnesota law); Or. Ins. Guar. Ass'n v. Thompson, 760 P.2d 890, 893 (Or. Ct. App. 1988) ("Without having knowledge that the counterclaim had been amended in a manner that could affect its contractual duty, [the insurer] had no reason or basis on which to reconsider its initial decision not to defend."); Weaver v. Hartford Accident & Indem. Co., 570 S.W.2d 367, 369 (Tex. 1978) ("[N]either the language of the policy, nor the construction made by any court . . . has imposed on the insurer, merely because it knows that an insured has been named as a defendant in an action, the sentry duty of tracking back and forth to the court house to keep a check on if or when he may be served with process." (quoting Campbell v. Cont'l Cas. Co., 170 F.2d 669, 671 (8th Cir. 1948))).

insurer is not required to thereafter monitor the lawsuit against the insured. To hold otherwise would impose an impossible burden on the insurer.[280]

Part of the forgoing discussion requires elaboration where California law controls. That is, it has long been suggested that California courts recognize that an insurer may have to defend what might be described as embedded claims or causes of action. As the California Supreme Court noted in *Scottsdale Insurance Co. v. MV Transportation*,[281] the fact "that the precise causes of action pled by the third-party complaint may fall outside policy coverage does not excuse the duty to defend where, under the facts alleged, reasonably inferable, or otherwise known, the complaint could fairly be amended to state a covered liability."[282] Although the *Scottsdale* court referred to the possible amendment of a complaint to trigger coverage, which violates the rule that speculation about amendments will not create a duty to defend, it is best to read *Scottsdale* simply as focusing the duty to defend analysis on the facts alleged or otherwise known to the insurer (that is, extrinsic evidence, as discussed later) rather than on the labels assigned to claims or causes of action. Where the facts pleaded or extrinsic evidence indicate the potential for coverage, the insurer has a duty to defend even though the claims or causes of action may need to be re-styled or pleaded differently. Indeed, that is the most reasonable reading given the multiple California cases stating that an insured may not speculate about unpled claims to manufacture a duty to defend.[283]

In the big picture, the eight corners rule has both positive and negative aspects. On the plus side of the ledger, the eight corners rule is simple and easy to apply. Courts that favor the rule further reason that it "serves a salutary purpose" by preventing courts "from conducting an intensive factual analysis at an early stage of the proceedings, which would only increase litigation costs and needlessly tax parties and courts before the underlying suit had barely begun."[284] The eight corners rule also aims to give effect to the contracting parties' intent and to lend predictability to the duty to defend. As the Texas Supreme Court has explained:

> The eight-corners rule does not arise merely from the courts' say-so. . . . The duty to defend is a creature of contract, "a valuable benefit granted to the insured by the policy." . . . The goal in interpreting the contractual duty to defend—as when interpreting any contract language—is to "ascertain the

280. Great Am. Ins. Co. v. McKemie, 259 S.E.3d 39, 40 (Ga. 1979).

281. 115 P.3d 460 (Cal. 2005).

282. *Id.* at 466.

283. *See, e.g.*, Shanahan v. State Farm Gen. Ins. Co., 122 Cal. Rptr. 3d 572, 577 (Ct. App. 2011) (stating that an insured may not speculate about unpled claims to manufacture coverage (quoting Michaelian v. State Comp. Ins. Fund, 58 Cal. Rptr. 2d 133, 141 (Ct. App. 1996))); Hurley Constr. Co. v. State Farm Fire & Cas. Co., 12 Cal. Rptr. 2d 629, 631 (Ct. App. 1992) ("[T]he insured may not speculate about unpled third party claims to manufacture coverage.").

284. CACI Int'l, Inc. v. St. Paul Fire & Marine Ins. Co., 566 F.3d 150, 155 (4th Cir. 2009).

> true intentions of the parties as expressed in the writing itself." . . . The eight-corners rule is not a judicial amendment to parties' agreements. Instead, its purpose is to effectuate those agreements, to enforce them consistently and predictably so that parties may write their agreements knowing how courts will interpret them.[285]

On the other hand, the eight corners rule places the insured at the mercy of the lawyer drafting the complaint or petition.[286] The drafting lawyer, whether through ignorance or carelessness, may not allege known facts potentially implicating coverage and thus triggering the insurer's duty to defend. An insured should not be denied a defense because of a plaintiff's haphazard pleading.[287] In short, a third-party claimant should not be allowed to determine the insured's rights under its insurance policy.

The eight corners rule also promotes collusion between insureds and plaintiffs.[288] An insured who fears being undefended can approach the plaintiff with a copy of her insurance policy and help the plaintiff craft a complaint or petition that is sure to trigger the insurer's duty to defend or amend an existing pleading to the same end. Such behavior has untold economic consequences for insurers.[289]

2. *The Extrinsic Evidence Approach*

In comparison to the eight corners rule, courts employing the extrinsic evidence approach hold that an insurer must look beyond the pleadings and consider any facts brought to its attention or any facts that it reasonably could discover at the time suit was filed in determining whether it has a duty to defend.[290]

---

285. Richards v. State Farm Lloyds, 597 S.W.3d 492, 499–500 (Tex. 2020) (citations omitted).

286. *See* Aetna Cas. & Sur. Co. v. Cochran, 651 A.2d 859, 865–66 (Md. 1995) ("[A]llowing an insurance company to refuse to defend an insured based solely on allegations in a complaint filed by an uninterested third-party leaves the insured with no choice but to rely on a plaintiff to file a well-pleaded complaint in order to establish a potentiality of coverage under the insured's insurance policy.").

287. *See* York Golf & Tennis Club v. Tudor Ins. Co., 845 A.2d 1173, 1175 (Me. 2004) ("[A]n insurer's duty should not depend on the skill of the drafter of the complaint against the insured.").

288. Jerry & Richmond, *supra* note 7, at 699.

289. *Id.*

290. *See, e.g.*, Att'ys Liab. Prot. Soc'y, Inc. v. Ingaldson Fitzgerald, P.C., 370 P.3d 1101, 1111–12 (Alaska 2016) ("[T]he duty to defend attaches, if at all, on the basis of the complaint and known or reasonably ascertainable facts at the time of the complaint."), *abrogated on other grounds by* Buntin v. Schlumberger Tech. Corp., 487 P.3d 595, 595 (Alaska 2021); Dua v. Stillwater Ins. Co., 308 Cal. Rptr. 3d 110, 118 (Ct. App. 2023) (stating that extrinsic facts known to the insurer at the inception of the lawsuit against the insured or upon tender of the defense, whether disputed or undisputed, may create a duty to defend); Smith v. Progressive Se. Ins. Co., 150 N.E.3d 192, 202 (Ind. Ct. App. 2020) ("When determining whether a duty to defend exists, the insurer must look to the allegations in the complaint coupled with the facts known to the insurer after reasonable investigation."); First Nat'l Bank of Mo. Valley v. Fid. & Deposit Co. of Md., 545 N.W.2d 332, 335 (Iowa Ct. App. 2006) (looking to the pleadings and all other relevant and admissible facts); Thornburg v. Schweitzer, 240 P.3d 969, 978 (Kan. Ct. App. 2010) (acknowledging that an insurer "must look beyond the effect of the pleadings

The reasoning behind the extrinsic evidence approach is straightforward: an insurer should not be able to avoid its duty to defend by ignoring facts relevant to the insured's potential liability and instead seizing on a pleading that may be inaccurate or falsified.[291] The insurer's sole concern when analyzing its duty to defend should be whether the judgment that may ultimately be entered against the insured might, either in whole or in part, be covered by the policy.[292] Although most courts base an insurer's duty to defend only on those facts known or reasonably ascertainable by the insurer at the time the lawsuit was filed, a few courts further base the duty to defend on facts revealed in discovery once litigation is underway.[293] Under no circumstances, though, can an insurer's duty to defend be based on facts first revealed at the trial of the third-party action.[294]

Where the insurer is unaware of extrinsic evidence that potentially triggers coverage, a court may not consider that evidence in determining the duty to defend.[295] A court deciding whether an insurer owed a duty to defend based on extrinsic evidence must evaluate the insurer's knowledge at the time the insured requested a defense; hindsight has no place in the analysis.[296]

---

and consider any facts brought to its attention or any facts which it could reasonably discover" in deciding whether to defend); Billings v. Com. Ins. Co., 936 N.E.2d 408, 414 (Mass. 2010) ("The duty to defend is determined based on the facts alleged in the complaint, and on facts known or readily knowable by the insurer that may aid in its interpretation of the allegations in the complaint."); Allen v. Cont'l W. Ins. Co., 436 S.W.3d 548, 553 (Mo. 2014) ("[T]he insurer's duty to defend arises only from potential coverage based on facts: (1) alleged in the petition; (2) the insurer knows at the outset of the case; or (3) that are reasonably apparent to the insurer at the outset of the case."); Huckins v. United Servs. Auto. Ass'n, 396 P.3d 121, 124 (Mont. 2017) (stating that an insurer's duty to defend may arise from its knowledge of facts outside the complaint); Merrick v. Fischer, Rounds & Assocs., Inc., 939 N.W.2d 795, 807 (Neb. 2020) ("An insurer has a duty to defend if (1) the allegations of the complaint, if true, would obligate the insurer to indemnify, or (2) a reasonable investigation of the facts by the insurer would or does disclose facts that would obligate the insurer to indemnify."); Sw. Steel Coil, Inc. v. Redwood Fire & Cas. Ins. Co., 148 P.3d 806, 812 (N.M. Ct. App. 2006) (recognizing that if the duty to defend does not arise from the face of the complaint, it may arise through extrinsic evidence); Riccobono v. State, 63 N.Y.S.3d 802, 808 (Ct. Cl. 2017) ("Under New York law, an insurer's duty to defend . . . is triggered whenever the four corners of a complaint, liberally construed, suggest a reasonable possibility of coverage, or when the insurance carrier has actual knowledge of facts establishing such a reasonable possibility. . . .") (citations omitted); Builders Mut. Ins. Co. v. Mitchell, 709 S.E.2d 528, 534–35 (N.C. Ct. App. 2011) (quoting cases); Nat'l Sur. Corp. v. Immunex Corp., 297 P.3d 688, 691 (Wash. 2013) ("Facts that are extrinsic to the pleadings, but readily available to the insurer, may give rise to the duty [to defend].").

291. 1 WINDT, *supra* note 229, § 4:3, at 4-88.

292. *Id.*

293. *See, e.g.*, Alticor, Inc. v. Nat'l Union Fire Ins. Co., 916 F. Supp. 2d 813, 826 (W.D. Mich. 2013) (applying Michigan law); W9/PHC Real Est. LP v. Farm Fam. Cas. Ins. Co., 970 A.2d 382, 391 (N.J. Super. Ct. App. Div. 2009).

294. Bos. Symphony Orchestra, Inc. v. Com. Union Ins. Co., 545 N.E.2d 1156, 1158 (Mass. 1989); *see, e.g.*, Brand v. Kan. City Gastroenterology & Hepatology, LLC, 414 S.W.3d 546, 555–56 (Mo. Ct. App. 2013) (holding that the insurer owed no duty to defend in this situation).

295. Pekin Ins. Co. v. McKeown Classic Homes, Inc., 161 N.E.3d 1059, 1068 (Ill. App. Ct. 2020).

296. *See* Harris v. Durham Enters., Inc., 586 F. Supp. 3d 856, 863 (S.D. Ill 2022) ("[W]hen an insured claims that facts showing coverage were ascertainable by the insurer through reasonable investigation, there must be evidence of what the insurer would have found in a reasonable investigation at

For courts following the extrinsic evidence approach, the allegations in the plaintiff's petition or complaint are but the starting point in analyzing the insurer's duty to defend.[297] The insurer's duty to defend still pivots on the potential for coverage, but the universe of information from which that potential must be ascertained is significantly greater. That universe is not limitless, however. Although the extrinsic approach does not allow an insurer to rely solely on the pleadings to determine its duty to defend, nor does it require an insurer to engage in conjecture or imagine facts to concoct a duty to defend.[298] Similarly, any extrinsic evidence that an insured wants to offer to prompt the insurer to provide a defense must relate in some manner to a cause of action actually alleged in the plaintiff's complaint or petition.[299] The insured cannot use extrinsic evidence to create a new, unpled claim that would give rise to a duty to defend.[300]

While courts often vaguely describe the extrinsic evidence an insurer should review when evaluating its duty to defend, it is important to remember that an insurer's obligation to consider extrinsic evidence is limited to facts that are brought to its attention or that it *reasonably* could discover in evaluating its duty to defend. Thus, while an insurer should invite the insured to provide information that may help it determine its defense obligation,[301] consider facts that the insured calls to its attention (whether independently or at the insurer's

that time that would have brought the claim within the policy's coverage.") (applying Missouri law); Great Am. Ins. Co. v. McKemie, 259 S.E.2d 39, 40 (Ga. 1979) ("[T]he correctness of an insurer's decision to defend or not cannot be determined by 'later-revealed facts' of which the insurer has no knowledge or notice. Under the later-revealed facts doctrine, even if an insurer justifiably refused to defend a case based on the information it had at the outset, it would have to monitor the case throughout to be sure that its duty did not arise later. Such a burden would be intolerable.").

297. *See, e.g.*, McMillin Homes Constr., Inc. v. Nat'l Fire & Marine Ins. Co., 247 Cal. Rptr. 3d 825, 830 (Ct. App. 2019) (citation omitted) ("To evaluate whether an insurer owes a duty to defend, we start by comparing the allegations of the complaint to the terms of the policy. . . . Extrinsic facts may give rise to a duty to defend where they reveal the possibility of coverage."); First Nat'l Bank of Mo. Valley v. Fid. & Deposit Co. of Md., 545 N.W.2d 332, 335 (Iowa Ct. App. 2006) (citations omitted) ("We look first and primarily to the petition for the facts at the outset of the case. . . . When necessary, we expand our scope of inquiry to any other admissible and relevant facts in the record. . . . Such expansion is especially necessary under 'notice pleading' petitions which often give few facts upon which to assess an insurer's duty to defend."); Sw. Steel Coil, Inc. v. Redwood Fire & Cas. Ins. Co., 148 P.3d 806, 812 (N.M. Ct. App. 2006) ("If the duty to defend does not arise from the complaint on its face, the duty may arise if the insurer is notified of factual contentions or if the insurer could have discovered facts, through reasonable investigation, implicating a duty to defend.").

298. LDF Food Grp., Inc. v. Liberty Mut. Fire Ins. Co., 146 P.3d 1088, 1093 (Kan. Ct. App. 2006).

299. Reames v. State Farm Fire & Cas. Ins., 683 A.2d 179, 186 (Md. Ct. Spec. App. 1996).

300. *Id.*

301. When denying coverage and thus declining to provide a defense, insurers typically include language in their denial letters inviting the insured to provide information that might lead to a different conclusion. Such language is not mere boilerplate; to the contrary, an insurer wants to be advised of facts that indicate the existence of coverage and similarly wants to be informed if it has allegedly misconstrued or misinterpreted facts of which it is aware. Regardless, the insurer's denial letter does not need to include such an invitation for the insured to have the right to provide information intended to change the insurer's decision.

invitation or request), analyze evidence that is revealed in its investigation of the underlying occurrence, consider facts that it learns from a third-party administrator or independent adjuster involved in the matter, and examine facts shared by the plaintiff or a co-defendant, the insurer need not endlessly investigate a loss to evaluate its defense obligation. There also may be cases where there is no relevant extrinsic evidence for the insurer to consider, where any extrinsic evidence is unpersuasive or confirms that there is no potential for coverage,[302] or where the facts alleged in the plaintiff's pleading are sufficiently clear or the applicable law is such that the insurer can properly determine its duty to defend simply by comparing the plaintiff's pleading to the terms of its policy.

The extrinsic evidence approach can trap an incautious insurer, as in *Travelers Property Casualty Co. of America v. Liberty Mutual Fire Insurance Co.*[303] The *Travelers* opinion is short on details because the court assumed readers' familiarity with the facts, but the case apparently arose out of a construction dispute. The Aldridge/Rosen Joint Venture (Aldridge) alleged that Liberty Mutual Fire Insurance Co. (Liberty Mutual) breached its duty to defend Aldridge in the underlying litigation. The key issue was whether property damage had occurred that would potentially implicate Liberty Mutual's coverage. The court agreed with Liberty Mutual that the relevant pleading in the underlying case, a cross-complaint, did not trigger its duty to defend because the allegations indicated only that defective work was performed and defective materials were installed—there was no suggestion of property damage.[304]

Unable to point to any facts in the cross-complaint that indicated the possibility of property damage, Aldridge leaned on language in the cross-complaint which stated that another insured knew or reasonably should have known that its misconduct "would give rise to economic damages, property damage, liquidated damages, and consequential damages."[305] The court rejected this argument as well, stating that this "boilerplate language," which had no factual support, did not trigger Liberty Mutual's duty to defend.[306]

Unfortunately for Liberty Mutual, while the allegations in the cross-complaint did not trigger its duty to defend, the court reasoned that they did place it "on inquiry notice."[307] Accordingly, Liberty Mutual was required to conduct a reasonable investigation before deciding whether to reject

302. *See, e.g.*, Talen v. Emps. Mut. Cas. Co., 703 N.W.2d 395, 406–07 (Iowa 2005) (explaining that the insurer's denial of coverage based on certain assumptions prior to obtaining more accurate information was "without significance in light of the fact that its assumptions proved to be correct").

303. No. 22-cv-05803-VC, 2023 WL 3510384 (N.D. Cal. May 16, 2023).

304. *Id.* at *1.

305. *Id.* (internal quotation marks omitted).

306. *Id.*

307. *Id.* at *2.

Aldridge's tender of its defense.[308] The *Travelers* court concluded that no reasonable juror could find that Liberty Mutual did so.

> In response to Aldridge's tender, Liberty Mutual sent an email acknowledging receipt and communicating that it would "need to review the file material in its entirety as well as the allegations pled in any complaint to determine whether [Aldridge] potentially would by [sic] covered" and that "[a]fter we have completed our review, we will provide you with a position on our defense and indemnity obligations to you." . . . Without asking Aldridge a single question or requesting a single piece of additional information, Liberty Mutual then sent a denial letter, explaining that neither the pleadings nor other publicly available information—such as press releases and reports made by [another party] to its board of directors—suggested that property damage had occurred.[309]

The court ordered Liberty Mutual to reimburse Aldridge for its defense costs in the underlying litigation since the date of its tender. The court further held that by breaching its duty to defend, Liberty Mutual had forfeited its right to control Aldridge's defense, including losing the right to negotiate the hourly rates paid to the defense lawyers Aldridge hired.

Travelers involved an insurer's lack of effort to discover extrinsic evidence that might give rise to a duty to defend. Extending the analysis, an insurer that either fails to consider relevant extrinsic evidence of which it is aware or that is unwilling to consider such evidence likewise risks liability for breach of contract and perhaps even exposes itself to liability for bad faith, as *Dua v. Stillwater Insurance Co.*[310] illustrates. *Dua* also demonstrates how an insurer can err when analyzing its duty to defend by confusing the potential for coverage with the potential for the insured to be held liable.

Poonam Dua was the named insured on a homeowners policy issued by Stillwater Insurance Co. (Stillwater). The policy contained two animal exclusions, both of which stated: "This insurance does not apply to any occurrence or damages caused by any animal, at any time, at any premises insured hereunder, or caused by, arising out of, or in any way related to any animal owned by or in the care, custody, or control of the insured, or any member of the insured's family or household."[311]

Simeon and Roslyn Peroff sued Dua and her boyfriend, Eric Taylor, for personal injuries and property damage caused by Taylor's dogs. In their complaint, the Peroffs alleged that Taylor's pit bulls attacked their dogs during a walk. The Peroffs alleged that as they neared Taylor, he turned his dogs loose,

308. *Id.* (citing Cal. Shoppers, Inc. v. Royal Globe Ins. Co., 221 Cal. Rptr. 171, 189 (Ct. App. 1985)).
309. *Id.* (citation to the court's docket omitted).
310. 308 Cal. Rptr. 3d 110 (Ct. App. 2023).
311. *Id.* at 114 (internal quotation marks omitted).

and Taylor's dogs then mauled their dogs. The Peroffs further alleged that they suffered emotional distress from witnessing the attack. They did not allege that Dua was present during the attack, nor did the complaint allege that she owned the pit bulls. The Peroffs alleged that Taylor owned the dogs and that the attack occurred on a public street. The Peroffs did allege, however, that Taylor and his dogs lived at Dua's home, that Dua knew the pit bulls were dangerous, and that the attack was reasonably foreseeable to her. The Peroffs claimed that Dua was therefore liable because she owned the property where the pit bulls were kept and breached her duty to prevent the attack.

Dua notified Stillwater of the Peroffs' lawsuit and sought a defense. She told Stillwater that she did not own the dogs and that the dogs were in her boyfriend's care, custody, and control when the attack occurred.[312] She also told Stillwater that Taylor owned the dogs.[313] Stillwater denied coverage based on one of the animal exclusions. Dua then settled with the Peroffs and sued Stillwater for breach of contract and for bad faith.

In her suit against Stillwater, Dua alleged that Stillwater did not adequately investigate the Peroff's claims and that it failed to defend and indemnify her because it unreasonably misinterpreted the policy. She asserted that had Stillwater reasonably investigated the Peroffs' claims, it would have learned that (1) she was not married to Taylor; (2) Taylor did not live with her nor was he staying with her at the time of the dog attack; (3) the attack occurred off her premises; and (4) at the time of the attack, the pit bulls were leashed and in Taylor's care, custody, and control.[314] Stillwater moved for summary judgment based on the animal exclusion in its policy. Stillwater argued that the exclusion defeated coverage, meaning that it did not breach its contract and that it was not liable for bad faith because its coverage denial was reasonable. The trial court agreed and awarded Stillwater summary judgment. Dua appealed to the California Court of Appeal.

In the *Dua* court's eyes, Stillwater ignored Dua's reports indicating that the policy's animal exclusions did not apply because she did not own the dogs, nor were they in her care, custody, or control.[315] Under California law, an insurer owes a duty to defend "where extrinsic facts, both disputed and undisputed, that the insurer knows or becomes aware of from any source at the time of the inception of the third party lawsuit or at the time of tender, suggest there may be coverage."[316] Here, there was no evidence that Stillwater attempted to investigate or otherwise negate the facts suggesting that an animal liability

312. *Id.* at 118.
313. *Id.* at 115.
314. *Id.* at 116.
315. *Id.* at 118.
316. *Id.* (citing Hartford Cas. Ins. Co. v. Swift Distrib., Inc., 326 P.3d 253, 258 (Cal. 2014)).

exclusion did not apply and there was potential coverage, and consequently it had a duty to defend Dua.[317]

Stillwater contended that the trial court correctly held that it had no duty to defend as a matter of law. It argued that if Dua lacked ownership, care, custody, or control of the dogs, then she could not possibly be held liable under the Peroffs' complaint. Stillwater also argued that if Dua did own the dogs or have care, custody, or control of them, then the animal exclusion would apply. As a result, there was no possibility of coverage under the policy.[318] The court rejected Stillwater's argument and illuminated the flaw in its reasoning:

> Stillwater conflates the possibility of Dua's liability with Stillwater's duty to defend. Even if Dua cannot be found legally liable under the Peroffs' complaint as pleaded, and is therefore not entitled to indemnity coverage under the policy, Stillwater may still be required to defend her. The Peroffs' claims, when evaluated in light of the facts presented by Dua to Stillwater when she tendered the claim, may have been frivolous and unmeritorious, but did not come within the animal liability exclusion. They thus created at least a possibility of coverage and the duty to defend.[319]

In sum, Stillwater did not establish "that there was no conceivable theory to bring the [Peroffs'] complaint within the possibility of coverage," and the facts Dua shared with it suggested that there may be coverage.[320] The *Dua* court accordingly concluded that the trial court erred in granting Stillwater summary judgment on Dua's breach of contract claim.[321] The court reached the same conclusion with respect to Dua's bad faith claim. It therefore reversed the trial court's judgment and remanded the case for further proceedings.

C. The Low Threshold of the Duty to Defend

When comparing the allegations in a plaintiff's pleading with insurance policy terms to decide whether the insurer has a duty to defend under either the eight corners rule or as the starting point under the extrinsic evidence approach, a court liberally construes the allegations in the pleading so that all doubts about their meaning are resolved in favor of finding a duty to defend.[322] Indeed, numerous courts have stated that when evaluating the duty to defend, doubts about the duty's existence must be resolved in the insured's favor.[323]

---

317. *Id.*
318. *Id.* at 119.
319. *Id.*
320. *Id.*
321. *Id.*
322. Farmers Union Mut. Ins. Co. v. Staples, 90 P.3d 381, 385 (Mont. 2004).
323. *See, e.g.*, Scottsdale Ins. Co. v. Columbia Ins. Grp., Inc., 972 F.3d 915, 919–20 (7th Cir. 2020) (applying Illinois law); *Dua*, 308 Cal. Rptr. 3d at 118; Stevens v. United Gen. Title Ins. Co., 801 A.2d

Courts similarly explain that when analyzing whether an insurer owes a duty to defend, they resolve any ambiguities in a plaintiff's complaint or petition in the insured's favor,[324] or that they resolve any uncertainties in a plaintiff's pleading in the insured's favor.[325] In fact, there may be no meaningful difference between "doubts," "ambiguities," and "uncertainties" when it comes to determining an insurer's duty to defend. Simply stated, the threshold for finding a duty to defend is low.[326]

Uncertainty as to whether a plaintiff's allegations trigger an insurer's duty to defend may be either factual or legal.[327] Factual uncertainty arises when it is unclear from the face of the complaint or petition whether there was an "occurrence" that caused covered damage.[328] Suppose, for example, that an insured has a policy in force for calendar year 2023; the policy expired by its terms on December 31, 2023. If, in March 2024, a plaintiff sues the insured for injuries suffered in an accident that allegedly occurred on the insured's property but does not specify in her complaint when she was injured, there would be factual uncertainty as to whether her claims are potentially covered because it is impossible to know from the face of the complaint whether she was injured during the policy period. This factual uncertainty would give rise to a duty to defend, at least until the insurer could establish that the plaintiff was injured sometime other than in 2023. Of course, an insurer may encounter any number of other factual uncertainties.

61, 67 (D.C. 2002); Flamingo Self Storage, LLC v. Travelers Indem. Co., 43 So. 3d 168, 170 (Fla. Dist. Ct. App. 2010); S. Tr. Ins. Co. v. Mountain Express Oil Co., 828 S.E.2d 455, 458 (Ga. Ct. App. 2019) (quoting Penn-Am. Ins. Co. v. Disabled Am. Veterans, Inc., 490 S.E.2d 374, 376 (Ga. Ct. App. 1997)); Nationwide Prop. & Cas. Ins. Co. v. State Farm Fire & Cas. Co., 208 N.E.3d 1106, 1113 (Ill. App. Ct. 2022); Walk v. Hartford Cas. Ins. Co., 852 A.2d 98, 107 (Md. 2004); Zurich Am. Ins. Co. v. Ironshore Specialty Ins. Co., 497 P.3d 625, 629 (Nev. 2021) (quoting United Nat'l Ins. Co. v. Frontier Ins. Co., 99 P.3d 1153, 1158 (Nev. 2004)); N.C. Farm Bureau Mut. Ins. Co. v. Cox, 823 S.E.2d 613, 636 (N.C. Ct. App. 2019); Tibert v. Nodak Mut. Ins. Co., 816 N.W.2d 31, 42 (N.D. 2012); Erie Ins. Exch. v. Moore, 228 A.3d 258, 265 (Pa. 2020); Demaray v. De Smet Farm Mut. Ins. Co., 801 N.W.2d 284, 287 (S.D. 2011); Travelers Indem. Co. of Am. v. Moore & Assocs., Inc., 216 S.W.3d 302, 305 (Tenn. 2007); Zurich Am. Ins. Co. v. Nokia, Inc., 268 S.W.3d 487, 491 (Tex. 2008); Choinsky v. Emps. Ins. of Wausau, 938 N.W.2d 548, 555 (Wis. 2020); Shoshone First Bank v. Pac. Emps. Ins. Co., 2 P.3d 510, 514 (Wyo. 2000).

324. *See, e.g.*, *Nationwide*, 208 N.E.3d at 1113; *Moore*, 228 A.3d at 265; Webb v. USAA Cas. Ins. Co., 457 P.3d 1258, 1266 (Wash. Ct. App. 2020); *see also* Smith v. Liberty Mut. Ins. Co., 201 A.3d 555, 573 (Del. 2019) (stating that ambiguities in pleadings must be "resolve[d] against the insurance company").

325. *See, e.g.*, Deutsche Bank Nat'l Ass'n v. First Am. Title Ins. Co., 991 N.E.2d 638, 642 (Mass. 2013).

326. Acuity v. M/I Homes of Chi., Inc., 205 N.E.3d 174, 185 (Ill. App. Ct. 2022); Irving Oil Ltd. v. ACE INA Ins. Co., 91 A.3d 594, 599 (Me. 2014).

327. Nash St., LLC v. Main St. Am. Assur. Co., 251 A.3d 600, 607 (Conn. 2020).

328. *See id.* (citing Hugo Boss Fashions, Inc. v. Fed. Ins. Co., 252 F.3d 608, 620–22 (2d Cir. 2001)).

As indicated earlier, an insurer evaluating its duty to defend must resolve any doubtful or uncertain factual issues in the insured's favor.[329] The insurer must treat all factual allegations in a complaint or petition as though they are true.[330] If there are inconsistencies between or among the factual allegations in the plaintiff's pleading, the allegations indicating a potential for coverage must be treated as if they are true.[331] If the case is in a jurisdiction that follows the extrinsic evidence approach when determining an insurer's duty to defend, the insurer must treat extrinsic evidence that indicates the potential for coverage as if it is true.[332]

Legal uncertainty for purposes of the duty to defend arises "when it is unclear how a court might interpret the policy language at issue, and, as a result, it is unclear whether the alleged injury falls within coverage."[333] Legal uncertainties, like factual uncertainties, work in favor of defending the insured.[334] Courts have recognized that legal uncertainty can arise in at least two ways. First, ambiguous policy language can spawn a duty to defend.[335] Second, a duty to defend may arise when there is a split of authority in other jurisdictions as to the interpretation of a certain policy provision, and no appellate court in the relevant jurisdiction has opined on the matter.[336] In any case of legal uncertainty, an insurer is wise to promptly pursue a declaratory judgment action.

Although the threshold for determining the duty to defend is low, that does not mean every case crosses it. This is because the duty to defend, although broad, is not limitless. Just as an insurer does not promise to indemnify an insured for any liability regardless of its nature, an insurer does not promise to defend an insured against all claims, whatever they might be.[337] Moreover, an insurer has a duty to defend only when the plaintiff's complaint or petition *reasonably* alleges a potentially covered claim.[338] A court will not torture a plaintiff's pleading to find a duty to defend.[339]

---

329. *See* Siplast, Inc. v. Emps. Mut. Cas. Co., 23 F.4th 486, 494 (5th Cir. 2022) ("For both the third-party complaint and the insurance policy, if there are any ambiguities, the tie goes to the insured.").

330. Restatement of the L. of Liab. Ins. § 13 cmt. a (Am. L. Inst. 2019).

331. *Id.*

332. *Id.*

333. Nash St., LLC v. Main St. Am. Assur. Co., 251 A.3d 600, 607 (Conn. 2020).

334. *Id.* at 613.

335. *Id.* at 607 (citing Wentland v. Am. Equity Ins. Co., 840 A.2d 1158, 1163 (Conn. 2004)).

336. *Id.* (citing Am. Best Food, Inc. v. Alea London, Ltd., 229 P.3d 693, 699 (Wash. 2010)).

337. Jerry & Richmond, *supra* note 7, at 692; *see also* Waller v. Truck Ins. Exch., 900 P.2d 619, 628 (Cal. 1995) ("[T]he duty to defend, although broad, is not unlimited; it is measured by the nature and kinds of risks covered by the policy.").

338. Stewart v. Old Republic Nat'l Title Ins. Co., 291 A.3d 1051, 1062 (Conn. App. Ct. 2023) (quoting Kling v. Hartford Cas. Ins. Co., 273 A.3d 717, 721 (Conn. App. Ct. 2022)).

339. *Id.* (quoting *Kling*, 273 A.3d at 721); *see, e.g.*, State of N.Y. v. AMRO Realty Corp., 936 F.2d 1420, 1428 (2d Cir. 1991) (citation omitted) ("While it is true that an insurer 'can be excused from its duty to defend only if it can be determined as a matter of law that there is no possible basis in law

In *Christian v. United Fire & Casualty Co.*,[340] for example, Clifford Christian contracted with Weatherall Builders to build four townhomes in Helena, Montana.[341] Albert and Linda Parisian bought one of the homes through a "Buy-Sell Agreement."[342] Weatherall contracted with Zachary Beveridge to landscape the Parisians' property. Beveridge was never paid for this work, and he thus sued Weatherall and the Parisians. Weatherall and the Parisians filed third-party claims against Christian.

Christian was an additional insured under Weatherall's CGL policy with United Fire & Casualty Co. (United Fire). Christian asked United Fire to defend and indemnify him with respect to the Parisians' claims. United Fire refused on the basis that the Parisians' complaint did not allege "property damage" as defined in its policy, and there was no "occurrence."[343] Christian then sued United Fire and lost at summary judgment in the trial court. Although the Parisians had alleged in their complaint that "Christian was negligent in failing to honor his contractual duties to pay his subcontractors," the trial court agreed with United Fire's rationale for denying coverage.[344] Christian appealed to the Montana Supreme Court.

On appeal, Christian argued from the position that a court must liberally construe the allegations in a plaintiff's complaint in favor of finding a duty to defend.[345] Thus, Christian asserted, the Parisians' allegation that they were damaged by "Mr. Christian's negligence and/or failure to perform his contractual obligations," should be construed to allege a property damage claim.[346] Specifically, Christian contended that the Parisians' complaint could only be interpreted to mean that they were asserting a construction defect claim based on the negligent construction of the townhomes, and were seeking both contract and tort damages.[347] The Montana Supreme Court disagreed.

Despite the Parisians' use of the term "negligence" in their complaint, their claims arose solely from Christian's breach of the Buy-Sell Agreement. The complaint alleged that, under the Buy-Sell Agreement, Christian was responsible for building the Parisians' home, and that Christian contracted with

or fact upon which the insurer might be held to indemnify' the insured, . . . we decline to obligate an insurer to extend coverage based on a reading of the complaint that is linguistically conceivable but tortured and unreasonable.").

340. 530 P.3d 456 (Mont. 2023).

341. Clifford Christian died while the case was still in the trial court. The case was thereafter prosecuted by his wife, Debra Christian, as the personal representative of the Estate of Clifford Christian. *Id.* at 457. We will refer to Mr. Christian and his estate collectively as Christian for ease of discussion.

342. *Id.*

343. *Id.* at 458.

344. *Id.* (internal quotation marks omitted).

345. *Id.* at 459 (citing Farmers Union Mut. Ins. Co. v. Staples, 90 P.3d 381, 385 (Mont. 2004)).

346. *Id.* (internal quotation marks omitted).

347. *Id.*

Weatherall, who, in turn, subcontracted with Beveridge to complete the work due the Parisians under the Buy-Sell Agreement. When Beveridge later sued Weatherall and the Parisians, the Parisians pleaded in their third-party complaint that Beveridge's damages "were solely due to Mr. Christian's negligence and/or his failure to perform his contractual obligations . . . owed to the Parisians and/or his subcontractual obligations owed to [Beveridge]."[348]

Christian tried to stretch the Parisians' reference to "negligence" to encompass a claim for property damage due to a construction defect; however, nowhere in their complaint did the Parisians allege a problem with their home itself, nor did they allege any harm beyond Christian's failure to pay Beveridge.[349] The Parisians' third-party complaint against Christian was wholly devoted to obtaining indemnity for Beveridge's claims against them.[350]

Even liberally construing the Parisians' complaint in Christian's favor, it was clear that the United Fire policy's definition of "property damage" caused by an "occurrence" did not fit the Parisians' claims, so United Fire had no duty to defend or indemnify Christian.[351] The *Christian* court therefore affirmed the trial court judgment for United Fire.

D. The Duty to Defend Mixed Actions

A plaintiff's complaint or petition may contain some claims that clearly are within coverage and other claims that are clearly outside coverage. Courts commonly describe these cases as mixed actions.[352]

Under the "entire-suit rule," also known as the "in for one, in for all rule," the "mixed-action rule," and the "complete defense rule," an insurer asked to defend an insured in a mixed action generally must defend the insured against *all* claims alleged in the lawsuit, including those that are not covered, so long as the insurer has an arguable duty to indemnify the insured on even one of the claims.[353] In other words, under the entire-suit rule, an insurer's duty to

---

348. *Id.* (internal quotation marks omitted).

349. *Id.* at 459–60.

350. *Id.* at 460.

351. *Id.*

352. *See, e.g.*, Gonzalez v. Fire Ins. Exch., 184 Cal. Rptr. 3d 394, 403 (Ct. App. 2015) ("When a complaint states multiple claims, some of which are potentially covered by the insurance policy and some of which are not, it is a mixed action."); Fire Ins. Exch. v. Weitzel, 371 P.3d 457, 461 (Mont. 2016) ("If a complaint states multiple claims, some of which are covered by the insurance policy and some of which are not, it is a mixed action.").

353. Mesa Labs., Inc. v. Fed. Ins. Co., 994 F.3d 865, 868 (7th Cir. 2021) (applying Illinois law); Teufel v. Am. Fam. Mut. Ins. Co., 419 P.3d 546, 549 (Ariz. 2018); Carter v. Pulte Home Corp., 266 Cal. Rptr. 3d 447, 455 (Ct. App. 2020); Mount Vernon Fire Ins. Co. v. Visionaid, Inc., 76 N.E.3d 204, 210 (Mass. 2017); Reinsurance Ass'n of Minn. v. Timmer, 641 N.W.2d 302, 307 (Minn. Ct. App. 2002); Murray-Kaplan v. NEC Ins., Inc., 617 S.W.3d 485, 493 (Mo. Ct. App. 2021); *Weitzel*, 371 P.3d at 461; Sammy v. First Am. Title Ins. Co., 168 N.Y.S.3d 519, 524 (App. Div. 2022); Tibert v. Nodak

defend is not limited to those claims for which it may have a duty to indemnify the insured, but continues as long as the insurer has a potential indemnification obligation with respect to any single claim asserted in the lawsuit.[354] This is true even where most of the plaintiff's claims are outside the policy's coverage.[355] Furthermore, and consistent with the duty to defend generally, the entire-suit rule requires the insurer to defend the suit as a whole, even where the covered claims are meritless.[356]

The entire-suit rule ensures that the insured receives a meaningful, immediate defense of the claims that are potentially covered under its policy consistent with insurer's contractual duty to defend.[357] In the same vein, the entire-suit rule recognizes that it is not feasible to parse multiple claims when an insurer must provide an immediate defense to fulfill its contractual obligation to its insured. Certainly, it is impossible to know at the outset of litigation what claims the plaintiff may ultimately prevail on, if any, or which claims it might amend. For these reasons, the insurer's duty to defend uncovered claims is expressly tethered to its contractual agreement to provide a defense for those claims that are covered.[358] So viewed, the entire-suit rule does not exist independently of the parties' contract (the insurance policy), but instead exists to fulfill it.[359] In addition, the entire-suit rule enhances efficiency for litigants, lawyers, and courts in cases where there are multiple claims and a question whether one or more of the claims is covered under a particular insurance policy.[360] It allows the parties to reach the merits of the third-party action quickly, rather than litigating the insurer's duty to defend and the extent of that duty before trying the third-party action to a court or jury.[361]

Mut. Ins. Co., 816 N.W.2d 31, 42 (N.D. 2012); Sharonville v. Am. Emps. Ins. Co., 846 N.E.2d 833, 837 (Ohio 2006); Rogowski v. Safeco Ins. Co. of Or., 473 P.3d 111, 114 (Or. Ct. App. 2020); Kramer v. Nationwide Prop. & Cas. Ins. Co., 271 A.3d 431, 435 (Pa. Super. Ct. 2021); Zurich Am. Ins. Co. v. Nokia, Inc., 268 S.W.3d 487, 491 (Tex. 2008); Anderson v. Kayser Ford, Inc., 925 N.W.2d 547, 554 (Wis. Ct. App. 2019). *But see* Passaic Valley Sewerage Comm'rs v. St. Paul Fire & Marine Ins. Co., 21 A.3d 1151, 1162 (N.J. 2011) (stating that in a mixed action, the insurer "may refuse defense on the uncovered counts and dispute coverage").

354. *Kramer*, 271 A.3d at 435; *Anderson*, 925 N.W.2d at 554.

355. Selective Way Ins. Co. v. Nationwide Prop. & Cas. Ins. Co., 219 A.3d 20, 42 (Md. Ct. Spec. App. 2019); *see also* Drexel Chem. Co. v. Bituminous Ins. Co., 933 S.W.2d 471, 480 (Tenn. Ct. App. 1996) ("If even one of the allegations is covered by the policy, the insurer has a duty to defend, irrespective of the number of allegations that may be excluded by the policy.").

356. Steadfast Ins. Co. v. Greenwich Ins. Co., 922 N.W.2d 71, 79 (Wis. 2019).

357. 24th & Hoffman Invs., LLC v. Northfield Ins. Co., 298 Cal. Rptr. 3d 816, 825 (Ct. App. 2022).

358. *Id.*

359. *Id.*

360. Mount Vernon Fire Ins. Co. v. Visionaid, Inc., 76 N.E.3d 204, 211 (Mass. 2017).

361. *Id.*

E. Groundless, False, or Fraudulent Claims

Some insurance policies include a groundless-claims clause, which provides that if the insured is sued, the insurer will furnish a defense by counsel of its choice "even if the suit is groundless, false or fraudulent."[362] A few courts continue to use the phrase in their discussion of the duty to defend to highlight the breadth of the duty regardless of whether the policies in question include that language.[363] Still other courts have said that a groundless-claims clause "heightens" an insurer's duty to defend.[364] In fact, an insurer's duty to defend is no different under a policy with a groundless-claims clause as compared to a policy without a groundless-claims clause.

To explain, the phrase "groundless, false or fraudulent" as used in a policy's insuring agreement or other provision promising a defense "refers to the quality of the factual and legal allegations against the insured on which the insured's liability to the plaintiff is said to rest."[365] In other words, an insurance company must defend an insured in a lawsuit in which the plaintiff's claims are meritless or are asserted for some improper purpose provided that the complaint or petition alleges facts that, if proven, would obligate the insurer to indemnify the insured. An insurer's duty to defend even groundless, false, or fraudulent actions does not, however, obligate the insurer to defend the insured where there is no potential for coverage.[366]

Insurers originally included "groundless, false or fraudulent" language in their policies to clarify for insureds the breadth of the duty to defend and, conjunctively, to highlight the difference between the duty to defend and the duty to indemnify.[367] Yet, the broad duty to defend that insurers once signaled

---

362. Ins. Servs. Off., Inc. Homeowners 3 – Special Form (HO 00 03 05 11), at 17 (2010).

363. *See, e.g.*, Gen. Agents Ins. Co. of Am., Inc. v. Midwest Sporting Goods Co., 828 N.E.2d 1092, 1098 (Ill. 2005); Am. & Foreign Ins. Co. v. Jerry's Sport Ctr., Inc., 2 A.3d 526, 542 (Pa. 2010).

364. *See, e.g.*, Gallagher Sharp, L.L.P. v. Miller Goler Faeges Lapine, L.L.P., 137 N.E.3d 647, 659 (Ohio Ct. App. 2019) (quoting Sharonville v. Am. Emps. Ins. Co., 846 N.E.2d 833, 837 (Ohio 2006)).

365. Jerry & Richmond, *supra* note 7, at 691–92 n.63.

366. ACE Am. Ins. Co. v. Rite Aid Corp., 270 A.3d 239, 252 (Del. 2022) ("[T]he requirement to defend against 'groundless, false, or fraudulent' claims applies when the facts underlying the claims are untrue or misleading—not when the claims do not, in fact, invoke coverage."); Merrick v. Fischer, Rounds & Assocs., Inc., 939 N.W.2d 795, 807 (Neb. 2020) (footnote omitted) ("Although an insurer is obligated to defend all suits against the insured, even if groundless, false, or fraudulent, the insurer is not bound to defend a suit based on a claim outside the coverage of the policy."); Waste Mgmt. of the Carolinas, Inc. v. Peerless Ins. Co., 340 S.E.2d 374, 378 (N.C. 1986) ("Even though the insurer is bound by the policy to defend 'groundless, false or fraudulent' lawsuits filed against the insured, if the facts are not even arguably covered by the policy, then the insurer has no duty to defend.").

367. *See generally* Hartford Accident & Indem. Co. v. Capitol Home Improvement Co., 205 A.2d 192, 195 (Conn. Cir. Ct. 1964) ("The obligation of the [insurer] to defend does not depend on whether the injured party will successfully maintain a cause of action. The policy requires the [insurer] to defend irrespective of the ultimate outcome."); Brodek v. Indem. Ins. Co. of N. Am., 11 N.E.2d 228, 237 (Ill. App. Ct. 1937) ("What is meant by the requirement that the insurer undertakes to defend the suit whether 'groundless, false or fraudulent'? If a plaintiff alleges in his pleadings that he is entitled to recover upon a ground of liability covered by the policy, then of course the defendant's insurance

by inserting groundless-claims clauses in their policies is the same duty that an insurer has under a policy that simply obligates it to defend any suit seeking the specified covered damages.[368]

Compare, for example, a former version of the CGL policy with the current version. The former version of the CGL policy provided in pertinent part:

> The company will pay on behalf of the insured all sums which the insured shall become legally obligated to pay as damages because of
>
> Coverage A bodily injury or
>
> Coverage B property damage
>
> to which this insurance applies, caused by an occurrence, and the company shall have the right and duty to defend *any* suit against the insured seeking damages on account of such bodily injury or property damage, even if any of the allegations of the suit are groundless, false, or fraudulent. . . .[369]

The current version of the CGL policy states:

> We will pay those sums that the insured becomes legally obligated to pay as damages because of "bodily injury" or "property damage" to which this insurance applies. We will have the right and duty to defend the insured against *any* "suit" seeking those damages. However, we will have no duty to defend the insured against any suit seeking damages for "bodily injury" or "property damage" to which this insurance does not apply.[370]

Under the former version of the CGL policy, the insurer promised to "defend *any* suit against the insured seeking damages on account of bodily

---

carrier must defend the suit; it cannot avoid that duty by determining upon its own investigation that the ground of liability alleged cannot be substantiated."); Danek v. Hommer, 100 A.2d 198, 203 (N.J. Super. Ct. App. Div. 1953) ("[T]he duty [to defend] is not abrogated by the fact that the cause of action stated cannot be maintained against the insured either in law or in fact—in other words, because the cause is groundless, false or fraudulent. Liability of the insured to the plaintiff is not the criterion; it is the allegation in the complaint of a cause of action which, if sustained, will impose a liability covered by the policy."); Zeitz v. Zurich Gen. Accident & Liab. Ins. Co., 67 A.2d 742, 746 (Pa. Super. Ct. 1949) (discussing the breadth of the insurer's duty to defend under a policy with a groundless-claims clause); Prashker v. U.S. Guar. Co., 144 N.Y.S.2d 451, 455 (Sup. Ct. 1955) (describing the phrase "groundless, false or fraudulent" as a "clear and explicit" expression of the insurer's broad duty to defend).

368. *See* United Fire & Cas. Co. v. Prate Roofing & Installations, LLC, 7 F.4th 573, 581 (7th Cir. 2021) (stating that an "insurer may not deny a defense on the ground that the suit against its insured is hopeless"); Hanover Ins. Co. v. Anova Food, LLC, 173 F. Supp. 3d 1008, 1020 (D. Haw. 2016) ("The insurer's duty to defend exists even if the facts alleged are untrue or the legal theories unsound."); Holyoke Mut. Ins. Co. v. Vibram USA, Inc., 106 N.E.3d 572, 576 (Mass. 2018) (stating that an insurer may have a duty to defend "notwithstanding the possibility that the underlying claim may ultimately fail, or that the merits of the claim are weak or frivolous").

369. Willets Point Contracting Corp. v. Hartford Ins. Grp., 429 N.Y.S.2d 230, 231 (App. Div. 1980) (emphasis added) (quoting the Hartford CGL policy at issue); Ins. Servs. Off., Inc., Standard Coverage Part Comprehensive General Liability Insurance (GL 00 02 01 73), at 2 (1973) (emphasis added).

370. Ins. Servs. Off., Inc., Commercial General Liability Coverage Form (CG 00 01 04 13), at 1 (2012) (emphasis added).

injury or property damage" to which the policy applied.[371] Under the current version of the CGL policy, the insurer must defend the insured against "*any* suit seeking damages because of 'bodily injury' or 'property damage' to which [its] policy applies."[372] The promise to defend *any* suit seeking covered damages in the current CGL policy is the same promise made in the former version of the CGL policy and necessarily includes groundless, false, or fraudulent suits; the "groundless, false or fraudulent" language in the former version of the CGL policy was redundant. Indeed, when it revised the standard CGL policy form in 1986, the Insurance Services Office (ISO) deleted the groundless, false, or fraudulent language for that reason. Where such language appears in other liability insurance policies still in circulation, it is equally redundant.

At least one court has reasoned that the purpose of a groundless-claims clause "is to guarantee that the purchaser of a policy of liability insurance will be protected from all expense."[373] Assuming that to be true, the "groundless, false or fraudulent" language remains redundant. This is because standard liability insurance policies with no groundless-claims clause provide that the insurer will pay defense costs in addition to the policy limits.[374]

In summary, a groundless-claims clause in a liability insurance policy does not alter in any way the insurer's duty to defend. The duty to defend under such a policy is the same as it is under a policy without a groundless-claims clause.

VI. Excess and Umbrella Insurers' Duty to Defend

A. Overview

Insureds often have more than one layer of liability insurance protection. For instance, an individual may have a personal umbrella policy that protects her against liability that exceeds the limits of her personal auto and homeowners policies. Commercial insureds may have excess or commercial umbrella policies to protect them against liability that exceeds their CGL policy limits. In

371. *Willets Point*, 429 N.Y.S.2d at 231 (emphasis added); Ins. Servs. Off., Inc., Standard Coverage Part Comprehensive General Liability Insurance (GL 00 02 01 73), at 2 (1973) (emphasis added).

372. Ins. Servs. Off., Inc., Commercial General Liability Coverage Form (CG 00 01 04 13), at 1 (2012) (emphasis added).

373. Conn. Fire Ins. Co. v. Reliance Ins. Co., 208 F. Supp. 20, 27 (D. Kan. 1962).

374. *See, e.g.*, Ins. Servs. Off., Inc., Commercial General Liability Coverage Form (CG 00 01 04 13), at 1 (2012) ("We will pay, with respect to . . . any 'suit' against an insured we defend: . . . All expenses we incur."); ISO Props., Inc., Personal Auto Policy (PP 00 01 09 18), at 2 (2017) ("In addition to our limit of liability, we will pay all defense costs we incur.").

fact, commercial insureds often have towers of excess insurance with different insurers issuing policies for different layers of coverage.

Although excess insurance policies and umbrella policies both protect insureds against liability that exceeds the limits of the insured's primary policy,[375] they are not identical forms of insurance. An excess policy provides specific coverage above a scheduled underlying limit of primary insurance.[376] A true excess policy does not broaden the underlying coverage.[377] An excess policy increases the *amount* of coverage available to indemnify an insured but it does not increase the *scope* of coverage.[378]

An umbrella policy is a form of excess insurance.[379] In contrast to a true excess policy, however, an umbrella policy typically insures against certain risks that an underlying primary policy does not cover.[380] An umbrella policy is thus a "gap filler";[381] by design it sometimes provides first dollar coverage where a primary policy and an excess policy do not.[382] In other words, an umbrella policy occasionally drops down to provide primary coverage.[383] This may happen several ways: an umbrella policy may not contain exclusions that are found in the underlying primary policy, it may have broader definitions that operate to expand coverage beyond the terms of the primary policy, it

---

375. *See generally* Deere & Co. v. Allstate Ins. Co., 244 Cal. Rptr. 3d 100, 105 (Ct. App. 2019) ("Primary insurance provides immediate coverage upon the happening of an occurrence that gives rise to liability."); Am. Guarantee & Liab. Ins. Co. v. EXP US Servs., No. 1-21-0821, 2023 WL 1881939, at *5 (Ill. App. Ct. Feb. 10, 2023) ("Primary insurance coverage is coverage whereby, under the terms of the policy, liability attaches immediately upon the happening of an event that gives rise to liability.").

376. In large insurance programs where a commercial insured or a professional services firm has multiple layers of excess coverage above its primary coverage, an excess policy may provide coverage above one or more underlying excess policies.

377. Wells Fargo Bank v. Cal. Ins. Guar. Ass'n, 45 Cal. Rptr. 2d 537, 539 n.2 (Ct. App. 1995) (differentiating between excess and umbrella policies); Certain Underwriters at Lloyd's, London v. Cent. Mut. Ins. Co., 12 N.E.3d 762, 765 (Ill. App. Ct. 2014); Or. Mut. Ins. Co. v. Those Certain Underwriters at Lloyd's London Subscribing to Policy No. OROAKG2-CNE, 437 P.3d 232, 237 (Or. Ct. App. 2019).

378. John Crane Inc. v. Admiral Ins. Co., No. 04CH8266, 2006 WL 1010495, at *7 (Ill. App. Ct. Apr. 12, 2006); Globe Indem. Co. v. Jordan, 634 A.2d 1279, 1283 (Me. 1993).

379. Fed. Deposit Ins. Corp. v. Arrillaga-Torrens, 212 F. Supp. 3d 312, 364 (D.P.R. 2016); *EXP US Servs.*, 2023 WL 1881939, at *5.

380. Legacy Vulcan Corp. v. Super. Ct., 110 Cal. Rptr. 3d 795, 803 (Ct. App. 2010); Apodaca v. Allstate Ins. Co., 255 P.3d 1099, 1103 (Colo. 2011); Fortunato v. Highlands Ins. Grp., 785 A.2d 963, 966 (N.J. Super. Ct. Law Div. 2001); Am. States Ins. Co. v. Md. Cas. Co., 628 A.2d 880, 886 (Pa. Super. Ct. 1993); Christal v. Farmers Ins. Co. of Wash., 135 P.3d 479, 483 (Wash. Ct. App. 2006). While umbrella policies frequently cover risks not insured under a primary policy, they do not necessarily do so. Selimanovic v. Finney, 337 S.W.3d 30, 40 (Mo. Ct. App. 2011).

381. Com. Union Ins. Co. v. Walbrook Ins. Co., 7 F.3d 1047, 1053 (1st Cir. 1993); *Arrillaga-Torrens*, 212 F. Supp. 3d at 364; Certain Underwriters at Lloyd's, London v. S. Natural Gas Co., 142 So. 3d 436, 463 (Ala. 2013); Wells Fargo Bank v. Cal. Ins. Guar. Ass'n, 45 Cal. Rptr. 2d 537, 539 n.2 (Ct. App. 1995) (quoting Rsrv. Ins. Co. v. Pisciotta, 640 P.2d 764 (Cal. 1982)); Piatt v. Ind. Lumbermen's Mut. Ins. Co., 461 S.W.3d 788, 793 (Mo. 2015).

382. Cincinnati Ins. Co. v. CPS Holdings, Inc., 875 N.E.2d 31, 33 (Ohio 2007) (quoting Am. Special Risk Ins. Co. v. A-Best Prods., Inc., 975 F. Supp. 1019, 1022 (N.D. Ohio 1997)).

383. *Legacy Vulcan Corp.*, 110 Cal. Rptr. 3d at 803.

may insure additional persons or entities, or it may provide an additional form of coverage. For example, an umbrella policy may insure against "personal injury" when a primary policy does not.

By providing primary coverage in certain circumstances, an umbrella policy broadens the insured's primary coverage where an excess policy does not.[384] Thus, the terms "excess policy" and "umbrella policy" are not synonymous, although an umbrella policy is far more like a true excess policy than it is a primary policy.

B. Excess Insurers' Defense Obligations

Generally, when an insured with excess coverage is sued, the primary insurer must defend the lawsuit.[385] An excess insurer typically has no duty to defend until the limits of the underlying primary coverage are exhausted;[386] until the primary insurer unequivocally tenders the liability limits of its policy to the excess insurer and the excess insurer accepts the tender; or, where an excess policy is written above the insured's self-insured retention (SIR), the SIR is exhausted.[387] This is true even where the amount of the plaintiff's claim against the insured exceeds the primary policy limits, such that any judgment might implicate the excess insurer's duty to indemnify the insured.[388]

Consistent with the rule that an excess insurer has no duty to defend until the primary insurer's policy limits are exhausted, an excess insurer's duty to

384. Benjamin v. Amica Mut. Ins. Co., 140 P.3d 1210, 1217 (Utah 2006) (involving an umbrella policy that the insurer branded as an "excess" policy).

385. Great Am. Ins. Co. v. Quintana Homeowners Ass'n, 291 F. Supp. 3d 1003, 1009 (N.D. Cal. 2018).

386. SRM, Inc. v. Great Am. Ins. Co., 798 F.3d 1322, 1327 (10th Cir. 2015) (applying Oklahoma law); Preferred Constr., Inc. v. Ill. Nat'l Ins. Co., 494 F. App'x 162, 164–65 (2d Cir. 2012) (applying New York law); Schneider Nat'l Transp. v. Ford Motor Co., 280 F.3d 532, 538 (5th Cir. 2002) (interpreting Texas law); Sacred Heart Health Servs. v. MMIC Ins., Inc., 575 F. Supp. 3d 1137, 1158 (D.S.D. 2021); Grace v. Ins. Co. of N. Am., 944 P.2d 460, 466 (Alaska 1997); Twin City Fire Ins. Co. v. Burke, 63 P.3d 282, 287 (Ariz. 2003); City of Oxnard v. Twin City Fire Ins. Co., 44 Cal. Rptr. 2d 177, 179 (Ct. App. 1995); Ticor Title Ins. Co. v. Emps. Ins. of Wausau, 48 Cal. Rptr. 2d 368, 373 (Ct. App. 1995); Cotter Corp. v. Am. Empire Surplus Lines Ins. Co., 90 P.3d 814, 834 (Colo. 2004); W. Bend Mut. Ins. Co. v. DJW-Ridgeway Bldg. Consultants, Inc., 40 N.E.3d 194, 205 (Ill. App. Ct. 2015); Associated Wholesale Grocers, Inc. v. Americold Corp., 934 P.2d 65, 81 (Kan. 1997); Frankenmuth Mut. Ins. Co. v. Cont'l Ins. Co., 537 N.W.2d 879, 881 (Mich. 1995); Fireman's Fund Ins. Co. v. TIG Ins. Co., 14 S.W.3d 230, 232 (Mo. Ct. App. 2000); Old Republic Ins. Co. v. Stratford Ins. Co., 132 A.3d 1198, 1199, 1202 (N.H. 2016); U.S. Fid. & Guar. Co. v. Federated Rural Elec. Ins. Corp., 37 P.3d 828, 832–35 (Okla. 2001); Weyerhaeuser Co. v. Com. Union Ins. Co., 15 P.3d 115, 134–36 (Wash. 2001).

387. Lasorte v. Those Certain Underwriters at Lloyd's Subscribing to Pol'y Nos. 115NAP108111970, 115NAP109111970, 995 F. Supp. 2d 1134, 1145–46 (D. Mont. 2014) (applying New York law); Gen. Star Indem. Co. v. Super. Ct., 55 Cal. Rptr. 2d 322, 325 (Ct. App. 1996).

388. *Sacred Heart*, 575 F. Supp. 3d at 1158; Vizio, Inc. v. Arch Ins. Co., No 2:20-CV-06864-ODW (ASx), 2021 WL 6135756, at *4 (C.D. Cal. Dec. 9, 2021) (applying California law); Travelers Cas. & Sur. Co. v. Am. Int'l Surplus Lines Ins. Co., 465 F. Supp. 2d 1005, 1022 (S.D. Cal. 2006) (applying California law).

defend does not come into play where the underlying primary insurer simply declines to defend the insured.[389] So long as the primary insurer's policy limits are payable, regardless of whether they have actually been paid, the excess insurer has no duty to defend.[390]

An excess insurer may, however, elect to participate in the insured's defense where its policy limits are potentially implicated even though the underlying primary policy has not been exhausted. This right is contractual. For example, an excess policy may provide:

> We will have the right and duty to defend the insured against any suit seeking damages for "such injury or damage" when the limits of "controlling underlying insurance" have been exhausted in accordance with the provisions of such "controlling underlying insurance."
>
> When we have no duty to defend, we will have the right to defend, or the right to participate in the defense of, the insured against any other suit seeking damages for "injury or damage."
>
> However, we will have no duty to defend the insured against any suit seeking damages for which insurance under this policy does not apply.[391]

An umbrella policy might provide:

> We will have the right and duty to defend the insured against any "suit" seeking damages for such "bodily injury" or "property damage" when the "underlying insurance" does not provide coverage or the limits of "underlying insurance" have been exhausted. When we have no duty to defend, we will have the right to defend, or to participate in the defense of, the insured against any other "suit" seeking damages to which this insurance may apply. However, we will have no duty to defend the insured against any "suit" seeking damages for "bodily injury" or "property damage" to which this insurance does not apply.[392]

Excess and umbrella insurers need an option to defend to protect themselves in cases where the insured's exposure exceeds its primary policy limits, and the primary insurer is not mounting a strong defense. Courts correctly hold that even where an excess policy gives the insurer the right and option to defend before an underlying primary policy is exhausted, such language does not create a *duty* to defend.[393] Policy provisions granting an excess insurer a

389. Republic W. Ins. Co. v. Fireman's Fund Ins. Co., 241 F. Supp. 2d 1090, 1096 (N.D. Cal. 2003) (applying California law).

390. *Id.* (citing *Ticor*, 48 Cal. Rptr. 2d at 374).

391. Ins. Servs. Off., Inc., Commercial Excess Liability Coverage Form (CX 00 01 04 13), at 1 (2012).

392. Ins. Servs. Off., Inc., Commercial Liability Umbrella Coverage Form (CU 00 01 04 13), at 1 (2013).

393. *See, e.g.*, Inst. of London Underwriters v. First Horizon Ins. Co., 972 F.2d 125, 126–27 (5th Cir. 1992) (applying Louisiana law); Schwinn Cycling & Fitness, Inc. v. Hartford Accident & Indem.

right and option to participate in its insured's defense are intended to protect the insurer, not the insured. The majority position also makes sense because an insurer's duty to defend is expressly contractual and if there is no policy language requiring an insurer to defend, there can be no duty to do so.[394]

Preferred Construction, Inc. v. Illinois National Insurance Co.[395] is informative. That case arose out of a construction accident. Kevin Kennedy, a Preferred Construction, Inc. (Preferred Construction) employee, was injured when he fell from a roof at the Holy Sepulchre Cemetery (the Cemetery) of the Diocese of Rockville Centre (the Diocese). Kennedy sued the Cemetery, the Diocese, and the general contractor that hired Preferred Construction for negligence and labor law violations. Preferred Construction was insured under a $1 million primary CGL policy issued by Nova Casualty Co. (Nova) and a $5 million excess policy with Illinois National Insurance Co. (Illinois National). Nova accepted the defense of the Cemetery, the Diocese, and the general contractor as additional insureds under its policy, and appointed defense counsel for all three.

The additional insureds subsequently filed a third-party complaint against Preferred Construction in Kennedy's case seeking indemnification for any recovery that Kennedy might obtain in excess of Preferred Construction's primary policy limits. Nova sent the third-party complaint to Illinois National and requested that it defend Preferred Construction. Illinois National declined to do so.

Preferred Construction and Nova filed a declaratory judgment action against Illinois National, seeking (1) a declaration that Illinois National had a duty to defend and indemnify Preferred Construction in the third-party action; and (2) recovery of Nova's costs incurred in defending the third-party claims. The parties filed cross-motions for summary judgment. The district court granted Illinois National's motion and denied the motion filed by Preferred Construction and Nova. The district court based its ruling on the language of the Illinois National excess policy, which stated that Illinois National had a duty to defend "only when 'the total applicable limits of Scheduled Underlying Insurance have been exhausted by payment of Loss to which this policy applies and the total applicable limits of other insurance have been exhausted.'"[396] Because the Nova primary policy was not exhausted, the district court held that Illinois National currently had no duty to defend Preferred Construction.

Co., 863 F. Supp. 784, 787 (N.D. Ill. 1994) (applying Illinois law); Grace v. Ins. Co. of N. Am., 944 P.2d 460, 466 (Alaska 1997); FMC Corp. v. Plaisted & Cos., 72 Cal. Rptr. 2d 467, 508–10 (Ct. App. 1998); Gen. Motors Acceptance Corp. v. Nationwide Ins. Co., 828 N.E.2d 959, 961 (N.Y. 2005).

394. Fireman's Fund Ins. Co. v. TIG Ins. Co., 14 S.W.3d 230, 232 (Mo. Ct. App. 2000).

395. 494 F. App'x 162 (2d Cir. 2012).

396. *Id.* at 163 (quoting the Illinois National policy).

Nova and Preferred Construction appealed to the Second Circuit, which affirmed the district court's judgment.

The *Preferred Construction* court began its analysis of the parties' respective positions by quoting the relevant portion of the Illinois National policy, which provided:

> We will have the right and duty to defend any Suit against the Insured that seeks damages for Bodily Injury, Property Damage or Personal Injury and Advertising Injury covered by this policy, even if the Suit is groundless, false or fraudulent *when the total applicable limits of Scheduled Underlying Insurance have been exhausted* by payment of Loss to which this policy applies and the total applicable limits of Other Insurance have been exhausted.[397]

The Illinois National policy clearly stated that the underlying primary insurance had to be exhausted before the excess policy would provide a defense. Everyone acknowledged that the Nova policy was not exhausted. The *Preferred Construction* court therefore agreed with the district court that Illinois National as yet had no duty to defend.[398] Pushing back, Preferred Construction and Nova argued that Illinois National had a duty to defend because the third-party complaint sought only damages above the "applicable limits" of the Nova policy.[399] But that argument was a loser because even though the third-party claim was confined to damages above the Nova policy limits, exhaustion was still a condition precedent to Illinois National's acceptance of the defense, and that condition had not been met.[400]

The fact that the third-party complaint sought indemnification "only for 'any recovery that plaintiff may obtain in excess of the primary policy limits'" did not change the result.[401] To require Illinois National to defend here would effectively permit any claim of excess liability to preemptively trigger the excess insurer's duty to defend regardless of whether the underlying primary policy limits were exhausted. To adopt that position would gut the general rule that an excess insurer may choose to participate in an insured's defense before primary coverage is exhausted to protect its interests but has no duty to do so.[402]

397. *Id.* at 164 (emphasis added by the court).
398. *Id.* at 165.
399. *Id.*
400. *Id.*
401. *Id.*
402. *Id.* (quoting Fieldston Prop. Owners Ass'n, Inc. v. Hermitage Ins. Co., 945 N.E.2d 1013, 1018 (N.Y. 2011)).

C. Umbrella Carriers' Duty to Defend Suits Not Covered by Underlying Primary Insurance

Where an umbrella policy provides excess coverage, the umbrella insurer—like a true excess insurer—has no duty to defend until the liability limits of the underlying primary policy are exhausted.[403] As noted earlier, however, unlike true excess policies, umbrella policies frequently provide that the umbrella policy will afford primary coverage for suits that are not within the ambit of the insured's primary policy in some circumstances. With primary coverage come a primary insurer's duties. Thus, an umbrella insurer may have a duty to defend its insured where a true excess carrier would not.[404] Of course, there must be a potential for coverage under the umbrella policy for the umbrella carrier to have a duty to defend.[405]

There is nothing remarkable about umbrella carriers' occasional duty to defend suits that primary policies do not cover. Excess and umbrella policies are different, and excess and umbrella carriers may have different obligations depending on the case. None of this should be understood to mean, however, that an umbrella insurer is obligated to assume a duty to defend whenever an underlying primary insurer denies coverage. *Travelers Indemnity Co. v. Northrop Grumman Corp.*[406] is an interesting case in point.

There, Northrop Grumman Corp. (Northrop Grumman) was insured over a period of years under primary CGL policies issued by Century Indemnity Co. (Century) and umbrella policies issued by Travelers Indemnity Co. (Travelers). Century denied coverage for a putative mass tort class action known as the *Romano* lawsuit based on late notice. While Northrop Grumman and Century were litigating Century's late notice defense, Northrop Grumman asserted that Travelers had a duty to defend it in the *Romano* lawsuit.

---

403. Johnson v. RLI Ins. Co., No. 3:14-cv-00095-SLG, 2016 WL 777885, at *5 (D. Alaska Feb. 29, 2016) (describing this principle as the majority rule); *see, e.g.*, Travelers Prop. Cas. Co. of Am. v. Amerisure Ins. Co., No. 21-cv-10969, 2022 WL 18957187, at *4 (E.D. Mich. Nov. 17, 2022) (footnote omitted) ("Because no settlement or judgment has been paid on behalf of [the insured], the CGL policy limits have not been exhausted, and the duty to defend [the insured] remains under the CGL policies; at this stage, no duty to defend under the umbrella policies has been triggered.").

404. *See, e.g.*, Fed. Ins. Co. v. Steadfast Ins. Co., 147 Cal. Rptr. 3d 363, 375 (Ct. App. 2012); Nat'l Union Fire Ins. Co. v. Glenview Park Dist., 594 N.E.2d 1300, 1306–08 (Ill. App. Ct. 1992), *aff'd in part, rev'd in part on other grounds*, 632 N.E.2d 1039 (Ill. 1994); Am. States Ins. Co. v. Md. Cas. Co., 628 A.2d 880, 886–88 (Pa. Super. Ct. 1993).

405. *See Am. States*, 628 A.2d at 887 (applying standard duty to defend analysis to an umbrella policy); *see, e.g.*, State Farm Fire & Cas. Co. v. Rodriguez, No. 19-00567 JMS-KJM, 2021 WL 412268, at *5–6 (D. Haw. Feb. 5, 2021) (finding no duty to defend under the insured's personal umbrella policy because there was no "loss" as defined in the policy); Cincinnati Ins. Co. v. CPS Holdings, Inc., 875 N.E.2d 31, 34–36 (Ohio 2007) (finding no duty to defend by the umbrella carrier where the primary policy was not "underlying insurance" within the meaning of the umbrella policy).

406. No. 16 Civ. 8778 (LGS), 2022 WL 4448502 (S.D.N.Y. Sept. 23, 2022).

The Travelers umbrella policies provided that Travelers had a duty to defend Northrop Grumman against "'any claim or suit alleging bodily injury, personal injury . . . or property damage . . . , insurance for which is not afforded by the underlying policies listed in . . . the declarations or any other applicable insurance . . . , but which is insured by the terms and conditions of this policy.'"[407] The parties' disagreement centered on the term "afforded" in the umbrella policies. Northrop Grumman argued that it was entitled to recoup its defense costs from Travelers because Century was not defending it under the primary CGL policies. According to Northrop Grumman, "afforded" as used in the umbrella policies referred to whether a defense was actually provided or furnished under the primary policies for a given lawsuit, not whether the primary policies generally included a duty to defend.[408] Travelers countered that it was not obligated to reimburse Northrop Grumman's defense costs under its umbrella policies because the Century primary policies "afforded" coverage; that is, the allegations in the *Romano* lawsuit were within the scope of the primary policies' coverage.[409]

Because the umbrella policies did not define "afforded," the court gave the word its ordinary meaning as supplied by a dictionary, which was "to make available, give forth, or provide naturally or inevitably."[410] Applying this definition, Travelers's duty to defend arose under the umbrella policies only if insurance was not "afforded"—meaning made available or provided—under the Century primary policies.[411]

Again, the Travelers umbrella policies provided coverage when "insurance . . . is not afforded by the underlying policies."[412] Northrop Grumman's proposed interpretation of "afforded" would have required the court to interpret "insurance" to mean "payment," which could not be justified by the umbrella policies' plain language.[413] Had the parties intended the umbrella policies to drop down and provide primary coverage when the Century policies were uncollectible, the umbrella policies would have expressly said so by referring to collection or recoverability.[414] Bolstering the court's interpretation, Northrop Grumman grudgingly acknowledged that when an excess insurer uses the

407. *Id.* at *6 (quoting the Travelers umbrella policies).
408. *Id.*
409. *Id.*
410. *Id.*
411. *Id.*
412. *Id.*
413. *Id.*
414. *Id.* (observing that the parties did precisely this in "clause (g) of Insuring Clause I, which states that indemnification coverage is not available to the extent 'any valid and *collectible* insurance . . . is available to the insured. . . .'").

terms "collectible" or "recoverable," it is promising to drop down if the primary coverage becomes uncollectible or unrecoverable.[415]

Furthermore, interpreting "afforded" to mean that the risk or loss was within the scope of the primary policies' coverage was also consistent with the use of the terms "afforded" and "insurance" elsewhere in the umbrella policies. For instance, the Limits of Liability section stated that, "with respect to any occurrence for which insurance is afforded hereunder . . . the company's liability is limited as follows."[416] If the court were to interpret "afforded" and "insurance" to mean whether defense or indemnity costs were actually provided under the umbrella policies, then this provision, which set the policy limits, would be meaningless.[417] That result would be contrary to basic principles of contract interpretation

Finally, Northrop Grumman argued in the alternative that the term "afforded" was ambiguous.[418] The court succinctly rejected this argument; the language in the umbrella policies that prescribed Travelers' duty to defend was unambiguous and had to be given its plain meaning.[419] The *Travelers Indemnity* court therefore held that Travelers had no duty to defend Northrop Grumman in the *Romano* lawsuit.

415. *Id.* (citing Garay v. Nat'l Grange Mut. Ins. Co., 117 F. App'x 785, 789 (2d Cir. 2004)).
416. *Id.* (quoting the Travelers umbrella policies).
417. *Id.*
418. *Id.* at *7.
419. *Id.*

CHAPTER 2
Reservations of Rights and Nonwaiver Agreements

Douglas R. Richmond

I. Introduction

An insurer's duty to defend its insured is assessed at the outset of a case.[1] Sometimes, a lawsuit against its insured may be the insurer's first notice of the claimed loss, such that the insurer knows only the facts of the loss alleged in the plaintiff's complaint or petition—and there is no assurance that those facts are accurate or complete. In other cases, the insurer may have investigated the underlying occurrence but may nonetheless be uncertain whether it will ultimately be obligated to indemnify the insured. In yet other cases, the plaintiff's complaint or petition may be sufficiently vague that the insurer cannot determine whether it will be obligated to indemnify the insured or the pleading may allege multiple claims or causes of action, some of which clearly are covered and others which clearly are not.

In these situations, the insurer faces a dilemma based on the differences between its duty to defend and its duty to indemnify the insured. Both duties are created when the contract between the insurer and insured (the policy) is formed. As explained in Chapter 1, however, the duty to indemnify is not due and owing until the insured's liability is established.[2] In contrast, the duty to

1. Liberty Ins. Underwriters, Inc. v. Cocrystal Pharma, Inc., No. 22-2242, 2023 WL 3067498, at *5 (3d Cir. Apr. 25, 2023); Bitco Gen. Ins. Corp. v. Monroe Guar. Ins. Co., 31 F.4th 325, 329 (5th Cir. 2022); McMillin Homes Constr., Inc. v. Nat'l Fire & Marine Ins. Co., 247 Cal. Rptr. 3d 825, 830 (Ct. App. 2019).

2. *Bitco*, 31 F.4th at 329; Buss v. Super. Ct., 939 P.2d 766, 993 (Cal. 1997); First Mercury Ins. Co. v. Nationwide Sec. Servs., Inc., 54 N.E.3d 323, 330 (Ill. App. Ct. 2016); Irving Oil Ltd. v. ACE INA Ins. Co., 91 A.3d 594, 599 (Me. 2014); Remodeling Dimensions, Inc. v. Integrity Mut. Ins. Co., 819

defend exists as soon as the insured is sued on a claim potentially within coverage, regardless of whether the insured is ultimately found to be liable. Plus, in determining whether an insurer owes a duty to defend, courts resolve any ambiguities or doubts in the insured's favor.[3] As a result, an insurer may have a duty to defend an insured in a case even though it ultimately has no duty to indemnify the insured.[4]

Often, and as the forgoing discussion suggests, the facts and allegations are such that an insurer that doubts whether its policy covers a loss cannot afford to flatly decline to defend its insured. After all, if the insurer is wrong about its potential indemnity obligation and is thereafter held to have breached its duty to defend, it faces a range of negative consequences. If, on the other hand, the insurer defends the insured without asserting its coverage position, it will likely be deemed to have waived any coverage defenses or will be estopped to assert them. Accordingly, to protect itself against breach allegations and preserve its ability to later deny coverage, the insurer normally defends the insured under a reservation of rights. That is, the insurer agrees to defend the insured while reserving its rights not to indemnify the insured under the terms of its policy.[5] The insurer may reserve its rights because the underlying occurrence arguably falls outside the policy's insuring agreements or at least some of the plaintiff's claims do, because the allegations against the insured implicate a policy exclusion, because legal principles preclude coverage, because the insured may have breached a policy condition, or because of some combination of these factors.

N.W.2d 602, 616 (Minn. 2012); Barron v. Shelter Mut. Ins. Co., 220 S.W.3d 746, 747 (Mo. 2007); Gem-Quality Corp. v. Colony Ins. Co., 177 N.Y.S.3d 133, 138 (App. Div. 2022) (quoting Am. Mfrs. Mut. Ins. Co. v. Quality King Distribs., Inc., 792 N.Y.S.2d 555, 556 (App. Div. 2005)); Bighorn Logging Corp. v. Truck Ins. Exch., 437 P.3d 287, 293 (Or. Ct. App. 2019); Choinsky v. Germantown Sch. Dist. Bd. of Educ., 926 N.W.2d 196, 203 (Wis. Ct. App. 2019).

3. Scottsdale Ins. Co. v. Columbia Ins. Grp., Inc., 972 F.3d 915, 919–20 (7th Cir. 2020) (applying Illinois law); 24th & Hoffman Inv., LLC v. Northfield Ins. Co., 298 Cal. Rptr. 3d 816, 823 (Ct. App. 2022); Nautilus Ins. Co. v. Access Med., LLC, 482 P.3d 683, 691 (Nev. 2021); N.C. Farm Bureau Mut. Ins. Co. v. Cox, 823 S.E.2d 613, 626 (N.C. Ct. App. 2019); Robbins v. Mason Cnty. Title Ins. Co., 425 P.3d 885, 893 (Wash. Ct. App. 2018); Grigg v. Aarrowcast, Inc., 909 N.W.2d 183, 191 (Wis. Ct. App. 2018).

4. Siplast, Inc. v. Emps. Mut. Ins. Co., 23 F.4th 486, 492 (5th Cir. 2022) (applying Texas law); Greene v. Westfield Ins. Co., 963 F.3d 619, 628 (7th Cir. 2020) (applying Indiana law); N. Counties Eng'g, Inc. v. State Farm Gen. Ins. Co., 169 Cal. Rptr. 3d 726, 739 (Ct. App. 2014); Sprint Lumber, Inc. v. Union Ins. Co., 627 S.W.3d 96, 114 (Mo. Ct. App. 2021) (quoting Arch Ins. Co. v. Sunset Fin. Servs., Inc., 475 S.W.3d 730, 733 (Mo. Ct. App. 2015)); Auto. Ins. Co. of Hartford v. Cook, 850 N.E.2d 1152, 1155 (N.Y. 2006); ZRZ Realty Co. v. Beneficial Fire & Cas. Ins. Co., 266 P.3d 61, 66 (Or. 2011).

5. *See* Hoover v. Maxum Indem. Co., 730 S.E.2d 413, 416 (Ga. 2012) (describing the purpose of a reservation of rights); Becker v. Bar Plan Mut. Ins. Co., 429 P.3d 212, 217 (Kan. 2018) (stating that a reservation of rights "allows an insurer to assume a defense of an insured without waiving noncoverage defenses"); Am. W. Home Ins. Co. v. Gjonaj Realty & Mgmt. Co., 138 N.Y.S.3d 626, 630 (App. Div. 2020) (explaining a reservation of rights); Mastellone v. Lightning Rod Mut. Ins. Co., 884 N.E.2d 1130, 1139–40 (Ohio Ct. App. 2008) ("By definition, a reservation of rights means that the insurer does not believe that coverage is available under the policy, but that it is proceeding to defend a claim in order to control the defense.").

II. Foundational Principles

A. The Purpose of a Reservation of Rights

A reservation of rights letter is a unilateral notice stating that the insurer reserves the right to deny coverage despite its initial decision to defend the insured.[6] A reservation of rights letter serves two important purposes. First, a reservation of rights letter alerts the insured that its interests and the insurer's interests are not necessarily aligned, and that the insured is potentially exposed to personal liability. Once alerted, the insured may be able to take steps to protect itself against any harm or prejudice that might otherwise result from the insurer's ultimate denial of coverage. At the very least, the insured might be prompted to retain a lawyer to advise it on relevant considerations. In the absence of a reservation of rights letter, on the other hand, the insurer's provision of a defense could lull the insured into a false sense of security with respect to the insurer's duty to indemnify it when the time comes. Second, assuming the reservation of rights letter is timely issued and properly drafted, it inoculates the insurer against claims that it has waived any policy defenses or is estopped from asserting them by controlling the insured's defense.

B. Oral versus Written Reservations of Rights

A reservation of rights may be oral,[7] but an insurer typically informs an insured of its reservation of rights by sending a reservation of rights letter. Insurers generally send reservation of rights letters by certified mail, and they often send a copy by email as well. An insurer that sends a reservation of rights letter as an email attachment can request a "delivery receipt," a "read receipt," or both to confirm that the insured received the email message and thus the letter.[8] By reserving its rights in writing, the insurer avoids the ambiguity or confusion that may accompany an oral reservation of rights and increases the likelihood that its reservation of rights will be effective because it adequately informed the insured of its coverage position.[9]

---

6. Landmark Am. Ins. Co. v. Esters, 600 F. Supp. 3d 677, 687 (W.D. La. 2022).

7. State Farm Fire & Cas. Co. v. Jioras, 29 Cal. Rptr. 2d 840, 844 (Ct. App. 1994); World Harvest Church, Inc. v. GuideOne Mut. Ins. Co., 695 S.E.2d 6, 10 (Ga. 2010).

8. A "read receipt" confirms only that the insured read the email message transmitting the reservation of rights letter; it does not establish that the insured read the reservation of rights letter that was attached to the message.

9. *See, e.g.*, Harleysville Lake States Ins. Co. v. Granite Ridge Builders, Inc., No. 1:06-CV-397-TS, 2009 WL 897412, at *7 (N.D. Ind. Mar. 31, 2009) (concluding that the adjuster's equivocal statement to the insured's representatives during a telephone conversation did not constitute a clear, unambiguous, or effective reservation of rights); ACCC Ins. Co. of Ga. v. Walker, 832 S.E.2d 878, 880 (Ga. Ct. App. 2019) (concluding that the adequacy of an insurer's reservation of rights delivered via voicemail was a question for the fact finder); Am. Safety Indem. Co. v. Sto Corp., 802 S.E.2d 448, 454 (Ga. Ct.

C. To Whom Must a Reservation of Rights Letter Be Sent?

An insurer is obligated only to send a reservation of rights letter to its insured. If multiple insureds may be owed coverage for a loss, the insurer generally must inform each insured of its reservation of rights to preserve its coverage defenses with respect to that insured.[10] There may be situations, however, where sending a reservation of rights letter to only some insureds is sufficient. Where the insured is a small company or a partnership, for example, sending a reservation of rights letter to one or two officers or partners may suffice to reserve the insurer's rights with respect to the remaining officers or partners.[11] In contrast, an insurer has no duty to inform the party suing its insured that there may be no coverage under the insured's policy.[12] Only the insured is a party to the contract—again, the insurance policy—and it is the insured to whom the insurer potentially owes a duty to indemnify. The plaintiff suing the insured is a stranger to the contract between the insurer and the insured, has no rights under the policy, and has no legitimate expectation that the policy will cover the insured for the accident at issue. There is thus no basis to argue that the insurer should send a reservation of rights letter to the plaintiff. Similarly, in the absence of a direct action statute,[13] only an insured has standing to complain that an insurer failed to reserve its rights or that a reservation of rights letter is somehow inadequate.[14]

App. 2017) (finding that an insurance adjuster's nonspecific recollection of undocumented quarterly calls with the insured to discuss coverage issues did not unambiguously convey a reservation of rights).

10. *See, e.g.*, Knox-Tenn Rental Co. v. Home Ins. Co., 2 F.3d 678, 682–84 (6th Cir. 1993) (estopping the insurer from denying coverage in a case involving an employee who was insured under an insurance agency's policy; the insurer did not send a reservation of rights letter to the employee and, while it did send a reservation of rights letter to the insurance agency and copied the lawyer who was representing both the agency and the employee, the letter did not mention the employee); Erie Ins. Exch. v. Lobenthal, 114 A.3d 832, 837–40 (Pa. Super. Ct. 2015) (concluding that a reservation of rights letter sent to parents, who were the named insureds, was ineffective toward an 18-year-old child who was also an insured under the policy; sending a copy of the letter to the defense lawyer was not effective because the letter did not refer to the child).

11. *See, e.g.*, Mendel v. Home Ins. Co., 806 F. Supp. 1206, 1214 (E.D. Pa. 1992) (discussing the insurer's reservation of rights letter sent to the president of a company with only five officers, directors, or shareholders and stating that the insurer "reasonably could conclude that notice to [the president] would be communicated among and between the officers, directors and shareholders"); *Jioras*, 29 Cal. Rptr. 2d at 846 (explaining that a reservation of rights letter sent to two partners provided constructive notice of the insurer's position to two other partners).

12. Chi. Ins. Co. v. Paulson & Nace, PLLC, 37 F. Supp. 3d 281, 296 n.15 (D.D.C. 2014) (applying D.C. law); Cincinnati Ins. Co. v. All Plumbing, Inc. Serv., Parts, Installation, 983 F. Supp. 2d 162, 167 (D.D.C. 2013) (applying D.C. law); Kirschner v. Process Design Assocs., Inc., 592 N.W.2d 707, 712 (Mich. 1999).

13. *See* FDIC v. Duffy, 47 F.3d 146, 150 (5th Cir. 1995) (reasoning that the Louisiana direct action statute grants a third-party standing to assert that an insurer has waived its coverage defenses).

14. *See, e.g.*, State Farm Mut. Auto. Ins. Co. v. Reynolds, No. 3:21-cv-05077-MDH, 2022 WL 4585833, at *2 (W.D. Mo. Sept. 29, 2022) (applying Missouri law and concluding that the tort claimants did not have standing to challenge the adequacy of a reservation of rights letter); Capitol Indem. Corp. v. Fraley, 597 S.E.2d 601, 603 (Ga. Ct. App. 2004) (concluding that a tort claimant lacked standing to assert waiver or estoppel based on the insurer's failure to reserve its rights); Am. Nat'l

D. No Duty to Reserve Rights Regarding Policy Limits and Deductibles

An insurer has no obligation to reserve its rights with respect to the liability limits of its policy.[15] This is because "limits of liability are not defenses to coverage and cannot be waived."[16] An insurer's defense of an action where coverage is questionable without reserving its rights does not rewrite the policy to remove the limits of liability.[17] Similarly, an insurer has no duty to reserve its rights where deductibles are concerned because deductibles are far more like policy limits than they are exclusions.[18]

E. Excess Letters as Compared to Reservation of Rights Letters

Where excess liability is a possibility, an insurer that advises its insured that a verdict or judgment may exceed the policy's liability limits has not reserved its rights and the letter it sends to the insured alerting the insured to the potential for excess liability is not a reservation of rights letter.[19] Rather, such a letter is properly described as an "excess letter."[20] In states that hold that a reservation of rights allows an insured to reject the defense offered by the insurer or creates a conflict of interest between the insurer and the insured, an excess letter does not have the same effect.[21] This makes sense because an excess letter does not reflect the insurer's assertion of possible coverage defenses. Furthermore, an insurer's failure to send an excess letter will not later estop it from

Prop. & Cas. Cos. v. Hearn, 93 A.3d 880, 887 (Pa. Super. Ct. 2014) (rejecting the plaintiffs' claim that the reservation of rights letter issued to the defendant was deficient).

15. Stacy v. Bar Plan Mut. Ins. Co., 621 S.W.3d 549, 565 (Mo. Ct. App. 2021); *see* Kannaday v. Ball, No. 09-2255-JWL, 2010 WL 2346368, at *4–5 (D. Kan. June 9, 2010) (applying Kansas law).

16. *Stacy*, 621 S.W.3d at 565; *see also* Chemstar, Inc. v. Liberty Mut. Ins. Co., No. 93-55555, 1994 WL 6540026, at *1 (9th Cir. Nov. 16, 1994) ("The mere fact that Liberty defended Chemstar without a reservation of rights did not cause Liberty to waive, or to become estopped from asserting, its policy limits as a defense to coverage."); Merrimack Mut. Fire Ins. Co. v. Nonaka, 606 N.E.2d 904, 907 (Mass. 1993) (stating that waiver does not apply to an insurer's policy limits); Rolan v. New W. Health Servs., 504 P.3d 464, 471 (Mont. 2022) (citation omitted) ("[A] policy's liability limits are not 'policy defenses' to coverage. . . . They are the monetary amounts potentially available to be paid for qualifying liability coverage upon a determination of the scope of an insurer's duty to indemnify.").

17. *Chemstar*, 1994 WL 6540026, at *1 (quoting 14 Couch on Insurance 2d § 51:93, at 595 (1982)).

18. W. Heritage Ins. Co. v. Asphalt Wizards, 795 F.3d 832, 837–38 (8th Cir. 2015) (predicting how the Missouri Supreme Court would rule); Cincinnati Ins. Co. v. All Plumbing, Inc., Serv., Parts Installation, 64 F. Supp. 3d 69, 79–80 (D.D.C. 2014); Pav-Lak Indus., Inc. v. Arch Ins. Co., 866 N.Y.S.2d 671, 673 (App. Div. 2008).

19. Marathon Ashland Pipe Line LLC v. Md. Cas. Co., 243 F.3d 1232, 1249 (10th Cir. 2001).

20. In addition to advising the insured that the value of the plaintiff's claims may exceed the insured's policy limits, a typical excess letter informs the insured that the insured will be responsible for paying any portion of a judgment that exceeds the policy limits; identifies the defense lawyer appointed by the insurer; informs the insured that it has the right to engage separate counsel at its own expense to advise it with respect to its potential excess exposure; and encourages the insured to notify its other insurers, if any, of the lawsuit.

21. *Marathon*, 243 F.3d at 1249.

asserting that the liability limits of its policy have been exhausted, nor can it through inaction waive exhaustion of the policy limits as a defense to an insured's indemnification claim.[22] This result reflects the oft-stated principle that estoppel and waiver cannot be used to create coverage where it would not otherwise exist.[23]

F. Reservations of Rights and the Duty to Defend

An insurer that defends under reservation of rights fulfills its duty to defend the insured.[24] Relatedly, because an insurer that defends under a reservation of rights is fulfilling its duty to defend, the insured generally remains obligated to cooperate in the defense.[25]

An insurer that defends under a reservation of rights generally is entitled to control the defense.[26] This rule makes perfect sense because a reservation of rights does not alter the insurer's duty to defend the insured; a reservation of rights relates only to the insurer's potential duty to indemnify the insured. An insurer that controls the insured's defense under a reservation of rights must defend the insured as competently and diligently as it would in a full coverage case.[27]

Finally, regardless of any benefit an insurer derives from a reservation of rights, a defense under reservation also benefits the insured. Even if the insurer ultimately disclaims its duty to indemnify, the insured received a defense paid

22. Gambino v. Lamulle, 715 So. 2d 574, 576 (La. Ct. App. 1998) (discussing waiver); Faber v. Roelofs, 250 N.W.2d 817, 825 (Minn. 1977) (discussing estoppel); Martin v. U.S. Fid. & Guar. Co., 996 S.W.2d 506, 511 (Mo. 1999) (referring to estoppel).

23. *Martin*, 996 S.W.2d at 511.

24. Sacred Heart Health Servs. v. MMIC Ins., Inc., 575 F. Supp. 3d 1137, 1186–87 (D.S.D. 2021) (applying South Dakota law); Becker v. Bar Plan Mut. Ins. Co., 429 P.3d 212, 219 (Kan. 2018); Passaic Valley Sewerage Comm'rs v. St. Paul Fire & Marine Ins. Co., 21 A.3d 1151, 1162 (N.J. 2011).

25. Douglas R. Richmond, *Independent Counsel in Insurance*, 48 San Diego L. Rev. 857, 890 n.205 (2011); Restatement of the L. of Liab. Ins. § 29 cmt. e (Am. L. Inst. 2019); *see, e.g.*, Vincent Soybean & Grain Co. v. Lloyd's Underwriters of London, 246 F.3d 1129, 1131–32 (8th Cir. 2001) (settling without the insurer's consent while being defended under a reservation of rights breached the insured's duty to cooperate); Emps. Reinsurance Corp. v. E. Miller Ins. Agency, Inc., 773 N.E.2d 707, 717–18 (Ill. App. Ct. 2002) (finding that the insureds' failure to cooperate while being defended under a reservation of rights breached the policy).

26. U.S. Underwriters Ins. Co. v. Kenfa Madison, LLC, No. 20-CV-2761 (NGG) (LB), 2023 WL 2710879, at *4 (E.D.N.Y. Mar. 30, 2023) (applying New York law); Great Am. Assur. Co. v. PCR Venture of Phoenix LLC, 161 F. Supp. 3d 778, 782–83 (D. Ariz. 2015) (applying Arizona law); Auto-Owners Ins. Co. v. Bolt Factory Lofts Owners Ass'n, Inc., 487 P.3d 276, 284 (Colo. 2021). *But see* John Moriarty & Assocs. v. Zurich Am. Ins. Co., 207 N.E.3d 542, 549 (Mass. App. Ct. 2023) (explaining that when an insurer defends under a reservation of rights, the insured is entitled to control the defense and to seek payment of its legal bills by the insurer).

27. *See* Willis Corroon Corp. v. Home Ins. Co., 203 F.3d 449, 452 (7th Cir. 2000) (stating that an insurer defending under a reservation of rights must provide an effective defense and cannot put its interests ahead of its insureds' interests); United Nat'l Ins. Co. v. Waterfront N.Y. Realty Corp., 948 F. Supp. 263, 268 (S.D.N.Y. 1996) (stating that an insurer defending under a reservation of rights "must conduct the defense of the insured with due care and good faith").

for by the insurer rather than having to fund its own defense. The value and importance of an insurer's defense under reservation of rights is magnified for insureds who cannot realistically afford to defend themselves. For that matter, in most cases defended under a reservation of rights, the reservation proves to be inconsequential. Insurers routinely indemnify insureds or settle cases against insureds after reserving their rights because (1) those approaches are preferable from a business standpoint, as where the judgment is acceptable in amount, or the settlement was nominal or at least lower than the cost of defense; or (2) the reserved coverage defenses never materialize or are too uncertain to support a reasonable denial of coverage.

III. Timeliness, Informational Adequacy, and Waiver and Estoppel

A. Introduction

An insurer must send a reservation of rights letter to the insured on a timely basis under the circumstances. The letter must also fairly or adequately inform the insured of the insurer's coverage position. If an insurer unreasonably delays in reserving its rights or issues a letter that is ambiguous or incomplete, it may be estopped from asserting any coverage defenses or may be held to have waived those defenses. The issues of timeliness, informational adequacy, and waiver and estoppel are interrelated.

B. The Timeliness of a Reservation of Rights

1. Fundamental Timing Issues

For an insurer to have an obligation to issue a reservation of rights letter with respect to a coverage defense, it must know of,[28] or at least be on notice of,[29] the coverage defense when it assumes the insured's defense.[30] Either way, an insurer is not obligated to speculate about all possible coverage defenses before it assumes an insured's defense.[31] Accordingly, where an insurer's alleged delay in reserving its rights is due to its lack of knowledge of facts that suggest a

28. Ill. Ins. Guar. Fund v. Nwidor, 105 N.E.3d 1035, 1043 (Ill. App. Ct. 2018); Federated Dep't Stores, Inc. v. Twin City Fire Ins. Co., 807 N.Y.S.2d 62, 66 (App. Div. 2006).

29. 1 Allan D. Windt, Insurance Claims and Disputes § 2:7, at 2-28 (6th ed. 2013 & Supp. 2023).

30. *See also* Restatement of the L. of Liab. Ins. § 15(1) (Am. L. Inst. 2019) ("An insurer may reserve the right to contest coverage for an action before undertaking the defense of the action if it gives timely notice to the insured of any ground for contesting coverage *of which it knows or should know*.") (emphasis added).

31. *Federated Dep't Stores*, 807 N.Y.S.2d at 66.

potential coverage defense, it should not be estopped to deny coverage or be held to have waived the coverage defense if it promptly reserves its rights upon acquiring the knowledge necessary to identify the defense.[32] This is especially true where the insured's conduct—such as delay in giving notice of a loss or providing incorrect or misleading statements about the facts of an accident, regardless of reason—deprives the insurer of information it needs to reserve its rights.[33]

In addition, an insurer must have reasonable time to evaluate coverage.[34] For example, an insurer may need to investigate the facts of an occurrence, or it may have to obtain a coverage opinion from outside counsel before it can properly reserve its rights. In such cases, the insurer's delay in issuing a reservation of rights letter is excusable. In *Certain Underwriters at Lloyd's London v. Covert Holdings, LLC*,[35] the insurer did not learn of facts that affected its coverage until after the underlying tort litigation was underway.

Covert Holdings arose out of Donald Howard's 2015 fall on a sidewalk that fronted property owned by Covert Holdings, LLC (Covert Holdings) and leased in part by an unnamed tenant. Certain Underwriters at Lloyd's London (Underwriters) insured the tenant and, while it is not clear from the opinion, apparently also insured Covert Holdings as an additional insured. Covert Holdings had its own coverage through DB Insurance, Ltd. (DB Insurance). Howard sued Covert Holdings and the tenant.

Underwriters defended Covert Holdings in Howard's lawsuit in addition to defending the tenant but, in early 2016, learned for the first time that Howard did not fall on the sidewalk fronting the portion of the premises leased by the tenant.[36] Underwriters thus demanded that DB Insurance assume Covert Holdings' defense. On December 20, 2016, Underwriters sent a letter to

32. AIG Haw. Ins. Co. v. Smith, 891 P.2d 261, 264 (Haw. 1995); *Federated Dep't Stores*, 807 N.Y.S.2d at 66 (quoting a treatise); *see* Med. Prot. Co. v. Pang, 606 F. Supp. 2d 1049, 1060 (D. Ariz. 2008) (stating that an insurer does not need to reserve its rights immediately upon learning of a lawsuit but can later reserve its rights upon learning new information that would provide a coverage defense).

33. *See, e.g.*, Moody v. Pa. Millers Mut. Ins. Co., 263 S.E.2d 495, 496 (Ga. Ct. App. 1979) ("Although the insurance company . . . did not assert a reservation of rights at the time it filed its answer to the personal injury suit . . . no estoppel resulted, since the insured's delay in notifying the company of the suit deprived the company of any prior opportunity to investigate the claim."); T.V. *ex rel.* Villnave v. Columbia Nat'l Ins. Co., 313 P.3d 1022, 1027 (Okla. Civ. App. 2013) (involving an insured who waited 45 days after being served with suit papers to notify his insurer of the underlying incident, leaving the insurer with no time to conduct a pre-suit investigation and forcing it to act quickly to defend the insured).

34. *See, e.g.*, Diamond Serv. Co. v. Utica Mut. Ins. Co., 476 A.2d 648, 656 (D.C. 1984) (explaining that "an insurer has a reasonable time to investigate the facts to determine its acceptance of liability"); Delmonte v. State Farm Fire & Cas. Co., 975 P.2d 1159, 1171 (Haw. 1999) (stating that an insurer "may initially assume an unconditional defense while it conducts its own reasonable investigation as to coverage").

35. 192 N.Y.S.3d 674 (App. Div. 2023).

36. *Id.* at 676.

Covert Holdings and DB Insurance in which it specifically reserved its rights to withdraw from its defense of Covert Holdings, deny coverage, and initiate a declaratory judgment action.[37] In its reservation of rights letter, Underwriters informed Covert Holdings and DB Insurance that it was basing its position on its recent discovery that Howard did not fall on the sidewalk in front of the portion of the premises leased by the tenant.[38]

In separate coverage litigation, Covert Holdings and DB Insurance asserted that Underwriters was estopped to deny coverage to Covert Holdings because the reservation of rights letter was untimely. The *Covert Holdings* court disagreed. Under the circumstances, it could not be said that Underwriters "lulled Covert Holdings into sleeping on its rights."[39] In other words, Covert Holdings was not prejudiced by the timing of Underwriters' reservation of rights.[40] As a result, the *Covert Holdings* court concluded that Underwriters had no duty to defend or indemnify Covert Holdings in Howard's lawsuit and remanded the case to the trial court handling the coverage litigation to enter judgment for Underwriters.

In *Covert Holdings*, Underwriters reserved its rights reasonably soon after discovering facts that jeopardized its coverage. Accordingly, the court correctly held that Underwriters was not estopped to deny coverage and withdraw its defense. In other cases, an insurer may reserve its rights at the outset based on one or more coverage defenses but be concerned that it may learn of additional coverage defenses as its investigation continues or as the litigation against the insured progresses. In that situation, the insurer may protect against allegations of waiver or estoppel regarding later-discovered coverage defenses by stating in its reservation of rights letter that it reserves its right to assert any defenses that are subsequently revealed.[41] On the other hand, if an insurer does not discover a coverage defense at the outset of a case because it inadequately investigated the underlying loss, it may be estopped to assert that defense when it eventually learns of it, if the insured is prejudiced by the delay.[42]

37. *Id.* at 676–77.

38. *Id.* at 677.

39. *Id.*

40. *See id.* (quoting Provencal, LLC v. Tower Ins. Co. of N.Y., 30 N.Y.S.3d 138, 141 (App. Div. 2016)).

41. Sayah v. Metro. Prop. & Cas. Ins. Co., 733 N.W.2d 192, 197 (Neb. 2007); *see, e.g.*, Pereira v. Gulf Ins. Co., 330 F. App'x 5, 6 (2d Cir. 2009) (applying New York Law); Nautilus Ins. Co. v. Worldwide Aeros Corp., 171 F. App'x 182, 185 (9th Cir. 2006) (applying California law).

42. *See* Westport Ins. Corp. v. McClellan, 493 F. Supp. 3d 315, 328–29 (E.D. Pa. 2020) (applying Pennsylvania law) ("[A]n insurer has a duty to investigate all circumstances bearing on coverage and reserve its rights in a timely manner. An insurer who fails to do so could face estoppel if it discovers a defense to coverage it should have discovered at the outset. But an insured cannot establish estoppel by merely showing an insurer should have discovered a defense to coverage and reserved its rights at an earlier date. The insured must also show he suffered 'actual prejudice' from the insurer's failure to timely discover and reserve its rights. . . ."); *see, e.g.*, Scottsdale Ins. Co. v. Casino Dev. Grp., Inc., 190 N.Y.S.3d 28, 30 (App. Div. 2023) (citations omitted) ("Scottsdale should have conducted an

So, when must an insurer that knows of possible coverage defenses send a reservation of rights letter?[43] An insurer should have no duty to issue a reservation of rights letter before an insured is sued, because it is the existence of a "suit" against the insured that triggers the insurer's duty to defend and thus its potential need to reserve its rights to disclaim coverage.[44] An insurer may choose to issue a reservation of rights before the insured is sued but that does not mean it must do so. Certainly, there is no generally applicable standard of care in this context. The best practice is for an insurer to reserve its rights as soon as practicable after identifying a coverage defense on which it may rely, but best practices are not a standard of care in insurance any more than they are in other industries or areas of the law.[45] Furthermore, case-specific facts and circumstances may affect the timing of a reservation of rights. In some instances, a state regulation or statute may dictate timing, as in Florida, where the claims administration statute provides that a liability insurer cannot "deny coverage based on a particular coverage defense" unless "[w]ithin 30 days after the liability insurer knew or should have known of the coverage defense,

investigation upon receiving a copy of the Trade Subcontract, which described the building project at issue as 'residential.' Even if this failure to investigate were justified, Scottsdale does not explain when its monitoring counsel had completed his evaluation of the underlying litigation or the necessity of any subsequent delay in disclaiming. . . . Scottsdale thus failed to meet its burden to show that its delay was reasonably related to necessary, prompt, and diligent investigation. . . .").

43. Courts evaluating insurers' reservation of rights sometimes distinguish between "coverage defenses" and "policy defenses." A coverage defense is one where the insurer asserts that a given claim or suit may not be covered by its policy as, for example, where an exclusion applies. A policy defense is one where the insurer acknowledges that its policy ordinarily would obligate it to indemnify the insured but asserts that the insured's breach of a policy condition, such as cooperation or notice, excuses its duty to indemnify the insured. *See* Yeagley v. Allstate Ins. Co., No. 1:09-CV-19-JOF, 2009 WL 2486320, at *6 (N.D. Ga. Aug. 12, 2009) (applying Georgia law). Depending on the jurisdiction, the proper characterization of a coverage issue may determine how a court treats an insurer's failure to reserve its rights.

44. The requirement of a "suit" to trigger the insurer's duty to defend is discussed in Chapter 1.

45. "Best practices" are aspirational ideals; they do not constitute standards of care. *See, e.g.*, Leibel v. City of Buckeye, 556 F. Supp. 3d 1042, 1082 (D. Ariz. 2021) (asserting that testimony on best practices does not establish the standard of care in a negligence action); MCI Commc'ns Servs., Inc. v. Maverick Cutting & Breaking LLC, 374 F. Supp. 3d 789, 808 (D. Minn. 2019) ("[I]ndustry best practices are aspirational, generally requiring a higher standard of care than the industry standard of care."), *vacated on other grounds by* 2019 WL 2082376 (D. Minn. Apr. 26, 2019); Gross v. Balt. Aircoil Co., No. 3:13cv423-DPJ-FKB, 2016 WL 10607176, at *5 (S.D. Miss. Aug. 30, 2016) (stating that "best practices are not the standard of care under a negligence theory"); Somerville v. United States, No. 6:08-cv-787-Orl-22KRS, 2010 WL 2643533, at *5 n.9 (M.D. Fla. June 30, 2010) ("The standard of care is not equivalent to 'best practices.'"); *In re* Walt Disney Co. Derivative Litig., 907 A.2d 693, 697 (Del. Ch. 2005) (failing to comply with "the aspirational ideal of best practices" is not a basis for liability); Green v. House of Wright Mortuary, Inc., No. 02C-11-242MMJ, 2005 WL 3194484, at *6 (Del. Super. Ct. Nov. 17, 2005) (criticizing an expert witness's opinion because it could "be read as evaluating the funeral director's conduct under a 'best practices' test, rather that the legal standard of care").

written notice of reservation of rights to assert a coverage defense is given to the named insured[.]"[46]

Although courts typically reason that an insurer should reserve its rights "reasonably promptly"[47] upon concluding that it has a policy defense that it may wish to assert, and insurers usually strive to do so, an insurer generally has no duty to issue a reservation of rights letter until it assumes control of the insured's defense.[48] With rare exception, however, an insurer must reserve its rights with respect to known coverage defenses at the time it assumes control of the insured's defense,[49] or within a reasonable time thereafter.[50] The

46. FLA. STAT. § 627.426(2)(a) (2022). The Florida Supreme Court explained the meaning of "coverage defense" under the statute in *AIU Insurance Co. v. Block Marina Investment, Inc.*, 544 So. 2d 998 (Fla. 1989):

> [W]e hold that the term "coverage defense," as used in section 627.426(2), means a defense to coverage that otherwise exists. We do not construe the term to include a disclaimer of liability based on a complete lack of coverage for the loss sustained. Under this construction, for example, if the insurer fails to comply with the requirements of the statute, it may not declare a forfeiture of coverage which otherwise exists based on a breach of a condition of the policy. However, its failure to comply with the requirements of the statute will not bar an insurer from disclaiming liability where a policy or endorsement has expired or where the coverage sought is expressly excluded or otherwise unavailable under the policy or under existing law.

Id. at 1000.

47. Am. Safety Indem. Co. v. Sto Corp., 802 S.E.2d 448, 454 (Ga. Ct. App. 2017).

48. St. Paul Fire & Marine Ins. Co. v. Children's Hosp. Nat'l Med. Ctr., 670 F. Supp. 393, 402 (D.D.C. 1987) (applying District of Columbia law); Jioras v. State Farm Fire & Cas. Co., 29 Cal. Rptr. 2d 840, 844 (Ct. App. 1994); Portal Pipe Line Co. v. Stonewall Ins. Co., 845 P.2d 746, 749–50 (Mont. 1993); *see also* Ortiz v. Biscanin, 122 P.3d 365, 377 (Kan. Ct. App. 2004) (explaining that an insurer has no duty to inform its insured of its pre-suit investigation into coverage).

49. *See* Cincinnati Ins. Co. v. All Plumbing, Inc. Serv., Parts Installation, 64 F. Supp. 3d 69, 77 (D.D.C. 2014) (explaining that under D.C. law, an insurer's assumption of the defense of an action without a reservation of rights creates a rebuttable presumption of prejudice to the insured). *But see* Becker v. Bar Plan Mut. Ins. Co., 429 P.3d 212, 220 (Kan. 2018) (declining to impose a "bright line rule" requiring an insurer to reserve its rights "contemporaneously or almost contemporaneously with its assumption of its insured's defense").

50. *See* Am. Home Assur. Co. v. Superior Well Servs., Inc., 75 F.4th 184, 186–87, 191 n.7 (3d Cir. 2023) (explaining that the insurer's reservation of rights three months after receiving notice of the claim was sufficient); Scottsdale Ins. Co. v. City of Hazelton, 400 F. App'x 626, 628–29 (3d Cir. 2010) (agreeing with the district court that Scottsdale's three-month delay in reserving its rights was not unreasonable as a matter of law); Pa. Nat'l Mut. Cas. Ins. Co. v. Beach Mart, Inc., No. 2:14-CV-08-FL, 2022 WL 4709249, at *8 (E.D.N.C. Sept. 30, 2022) ("[P]laintiff sent the first reservation of rights letter one month after tender of the underlying counterclaims, and a third reservation of rights letter the month defendant received notice that plaintiff would defend it against [the] underlying counterclaims. . . . The letters therefore cannot reasonably be considered untimely."); Peleus Ins. Co. v. Atl. State Dev. Corp., 587 F. Supp. 3d 7, 22 (S.D.N.Y. 2022) (deciding that sending a reservation of rights letter less than two weeks after learning of a claim was timely); Hollyway Cleaners & Laundry Co. v. Cent. Nat'l Ins. Co. of Omaha, Inc., No. 2:13-cv-07497-ODW (Ex), 2015 WL 1884311, at *6 (C.D. Cal. Apr. 23, 2015) ("Plaintiffs do not offer any authority that requires an insurer reserve its right to contest coverage the instant it agrees to defend an insured. . . . Furthermore, Plaintiffs do not claim that they suffered prejudice or any other harm because [the insurer] reserved its right to contest coverage three weeks after agreeing to defend. Therefore, the [c]ourt finds that [the insurer] timely

reasonableness of any alleged delay in issuing a reservation of rights letter depends on the case.[51] In other words, whether an insurance company acted reasonably promptly in reserving its rights or, alternatively, unreasonably delayed in doing so, usually is a question of fact. Regardless of how the issue is framed, the longer the insurer waits to reserve its rights, the greater the likelihood that the insured will be prejudiced by the delay and that the insurer will be estopped to deny coverage as a result.[52]

Along the timeliness spectrum, is it possible for an insurer to issue a reservation of rights letter too early? The short answer to that question is "no," as an Illinois court properly concluded in *American Family Mutual Insurance Co. v. Westfield Insurance Co.*[53] There, 13-year old Shannon Dennis was playing with friends when she threw a lit match through a cracked window of the

reserved its right to contest coverage."); Rector of St. Peter's Church in the City of Phila. v. Am. Nat'l Fire Ins. Co., No. Civ. A. 00-2806, 2002 WL 59333, at *8 (E.D. Pa. Jan. 14, 2002) (concluding that a 90-day delay in issuing a reservation of rights letter was "not sufficient to deem the reservation of rights letter invalid"); Builders Ins. v. Tenenbaum, 757 S.E.2d 669, 675 (Ga. Ct. App. 2014) (stating that an insurer "must act reasonably promptly upon learning of a policy defense"); Fisher v. Moore, No. 117,797, 2019 WL 406513, at *11 (Kan. Ct. App. Feb. 1, 2019) (reasoning that a reservation of rights sent within a month of the insurer learning of its coverage defense was timely); Dale Osburn, Inc. v. Auto Owners Ins. Co., No. 242313, 2003 WL 22718194, at *3 (Mich. Ct. App. Nov. 18, 2003) (stating that 120 days between the initiation of the third-party action and the issuance of a reservation of rights is reasonable as a matter of law); Selective Way Ins. Co. v. MAK Servs., Inc., 232 A.3d 762, 768 (Pa. Super. Ct. 2020) (determining that a reservation of rights letter sent within three weeks of the insured being served with the plaintiff's complaint and before the insurer assumed the insured's defense was timely); Paradigm Ins. Co. v. Tex. Richmond Corp., 942 S.W.2d 645, 652–53 (Tex. App. 1997) (determining that it was reasonable for an insurer to send a reservation of rights letter 15 days after causing an answer to be filed in the underlying action).

51. *See Becker*, 429 P.3d at 220 (explaining that the timeliness of a reservation of rights is a question of fact); Fisher v. Moore, No. 117,797, 2019 WL 406513, at *9 (Kan. Ct. App. Feb. 1, 2019) ("Timeliness of a reservation of rights letter depends on the particular facts of the case.").

52. *See, e.g.*, Interstate Fire & Cas. Co. v. Apt. Mgmt. Consultants LLC, 824 F. App'x 565, 570–72 (10th Cir. 2020) (explaining that the insurer's 18-month delay in issuing a reservation of rights letter and finally reserving its rights only 11 days before trial prejudiced the insured and estopped the insurer from denying coverage for punitive damages); Westport Ins. Corp. v. McClellan, 493 F. Supp. 3d 315, 326–28 (E.D. Pa. 2020) (determining that the insurer's defense of the insured for 20 months without reserving its rights supported estoppel); RLI Ins. Co. v. AST Eng'g Corp., No. 19cv1649 (DLC), 2019 WL 7114986, at *7 (S.D.N.Y. Dec. 20, 2019) (applying New Jersey law and holding that the insurer's nearly three-year delay in reserving its rights was unreasonable and presumptively prejudicial, such that it was estopped from denying coverage); Penn-Am. Ins. Co. v. Morgan Fleet Servs., Inc., 847 S.E.2d 378, 382 (Ga. Ct. App. 2020) (waiting six months after appointing defense counsel to reserve its rights cost the insurer its coverage defense); Ohio Cas. Ins. Co. v. Wellington Place Council of Co-Owners Homeowners Ass'n, Inc., No. 2012-CA-000382-MR, 2014 WL 97395, at *2–4 (Ky. Ct. App. Jan. 10, 2014) (reasoning that a two-year delay in reserving rights was unreasonable); Hiser v. Rajki, 700 So. 2d 1302, 1302 (La. Ct. App. 1997) (determining that the insurer could not assert coverage defenses for the first time 22 days before trial); Home-Owners Ins. Co. v. Fourment, Nos. 327751 & 330269, 2017 WL 781596, at *3 (Mich. Ct. App. Feb. 21, 2017) (concluding that a one-year delay in issuing a reservation of rights was unreasonable and prejudiced the insured); *see generally* Penn-Am. Ins. Co. v. Sanchez, 202 P.3d 472, 478 (Ariz. Ct. App. 2008) ("[U]nreasonable delay without prejudice to the insured will not cause loss of the insurer's coverage defenses. Prejudice to the insured is required.").

53. 962 N.E.2d 993 (Ill. App. Ct. 2011).

Central Supply Co. (Central) and started a fire. In September 2005, she was convicted of criminal damage to property. Central's insurer, Westfield Insurance Co. (Westfield), paid the loss and then looked to recover its funds through subrogation. At the time of the fire, Shannon was insured under her grandparents' American Family Mutual Insurance Co. (American Family) farm-ranch policy.

In June 2006, Westfield sent American Family a copy of the complaint it planned to file against Patrick Dennis, Shannon's father, on account of the fire.[54] Ninety days later, in late September 2006, James Keane, an American Family in-house lawyer, sent a reservation of rights letter to Patrick focused on the intentional injury exclusion in the American Family policy.[55] In late October 2006, Westfield sued Patrick Dennis as Shannon's parent and guardian. Patrick was served with the lawsuit in mid-December 2006. American Family defended the lawsuit, which concluded in May 2009 when the trial court found that Shannon negligently caused the fire and awarded Westfield damages of nearly $466,000. The next day, American Family declined to indemnify Shannon.[56] Just days later, American Family filed a declaratory judgment action to establish that it was not obligated to indemnify Shannon based on the intentional injury exclusion in its policy.

In the declaratory judgment action, Shannon moved for summary judgment, arguing that American Family was collaterally estopped from asserting the intentional acts exclusion based on an improper reservation of rights.[57] The trial court granted her motion. In doing so, the trial court also determined that American Family sent its reservation of rights letter "so prematurely 'that [Shannon] could not possibly be properly informed as to her rights under a proper reservation of rights, and any potential for conflict which would exclude American Family from indemnification of its insured.'"[58] American Family appealed.

On appeal, Shannon apparently argued that rather than sending its reservation of rights letter in late September 2006, American Family should have waited until her father was served with suit papers in mid-December 2006.[59] American Family countered that it is better to send a reservation of rights letter earlier rather than later.[60] The court agreed with American Family. The *American Family* court observed that there was no requirement that a reservation

54. *Id.* at 996.
55. *Id.*
56. *Id.* at 997.
57. *Id.*
58. *Id.* (quoting the trial court).
59. *Id.* at 998.
60. *Id.*

of rights letter be sent after a complaint is filed.[61] Although an insurer that reserves its rights before suit is filed may have to send another reservation of rights letter if the complaint alleges facts suggesting new coverage defenses, that was not the case here.[62] In the end, the *American Family* court reversed the trial court and remanded the case for further proceedings.

2. *Supplemental Reservation of Rights Letters*

Interestingly, the reservation of rights in *American Family* arguably was premature as a matter of law, although that certainly was no basis to fault American Family. As noted earlier, an insurer generally does not have to reserve its rights until it agrees to defend the insured.[63] At the same time, American Family had a copy of Westfield's draft complaint and thus could confidently evaluate coverage pre-suit. American Family's prompt reservation of its rights could only have benefited the insureds. Had Westfield filed a complaint that differed from the draft version, American Family could have issued a supplemental reservation of rights letter if the complaint that was eventually filed pleaded facts that raised additional or different coverage defenses.[64]

Insurers often send supplemental reservation of rights letters. In doing so, there is no requirement for a prior reservation of rights letter to have included a reservation of the insurer's "other rights" or to have stated that the insurer reserved the right to assert additional coverage defenses of which it might subsequently learn.[65] While insurers usually include such clauses in their reservation of rights letters as a best practice, the failure to do so generally will not support waiver or estoppel claims. With respect to waiver, the insurer's failure to include such a clause cannot be construed as the knowing and voluntary relinquishment of an unknown coverage defense.[66] Estoppel presents a closer call, but it is difficult to see how the insured could have reasonably relied on the absence of a qualifier to indicate that no other coverage defenses might later surface. Of course, by including such a clause in a reservation of rights letter as a precaution, an insurer generally preempts a related estoppel claim.

Hernandez v. Great American Alliance Insurance Co.[67] exemplifies an insurer's prudent use of supplemental reservation of rights letters. The case

61. *Id.*

62. *Id.*

63. St. Paul Fire & Marine Ins. Co. v. Children's Hosp. Nat'l Med. Ctr., 670 F. Supp. 393, 402 (D.D.C. 1987) (applying D.C. law); Jioras v. State Farm Fire & Cas. Co., 29 Cal. Rptr. 2d 840, 844 (Ct. App. 1994); Portal Pipe Line Co. v. Stonewall Ins. Co., 845 P.2d 746, 749–50 (Mont. 1993).

64. *Am. Family Mut. Ins. Co.*, 962 N.E.2d at 998; *see also* Amerisure Mut. Ins. Co. v. Carey Transp., Inc., 578 F. Supp. 2d 888, 904 (W.D. Mich. 2008) (concluding that an insurer's supplemental reservation of rights letter based on facts learned after it first reserved its rights was timely and substantively adequate).

65. 1 Windt, *supra* note 29, § 2:16, at 2-71.

66. *Id.*

67. 879 S.E.2d 522 (Ga. Ct. App. 2022).

also illustrates the timeliness and informational adequacy aspects of an effective reservation of rights letter.

Hernandez began when Manuel Hernandez was shot at an apartment complex operated by Star Residential, LLC (Star) and owned by Terraces at Brookhaven, LLC (Terraces). Star promptly notified Terraces of the shooting, and notified its primary insurer, Associated Industries Insurance Co. (AIIC). Terraces apparently was an additional insured under Star's policy with AIIC and under Star's umbrella policy with Great American Alliance Insurance Co. (GAAIC). Neither Star nor Terraces notified GAAIC of any potential claim.

In December 2017, Hernandez's lawyer sent a $1.5 million settlement demand to AIIC. The insureds notified GAAIC of Hernandez's claim in early February 2018. GAAIC acknowledged the notice and stated that it had logged the matter as "incident only" because it did not expect Hernandez's claim to exceed the AAIC primary policy's $1 million liability limit.[68]

In March 2018, Hernandez sued the insureds and served them in April 2018. In May 2018, AIIC denied coverage and declined to defend the insureds. In June 2018, GAAIC began defending the insureds. On June 20, 2018—one day after agreeing to assume the defense—GAAIC sent Star and Terraces the first of three reservation of rights letters.[69]

GAAIC's first reservation of rights letter noted AIIC's denial of coverage because Hernandez was intentionally injured and because AIIC's policy included a firearms exclusion.[70] The letter further stated that the GAAIC umbrella policy did not cover punitive damages, that the umbrella policy would only cover that portion of any damages that exceeded the $1 million AIIC policy limit, and that the insured would owe the first $1 million of any judgment that Hernandez might obtain.[71] The letter also quoted the GAAIC policy's insuring agreement, which provided that "the coverage applied to 'bodily injury' . . . caused by an 'occurrence,'" without also quoting the definition of "occurrence," and stated that coverage would be subject to the policy's "exclusions, terms, and conditions."[72] Continuing, the letter asserted "that GAAIC 'reserve[d]' the right to rely upon all the terms, provisions[,] and exclusions in its Umbrella Policy and in the underlying primary policy."[73] One of the GAAIC policy provisions encompassed by the reservation of rights letter but not highlighted there was a portion of the definition of "Insured" which stated that "'coverage applies only if the [underlying insurance] organization is included under the coverage provided by the policies listed in the Schedule of

68. *Id.* at 524 & 525 n.7.
69. *Id.* at 524.
70. *Id.*
71. *Id.*
72. *Id.*
73. *Id.* (first alteration added).

Underlying Insurance and then for no broader coverage than is provided under such 'underlying insurance.'"[74]

In May 2019, GAAIC sent a supplemental reservation of rights letter after Hernandez amended his complaint. That letter noted that the same AAIC and GAAIC policy provisions discussed in the initial reservation of rights letter applied to Hernandez's new claims. The letter additionally highlighted the definitions of "bodily injury" and "occurrence" in the GAAIC policy and stated that the policy defined "occurrence" as an "accident."[75]

In May 2020, GAAIC sent a second supplemental reservation of rights letter. There, GAAIC explained that its umbrella policy applied only if an organization was covered by the underlying primary policy and then for no broader coverage than that provided by the underlying insurance. Therefore, the letter explained, the AIIC policy exclusions—including the firearms exclusion—applied equally to preclude coverage under the GAAIC policy.[76]

GAAIC subsequently filed a declaratory judgment action. In time, GAAIC moved for summary judgment and Star and Terraces filed a cross-motion for partial summary judgment. The trial court granted GAAIC's motion and denied the insureds' cross-motion. Hernandez, Star, and Terraces (collectively the claimants) then appealed to the Georgia Court of Appeals.

The claimants argued on appeal that GAAIC waived its coverage defenses when it assumed their defense without timely and specifically reserving its right to assert its policy defenses. The *Hernandez* court disagreed.

The court stated that an insurer is not required to list all bases for disputing coverage in its initial reservation of rights letter to preserve its right to later assert a particular ground for denying coverage, but it must act reasonably promptly when it learns of a policy defense.[77]

Here, GAAIC sent its first reservation of rights letter within 24 hours of agreeing to defend the insureds, which was "sufficiently prompt."[78] The letter quoted the AIIC policy's firearms exclusion, as well as the GAAIC policy's requirement of an "occurrence," which the policy defined as an "accident."[79] Further, the letter explicitly stated that GAAIC reserved the right to rely upon all the terms, provisions, and exclusions in its umbrella policy and in the AIIC primary policy and that no current or subsequent action on its part should be construed as a waiver of any coverage defense it might have.[80] According to the court:

74. *Id.* (emphasis and footnote omitted).
75. *Id.*
76. *Id.* at 525.
77. *Id.* (quoting Builders Ins. v. Tenenbaum, 757 S.E.2d 669, 675 (Ga. Ct. App. 2014)).
78. *Id.*
79. *Id.* at 525–26.
80. *Id.* at 526 (footnote omitted).

> This prompt reservation of rights letter was sufficient to notify the Insureds that even though GAAIC had initiated its coverage of a legal defense, it would still rely on the terms, definitions, and provisions of the umbrella policy; that the underlying insurance (quoted in the reservation of rights letter) likely did not cover injuries caused by firearms; and that GAAIC was not waiving its policy defenses implicated by the terms of the GAAIC policy *or the underlying AIIC policy*, which policy GAAIC quoted in the reservation of rights letter.[81]

Although GAAIC's third reservation of rights letter in May 2020 better articulated the fact that the GAAIC umbrella policy followed form to the firearms exclusion in the AIIC primary policy, GAAIC's initial reservation of rights letter in June 2018 quoted the firearms exclusion and reserved GAIC's right to rely on provisions in the AIIC policy. "Thus, this was more than a mere boilerplate recitation that GAAIC reserved the right to rely on some unidentified defense in the future."[82] In addition, the policy provisions that the claimants argued GAAIC had waived were basic terms and definitions that established the coverage Star and Terrace purchased. As the court saw matters, a reservation of rights letter "should operate to inform the insured, not create a trap for the insurer by reforming the insurance contract to provide coverage never bargained for by the parties."[83]

In the end, the *Hernandez* court reasoned that GAAIC acted in good faith in defending Star and Terrace under a reservation of rights and that, given the language in the initial reservation of rights letter, it would be imprudent to effectively penalize GAAIC for clarifying its coverage positions in its supplemental reservation of rights letters.[84] Consequently, the court affirmed the trial court judgment for GAAIC.

3. *Summary*

Numerous issues may affect the timing of an insurer's reservation of rights, including when the insurer is notified of a loss or lawsuit; who gives the insurer notice; the information contained in the notice of the loss or lawsuit; whether an investigation is required before the insurer can reasonably evaluate coverage and the extent of any necessary investigation; when the first notice of the loss is a lawsuit, the clarity of the plaintiff's complaint or petition; and whether the insurer needs to consult with coverage counsel or obtain a coverage opinion to determine its duty to indemnify the insured. The sooner the insurer can inform the insured of its coverage position, the better. Basically, the insurer must reserve it rights reasonably promptly under the circumstances and generally

81. *Id.*
82. *Id.*
83. *Id.* (citing Am. Safety Indem. Co. v. Sto Corp., 802 S.E.2d 448, 453 (Ga. Ct. App. 2017)).
84. *Id.*

upon assuming the insured's defense. If the insurer learns of information after issuing a reservation of rights letter that suggests new coverage defenses, the plaintiff files an amended pleading that asserts new claims or causes of action, or other circumstances require the insurer to amend or clarify its position, the insurer should send a supplemental reservation of rights letter. If necessary, an insurer may issue more than one supplemental reservation of rights letter.

C. The Informational Adequacy of Reservation of Rights Letters

1. *Essential Principles for Fairly or Adequately Informing an Insured of the Insurer's Coverage Position*

In addition to being timely, and as *Hernandez* illustrates, a reservation of rights letter must fairly or adequately inform the insured of the insurance company's coverage position to be effective.[85] ("Fairly" and "adequately" describe the same standard and courts use the terms interchangeably, as will we.) Only if the letter fairly expresses the insurer's coverage position can the insured reasonably evaluate whether it should accept the insurer's offer of a defense, seek independent counsel, or consider whether there might be other steps it could take to protect its interests. For these reasons, courts generally hold that "bare notice" of the insurer's reservation of rights will not preserve the insurer's coverage defenses.[86]

Illinois Insurance Guaranty Fund v. Nwidor[87] offers examples of the sort of "bare notice" that most courts abhor. In *Nwidor*, the Illinois Insurance Guaranty Fund (IIGF) stepped into the shoes of an insolvent insurer, Ullico, and thus became responsible for defending Ullico's insured, Chicago Cab, in a personal injury action. IIGF sent Chicago Cab three reservation of rights letters. In the first letter, IIGF wrote: "IIGF specifically asserts and maintains a reservation of rights related to any payments it may make in respect to your company. IIGF also asserts and maintains an absolute reservation of rights in respect to any policy related issues which may be discovered or disclosed."[88]

85. *See* State Farm Mut. Auto. Ins. Co. v. Dabbene, 511 F. Supp. 3d 600, 621 (E.D. Pa. 2021) (using "fairly inform" (quoting Selective Way Ins. Co. v. MAK Servs., Inc., 232 A.3d 762, 768 (Pa. Super. Ct. 2020))); Hoover v. Maxum Indem. Co., 730 S.E.2d 413, 417 (Ga. 2012) (referring to the insurer's duty to "fairly inform" the insured); Ill. Ins. Guar. Fund v. Nwidor, 105 N.E.3d 1035, 1043 (Ill. App. Ct. 2018) ("A reservation of rights must adequately inform the insured of the rights which the insurer intends to reserve.").

86. *See, e.g.*, Std. Mut. Ins. Co. v. Lay, 989 N.E.2d 591, 596 (Ill. 2013) ("Bare notice of a reservation of rights is insufficient."); Doctors' Co. v. Ins. Corp. of Am., 864 P.2d 1018, 1030 (Wyo. 1993) ("A bare notice of reservation of rights is insufficient."). *But see* Marentes v. State Farm Mut. Auto. Ins. Co., 224 F. Supp. 3d 891, 914 (N.D. Cal. 2016) (explaining that under California law, the insurer's statement that its defense would be "subject to 'a full reservation of rights'" was sufficient to preserve its coverage defenses).

87. 105 N.E.3d 1035 (Ill. App. Ct. 2018).

88. *Id.* at 1040.

IIGF repeated that language in its second reservation of rights letter. In its third letter, IIGF stated:

> In addition to any prior reservation of rights issued by Ullico . . . , IIGF is conducting the handling of the above referenced matter under a full and complete reservation of rights under the terms and conditions of the Ullico insurance policy. . . . Nothing in this letter should be viewed as a waiver of any rights or defenses IIGF may have under the Illinois Insurance Code, under the pertinent insurance policies or otherwise which rights and defenses are hereby reserved.[89]

The *Nwidor* court noted that IIGF's three letters each expressed a "bare, boilerplate" reservation of rights and thus preserved no coverage defenses.[90] Luckily for IIGF, it sent a fourth reservation of rights letter that the court found to be adequate, and the court ultimately held that Chicago Cab suffered no prejudice that would support estoppel.

The reservation of rights in *Selective Way Insurance Co. v. MAK Services, Inc.*[91] further illustrates a bare notice of coverage defenses that failed judicial scrutiny. In that case, MAK Services, Inc. (MAK), which was exclusively in the snow and ice removal business, was sued by a pedestrian who slipped and fell on ice on property that MAK maintained. MAK's policy with Selective Way Insurance (Selective) contained a snow and ice removal exclusion. In its reservation of rights letter, however, Selective did not mention the exclusion. Instead, it "reserve[d] all rights reserved to it under applicable law, insurance regulations and policy provisions that may become relevant as this matter continues to develop. Those rights include, but are not limited to, the rights to decline coverage for this claim and to withdraw assigned defense counsel."[92]

The *Selective Way* court understandably concluded that the reservation of rights letter failed to clearly communicate the extent of the rights that Selective was reserving, and that MAK was prejudiced as a result.[93] Thus, Selective was estopped from relying on the snow and ice exclusion when it invoked the exclusion 18 months into the underlying case.

In *SavaSeniorCare, LLC v. Starr Indemnity & Liability Co.*,[94] the court expressed its dislike for "boilerplate" reservation of rights letters, which other courts might describe as providing "bare notice" of the insurer's reservation of rights. There is no material difference between these unflattering characterizations.

---

89. *Id.* at 1040–41 (internal quotation marks omitted).
90. *Id.* at 1043.
91. 232 A.3d 762 (Pa. Super. Ct. 2020).
92. *Id.* at 765.
93. *Id.* at 772.
94. 491 F. Supp. 3d 1275 (N.D. Ga. 2020).

In *SavaSeniorCare*, Starr Indemnity & Liability Co. (Starr) attempted to deny coverage based on late notice of the plaintiffs' claims. In its initial "coverage letter" to the insured, Starr wrote:

> Starr continues to reserve all of its rights, remedies, and defenses for this matter under the Policy, in equity, and at law. Neither this letter nor any other prior or future act by or on behalf of Starr shall constitute a waiver of any of Starr's rights, remedies, or defenses. Please note that the foregoing analysis is not meant to be exhaustive as certain other potentially applicable provisions of the Policy that may similarly preclude or limit coverage under the Policy have not been addressed herein.[95]

Four subsequent letters from Starr contained the same or similar language. In one of the letters, Starr tried to reserve its rights "with respect to the date that this matter first became a Claim first made against an Insured,"[96] but it never cited the notice provision in its policy or indicated that it might assert a late notice defense.

The *SavaSeniorCare* court declared Starr's "boilerplate reservation of rights disclaimer" to be ineffective as a matter of law.[97] The court further stated that Starr's passing reference to the date that the underlying matter became a claim in one letter did not unambiguously inform SavaSeniorCare of Starr's late notice defense nor did it fairly inform the company of Starr's coverage position.[98] Consequently, Starr waived its late notice defense.

Although bare notice of an insurer's coverage defenses generally will not suffice, there are no specific requirements for a valid reservation of rights letter. The key is that the letter adequately informs the insured of the insurer's coverage position. Thus, a reservation of rights letter does not necessarily need to specify every ground for contesting coverage if it fairly informs the insured that the insurer is not waiving its coverage defenses despite its provision of a defense.[99] An insurer is not required to reserve its rights regarding coverage defenses that have yet to be revealed in its investigation or which might rest on facts of which it is otherwise unaware.[100] Analogously, an insurer is not

95. *Id.* at 1279 (footnote omitted).
96. *Id.* at 1280 (footnote omitted).
97. *Id.* at 1286.
98. *Id.*
99. Wellons, Inc. v. Lexington Ins. Co., 566 F. App'x 813, 821–22 (11th Cir. 2014) (interpreting Georgia law); Selective Way Ins. Co. v. MAK Servs., Inc., 232 A.3d 762, 770 (Pa. Super. Ct. 2020).
100. *See* Ill. Ins. Guar. Fund v. Nwidor, 105 N.E.3d 1035, 1043 (Ill. App. Ct. 2018) ("[A]n insurer cannot assert a policy defense until it is aware of the facts giving rise to that defense, and an insurer will not be found to have waived rights of which it was unaware."); Am. States Ins. Co. v. Nat'l Cycle, Inc., 631 N.E.2d 1292, 1298 (Ill. App. Ct. 1994) (citation omitted) ("[A] party cannot assert a policy defense until it is aware of the facts giving rise to that defense . . . and . . . a party will not be found to have waived rights of which it was ignorant.").

obligated to reserve its right to contest coverage for claims that a plaintiff has not pleaded. For example, an insurer need not reserve its rights with respect to punitive damages where the plaintiff's complaint or petition does not seek them. Nor must an insurer specify legal doctrines or terms of art on which it is predicating its coverage defenses so long as it adequately explains the factual basis for the defenses to the insured.[101] Again, and at the risk of sounding like a broken record, the standard by which a reservation of rights is measured is whether the insurer fairly or adequately informed the insured of its coverage position.[102]

An insurer's mere recitation of insurance policy provisions in a reservation of rights letter without accompanying explanation or application to the facts of the case is generally not sufficient to preserve the insurer's coverage defenses.[103] Rather, to reliably avoid estoppel or waiver arguments premised on the informational inadequacy of a reservation of rights letter, the insurer should specify in the letter the coverage defenses it is asserting, and the policy provisions and facts on which those defenses rest.[104] If a reservation of rights creates a conflict of interest, the insurer generally must alert the insured.[105] In that situation, the insurer should also inform the insured of her right to independent counsel.[106]

In short, clarity in a reservation of rights letter is critical. Consistent with fundamental principles of insurance policy interpretation, courts resolve ambiguities in a reservation of rights letter against the insurer.[107]

---

101. *See, e.g.*, Am. & Foreign Ins. Co. v. Sequatchie Concrete Servs., Inc., 441 F.3d 341, 347 (6th Cir. 2006) (holding the insurer's failure to use the term of art "loss-in-progress doctrine" in its reservation of rights letter did not waive that defense in later coverage litigation because the insurer had clearly informed the insured of the factual basis for its eventual coverage denial); Richards Mfg. Co. v. Great Am. Ins. Co., 773 S.W.2d 916, 919 (Tenn. Ct. App. 1988) ("It is the insurer's conclusion regarding the existence or non-existence of certain coverage that must be clearly and fairly communicated to the insured, not its legal reasons therefor.").

102. *See, e.g.*, Peleus Ins. Co. v. Atl. State Dev. Corp., 587 F. Supp. 3d 7, 21–22 (S.D.N.Y. 2022) (stating that because the insurer's timely reservation of rights letter gave the insured "fair and explicit notice" of the insurer's coverage defense, there was no basis for estoppel).

103. Advantage Bldgs. & Exteriors, Inc. v. Mid-Continent Cas. Co., 449 S.W.3d 16, 23–24 (Mo. Ct. App. 2014); Harleysville Grp. Ins. v. Heritage Cmtys., Inc., 803 S.E.2d 288, 297 (S.C. 2017).

104. Am. Fam. Mut. Ins. Co. v. Westfield Ins. Co., 962 N.E.2d 993, 999 (Ill. App. Ct. 2011); *Advantage Bldgs. & Exteriors*, 449 S.W.3d at 24–25; *Harleysville Grp. Ins.*, 803 S.E.2d at 297–301; Doctors' Co. v. Ins. Corp. of Am., 864 P.2d 1018, 1030 (Wyo. 1993).

105. Std. Mut. Ins. Co. v. Lay, 989 N.E.2d 591, 596 (Ill. 2013); *Doctors' Co.*, 864 P.2d at 1030.

106. Starr Indem. & Liab. Co. v. Young, 379 F. Supp. 3d 1103, 1108–09 (D. Nev. 2019).

107. Select Comfort Corp. v. Arrowood Indem. Co., No. 13-2975 (JNE/FLN), 2014 WL 4232334, at *7 (D. Minn. Aug. 26, 2014) (applying Minnesota law); Canal Ins. Co. v. Flores, 524 F. Supp. 2d 828, 834 (W.D. Tex. 2007) (quoting Farmers Tex. Cnty. Mut. Ins. Co. v. Wilkinson, 601 S.W.2d 520, 523 (Tex. App. 1980)); Penn-Am. Ins. Co. v. Morgan Fleet Servs., Inc., 847 S.E.2d 378, 381 (Ga. Ct. App. 2020) (quoting World Harvest Church, Inc. v. GuideOne Mut. Ins. Co., 695 S.E.2d 6, 10 (Ga. 2010)); *Harleysville Grp. Ins.*, 803 S.E.2d at 298 (quoting *World Harvest Church*, 695 S.E.2d at 10).

2. *Illustrative Cases on the Informational Adequacy of Reservation of Rights Letters*

Insureds regularly challenge the adequacy of reservation of rights letters. Although courts frequently hold that a reservation of right letters adequately informed the insured of the insurer's coverage defenses,[108] they also find reservation of rights letters to be deficient more often than might be expected given the clarity of the law on this issue.[109]

World Harvest Church, Inc. v. GuideOne Mutual Insurance Co.[110] is perhaps the leading case on the informational adequacy—or inadequacy—of reservation of rights letters. *World Harvest Church* traced back to a Ponzi scheme orchestrated by Michael Gause. Before the scheme was exposed, Gause donated generously to the World Harvest Church. After the scheme was exposed, the Securities and Exchange Commission appointed a receiver to recover funds belonging to Gause's victims. The receiver demanded that the church return $1.8 million it had received from Gause and, in November 2002, sued the church in an Illinois federal court to recover that money when the church decided that receiving was preferable to giving. The church was insured under a commercial general liability (CGL) policy issued by GuideOne Mutual Insurance Co. (GuideOne). A GuideOne sister company issued a reservation of rights letter in connection with the Illinois federal action before ultimately denying coverage for the receiver's lawsuit.[111]

The Illinois federal court dismissed the receiver's case against the church for lack of personal jurisdiction, so, in November 2004, the receiver sued the church in the U.S. District Court for the Northern District of Georgia. The church notified GuideOne of the new case. GuideOne split its file between two adjusters, assigning coverage issues to Dale Hubbell and liability issues to another adjuster. Hubbell told the church's counsel in a conversation that GuideOne "'didn't see coverage but [GuideOne] would have to evaluate what

108. *See, e.g.*, Indem. Ins. Co. of N. Am. v. Westfield Ins. Co., 58 F.4th 276, 283 (7th Cir. 2023) (holding that the insurer's reservation of rights letter was adequate even though it referred to only one policy year rather than both years at issue because the policy language in both years was identical); Pa. Nat'l Mut. Cas. Ins. Co. v. Beach Mart, Inc., No. 2:14-CV-08-FL, 2022 WL 4709249, at *8 (E.D.N.C. Sept. 30, 2022) (stating that the insurer's letters asserted "a clear, unequivocal reservation of rights" that provided the insured "with full knowledge" that the insurer disputed coverage); Peleus Ins. Co. v. Atl. State Dev. Corp., 587 F. Supp. 3d 7, 21–22 (S.D.N.Y. 2022) (finding that the reservation of rights letter gave the insured "fair and explicit notice" of the insurer's coverage defense); Nationwide Affinity Ins. Co. v. Laderoute, 293 F. Supp. 3d 870, 877–78 (W.D. Mo. 2017) (listing the elements that validated Nationwide's reservation of rights letter).

109. *See, e.g.*, Stoneledge at Lake Keowee Owners' Ass'n, Inc. v. Cincinnati Ins. Co., No. 19-2009, 2022 WL 17592121, at *2–4 (4th Cir. Dec. 13, 2022) (applying South Carolina law and finding that reservation of rights letters that "fail[ed] to inform the insureds that the insurers intend[ed] to litigate coverage issues and [did] not apprise the insureds of potential conflicts of interest" were inadequate).

110. 695 S.E.2d 6 (Ga. 2010).

111. *Id.* at 8.

[it had] currently to see if there would be coverage issues.'"[112] Then, without issuing a reservation of rights letter, GuideOne appointed defense counsel for the church and defended the Georgia federal action for over ten months.[113]

In late January 2005, GuideOne informed the church that it would soon withdraw its defense because there was no coverage for the receiver's claims. The church hired its own lawyers to defend the suit and eventually settled the receiver's lawsuit for $1 million. The church then sued GuideOne in the Northern District of Georgia for breach of contract. On cross-motions for summary judgment, the district court rejected the church's argument that GuideOne should be estopped from denying coverage because there was no evidence that GuideOne's defense of the church without a written reservation of rights had prejudiced the church.[114] The church appealed to the Eleventh Circuit, which certified the following question to the Georgia Supreme Court:

> Does an insurer effectively reserve its right to deny coverage if it informs the insured that it "does not see coverage," after the insured had received a written reservation of rights from the insurer's sister company in a similar lawsuit in another jurisdiction, or is a written or more unequivocal reservation of rights required?[115]

The Georgia Supreme Court reasoned that while "written notification is preferable," the church's position that an oral reservation of rights is ineffective was unsupportable.[116] But the court's conclusion that a reservation of rights need not be in writing still left open the adequacy of GuideOne's oral reservation of rights. Here GuideOne fell short.

> [A] "mere allegation that the insurer contended that [the insured] was not covered by the policy, without more, [does] not show any reservation on its part of a right to insist that the coverage of the policy was not extended to him." . . . At a minimum, the reservation of rights must fairly inform "the insured that, notwithstanding [the insurer's] defense of the action, it disclaims liability and does not waive the defenses available to it against the insured." . . . The reservation of rights should also inform the insured of the specific "basis for [the insurer's] reservations about coverage". . . . The statement of a claims adjuster for GuideOne that it did not see coverage but would have to see if there would be coverage issues failed to comply with those requirements and, therefore, failed to "fairly inform" the Church of GuideOne's position.[117]

---

112. *Id.* (quoting Hubbell).
113. *Id.*
114. *Id.* at 9.
115. *Id.*
116. *Id.* (quoting State Farm Fire & Cas. Co. v. Jioras, 29 Cal. Rptr. 2d 840, 846 n.12 (Ct. App. 1994)).
117. *Id.* (citations omitted).

The inadequacy of GuideOne's oral reservation of rights was not cured by its sister company's written reservation of rights in the Illinois federal case.[118] That reservation of rights involved a different lawsuit and a different policy, although the policy was substantively identical to GuideOne's policy.[119] Even if the sister company's written reservation of rights was paired with GuideOne's oral reservation, the two communications were at best ambiguous because only the sister company's written reservation asserted the right to withdraw the church's defense.[120] This ambiguity doomed GuideOne, the court reasoned, because to be effective an insurer's reservation of rights must be unambiguous.[121] In the end, the *World Harvest Church* court held that GuideOne was estopped from denying coverage.

Advantage Buildings & Exteriors, Inc. v. Mid-Continent Casualty Co.[122] is another notable case on the informational adequacy of reservation of rights letters. *Advantage Buildings* began in July 2008, when Alsation Land Company, Vallejo, LLC (Alsation) sued Advantage Buildings & Exteriors, Inc. (Advantage) on various theories due to construction defects in a building for which Advantage had supplied materials. Advantage sent the suit papers to Mid-Continent Casualty Co. (Mid-Continent), with which it had a $1 million CGL policy and a $2 million umbrella policy. On August 12, Mid-Continent wrote Advantage to say that it would investigate Alsation's claims and analyze coverage, but further stated in the letter that it was reserving its rights to disclaim its duties to defend and indemnify Advantage. The letter finished by stating that Mid-Continent would "'promptly advise [Advantage] of the outcome of our coverage analysis.'"[123] On September 2, Mid-Continent sent Advantage a second letter in which it agreed to defend Advantage under a reservation of rights and informed Advantage that it had appointed lawyer Eric Swanson to represent the company. The letter also advised Advantage that "'[i]f other facts come to our attention, we will promptly inform you of them.'"[124]

The litigation went badly for Advantage, but despite Swanson's warning that Advantage could face excess liability and his recommendation that Mid-Continent settle the case within its primary policy limits, Mid-Continent refused to offer more than $50,000 to settle. Then, after the litigation had been underway for two years and a mere four days before trial was set to begin, Mid-Continent finally told Advantage that its policy covered only about $53,000 of

118. *Id.*
119. *Id.*
120. *Id.*
121. *Id.* (quoting Canal Ins. Co. v. Flores, 524 F. Supp. 2d 828, 834 (W.D. Tex. 2007)).
122. 449 S.W.3d 16 (Mo. Ct. App. 2014).
123. *Id.* at 19.
124. *Id.*

Alsation's claimed damages.[125] After some frantic procedural maneuvers, Alsation obtained a $4.6 million judgment against Advantage.[126]

Meanwhile, Mid-Continent was pursuing a declaratory judgment action against Advantage. In the declaratory judgment action, Advantage counterclaimed for bad faith. Mid-Continent moved for summary judgment on its claims and on Advantage's bad faith counterclaim. The trial court held that Mid-Continent's policy did not cover Alsation's claims against Advantage and awarded Mid-Continent partial summary judgment.[127] The court denied Mid-Continent's summary judgment motion with respect to Advantage's counterclaim, however, so the bad faith claim went to trial. Advantage won a $5 million judgment split between compensatory and punitive damages. Mid-Continent appealed.

On appeal, Mid-Continent contended that Advantage's bad faith claim was baseless because it had agreed to defend Advantage under a reservation of rights while it investigated Alsation's claim and analyzed coverage, and because the trial court determined that there was no coverage for Alsation's lawsuit.[128] The *Advantage Buildings* court rejected Mid-Continent's argument based on the inadequacy of its reservation of rights letters.

The court acknowledged that Missouri law permits an insurer to defend an insured under a reservation of rights but further stated that "the insurer owes the insured a duty to assert a proper reservation of rights that is timely and clear and that fully informs the insured of its position."[129] That was not the situation here. Rather, Mid-Continent's reservation of rights letters only vaguely informed Advantage of Mid-Continent's position with respect to its defense and indemnity obligations.[130] The letters generally discussed Alsation's lawsuit and quoted provisions of Advantage's primary CGL policy but neither letter clearly explained how the quoted policy language pertained to Advantage's situation or how it potentially created coverage issues.[131]

The first reservation of rights letter stated that Advantage would be promptly advised of the result of Mid-Continent's coverage analysis.[132] The

125. *Id.* at 20.

126. Advantage entered into an agreement with Alsation under which it agreed to pay Alsation $500, to sue Mid-Continent for any claims it might have, and to give Alsation the proceeds of those claims. Alsation agreed to not execute on any judgment against Advantage, to fund Advantage's suit against Mid-Continent, and to accept any damages Advantage recovered from Mid-Continent in satisfaction of its claims against Advantage. The parties then tried their case to the court. *Id.* at 21. Agreements like the one entered into here are statutorily permitted in Missouri. *See* Mo. Rev. Stat. § 537.065 (2022).

127. *Advantage Bldgs.*, 449 S.W.3d at 21.

128. *Id.* at 23.

129. *Id.* at 22.

130. *Id.* at 23.

131. *Id.* (internal quotation marks omitted).

132. *Id.* at 23–24.

second letter promised that Mid-Continent would promptly inform Advantage "[i]f other facts come to our attention."[133] Despite "not actually analyzing anything" or explaining any coverage issues, both letters stated: "The above analysis constitutes our best efforts to inform you of all factors, which we are currently aware of, that may affect our ultimate responsibility to provide a defense and/or indemnification for damages that may be imposed against you in this litigation."[134] Mid-Continent's letters quite simply did not constitute an effective reservation of rights.[135]

Continuing, the court explained that an insurer that defends its insured in a case where coverage is doubtful without properly reserving its rights cannot later deny liability based on a lack of coverage.[136] Here, Mid-Continent's reservation of rights was neither timely nor clear, nor did Mid-Continent fully and unambiguously inform Advantage of its coverage position. Furthermore, Mid-Continent did not promptly inform Advantage of its coverage position as it twice promised to do. Rather, Mid-Continent failed to advise Advantage of its final coverage decision for two years and then did so a mere four days before the Alsation trial was to begin. Thus, despite the trial court's ruling in the declaratory judgment action that Mid-Continent's policy did not cover Alsation's claims, Mid-Continent was estopped from denying coverage up to its policy limits.[137] Consequently, the trial court did not err in submitting Advantage's bad faith claim to the jury despite holding that the Mid-Continent policy did not afford coverage for the underlying lawsuit.

In another case, *Harleysville Group Insurance v. Heritage Communities, Inc.*,[138] Harleysville Group Insurance (Harleysville) issued CGL policies to the developers of two condominium complexes known jointly as Heritage. The complexes were plagued by construction defects, including building code violations, structural flaws, and water intrusion. A few years after the complexes were built, the buyers sued to recover damages for repairs to their homes.

The lawsuits were filed by the respective property owners' associations (POAs), which sought compensatory and punitive damages under theories of negligent construction, breach of fiduciary duty, and breach of warranty. Harleysville informed Heritage that it would provide a defense "under a full reservation of rights."[139] In fact, Harleysville's reservations of rights "were generic statements of potential non-coverage coupled with furnishing most of the Heritage entities with copies (through a cut-and-paste method) of the insur-

133. *Id.* at 24 (internal quotation marks omitted).
134. *Id.*
135. *Id.*
136. *Id.*
137. *Id.*
138. 803 S.E.2d 288 (S.C. 2017).
139. *Id.* at 293.

ance policies."[140] Harleysville was, however, more specific with respect to the punitive damage claims:

> The complaint filed against you seeks punitive damages. [Harleysville] reserves the right to disclaim coverage for these since under all of your policies, they would not arise from an "occurrence," do not fit the definition of "bodily injury" or "property damage," and/or were "expected and intended" within the meaning of exclusions in the policies.[141]

The POAs won their cases against Heritage and were awarded judgments totaling $14 million. Harleysville filed declaratory judgment actions to determine what portion of the judgments in the underlying lawsuits would be covered under Heritage's CGL policies. The cases ultimately reached the South Carolina Supreme Court, which addressed them in a single opinion given the nearly identical issues they raised.

The first question for the *Harleysville* court was "whether a reservation of rights letter that merely provides the insured with a copy of the policy, coupled with a general statement that the insurer reserves all of its rights, is sufficient."[142] The court answered that it was not:

> [The reservation of rights] letters explained that Harleysville would provide a defense in the underlying suits and listed the name and contact information for the defense attorney Harleysville had selected to represent Heritage in each matter. These letters identif[ied] the particular insured entity and lawsuit at issue, summarize[d] the allegations in the complaint, and identif[ied] the policy numbers and policy periods for policies that potentially provided coverage. Additionally, each of these letters (through a cut-and-paste approach) incorporated a nine- or ten-page excerpt of various policy terms, including the provisions relating to the insuring agreement, Harleysville's duty to defend, and numerous policy exclusions and definitions. *Despite these policy references, the letters included no discussion of Harleysville's position as to the various provisions or explanation of its reasons for potentially denying coverage. With the exception of the claim for punitive damages, the letters failed to specify the particular grounds upon which Harleysville did, or might thereafter, dispute coverage.*
>
> The fact that Harleysville stated the specific grounds for contesting coverage for punitive damages stands in stark contrast to the otherwise nonspecific—"we will let you know later"—purported reservation of rights. It is reasonable to conclude that Harleysville knew precisely how to protect its interests, but elected to be purposefully vague on all coverage matters except punitive damages.

140. *Id.*
141. *Id.* at 299.
142. *Id.* at 296.

> Significantly, none of the reservation letters advised Heritage of the need for allocation of damages between covered and non-covered losses or referenced a possible conflict of interest or Harleysville's intent to pursue a declaratory judgment action following any adverse jury verdicts in the underlying lawsuits.[143]

Not surprisingly, the court concluded that except for punitive damages, Harleysville had not effectively reserved its rights. A dissenting justice disagreed and would have found the reservation of rights letters to be sufficient.[144]

3. *Summary*

Harleyesville is an unremarkable decision with one exception: the court's criticism of Harleysville for not discussing its intent to file a declaratory judgment action in its reservation of rights letter. A declaratory judgment action is not a policy-based defense to coverage; an insurer therefore should have no duty to reserve its right to pursue a judicial determination of its duty to indemnify its insured. That said, some other courts are aligned with the *Harleysville* court on this issue,[145] and insurers are well-advised to inform insureds of that possibility given the ease of doing so.

In *World Harvest Church*, while the Georgia Supreme Court *required* an insurer to fairly inform an insured of its coverage defenses under a reservation of rights, the court only *recommended* that the insurer provide the insured with the specific bases for its reservation.[146] Thus, as the Eleventh Circuit reasoned in a 2014 opinion applying Georgia law, an insurer need not specify in a reservation of rights letter all possible bases for disputing coverage "as long as the reservation fairly informs the insured that, notwithstanding the defense of the insured, the insurer does not waive its coverage defenses."[147]

Many courts employ similar approaches. In *Starr Indemnity & Liability Co. v. i3 Verticals, LLC*,[148] for example, the court explained that Tennessee law does not require that the reasons an insurer gives for its coverage position in a reservation of rights letter "be legally correct."[149] Rather, the insurer's position on coverage "may be correct, but for other legal reasons. It is the insurer's conclusion regarding the existence or non-existence of certain coverage that

143. *Id.* at 298–99 (footnote omitted) (emphasis added).

144. *Id.* at 310–11 (Pleicones, Acting J., dissenting).

145. *See, e.g.*, United Nat'l Ins. Co. v. Waterfront N.Y. Realty Corp., 948 F. Supp. 263, 268 (S.D.N.Y. 1996) ("A reservation of rights letter must give fair notice to the insured that the insurer intends to assert defenses to coverage or to pursue a declaratory relief action at a later date.").

146. Wellons, Inc. v. Lexington Ins. Co., 566 F. App'x 813, 821–22 (11th Cir. 2014).

147. *Id.* at 821.

148. No. 3:16-cv-2832, 2018 WL 5266588 (M.D. Tenn. Oct. 23, 2018).

149. *Id.* at *4 (quoting Richards Mfg. Co. v. Great Am. Ins. Co., 773 S.W.2d 916, 919 (Tenn. Ct. App. 1988)).

must be clearly and fairly communicated to the insured, not its legal reasons therefor."[150]

Thus, whether a reservation of rights letter is sufficiently clear pivots on whether the insurer "provided adequate notice of its ultimate position" on coverage.[151] In other words, so long as the insurer clarifies that it disputes any duty to indemnify the insured notwithstanding its provision of a defense, a reservation of rights letter is suitably informative under Tennessee law. Likewise, California courts have long held that a "generalized reservation of rights" or "global reservation of rights" will preserve an insurer's coverage defenses.[152]

As *Advantage Buildings* illustrates, however, many courts will not enforce generalized reservations of rights. In these courts, an insurer that quotes policy language in a reservation of rights letter, without applying the language to the facts of the case and without clearly explaining how coverage might be affected, does not preserve its ability to contest coverage.

It is good practice—and in many courts essential—for insurers to specifically inform insureds of the contractual and factual bases for a reservation of rights. An insurer should explain how its policy language applies to the facts of the loss and how coverage is potentially affected as a result. In addition to benefiting the insured by fully informing it of the insurer's coverage position, an insurer that details the reasons for its reservation increases the likelihood that a court will hold that its reservation of rights letter preserved its coverage defenses. At the same time, whether a court will determine that a reservation of rights letter adequately informed the insured of the insurer's coverage position generally depends on the facts. This is an area in which context counts.[153]

D. Waiver and Estoppel

Regardless of whether an insurer's reservation of rights letter is allegedly untimely or is said to be deficient because it does not fairly or adequately express the insurer's coverage position, the ultimate issue is whether the insurer has thereby waived any coverage defenses or should be estopped from asserting them. Although "waiver" and "estoppel" are separate legal doctrines, courts occasionally blend them or use the terms interchangeably.[154]

---

150. *Id.* (quoting *Richards*, 773 S.W.2d at 919).

151. *Id.*

152. *See, e.g.*, State Farm Fire & Cas. Co. v. Jioras, 29 Cal. Rptr. 2d 840, 844 (Ct. App. 1994); *see also* Marentes v. State Farm Mut. Auto. Ins. Co., 224 F. Supp. 3d 891, 913 (N.D. Cal. 2016) ("A reservation of rights does not need to specifically address each coverage defense, but can be general.").

153. *See* Liberty Ins. Corp. v. HNTB Corp., No. 21-cv-00641-SRB, 2022 WL 16713024, at *4 (W.D. Mo. Sept. 22, 2022) (stating that "a reservation of rights letter can only be as specific and helpful as language in the underlying complaints and the information relayed to the insurer by the insured").

154. ISCO Indus., Inc. v. Fed. Ins. Co., 587 F. Supp. 3d 558, 578 (W.D. Ky. 2022) ("Waiver and estoppel are terms often misused interchangeably despite the clear distinction between them."); *see*

1. *Understanding Waiver*

"Waiver" is the intentional or voluntary relinquishment of a known right.[155] A party's negligence or mistake will not support a finding of waiver.[156] A party cannot waive a right where it is unaware of facts supporting or giving rise to that right. Waiver does not require detrimental reliance by the party asserting the doctrine.[157]

A waiver may be express or implied.[158] For express waiver, an insurer must—obviously enough—expressly relinquish its rights; silence or inaction by the insurer is not sufficient.[159] For waiver to be implied, the party's conduct must be "inconsistent with any intention other than to waive" the right in question.[160] Courts sometimes equate implied waiver with estoppel,[161] although they are different doctrines.

In some jurisdictions, waiver applies only where an insurer attempts to deny coverage based on an exclusion without reserving its rights; waiver does not apply where coverage never existed in the first place.[162] This approach reflects the oft repeated saying that waiver cannot be used to create or expand coverage that does not otherwise exist.

Because waiver requires the intentional or voluntary relinquishment of a known right, the doctrine should seldom apply to reservations of rights. After all, it is nonsensical to think that an insurer that sent a reservation of rights letter—even if the letter was somehow deficient—intentionally or voluntarily

---

also Secura Supreme Ins. Co. v. Differding, 988 N.W.2d 580, 583 (N.D. 2023) ("Waiver and estoppel are distinct but related concepts."); Chubb v. Ohio Bureau of Workers' Comp., 690 N.E.2d 1267, 1270 (Ohio 1998) ("Although waiver is typical of estoppel, estoppel is a separate and distinct doctrine. With estoppel, it is not necessary to intend to relinquish a right.").

155. Divino Plastic Surgery, Inc. v. Super. Ct., 293 Cal. Rptr. 3d 47, 63 (Ct. App. 2022); Studio WTA, LLC v. Pruco Life Ins. Co., 368 So. 3d 630, 642 (La. Ct. App. 2023); Kingery Constr. Co. v. 6135 O St. Car Wash, LLC, 979 N.W.2d 762, 771 (Neb. 2022); Kellogg v. Nat'l R.R. Passenger Corp., 504 P.3d 796, 810 (Wash. 2022).

156. *See* Saunders v. Lloyd's of London, 779 P.2d 249, 254 (Wash. 1989) (citation omitted) ("[C]onduct giving rise to a waiver argument cannot be consistent with any other interpretation than intent to waive. . . . A person must know that certain conduct has the effect of relinquishing a right.").

157. Ill. Ins. Guar. Fund v. Nwidor, 105 N.E.3d 1035, 1043 (Ill. App. Ct. 2018); UMIA Ins., Inc. v. Saltz, 515 P.3d 406, 415 (Utah 2022); Potesta v. U.S. Fid. & Guar. Co., 504 S.E.2d 135, 144 (W. Va. 1998). *But see* Shake Out, LLC v. Clearwater Constr., LLC, 535 P.3d 598, 604 (Idaho 2023) (requiring detrimental reliance for a party to succeed in asserting waiver).

158. State Farm Mut. Auto. Ins. Co. v. Easterling, 19 N.E.3d 156, 163 (Ill. App. Ct. 2014); Smith v. Md. Cas. Co., 500 S.W.3d 244, 250 (Mo. Ct. App. 2015).

159. CMW Int'l LLC v. Amerisure Ins. Co., No. 1:16-cv-01384-TWP-DKL, 2016 WL 7438846, at *5 (S.D. Ind. Dec. 27, 2016) (applying Indiana law); Peck v. Peck, 649 N.Y.S.2d 22, 23 (App. Div. 1996).

160. *Easterling*, 19 N.E.3d at 163; *see also* Cutcher v. MultiPlan, Inc., 22 F.4th 756, 766 (8th Cir. 2022) (reciting a similarly high standard under Missouri law).

161. *See, e.g.*, Morgan v. Millstone Res. Ltd., 267 A.3d 1235, 1249 (Pa. Super. Ct. 2021) ("Regarding the doctrine of implied waiver, '[it] applies only to situations involving circumstances equivalent to an estoppel, and the person claiming the waiver to prevail must show that he was misled and prejudiced thereby[.]'" (quoting Brown v. City of Pittsburgh, 186 A.2d 399, 401 (Pa. 1962))).

162. *See, e.g.*, Associated Indem. Corp. v. Miller-Campbell Co., 596 S.W.2d 383, 389 (Mo. 1980).

elected to grant the insured coverage for which it did not pay.[163] Accordingly, equitable estoppel represents the better approach when basing coverage on an insurer's failure to reserve its rights properly or at all.[164] Nonetheless, some courts hold that an insurer that defends its insured without reserving its rights despite knowing of facts that suggest it may not owe a duty to indemnify the insured waives any coverage defenses.[165]

2. *Understanding Estoppel*

As with waiver, it is often said that estoppel cannot be used to create coverage under an insurance policy where it would not otherwise exist.[166] That is true with respect to what might be called "general estoppel." As the Illinois Supreme Court once explained, general estoppel cannot be used to create coverage "where the insurer was given no opportunity to defend; where there was no insurance policy in existence; and where, when the policy and the complaint are compared, there clearly was no coverage or potential for coverage."[167] The rationale for the rule that estoppel cannot be used to create coverage is that courts should not rewrite parties' contracts to force an insurer to cover a loss for which the insured paid no premium.[168] But there is another form of estoppel—equitable estoppel—that can compel an insurer to do what general estoppel cannot: pay a claim that falls outside the terms of its policy.[169] Numerous courts recognize equitable estoppel in connection with reservations of rights.[170]

---

163. *See, e.g.*, Perini/Tompkins Joint Venture v. Ace Am. Ins. Co., 738 F.3d 95, 106–07 (4th Cir. 2013) (interpreting Tennessee and Maryland law); Metro Prop. & Cas. Ins. Co. v. Gilson, 458 F. App'x 609, 612 (9th Cir. 2011) (applying New Hampshire law); St. Paul Fire & Marine Ins. Co. v. Albany Cnty. Sch. Dist. No. 1, 763 P.2d 1255, 1262 (Wyo. 1988) (rejecting the insured's waiver claim predicated on the insurer's allegedly deficient reservation of rights letter).

164. Becker v. Bar Plan Mut. Ins. Co., 429 P.3d 212, 219 (Kan. 2018); Morgan v. State Farm Fire & Cas. Co., 344 S.W.3d 771, 777 (Mo. Ct. App. 2011).

165. *See, e.g.*, Jeffries v. Prime Ins. Co., 334 So. 3d 761, 777–78 (La. Ct. App. 2021); Collins v. Grange Mut. Cas. Co., 706 N.E.2d 856, 859 (Ohio Ct. App. 1997).

166. *See, e.g.*, United Heritage Prop. & Cas. Co. v. Zech, 516 P.3d 1035, 1046 (Idaho 2022) (referring to equitable estoppel); Burdette v. Bell, 137 N.E.3d 1236, 1243 (Ohio Ct. App. 2019) ("Waiver and estoppel cannot be invoked to create coverage under an insurance policy where coverage otherwise does not exist."); Prime Time Fam. Ent. Ctr., Inc. v. AXIS Ins. Co., 630 S.W.3d 226, 232 (Tex. App. 2020) ("The contractual coverage of an insurance policy cannot be expanded by waiver or estoppel on the part of the insurer.").

167. Emps. Ins. of Wausau v. Ehlco Liquidating Tr., 708 N.E.2d 1122, 1135 (Ill. 1999).

168. Secura Supreme Ins. Co. v. Differding, 988 N.W.2d 580, 584 (N.D. 2023).

169. Essex Ins. Co. v. Blue Moon Lofts Condo. Ass'n, 927 F.3d 1007, 1012–13 (7th Cir. 2019) (applying Illinois law).

170. *See, e.g.*, Westport Ins. Corp. v. McClellan, 493 F. Supp. 3d 315, 326–28 (E.D. Pa. 2020) (applying Pennsylvania law); Komorsky v. Farmers Ins. Exch., 245 Cal. Rptr. 3d 623, 633–34 (Ct. App. 2019) ("An exception to the rule against coverage by estoppel applies where a liability insurer defends an action against its insured without reserving the right to deny coverage."); Facility Invs., LP v. Homeland Ins. Co. of N.Y., 741 S.E.2d 228, 233 (Ga. Ct. App. 2013) (mentioning both estoppel and waiver); *Burdette*, 137 N.E.3d at 1243 ("One exception to that general rule [that estoppel cannot be used to create coverage] is when the insurer provides a defense to the insured without reserving its rights under the policy for such a period of time as to prejudice the insured."); Tull v. Chubb Grp. of

Equitable estoppel requires an inducement or misrepresentation by the party against whom the doctrine is asserted.[171] As one court put it, equitable estoppel prevents a party "who has made certain representations from taking unfair advantage of another when the party making the representations changes its position to the prejudice of the party who relied upon the representations."[172] In other words, equitable estoppel requires detrimental reliance by the party invoking the doctrine.[173] Furthermore, the claiming party's detrimental reliance must have been reasonable for equitable estoppel to apply.[174]

In the reservation of rights context, the representation or inducement on which estoppel rests is the insurer's defense of the insured with knowledge of possible coverage defenses but without a reservation of rights or absent a proper reservation of rights. So, if an insurer assumes control of the defense of an action against its insured with knowledge of facts that would permit it to disclaim coverage but does not reserve its right to do so, or if the insurer issues a reservation of rights letter that does not adequately inform the insured of the insurer's coverage defenses, the insurer may be estopped from subsequently denying coverage if the insured was prejudiced by the insurer's conduct.[175] If an insurer has issued multiple concurrent policies to an insured, as may be the case where an insurer is providing different types of primary liability insurance via separate policies (such as CGL and employment practices liability) or is providing both primary and excess or umbrella coverage, estoppel will apply, if at all, only to the policy under which the insurer is providing the defense.[176]

Ins. Cos., 146 S.W.3d 689, 694 (Tex. App. 2004) (referring to estoppel and waiver where an insurer fails to reserve its rights).

171. *See* Felder v. Cent. Masonry, Inc., 864 S.E.2d 906, 908 (S.C. Ct. App. 2021) ("Estoppel applies if an insurer has misled the insured into believing a particular risk is within an insurance policy's coverage.").

172. ABC Disposal Sys., Inc. v. Dep't of Nat. Res., 681 N.W.2d 596, 606 (Iowa 2004).

173. *See, e.g.*, Am. Home Assur. Co. v. Superior Well Servs., Inc., 75 F.4th 184, 191 n.7 (3d Cir. 2023) (rejecting the insured's estoppel claim because it did not establish detrimental reliance on the insurer's alleged failure to reserve its rights).

174. Santa Clara Valley Water Dist. v. Century Indem. Co., 306 Cal. Rptr. 3d 724, 752 (Ct. App. 2023).

175. Founders Ins. Co. v. Olivares, 894 N.E.2d 586, 592 (Ind. Ct. App. 2008) (quoting Emps. Ins. of Wausau v. Recticel Foam Corp., 716 N.E.2d 1015, 1028 (Ind. Ct. App. 1999)); Breci v. St. Paul Mercury Ins. Co., 849 N.W.2d 523, 535 (Neb. 2014); Temple Beth Sholom, Inc. v. Commerce & Indus. Ins. Co., 103 N.Y.S. 3d 413, 414 (App. Div. 2019); *Burdette*, 137 N.E.3d at 1243; Paradigm Ins. Co. v. Tex. Richmond Corp., 942 S.W.2d 645, 652–53 (Tex. App. 1997).

176. *See, e.g.*, N. Am. Specialty Ins. Co. v. Bull River Marina, LLC, 709 F. App'x 623, 629–31 (11th Cir. 2017) (concluding that the insurer was not estopped to deny coverage under the insured's marina operator's policy when it defended the insured under its CGL policy); Capitol Specialty Ins. Corp. v. Higgins, 203 F. Supp. 3d 200, 215–16 (D. Mass. 2016) (explaining that Capitol had no duty to reserve its rights under its CGL policy when it defended under a liquor liability policy and coverage under the CGL policy was never in question until Capitol offered to pay the remaining liability limit of its liquor liability policy in settlement); St. Paul Fire & Marine Ins. Co. v. Children's Hosp. Nat'l Med. Ctr., 670 F. Supp. 393, 402 (D.D.C. 1987) (explaining that St. Paul's obligation to reserve its rights applied only

As indicated earlier, an insured asserting estoppel generally must establish that it was prejudiced by the insurer's failure to reserve its rights, or by the insurer's failure to do so adequately or timely.[177] A few courts, however, presume prejudice to the insured in these situations, sometimes with any presumption depending on the insurer's degree of control over the insured's defense.[178]

An insurer's mere acceptance of an insured's defense without a reservation of rights or pursuant to a deficient or untimely reservation of rights does not constitute prejudice to the insured.[179] Rather, for there to be prejudice, the insurer must induce the insured to surrender its right to control its own defense,[180] leaving control exclusively in the insurer's hands.[181] There is no prejudice, and thus no basis for estoppel, where the insured controls or shares control of its defense.[182] Nor can the insured demonstrate prejudice where the insured was satisfied with the performance of the defense lawyer appointed by the insurer or where the insured cannot point to anything that independent counsel would have done differently.[183]

---

to the primary policy under which it was defending the hospital; it had no duty to reserve its rights under excess policies it also issued to the hospital).

177. *See, e.g.*, Templin v. Catlin Specialty Ins. Co., 612 F. App'x 940, 959 (10th Cir. 2015) (applying New York law); Penn-Am. Ins. Co. v. Sanchez, 202 P.3d 472, 478 (Ariz. Ct. App. 2008); Bishop v. Progressive Express Ins. Co., 154 So. 3d 467, 468 (Fla. Dist. Ct. App. 2015); Std. Mut. Ins. Co. v. Lay, 989 N.E.2d 591, 596 (Ill. 2013); *Olivares*, 894 N.E.2d at 593; Westfield Ins. Cos. v. Econ. Fire & Cas. Co., 623 N.W.2d 871, 880 (Iowa 2001); Ky. Farm Bureau Mut. Ins. Co. v. Brewer, 596 S.W.3d 620, 623 (Ky. Ct. App. 2020); *Breci*, 849 N.W.2d at 535; Ulico Cas. Co. v. Allied Pilots Ass'n, 262 S.W.3d 773, 787 (Tex. 2008).

178. *See, e.g.*, Athridge v. Aetna Cas. & Sur. Co., 604 F.3d 625, 629 (D.C. Cir. 2010) (applying D.C. law and observing that an insured may be entitled to a rebuttable presumption of prejudice depending on the amount of control over the defense the insurer exercised); World Harvest Church, Inc. v. Guide-One Mut. Ins. Co., 695 S.E.2d 6, 10–13 (Ga. 2010) (reasoning that where an insurer assumes exclusive control of the insured's defense without effectively reserving its rights, prejudice to the insured should be conclusively presumed); Becker v. Bar Plan Mut. Ins. Co., 429 P.3d 212, 219 (Kan. 2018) (presuming prejudice once the insured establishes reliance).

179. *Lay*, 989 N.E.2d 596; *see* Mgmt. Specialists, Inc. v. Northfield Ins. Co., 117 P.3d 32, 38 (Colo. App. 2004) (declining to apply estoppel where the insurer defended the insured without a reservation of rights for several months but the insured could not demonstrate any resulting prejudice); Tarry Realty LLC v. Utica First Ins. Co., 980 N.Y.S.2d 441, 443 (App. Div. 2014) (refusing to invoke estoppel simply because the insurer assumed the insured's defense without reserving its rights).

180. *Lay*, 989 N.E.2d 596.

181. *See, e.g.*, Temple Beth Sholom, Inc. v. Com. & Indus. Ins. Co., 103 N.Y.S.3d 413, 414 (App. Div. 2019) ("Temple relied to its detriment on the defense provided by defendant Commerce, which was in conflict with the defense Commerce provided to the general contractor, and as a result, Temple lost control of its defense. Commerce was properly estopped from denying coverage by virtue of its conduct in handling the underlying claim[.]").

182. *See, e.g.*, Essex Ins. Co. v. Blue Moon Lofts Condo. Ass'n, 927 F.3d 1007, 1013 (7th Cir. 2019) (explaining that the insurer did not prejudice the insured because it was the insured's chosen counsel and not Essex that controlled the litigation); Nutmeg Ins. Co. v. Clear Lake City Water Auth., 229 F. Supp. 2d 668, 696 (S.D. Tex. 2002) (finding no prejudice where the insured was defended by independent counsel at the insurer's expense); Rosalind Franklin Univ. of Med. & Sci. v. Lexington Ins. Co., 8 N.E.3d 20, 33–36 (Ill. App. Ct. 2014) (finding no prejudice where the insured's general counsel was actively involved in the defense).

183. Evanston Ins. Co. v. Law Off. of Michael P. Medved, P.C., 890 F.3d 1195, 1201 (10th Cir. 2018); Nat'l Sur. Corp. v. Dustex Corp., No. C13-2004, 2015 WL 1057506, at *15 (N.D. Iowa Mar. 10, 2015).

The best example of a case in which the insurer induces the insured to surrender control of its defense is one where the insurer defends the insured through judgment without advising the insured of a conflict of interest affecting the manner in which the defense might be conducted. Or, an insurer might defend an insured without advising her of a conflict of interest affecting the defense short of judgment, but until it is too late for the insured to avoid the consequences of the conflict.[184] In either case, the insured would have been denied the valuable right to control the defense by engaging independent counsel at the insurer's expense. That deprivation alone establishes prejudice.[185]

Prejudice may further exist where "the insurer's control of the defense is such that the character and strategy of the lawsuit can no longer be altered."[186] In *Brecek & Young Advisors, Inc. v. Lloyds of London Syndicate 2003*,[187] for example, the court found that the insured was prejudiced when the insurer defended the case to conclusion and contributed to the settlement of a group of claims before trying to deny coverage for those claims.[188] But litigation strategy and the substantive or tactical contours of a lawsuit may be cemented short of settlement or judgment.[189] Consider a case where the insurer controls the defense until discovery has closed or key deadlines, such as dates for amending pleadings, disclosing expert witnesses, or filing dispositive motions have passed, and only then reserves its rights. Finally, think of a case in which the insurer reserves its rights on the eve of trial or shortly before a pre-trial settlement conference,[190] or after reasonable settlement opportunities that the insured had the financial ability to seize have passed.[191]

184. *See, e.g.*, Interstate Fire & Cas. Co. v. Apt. Mgmt. Consultants LLC, 824 F. App'x 565, 571 (10th Cir. 2020) (sending a reservation of rights letter after defending the case for over 18 months and only 11 days before the start of a jury trial); Erie Ins. Exch. v. Lobenthal, 114 A.3d 832, 839–40 (Pa. Super. Ct. 2015) (delaying in reserving rights until only noncovered claims remained).

185. Royal Ins. Co. v. Process Design Assocs., Inc., 582 N.E.2d 1234, 1240 (Ill. App. Ct. 1991).

186. Federated Dep't Stores, Inc. v. Twin City Fire Ins. Co., 807 N.Y.S.2d 62, 68 (App. Div. 2006).

187. 715 F.3d 1231 (10th Cir. 2013) (applying New York law).

188. *Id.* at 1239–42.

189. *See, e.g.*, SPARTA Ins. Co. v. Tech. Ins. Co., 751 F. App'x 32, 35 (2d Cir. 2018) (finding prejudice where the general contractor, in reliance on the insurer's defense, lost the opportunity to file a third-party complaint against a subcontractor for indemnification in the underlying tort suit); Bluestein & Sandler v. Chi. Ins. Co., 276 F.3d 119, 122–23 (2d Cir. 2002) (finding prejudice where important discovery "was no longer possible, or, at the very least, was seriously compromised").

190. *See, e.g.*, Interstate Fire & Cas. Co. v. Apt. Mgmt. Consultants LLC, 824 F. App'x 565, 572 (10th Cir. 2020) ("Interstate failed to reserve its rights until eleven days before trial, past the point where [the insured] could have hired independent counsel to represent its interests on the purportedly uncovered claims, have them dismissed as a matter of law at summary judgment, or to attempt to settle them prior to trial."); U.S. Fid. & Guar. Co. v. N.Y. Susquehanna & W. Ry. Corp., 713 N.Y.S.2d 624, 625–26 (App. Div. 2000) (citations omitted) ("[The] [p]laintiff's first assertion of a possible disclaimer on the eve of the settlement conference placed in jeopardy a favorable settlement . . . and forced [the] defendant to agree to litigate the coverage issues in order to save the settlement. In our view, [the] defendant demonstrated prejudice. . . .").

191. Dietz-Britton v. Smythe, Cramer & Co., 743 N.E.2d 960, 968 (Ohio 2000).

Depending on the facts, the insureds in these cases may be able to establish that they were prejudiced by the insurer's failure to reserve its rights, or by its failure to do so timely or adequately. The argument for prejudice in these circumstances is stronger where there is a conflict of interest that entitles the insured to independent counsel or where the applicable law permits the insured to reject a defense under a reservation of rights, but courts may apply estoppel even when that is not the case.[192] Whether they should do so, however, is another story. If defense counsel appointed by the insurer has defended the case appropriately, the mere passage of time should not support a finding of prejudice.[193] The insured's satisfaction with the representation furnished by the lawyer appointed by the insurer should also defeat any prejudice claim.[194]

Prejudice may further be found where an insurer's delay in reserving its rights, or its ambiguous or incomplete reservation of rights, deprives the insured of coverage under another insurance policy. In *Penn-America Insurance Co. v. Sanchez*,[195] for instance, Penn-America defended the insured, Inside Arizona, under a CGL policy for ten months before reserving its rights.[196] Allegedly lulled into a false sense of security by Penn-America's extended defense without a reservation of rights, Inside Arizona delayed in notifying its auto insurer, National American Insurance Co. of California (NAICC), of the lawsuit.[197] When finally notified, NAICC refused to commit to Inside Arizona's defense or indemnity based on late notice of the suit. The *Sanchez* court concluded that "the[se] facts and reasonable inferences [would] support a finding of prejudice to the insured by a reasonable trier of fact."[198]

192. *See, e.g.*, *N.Y. Susquehanna & W. Ry. Corp.*, 713 N.Y.S.2d at 625–26 (finding prejudice where the insured was defended by counsel of its choice, and coverage and liability did not pivot on the same facts).

193. *See* Capitol Specialty Ins. Corp. v. Sanford Wittels & Heisler, LLP, 793 F. Supp. 2d 399, 412–13 (D.D.C. 2011) (finding no prejudice that would support estoppel, in the process noting that "[a]ctual prejudice may be shown if the insurer's participation in the defense harmed or hindered the insured by undermining their ability to defend themselves" but observing that "tellingly, defendants offer no criticism of [defense counsel appointed by the insurer] nor do they allege any facts of poor representation or malpractice"); Merchants Mut. Ins. Co. v. Artis, 907 F. Supp. 886, 892–93 (E.D. Pa. 1995) (finding no prejudice where defense counsel provided a thorough and competent defense up until the time the insurer withdrew the defense and further concluding that the insured's entry into a consent judgment weighed against any claim of prejudice); Ky. Farm Bureau Mut. Ins. Co. v. Brewer, 596 S.W.3d 620, 623 (Ky. Ct. App. 2020) (concluding that the trial court erred by holding that the mere passage of time estopped the insurer from asserting a coverage defense and remanding the case for factual findings as to any potential prejudice).

194. Evanston Ins. Co. v. Law Off. of Michael P. Medved, P.C., 890 F.3d 1195, 1201 (10th Cir. 2018).

195. 202 P.3d 472 (Ariz. Ct. App. 2008).

196. *Id.* at 476–78, 480.

197. *Id.* at 478–80.

198. *Id.* at 481.

3. *Only an Insured May Invoke Estoppel or Waiver*

Where a reservation of rights is concerned, a party must be an insured under the policy to invoke waiver or equitable estoppel to overcome the insurer's coverage defense.[199] *Secura Supreme Insurance Co. v. Differding*[200] illustrates this principle's application in a slightly muddled factual scenario.

In *Differding*, Aaron Greterman sued the Oxbow Golf and Country Club (Oxbow) and some of its board members in both their official and individual capacities. Oxbow had a CGL policy with Secura Supreme Insurance Co. (Secura) that included coverage for its directors, but only with respect to their duties as officers or directors. Secura agreed to defend the directors under a reservation of rights but advised them to request a defense under any other policies they may have. Greterman later amended his complaint to add Scott Differding as a defendant in both his capacity as a director and as an individual.

Secura hired a lawyer to represent Oxbow and the board members in their dual capacities. Greterman's case went to trial and Secura issued another reservation of rights letter to Oxbow and the directors during trial. The jury thereafter returned a verdict for Greterman. The trial court entered judgment against Oxbow for over $430,000 and against Differding in his individual capacity for over $540,000.[201] Differding's homeowners carrier, Nationwide Insurance, satisfied the judgment against him.

Secura filed a declaratory judgment action seeking a ruling that it was not obligated to indemnify Differding in his individual capacity. Differding and Nationwide responded that Secura had waived any coverage defenses or was estopped from asserting them because it defended Differding without properly reserving its rights. The trial court held that Secura's policy did not cover Differding individually but further held that it had waived its right to deny coverage and was also equitably estopped from doing so because it had defended

199. W. Va. Mut. Ins. Co. v. Vargas, 933 F. Supp. 2d 847, 859 (N.D. W. Va. 2013) (applying West Virginia law); St. Paul Fire & Marine Ins. Co. v. Nat'l Real Est. Clearinghouse Inc., 957 F. Supp. 187, 191 (D. Minn. 1997) (applying Minnesota law); Capitol Indem. Corp. v. Fraley, 597 S.E.2d 601, 603 (Ga. Ct. App. 2004); W. Cas. & Sur. Co. v. Am. Nat'l Fire Ins. Co., 318 N.W.2d 126, 128 (S.D. 1982). The approach may be different in some jurisdictions with direct action statutes. See *supra* notes 13–14 and accompanying text. It is also possible that in some states, a party that takes an assignment of an insured's rights against its insurer may be able to invoke estoppel based on the insurer's failure to properly reserve its rights. *See, e.g.*, Pueblo Santa Fe Townhomes Owners' Ass'n v. Transcon. Ins. Co., 178 P.3d 485, 492 (Ariz. Ct. App. 2008) ("If Pueblo were barred from asserting whatever estoppel rights PVP acquired by virtue of CNA's delay, CNA would be able to avoid the consequences of its conduct simply because its insured chose to protect itself from the risk of the litigation—risk that may have been enhanced by CNA's delay in reserving its rights—by entering a *Morris* agreement. We decline to adopt a rule that would enable an insurer to avoid responsibility in that manner for failing to promptly notify its insured of its reservation of rights to deny coverage.").

200. 988 N.W.2d 580 (N.D. 2023).

201. *Id.* at 582.

him without properly reserving its rights.[202] Secura appealed the trial court's decision.

The North Dakota Supreme Court easily rejected Differding's and Nationwide's claims. Although the Secura policy extended coverage to Oxbow's directors, it did so only in their official capacities.[203] Secura did not insure Differding in his individual capacity, as Differding himself conceded.[204] As a matter of law, Differding could not invoke waiver or estoppel to create coverage under an insurance policy to which he was not a party and which he had no right to enforce.[205] The *Secura* court thus reversed the trial court judgment.

IV. Effectively Reserving Rights

In addition to complying with any state-specific statutes or administrative regulations governing reservations of rights, insurers should follow some basic guidelines to ensure that their reservation of rights letters serve their interests as well as their insureds' interests. The following nonexclusive list of steps to take or issues to address in a reservation of rights letter is intended to either ensure or enhance the effectiveness of insurers' reservations of rights, keeping in mind that every case is different.[206]

1. An insurer that knows of coverage defenses should send a reservation of rights letter asserting those defenses as soon as reasonably practicable. The insurer should reserve its rights before or upon assuming the insured's defense. If that timing is not feasible, the insurer should reserve its rights as soon after assuming the defense as is reasonably possible.
2. The insurer should pay careful attention to the seemingly mundane details that may generate ambiguity allegations if they are inaccurate. For example, the reservation of rights letter (a) should specify the policy at issue; (b) correctly state the policy number;[207] (c) correctly state the

202. *Id.* at 582–83.
203. *Id.* at 585.
204. *Id.*
205. *Id.*
206. An insurer's failure to include or address any of the listed issues in a reservation of rights letter does not necessarily render the reservation of rights deficient or ineffective. *See* Smith v. Md. Cas. Co., 500 S.W.3d 244, 250–51 (Mo. Ct. App. 2015) (rejecting the insured's list of specific elements that an insurer supposedly must include in a "proper" reservation of rights letter and stating that the test for an adequate reservation of rights letter is whether it "fully informed" the insured of the insurer's coverage position).
207. In *Country Mutual Insurance Co. v. Jackson*, No. 2:20-CV-00150-SAB, 2022 WL 187808 (E.D. Wash. Jan. 20, 2022), the insureds contended that Country Mutual's reservation of rights letter was deficient because it listed the wrong insurance policy number on one page. The court rejected this

policy period; (d) correctly identify the insured; (e) accurately state the policy's limits of liability; (f) identify the right insurer if the insurance company is one of several affiliated companies;[208] (g) use the words "reservation of rights"; and (h) clarify that the insurer is reserving its rights and not denying coverage.

3. If the plaintiff has amended its complaint or petition, the reservation of rights letter must relate and refer to the controlling pleading.
4. The insurer should acknowledge that it will be providing a defense and state how it intends to do so, such as by identifying the defense lawyer it is appointing for the insured. If the insurer will be defending through staff counsel, the letter should say so.
5. If the insurer will be appointing defense counsel for the insured, the letter should inform the insured that it has the right to retain personal counsel at its expense.
6. If multiple insureds are involved, the insurer should (a) identify in the reservation of rights letter all insureds to which the reservation of rights applies; (b) state which coverage defenses apply to each of them; and (c) send each of them a reservation of rights letter.
7. An insurer should reserve all known rights that it may wish to assert in its initial reservation of rights letter. Although an insurer may issue supplemental reservation of rights letters as it acquires new information, asserting a policy defense known at the outset of a case for the first time in a supplemental letter invites unnecessary confusion or controversy.
8. In any reservation of rights letter, the insurer should state that it reserves its right to assert coverage defenses of which it subsequently becomes aware and to adjust its position based on new information or developments in the case. The insurer may further wish to broadly state that it reserves the right to assert all other terms, provisions, conditions, and exclusions in its policy that may apply to the underlying action.[209] Such language alerts the insured to the possibility that additional coverage issues may arise.
9. An insurer should avoid "general" or "global" reservations of rights other than as a placeholder for a detailed reservation of rights to

argument because the letter quoted the correct policy and enumerated the precise exclusions at issue and specified the correct policy number elsewhere in the letter. *Id.* at *6.

208. Similarly, insurance companies sometimes administer policies issued by other insurance companies. In such a case, the company that is administering the policy and preparing the reservation of rights letter needs to make clear that it is the company that issued the policy whose rights are being reserved.

209. *See* Street Surfing, LLC v. Great Am. E & S Ins. Co., 776 F.3d 603, 609 n.6 (9th Cir. 2014) (stating that nearly identical language was sufficient under California law to defeat the insured's estoppel argument).

follow. The insurer should instead clearly articulate in its reservation of rights letter all the reasons why coverage may be denied or limited. If an insurer sends a general or global reservation of rights letter, it should explain in the letter that a detailed reservation of rights will follow.

10. In explaining why coverage might be denied or limited, the insurer should quote the applicable policy language and specifically apply it to the material facts of the case as then known. The insurer should avoid paraphrasing policy language.
11. The insurer should not quote, cite, or refer to inapplicable policy language.
12. The insurer should specifically explain the basis for its coverage position. If the insurer is relying on allegations in pleadings as the basis for its coverage determination, it should either quote or be careful to accurately state or summarize the allegations when linking them to policy language. If the insurer is instead or additionally relying on extrinsic evidence, it should identify that evidence and explain its relation to the policy language. In sum, the insurer should do its best to link the material facts of the case to the applicable policy language in a fashion calculated for an average consumer.
13. If the plaintiff's complaint or petition pleads some claims or causes of action that clearly are covered and others that plainly are not covered or may not be, the insurer should specifically categorize each claim or cause of action.
14. If a special verdict form or special interrogatories may be needed to allocate any damages between covered and uncovered claims or causes of action, or may otherwise be needed to address coverage issues, the reservation of rights letter should inform the insured of these possibilities and reserve the insurer's right to intervene in the case or take other steps to accomplish these purposes. The letter should also inform the insured that the insurer may require it to pursue the use of a special verdict form or special interrogatories.
15. The insurer should reserve its right to withdraw its defense if it determines that there is no possibility of coverage.[210]

---

210. An insurer's failure to specifically reserve its right to withdraw its defense does not necessarily prevent the insurer from withdrawing its defense if the reservation of rights letter is otherwise broad enough to encompass that right. *See, e.g.*, U.S. Underwriters Ins. Co. v. Kenfa Madison, LLC, No. 20-CV-2761 (NGG) (LB), 2023 WL 27010879, at *4 (E.D.N.Y. Mar. 30, 2023) (concluding that the insurer's statement that it "reserve[d] all of our rights under the policy" put the insured on notice that the insurer reserved its right to withdraw a defense); Integris Ins. Co. v. Tohan, No. HHD CV21-6141816, at *14 (Conn. Super. Ct. Nov. 8, 2023) (allowing Integris to withdraw its defense because, while its reservation of rights letter did not explicitly list the right to withdraw its defense as one of the rights reserved, "the inclusion of the phrase '[o]ur rights include, but are not limited to' necessarily

16. In an appropriate case, the insurer should reserve its right to seek reimbursement of defense costs or indemnity payments associated with uncovered claims or causes of action.[211]
17. The insurer must advise the insured if its reservation of rights creates a conflict of interest.[212] If the insurer fails to do so, that failure generally should not prejudice the insured where the defense lawyer appointed by the insurer recognizes the conflict and explains the conflict to the insured upon being appointed to represent the insured or very soon thereafter.[213] Even so, the insurer needs to make the disclosure in its reservation of rights letter.[214]
18. In an appropriate case, the reservation of rights letter should inform the insured of its right to a defense by independent counsel at the insurer's expense.[215]
19. In a jurisdiction where the insured has the right to reject a defense under reservation of rights and courts require the insurer to inform the insured of that right,[216] the insurer must comply.[217] In these jurisdictions, the insurer must further explain to the insured the effect of accepting the defense under reservation.[218]

---

implie[d] that the rights listed [in the reservation of rights letter] [were] not exhaustive"). Nonetheless, explicitly reserving the right to withdraw a defense clearly is the better practice.

211. *See* Equitable Life Assur. Soc'y of the U.S. v. Schwartz, 291 F. App'x 25, 27 (9th Cir. 2008) ("The reservation of rights requirement [with respect to recoupment] is important in the third party defense context because it puts the insured on notice that he has to protect his interests where they differ from the insurance company's interests. The insurer's control of his defense against the third party claim may run counter to how the insured would manage defense and settlement if he knew that the insurer might not pay the judgment or settlement.").

212. Landmark Am. Ins. Co. v. Esters, 600 F. Supp. 3d 677, 688 (W.D. La. 2022); Starr Indem. & Liab. Co. v. Young, 379 F. Supp. 3d 1103, 1108–09 (D. Nev. 2019) (applying Nevada law); Md. Cas. Co. v. Nestle, No. 1:09cv644-LG-RHW, 2010 WL 3735756, at *6 (S.D. Miss. Sept. 17, 2010) (applying Mississippi law); Std. Mut. Ins. Co. v. Lay, 989 N.E.2d 591, 596 (Ill. 2013).

213. *See* Ind. Ins. Co. v. CE Design Ltd., 6 F. Supp. 3d 858, 863 (N.D. Ill. 2013) ("Upon learning of a possible conflict of interest between the insurer and the insured, it is the duty of the attorneys to notify the insured immediately of that fact."); Model Rules of Pro. Conduct r. 1.4 (Am. Bar Ass'n 2023) (governing lawyers' duty to communicate with clients).

214. *Starr Indem.*, 379 F. Supp. 3d at 1108–09.

215. *See, e.g.*, Grain Dealers Mut. Ins. Co. v. Cooley, 734 F. App'x 223, 225–27 (5th Cir. 2018) (concluding because the insurer's failure to advise the insureds of their right to independent counsel when it reserved its rights prejudiced the insureds, the insurer was estopped to deny coverage).

216. *See, e.g.*, Moses v. Halstead, 477 F. Supp. 2d 1119, 1127 (D. Kan. 2007) (discussing Kansas law); Gomez v. First Jersey Cas. Ins. Co., 2010 WL 1330838, at *2 (N.J. Super. Ct. App. Div. Apr. 1, 2010).

217. The failure to do so may estop the insurer from later denying coverage. *See, e.g.*, RLI Ins. Co. v. AST Eng'g Corp., No. 19cv1649, 2019 WL 7114986 (DLC), at *7 (S.D.N.Y. Dec. 20, 2019) (applying New Jersey law); Nazario v. The Lobster House, 2009 WL 1181620, at *8 (N.J. Super. Ct. App. Div. Mar. 4, 2009) (rejecting the insurers' argument that the insured had acquiesced to their control of the defense under reservation because they did not inform the insured that it could either accept or reject a defense under reservation).

218. *See, e.g.*, *Moses*, 477 F. Supp. 2d at 1127.

20. The insurer should state that it reserves the right to pursue a declaratory judgment action to determine its obligations under its policy.[219]
21. If the insurer recognizes that the insured may have an affirmative claim against the plaintiff or another party in the case (such as a counterclaim or crossclaim), it should advise the insured of that possibility, state that it will not pay the defense lawyer it appoints for the insured to prosecute any affirmative claim, and advise the insured to promptly consult separate counsel at its own expense concerning any such claims.
22. The insurer should state that nothing in its reservation of rights letter changes or modifies any of the policy's provisions.
23. The insurer should state that nothing in the letter nor any other actions it may take should be construed as a waiver of any rights or defense that the insurer may currently have or that may be available to it at any other time.[220]
24. The insurer should invite the insured to bring to its attention any facts that might cause the insurer to revisit its coverage positions or that the insured otherwise wants it to know. Such language is not mere boilerplate; to the contrary, an insurer wants to be advised of facts that indicate the existence of coverage and similarly wants to be informed if it has allegedly misconstrued or misinterpreted facts of which it is aware.
25. The insurer should send a copy of the reservation of rights letter—and any supplemental reservation of rights letters—to the insured's defense lawyer. In any case where the insurer is controlling the defense, the defense lawyer needs to know the grounds for the insurer's reservation of rights to spot conflicts of interest. If the insured has personal counsel, the insurer should also send a copy of the reservation of rights letter to that lawyer.

Once an insurer has adequately reserved its rights, it need not renew its reservation of rights in subsequent communications with the insured.[221] Having reserved its rights, the insurer may communicate with the insured in the course of the defense without prejudicing its ability to later deny coverage.

---

219. *See, e.g.*, U.S. Underwriters Ins. Co. v. Kenfa Madison, LLC, No. 20-CV-2761 (NGG) (LB), 2023 WL 2710879, at *4 (E.D.N.Y. Mar. 30, 2023) (finding such language persuasive in rejecting the insured's argument that the insurer was estopped from withdrawing its defense).

220. *See, e.g.*, Hemphill v. Landmark Am. Ins. Co., No. 20-2544, 2023 WL 2783249, at *4 (3d Cir. Apr. 5, 2023) (relying on similar language to hold that the insured could not have reasonably expected the insurer to defend it in a subsequent, unrelated lawsuit).

221. KitBar Enters., LLC v. Liberty Ins. Underwriters, Inc., 291 F. Supp. 3d 758, 768 (E.D. Va. 2018); *see, e.g.*, ISCO Indus., Inc. v. Fed. Ins. Co., 587 F. Supp. 3d 558, 579 (W.D. Ky. 2022) ("Having explicitly reserved its rights twice . . . , Federal's failure to reiterate that reservation a third time in response to an inquiry regarding providing a defense for the underlying suit cannot support a claim of waiver by Federal.").

V. Reservations of Rights under Excess and Umbrella Policies

We have so far been analyzing reservations of rights in the primary insurance context. An insured may also purchase excess or umbrella coverage. As a rule, it is a primary insurer's duty to defend an insured against a potentially covered claim or suit. An excess or umbrella insurer normally has no duty to defend the insured until the underlying primary policy limits are exhausted in accordance with the primary policy's terms.[222]

Because an excess insurer has no duty to defend its insured until the underlying limits of insurance are exhausted, it cannot be estopped from raising coverage defenses or be said to have waived those defenses where there is nothing to indicate that the underlying primary policies have been, or will be, exhausted.[223] Nor can an excess insurer be held to have waived its coverage defenses or be estopped to assert those defenses if it does not reserve its rights when notified of a lawsuit that may reach its coverage.[224] It is, after all, a liability insurer's duty to defend that requires it to reserve its rights, and absent a duty to defend an excess insurer is not obligated to issue a reservation of rights letter.[225] Although an excess carrier is free to reserve its rights at any time and may decide to do so if it participates in settlement negotiations, that choice does not equal a duty to issue a reservation of rights letter to the insured.[226] The same principles apply where an umbrella policy affords excess coverage.[227]

An excess or umbrella insurer that wishes to preserve coverage defenses will have to reserve its rights, however, when it assumes the insured's defense upon exhaustion of the underlying limits of insurance.[228] Furthermore, it is

222. John M. O'Quinn, P.C. v. Lexington Ins. Co., 906 F.3d 363, 372 (5th Cir. 2018); Sacred Heart Health Servs. v. MMIC Ins., Inc., 575 F. Supp. 3d 1137, 1158 (D.S.D. 2021); Selective Way Ins. Co. v. Nationwide Prop. & Cas. Ins. Co., 219 A.3d 20, 46 (Md. Ct. Spec. App. 2019).

223. Santa Clara Valley Water Dist. v. Century Indem. Co., 306 Cal. Rptr. 3d 724, 753 (Ct. App. 2023).

224. Cincinnati Ins. Co. v. All Plumbing, Inc., 64 F. Supp. 3d 69, 80 (D.D.C. 2014) (applying D.C. law); TIG Ins. Co. v. Tyco Int'l Ltd., 919 F. Supp. 2d 439, 458–59 (M.D. Pa. 2013) (quoting a treatise); Wellons, Inc. v. Lexington Ins. Co., 931 F. Supp. 2d 1228, 1243–47 (N.D. Ga. 2013), *aff'd*, 566 F. App'x 813 (11th Cir. 2014); U.S. Fire Ins. Co. v. Vanderbilt Univ., 82 F. Supp. 2d 788, 794 (M.D. Tenn. 2000); Interstate Fire & Cas. Co. v. Archdiocese of Portland, 899 F. Supp. 498, 501 (D. Or. 1995), *aff'd sub nom.* Interstate Fire & Cas. Co. v. Underwriters at Lloyd's, London, 139 F.3d 1234 (9th Cir. 1998); Phila. Indem. Ins. Co. v. Barrera, 998 P.2d 1064, 1069 (Ariz. Ct. App. 1999); State Farm Fire & Cas. Co. v. Jioras, 29 Cal. Rptr. 2d 840, 844 (Ct. App. 1994); N. River Ins. Co. v. Grinnell Mut. Reinsurance Co., 860 N.E.2d 460, 467 (Ill. App. Ct. 2006).

225. *TIG Ins. Co.*, 919 F. Supp. 2d at 458–59; Int'l Ins. Co. v. Sargent & Lundy, 609 N.E.2d 842, 855 (Ill. App. Ct. 1993); Portal Pipe Line Co. v. Stonewall Ins. Co., 845 P.2d 746, 750 (Mont. 1993).

226. *Portal Pipe Line Co.*, 845 P.2d at 750.

227. State Farm Fire & Cas. Co. v. Jioras, 29 Cal. Rptr. 2d 840, 844 (Ct. App. 1994); McGuffin v. Zaremba Contracting, 849 N.E.2d 315, 319 (Ohio Ct. App. 2006).

228. Sinclair Oil Corp. v. Allianz Underwriters Ins. Co., 39 N.E.3d 570, 586 (Ill. App. Ct. 2015); *see, e.g.*, W. Side Salvage, Inc. v. RSUI Indem. Co., 878 F.3d 219, 225–26 (7th Cir. 2017) (explaining

important to remember that unlike true excess policies, umbrella policies may afford primary coverage for some claims that are not within the ambit of the primary policy. Thus, an umbrella insurer may have a duty to defend where a true excess carrier would not. If an umbrella insurer must defend as a primary insurer, then reservation of rights principles applicable to primary insurers apply equally to it. To illustrate this point, recall the earlier discussion of *Hernandez v. Great American Alliance Insurance Co.*[229] In *Hernandez*, the umbrella carrier, Great American Alliance Insurance Co. (GAAIC), did not reserve its rights when it was first notified of the underlying claim.[230] Then, when the insureds were sued and their primary insurer denied coverage, GAAIC assumed the defense and immediately reserved its rights.[231] In other words, when GAAIC was forced to defend the lawsuit against its insureds as though it was a primary insurer, it reserved its rights just as a responsible primary insurer would.

Lastly, excess and primary insurers have no duty to reserve their rights against one another,[232] as *National Union Fire Insurance Co. v. American Motorist Insurance Co.*[233] illustrates. In *National Union*, the excess insurer, National Union Fire Insurance Co. (National Union), accepted the primary insurer's tender of the insured's defense. The primary insurer, American Motorists Insurance Co. (American Motorists), had issued two policies that applied to the underlying litigation. National Union settled that case and then sued American Motorists to recover part of the settlement. American Motorists contended that National Union had waived its right to recover or should be estopped from asserting its right because it failed to reserve its rights to deny coverage when American Motorists tendered the defense.[234] The Georgia Court of Appeals ruled for American Motorists and National Union appealed to the Georgia Supreme Court.

As an initial matter, the *National Union* court stated that American Motorists' attempt to label National Union's actions below as a denial of coverage was

that an excess insurer was not estopped from asserting a coverage defense where it assumed the insured's defense under a reservation of rights after the primary insurer's policy limits were exhausted).

229. 879 S.E.2d 552 (Ga. Ct. App. 2022).

230. *Id.* at 524.

231. *Id.*

232. *See, e.g.*, Alliance Gen. Ins. Co. v. Ins. Co. of the State of Pa., Nos. 97-1475, 97-1432, 1998 WL 31744, at *3 (4th Cir. Jan. 29, 1998) ("The estoppel rule is to protect the insured once she has given up all control of her defense in the lawsuit, and as such does not apply between insurers."); St. Paul Mercury Ins. Co. v. Lexington Ins. Co., 78 F.3d 202, 207–08 (5th Cir. 1996) (applying Texas law and discussing waiver); Chubb Custom Ins. Co. v. Burnett & Co., No. 04-0950, 2006 WL 1663820, at *6 (E.D. La. June 15, 2006) (finding that waiver and estoppel principles do not apply between insurers); Am. Gen. Fire & Cas. Co. v. Progressive Cas. Co., 799 P.2d 1113, 1117 (N.M. 1990) (explaining why estoppel does not operate to preclude one insurer from attempting to assert that another insurer provided primary coverage).

233. 504 S.E.2d 673 (Ga. 1998).

234. *Id.* at 674.

a mischaracterization. The fact that National Union was attempting to recoup its settlement outlay did not mean that it was denying coverage. National Union accepted American Motorists' tender of their common insured's defense, assumed the defense, and settled the lawsuit. Because National Union did not attempt to deny coverage it was not required to reserve its rights to do so.[235]

The court further reasoned that even if National Union were denying coverage, its failure to reserve its rights would not bar recovery from American Motorists.[236] National Union had a contract only with its insured. Accordingly, only the insured could complain about National Union's failure to reserve its rights.[237]

Finally, the *National Union* court considered whether public policy considerations might require an excess insurer to reserve its rights vis-à-vis a primary insurer in the absence of a contract between them. The court concluded that there was no public policy basis for imposing such a requirement on excess insurers.

> The public policy interest . . . where insurance companies are arguing over which should cover a claim rests with neither insurer, but with the insured. By requiring an excess insurer to . . . notify a primary carrier of any claim for subrogation, we would be placing the insurer's interest ahead of the insured because the excess insurer would be required to delay action until it completed an investigation. . . . [T]he better policy is to encourage insurers to promptly protect their insureds' interests and to hold disputes among themselves in abeyance. Therefore, we decline to impose a notice requirement.[238]

The Georgia Supreme Court thus reversed the Court of Appeals.

VI. The Insured's Ability to Reject a Defense under a Reservation of Rights

A. Overview

In a few jurisdictions, insureds may reject a defense under reservation of rights.[239] In these jurisdictions, the insured has the option of accepting the defense under reservation if it wishes, but the insurer cannot compel it to do so.

---

235. *Id.*
236. *Id.*
237. *Id.* at 675.
238. *Id.*
239. *See, e.g.*, Mid-Continent Cas. Co. v. Am. Pride Bldg. Co., 601 F.3d 1143, 1149 (11th Cir. 2010) (discussing Florida law); United Nat'l Ins. Co. v. SST Fitness Corp., 309 F.3d 914, 921 (6th Cir. 2002) (applying Ohio law); Rhodes v. Chi. Ins. Co., 719 F.2d 116, 120 (5th Cir. 1983) (applying Texas law); Sauer v. Home Indem. Co., 841 P.2d 176, 182–83 (Alaska 1992); Finley v. Home Ins. Co., 975 P.2d 1145, 1155 (Haw. 1998); Ky. Farm Bureau Mut. Ins. Co. v. Brewer, 596 S.W.3d 620, 622 (Ky. Ct.

This right gives an insured tremendous leverage in negotiating with its insurer. Indeed, the insured can impale the insurer on the horns of a dilemma. To explain, if the insured rejects a defense under reservation of rights, it forces the insurer to choose between (1) withdrawing its reservation of rights and thereby surrendering its coverage defenses to retain control of the insured's defense; or (2) standing on its coverage defenses and losing control of the defense of the third-party action. The second option is unappealing because it leaves the insurer exposed to allegations that it breached its duty to defend and, in any event, may leave the insurer bound by the facts as determined in the third-party action.[240] It is also likely that the insured and plaintiff will stipulate to a judgment that is to be collected, if at all, from the insurer alone. Alternatively, or conjunctively, the insured and plaintiff will enter into an agreement whereby the insured is insulated from personal liability in exchange for its right to sue the insurance company or its promise to sue the insurer for bad faith with any recovery going to the plaintiff.[241]

Insurers can sometimes avoid this dilemma by not reserving their rights or by preemptively withdrawing a reservation of rights where a coverage defense is weak or the likelihood of prevailing on the merits in the third-party action is strong. By controlling the defense, an insurer can often defeat a plaintiff's claim against the insured or settle with the plaintiff on favorable terms. For that matter, insurers probably reserve their rights more often than they should in jurisdictions that allow insureds to reject a defense under reservation, given that the chances of winning the third-party action often outweigh the likelihood of avoiding coverage. Be that as it may, insurers should not be leveraged into waiving coverage defenses when insureds (1) benefit from a defense under a reservation of rights and (2) are not entitled to indemnification for uncovered claims. Plus, as explained later, none of the reasons courts offer for allowing insureds to reject defenses under reservations of rights justify that approach.

B. The Flawed Justifications for the Minority Approach

Jurisdictions that permit insureds to reject defenses under reservations of rights do so for one or more of the following reasons: (1) by defending under a reservation of rights the insurer is conditioning the insured's defense; (2) a

App. 2020); Herbert A. Sullivan, Inc. v. Utica Mut. Ins. Co., 788 N.E.2d 522, 539 (Mass. 2003); Allen v. Bryers, 512 S.W.3d 17, 32 (Mo. 2016); First United Bank of Bellevue v. First Am. Title Ins. Co., 496 N.W.2d 474, 481 (Neb. 1993) (quoting City of Carter Lake v. Aetna Cas. & Sur. Co., 604 F.2d 1052, 1060 n.7 (8th Cir. 1979)); Merch. Indem. Corp. v. Eggleston, 179 A.2d 505, 512 (N.J. 1962); Nat'l Mortg. Corp. v. Am. Title Ins. Co., 255 S.E.2d 622, 629–30 (N.C. Ct. App. 1979), *rev'd on other grounds*, 261 S.E.2d 844 (N.C. 1980).

240. *See* Metro. Prop. & Cas. Ins. Co. v. Morrison, 951 N.E.2d 662, 668–70 (Mass. 2011).

241. This scenario and the prior one in which the insured and the plaintiff stipulate to a judgment to be collected solely from insurance proceeds are discussed in Chapter 11.

reservation of rights defense amounts to a breach of the duty to defend; (3) an insurer's defense under a reservation of rights amounts to a denial of its duty to indemnify the insured and deprives the insurer of its right to control the defense; and (4) allowing an insured to reject a reservation of rights defense is necessary to protect the insured against conflicts of interest. These rationales are not persuasive.

1. *A Reservation of Rights Allegedly Is a Conditional Defense*

Over time, a few courts have reasoned that by reserving its rights to contest coverage, an insurer is imposing conditions on an insured's defense.[242] Therefore, the insured should be allowed to reject the defense. To the contrary, an insurer defending under reservation of rights is imposing no conditions or limitations on the insured's defense. In fact, the insurer's duty to defend is unaltered by its reservation; the insurer is simply advising the insured that the insurer's separate duty to indemnify may not attach based on the allegations or facts then known to the insurer. It is the insurer's duty to indemnify the insured that is conditioned by a reservation of rights—not its duty to defend. A defense under reservation of rights is no different from an unconditional or unqualified defense.[243] In fact, a defense under reservation of rights *is* an unconditional or unqualified defense, because the insurer remains obligated to defend the insured reasonably, responsibly, and in good faith.

2. *A Reservation of Rights as an Alleged Breach of the Duty to Defend*

Other courts reason that an insured should be able to reject a defense under reservation of rights because it is akin to a breach of the insurer's duty to defend. As a Florida court stated, a defense under a reservation of rights "is similar to a refusal to provide any defense at all in its effect on the insured. In either case, the carrier has violated its duties under the policy unconditionally to defend and indemnify its insured within specified limits."[244] That is not so.

242. *See, e.g.*, Charles J. King, Inc. v. U.S. Fid. & Guar. Co., 264 F. Supp. 703, 708 (S.D.N.Y. 1967) (applying New York law).

243. *See* Willis Corroon Corp. v. Home Ins. Co., 203 F.3d 449, 452 (7th Cir. 2000) (applying Illinois law and stating that an insurer defending under a reservation of rights must provide an effective defense and cannot put its interests ahead of the insured's); United Nat'l Ins. Co. v. Waterfront N.Y. Realty Corp., 948 F. Supp. 263, 268 (S.D.N.Y. 1996) (stating that an insurer defending under a reservation of rights "must conduct the defense of the insured with due care and good faith"); Twin City Fire Ins. Co. v. Colonial Life & Accident Ins. Co., 839 So. 2d 614, 616 (Ala. 2002) (quoting Tank v. State Farm Fire & Cas Co., 715 P.2d 1133, 1137 (Wash. 1986)); Nautilus Ins. Co. v. Access Med., Inc., 482 P.3d 683, 687 n.3 (Nev. 2021) ("When an insurer has a contractual duty to defend, the law implies a duty to do so in a reasonable manner.").

244. Nationwide Mut. Fire Ins. Co. v. Beville, 825 So. 2d 999, 1003 (Fla. Dist. Ct. App. 2002).

A defense under reservation of rights is neither a refusal to defend nor a breach of the duty to defend.[245] A breach of contract occurs when a party fails to do something it promised to do,[246] and an insurer that defends under a reservation of rights is providing the insured with the defense it contractually promised.

Nor is an insurer's defense under a reservation of rights an anticipatory breach of the insurer's duty to defend. An anticipatory breach or anticipatory repudiation of a contract occurs when a party to a contract refuses to perform under the contract's terms before the time for performance is due.[247] An anticipatory breach must be an unequivocal repudiation of the contract.[248] Or, stated slightly differently, the repudiation of the contract must be "absolute and unconditional."[249] Furthermore, a party must refuse to perform the *entire* contract to be guilty of an anticipatory breach.[250]

A defense under reservation of rights meets none of the requirements for an anticipatory breach of contract. The insurer cannot be said to have breached its duty to indemnify by reserving its rights because the reservation is not an absolute, unconditional, or unequivocal refusal to indemnify the insured. The insurer clearly has not breached the entire contract because it is defending the insured. If damages factor into the analysis, the insured is not damaged by the reservation of rights because the insurer is providing a free defense. Finally, an insurer's defense of the insured under a reservation of rights is not an anticipatory breach of contract because there can be no anticipatory breach if the allegedly breaching party has a just excuse for its actions.[251]

---

245. Cont'l Cas. Co. v. City of Jacksonville, 283 F. App'x 686, 690 (11th Cir. 2008) (quoting First Am. Title Ins. Co. v. Nat'l Union Fire Ins. Co., 695 So. 2d 475, 477 (Fla. Dist. Ct. App. 1997)); Hanover Ins. Co. v. Anova Food, LLC, 173 F. Supp. 3d 1008, 1025 (D. Haw. 2016) (explaining Florida law); Am. Fam. Mut. Ins. Co. v. C.M.A. Mortg., Inc., 682 F. Supp. 2d 879, 891 (S.D. Ind. 2010) (interpreting Indiana law); TIG Ins. Co. v. Chapman & Chapman, P.C., 436 F. Supp. 2d 1047, 1054 (D.N.D. 2006) (applying North Dakota law); Kelly v. Iowa Mut. Ins. Co., 620 N.W.2d 637, 642 (Iowa 2000); Ramsey v. Lee Builders, Inc., 95 P.3d 1033, 1041 (Kan. Ct. App. 2004); Patrons Oxford Ins. Co. v. Harris, 905 A.2d 819, 825 (Me. 2006); Pink v. Knoche, 103 S.W.3d 221, 228 (Mo. Ct. App. 2003); Passaic Valley Sewerage Comm'rs v. St. Paul Fire & Marine Ins. Co., 21 A.3d 1151, 1162 (N.J. 2011); Babcock & Wilcox Co. v. Am. Nuclear Insurers, 131 A.3d 445, 454 (Pa. 2015).

246. Dorsett v. Cross, 106 S.W.3d 213, 217 (Tex. App. 2003).

247. Stephens & Stephens XII, LLC v. Fireman's Fund Ins. Co., 180 Cal. Rptr. 3d 683, 699–700 (Ct. App. 2014); Park Nicollet Clinic v. Hamann, 808 N.W.2d 828, 837 (Minn. 2011); Schafer v. Soderberg & Schafer CPAs, LLC, 964 N.E.2d 24, 38 (Ohio Ct. App. 2011).

248. Hefner v. Deutscher, 464 P.3d 367, 378 (Kan. Ct. App. 2020); TNT Cattle Co. v. Fife, 937 N.W.2d 811, 830 (Neb. 2020).

249. Kartsotis v. Bloch, 503 S.W.3d 506, 523 (Tex. App. 2016).

250. Chaudhuri v. Fannin Reg'l Hosp., 730 S.E.2d 425, 428 (Ga. Ct. App. 2012); O'Connor v. Sleasman, 830 N.Y.S.2d 377, 379 (App. Div. 2007) (quoting DeLorenzo v. Bac Agency, 681 N.Y.S.2d 846, 848 (App. Div. 1998)); Bennett v. Sage Payment Sols., Inc., 710 S.E.2d 736, 742 (Va. 2011) (quoting Vahabzadeh v. Mooney, 399 S.E.2d 803, 805 (Va. 1991)).

251. Berg v. Wilson, 353 S.W.3d 166, 174 n.11 (Tex. App. 2011).

3. A Reservation of Rights as a Denial of Coverage

Courts occasionally reason that a reservation of rights amounts to the insurer's denial of its duty to indemnify the insured, so the insurer should consequently lose the right to control the insured's defense. The Kentucky Court of Appeals expressed this view in *Medical Protective Co. v. Davis*:[252]

> When the insurer has the obligation to pay the judgment, it surely is entitled to control the defense of the claim. But when the insurer reserves a right to assert its nonliability for payment there is little or no reason to require the insured to surrender defense of the claim *to a company which asserts that it has no obligation to satisfy the claim*. Under such conditions the insured has the right to refuse the proffered defense. . . .[253]

The *Davis* court misunderstood the effect of a reservation of rights. An insurer that reserves its rights has not disclaimed its duty to indemnify the insured. A reservation of rights is not a denial of coverage.[254] A reservation of rights letter does not evidence the insurer's abandonment of the insured.[255] A reservation of rights deprives the insured of no policy benefits. All the insurer has done by reserving its rights is advise the insured of the insurer's rights under the policy as they may apply in the future. Indeed, the insurer may well indemnify the insured when the time comes. Additionally, any assertion that an insurer's reservation of rights is a denial of coverage must fail because the insurer is providing a defense. If the insurer is defending the insured, it plainly has not denied coverage.

4. Protecting the Insured against Conflicts of Interest

Another reason offered for allowing insureds to reject a defense under reservation of rights is that a reservation of rights may chill a zealous defense and thus presents a conflict of interest because the insurer may be more interested in developing facts to defeat coverage rather than facts defeating liability. This argument fails on multiple grounds.

First, speculation that an insurer may breach its contract in the future does not justify denying the insurer its contractual right to defend its insured as though the insurer were already in breach. Second, it is wrong to speculate that a defense lawyer hired by an insurer to defend an insured under a reservation of rights will in any way compromise the insured's defense to advance the

252. 581 S.W.2d 25 (Ky. Ct. App. 1979).
253. *Id.* at 26 (emphasis added).
254. Fuller-Austin Insulation Co. v. Highlands Ins. Co., 38 Cal. Rptr. 3d 716, 736 (Ct. App. 2006); Tran v. Com. Ins. Co., No. CIV. A. 01-0129, 2001 WL 1517580, at *3 (Mass. Super. Ct. Nov. 21, 2001); Pink v. Knoche, 103 S.W.3d 221, 228 (Mo. Ct. App. 2003).
255. N.J. Eye Ctr., P.A. v. Princeton Ins. Co., 928 A.2d 25, 32 (N.J. Super. Ct. App. Div. 2007).

insurer's coverage position.[256] Third, not every reservation of rights creates a conflict of interest. As explained in Chapter 3, the majority rule holds that a reservation of rights creates a conflict of interest only when the outcome of a coverage issue can be affected by the defense of the third-party action. In other words, a conflict exists only when the facts on which liability will be adjudicated are the same facts on which coverage depends. Fourth, even where a reservation of rights creates a conflict of interest, a better solution is to make the insurer provide the insured with independent counsel at the insurer's expense. The independent counsel approach assures the insured of an adequate defense without forcing unreasonable choices on the insurer.

C. Summary

Most courts do not permit an insured to reject a defense under reservation of rights.[257] Notably, the Restatement of the Law of Liability Insurance recognized insureds' ability to reject a reservation of rights defense as a minority rule and declined to adopt it.[258]

Where the insured is permitted to reject a defense under reservation and does so, an insurer may opt to withdraw its reservation of rights and thus retain control of the defense of the litigation against the insured.[259] Alternatively, the insurer might elect to stand on its coverage defenses, withdraw its defense of the insured, and file a declaratory judgment action. Before choosing this course, however, the insurer should check the law of the jurisdiction to ascertain any potential negative consequences of this approach. Finally, the insurer might attempt to negotiate a compromise with the insured whereby it cedes control of the defense to the insured who will then be defended by independent counsel of its choice at the insurer's expense while the insurer maintains its reservation of rights.

256. *See* Twin City Fire Ins. Co. v. Ben Arnold-Sunbelt Beverage Co. of S.C., 433 F.3d 365, 372–74 (4th Cir. 2005) (discussing insurance defense lawyers' ethical duties under South Carolina law and the incentives for them to fulfill their duties); Fed. Ins. Co. v. X-Rite, Inc., 748 F. Supp. 1223, 1229 (W.D. Mich. 1990) (footnote omitted) ("To hold that the insurer who, under reservation of rights, participates in selection of counsel, automatically breaches its duty of good faith is to indulge the conclusive presumption that counsel is unable to fully represent its client, the insured, without consciously or unconsciously compromising the insured's interests. The [c]ourt is unable to conclude that Michigan law professes so little confidence in the integrity of the bar of this state."); Eckman v. Erie Ins. Exch., 21 A.3d 1203, 1209 (Pa. Super. Ct. 2011) ("The categorical supposition that all attorneys compensated by a third party will breach their ethical duties is undeveloped, unsupported, and not cognizable under established principles of law.").

257. *See, e.g.*, McGough v. Ins. Co. of N. Am., 691 P.2d 738, 745 (Ariz. Ct. App. 1984) (holding that an insured may not condition an insurer's right to defend on the insurer's agreement to waive its right to later litigate coverage).

258. Restatement of the L. of Liab. Ins. § 15 cmt. e (Am. L. Inst. 2019).

259. *See* Heubel Material Handling, Inc. v. Universal Underwriters Ins. Co., 861 F. Supp. 2d 1003, 1011 (W.D. Mo. 2012), *aff'd*, 704 F.3d 558 (8th Cir. 2013).

An insured should also think carefully before exercising its right to reject a reservation of rights defense. Although the insured may thereafter be able to consent to a judgment to be collected solely out of insurance proceeds or reach an agreement with the plaintiff to the same effect and thereby insulate itself against personal liability, those deals come at a cost. Among other things, they are almost certain to mire the insured in continued litigation and they may have financial downsides. On the other hand, and as noted earlier, a defense at the insurer's expense even under a reservation of rights is a valuable benefit and insurers often end of indemnifying insureds or settling on their behalf rather than denying coverage.

VII. Discovery of Reservation of Rights Letters in the Third-Party Action against the Insured

A. Discovery of Insurance Agreements in Litigation

In federal courts, parties are generally entitled to discover any non-privileged matters that are relevant to the claims or defenses of any party in the litigation and proportional to the needs of the case.[260] This includes insurance policies under which an insurance company may be obligated to satisfy all or part of a possible judgment in the action. In fact, in federal court, parties must provide copies of applicable insurance agreements in their initial disclosures.[261] Many state courts have similar rules of civil procedure, at least so far as the discovery (if not the initial disclosure) of insurance policies is concerned.[262] Requirements that parties produce their insurance policies in discovery are intended to facilitate settlement.[263]

260. *See* FED. R. CIV. P. 26(b)(1).

261. FED. R. CIV. P. 26(a)(1)(A)(iv).

262. *See, e.g.*, KAN. STAT. ANN. 60-226(b)(3) (2023) ("A party may obtain discovery of the existence and contents of any insurance agreement under which an insurance business may be liable to satisfy part or all of a possible judgment in the action or to indemnify or reimburse for payments made to satisfy the judgment. Information concerning the insurance agreement is not by reason of disclosure admissible in evidence at trial. For purposes of this paragraph, an application for insurance is not a part of an insurance agreement."); MO. SUP. CT. R. 56.01(b)(4) ("A party may obtain discovery of the existence and contents, including production of the policy and declaration page, of any insurance agreement under which any person carrying on an insurance business may be liable to satisfy part or all of a judgment that may be entered in the action or to indemnify or reimburse for payments made to satisfy the judgment.").

263. Moslimani v. Union Valley Corp., 638 A.2d 171, 172 (N.J. Super. Ct. Law Div. 1993); *In re* Dana Corp., 138 S.W.3d 298, 303–04 & n.2 (Tex. 2004).

B. Reservation of Rights Letters Generally Are Not Discoverable

In addition to copies of defendants' insurance policies, plaintiffs in third-party actions sometimes attempt to obtain copies of any reservation of rights letters related to the lawsuit. Plaintiffs argue that they need the letters to evaluate settlement consistent with the purpose of allowing the discovery of insurance agreements, while defense lawyers and insurers counter that plaintiffs have no need for reservation of rights letters because they are neither relevant to any party's claim or defense nor likely to lead to the discovery of admissible evidence. If a plaintiff seeks any reservation of rights letters on the basis that they are needed to evaluate the collectability of any judgment, defendants and insurers argue that discovery is improper again on relevance grounds because, as federal courts have noted,[264] a plaintiff's discovery into a defendant's ability to satisfy a judgment generally must be conducted post-judgment.[265]

Discovery of reservation of rights letters generally is impermissible for several reasons. First, rules of civil procedure governing discovery typically mandate that parties produce "insurance agreements,"[266] meaning an agreement "under which any person carrying on an insurance business may be liable to satisfy part or all of a possible judgment which may be entered in the action or to indemnify or reimburse for payments made to satisfy the judgment."[267]

---

264. *See* Sierrapine v. Refiner Prods. Mfg., Inc., 275 F.R.D. 604, 609 (E.D. Cal. 2011) (observing that "district courts . . . generally do not allow pre-judgment discovery regarding a defendant's financial condition or ability to satisfy a judgment—aside from those insurance-related disclosures made pursuant to Rule 26(a)(1)(A)(iv), or where punitive damages are available—on the grounds that such discovery is not relevant to the parties' claims or defenses and is not reasonably calculated to lead to the discovery of admissible evidence").

265. *See, e.g.*, FED. R. CIV. P. 69(a)(2) (providing for discovery in aid of judgment or execution).

266. *See, e.g.*, FED. R. CIV. P. 26(a)(1)(A)(iv); KAN. STAT. ANN. § 60-226(b)(3); MO. SUP. CT. R. 56.01(b)(4). *Cf.* CAL. CODE CIV. P. 2017.210 ("A party may obtain discovery of the existence and contents of any agreement under which any insurance carrier may be liable to satisfy in whole or in part a judgment that may be entered in the action or to indemnify or reimburse for payments made to satisfy the judgment. This discovery may include the identity of the carrier and the nature and limits of the coverage. A party may also obtain discovery as to whether that insurance carrier is disputing the agreement's coverage of the claim involved in the action, *but not as to the nature and substance of that dispute*. . . .") (emphasis added). *But see* NEV. R. CIV. P. 16.1(a)(1)(v) (emphasis added) (requiring a party to provide as part of its initial disclosures "for inspection and copying as under Rule 34, any insurance agreement under which an insurance business may be liable to satisfy all or part of a possible judgment in the action or to indemnify or reimburse for payments made to satisfy the judgment and any disclaimer or limitation of coverage or *reservation of rights* under any such insurance agreement"); WASH. R. CIV. P. 26(b)(2) ("A party may obtain discovery and production of: (i) the existence and contents of any insurance agreement . . . and (ii) any documents affecting coverage (such as denying coverage, extending coverage, or *reserving rights*) from or on behalf of such person to the covered person or the covered person's representative.") (emphasis added).

267. FED. R. CIV. P. 26(a)(1)(A)(iv); *see also* KAN. STAT. ANN. § 60-226(b)(3) (using identical language); MO. SUP. CT. R. 56.01(b)(4) (omitting the word "possible").

Reservation of rights letters clearly do not fit that description.[268] For one thing, a reservation of rights letter is not an insurance *agreement*; rather, it is the insurer's *unilateral* declaration of its intent to defend the insured without promising to indemnify the insured. For another thing, while a reservation of rights letter concerns the insurer's duty to indemnify the insured, it does not create, embody, or impose on the insurer potential liability to satisfy or reimburse a judgment that may be entered against the insured. That is a fundamental and critical difference between a reservation of rights letter and an insurance policy.

Second, for a document to be discoverable (1) in federal courts, it must be relevant to a party's claim or defense; or (2) in some states, it must be reasonably calculated to lead to the discovery of admissible evidence. A reservation of rights letter fails both tests. The letter is not relevant to the subject of the action because the insured's potential liability to the plaintiff has nothing to do with insurance coverage.[269] This is true even where the plaintiff seeks to discover the defendant's ability to satisfy any judgment.[270] Bottom line, the letter itself is irrelevant and will be inadmissible at trial because its existence does not tend to make any fact consequential to the determination of the action more or less probable than it would be otherwise.

Third, in some cases, reservation of rights letters are privileged communications.[271] In others, they may qualify as the insurance company's work product.[272] Both privilege and work product immunity are, with limited exceptions, strong barriers to discovery.

---

268. Coe v. Cross-Lines Ret. Ctr., Inc., 342 F.R.D. 539, 544 (D. Kan. 2022); Sea Salt, LLC v. Bellerose, No. 2:18-cv-00413, 2020 WL 5032466, at *2 (D. Me. Aug. 5, 2020); Excelsior Coll. v. Frye, 233 F.R.D. 583, 585–86 (S.D. Cal. 2006); Native Am. Arts, Inc. v. Bundy-Howard, Inc., No. 01 C 16182003, WL 1524649, at *1–2 (N.D. Ill. Mar. 20, 2003); S. Rehab. Network, Inc. v. Sharpe, No. 5:99CV353-BR, 2000 WL 33682699, at *4 (E.D.N.C. Jan. 14, 2000); Foster v. Power Sales & Leasing, Inc., No. BDV-97-771, 1998 Mont. Dist. LEXIS 459, at *2 (Mont. Dist. Ct. Apr. 14, 1998).

269. *See Foster*, 1998 Mont. Dist. LEXIS 459, at *2 (refusing to allow discovery of a reservation of rights letter because it was not relevant to the plaintiff's claims).

270. *See, e.g.*, Dickson v. Nat'l Maint. & Repair of Ky., Inc., No. 5:08-CV-8, 2011 WL 2610195, at *1–2 (W.D. Ky. July 1, 2011) (refusing to reopen discovery to allow the plaintiff to discover the defendant's assets and reservation of rights letters from its two insurers after the defendant revealed the existence of the reservation of rights letters); Sierrapine v. Refiner Prods. Mfg., Inc., 275 F.R.D. 604, 609 (E.D. Cal. 2011) (observing that federal courts generally do not allow prejudgment discovery regarding a defendant's financial condition or ability to satisfy a judgment on the grounds that such discovery is not relevant to the parties' claims or defenses and is not reasonably calculated to lead to the discovery of admissible evidence).

271. *See, e.g.*, May Dep't Stores Co. v. Ryan, 699 S.W.2d 134, 136 (Mo. Ct. App. 1985) ("Any communication between insured and insurer which relates to the former's duty to report incidents and the latter's duty to defend and indemnify falls within the attorney-client privilege and is excluded from discovery. . . .").

272. *See, e.g.*, Midwest Feeders, Inc. v. Bank of Franklin, No. 5:14cv78-DCB-MTP, 2016 WL 7422561, at *5 (S.D. Miss. June 28, 2016) (concluding that a reservation of rights letter was shielded from discovery as work product); *In re* Madrid, 242 S.W.3d 563, 568–69 (Tex. App. 2007) (finding that the reservation of rights letter constituted fact or tangible work product).

The best argument for discovery is that a reservation of rights letter will lead to the discovery of admissible evidence even though the letter itself will not be admissible at trial. Even that argument is not good enough.[273] If the contention is that a reservation of rights letter contains facts that might further discovery, those facts almost certainly derive from the plaintiff's complaint or petition, making their discovery via a reservation of rights letter cumulative and unnecessary. Furthermore, assuming that the plaintiff obtained a copy of the defendant's insurance policy in discovery, it can evaluate any coverage concerns it may have by reviewing the policy; it does not need to see any reservation of rights letter.[274]

The fact that reservation of rights letters are generally not discoverable does not mean that they are always off-limits. For example, a reservation of rights letter may be discoverable in a direct action jurisdiction.[275]

C. Analyzing the Case Law

1. *Cases Permitting Discovery of Reservation of Rights Letters*

Despite good arguments against the discovery of reservation of rights letters in third-party actions, there are at least two reported decisions where the courts permitted their discovery in the absence of a rule of civil procedure specifically providing for the discovery of reservation of rights letters. Neither decision is persuasive or precedential.

In *Weiner v. Charny*,[276] the defendant, Psychiatric Medical Associates (PMA), revealed that its insurer had reserved its rights to deny coverage under a reservation of rights provision in its policy.[277] The plaintiffs requested a copy of PMA's policy so that they could examine the reservation of rights provision. In response, PMA identified its insurer and the liability limits of the policy, but it refused to produce a copy of the policy on relevance grounds.[278]

The plaintiff moved to compel production of the policy. A Pennsylvania rule of civil procedure stated that a party could "'obtain discovery of the existence and terms of any insurance agreement under which any person carrying

---

273. This argument has no application in federal court. Although under both the current and prior versions of Federal Rule of Civil Procedure 26(b)(1) evidence need not be admissible at trial to be discoverable, it is important to remember that following the 2015 amendments to Rule 26(b)(1), the test for discovery is "whether evidence is 'relevant to any party's claim or defense,' not whether it is 'reasonably calculated to lead to admissible evidence.'" *In re* Bard IVC Filters Prods. Liab. Litig., 317 F.R.D. 562, 564 (D. Ariz. 2016).

274. S. Rehab. Network, Inc. v. Sharpe, No. 5:99CV353-BR, 2000 WL 33682699, at *4 (E.D.N.C. Jan. 14, 2000); *Foster*, 1998 Mont. Dist. LEXIS 459, at *2.

275. *See* Blockbuster Ent. Corp. v. McComb Video, Inc., 145 F.R.D. 402, 404–05 (M.D. La. 1992).

276. No. G.D. 81-13282, 1982 WL 643 (Pa. Ct. Comm. Pl. Nov. 18, 1982).

277. *Id.* at *1.

278. *Id.*

on an insurance business may be liable to satisfy part or all of a judgment which may be entered in the action or to satisfy or reimburse for payments made to satisfy the judgment.'"[279] Relying on this language, the court concluded that the plaintiffs were entitled to the policy. PMA continued to resist on relevance grounds, however, arguing that the issue of coverage could only be resolved in a separate declaratory judgment action or garnishment proceeding. The court disagreed:

> While [PMA's statement about declaratory relief or garnishment litigation] is true, knowledge of the reservation of rights provision assists a plaintiff in evaluating the merits of the carrier's assertion that it is protected by a reservation of rights provision and, consequently, will promote the purposes for requiring disclosure of insurance matters. . . .[280]

Accordingly, the court ordered PMA to produce a copy of its policy.

Weiner is valueless as authority for the discovery of reservation of rights letters for the simple reason that the reservation of rights oddly was contained in the policy. Thus, *Weiner* merely reinforces parties' obligation to produce copies of their insurance policies when rules of civil procedure require.[281]

In *Wood v. Campbell*,[282] plaintiff Nancy Wood propounded an interrogatory asking one of the defendants, Robert Campbell, whether he had received a reservation of rights letter from his auto insurer, State Farm Insurance Co. (State Farm). In fact, State Farm had reserved its rights based on late notice of the suit. A Virginia court rule permitted the discovery of insurance agreements and further permitted the discovery of "'any matter, not privileged, which [was] relevant to the subject matter involved in the pending action, whether it relate[d] to the claim or defense of the party seeking discovery or to the claim or defense of any other party.'"[283]

Campbell objected to the interrogatory on the basis that a reservation of rights letter was not within the scope of the rule and was irrelevant at least until he was held liable, and State Farm became obligated to indemnify him.[284] Wood moved to compel Campbell's answer. In a cursory opinion, the court sided with Wood, reasoning that the reservation of rights letter was not a privileged communication and was relevant to the subject of the pending action. According to the court, "[Wood's] course of action in the pursuit of the instant case may be materially affected by the weight [she] may independently ascribe to the reservation claim of the insurer."[285]

279. *Id.* (quoting the Pennsylvania rule).
280. *Id.* at *2.
281. *See id.* at *1 (making this point).
282. No. 31066, 2006 WL 2590479 (Va. Cir. Ct. Sept. 6, 2006).
283. *Id.* at *1 (quoting the Virginia rule).
284. *Id.*
285. *Id.*

The *Wood* court erred in its relevance analysis. The fact that a reservation of rights may affect a plaintiff's case analysis does not necessarily make it relevant. The "subject" of the case was Campbell's alleged negligence and the other defendants' attendant liability. Wood's "claim" to which her discovery request related was the defendants' tort liability and her damages. A reservation of rights does not tend to make any liability-related fact more or less true. Nor does a reservation of rights letter bear on a plaintiff's damages. While an insurer's coverage defenses expressed in a reservation of rights letter may someday make collection of a judgment difficult, they are immaterial from an evidentiary standpoint in the case against the insured. The *Wood* court should not have found that the reservation of rights letter was discoverable even under a generous reading of the Virginia rule.

2. *Illustrative Cases Rejecting Discovery of Reservation of Rights Letters*

In contrast to the decisions in *Weiner* and *Wood*, a Texas appellate court rejected an attempt to discover a reservation of rights letter in *In re Madrid*.[286] In that case, Ector Calvillo sued Edward Madrid for negligence following an accident caused by Madrid's drunk driving. Calvillo pleaded his entitlement to punitive damages and soon made a policy limits settlement demand. In discovery, he sought the production of a reservation of rights letter sent by Madrid's insurer, Mid-Century Insurance Co. (Mid-Century). Mid-Century sent the letter to Madrid and his lawyer after the suit was filed. Madrid declined to produce the letter, asserting that it was work product, was beyond the scope of discovery permitted for insurance agreements, and was neither relevant nor reasonably calculated to lead to the discovery of admissible evidence.[287] Madrid further pointed out that he had produced a copy of his insurance policy.[288] The trial court nonetheless ordered that Madrid produce the letter. Madrid then petitioned for a writ of mandamus.

The dispute in *In re Madrid* pivoted on Texas Rule of Civil Procedure 192.3, which governed the scope of discovery. Rule 192.3 provided in pertinent part:

> (a) *Generally.* In general, a party may obtain discovery regarding any matter that is not privileged and is relevant to the subject matter of the pending action, whether it relates to the claim or defense of the party seeking discovery or the claim or defense of any other party. It is not a ground for objection that the information sought will be inadmissible at trial if the information sought appears reasonably calculated to lead to the discovery of admissible evidence.
>
> * * *

286. 242 S.W.3d 563 (Tex. App. 2007).
287. *Id.* at 565.
288. *Id.* at 568.

> (f) *Indemnity and Insuring Agreements.* Except as otherwise provided by law, a party may obtain discovery of the existence and contents of any indemnity or insurance agreement under which a person may be liable to satisfy part or all of a judgment rendered in the action or to indemnify or reimburse for payments made to satisfy the judgment. . . .[289]

Calvillo contended that the reservation of rights letter was necessarily a part of the Mid-Century policy, thus making it discoverable under Rule 192.3(f).[290] The *In re Madrid* court rejected that argument, explaining the purpose of a reservation of rights letter and noting that "[a] unilateral reservation of rights letter cannot create rights not contained in [an] insurance policy."[291] As a result, Calvillo was not entitled to see the letter unless it related to his claim and thus fell within the broad general discovery standard set forth in Rule 192.3(a).

Calvillo argued that the reservation of rights letter related to his claim because he needed it to evaluate the availability of insurance coverage, which would, in turn, affect the settlement value of the case.[292] The court disagreed. Determining the case's settlement value was not related to the merits of Calvillo's claim or to Madrid's defense, and there was no showing that the letter was reasonably calculated to lead to the discovery of admissible evidence.[293] Besides, Calvillo had been provided with the policy and its liability limits as the rule required. Thus, the trial court had clearly erred in ordering the letter's production.

The final question was whether the work product doctrine prevented discovery of the reservation of rights letter. The court did not need to reach this issue because it had already determined that the letter should not have been produced under Rule 192.3, but it nonetheless found that the letter constituted "fact" or "tangible" work product.[294] As the court explained:

> The reservation of rights letter was prepared by Madrid's insurer after suit was filed and while the insurer was in communication with Calvillo's attorney and Madrid's attorney. It was sent to Madrid and a copy was sent to Madrid's attorney. As such, it [was] a communication between a party, the party's insurer, and the party's attorney. Calvillo contends, however, that the letter is not work product because it was not prepared in anticipation of the instant negligence suit but was rather prepared in anticipation of a future coverage

289. *Id.* at 567 (quoting the Texas rule).
290. *Id.* at 568.
291. *Id.* (citing Tex. Ass'n of Cntys. Gov't Risk Mgmt. Pool v. Matagorda Cnty., 52 S.W.3d 128, 131 (Tex. 2000)).
292. *Id.*
293. *Id.*
294. *Id.* at 569.

> suit. While it may be true that the insurer's reservation of rights stated in the letter will be significant in the event of a future coverage suit, the reservation of rights letter relates directly to the insurer providing Madrid a defense in the instant case. Thus . . . the reservation of rights letter is work product. . . .[295]

For Calvillo to discover the letter as tangible work product, he had to demonstrate that he had a substantial need for it to prepare his case and that he was unable to obtain the substantial equivalent of the letter's contents through other means.[296] He made no such showing below. Accordingly, the trial court erred by requiring the letter's disclosure.[297]

In *Foster v. Power Sales & Leasing, Inc.*,[298] the plaintiff sued the defendants on various theories. In discovery, he requested a copy of a reservation of rights letter issued by the defendants' insurance company. The defendants refused to provide the letter, claiming that it was irrelevant and was shielded from discovery by the attorney-client privilege and work product immunity. The parties filed cross-motions concerning discovery of the letter. The court agreed with the defendants that the reservation of rights letter was irrelevant.[299]

The *Foster* court noted that under Montana Rule of Civil Procedure 26(b), a party may obtain discovery regarding any non-privileged matter which is relevant to the subject of the action; that even if the material sought is inadmissible, it must still be disclosed if it appears to be reasonably calculated to lead to the discovery of admissible evidence; and that a defendant must disclose insurance agreements that may serve to satisfy a judgment against it.[300] But while the plaintiff was entitled to a copy of the defendants' insurance policy, Montana's discovery rules did not compel disclosure of the reservation of rights letter. The reservation of rights letter was separate from the insurance policy and reflected the insurer's interpretation of the policy.[301] In addition, the plaintiff had a copy of the defendants' insurance policy and could evaluate it for himself.[302] Finally, the court reasoned that the reservation of rights letter was irrelevant to the plaintiff's claims and was not reasonably calculated to lead to the discovery of admissible evidence.[303] The court therefore held that the defendants did not have to produce the letter.

---

295. *Id.*
296. *Id.*
297. *Id.*
298. No. BDV-97-771, 1998 Mont. Dist. LEXIS 459 (Mont. Dist. Ct. Apr. 14, 1998).
299. *Id.* at *1.
300. *Id.*
301. *Id.*
302. *Id.*
303. *Id.*

D. Summary

In re Madrid and *Foster* are correctly decided. Again, reservation of rights letters are not insurance agreements. A reservation of rights does not relate to the merits of a third-party action. If a plaintiff is concerned about the availability of insurance to satisfy any judgment it may obtain, it can review the insured's insurance policy and formulate any related opinions or conclusions based on the policy language—it does not need a copy of the reservation of rights letter. In short, absent a contrary rule of civil procedure, there is generally no reason to permit the discovery of reservation of rights letters in third-party actions against insureds.

VIII. Nonwaiver Agreements

Although insurers looking to preserve coverage defenses while defending insureds in litigation generally rely on reservation of rights letters for that purpose, they have another option. Instead of issuing a reservation of rights letter, an insurer might ask an insured to sign a nonwaiver agreement. Under a nonwaiver agreement, the insured agrees that the insurer may investigate an occurrence or defend the insured in litigation while preserving the right to contest coverage.

Like a reservation of rights letter, a nonwaiver agreement inoculates the insurer against estoppel and waiver claims. In contrast, where a reservation of rights letter is unilateral, a nonwaiver agreement is bilateral.[304] A nonwaiver agreement is basically a reservation of rights to which the insured consents.

Nonwaiver agreements often are standard forms prepared by the insurance company. For example, a nonwaiver agreement's essential terms might provide:

> It is hereby agreed by and between the Insured and the Company that any action taken by the Company, by and through its representatives, and at such time and in such manner as it deems advisable, in investigating said accident, shall not operate in any way as a waiver, or invalidate any of the conditions, of said policy nor any of the rights of either party hereto under said policy; and in the event any suit has been or shall be filed against the Insured growing out of a said accident or occurrence should the Company elect to defend said suit, such defense by it shall not be construed as a waiver of any of the conditions of said policy.
>
> Nothing herein shall be construed as a waiver of any rights which the Insured has under said policy.[305]

304. Landmark Am. Ins. Co. v. Esters, 600 F. Supp. 3d 677, 687 (W.D. La. 2022).
305. Shelby Steel Fabricators Inc. v. U.S. Fid. & Guar. Co., 569 So. 2d 309, 311 (Ala. 1990).

Alternatively, a nonwaiver agreement might provide:

> Any action that [Insurance Company] takes, including signing this agreement determining actual cash value or the amount of the damage that occurred on [date] to [the insured] or investigating this loss will not waive any of the policy's provisions and preserves all the insured's and [Insurance Company's] rights.
>
> We agree that no representative of [Insurance Company] has any authority to waive any of the policy's provisions, unless that waiver is written.
>
> The sole object and intent of this agreement is to allow [Insurance Company] to determine the actual cash value, the amount of damages, and to investigate this loss, without regard to [Insurance Company's] liability and to preserve all the insured's and [Insurance Company's] rights.

Rather than employing a standardized nonwaiver agreement, an insurer could create a case-specific nonwaiver agreement by preparing a reservation of rights letter, adding language about the insured's agreement to its terms, otherwise editing the letter so that it makes grammatical sense given its purpose, and then having the insured countersign, date, and return the letter to the insurer. An insurer and insured could also reach a nonwaiver agreement through an exchange of correspondence.[306]

Because a nonwaiver agreement is bilateral, it might seem that one offers an insurer greater protection against waiver and estoppel allegations than does a reservation of rights letter. In fact, a nonwaiver agreement generally affords an insurer no greater protection against estoppel or waiver claims than does a properly drafted reservation of rights letter. An insurer needs to obtain a nonwaiver agreement from the insured on a timely basis just as an insurer must reserve its rights reasonably promptly under the circumstances.[307] The insurer generally must specify coverage defenses about which it knows in a nonwaiver agreement just as it would in a reservation of rights letter.[308] For instance, in many states, the nonwaiver agreements quoted earlier would be considered

---

306. Merchants Indem. Corp. v. Eggleston, 179 A.2d 505, 511 (N.J. 1962); W. Cas. & Sur. Co. v. Newell Mfg. Co., 566 S.W.2d 74, 76 (Tex. App. 1978).

307. Peavey Co. v. M/V ANPA, 971 F.2d 1168, 1175 (5th Cir. 1992); Casey v. Stewart, 727 So. 2d 655, 658 (La. Ct. App. 1999).

308. *See, e.g.*, *In re* Lynch, 226 B.R. 813, 816–17 (Bankr. D. Vt. 1998) (holding that the insurer waived its coverage defenses because it did not specify them in its nonwaiver agreements); Nw. Nat'l Ins. Co. v. R.S. Armstrong & Bros. Co., 627 F. Supp. 951, 954–56 (D.S.C. 1985) (concluding that insurer was estopped from raising coverage defenses that it did not identify in its nonwaiver agreement); Bogle v. Conway, 433 P.2d 407, 412 (Kan. 1967) (citation omitted) ("It matters little . . . whether the insurer states that position in a unilateral notice to its insured or in a bilateral agreement with the insured. . . . In either case, the insured must be fairly and timely informed of the insurer's position."); Cincinnati Ins. Co. v. Hall, No. 297600, 2011 WL 2342704, at *2 (Mich. Ct. App. June 14, 2011) (stating that a nonwaiver agreement's reservation of "any defense" to coverage was insufficient); YMCA of Metro. Ft. Worth v. Com. Std. Ins. Co., 552 S.W.2d 497, 503–04 (Tex. App. 1977) (determining that an inadequate nonwaiver agreement estopped the insurer from asserting late notice as a defense to coverage).

ineffective boilerplate absent additional language specifying applicable policy provisions and tying those provisions to the facts of the case. Many courts would further consider those agreements to be ambiguous.[309] Naturally, there are differences in the law between jurisdictions, and there is authority for the proposition that a nonwaiver agreement that provides only that the insurer will undertake the defense "without waiver of any right or admission of any obligation under the policies" is sufficient to preserve the insurer's coverage defenses.[310]

Although a nonwaiver agreement is bilateral, it still only operates prospectively. If an insurer has waived a defense to coverage, it cannot cure the waiver and reclaim or retain the defense by thereafter entering into a nonwaiver agreement with the insured.[311]

An insured is not obligated to enter into a nonwaiver agreement.[312] In many situations, an insured arguably is justified in not doing so. An insured certainly is justified in not doing so where the proposed nonwaiver agreement is ambiguous. Regardless, an insurer cannot compel an insured to sign a nonwaiver agreement in exchange for a defense. An insurer's duty to defend is not subject to such a condition precedent.[313] If an insured refuses to enter into a nonwaiver agreement or unreasonably delays in doing so, an insurer may send a reservation of rights letter as a fall back measure and thereby preserve its coverage arguments while defending the insured.[314] In states where the insured is entitled to reject a reservation of rights defense, however, an insurer's attempt to impose a unilateral reservation of rights on an insured who declined to enter into a nonwaiver agreement will be ineffective unless the insured acquiesces.[315]

As for enforceability, there is little an insurer can do if an insured who enters into a nonwaiver agreement later repudiates it. One school of thought holds that the insurer cannot enforce the agreement because the insurer gave no consideration for it; the insurer merely agreed to perform its pre-existing duty to defend the insured. Indeed, it is a basic principle of contract law that

309. Courts strictly construe a nonwaiver agreement against the insurer. Conn. Fire Ins. Co. v. Fox, 361 F.2d 1, 7 (10th Cir. 1966) (applying Wyoming law); Millers Mut. Fire Ins. Co. v. Alamo Express, 548 S.W.2d 85, 89 (Tex. App. 1977).

310. Vt. Ins. Mgmt., Inc. v. Lumbermens' Mut. Cas. Co., 764 A.2d 1213, 1215 (Vt. 2000); *see also* Moon v. Cincinnati Ins. Co., 975 F. Supp. 2d 1326, 1330–31 (N.D. Ga. 2013) (enforcing similarly broad language).

311. Sargent v. Allstate Ins. Co., 303 S.E.2d 43, 47 (Ga. Ct. App. 1983).

312. *See, e.g.*, Charlton v. U.S. Fire Ins. Co., 627 N.Y.S.2d 221, 224 (Sup. Ct. 1995) (pointing out that no policy provision required the insureds to sign a nonwaiver agreement); Motorists Mut. Ins. Co. v. Trainor, 294 N.E.2d 874, 877 (Ohio 1973) (stating that the insureds were under no obligation to either assent to or reject the insurer's alleged nonwaiver agreement).

313. 1 Windt, *supra* note 29, § 2:19, at 2-77.

314. *See* Diamond Serv. Co. v. Utica Mut. Ins. Co., 476 A.2d 648, 654–56 (D.C. 1984).

315. Pac. Indem. Co. v. Acel Delivery Serv., Inc., 485 F.2d 1169, 1171, 1173–74 (5th Cir. 1973) (quoting 7A J. Appleman, Insurance Law and Practice § 4694, at 547 n.32.5 (1962)).

a promise to perform an existing obligation is not valid consideration.[316] That is contract law's "pre-existing duty rule."[317] But even assuming a valid contract, an insurer would be unlikely to sue the insured for breach and seek specific performance. An insurer that did so probably would lose given that (1) nonwaiver agreements lack the definite and certain terms required to compel specific performance; and (2) courts tend to balance the equities in specific performance cases, and it is difficult to see how any claimed equities would favor the insurer. Finally, were an insured to back out of a nonwaiver agreement in a state that does not allow an insured to reject a defense under reservation of rights, the insurer could send the insured a reservation of rights letter and obtain unilaterally the protection against potential estoppel and waiver allegations it once sought to achieve bilaterally.[318]

Given that courts uniformly recognize the purpose and effect of reservation of rights letters, it is generally easier and more efficient for an insurer to send a reservation of rights letter than it is to obtain a nonwaiver agreement. For this reason, insurers employ reservation of rights letters far more often than they do nonwaiver agreements. An insurer may opt to send a reservation of rights letter even where the insured is willing to execute a nonwaiver agreement.[319]

Finally, like reservation of rights letters, nonwaiver agreements should not normally be discoverable in the third-party action against the insured. Nonwaiver agreements are not insurance agreements within the meaning of rules of civil procedure. They are not relevant to either liability or damages. Nor are they likely to lead to the discovery of admissible evidence in jurisdictions where that is the test for discoverability.

---

316. San Luis Obispo Loc. Agency Formation Comm'n v. City of Pismo Beach, 275 Cal. Rptr. 3d 827, 840 (Ct. App. 2021); Mosier v. Vill. of Holliday Hills, 128 N.E.3d 1210, 1217 (Ill. App. Ct. 2019); Zheng v. City of N.Y., 940 N.Y.S.2d 582, 584 (App. Div. 2012).

317. BMO Harris Bank, N.A. v. Porter, 106 N.E.3d 411, 423 (Ill. App. Ct. 2018); Yerkovich v. AAA, 610 N.W.2d 542, 546 (Mich. 2000).

318. *See Diamond Serv. Co.*, 476 A.2d at 656 (holding that an insurer preserves its coverage defenses by issuing a reservation of rights letter after an insured fails to timely enter into a nonwaiver agreement); Richmond v. Ga. Farm Bureau Mut. Ins. Co., 231 S.E.2d 245, 248 (Ga. Ct. App. 1976) (stating that where the insured refuses to consent to a defense under a bilateral reservation of rights, the insurer must (1) properly reserve its rights unilaterally, (2) take steps to prevent the insured from being prejudiced in the underlying action, and (3) seek immediate declaratory relief, including a stay of the underlying case).

319. Williams v. Ala. Farm Bureau Mut. Cas. Ins. Co., 416 So. 2d 744, 748 (Ala. 1982).

CHAPTER 3
Conflicts of Interest in Insurance Defense

Douglas R. Richmond

I. Introduction

Standard liability insurance policies grant the insurance company the right to defend a lawsuit against an insured in addition to imposing on the insurer the duty to defend the insured.[1] The insurer's duty to defend the insured and its right to do so go hand-in-hand.[2]

1. *See, e.g.*, INS. SERVS. OFF., INC., PERSONAL AUTO POLICY (PP 00 01 09 18), at 2 (2017) ("We will pay damages for 'bodily injury' or 'property damage' for which any 'insured' becomes legally responsible because of an auto accident. . . . We will settle or defend, as we consider appropriate, any claim or suit asking for these damages."); INS. SERVS. OFF., INC., COMMERCIAL GENERAL LIABILITY COVERAGE FORM (CG 00 01 04 13), at 1 (2012) ("We will pay those sums that the insured becomes legally obligated to pay as damages because of 'bodily injury' or 'property damage' to which this insurance applies. We will have the right and duty to defend the insured against any 'suit' seeking those damages."); INS. SERVS. OFF., INC., HOMEOWNERS 3 – SPECIAL FORM (HO 00 03 05 11), at 17 (2010) ("If a claim is made or a suit is brought against an 'insured' . . . we will . . . [p]rovide a defense at our expense by counsel of our choice, even if the suit is groundless, false or fraudulent."). The insurer's right to defend is most clearly and explicitly stated in the standard commercial general liability policy; standard personal auto and homeowners policies are less specific with respect to the insurer's right to defend. The latter lack of specificity in unimportant, however, because the insurer's right to defend is implied in policies that include a duty to defend. *See* Nat'l Cas. Co. v. Forge Indus. Staffing Inc., 567 F.3d 871, 874 (7th Cir. 2009) ("Along with an insurer's obligation to defend its insured comes its right to control and direct the defense."); Peterson v. Reliance Ins. Co., 5 F. App'x 687, 688 (9th Cir. 2001) ("The duty to defend gives the insurer absolute right to control the defense and the insured is required to surrender all control over the defense."); Joseph T. Ryerson & Son, Inc. v. Travelers Indem. Co. of Am., 165 N.E.3d 439, 458 (Ill. App. Ct. 2020) ("Ordinarily, an insurer's duty to defend its insured includes the right to control the defense, which allows insurers to protect their financial interest in the outcome of the litigation."); Kelly v. Iowa Mut. Ins. Co., 620 N.W.2d 637, 643 (Iowa 2000) ("When an insurer defends an insured, it has control over the defense and over settlement."); McCormack Baron Mgmt. Servs., Inc. v. Am. Guarantee & Liab. Ins. Co., 989 S.W.2d 168, 170 n.2 (Mo. 1999) (noting that "an insurer's obligation to defend is also a right to defend"); Milroy v. Allstate Ins. Co., 151 P.3d 922, 927 (Okla. Civ. App. 2006) ("The contractual duty to defend includes the right to control the course of the defense of the liability claim and to decide on litigation strategy."); Pa. Mfrs. Ass'n Ins. Co. v. Johnson Matthey, Inc., 243 A.3d 298, 315 (Pa. Commw. Ct. 2020) (agreeing that an insurer's duty to defend is also a right to defend).

2. *See Nat'l Cas. Co.*, 567 F.3d at 874; *Peterson*, 5 F. App'x at 688; *Joseph T. Ryerson & Son, Inc.*, 165 N.E.3d at 458; *McCormack Baron Mgmt. Servs., Inc.*, 989 S.W.2d at 170 n.2; Bruce v. Junghun,

An insurer's right to defend its insured entitles it to control the insured's defense,[3] including the right to select defense counsel for the insured.[4] The selection of counsel is important to an insurer first because it allows the insurer to select proven and capable defense counsel and thereby either win the case against the insured or minimize any potential damage award should the case be lost. By controlling the defense, an insurer is also able to seize settlement opportunities and control settlement negotiations to the extent possible. Insurers' control of the defense additionally allows them to participate in strategic decisions that might otherwise be made solely by defense counsel or the insured, to reasonably manage litigation costs, and to prevent collusion between claimants and insureds. Boiled down, control of the defense allows insurers to minimize overall liability costs.

An insurer's control of its insured's defense generally benefits the insured as well. Few policyholders have the ability or desire to competently manage litigation. As the Restatement of the Law of Liability Insurance explains, "insurers have greater capacity to direct the defense of a legal action than all but the most sophisticated insureds."[5] That is especially true where individual insureds and small businesses are concerned. Furthermore, in almost all cases, insurers satisfactorily manage the defense of lawsuits brought against their insureds and the exercise of their duty and right to defend presents no problems. Finally, insurers' ability to minimize liability costs by controlling the defense of third-party litigation benefits all insureds by helping to hold down premiums.

At the same time, the language in standard liability insurance policies that generally vests control of the insured's defense in the insurer has long fostered concern about conflicts of interest between insureds and the defense lawyers appointed by insurers. The essential concern has always been that because insurance defense attorneys normally enjoy ongoing relationships with the insurers that engage them but seldom have continuing relationships with the insureds they are hired to represent, they are predisposed to favor the insurer

---

912 N.E.2d 1144, 1148 (Ohio Ct. App. 2009); *Milroy*, 151 P.3d at 927; *Pa. Mfrs. Ass'n Ins. Co.*, 243 A.3d at 315.

3. *Peterson*, 5 F. App'x at 688; Valenzuela v. Mt. Hawley Ins. Co., 536 F. Supp. 3d 1217, 1223 (D.N.M. 2021) (applying New Mexico law); Centex Homes v. St. Paul Fire & Marine Ins. Co., 187 Cal. Rptr. 3d 542, 548 (Ct. App. 2015); Auto-Owners Ins. Co. v. Bolt Factory Lofts Owners Ass'n, Inc., 487 P.3d 276, 283–84 (Colo. 2021) (quoting Farmers Ins. Grp., Inc. v. Trimble, 691 P.2d 1138, 1141 (Colo. 1984)); *Joseph T. Ryerson & Son, Inc.*, 165 N.E.3d at 458.

4. DePasquale Steel Erectors Inc. v. Gemini Ins. Co., 249 F. Supp. 3d 899, 902 (N.D. Ill. 2017) (applying Illinois law); OneBeacon Am. Ins. Co. v. Celanese Corp., 84 N.E.3d 867, 872 (Mass. App. Ct. 2017); Moeller v. Am. Guarantee & Liab. Ins. Co., 707 So. 2d 1062, 1068 (Miss. 1996); *In re* Farmers Tex. Cnty. Mut. Ins. Co., 621 S.W.3d 261, 269 (Tex. 2021); Restatement of the L. of Liab. Ins. § 10(1) (Am. L. Inst. 2019).

5. Restatement of the L. of Liab. Ins. § 10 cmt. b (Am. L. Inst. 2019).

over the insured in any case where their interests diverge.[6] In fact, and as indicated earlier, it is a rare case in which the insurer's and insured's interests in a lawsuit against the insured are not aligned. Third-party claims against insureds typically are within policy limits, do not spawn coverage issues, and do not involve a situation where the insured has an independent, non-economic interest at stake in the litigation. It is also wrong to presume that a lawyer hired by an insurer to defend an insured will somehow favor the insurer's interests over the insured's interests because of the lawyer's business relationship with the insurer.[7] Nonetheless, conflicts of interest occasionally arise in insurance defense just as they do in other litigation practice areas. In such cases, the insured may be entitled to representation by independent counsel at the insurer's expense. This chapter examines common conflicts of interest in the tripartite relationship between the insured, insurer, and defense counsel that characterizes insurance defense practice.

II. The Attorney-Client Relationship in Insurance Defense

A. The Question of Client Identity

It is first critical to understand who a lawyer hired by an insurance company to defend an insured represents. This knowledge is critical because client status determines, among other things, whether the lawyer owes the person or entity a fiduciary duty; whether the lawyer owes the person or entity ethical duties that flow exclusively to clients, such as competence, communication, confidentiality, diligence, and loyalty; and whether their confidential communications may be protected by the attorney-client privilege. Moreover, lawyers' duties of confidentiality and loyalty undergird conflict of interest rules. So, whom does a lawyer engaged by an insurer to defend its insured represent? There are two possible answers to this question: (1) both the insured and the insurer or (2) the insured alone.

6. *See* Nat'l Cas. Co. v. Forge Indus. Staffing Inc., 567 F.3d 871, 874 (7th Cir. 2009).

7. *See* Twin City Fire Ins. Co. v. Ben Arnold-Sunbelt Beverage Co. of S.C., 433 F.3d 365, 372–74 (4th Cir. 2005) (discussing insurance defense lawyers' ethical duties under South Carolina law and the incentives for them to fulfill their duties); Fed. Ins. Co. v. X-Rite, Inc., 748 F. Supp. 1223, 1229 (W.D. Mich. 1990) (footnote omitted) ("To hold that the insurer who, under reservation of rights, participates in selection of counsel, automatically breaches its duty of good faith is to indulge the conclusive presumption that counsel is unable to fully represent its client, the insured, without consciously or unconsciously compromising the insured's interests. The [c]ourt is unable to conclude that Michigan law professes so little confidence in the integrity of the bar of this state."); Eckman v. Erie Ins. Exch., 21 A.3d 1203, 1209 (Pa. Super. Ct. 2011) ("The categorical supposition that all attorneys compensated by a third party will breach their ethical duties is undeveloped, unsupported, and not cognizable under established principles of law.").

1. *The Dual Client Doctrine*

Under the dual client doctrine, a lawyer appointed by an insurance company to defend its insured represents both the insurer and the insured, meaning that the defense lawyer has an attorney-client relationship with both. As a California court famously explained: "As long as the interests of the insurer and the insured coincide, they are both clients of the defense attorney and the defense attorney's fiduciary duty runs to both the insurer and the insured."[8] The dual client doctrine represents the majority rule.[9]

There are good reasons for an insurance company to want an attorney-client relationship with the lawyer it hires to defend its insured. As a client, the insurer has as much right as any other client to instruct the lawyer it hires in the conduct of the litigation and that ability exists apart from the right to defend under its policy. As a client of the defense lawyer, the insurer also acquires the benefits of the ethical and fiduciary duties that lawyers owe to clients, it best assures that its confidential communications with defense counsel concerning the litigation against the insured will be shielded from discovery by the attorney-client privilege, and it enjoys the right to sue defense counsel for professional negligence (generally described as legal malpractice) in the rare and unfortunate case where the lawyer seriously mishandles the insured's defense and the insurer is damaged as a result.

2. *The Flawed Concept of the Insured as the Primary Client*

Some courts that recognize the dual client doctrine further hold that a defense lawyer owes "primary allegiance" to the insured.[10] This simply cannot be. A

8. Nat'l Union Fire Ins. Co. v. Stites Pro. Law Corp., 1 Cal. Rptr. 2d 570, 575 (Ct. App. 1991).

9. *See, e.g.*, Mt. Vernon Fire Ins. Co. v. VisionAid, Inc., 875 F.3d 716, 724 (1st Cir. 2017) (interpreting Massachusetts law); Home Indem. Co. v. Lane Powell Moss & Miller, 43 F.3d 1322, 1331 (9th Cir. 1995) (interpreting Alaska law); Lee v. Med. Prot. Co., 858 F. Supp. 2d 803, 806 (E.D. Ky. 2012) (interpreting Kentucky law); Mitchum v. Hudgens, 533 So. 2d 194, 198 (Ala. 1988); Bank of Am., N.A. v. Super. Ct., 151 Cal. Rptr. 3d 526, 536 (Ct. App. 2013); Pa. Ins. Guar. Ass'n v. Sikes, 590 So. 2d 1051, 1052 (Fla. Dist. Ct. App. 1991); Coscia v. Cunningham, 299 S.E.2d 880, 881 (Ga. 1983); Huang v. Brenson, 7 N.E.3d 729, 739 (Ill. App. Ct. 2014); Cincinnati Ins. Co. v. Wills, 717 N.E.2d 151, 161 (Ind. 1999); Teague v. St. Paul Fire & Marine Ins. Co., 10 So. 3d 806, 832 (La. Ct. App. 2009); McCourt Co. v. FPC Props., Inc., 434 N.E.2d 1234, 1235 (Mass. 1982); State Farm Mut. Auto. Ins. Co. v. Jones, 37 So. 3d 87, 93–94 (Miss. Ct. App. 2009); State Farm Mut. Auto. Ins. Co. v. Hansen, 357 P.3d 338, 343 (Nev. 2015); Lieberman v. Emps. Ins., 419 A.2d 417, 423–25 (N.J. 1980); Nationwide Mut. Fire Ins. Co. v. Bourlon, 617 S.E.2d 40, 45–46 (N.C. Ct. App. 2005); U.S. Fid. & Guar. Co. v. Pietrykowski, No. E99-38, 2000 WL 204475, at *3–4 (Ohio Ct. App. Feb. 11, 2000); Spratley v. State Farm Mut. Auto. Ins. Co., 78 P.3d 603, 607 (Utah 2003); *In re* Illuzzi, 616 A.2d 233, 236 (Vt. 1992); Barry v. USAA, 989 P.2d 1172, 1175 (Wash. Ct. App. 1999); Juneau Cnty. Star-Times v. Juneau Cnty., 824 N.W.2d 457, 467 (Wis. 2013).

10. Paradigm Ins. Co. v. Langerman Law Off., P.A., 24 P.3d 593, 598 (Ariz. 2001) ("[I]n the unique situation in which the lawyer actually represents two clients, he must give primary allegiance to one (the insured) to whom the other (the insurer) owes a duty of providing not only protection, but of doing so fairly and in good faith."); *see also* Thompson v. Dennis Widmer Constr., Inc., No. 3:20-cv-01145-IM, 2021 WL 5235974, at *3 (D. Or. Nov. 10, 2021) (quoting Or. State Bar, Formal

lawyer generally cannot favor one co-client over another absent the co-clients' informed consent without suffering a conflict of interest. Co-clients have a right to expect that their common lawyer is equally loyal. Furthermore, this approach is unnecessary considering general conflict of interest rules, which protect insureds in cases where their interests and those of their insurers are not aligned. Finally, the primary allegiance approach is insidious from insurers' perspective because an insurer relying on a defense lawyer to protect its interests along with the insured's interests may unknowingly be vulnerable on several fronts.[11] This approach also is insidious from insureds' standpoint, because if you embrace the dubious concern that a lawyer hired by an insurer will favor the insurer out of economic self-interest, then an insured in a case presenting a conflict of interest should be defended by independent counsel owing it undivided loyalty rather than by a lawyer owing it "primary allegiance."

3. *The Sole Client Model*

A lawyer appointed by an insurer to defend its insured always represents the insured.[12] The issue then becomes whether the lawyer can jointly represent the insurer or whether the insured is the lawyer's sole client.[13] Although the dual client doctrine represents the majority rule, a significant minority of jurisdictions hold that the insured is the defense lawyer's sole client.[14] At least two courts have held that in a case defended under a reservation of rights,

Op. 2005-121 (2016)); *Spratley*, 78 P.3d at 607 ("[W]here no actual conflict exists or is foreseeable, an attorney will ordinarily represent both the interests of the insured and the insurer. However, where actual conflict exists or is likely to arise, the attorney's allegiance is to the insured because of an insurer's duty to provide a defense in good faith.").

11. *See* William T. Barker & Charles Silver, Professional Responsibilities of Insurance Defense Counsel § 5.04, at 5-34 to -35 (2012 & Supp. 2017) (explaining several ways in which the primary client approach may prejudice insurers).

12. *See* Remodeling Dimensions, Inc. v. Integrity Mut. Ins. Co., 819 N.W.2d 602, 613 (Minn. 2012).

13. *See id.* (citations omitted) ("It is well established that an attorney hired by an insurer to defend a claim against its insured represents the insured. . . . But we have not held that an attorney cannot have an attorney-client relationship with both the insured and the insurer.").

14. *See, e.g.*, Cont'l Cas. Co. v. Pullman, Comley, Bradley & Reeves, 929 F.2d 103, 108 (2d Cir. 1991); *In re* A.H. Robins Co., 880 F.2d 694, 751 (4th Cir. 1989); U.S. Underwriters Ins. Co. v. Tauber, 604 F. Supp. 2d 521, 532 (E.D.N.Y. 2009); Gen. Sec. Ins. Co. v. Jordan, Coyne & Savits, LLP, 357 F. Supp. 2d 951, 957 (E.D. Va. 2005) (discussing Virginia law); Essex Ins. Co. v. Tyler, 309 F. Supp. 2d 1270, 1272 (D. Colo. 2004) (discussing Colorado law); Gibbs v. Lappies, 828 F. Supp. 6, 7 (D.N.H. 1993); First Am. Carriers, Inc. v. Kroger Co., 787 S.W.2d 669, 671 (Ark. 1990); Higgins v. Karp, 687 A.2d 539, 543 (Conn. 1997); Franco v. Reinhardt, 539 P.3d 934, 941 (Haw. 2023); Hackman v. W. Agric. Ins. Co., No. 104,786, 2012 WL 1524060, at *15 (Kan. Ct. App. Apr. 27, 2012); Kirschner v. Process Design Assocs., Inc., 592 NW.2d 707, 711 (Mich. 1999); *In re* Rules of Pro. Conduct & Insurer Imposed Billing Rules & Proc., 2 P.3d 806, 814 (Mont. 2000); Feliberty v. Damon, 527 N.E.2d 261, 265 (N.Y. 1988); Sentry Select Ins. Co. v. Maybank Law Firm, LLC, 826 S.E.2d 270, 272 (S.C. 2019); Givens v. Mullikin, 75 S.W.3d 383, 396 (Tenn. 2002); Stewart Title Guar. Co. v. Sterling Sav. Bank, 311 P.3d 1, 3 (Wash. 2013); Barefield v. DPIC Cos., 600 S.E.2d 256, 270 (W. Va. 2004).

the insurer's reservation trumps otherwise permissible dual representation and transforms the insured into the defense lawyer's sole client.[15]

4. *The Proper Approach: Client Identity Is a Question of Fact*

In fact, the dual client and sole client models are best seen as default rules. Generally, whether a defense lawyer represents the insurer in addition to the insured—again, the insured is always the defense lawyer's client—is a matter of contract.[16] In other words, the insurer and defense lawyer may agree that the lawyer represents the insurer as well as the insured.

Moreover, some states that might be classified as recognizing the dual client doctrine in fact hold a slightly more nuanced view. In these states, while the law permits a lawyer to jointly represent an insured and an insurer,[17] that allowance does not mean a defense lawyer always engages in dual representation.[18]

Cutting to the chase, the existence of an attorney-client relationship is a question of fact.[19] An attorney-client relationship may arise in the absence of an express agreement between the lawyer and the client.[20] Indeed, an express agreement is not necessary; an attorney-client relationship may be implied or inferred from the parties' conduct.[21] An implied attorney-client relationship may be formed when (1) a person seeks the lawyer's advice or assistance; (2) the requested advice or assistance relates to matters within the lawyer's professional competence; and (3) the lawyer expressly or impliedly agrees to provide or actually furnishes the desired advice or assistance.[22] In some cases, the third element may be established by proof of detrimental reliance, meaning that the person seeking legal services reasonably relied on the lawyer to provide those services, and the lawyer, who recognized the person's reliance,

---

15. Lifestar Response of Ala., Inc. v. Admiral Ins. Co., 17 So. 3d 200, 217 (Ala. 2009); Mut. of Enumclaw Ins. Co. v. Dan Paulson Constr., Inc., 169 P.3d 1, 8 n.10 (Wash. 2007).

16. Unauthorized Prac. of Law Comm. v. Am. Home Assur. Co., 261 S.W.3d 24, 42 (Tex. 2008).

17. *See, e.g.*, Pa. Nat'l Mut. Cas. Ins. Co. v. Perlberg, 819 F. Supp. 2d 449, 454 (D. Md. 2011) (discussing Maryland law); *In re* Allstate Ins. Co., 722 S.W.2d 947, 952 (Mo. 1987) (stating that "there is no reason why the same lawyer may not represent both" the insured and the insurer).

18. *Perlberg*, 819 F. Supp. 2d at 454.

19. Jarquin v. Blanks, 364 So. 3d 330, 332 (La. Ct. App. 2019); Savell v. Duddy, 147 A.3d 1179, 1185 (Me. 2016); Newsome v. Peoples Bancshares, 269 So. 3d 19, 31 (Miss. 2018); N.C. State Bar v. Merritt, 877 S.E.2d 892, 901 (N.C. Ct. App. 2022) (quoting Cornelius v. Helms, 461 S.E.2d 338, 339 (N.C. Ct. App. 1995)); Rice v. Neether, 888 N.W.2d 749, 755 (N.D. 2016).

20. Bistline v. Parker, 918 F.3d 849, 864 (10th Cir. 2019) (applying Utah law); Att'y Grievance Comm'n of Md. v. Shoup, 979 A.2d 120, 136 (Md. 2009); Ripa v. Petrosyants, 164 N.Y.S.3d 168, 170 (App. Div. 2022).

21. Est. of Nixon v. Barber, 796 S.E.2d 489, 492 (Ga. Ct. App. 2017); *In re* Hodge, 407 P.3d 613, 648 (Kan. 2017); Patel v. Martin, 111 N.E.3d 1082, 1093 (Mass. 2018); State *ex rel.* Couns. for Discipline of the Neb. Sup. Ct. v. Chvala, 935 N.W.2d 446, 471 (Neb. 2019).

22. *Chvala*, 935 N.W.2d at 471–72; Chem-Age Indus., Inc. v. Glover, 652 N.W.2d 756, 768 (S.D. 2002).

did not dispel it.[23] In contrast, a person or entity's payment of a lawyer's fees, standing alone, does not create an attorney-client relationship.[24]

The existence of an implied attorney-client relationship is determined on a case-by-case basis.[25] When deciding whether an implied attorney-client relationship exists, courts focus on the putative client's expectations.[26] As important as a would-be client's perspective may be, however, a person's unilateral belief that an attorney-client relationship exists does not make it so.[27] Rather, a putative client's subjective belief that an attorney-client relationship has been formed must be accompanied by facts indicating that such belief is objectively reasonable.[28] At base, then, the existence of an implied or de facto attorney-client relationship is governed by an objective standard.[29]

In most cases, defense lawyers likely will be deemed to have an attorney-client relationship with insurers that engage them. Defense lawyers supply insurers with legal advice intended to benefit them in conducting the insured's defense. For instance, defense lawyers advise insurers on the applicable law, possible verdict value, settlement value, the likelihood that an insured will be found liable if the case is tried, the assessment of comparative fault, whether there are other potential defendants to be joined or against whom crossclaims might be asserted, the prospects for winning by dispositive motion, whether the case should be settled or tried, the expected composition of the jury pool, the judge's reputation, the skill of the plaintiff's lawyer, prospects on appeal in the event of an unfavorable trial outcome, and more. Insurers expect to receive such advice from defense counsel and incorporate it when making critical

---

23. Cesso v. Todd, 82 N.E.3d 1074, 1078–79 (Mass. App. Ct. 2017) (quoting DeVaux v. Am. Home Assur. Co., 444 N.E.2d 355, 357 (Mass. 1983)); *Chvala*, 935 N.W.2d at 472.

24. Palmer v. Super. Ct., 180 Cal. Rptr. 3d 620, 628 (Ct. App. 2014); Rubin & Norris, LLC v. Panzarella, 51 N.E.3d 879, 891 (Ill. App. Ct. 2016); State *ex rel.* Stovall v. Meneley, 22 P.3d 124, 140 (Kan. 2001); Att'y Grievance Comm'n of Md. v. Brooke, 821 A.2d 414, 424 (Md. 2003); State *ex rel.* Thompson v. Dueker, 346 S.W.3d 390, 394 (Mo. Ct. App. 2011); *In re* Disciplinary Action Against Ward, 881 N.W.2d 226, 230 (N.D. 2016).

25. Azarax, Inc. v. Syverson, 398 F. Supp. 3d 425, 436 (D. Minn. 2019) (applying Minnesota law).

26. *See, e.g.*, People v. Bennett, 810 P.2d 661, 664 (Colo. 1991) ("The proper test is a subjective one, and an important factor is whether the client believes that the relationship existed."); *Rubin & Norris*, 51 N.E.3d at 891 (stating that the analysis of whether an attorney-client relationship exists focuses on the client's viewpoint rather than the lawyer's); Barkerding v. Whittaker, 263 So. 3d 1170, 1181 (La. Ct. App. 2018) ("[T]he existence of an attorney-client relationship turns largely on the client's subjective belief that such a relationship exists.").

27. Belliveau v. Barco, Inc., 987 F.3d 122, 133 (5th Cir. 2021) (applying Texas law); *In re* Grand Jury Subpoena: Under Seal, 415 F.3d 333, 339 (4th Cir. 2005); *In re* Robbins, 192 A.3d 558, 563 (D.C. 2018); Moran v. Hurst, 822 N.Y.S.2d 564, 566 (App. Div. 2006).

28. Kemp Inv. N., LLC v. Englert, 314 So. 3d 734, 738 (Fla. Dist. Ct. App. 2021); Murphy v. MKS Plastics, L.L.C., 314 So. 3d 65, 71 (La. Ct. App. 2020); Hinerman v. Grill on Twenty First, LLC, 112 N.E.3d 1273, 1275–76 (Ohio Ct. App. 2018); O'Kain v. Landress, 450 P.3d 508, 516 (Or. Ct. App. 2019).

29. *Barkerding*, 263 So. 3d at 1182; Flores v. Branscomb PC, No. 13-18-00411-CV, 2021 WL 2371517, at *4 (Tex. App. June 10, 2021).

decisions in the litigation, both points being known to the defense lawyers willingly supplying the advice.[30]

Courts increasingly recognize the importance of fact-specific inquiry into the existence of an attorney-client relationship between an insurer and the lawyer the carrier hires to defend its insured.[31] In *Paradigm Insurance Co. v. Langerman Law Offices*,[32] for example, the Arizona Supreme Court embraced the general rule that the existence of an attorney-client relationship turns on whether (1) the would-be client has manifested to the lawyer its intent that the lawyer provide legal services for it; and (2) the lawyer manifests her consent to do so.[33]

The Minnesota Supreme Court modified the general rules concerning the creation of attorney-client relationships in *Pine Island Farmers Coop v. Erstad & Riemer, P.A.*,[34] to provide a "bright-line rule to determine whether defense counsel represents the insurer as well as the insured."[35] Under the *Pine Island* approach:

> [I]n the absence of a conflict of interest . . . , the insurer can become a co-client of defense counsel based on contract or tort theory if two conditions are satisfied. First, defense counsel or another attorney must consult with the insured, explaining the implications of dual representation and the advantages and risks involved. . . . Second, after consultation, the insured must give its express consent to the dual representation.[36]

Without this consultation and the insured's consent to dual representation, the insured is the defense lawyer's sole client.[37]

The *Pine Island* approach is flawed for three reasons. First, it is by no means apparent why the insured alone should control whether the insurer should enjoy the benefits of an attorney-client relationship with the defense lawyer. In most cases, only the insurer's money is at stake either when negotiating a settlement or where the plaintiff wins a judgment against the insured.

---

30. A defense lawyer might argue that in furnishing such information, she is simply evaluating the case for the insurer in the justifiable belief that offering the evaluation is compatible with her relationship with the insured, and that no attorney-client relationship results. *See* Model Rules of Pro. Conduct r. 2.3(a) (Am. Bar Ass'n 2023) ("Evaluation for Use by Third Persons"). That argument is not persuasive in the absence of the defense lawyer's express disclaimer of an attorney-client relationship with the insurer, however, because it does not account for the insurer's expectations.

31. *See, e.g.*, CAMICO Mut. Ins. Co. v. Heffler, Radetich & Saitta, LLP, No. 11-4753, 2013 WL 315716, at *2–5 (E.D. Pa. Jan. 28, 2013) (discussing Pennsylvania law); Pa. Nat'l Mut. Cas. Ins. Co. v. Perlberg, 819 F. Supp. 2d 449, 454–55 (D. Md. 2011) (applying Maryland law); Swiss Reinsurance Am. Corp. v. Roetzel & Andress, 837 N.E.2d 1215, 1220–21 (Ohio Ct. App. 2005).

32. 24 P.3d 593 (Ariz. 2001).

33. *Id.* at 595–96 (quoting the Restatement (Third) of the L. Governing Laws. § 14 (Am. L. Inst. 2000)).

34. 649 N.W.2d 444 (Minn. 2002).

35. *Id.* at 451.

36. *Id.* at 452 (citations omitted).

37. *Id.* at 451.

Second, the *Pine Island* approach ignores the view that the insured consented to dual representation when it purchased an insurance policy that granted the insurer the right to defend.[38] Third, if there is no conflict of interest, the insured has no right to independent counsel at the insurer's expense.[39] By extension, an insured cannot be entitled to withhold consent to dual representation if there is no conflict of interest.

If an insurer that wants to claim an implied attorney-client relationship with a defense lawyer, it must be prepared to prove the relationship's existence. The insurer in *Pennsylvania National Mutual Insurance Co. v. Perlberg*[40] could not carry that burden.

In *Perlberg*, Penn National filed a declaratory judgment action to establish that it owed no duty to defend or indemnify its insureds, the Perlberg Parties, in connection with a lawsuit in which the plaintiffs alleged that they were poisoned by exposure to lead paint while residing in property the Perlberg Parties owned. The Perlberg Parties were represented in the declaratory judgment action by lawyers from Hodes, Pessin & Katz (HPK), including Natalie Magdeburger. Before joining HPK, Magdeburger practiced at Whiteford, Taylor & Preston (WTP), which Penn National often hired to defend its insureds in third-party actions, including lead paint exposure cases. When Penn National alerted HPK to its prior relationship with Magdeburger, the firm investigated. Magdeburger responded with an affidavit in which she acknowledged that she had defended Penn National's insureds in auto accident and lead paint cases while at WTP, but she denied any role in coverage matters for Penn National, disclaimed any knowledge of Penn National's coverage practices, and asserted that she learned nothing at WTP related to the current case.[41] Magdeburger further stated that she had only represented Penn National's insureds—never Penn National.[42] Penn National nevertheless moved to disqualify her from representing the Perlberg Parties.

In arguing for Magdeburger's disqualification, Penn National asserted that it was a former client of hers because, under Maryland law, a lawyer hired

38. *See* Mora v. Lancet Indem. Risk Retention Grp., Inc., 773 F. App'x 113, 117–18 (4th Cir. 2019) (quoting Fid. & Cas. Co. v. McConnaughey, 179 A.2d 117, 121 (Md. 1962)).

39. *See, e.g.*, Cont'l Cas. Co. v. Nat'l Union Fire Ins. Co., 940 F. Supp. 2d 898, 928 (D. Minn. 2013) (applying Minnesota law); Coregis Ins. Co. v. Lewis, Johns, Avallone, Aviles & Kaufman, LLP, No. 01 CV 3844(SJ), 2006 WL 2135782, at *15 (E.D.N.Y. July 28, 2006) ("In the absence of . . . a conflict, [the insured] is not entitled to independent counsel."); Swanson v. State Farm Gen. Ins. Co., 162 Cal. Rptr. 3d 477, 483–85 (Ct. App. 2013) (explaining that the insured lost the right to independent counsel when the insurer withdrew its coverage defenses that created a conflict of interest); Rainey v. Ind. Ins. Co., No. 1-15-0862, 2016 WL 2841285, at *9 (Ill. App. Ct. May 11, 2016) ("Absent a conflict of interest . . . Indiana [Insurance Co.] was not obligated to pay for independent counsel and did not breach its duty to defend by failing to do so.").

40. 819 F. Supp. 2d 449 (D. Md. 2011).

41. *Id.* at 452.

42. *Id.* at 454.

by an insurer to defend an insured in a third-party action represents both the insurer and the insured.[43] Penn National supported its argument with citations to Maryland cases where the courts concluded that a lawyer's dual representation of an insurer and its insured was ethically permissible and, indeed, was the typical result of insurance policy language permitting the insurer to control the insured's defense.[44] As noted earlier, however, the fact that a lawyer "*may*, in conformance with ethical rules, simultaneously represent an insurer and its insured does not establish . . . that in all cases in which an attorney is hired by an insurer to represent an insured, the attorney *does* engage in such dual representation."[45]

Here, Penn National demonstrated only that it formerly hired Magdeburger to defend its insureds.[46] It submitted no insurance policies from Magdeburger's cases to show that the insureds there consented to dual representation, nor did it provide retainer agreements from those cases that would reflect the relationships between itself, its insureds, and the lawyers at WTP.[47] Penn National further failed to offer any evidence of "the circumstances under which Magdeburger performed work for its insureds."[48] Consequently, the *Perlberg* court concluded that Penn National had not established that it shared an attorney-client relationship with Magdeburger, so her disqualification would be inappropriate.

5. *Structuring the Relationship So the Insured Is the Defense Lawyer's Sole Client*

Defense lawyers who do not want an attorney-client relationship with an insurance company are free to structure their engagements so that the insured is their sole client. Just as an insurer and defense lawyer can agree that the lawyer represents both the insurer and the insured in litigation against the insured, so can they agree that the insured will be the defense lawyer's sole client. This can be accomplished in an engagement letter sent to the insurer in which the lawyer specifies that the insured is her sole client.[49] The use of such an engagement letter is important given that an attorney-client relationship between the defense lawyer and the insurer can generally be implied from their conduct. Even if the defense lawyer gives the insurer the sort of advice described earlier, the insurer should not be able to claim an implied attorney-client relationship with

43. *Id.*
44. *Id.*
45. *Id.*
46. *Id.* at 455.
47. *Id.* (citing Charles Silver & Kent Syverud, *The Professional Responsibilities of Insurance Defense Lawyers*, 45 Duke L.J. 255, 270 (1995)).
48. *Id.*
49. The insurer could also establish that the insured is the defense lawyer's sole client through language in its outside counsel guidelines or in a letter assigning a case to defense counsel.

the lawyer because the engagement letter's contrary terms render the insurer's expectation of an attorney-client relationship objectively unreasonable.

Where the defense lawyer has expressly disclaimed an attorney-client relationship with the insurer, a court evaluating the relationship between the two should conclude that the defense lawyer is merely evaluating the matter for the insurer in furtherance of the lawyer's representation of the insured.[50] Alternatively, a court might reason that the lawyer is providing the information to the insurer as the insured's agent in fulfilling the insured's duty to cooperate with the insurer in the defense rather than as the insurer's lawyer.

Although there are good reasons for an insurer to want an attorney-client relationship with the defense lawyers it hires for its insureds, there are also sound reasons for an insurer to agree that an insured will be a defense lawyer's sole client. By treating the insured as the defense lawyer's sole client, the insurer reduces the opportunities for conflicts of interest that will rob it of defense control. Depending on the facts, a sole client relationship between the insured and defense counsel may minimize the prospects of a bad faith claim if the litigation against the insured turns out badly. Plus, while an attorney-client relationship with the defense lawyer best assures the confidentiality protections of the attorney-client privilege, the insurer's communications with the defense lawyer in case where the insured is the defense lawyer's sole client should still be shielded from discovery by extension of the insured's attorney-client privilege and by the defense lawyer's work product immunity.[51] The communications should also be protected by the insured-insured privilege in states that recognize the doctrine.[52]

50. *See* Model Rules of Pro. Conduct r. 2.3(a) (Am. Bar Ass'n 2023) (stating when a lawyer may provide an evaluation of a client matter for someone other than the client).

51. *See* Bredice v. Doctors Hosp., Inc., 50 F.R.D. 249, 251 (D.D.C. 1970) ("Reports from the insured to its insurance carrier subsequent to the institution of a suit are in furtherance of and for the purpose of aiding in the defense of its case and in the preparation of its attorney for trial. Such reports are part of the attorney's 'work product' and are precluded from discovery."); Kenneson v. Eggert, 170 A.3d 14, 25 n.7 (Conn. App. Ct. 2017) (citations omitted) ("[W]hen an insurer engages an attorney to represent an insured, the resultant attorney-client privilege belongs to the insured. . . . There is, however, 'a common interest among the insured, the attorney and the insurer, and ordinarily the insured's privilege is not waived because of disclosure to the insurer.'"); United Servs. Auto. Ass'n v. Law Off. of Herssein & Herssein, P.A., 233 So. 3d 1224, 1230–31 (Fla. Dist. Ct. App. 2017) (footnote omitted) ("While the insured is the attorney's client when an attorney is hired by an insurance company to represent an insured in a liability case, it is well settled that communications between an insurer and the lawyer hired by the insurer to protect the insured's interests are protected by the attorney-client privilege because the insurer and insured share a common interest in the outcome of the case."); Zurich Am. Ins. Co. v. Circle Centre Mall, LLC, 113 N.E.3d 1220, 1228–30 (Ind. Ct. App. 2018) (upholding work product immunity and the attorney-client privilege common interest doctrine); Kohl's Dep't Stores v. Liberty Mut. Ins. Co., No. BCD-CV-12-13, 2012 Me. Bus. & Consumer LEXIS 44, at *17 (Me. Bus. & Consumer Ct. Oct. 11, 2012) (recognizing the attorney-client privilege's common interest doctrine); 1415, LLC v. N.Y. Marine & Gen. Ins. Co., 121 N.Y.S.3d 118, 120 (App. Div. 2020) (enforcing the attorney-client privilege and, less obviously, work product immunity).

52. *See* Pietro v. Marriott Senior Living Servs., Inc., 810 N.E.2d 217, 226 (Ill. App. Ct. 2004); Ratcliff v. Sprint Mo., Inc., 261 S.W.3d 534, 548 (Mo. Ct. App. 2008).

B. The Role of the Insurance Policy in the Attorney-Client Relationship

1. *The Insured's Consent to Representation by Appointed Defense Counsel*

When considering attorney-client relationships in insurance defense, it is necessary to distinguish between the insurance policy and the defense lawyer's engagement agreement with the insurer. The insurance policy does not determine who the defense lawyer represents, nor does it control the lawyer's professional responsibilities. The policy cannot impose these terms because the defense lawyer is not a party to it; only the insured and the insured are and only they have rights and duties under it. The defense lawyer is a party to the engagement agreement with the insurer, however, and it is this document that governs who the defense lawyer represents, the scope of the representation, and other representation-related details, such as the lawyer's compensation.

Yet, the insurance policy is essential to the attorney-client relationship between the defense lawyer and the insured.[53] An attorney-client relationship is, among other things, a voluntary relationship.[54] The lawyer and the client must both agree to the representation to form an attorney-client relationship.[55] The defense lawyer consents to an attorney-client relationship with the insured when the lawyer agrees with the insurer to represent the insured. But when does the insured consent to representation by the lawyer selected by the insurer?

Courts commonly reason that an insured consents to representation by the defense lawyer retained by the insurer when it purchases a policy that grants the insurance company a duty and right to defend.[56] Were the rule otherwise, an insurer would not be able to fulfill its duty to defend in a case where the insured could not be found, was temporarily unavailable, or was uncooperative.[57] Nor might an insurer be able to satisfy its duty to defend in a case that required swift action to protect the insured's interests.

53. *See* Robert H. Jerry, II & Douglas R. Richmond, Understanding Insurance Law 751 (6th ed. 2018) (stating that the relationship between the insured and the defense lawyer is "affected greatly" by the insurance policy); Barker & Silver, *supra* note 11, § 3.02, at 3-5 (explaining that the insurance policy "bleed[s] into" the defense lawyer's retainer agreement).

54. Wilmington Tr. Co. v. Varan, Nos. 2-20-0211 & 20-0465 cons., 2021 WL 4352741, at *2 (Ill. App. Ct. Sept. 24, 2021); Arabzadegan v. State, 240 S.W.3d 44, 51 (Tex. App. 2007).

55. *Wilmington Tr. Co.*, 2021 WL 4352741, at *2; *Arabzadegan*, 240 S.W.3d at 51.

56. *See, e.g.*, Mora v. Lancet Indem. Risk Retention Grp., Inc., 773 F. App'x 113, 117–18 (4th Cir. 2019) (applying Maryland law); Maple Wood Partners, L.P. v. Indian Harbor Ins. Co., 295 F.R.D. 550, 601 (S.D. Fla. 2013); Kruger-Willis v. Hoffenburg, 393 P.3d 844, 849 (Wash. Ct. App. 2017).

57. *Kruger-Willis*, 393 P.3d at 849; *see also* S.C. Adv. Op. 1904, 2019 WL 5853809, at *1 (S.C. Bar, Ethics Advisory Comm. 2019) [hereinafter S.C. Adv. Op. 1904] ("Attorney may appear for and defend an Insured who cannot be located . . . if Insurance Carrier's insurance contract with the Insured gives it the right to retain counsel to defend claims made against the Insured. Where a person has, by contract, including insurance contract, delegated authority to another to choose counsel, conduct the defense of a claim, and perhaps even settle a matter within certain boundaries, an attorney may reasonably rely upon the instruction of the person's agent, in this situation Insurance Carrier, to appear

An insured's advance consent to representation by a lawyer appointed by the insurer is revocable.[58] For example, an insured may elect to be represented by independent counsel where the lawyer appointed by the insurer has a conflict of interest. Less likely, but still possible, an insured could reject the defense lawyer appointed by the insurer in a case where there is no conflict of interest and pay for its own defense by a lawyer of its choice.

Alternatively, it might be argued that insureds likely do not understand when they purchase a policy that the insurer has the right to defend them, including the right to appoint a lawyer for them.[59] Following this approach, the defense lawyer at the time of her appointment must inform the insured about the nature of the representation and secure the insured's informed consent to it.[60] In most cases, the extent of the disclosure required to obtain the insured's informed consent to the appointed lawyer's representation is modest:

> A short letter clearly stating that the lawyer intends to proceed at the direction of the insurer in accordance with the terms of the insurance contract and what this means to the insured is sufficient. . . . We do not believe extended discussion is required or, indeed, that any oral communication is necessary. As long as the insured is clearly apprised of the limitations on the representation being offered by the insurer and that the lawyer intends to proceed in accordance with the directions of the insurer, the insured has sufficient information to decide whether to accept the defense offered by the insurer or to assume responsibility for his own defense at his own expense. No formal acceptance or written consent is necessary. The insured manifests consent to the limited representation by accepting the defense offered by the insurer after being advised of the terms of the representation being offered.[61]

---

and conduct the defense of the case in the absence of any direction from the missing Insured to the contrary."). In contrast, when asked whether a lawyer hired by an insurer to defend a missing insured could undertake the representation, the North Carolina State Bar stated in a 2010 ethics opinion that "unless allowed by statute, court order, or subsequent case law, a lawyer may not appear in court for a party who has not authorized the representation and with whom the lawyer has not established a client-lawyer relationship." 2010 N.C. Eth. Op. 1, N.C. State Bar, 2010 WL 2020508, at *1 (N.C. State Bar 2010). The North Carolina Bar further opined that this rule applies even if the policy specifies that the insurer is authorized to appoint counsel for the insured and to control settlement. *Id.*

58. *See* Twin City Fire Ins. Co. v. Ben Arnold-Sunbelt Beverage Co. of S.C., 433 F.3d 365, 374 (4th Cir. 2005) (citations omitted) ("Of course, an insured must consent to the counsel assigned by the insurance company. . . . If the insured does not consent to counsel selected by the insurance company, the insured may refuse the defense and pay for its own defense."); Henke v. Iowa Home Mut. Cas. Co., 87 N.W.2d 920, 923 (Iowa 1958) ("Nothing in the policy compels the insured or his representative to accept the attorney selected by the insurer. He may reject such attorney and thus relieve the insurer from the obligation.").

59. *See* Am. Bar Ass'n, Comm. on Ethics & Pro. Resp., Formal Op. 94-403, at 3 (1996) [hereinafter ABA Formal Op. 96-403].

60. *Id.* ("If the lawyer is to proceed with the representation of the insured at the direction of the insurer, the lawyer must make appropriate disclosure sufficient to apprise the insured of the limited nature of his representation as well as the insurer's right to control the defense in accordance with the terms of the insurance contract.").

61. *Id.* at 3–4.

In terms of choosing between the two approaches, the first one—which holds that an insured consents to representation by the lawyer hired by the insurer when it buys a policy that grants the insurer a duty and right to defend—is preferable because it accounts for situations where the insured's interests must be protected, but consent to the representation cannot be obtained. Again, if an insured objects to representation by its insurer-appointed defense lawyer, it can revoke its advance consent and either engage independent counsel at the insurer's expense or litigate on its own, depending on the circumstances.[62] In a case where urgent action was required to protect the insured's interests, the insured will, in the meantime, have received the benefit of the defense it was owed under the policy.

2. *The Insured's Consent to Dual Representation*

Accepting that an insured consents to representation by the defense lawyer appointed by the insurer either by purchasing an insurance policy that grants the insurer a right to defend or by accepting the defense offered by the insurer after the appropriate disclosures by the defense lawyer, the next question is whether the insured also consents to the lawyer's dual representation of both it and the insurer. That is the conclusion of some courts.[63] That is also a reasonable approach, at least where there is no conflict of interest that entitles the insured to independent counsel. Again, the insured's consent must be considered revocable, as where the defense lawyer has a conflict.

In a case where there is no conflict of interest and the insured refuses to consent to dual representation, it is arguable that the insured has thereby breached the contract and breached its duty to cooperate with the insurer.[64] As a practical matter, this situation should rarely present itself. The vast majority of insureds rightly trust the defense lawyers that their insurers hire for them. A defense lawyer should be able to explain dual representation to an insured in a fashion that persuades the insured that the arrangement poses no threat to its defense or to the ultimate resolution of the litigation. For that matter, an insurer has little incentive to get into a dispute with the insured in this context because allowing the defense lawyer to treat the insured as the lawyer's sole client is generally uncontroversial and offers the insurer some advantages, as outlined earlier.

---

62. The defense lawyer appointed by the insurer can and should be expected to explain the scope of her representation to the insured as well as conveying other information necessary for the insured to make informed decisions regarding the representation during their earliest communications about the case. *See* MODEL RULES OF PRO. CONDUCT r. 1.4(b) (AM. BAR ASS'N 2023) (governing client communications).

63. *See, e.g.*, Mora v. Lancet Indem. Risk Retention Grp., Inc., 773 F. App'x 113, 117–18 (4th Cir. 2019) (quoting Fid. & Cas. Co. v. McConnaughey, 179 A.2d 117, 121 (Md. 1962)).

64. *See* BARKER & SILVER, *supra* note 11, § 4.05[1], at 4-25.

3. *The Scope of the Defense Lawyer's Representation*

In addition to evidencing the insured's consent to representation by the defense lawyer hired by the insurer, the insurance policy also affects the scope of the lawyer's representation of the insured. A standard liability insurance policy grants the insurance company the right to defend the insured in litigation seeking covered damages. The insurer has no contractual obligation to appoint a lawyer for an insured for any other purpose.[65] More to the immediate point, the policy grants the insurer no authority or right to appoint a lawyer for the insured for any other purpose. If the insurance company wanted to engage a lawyer to represent the insured in criminal litigation arising out of the occurrence that spawned the lawsuit against the insured that the insurer was defending, for example, it would need the insured's explicit consent to do so.

The scope of the defense lawyer's representation of the insured also depends on the terms of its engagement agreement with the insurer. For example, the engagement agreement will generally limit the scope of the lawyer's representation to defending the insured in the third-party action. Thus, the fact that a lawyer is representing the insured in litigation against it does not mean that the lawyer is representing the insured for all purposes. But here, too, the insurance policy bleeds into the retainer agreement to contractually limit the scope of the lawyer's representation of the insured to the defense of the third-party action.

Scope limitations sometimes lead to controversies involving all parties to the tripartite relationship, as in *Flexi-Van Leasing, Inc. v. Travelers Indemnity Co.*[66] There, a mechanic, Charles Vititoe, was injured when a wheel rim assembly on a semi-trailer chassis owned by Flexi-Van Leasing, Inc. (Flexi-Van) exploded while he was changing a tire. Flexi-Van leased the chassis to the South Atlantic Consolidated Chassis Pool (the Pool).

In addition to owning the chassis, Flexi-Van managed the Pool. In that capacity, it contracted with Interstar North America, Inc. (Interstar) to maintain and repair chassis in the Pool. It was Interstar that hired Vititoe to replace the tire on the Flexi-Van chassis. Under their contract, Interstar agreed to defend and indemnify Flexi-Van and the Pool against lawsuits arising out of Interstar's negligence. Interstar also had the Pool and Flexi-Van named as additional insureds on its policy with Travelers Indemnity Co. (Travelers).

Vititoe sued Flexi-Van for its role in his accident. Flexi-Van tendered its defense to Travelers, which questioned whether it owed coverage, but nonetheless hired lawyer Mark Wall to represent Flexi-Van.[67] Travelers subsequently

65. *See, e.g.*, Red Head Brass, Inc. v. Buckeye Union Ins. Co., 735 N.E.2d 48, 57 (Ohio Ct. App. 1999) (holding that Buckeye Union's policy did not require it to pay for the insured's pursuit of a counterclaim).

66. 837 F. App'x 141 (4th Cir. 2020).

67. *Id.* at 143.

sent Flexi-Van a reservation of rights letter that caused Flexi-Van to doubt whether it had coverage under the Travelers policy. Flexi-Van thus asked Wall to file a third-party complaint against Interstar. Wall informed Flexi-Van he was willing to do so but said that Flexi-Van would have to pay him to bring the third-party action because Travelers would not.[68] Consequently, Flexi-Van accused Wall of having a conflict of interest, fired him, and hired substitute counsel.[69] When Travelers refused to pay for substitute counsel, Flexi-Van sued Travelers in a South Carolina federal court. Flexi-Van sought a declaratory judgment that Travelers owed it a defense and indemnity, and asserted breach of contract and bad faith claims. All Flexi-Van's claims were based on Wall's alleged conflict of interest in failing to file a third-party complaint against Interstar.[70]

The district court awarded Travelers summary judgment. Flexi-Van appealed to the U.S. Court of Appeals for the Fourth Circuit.

On appeal, Flexi-Van's argument that Wall had a conflict of interest based on his failure to file a third-party complaint against Interstar failed on the facts. Wall never refused to sue Interstar; to the contrary, he expressly agreed that he would do so.[71] He simply insisted that Flexi-Van pay him to prosecute its claim against Interstar, inasmuch as Travelers would not because it believed it had no duty to pay for Flexi-Van's third-party claim under its policy and controlling South Carolina law.[72] Furthermore, the *Flexi-Van* court agreed with the district court that recognizing a conflict of interest in these circumstances would cripple an insurer's ability to hire a lawyer to defend its insured "solely within the scope of an insurance policy."[73] The *Flexi-Van* court accordingly affirmed summary judgment for Travelers.

C. Summary

The existence of an attorney-client relationship is a question of fact. That principle is as true in insurance defense as elsewhere. Courts should therefore treat the dual client and sole client models as default rules. When determining who a defense lawyer represents, a court should begin its analysis by studying the engagement agreement between the lawyer and the insurance company. Depending on the case, the court may also need to scrutinize the parties' conduct.

68. *Id.* at 144.
69. *Id.*
70. *Id.*
71. *Id.* at 147.
72. *Id.*
73. *Id.* (internal quotation marks omitted).

Insurers and defense lawyers are free to structure their relationship so that either the lawyer represents both the insurer and the insured or the insured is the lawyer's sole client. Adopting a sole client approach reduces the chances of a conflict of interest but it does not eliminate all conflicts because, as we will see later, a conflict arises where there is a significant risk that a lawyer's representation of a client will be materially limited by the lawyer's responsibilities to a former client, a third person or by the lawyer's personal interests. Lawyers may have conflicts of interest in cases where they have only one client.

Regardless of whether a defense lawyer represents both the insurer and the insured or solely the insured, the scope of the lawyer's representation is limited to defending the lawsuit against the insured.[74] An insurance company lacks the authority or right to appoint a lawyer for the insured for any other purpose.

A defense lawyer must explain to an insured at the outset of a case that the scope of the lawyer's representation is limited to providing a defense. In the overwhelming majority of cases, the insured will have no objection to that limitation and, in fact, will be anticipating nothing else. Nonetheless, the lawyer's communication of the scope limitation is required.[75] If an insured wishes to expand the scope of an insurer-appointed lawyer's representation beyond defending the third-party action and the lawyer agrees to the expansion, the insured must be prepared to pay for the additional services.[76]

III. Conflict of Interest Essentials

A. Applying Insurance Law, Professional Responsibility Law, or Both

With client identity issues framed, basic conflict of interest principles come into focus. Deciding whether a conflict of interest exists requires the application of a standard of conduct as a matter of insurance law, the law of lawyering, or both. As a matter of insurance law, it is sometimes said that there is a conflict of interest between the insurer and the insured when the insurer's interests "would be furthered by providing a less than vigorous defense to the allegations against the insured."[77] At the same time, the insurance policy does not govern the defense lawyer's relationship with either the insured or the insurer, although it bleeds into those relationships. Nor does an insurance policy identify conflicts of interest or explain how they should be resolved.

---

74. As explained in Chapter 4, there occasionally are cases where the defense of the insured requires the insurer to pursue an insured's affirmative claim at the insurer's expense.

75. ABA Formal Op. 96-403, *supra* note 59, at 3.

76. *See generally* MODEL RULES OF PRO. CONDUCT r. 1.4(a)(2) & (b) (AM. BAR ASS'N 2023) (governing the lawyer's duty to communicate with the client about such an arrangement).

77. Mobil Oil Corp. v. Md. Cas. Co., 681 N.E.2d 552, 561 (Ill. App. Ct. 1997).

Instead, insurance law (in some states, such as Alaska and California, a statute[78]) provides the remedy of independent counsel for the insured where a lawyer cannot represent both the insurer and insured because their divergent interests create a conflict of interest for the lawyer under rules of professional conduct.[79] As the *Nede Mgmt., Inc. v. Aspen American Insurance Co.*[80] court stated in connection with California's independent counsel statute, an insured is entitled to independent counsel at the insurance company's expense "when their competing interests create an ethical conflict for the insurer-appointed counsel."[81] The court in *Xtreme Protection Services LLC v. Steadfast Insurance Co.*[82] more subtly noted that the ultimate issue in a case where the insurer faces the loss of the right to control the defense is the defense lawyer's conflict of interest under rules of professional conduct. Specifically, the *Xtreme Protection* court wrote that when the insurer's and insured's interests are misaligned, "ethical issues regarding the insured's representation may arise."[83]

B. Concurrent Conflicts of Interest under the Model Rules of Professional Conduct

Because the essential issue in determining whether a conflict of interest deprives the insurer of defense control and entitles the insured to representation by independent counsel at the insurer's expense is the defense lawyer's conflict of interest under ethics rules, courts look to Rule 1.7(a) of the American Bar Association's Model Rules of Professional Conduct and state analogs to decide if a conflict exists.[84] Model Rule 1.7(a)(2), which encompasses insurance defense representations, provides that a concurrent conflict of interest exists if "there is

78. Alaska Stat. § 21.96.100 (2023–2024); Cal. Civ. Code § 2860 (2022).

79. *See* Golden Eagle Ins. Co. v. Foremost Ins. Co., 25 Cal. Rptr. 2d 242, 257 (Ct. App. 1993) (stating that an insured's right to independent counsel "is not based on insurance law but on the ethical duty of an attorney to avoid representing conflicting interests").

80. 284 Cal. Rptr. 3d 122 (Ct. App. 2021).

81. *Id.* at 130; *see also* Centex Homes v. St. Paul Fire & Marine Ins. Co., 187 Cal. Rptr. 3d 542, 547 (Ct. App. 2015) ("Civil Code section 2860 (Section 2860) and California case law provide Centex, as an insured, with the right to obtain independent counsel paid for by Travelers, as Centex's insurer, whenever their competing interests create an ethical conflict for counsel."); Swanson v. State Farm Gen. Ins. Co., 162 Cal. Rptr. 3d 477, 485 (Ct. App. 2013) (explaining that it is "the ethical bar to dual representation" that entitles an insured to representation by independent counsel).

82. 140 N.E.3d 128 (Ill. App. Ct. 2019).

83. *Id.* at 134–35.

84. *See, e.g.*, Valley Forge Ins. Co. v. Hartford Iron & Metal, Inc., 148 F. Supp. 3d 743, 749–52 (N.D. Ind. 2015) (applying Indiana's version of Rule 1.7); Armstrong Cleaners, Inc. v. Erie Ins. Exch., 364 F. Supp. 2d 797, 807–17 (S.D. Ind. 2005) (applying Indiana's version of Rule 1.7(a)(2)); Franco v. Reinhardt, 539 P.3d 934, 941–42 (Haw. 2023) (finding no conflict under Rule 1.7); Belanger v. Gabriel Chems., Inc., 787 So. 2d 559, 565 (La. Ct. App. 2001) (discussing material limitation conflicts under Louisiana's version of Rule 1.7); State Farm Mut. Auto. Ins. Co. v. Hansen, 357 P.3d 338, 343 (Nev. 2015) (concluding that whether a conflict of interest exists for insurance defense purposes is determined by reference to Rule 1.7).

a significant risk that the representation of one or more clients will be materially limited by the lawyer's responsibilities to another client, a former client or a third person or by a personal interest of the lawyer."[85] The restrictions that Model Rule 1.7(a)(2) imposes on individual lawyers generally apply equally to their law firms because, with some exceptions, lawyers' conflicts of interest are imputed to all other lawyers in the same firm.[86]

It is important to understand that the reference in Model Rule 1.7(a)(2) to "a significant risk" of a material limitation on a lawyer's ability to represent a client should not be read to mean that there is a *potential* conflict of interest in that scenario. Rather, when a lawyer recognizes that there is a significant risk that her representation of a client will be materially limited by her responsibilities to another client, a former client, or a third person, or by her personal interests, she has an *actual* conflict of interest.[87] Any harm or prejudice to the client attributable to the conflict may only be prospective, but the conflict of interest under Model Rule 1.7(a)(2) is real and immediate.

At the same time, the Model Rule 1.7(a)(2) requirement of a significant risk of a material limitation on a lawyer's representation clarifies that the mere potential for, or possibility of, a conflict of interest is no basis for disqualifying a lawyer. Conflict of interest allegations cannot rest on conjecture or speculation. Numerous courts have stressed this point in the insurance defense context.[88]

Simonyan v. Nationwide Insurance Co. of America[89] is a recent case in which a speculative conflict of interest did not merit the appointment of independent counsel. In *Simonyan*, plaintiff Nshan Simonyan was rear-ended by a truck while stopped at an intersection. The impact forced his car into the car in front of him. At the time of the accident, he was insured by Nationwide. Nationwide initially concluded internally that Simonyan was liable for the accident based on a statement he gave.

Simonyan, represented by the law firm of Gabrilov & Brooks, sued the driver of the truck that hit him. The driver of the car that Simonyan struck

---

85. Model Rules of Pro. Conduct r. 1.7(a)(2) (Am. Bar Ass'n 2023).

86. *Id.* r. 1.10(a); *see also Ex parte* Osbon, 888 So. 2d 1236, 1238 (Ala. 2004) (asserting that "Rule 1.10(a) requires a law firm to be treated as a single attorney").

87. Bottoms v. Stapleton, 706 N.W.2d 411, 417 (Iowa 2005).

88. *See, e.g.*, Nat'l Cas. Co. v. Forge Indus. Staffing Inc., 567 F.3d 871, 874 (7th Cir. 2009) (applying Illinois law) ("An actual, not merely potential, conflict of interest is required to trigger the insured's right to conflict counsel."); Dynamic Concepts, Inc. v. Truck Ins. Exch., 71 Cal. Rptr. 3d 882, 887 (Ct. App. 1998) ("A mere possibility of an unspecified conflict does not require independent counsel. The conflict must be significant, not merely theoretical, actual, not merely potential."); Quality Concrete Corp. v. Travelers Prop. Cas. Co. of Am., 43 A.3d 16, 22 (R.I. 2012) (reiterating that the mere potential for a future conflict of interest does not entitle the insured to independent counsel); Allstate Cnty. Mut. Ins. Co. v. Wootton, 494 S.W.3d 825, 837 (Tex. App. 2016) (stating that a potential conflict of interest does not entitle an insured to independent counsel).

89. 293 Cal. Rptr. 3d 555 (Ct. App. 2022).

then sued him. Simonyan asked Nationwide to hire Gavrilov & Brooks as independent counsel to defend him in the second driver's lawsuit. He argued that Nationwide had a conflict of interest because it had prejudged his fault for the accident.[90] Nationwide denied there was a conflict and appointed the law firm of Porter Scott to defend him. Simonyan complained that Porter Scott's appointment did not cure the alleged conflict of interest and further created a new conflict because Nationwide frequently retained Porter Scott, "and the law firm 'would have an incentive to litigate in a way that would cause [Nationwide] to send the firm more work.'"[91]

Nationwide refused to pay for independent counsel and demanded that Simonyan cooperate with both it and Porter Scott. Nationwide also stated that its internal decision that Simonyan bore fault for the collision was not final and that it had a financial interest in zealously defending him.[92] Nationwide later raised Simonyan's premiums and eliminated various policy discounts based on its determination that he was at fault for the collision.

Simonyan sued Nationwide for bad faith and breach of contract. The trial court sustained Nationwide's demurrer and dismissed the case. Simonyan appealed and lost again.

Simonyan argued that a conflict of interest existed because there was a significant risk that Porter Scott's representation of him would be materially limited.[93] He lifted that standard from California Rule of Professional Conduct 1.7(b), which tracks Model Rule 1.7(a)(2).[94] His allegations, however, did not measure up. As a comment to California's Rule 1.7 explains, in deciding whether a conflict exists, "[t]he critical questions are the likelihood that a difference in interests exists or will eventuate and, if it does, whether it will materially interfere with the lawyer's independent professional judgment in considering alternatives or foreclose courses of action that reasonably should be pursued on behalf of each client."[95] Simonyan offered no evidence of such a likelihood.

Simonyan contended there was a conflict because he believed the driver who rear-ended him was at fault for the collision and sued that driver, while Nationwide determined that he was at fault.[96] While Simonyan complained that Nationwide raised his premiums and removed his driving discounts based on this finding, Nationwide was contractually bound to defend and indemnify him regardless of whether it thought he caused the wreck. Indeed, he acknowl-

90. *Id.* at 558.
91. *Id.*
92. *Id.* at 559.
93. *Id.* at 561.
94. *See* Cal. Rules of Pro. Conduct r. 1.7(b) (State Bar of Cal. 2018).
95. *Id.* r. 1.7 cmt. 4.
96. *Simonyan*, 293 Cal. Rptr. 3d at 561.

edged Nationwide had never reserved its rights. Thus, Nationwide's interest in the case was to defeat his alleged liability and minimize any damages.[97] Simonyan's suggestion that Porter Scott would act contrary to his interests because Nationwide raised his premiums based on its assessment of his fault was "no more than a mere possibility."[98]

Hanging on by a thread, Simonyan argued that his duty to cooperate animated the conflict. He posited a scenario where a Porter Scott lawyer would "prepare him to testify one way based on Nationwide's belief that he was at fault," thereby forcing him to choose between agreeing with Nationwide that the accident was his fault or testifying truthfully and losing his lawyer for failing to cooperate in his defense.[99] As the *Simonyan* court observed, however, "[a]lleging 'anticipated circumstances' that 'have not occurred yet in the underlying litigation' is insufficient to state a claim that independent counsel is required."[100] In other words, a speculative or potential future conflict of interest was not sufficient to require Porter Scott's replacement by independent counsel.

C. Consent to a Conflict of Interest

Under Model Rule 1.7(b), a lawyer may represent a client despite a concurrent conflict of interest if (1) the lawyer reasonably believes that she will be able to provide competent and diligent representation to each affected client; (2) the representation is not prohibited by law; (3) the representation does not involve the assertion of a claim by one client against another client represented by the lawyer in the same litigation or other proceeding before a tribunal; and (4) each affected client gives informed consent, confirmed in writing.[101] In most cases, including insurance defense representations, the first and fourth requirements for consent are critical.

With respect to Model Rule 1.7(b)(1), whether lawyers reasonably believe that they can competently and diligently represent each affected client is measured objectively.[102] Lawyers' subjective, good faith beliefs that they can fulfill their professional obligations to affected clients despite competing interests

97. *Id.*

98. *Id.* at 562.

99. *Id.* (internal quotation marks omitted).

100. *Id.* (quoting Centex Homes v. St. Paul Fire & Marine Ins. Co., 187 Cal. Rptr. 3d 542, 548 (Ct. App. 2015)).

101. Model Rules of Pro. Conduct r. 1.7(b) (Am. Bar Ass'n 2023).

102. Federico v. Lincoln Military Hous., LLC, No. 2:12cv80, 2014 WL 12613388, at *2 (E.D. Va. May 23, 2014); People v. Mason, 938 P.2d 133, 136 (Colo. 1997); *In re* Stein, 177 P.3d 513, 519 (N.M. 2008); *In re* Anonymous Member of the S.C. Bar, 432 S.E.2d 467, 468 (S.C. 1993); Ill. Adv. Op. 09-02, 2009 WL 8559340, at *3 (Ill. State Bar Ass'n 2009).

or obligations is therefore immaterial.[103] If the lawyer cannot clear this initial hurdle, client consent is impossible; indeed, the lawyer cannot even seek the client's consent.[104] As for Model Rule 1.7(b)(4), "informed consent" describes a person's agreement "to a proposed course of conduct after the lawyer has communicated adequate information and explanation about the material risks of and reasonably available alternatives to the proposed course of conduct."[105] The disclosures and explanation required to achieve the client's informed consent necessarily depend on the nature of the conflict of interest and the nature of the risks involved in the representation.[106]

Courts recognize that insureds may consent to defense lawyers' conflicts of interest.[107] To obtain the insured's consent, the lawyer must comply with the jurisdiction's equivalent of Model Rule 1.7(b).

Interestingly, the court in *Starr Indemnity & Liability Insurance Co.*[108] asserted that the insurer has an independent duty to obtain a waiver of the right to independent counsel in the face of a conflict of interest.[109] The court reasoned:

> [T]he insured at the time a conflict arises will be in the confusing position, for one unversed in the law, with trying to understand a.) what it actually means to have an actual conflict with the insurer, b.) how they may not have actually received advice from the shared attorney if such advice conflicted with the interests of the insurer, c.) what it means to have an attorney who is not representing the insurer in the context of settlement negotiations, discovery and trial, and d.) how an independent attorney's fees and expenses will be paid by the insurer while the attorney's loyalty is only to the insured. This complex yet quite substantive—possibly dispositive—set of considerations does not lend itself to written notice or explication from the very attorney who has the actual conflict.[110]

Accordingly, if an insurer is to fulfill its duty to adequately protect its insured's interests, it must obtain the insured's explicit waiver to its right to independent counsel where a conflict of interest exists before dual representation by a defense lawyer may proceed.[111]

103. *In re Stein*, 177 P.3d at 519.
104. Carnegie Cos. v. Summit Props., Inc., 918 N.E.2d 1052, 1067 (Ohio Ct. App. 2009).
105. Model Rules of Pro. Conduct r. 1.0(e) (Am. Bar Ass'n 2023).
106. *Id.* r. 1.7 cmt. 18.
107. *See, e.g.*, Fulton v. Woodford, 545 P.2d 979, 982 (Ariz. Ct. App. 1976); Rainey v. Ind. Ins. Co., No. 1-15-0862, 2016 WL 2841285, at *7 (Ill. App. Ct. May 11, 2016); Country Mut. Ins. Co. v. Olsak, 908 N.E.2d 1091, 1099 (Ill. App. Ct. 2009); *In re* Sassin, 511 S.W.3d 121, 126 (Tex. App. 2014).
108. 379 F. Supp. 3d 1103 (D. Nev. 2019).
109. *Id.* at 1108.
110. *Id.* (citing Leo P. Martinez, *Coverage Advice: The Missing Piece of the* Cumis *Puzzle*, 43:4/44:1 Tort Trial & Ins. Prac. L.J. 63 (2008)).
111. *Id.* at 1109.

The *Starr Indemnity* court did note that a defense lawyer has a duty under Rule 1.7 to obtain the insured's consent to a conflict.[112] But the court figured "that whatever obligation the attorney in a dual representation case would have as to obtaining a waiver is separate and distinct from the insurer's obligation to obtain a waiver."[113] The court reached this conclusion because the insurer's obligation to obtain a waiver flows from its contractual duty to defend while the lawyer's obligation is a matter of legal ethics.[114] "Thus, the nature of the waiver in terms of what is being knowingly relinquished [by the insured] is different for the attorney versus the insurer."[115]

The *Starr Indemnity* court's reliance on insurance law to impose a duty on the insurer and its choice to separate the insurer's duty to obtain a waiver from the defense lawyer's ethical duty to obtain the insured's consent to the conflict was unremarkable.[116] It is certainly possible to conceive of such an obligation as an aspect of the insurer's right or duty to defend the insured or perhaps as an aspect of the insurer's duty of good faith and fair dealing. At the same time, the court's reasoning that imposing a separate duty on the insurer is necessary because the defense lawyer is not well-suited to explain matters to the insured was shaky. The information the court said an insured would need to consent to dual representation despite a conflict of interest is among that which a defense lawyer would be expected to share with an insured to obtain informed consent to the conflict. Courts generally trust lawyers to make appropriate disclosures to obtain clients' informed consent to conflicts, so why, in insurance defense, does the information necessary to achieve the insured's consent "not lend itself" to "explication from the very attorney who has the actual conflict"? In fact, the information does so lend itself, and the *Starr Indemnity* court's contrary conclusion was wrong.

If the insurer does not secure the insured's explicit waiver of the right to independent counsel but the insurer-appointed defense lawyer obtains the insured's informed consent to the lawyer's continued representation despite the conflict of interest, it should not matter in any later dispute between the insurer and the insured that the insurer's and the lawyer's waiver or consent obligations have different sources. The insured's informed consent to the defense lawyer's representation should defeat any claim that the insured was damaged by the insurer's failure to obtain an explicit waiver of the insured's right to independent counsel or that the insurer's failure proximately caused the insured any

112. *Id.* at 1108 n.1.
113. *Id.*
114. *Id.*
115. *Id.*
116. *But see* Tower Ins. Co. of N.Y. v. Sanita Constr. Co., 11 N.Y.S.3d 122, 123 (App. Div. 2015) (stating that "the right to independent counsel does not establish an affirmative duty on [the insurer's] part to advise its insured of that right").

harm. There certainly can be no harm to the insured where the insurer fails to inform the insured of its right to independent counsel but allows the insured to be represented by counsel of its choice at the insurer's expense.[117]

IV. Recurring Conflict of Interest Scenarios

Although conflicts of interest arise in various circumstances, conflicts are most often alleged to arise in cases where (1) the insurer is defending under a reservation of rights; (2) the plaintiff's claimed damages exceed the liability limits of the insured's policy; (3) the plaintiff seeks punitive damages; (4) the defense lawyer represents multiple insureds; (5) the insured shares confidential information with defense counsel that it does want the lawyer to share with the insurer, such as information affecting coverage; (6) the insurer and insured disagree over litigation strategy; (7) the insurer declines to fund the pursuit of an insured's affirmative claim for relief; and (8) either the defense lawyer or other lawyers in her law firm represent the insurer in unrelated coverage matters. Whether there is, in fact, a conflict of interest that entitles the insured to independent counsel must be determined on a case-by-case basis.

A. A Defense under a Reservation of Rights

An insurer that defends an insured under a reservation of rights generally retains the right to control the insured's defense.[118] In theory, however, an insurer's reservation of rights presents a conflict of interest because the insurer may be more concerned with developing facts showing the absence of coverage than facts defeating liability.[119] Yet, an insurer's interest in defeating coverage does not alone create a conflict of interest.[120] It is therefore necessary to strike some sort of balance when weighing insurers' and insureds' competing rights in cases where coverage is in doubt.

---

117. *See, e.g.*, Weinstein & Riley PS v. Westport Ins. Corp., 484 F. App'x 121, 123 (9th Cir. 2012) (finding that the insurer's failure to inform the insureds of their right to independent counsel did not harm them because they were always represented by counsel of their choice); Ledcor Indus. (USA), Inc. v. Mut. of Enumclaw Ins. Co., 206 P.3d 1255, 1261 (Wash. Ct. App. 2009) (finding no bad faith liability where the insured was represented by competent counsel who aggressively defended its interests, there was no evidence that the insured wanted the insurer to take over its defense, and the insurer stood ready to pay its share of defense costs).

118. U.S. Underwriters Ins. Co. v. Kenfa Madison, LLC, No. 20-CV-2761 (NGG) (LB), 2023 WL 2710879, at *4 (E.D.N.Y. Mar. 30, 2023) (applying New York law); Great Am. Assur. Co. v. PCR Venture of Phoenix LLC, 161 F. Supp. 3d 778, 782–83 (D. Ariz. 2015) (applying Arizona law); Auto-Owners Ins. Co. v. Bolt Factory Lofts Owners Ass'n, Inc., 487 P.3d 276, 284 (Colo. 2021).

119. State *ex rel.* Rimco, Inc. v. Dowd, 858 S.W.2d 307, 308 (Mo. Ct. App. 1993).

120. Flexi-Van Leasing, Inc. v. Travelers Indem. Co., 837 F. App'x 141, 147 (4th Cir. 2020); Nat'l Cas. Co. v. Forge Indus. Staffing, Inc., 567 F.3d 871, 874 (7th Cir. 2009).

Under the majority approach, courts reason that not every reservation of rights creates a conflict of interest requiring the insurer to provide the insured with independent counsel.[121] Rather, an insurer must provide the insured with independent counsel only when the outcome of a coverage issue can be affected by the defense of the third-party action.[122] Phrased another way, a conflict of interest exists when the insurance company defends under a reservation of rights and the facts on which the insured's liability will be adjudicated are the same facts on which coverage depends.[123]

So, in what circumstances might the conduct of the defense be able to affect coverage? One example is a case in which the insurer is defending under a reservation of rights because the insured's alleged conduct may have been intentional.[124] In that scenario, if the insured can be shown to have intentionally injured the plaintiff rather than having acted negligently, there will have been no "occurrence" within the meaning of the policy's insuring agreement and the policy's exclusion for expected or intended injury will additionally foreclose coverage. To be sure, the insurer and the insured share a common interest in defeating the plaintiff's claims, but if the insured is found to be liable, their interests diverge in establishing the basis for liability. Accordingly, the insured is owed a defense by independent counsel.[125]

A defense lawyer also may be able to affect coverage in a mixed action, that is, a case in which the plaintiff pleads multiple claims against the insured

121. Exec. Risk Indem. Inc. v. Icon Title Agency, LLC, 739 F. Supp. 2d 446, 450 (S.D.N.Y. 2010) (applying New York law); Centex Homes v. St. Paul Fire & Marine Ins. Co., 187 Cal. Rptr. 3d 542, 548 (Ct. App. 2015); Fed. Ins. Co. v. MBL, Inc., 160 Cal. Rptr. 3d 910, 920 (Ct. App. 2013); Findlay v. Chi. Title Ins. Co., 215 N.E.3d 1006, 1018 (Ill. App. Ct. 2022); State Farm Mut. Auto. Ins. Co. v. Hansen, 357 P.3d 338, 343 (Nev. 2015).

122. G&J Heavy Haul, Inc. v. Williamsburg Nat'l Ins. Co., No. 21-55297, 2021 WL 5564627, at *1 (9th Cir. Nov. 15, 2021) (applying California law); Downhole Navigator, L.L.C. v. Nautilus Ins. Co., 686 F.3d 325, 328–29 (5th Cir. 2012) (applying Texas law); *Centex Homes*, 187 Cal. Rptr. 3d at 548; *Fed. Ins. Co.*, 160 Cal. Rptr. 3d at 920; Nisson v. Am. Home Assur. Co., 917 P.2d 488, 490 (Okla. Ct. App. 1996); *see also* Restatement of the L. of Liab. Ins. § 16 (Am. L. Inst. 2019) ("When an insurer with the duty to defend provides the insured with notice of a ground for contesting coverage . . . and there are facts at issue that are common to the legal action for which the defense is due and to the coverage dispute, such that the action could be defended in a manner that would benefit the insurer at the expense of the insured, the insurer must provide an independent defense of the action.").

123. Graper v. Mid-Continent Cas. Co., 756 F.3d 388, 392 (5th Cir. 2014); Allstate Cnty. Mut. Ins. Co. v. Wootton, 494 S.W.3d 825, 837 (Tex. App. 2016).

124. Great Am. Ins. Co. v. Houlihan Lawrence, Inc., 449 F. Supp. 3d 354, 373–74 (S.D.N.Y. 2020) (applying New York law); Select Comfort Corp. v. Arrowood Indem. Co., No. 13-2975 (JNE/FLN), 2014 WL 4232334, at *6–7 (D. Minn. Aug. 26, 2014) (applying Minnesota law); Auto-Owners Ins. Co. v. Lake Erie Land Co., No. 2:12-CV-184 JD, 2013 WL 4401834, at *5–7 (N.D. Ind. Aug. 13, 2013); Utica Mut. Ins. Co. v. David Agency Ins., Inc., 327 F. Supp. 2d 922, 928 (N.D. Ill. 2004) (applying Illinois law); Long v. Century Indem. Co., 78 Cal. Rptr. 3d 483, 491 (Ct. App. 1998); Satterwhite v. Stolz, 442 P.2d 810, 813–14 (N.M. Ct. App. 1968); State Farm Fire & Cas. Co. v. Mabry, 497 S.E.2d 844, 847 (Va. 1998).

125. *Great Am. Ins. Co.*, 449 F. Supp. 3d at 373–74; *Select Comfort Corp.*, 2014 WL 4232334, at *6–7; *Lake Erie Land Co.*, 2013 WL 4401834, at *5–7.

but only some are covered.[126] The archetypal mixed action creating a conflict of interest is one where some causes of action allege negligence and others allege intentional torts.[127] The concern there is that a defense lawyer could through discovery steer the case out of coverage, successfully move for summary judgment on covered claims and leave the insured exposed to liability on uncovered causes of action, or submit special interrogatories or a special verdict form to enable the jury to allocate damages between covered and uncovered claims. The Restatement of the Law of Liability Insurance furnishes an example of a mixed action that creates a conflict of interest:

> Insured is sued for bodily injury sustained during a fight in a bar. The complaint alleges two counts. In the first count, the plaintiff alleges that Insured intentionally assaulted the plaintiff. In the second count, the plaintiff alleges that Insured negligently struck the plaintiff on the head. The insurer reserves the right to contest coverage for the suit based on the "expected or intended" exclusion in the policy. The insurer must provide an independent defense because the intent of the insured is a fact that may affect liability and damages in the suit against the insured as well as the potential coverage contest, thereby creating a risk that the defense of the suit may be handled in a manner that increases the likelihood that the insurer will be able to avoid coverage through the application of the intentional-harm exclusion.[128]

Conversely, there is no conflict of interest, and an insurer consequently has no duty to provide independent counsel for the insured, when the manner in which the third-party action is defended cannot affect coverage.[129] Lawyers must keep in mind, though, that the essential conflict of interest inquiry in all cases is not whether they *intend* their actions to affect coverage but whether they *could* influence coverage by their conduct or decisions.[130]

---

126. *See* Gonzalez v. Fire Ins. Exch., 184 Cal. Rptr. 3d 394, 403 (Ct. App. 2015) ("When a complaint states multiple claims, some of which are potentially covered by the insurance policy and some of which are not, it is a mixed action."); Fire Ins. Exch. v. Weitzel, 371 P.3d 457, 461 (Mont. 2016) ("If a complaint states multiple claims, some of which are covered by the insurance policy and some of which are not, it is a mixed action.").

127. Roussos v. Allstate Ins. Co., 655 A.2d 40, 44 (Md. Ct. Spec. App. 1995); *see, e.g.*, Aquino v. State Farm Ins. Cos., 793 A.2d 824, 830 (N.J. Super. Ct. App. Div. 2002); State Farm Mut. Auto. Ins. Co. v. Van Dyke, 668 N.Y.S.2d 821, 822–23 (App. Div. 1998).

128. Restatement of the L. of Liab. Ins. § 16 cmt. a, illus. 2 (Am. L. Inst. 2019).

129. *See, e.g.*, Sovereign Gen. Servs., Inc. v. Nat'l Cas. Co., 359 F. App'x 705, 707 (9th Cir. 2009) (seeing no conflict of interest where the defense firm could not control the determination of whether Sovereign was acting as a managing general agent for Lloyd's underwriters, which implicated an exclusion in the National Casualty policy); Fed. Ins. Co. v. MBL, Inc., 160 Cal. Rptr. 3d 910, 922 (Ct. App. 2013) (agreeing with the insurer that the insured was not entitled to independent counsel because the applicability of the insurer's absolute pollution exclusion would not be litigated in the underlying actions and defense counsel could not influence the outcome of this coverage issue, which was strictly a matter of contract interpretation).

130. *See* Gafcon, Inc. v. Ponsor & Assocs., 120 Cal. Rptr. 2d 392, 418–19 (Ct. App. 2002).

Peleus Insurance Co. v. Atlantic State Development Corp.[131] is instructive. In *Peleus*, Atlantic State Development Corp. (Atlantic) was the general contractor for a construction project in New York City. Atlantic hired Taconic Builders, Inc. (Taconic) as a subcontractor. Michael Winters, a Taconic employee, was injured when he fell at the construction site. He sued Atlantic and the property owner, Lauran Walk, for negligently causing his fall.

Atlantic notified its insurer, Peleus Insurance Co. (Peleus), of Winters's lawsuit. Peleus agreed to defend Atlantic but reserved its rights based on the "Contractors Condition Endorsement" to its policy.[132] The endorsement provided that for coverage to apply, any contractor hired by Atlantic must have executed an agreement to defend and indemnify Atlantic for all losses arising out of the contractor's work. The endorsement also mandated that Atlantic's agreements with its contractors require the contractors to name Atlantic as an additional insured on their commercial general liability (CGL) policies. Atlantic did not sign such an agreement with Taconic.[133] When Atlantic's defense lawyer told Peleus that Atlantic lacked the requisite contract with Taconic, Peleus denied coverage for Winters's lawsuit. Peleus then filed a declaratory judgment action in the Southern District of New York.

When Peleus moved for summary judgment, Atlantic resisted in part on the basis that Peleus was estopped from denying coverage for Winters's lawsuit. To supply the prejudice necessary for estoppel, Atlantic asserted that Peleus prejudiced it by failing to advise it of its right to independent counsel.[134] Atlantic contended that it had a right to independent counsel because Peleus's reservation of rights created a conflict of interest.[135] The court disagreed.

Peleus's reservation of rights rested on Atlantic's failure to comply with the Contractor Conditions Endorsement, which was unrelated to Atlantic's defense in Winters's lawsuit. Moreover, when Peleus appointed defense counsel for Atlantic, Atlantic had already failed to meet the Contractor Conditions Endorsement's requirements.[136] The defense lawyers hired by Peleus "could have done nothing to craft a liability defense to avoid coverage under these circumstances."[137] Thus, there was no conflict of interest that might have entitled Atlantic to independent counsel. In the end, the court awarded Peleus summary judgment.

---

131. 587 F. Supp. 3d 7 (S.D.N.Y. 2022).
132. *Id.* at 14.
133. *Id.*
134. *Id.* at 23.
135. *Id.*
136. *Id.*
137. *Id.*

Partain v. Mid-Continent Specialty Insurance Services, Inc.[138] is another instructive case. *Partain* also illustrates the principle that speculative or conjectural conflicts of interest do not entitle an insured to representation by independent counsel.

Partain arose out of a copyright infringement lawsuit by an architectural firm against two homebuilders known collectively as Hallmark. Hallmark tendered the defense of the lawsuit to Mid-Continent and asked that Mid-Continent appoint the law firm of Adair & Myers to defend it. Mid-Continent agreed to defend the lawsuit under a reservation of rights but appointed the law firm of Cooper & Scully as defense counsel. This was not acceptable to Hallmark, which claimed that Mid-Continent and Cooper & Scully had a conflict of interest that entitled it to a defense by counsel of its choice because Mid-Continent had reserved its rights in part based on Hallmark's late notice of the lawsuit. The court was not convinced.

Under Texas law, the insurer must prove that it was prejudiced by the insured's late notice.[139] Hallmark argued that a bad result in the underlying case could be blamed on their late notice of the suit to Mid-Continent. Hallmark contended that because the facts to be developed and presented in the underlying litigation would control whether they received a favorable result, those facts would also determine whether Mid-Continent was prejudiced by Hallmark's late notice of the suit.[140]

From the court's perspective, Hallmark was basically arguing that "Mid-Continent's lawyers would have an incentive to throw the entire case so that they could later argue that [Hallmark] late tender of the claim prevented them providing an effective defense."[141] But Hallmark offered no support for the conclusion that defense counsel would take such a risk, nor were there any "matching 'facts'" to be adjudicated in both the underlying case and the coverage dispute.[142] Although some of the same facts might be at issue in both cases, Texas law requires that for there to be a conflict of interest that warrants independent counsel for the insured, the facts to be actually adjudicated in the liability case must be the same facts on which coverage depends.[143] Because that was not the situation at hand, Mid-Continent's late notice defense did not create a disqualifying conflict of interest.[144]

138. 838 F. Supp. 2d 547 (S.D. Tex. 2012).
139. *Id.* at 571 (citing Members Ins. Co. v. Branscum, 803 S.W.2d 462, 467 (Tex. App. 1991)).
140. *Id.*
141. *Id.*
142. *Id.*
143. *Id.* (referring to N. Cnty. Mut. Ins. Co. v. Davalos, 140 S.W.3d 685, 689 (Tex. 2004)).
144. *Id.*

In conclusion, the majority rule provides that no conflict of interest necessarily exists in a reservation of rights defense.[145] An insurer defending under a reservation of rights retains the right to control the insured's defense.[146] The same rules apply where the insurer defends under a nonwaiver agreement. A few courts hold that an insurer's reservation of rights does create a conflict of interest that entitles the insured to independent counsel,[147] but the minority approach is unsupportable for two reasons. First, as explained in Chapter 2, an insurer defending under a reservation of rights must still defend the insured reasonably, responsibly, and in good faith. Indeed, the insurer must defend the insured just as zealously as it would if it had not reserved its rights. If the insurer does not do so, it risks liability for breaching its duty to defend. The insured is thus adequately protected against the risk that the insurer will defend half-heartedly based on the possible lack of coverage. Second, defense lawyers hired by insurers are called upon daily to handle cases in which the insured's and insurer's interests do not fully coincide. The defense bar has consistently shown the ability to zealously defend insureds (their clients) in those cases. Nearly all defense lawyers capably defend the insureds they represent without regard for insurers' coverage positions. Nevertheless, if the lawyer can affect coverage through the litigation of the third-party action, the insured is owed a defense by independent counsel at the insurer's expense.[148]

145. Graper v. Mid-Continent Cas. Co., 756 F.3d 388, 392 (5th Cir. 2014) (applying Texas law); Downhole Navigator, L.L.C., 686 F.3d at 328–31 (applying Texas law); Twin City Fire Ins. Co. v. Ben Arnold-Sunbelt Beverage Co. of S.C., LP, 433 F.3d 365, 366, 372 (4th Cir. 2005) (discussing South Carolina law and collecting cases); Tyson v. Equity Title & Escrow Co. of Memphis, LLC, 282 F. Supp. 2d 829, 831–32 (W.D. Tenn. 2003) (applying Tennessee law); MetLife Capital Corp. v. Water Quality Ins. Synd., 100 F. Supp. 2d 90, 94 (D.P.R. 2000); Bank of Am., N.A. v. Super. Ct., 151 Cal. Rptr. 3d 526, 537 (Ct. App. 2013); Delmonte v. State Farm Fire & Cas. Co., 975 P.2d 1159, 1174 (Haw. 1999); Mut. Serv. Cas. Ins. Co. v. Luetmer, 474 N.W.2d 365, 368–69 (Minn. Ct. App. 1991); State Farm Mut. Auto. Ins. Co. v. Hansen, 357 P.3d 338, 342–43 (Nev. 2015); Twp. of Readington v. Gen. Star Ins. Co., 2006 WL 551404, at *4 (N.J. Super. Ct. App. Div. Mar. 3, 2006); Nisson v. Am. Home Assur. Co., 917 P.2d 488, 490 (Okla. Ct. App. 1996); Eckman v. Erie Ins. Exch., 21 A.3d 1203, 1208–09 (Pa. Super. Ct. 2011); Unauthorized Prac. of Law Comm. v. Am. Home Assur. Co., 261 S.W.3d 24, 40 (Tex. 2008); Johnson v. Cont'l Cas. Co., 788 P.2d 598, 600 (Wash. Ct. App. 1990).

146. Auto-Owners Ins. Co. v. Bolt Factory Lofts Owners Ass'n, Inc., 487 P.3d 276, 282 (Colo. 2021).

147. Maister Assocs. v. State Farm Fire & Cas. Co., 350 F. App'x 978, 979 (5th Cir. 2009) (applying Louisiana law); Hartford Underwriters Ins. Co. v. Found. Health Servs., Inc., 524 F.3d 588, 592–93 (5th Cir. 2008) (applying Mississippi law); Am. Nat'l Prop. & Cas. Co. v. Est. of Farese, 530 F. Supp. 3d 655, 674 (S.D. Miss. 2021) (stating that when an insurer defends under a reservation of rights there is built-in conflict of interest); Hartford Cas. Ins. Co. v. A & M Assocs., Ltd., 200 F. Supp. 2d 84, 89–90 (D.R.I. 2002) (applying Rhode Island law for conflict of interest purposes); Great Divide Ins. Co. v. Carpenter *ex rel.* Reed, 79 P.3d 599, 604 (Alaska 2003); Hackman v. W. Agric. Ins. Co., No. 104,786, 2012 WL 1524060, at *14 (Kan. Ct. App. Apr. 27, 2012); Federated Dep't Stores, Inc. v. Twin City Fire Ins. Co., 807 N.Y.S.2d 62, 66 n.1 (App. Div. 2006); *see also Twin City*, 433 F.3d at 370–71 (collecting cases holding that a reservation of rights creates conflict of interest entitling insured to independent counsel).

148. Great W. Cas. Co. v. Dekeyser Express, Inc., 475 F. Supp. 2d 772, 778–80 (C.D. Ill. 2006) (applying Illinois law); Am. Fam. Mut. Ins. Co. v. W.H. McNaughton Builders, Inc., 843 N.E.2d 492,

B. The Potential for Excess Liability

Cases in which potential damages exceed the liability limits of the insured's policy are sometimes said to create conflicts of interest. A conflict allegedly arises when a plaintiff offers to settle within policy limits. As soon as a policy limits settlement offer is made, the reasoning goes, the insured's and insurer's interests diverge. The insured wants the insurer to settle to avoid possible excess liability, but settlement is not necessarily in the insurer's best interests.[149] By going to trial, the insurer may escape liability altogether, or obtain a judgment lower than the plaintiff's settlement offer. The insurer might therefore be tempted to gamble with the insured's money. Precisely to avoid this problem, however, insurance law obligates insurers to make reasonable settlement decisions as an aspect of their implied duty of good faith and fair dealing.[150] And, because insurance law addresses this adversity of interests through the duty to make reasonable settlement decisions, there normally is no conflict of interest that requires independent counsel for the insured.[151] Certainly, no conflict of interest exists where the insurer timely offers its policy limits in settlement or, in an appropriate case, interpleads its policy limits to achieve a settlement.[152]

Allstate Insurance Co. v. Campbell[153] is a leading case upholding the majority rule. In *Campbell*, Maryland's highest court concluded that potential excess liability alone does not create a conflict of interest that requires the insurer to surrender control of the defense and pay for the insured's representation by independent counsel.[154] The court acknowledged the adversity between the insurer and the insured in an excess liability scenario, but observed that the insured's and insurer's interests "are in no way adverse to the extent that exists where coverage is an issue."[155] The court concluded that any conflict of interest

498 (Ill. App. Ct. 2006); Roussos v. Allstate Ins. Co., 655 A.2d 40, 44 (Md. Ct. Spec. App.1995); *Nisson*, 917 P.2d at 490.

149. Myers v. Ambassador Ins. Co., 508 A.2d 689, 691 (Vt. 1986).

150. *See* State Farm Mut. Auto. Ins. Co. v. Mendoza, No. CIV-02-1141-PHX-ROS, 2006 WL 44376, at *9 (D. Ariz. Jan. 5, 2006) (citation omitted) ("This conflict of interest is remedied by requiring the insurance company to act as if there were no insurance limits when evaluating a settlement proposal. . . . If the company breaches its duty, it will be liable for the full amount of any subsequent judgment . . . against the insured.").

151. Restatement of the L. of Liab. Ins. § 16 cmt. c (Am. L. Inst. 2019).

152. *See* Lehto v. Allstate Ins. Co., 36 Cal. Rptr. 2d 814, 820 (Ct. App. 1994) (involving an interpleader action by the insurer and stating that "[w]here, as here, the insurer early on decides to offer the policy limits in settlement of its insureds' claims, no conflict of interest arises"); Bar Plan Mut. Ins. Co. v. Chesterfield Mgmt. Assocs., 407 S.W.3d 621, 631–32 (Mo. Ct. App. 2013) ("There was no bad faith where the insurer offered to settle for the full policy limits for an unconditional release of all claims, and it is difficult to see how offering to settle for the policy limits would constitute the intentional disregard of the plaintiff's financial interests in the hope of escaping full responsibility under the policy [as required for bad faith liability in Missouri].").

153. 639 A.2d 652 (Md. 1994).

154. *Id.* at 659.

155. *Id.*

was mitigated by the insured's ability to pursue a bad faith claim and recover the amount of any excess judgment should the insurer unreasonably reject a policy limits settlement offer. Absent a separate conflict of interest that necessitates independent counsel for the insured, the insurer retains the right to control the defense of a potential excess verdict case.[156]

Campbell is a sound decision.[157] An insurer must competently defend a potential excess verdict case to minimize its potential indemnity obligation up to the policy limits, and to avoid bad faith liability. As noted earlier, the latter factor provides special incentive. Again, the prospect of an excess verdict, standing alone, does not constitute a conflict of interest that deprives an insurer of the right to control the defense.[158]

New York Marine and General Insurance Co. v. Lafarge North America, Inc.[159] is a more recent case enforcing the majority rule. The insured in that case, Lafarge North America, Inc. (Lafarge), operated a barge terminal near New Orleans. Another company's barge that was moored at Lafarge's terminal during Hurricane Katrina broke free of its moorings and smashed through a levee, potentially causing the disastrous flooding in New Orleans' Lower Ninth Ward. As news accounts about the barge's possible role in the flooding proliferated, Lafarge recognized that its potential liability threatened the company's existence. Lafarge thus retained three law firms to represent it in connection with the levee breach: Goodwin Procter LLP (Goodwin Procter), Holland & Knight LLP (H&K), and Chaffe McCall LLP (Chaffe McCall). Lafarge also notified its primary liability insurer, New York Marine and General Insurance Co. (NYMAGIC), about the possibility of claims arising out of the levee breach potentially attributable to the barge.

NYMAGIC wanted to appoint the law firm of Sutterfield & Webb or one of its other New Orleans panel firms to represent Lafarge. Lafarge refused to accept any of NYMAGIC's proposed firms and continued with its representation by its three chosen firms, although it did tell Goodwin Procter to cooperate with Sutterfield & Webb when NYMAGIC nonetheless appointed Sutterfield & Webb as defense counsel.[160]

---

156. *Id.* at 659–60.

157. *See also* Valdez v. Ill. Cas. Co., No. 1-20-1121, 2022 WL 3026378, at *6 (Ill. App. Ct. Aug. 1, 2022) (observing that an insured's exposure to excess liability does not simultaneously establish that the insurer has an incentive to defend the insured less than vigorously, which is required for a conflict of interest).

158. Nede Mgmt., Inc. v. Aspen Am. Ins. Co., 284 Cal. Rptr. 3d 122, 130 (Ct. App. 2021) (quoting Cal. Civ. Code § 2860(b)); Joseph T. Ryerson & Son, Inc. v. Travelers Indem. Co. of Am., 165 N.E.3d 439, 460 (Ill. App. Ct. 2020); OneBeacon Am. Ins. Co. v. Celanese Corp., 84 N.E.3d 867, 874, 876 (Mass. App. Ct. 2017).

159. 599 F.3d 102 (2d Cir. 2010).

160. *Id.* at 109.

Subsequently, Lafarge was sued in four class actions related to its alleged role in the levee breach. In addition, NYMAGIC, as both Lafarge's primary insurer and one of its excess insurers, and two of Lafarge's other excess insurers filed declaratory judgment actions against Lafarge on various coverage issues. One of the issues to be decided when those cases reached the Second Circuit was responsibility for the payment of Goodwin Procter's, H&K's, and Chaffe McCall's legal fees, which, in the aggregate, exceeded $10 million.

Lafarge contended that NYMAGIC was not entitled to appoint defense counsel for it and therefore was required to pay the fees of the firms it selected "because a conflict of interest [was] inherent" in its relationship with NYMAGIC.[161] Lafarge contended that because the billions of dollars potentially at stake in the barge litigation dwarfed the combined liability limits of NYMAGIC's primary and excess policies (approximately $30 million), controlling New York law permitted Lafarge to retain its own counsel and bill NYMAGIC for those firms' fees under NYMAGIC's primary policy.[162] The *New York Marine* court rejected this argument because Lafarge's purported conflict of interest with NYMAGIC was "not of the type recognized to confer an independent right on the insured to retain counsel at the insurer's expense."[163]

Rather than alleging a conflict of interest based on differing theories of defense between NYMAGIC and Lafarge that might affect coverage for any damages that might be awarded in the barge litigation, Lafarge contended that the gulf between the amounts at stake in the barge litigation and NYMAGIC's primary policy limits created a conflict of interest.[164] But in fact, the Second Circuit observed, NYMAGIC and Lafarge shared a common interest in defeating Lafarge's alleged liability in the barge litigation.[165] Thus, as already noted, Lafarge's conflict claim was destined to fail under New York law.[166] Nor could Lafarge point to any other situation where its potential liability and coverage under the NYMAGIC primary policy were intertwined so as to support a conflict.[167] The *New York Marine* court thus reiterated that the mere prospect of excess liability did not create a conflict of interest that entitled Lafarge to independent counsel at NYMAGIC's expense.[168]

161. *Id.* at 124.
162. *Id.*
163. *Id.*
164. *See id.* at 125.
165. *Id.*
166. *See id.* (quoting Pub. Serv. Mut. Ins. Co. v. Goldfarb, 425 N.E.2d 810, 815 n.* (N.Y. 1981)).
167. *See id.* (footnote omitted) ("Of course, we observe that settlement negotiations may raise a conflict of interest even between an insured and an insurer sharing a common goal of defending against liability, but such a potential or actual conflict is not apparent in this case.").
168. *Id.*

The majority rule may yield where the insured's excess liability combines with other facts. In *Ladner v. American Home Assurance Co.*,[169] for example, the insured's potential excess liability blended with the nature of her alleged misconduct to create a conflict of interest. In a twist, the excess liability in *Ladner* related to a policy sublimit.

Dr. Judith Ladner was a psychologist who was sued for malpractice. The plaintiffs alleged that she had negligently treated, tested, and counseled a patient. They also claimed that she engaged in various acts of sexual misconduct with the patient. Ladner's malpractice insurer, American Home, provided general liability coverage of $1 million, but the policy also provided that claims for "erotic physical contact" were subject to a $25,000 sublimit.[170]

Ladner contended that defense counsel hired by American Home could not represent her because of a conflict of interest. Specifically, the policy provisions governing sexual misconduct claims made it desirable for American Home to have all the claims against her tied to sexual misconduct, thus subjecting them to the $25,000 sublimit. The court agreed.

> [C]ounsel for [Ladner] could conceivably decide that the best defense would be to argue that, as a factual matter, the allegations of sexual misconduct were untrue, while less vigorously contesting the allegations of other types of malpractice. Such an outcome would be beneficial to [Ladner], since any damages arising out of the malpractice would in that case be subject only to the $1,000,000 limit, but for the same reason would not be beneficial to [American Home]. Clearly, such tactical decisions should be in the hands of an attorney whose loyalty to [Ladner] is unquestioned and not an attorney employed by [American Home] with a potential for a conflict of interest.[171]

The court therefore concluded that Ladner was entitled to counsel of her choice to be paid by American Home.[172]

It is also possible that on the right facts, a court may disregard the majority rule, as in *R.C. Wegman Construction Co. v. Admiral Insurance Co.*[173] In that case, Brian Budrik was hurt in a fall on a construction site that the R.C. Wegman Construction Co. (Wegman) managed. Budrik was employed by one of Wegman's subcontractors. He sued Wegman in 2003. Wegman was an additional insured under the subcontractor's $1 million CGL policy with Admiral Insurance Co. (Admiral). The defense lawyer hired by Admiral to defend Wegman deposed Budrik in May 2005 and, as a result of the deposition, Admiral knew that Budrik was seriously injured in the accident and had lost substantial

169. 607 N.Y.S.2d 296 (App. Div. 1994).
170. *Id.* at 297.
171. *Id.* at 298.
172. *Id.* at 298–99.
173. 629 F.3d 724 (7th Cir. 2011).

income as a result. According to Wegman's complaint, at around the same time, Admiral knew that Burdrik wanted $6 million to settle and that his lawsuit realistically posed a risk of an excess verdict. Yet Admiral did not inform Wegman of the risk of an excess verdict.[174] Wegman learned of the substantial risk of an excess verdict only by happenstance on the eve of the trial of Budrik's lawsuit in 2007. Wegman then notified its excess insurer of Budrik's claim, but the excess insurer denied coverage based on late notice. Budrik's suit went to trial and the jury returned a verdict of slightly more than $2 million. Wegman sued Admiral for bad faith in an Illinois federal court, alleging that Admiral committed bad faith by failing to inform it of its potential excess exposure in time to notify its excess insurer and thus protect itself against uninsured liability.[175] The district court dismissed Wegman's lawsuit and Wegman appealed to the Seventh Circuit.

The Seventh Circuit reasoned that when a conflict of interest between an insurer and insured arises, the insurer's duty of good faith and fair dealing requires it to notify the insured.[176] A conflict may arise "from the relation of the policy limit to the insured's potential liability."[177] Once notified of the conflict, the insured has the right to hire independent counsel at the insurer's expense. "Had Wegman hired a new lawyer upon being promptly informed of the conflict back in May 2005, that lawyer would have tried to negotiate a settlement with Budrik that would not exceed the policy limit; and if the settlement was reasonable given the risk of an excess judgment, Admiral would [have been] obligated to pay."[178] Moreover, since Wegman had excess insurance, timely notice of the risk of an excess verdict would have enabled to notify its excess insurer in a fashion that would have preserved the protection afforded by its excess coverage.[179] Thus, the district court's dismissal of Wegman's lawsuit against Admiral was premature. The Seventh Circuit reversed the district court and remanded the case for further proceedings.

Wegman is an unusual decision in several respects and for that reason the holding is best limited to its facts.[180] To start, because the case came to the

174. *Id.* at 727.
175. *Id.*
176. *Id.* at 729.
177. *Id.*
178. *Id.*
179. *Id.*
180. Among other things, at oral argument Admiral's lawyer reportedly "confessed that his client had been gambling on minimizing its liability at the expense, if necessary, of Wegman." *Id.* at 728. In fact, the lawyer apparently stated that he believed that if the case went to trial, Wegman would be found to be no more than 25 percent at fault and thus would become obligated to pay—if it were held liable—no more than 25 percent of Budrik's damages. *Id.* Such a judgment apparently would have been within the Admiral policy limits based on the defense lawyer's calculation of Budrik's damages. Additionally, the lawyer pointed out that Budrik's $6 million settlement demand did not necessarily mean his case was worth that much; plaintiffs routinely make unrealistic settlement demands. *Id.*

Seventh Circuit on a motion to dismiss, the court was required to accept the allegations in Wegman's complaint as true.[181] Beyond that, the Seventh Circuit overstated the role potentially played by independent counsel. To explain, Admiral was defending Wegman without a reservation of rights, such that it had the right to control settlement. As a result, any lawyer hired as independent counsel could not have negotiated a policy limits settlement with Budrik without Admiral's consent.[182] Had independent counsel demanded that Admiral settle within policy limits and Admiral refused the insurer might have been liable for bad faith, but the result would be no different had Wegman known of the potential for an excess verdict and made a similar demand itself.[183] The essential problem was thus the communication breakdown between Admiral and Wegman that deprived Wegman of important facts concerning its potential liability, not a conflict of interest. Moreover, in denying Admiral's petition for rehearing, the *Wegman* court retreated somewhat, succinctly explaining that it had not broadly held that conflict of interest exists any time there is a possibility of an excess verdict, but only that it had so held based on the facts of this case.[184]

Wegman is much more about an insurer's duty to communicate settlement offers to its insured and the duty to make reasonable settlement decisions than it is about the defense lawyer's supposed conflict of interest. Neither Admiral nor the defense lawyer had any interest in preventing Wegman from notifying its excess insurer about Budrik's lawsuit. If the result in *Wegman* is supportable, it is on the basis that Admiral unreasonably failed to settle Budrik's lawsuit within its policy limits or that it unreasonably failed to timely communicate Budrik's settlement demand to Wegman so that Wegman could notify its excess insurer—not because there was a conflict of interest.

C. The Plaintiff Seeks Punitive Damages

Plaintiffs often plead claims for punitive damages. States are divided on the insurability of punitive damages. Some states prohibit the insurability of punitive damages on public policy grounds. Courts in these states reason that allowing insurance for punitive damages would undermine the goals of punishment and deterrence, or that insurers would unfairly shift the burden of

181. *Id.* at 726.

182. *See, e.g.*, Ins. Servs. Off., Inc., Commercial General Liability Coverage Form (CG 00 01 04 13), at 11 (2012) ("No insured will, except at that insured's own cost, voluntarily make a payment, assume any obligation, or incur any expense, other than for first aid, without our consent.").

183. For that matter, while Budrick apparently wanted $6 million to settle, Admiral could never have met that demand and it does not appear that Budrick ever offered to compromise his claim for an amount within Admiral's policy limits. Thus, Admiral never had the opportunity to settle Budrick's suit within its policy limits. That militates against the finding of a conflict of interest.

184. R.C. Wegman Constr. Co. v. Admiral Ins. Co., 634 F.3d 371, 371–72 (7th Cir. 2011).

punitive damage awards to the public through increased premiums. Of those states that generally prohibit the insurability of punitive damages, some make an exception for punitive damages awarded solely under vicarious liability principles. Other states allow insurance for punitive damages. In these states, standard policy language providing that the insurer will pay "all sums which the insured shall become legally obligated to pay as damages" is sufficiently broad to insure punitive damages.[185]

In jurisdictions that prohibit the insurability of punitive damages, or where a policy excludes coverage for punitive damages or does not cover them for some other reason, an insurance company may be thought to have no interest in defending punitive damage claims against insureds. On the other side of the coin, insureds are vitally interested in avoiding liability for punitive damages. Hence defense lawyers' perceived conflict of interest where punitive damages are in play.

1. *The Majority Rule: A Punitive Damages Claim Does Not Create a Conflict of Interest*

Despite these concerns, the majority rule holds that a punitive damage claim does not alone create a conflict of interest that entitles the insured to independent counsel.[186] This is a sensible approach because aggravating circumstances that spawn punitive damages also increase a defendant's compensatory damage exposure. An insurer must vigorously defend a case where punitive damages are sought to reduce its potential indemnity obligation to its insured. *Foremost Insurance Co. v. Wilks*[187] illustrates the majority rule and its rationale.

In *Wilks*, Delmar Brey sued Diana Wilks for defamation. Brey sought injunctive relief, compensatory damages of $100,000, and punitive damages of $250,000. California public policy prohibits insurance coverage for punitive damages. Wilks tendered the defense of Brey's lawsuit to her insurer, Foremost Insurance Co. (Foremost), which agreed to defend her. In its letter accepting her defense, however, Foremost informed her that under California law, its policy would not cover any punitive damages that Brey might be awarded,

185. *See, e.g.*, Shelter Mut. Ins. Co. v. Dale, 914 So. 2d 698, 701 (Miss. 2005) (discussing a Mississippi statute and an auto liability insurer's ability to exclude coverage for punitive damages). *But see* Heartland Stores, Inc. v. Royal Ins. Co., 815 S.W.2d 39, 42–43 (Mo. Ct. App. 1991) (stating that punitive damages were not covered because they were not attributable to "personal injury").

186. *See, e.g.*, Fox v. Am. Alt. Ins. Corp., 757 F.3d 680, 685 (7th Cir. 2014) ("A conflict does not arise simply because a plaintiff seeks both punitive and compensatory damages.") (applying Illinois law); Bean Prods., Inc. v. Scottsdale Ins. Co., No. 1-17-0421, 2018 WL 522627, at *7 (Ill. App. Ct. Jan. 22, 2018) ("[N]o actual conflict of interest existed to entitle Bean to independent counsel based simply on the fact that the complaint sought punitive damages."). *But see* Med-Plus, Inc. v. Am. Cas. Co., No. 16-CV-2985 (NGG) (JO), 2017 WL 3393824, at *8 (E.D.N.Y. Aug. 4, 2017) (stating that the possibility of punitive damages created a conflict of interest under both New York and New Jersey law).

187. 253 Cal. Rptr. 596 (Ct. App. 1989).

and further suggested that she might want to engage personal counsel to protect her interests with respect to a potential punitive damage award.[188] Wilks claimed that Foremost's advice created a conflict of interest that entitled her to independent counsel, but the court disagreed.

> Under the policy issued to Wilks, Foremost is obligated to indemnify for damages up to $1,000,000 sustained in a personal injury action, which is defined by the policy to include defamation actions. Foremost is prohibited from indemnifying Wilks from any punitive damages pursuant to Civil Code section 1668 and Insurance Code section 533. However, Foremost will be liable for indemnification of compensatory damages if the trier of fact in the *Brey* action finds Wilks defamed Brey regardless of whether her conduct was done with malice or reckless disregard for the truth. Contrary to Wilks' assertions, *it is in Foremost's interest to vigorously defend the suit to avoid liability for indemnification of compensatory damages. Although the nature of Wilks' conduct as developed at trial will determine whether punitive damages are awarded, under the facts of this case and the coverage afforded Wilks under the policy, Foremost gains no benefit from pursuing a theory that Wilks acted with malice or reckless disregard for the truth. Ergo, there is no conflict of interest.*[189]

Other courts have employed similar reasoning to the same end. In *Pennbank v. St. Paul Fire & Marine Insurance Co.*,[190] the court banked on the insurer's interest in minimizing compensatory damages in rejecting the insured's argument that the plaintiffs' punitive damage claims created a conflict of interest that entitled it to independent counsel. As the *Pennbank* court explained:

> The interests of insurer and insured in defense of the underlying suits were the same—prevent a finding of liability or failing that, minimize damages. Punitive damages can only be awarded where compensatory damages have been awarded and the punitives must have some relation to the compensatory award. . . . For St. Paul to admit outrageous, intentional and reckless conduct on the part of its insured, or to fail to vigorously defend such charges, would guarantee a large award of compensatory damages as well as punitive damages.
>
> This is not a case where liability can rest on either of two causes of action, one of which is covered and the other not (e.g., negligence and intentional tort). There an insurer would be tempted to construct a defense which would place any damage award outside policy coverage. That is not the case here. Any award of punitive damages would necessarily occasion the overwhelming

---

188. Both the trial court and appellate court concluded that Foremost's letter accepting Wilks's defense but further informing her that California law prohibited the insurability of punitive damages did not constitute a reservation of rights. Even if the letter could have been construed as a reservation of rights letter, however, the *Wilks* court still would not have found a conflict of interest. *Id.* at 602.

189. *Id.* (emphasis added).

190. 669 F. Supp. 122 (W.D. Pa. 1987).

> likelihood of a large compensatory award. Both parties shared the desire to prevent a finding which would justify punitive damages. For this reason, the rationale in *Cumis* is inapplicable here.[191]

The Restatement of the Law of Liability Insurance likewise recognizes that a punitive damage claim generally does not create a conflict of interest absent a reservation of rights to contest coverage more broadly.[192] In doing so, the Restatement embraces the majority view that the insurer's litigation efforts to minimize compensatory damages simultaneously reduce the insured's exposure to punitive damages.[193]

2. *The Punitive-to-Compensatory Damages Ratio Exception*

Although the Restatement generally embraces the majority position that a punitive damage claim does not create a conflict of interest, it further reasons that a punitive damage claim could create a conflict where the compensatory damages sought are so small in relation to the potential punitive damages that the defense of the action "might be handled in a hard-edged manner that disproportionately risks exacerbating the punitive-damages exposure or if there was a realistic possibility that the manner of presentation at trial could affect the jury's allocation between pain-and-suffering damages and punitive damages."[194] This exception to the general rule that a punitive damage claim does not create a conflict of interest is principally rooted in an Illinois appellate decision, *Nandorf v. CNA Insurance Cos.*[195]

Nandorf arose out of a lawsuit filed by Delores Scott and several other plaintiffs against Nandorf, Inc. (Nandorf), which owned a thrift shop, for false imprisonment. Each plaintiff sought $5,000 in compensatory damages and $100,000 in punitive damages.[196] Nandorf's insurer, CNA, appointed the law firm of Baker & McKenzie to defend Nandorf. CNA also reserved its right not to indemnify Nandorf for any punitive damage award based on Illinois public policy. Nandorf's counsel asked CNA to waive its reservation of rights and informed CNA that they planned to control the defense of the *Scott* case

---

191. *Id.* at 126–27.
192. Restatement of the L. of Liab. Ins. § 16 cmt. d (Am. L. Inst. 2019).
193. *Id.*
194. *Id.*
195. 479 N.E.2d 988 (Ill. App. Ct. 1985); *see also* Parker v. Agric. Ins. Co., 440 N.Y.S.2d 964, 968 (Sup. Ct. 1981) ("Indisputedly, the great bulk of litigation involving insureds, wherein punitive damages may be routinely tacked onto the ad damnum clause, may be predictably, regularly and properly defended and controlled by the insurer. . . . If punitive damages were a negligible or co-equal portion of the total damages sought, defendants' disclaimers therefor might not be of great significance. But in five actions discussed at the outset punitive damages totally [sic] 169 million dollars exceed compensatory damages more than sixfold. . . . Without doubting the sincerity of Agricultural's commitment to defend plaintiff, we must recognize the existence of a conflict of economic interests.").
196. *Nandorf*, 479 N.E.2d at 990.

if CNA refused. CNA declined to waive its reservation of rights and refused to relinquish control of the litigation.

Nandorf later sued CNA. Nandorf claimed that CNA's reservation of rights based on the plaintiffs' punitive damage claims created a conflict of interest that obligated CNA to provide it with independent counsel. The *Nandorf* court agreed:

> [T]he complaint . . . sought a large amount of punitive damages and a relatively small amount of compensatory damages. CNA disclaimed liability only for punitive damages. The insurer and the insured shared a common interest in a finding of no liability. However, if Nandorf was found liable, their interests diverged. CNA's interests would have been just as well served by an award of minimal compensatory damages and substantial punitive damages. Such an award is not inconceivable. As a result of its reservation of rights, CNA had an interest in providing a less than vigorous defense to allegations in the *Scott* complaint which, if proven, would have supported . . . punitive damages. . . . CNA's failure to vigorously defend those allegations would have had the effect of subjecting its insured to greater liability. Clearly, the insurer's fidelity to its insured was hampered by its own interests in this case.
>
> In contrast, Nandorf's interest lay in reducing any potential punitive damages award, regardless of the compensatory damages awarded. Therefore, if liability was imposed, it would have been in Nandorf's interest to have a determination that its employees acted in good faith. A finding of good faith would not have prevented an award of compensatory damages but would have precluded an award of punitive damages. . . . CNA would have had little interest in seeking such a finding. Because CNA's reservation of rights placed the insurer and insured at cross purposes with respect to allegations in the *Scott* complaint, we find that an actual conflict of interests existed between Nandorf and CNA which rendered it improper for CNA to retain control of the litigation.[197]

The *Nandorf* court cautioned readers that its holding was not meant to imply that an insured is entitled to independent counsel every time a plaintiff seeks punitive damages.[198] Rather, the "peculiar facts and circumstances of this litigation," where "punitive damages formed a substantial portion of the potential liability" and "CNA's disclaimer of liability for punitive damages left Nandorf with the greater interest and risk in the litigation," created an ethical conflict of interest that warranted Nandorf's representation by independent counsel at CNA's expense.[199]

---

197. *Id.* at 992 (citations omitted).

198. *Id.* at 993; *see also* Fox v. Am. Alt. Ins. Corp., 757 F.3d 680, 685 (7th Cir. 2014) ("A conflict does not arise [under Illinois law] simply because a plaintiff seeks both punitive and compensatory damages.").

199. *Nandorf*, 479 N.E.2d at 993–94.

Xtreme Protection Services, Inc. v. Steadfast Insurance Co.[200] is a recent case where the court found a right to independent counsel based on the ratio of compensatory damages to possible punitive damages. In *Xtreme*, David Israel sued Xtreme Protection Services, Inc. (Xtreme) after Xtreme's agent, Michael Bucon, allegedly bugged Israel's office, attached GPS devices to his cars, and sent him threatening and harassing text messages. Israel's third amended complaint, which was the operative pleading, sought no less than $120,000 in compensatory damages and no less than $2.1 million in punitive damages.[201]

Xtreme defended Israel's lawsuit through its own counsel while its insurer, Steadfast, evaluated coverage. After a few months, Steadfast agreed to indemnify Xtreme for any award of compensatory damages up to its policy limits and waived its right to deny coverage for any compensatory damage award, but reserved its right to deny coverage for punitive damages.[202] The Steadfast policy explicitly excluded coverage for punitive damages.[203]

Xtreme and Steadfast disagreed over whether Steadfast's reservation of rights created a conflict of interest that entitled Extreme to independent counsel. Coverage litigation between the two followed. The trial court in the coverage case held that Xtreme was entitled to select its own counsel due to Steadfast's reservation of rights regarding punitive damages and the potential for a substantial punitive award. Steadfast appealed.

Steadfast argued on appeal that there was no conflict of interest because it had waived its right to deny coverage for compensatory damages.[204] The *Xtreme* court was not persuaded, however, because while Steadfast's waiver may have resolved one type of conflict of interest, its refusal to accept coverage for punitive damages presented another conflict.[205]

The *Xtreme* court observed that Israel's third amended complaint requested no less than $120,000 in compensatory damages and no less than $ 2.1 million in punitive damages. Here, as in *Nandorf*, the underlying complaint sought substantially more in punitive damages than in compensatory damages but there was no coverage for punitive damages, and Steadfast had reserved its rights regarding punitive damages.[206] Plus, an award of punitive damages was certainly possible given the allegations in Israel's third amended complaint. In sum, because punitive damages formed a substantial portion of the potential liability in Israel's lawsuit and Steadfast disclaimed any related liability, Xtreme was left with the greater interest and risk in the litigation.[207]

200. 143 N.E.3d 128 (Ill. App. Ct. 2019).
201. *Id.* at 137.
202. *Id.* at 133.
203. *Id.* at 132.
204. *Id.* at 135.
205. *Id.*
206. *Id.* at 137.
207. *Id.*

Furthermore, while compensatory and punitive damage claims arise from the same misconduct, more evidence is necessary to recover punitive damages.[208] Punitive damages are awarded not as compensation but instead to punish the offender and to deter similar wrongful conduct in the future.[209] Punitive damages are appropriate "'when the defendant's tortious conduct evinces a high degree of moral culpability, that is, when the tort is committed with fraud, actual malice, deliberate violence or oppression, or when the defendant acts willfully, or with such gross negligence as to indicate a wanton disregard of the rights of others.'"[210] The court reasoned that because Steadfast had denied coverage for punitive damages, it had little incentive to defend Xtreme against Israel's punitive damages claims.[211]

The *Xtreme* court concluded that Xtreme was owed a defense by independent counsel at Steadfast's expense.[212] It therefore affirmed the trial court's judgment for Xtreme.

The *Nandorf* and *Xtreme* approach is not persuasive. The fact that a potential punitive damage award may far exceed a compensatory damage award does not mean that an insurer lacks an interest in resisting punitive damages. At least one court has reasoned that where compensatory and punitive damages arise out of the same conduct, the insurer's interest in defeating the insured's alleged liability means that the insurer will necessarily protect the insured's interests with respect to both categories of damages.[213] As noted earlier, if potential compensatory damages are significant—even if any punitive damages will probably be much greater—the insurer will be heavily invested in defeating or minimizing the plaintiff's claims for compensatory damages and, by extension, the punitive damage claims. Finally, the insurer's duty to defend the insured reasonably notwithstanding its reservation of rights should ensure that the defense will be conducted in a fashion that protects the insured against liability for both punitive damages and compensatory damages. For these reasons, the defense lawyer in such a case should not suffer a conflict of interest.

If it is accepted, application of the punitive-to-compensatory damages ratio exception requires careful case-by-case analysis that will depend on various factors, including the nature of the allegations against the insured, the amount of the compensatory damages sought, the policy limits, the likelihood of a punitive damage award, and the size of any potential punitive damage award. Finally, a court should not recognize this exception to the general rule that a

208. *Id.*

209. *Id.* (quoting Loitz v. Remington Arms Co., 563 N.E.2d 397, 402 (Ill. 1990)).

210. *Id.* (quoting Slovinski v. Elliot, 927 N.E.2d 1221, 1225 (Ill. 2010)) (internal quotation marks omitted).

211. *Id.*

212. *Id.*

213. Nat'l Cas. Co. v. Forge Indus. Staffing, Inc., 567 F.3d 871, 876 (7th Cir. 2009).

punitive damages claim does not create a conflict of interest until a plaintiff pleads its right to punitive damages and the court allows the claim.[214] The mere threat of a punitive damage claim where one has not been pleaded does not create a conflict of interest.[215]

D. The Defense Lawyer Represents Multiple Insureds

In a case where multiple defendants are insured by the same insurance company, it is common for the insurer to at least initially consider whether it may appoint a single lawyer to represent all the defendants. The appointment of a single lawyer has economic benefits and may afford strategic or tactical advantages through a consistent defense. Where there are no conflicts of interest, a single lawyer may represent multiple defendants. In fact, lawyers often represent multiple defendants in litigation with no problems. Yet, a lawyer's representation of multiple defendants can lead to conflicts of interest based on the co-defendants adversity in one form or another.[216] For example, a landowner is typically an additional insured under a general contractor's CGL policy. A lawyer hired by the general contractor's CGL insurer to defend a premises liability case may be asked to also defend the landowner; however, the doctrine of comparative fault makes the landowner and general contractor potential adversaries even though they have a common interest in defeating the plaintiff's claims. If an injured automobile passenger sues both the owner and the driver of the car, the owner and driver may be on opposing sides. It may be in the driver's best interest to argue that she is the owner's agent, while the owner may benefit by arguing that the driver was impermissibly operating the vehicle.[217] Representing a corporate insured and its employee is sometimes problematic because of course and scope of employment issues. Co-defendants may have indemnification agreements or common law indemnity rights that effectively

214. *Id.*

215. Rainey v. Ind. Ins. Co., No. 1-15-0862, 2016 WL 2841285, at *8 (Ill. App. Ct. May 11, 2016).

216. *See, e.g.*, L.A. Terminals, Inc. v. United Nat'l Ins. Co., 608 F. Supp. 3d 968, 979–80 (C.D. Cal. 2022) ("United agreed to provide a defense to adversary-insureds in direct litigation conflict, each seeking to find the other liable for all or part of the alleged contamination. The Court previously found such a direct conflict supports the need for Plaintiffs' independent counsel, and the Court reaffirms that finding here."); Univ. of Miami v. Great Am. Assur. Co., 112 So. 3d 504, 508 (Fla. Dist. Ct. App. 2013) (requiring separate lawyers where a single defense lawyer would "have had to necessarily imply blame to one co-defendant to the detriment of the other"); Country Mut. Ins. Co. v. Olsak, 908 N.E.2d 1091, 1099–1100 (Ill. App. Ct. 2009) (concluding that there was a conflict of interest requiring separate counsel where the two co-defendants had different interests when it came to characterizing one's conduct as either negligent or intentional); Murphy v. Nutmeg Ins. Co., 773 N.Y.S.2d 413, 415 (App. Div. 2004) (stating that insurer had to provide separate counsel for multiple insureds with potential contribution claims against each other).

217. *See, e.g.*, Murphy v. Urso, 430 N.E.2d 1079, 1083–84 (Ill. 1981). *But see* Allied Am. Ins. Co. v. Ayala, 616 N.E.2d 1349, 1358 (Ill. App. Ct. 1993) (finding no conflict where permissive use was acknowledged).

require defense counsel to assert crossclaims. In a direct action jurisdiction, where the plaintiff may sue the insured and its insurer in the same action, the insurer must provide the insured with separate counsel.[218]

Wolpaw v. General Accident Insurance Co.[219] exemplifies the conflicts of interest that a single defense lawyer's representation of multiple insureds can pose. In *Wolpaw*, Saranne Frew was insured under a $50,000 homeowners policy issued by General Accident Insurance Co. (General Accident). The policy also covered members of Frew's household, including her sister Karanne Wolpaw, and Karanne's son, Heath. Heath Wolpaw blinded a playmate, Michael Heim, when he shot him in the eye with a BB gun. Heim and his parents sued Heath, his mother, his father Ivan, and Frew. General Accident hired a single law firm to represent all the defendants except Ivan.

General Accident immediately paid its $50,000 policy limits into court as a settlement offer. The Heims rejected the offer. A jury awarded the Heims $502,000 after finding Michael Heim fifty percent at fault, Heath Wolpaw twenty percent at fault, and Ivan Wolpaw thirty percent at fault. By then, Frew was out of the case on summary judgment. Post-judgment interest brought the total judgment to over $700,000. Karanne Wolpaw then sued General Accident, alleging that its failure to provide separate counsel for each defendant was a breach of contract.[220]

The *Wolpaw* court noted the general rule that an insurer of co-defendants with conflicting interests must retain independent counsel for each insured, or permit each insured to do so at the company's expense.[221] That was the situation here.[222]

> The three insureds had the common interests of minimizing the amount of the Heims's judgment and maximizing the percentage of fault attributable to the other defendants. However, their interests in maximizing the percentage of the other insureds' fault and minimizing their own was clearly in conflict. For instance, it was in plaintiff's interest to argue that she adequately had secured the rifle from Heath's unattended use and had carefully instructed him in its safe use, which he negligently disregarded; on the other hand, it was in Heath's interest to argue that [his mother] negligently failed to secure the rifle, and that he was not negligent in view of his mother's negligence and his youth.
>
> With the general abolition of parental immunity, . . . and in the absence of sufficient liability insurance coverage, separate attorneys representing . . . plaintiff and Heath might well have asserted cross-claims for contribution

218. *See, e.g.*, Emery v. Progressive Cas. Ins. Co., 49 So. 3d 17, 21–22 (La. Ct. App. 2010) (holding that the insurer waived its coverage defenses by virtue of conflict of interest that resulted when it hired a single lawyer to represent both it and its insured).

219. 639 A.2d 338 (N.J. Super. Ct. App. Div. 1994).

220. *Id.* at 339.

221. *Id.* at 340.

222. *Id.*

> against the other's client. That was not done . . . . It was also in plaintiff's interest to assert a cross-claim against her sister and that she remain a codefendant to share the liability burden. Yet the single firm of attorneys, discharging its duty to her sister, not only did not file a cross-claim for contribution on plaintiff's behalf, but successfully moved to have Frew dismissed from the case.[223]

The court termed the conflict of interest "obvious," and concluded that General Accident breached its policy by virtue of its failure to provide independent counsel for its insureds.[224] The court then remanded the case to the trial court so that damages attributable to the conflict could be apportioned in a separate trial.

The *Wolpaw* court reached the right result. A defense lawyer generally cannot represent multiple insureds in a comparative fault case. Although the insureds' interests may appear to be harmonious in the sense that they all want to defeat the plaintiff's claims, there is a significant risk that one insured will at some point have to blame the other for causing or contributing to the plaintiff's injuries.

On another point, in concluding that General Accident had a conflict of interest, the *Wolpaw* court was strongly influenced by the prospect of excess liability.[225] The prospect of excess liability unquestionably was a complicating factor, but the defense firm had a conflict of interest even if the policy limits were sufficient to cover any potential judgment given Heath Wolpaw's obvious fault for Michael Heim's injury unless the other defendants were willing not to contest their individual liability. Any one insured's insistence on an allocation of fault would create a conflict of interest for the defense lawyer even in a case where the policy limits were sufficient to fully indemnify each insured.[226] Whether the insured's stance in that scenario might constitute a breach of the duty to cooperate is a separate issue. In contrast, where the insurer's policy limits are sufficient to fully indemnify each insured and there is no need to litigate their respective fault, there is no conflict of interest requiring independent counsel.[227] Even in a case of potential excess liability, where there is no need to allocate fault between the insured defendants or where their theories of defense

223. *Id.*
224. *Id.*
225. *See id.*
226. *See* Model Rules of Pro. Conduct r. 1.7(a)(2) (Am. Bar Ass'n 2023).
227. *See, e.g.*, Davenport v. St. Paul Fire & Marine Ins. Co., 978 F.2d 927, 932 (5th Cir. 1992) ("[W]here, as here, a carrier insures codefendants, if their coverage is sufficient to relieve each defendant of any possible personal liability and there are no cross-claims between the two insureds that require separate representation, it is difficult to conceive of any conflict of interest that would require separate legal representation."); Kaufman v. Med. Liab. Mut. Ins. Co., 938 N.Y.S.2d 367, 369–70 (App. Div. 2012) (finding no conflict where the policy limits were adequate to protect all the insureds and there was no suggestion that any of the defendants were more culpable than another).

are the same, there is no conflict of interest that requires the appointment of independent counsel.[228]

An insurer does not necessarily breach its duty to defend or its duty of good faith and fair dealing by failing to spot conflicts of interest in a case involving multiple insureds.[229] But an insurer that knowingly disregards a lawyer's conflict in defending multiple insureds does so at its peril. Medical Protective Co. (Med Pro) learned this lesson the hard way in *Jurinko v. Medical Protective Co.*[230]

In *Jurinko*, Med Pro appointed a lawyer, Kilcoyne, to represent two physicians—Dr. Marcincin and Dr. Edelman—in a malpractice action arising out of their alleged failure to diagnose plaintiff Stephen Jurinko's skin cancer. The doctors' interests were incompatible because either one could escape liability by blaming the other for the claimed diagnostic failure. The medical malpractice case went to trial and Jurinko and his wife won a verdict against Dr. Marcincin that exceeded the liability limit of his Med Pro policy by $1.3 million. Dr. Marcincin assigned to the Jurinkos his right to sue Med Pro for bad faith. The Jurinkos followed through and the jury in the bad faith case awarded them approximately $1.65 million in compensatory damages and $6.25 million in punitive damages. Med Pro then moved for judgment as a matter of law or, in the alternative, for a new trial.

One of the issues Med Pro raised in its motion was whether the plaintiffs' expert witness, James Griffith, should have been permitted to testify that Med Pro acted in bad faith and that its bad faith injured Dr. Marcincin. In concluding that Griffith's testimony was proper, the district court noted that the Med Pro claims handler, James Alff, testified that he appointed Kilcoyne to represent both doctors despite knowing it would create a conflict of interest that would undermine Kilcoyne's defense of Dr. Marcinin, and that he was fully aware that Kilcoyne's joint representation of the doctors was unethical.[231] Alff

228. *See, e.g.*, Fox v. Am. Alt. Ins. Corp., 757 F.3d 680, 686 (7th Cir. 2014) (seeing no conflict where the defendants pursued a joint defense at trial); Stevenson v. Corp. of Lloyd's, No: 8:15-cv-2745-T-30, 2016 WL 524735, at *7 (M.D. Fla. Feb. 10, 2016) (finding no conflict of interest where the insureds were members of the same family and their company and their defenses were aligned); *see also* Progressive Nw. Ins. Co. v. Gant, 957 F.3d 1144, 1153–54 (10th Cir. 2020) (concluding that the insurer could not be liable for negligently hiring the defense lawyer to represent multiple insureds where the insureds had no desire to blame one another for the underlying accident, they wanted to present a unified defense, and they all signed a conflict waiver).

229. *See* Marquis Acquisitions, Inc. v. Steadfast Ins. Co., 409 S.W.3d 808, 816–17 (Tex. App. 2013) (citation omitted) ("With respect to a claim for a defense, an insurer must act with reasonable care. . . . But it has no duty to independently identify conflicts among the insureds when appointing legal counsel.").

230. No. 03-CV-4053, 2006 WL 785234 (E.D. Pa. Mar. 29, 2006), *aff'd in part, rev'd in part*, 305 F. App'x 13 (3d Cir. 2008).

231. *Id.* at *4–5.

also testified that he appointed a single lawyer to defend both doctors despite the obvious conflict of interest "to save [Med Pro] money."[232]

The court considered Alff's conduct again in assessing the reprehensibility of Med Pro's conduct with respect to the jury's punitive damage award.[233] In this context, the court found that Med Pro intentionally harmed Dr. Marcinin based partly on Alff's testimony that he appointed Kilcoyne to jointly represent Drs. Marcincin and Edelman even though he knew that their joint representation posed a conflict of interest, and that he did so for Med Pro's financial benefit.[234]

The district court denied Med Pro's post-trial motion. On appeal, the Third Circuit let the bad faith verdict stand, but reduced the punitive damage award to just under $2 million on the basis that the original award was unconstitutionally excessive.[235]

E. Conflicts Attributable to the Insured's Confidential Information

1. *General Confidentiality Principles*

Conflicts of interest are partly predicated on lawyers' duty of confidentiality. A lawyer's duty to maintain client confidences is essential to the attorney-client relationship.[236] Almost all jurisdictions have adopted Model Rule 1.6(a), which provides that "[a] lawyer shall not reveal information relating to representation of a client" unless the client gives informed consent, the disclosure is impliedly authorized to carry out the representation, or one of the exceptions listed in Model Rule 1.6(b) applies.[237] Lawyers' duty of confidentiality

232. *Id.* at *5.

233. *Id.* at *6–7.

234. *Id.* at *7.

235. Jurinko v. Med. Prot. Co., 305 F. App'x 13, 25–30 (3d Cir. 2008).

236. *See In re* Skinner, 740 S.E.2d 171, 173 (Ga. 2013) (stating that a lawyer's duty of confidentiality "is a fundamental principle in the client-lawyer relationship."); Commonwealth v. Downey, 793 N.E.2d 377, 381 (Mass. App. Ct. 2003) (branding confidentiality one of lawyers' "highest duties"); *In re* Lane's Case, 889 A.2d 3, 12–13 (N.H. 2005) (describing a lawyer's duty of confidentiality as "the foundation of the attorney-client relationship"); State v. Aiken, 129 A.3d 87, 92 (Vt. 2015) (calling confidentiality the "cornerstone of the attorney-client relationship"); State *ex rel.* Ash v. Swope, 751 S.E.2d 751, 756 (W. Va. 2013) ("[I]t is a fundamental principle in the lawyer-client relationship that the lawyer maintain the confidentiality of information relating to the representation of a client.").

237. Model Rules of Pro. Conduct r. 1.6(a) (Am. Bar Ass'n 2023). A few jurisdictions have varied their confidentiality rules. For example, California's version of Rule 1.6(a) states: "A lawyer shall not reveal information protected from disclosure by Business and Professions Code section 6068, subdivision (e)(1) unless the client gives informed consent, or the disclosure is permitted by paragraph (b) of this rule." Cal. Rules of Pro. Conduct r. 1.6(a) (2022). The statute cited in the rule makes it a lawyer's duty "[t]o maintain inviolate the confidence, and at every peril to himself or herself to preserve the secrets, of his or her client.'" Cal. Bus. & Prof. Code § 6068(e)(1) (2022). New York's version of Rule 1.6(a) prohibits lawyers from "knowingly reveal[ing] confidential information," subject to certain exceptions. N.Y. Rules of Pro. Conduct r. 1.6(a) (2022). The rule defines confidential information as "information gained during or relating to the representation of a client, whatever its source, that is (a) protected by the attorney-client privilege, (b) likely to be embarrassing

under Model Rule 1.6(a) and equivalent state rules, although not absolute,[238] is very broad.[239] The duty applies to *all* information related to a client's representation.[240] Any exceptions that rules of professional conduct provide are narrow.[241]

A lawyer with multiple clients in a matter owes each client an equal and undivided duty of confidentiality. Unlike the attorney-client privilege, there is no co-client exception to the duty of confidentiality. Generally, for a lawyer to be able to share a co-client's confidential information with another co-client, the clients must so agree.[242] The clear lesson for a lawyer representing joint clients is to explain to the clients at the outset of the representation the need to share information that is material to their representations and obtain their consent to do so. In most cases, it is sufficient for the lawyer to state in the engagement letter for the matter that there will be no confidences between the co-clients and then explain what this means from a practical perspective. The clients' agreement to the lawyer's joint representation after being so informed reflects their consent to the sharing of their confidences related to the matter.

---

or detrimental to the client if disclosed, or (c) information that the client has requested be kept confidential." *Id.*

238. *In re* Est. of Rabin, 474 P.3d 1211, 1221 (Colo. 2020); *Downey*, 793 N.E.2d at 382.

239. People v. Braham, No. 15PDJ095, 2017 WL 1046460, at *12 (Colo. Jan. 23, 2017); *In re* Bryan, 61 P.3d 641, 656 (Kan. 2003).

240. State v. Gonzalez, 234 P.3d 1, 11 (Kan. 2010); State Bar of Nev., Comm. on Ethics & Pro. Resp., Formal Op. No. 41, at 3 (2009).

241. *In re Bryan*, 61 P.3d at 656 (discussing the Kansas version of Rule 1.6).

242. Some authorities essentially presume that a lawyer may share co-clients' confidential information with each other. *See* Barker & Silver, *supra* note 11, § 10.02, at 10-7 (stating that "the normal rule is that (unless the clients agree otherwise) all information may be shared with both clients"); Restatement (Third) of the L. Governing Laws. § 61 cmt. l (Am. L. Inst. 2000) ("Sharing of information among the co-clients with respect to the matter involved in the representation is normal and typically expected."). These authorities reason that this approach is consistent with the co-client exception to the attorney-client privilege. There are several problems with this position. First, this presumption contradicts Model Rule 1.6(a). In fact, as a comment to Model Rule 1.6 explains, "[a] fundamental principle in the client-lawyer relationship is that, in the absence of the client's informed consent, the lawyer must not reveal information relating to the representation." Model Rules of Pro. Conduct r. 1.6 cmt. 2 (Am. Bar Ass'n 2023). The counterargument is that a presumption of shared confidence exists because the lawyer owes each client an equal duty of loyalty and each client has the right to be told about anything bearing on the representation that might affect that client's interests. But it is because of this bilateral duty of loyalty that a lawyer should "advise each client that information will be shared and that the lawyer will have to withdraw if one client decided some matter material to the representation should be kept from the other." *Id.* r. 1.6 cmt. 31. Counseling lawyers to so advise clients and telling them that failing to consent to the sharing of information related to the representation may result in the lawyer's disqualification, refutes the notion that lawyers may presume that co-clients' confidences may be shared. Second, accurately predicting a typical client's expectations in any given situation "is risky business." Fla. Eth. Op. 95-4, 1997 WL 307142, at *5 (Fla. State Bar Ass'n, Comm. on Pro. Ethics 1997). Third, even where one client's information is material to the joint representation, it may be detrimental to that client or adverse to the other client, such that the first client does not want the lawyer to share it with the other client. To recognize the claimed presumption in that circumstance would gut the first client's expectation of confidentiality, destroy the clients' community of interests, place the lawyer squarely in a conflict of interest, and harm the client whose information was revealed in the process. *Id.* at *4.

The better practice is for the lawyer to also personally explain to the clients how the duty of confidentiality operates.

2. *Confidentiality in the Insurance Defense Context*

Independent duties to multiple clients may become a problem in the insurance defense context, where a defense lawyer must keep both the insurer and the insured informed about the status of a case. Even where the insured is the defense lawyer's sole client, insurers' outside counsel guidelines typically require defense lawyers to inform the insurer of significant case developments and to report after specified events, such as depositions. If the insured reveals confidential information to the defense lawyer, can the lawyer pass along that information to the insurer? Two situations stand out: First, the insured shares with the lawyer information the insured considers confidential that does not affect coverage but is material to the defense of the case. Second, the insured shares with the lawyer information that affects coverage.

Foundationally, a defense lawyer should explain to the insured up front the lawyer's relationship with the insurer and the lawyer's obligation to keep the insurer informed about the status of the case. This is a logical component of the lawyer's explanation to the insured of the scope of the representation. The lawyer should also outline her duty of confidentiality and how that duty may factor into the insured's representation. For instance, the insured needs to understand that the lawyer is impliedly authorized to disclose to the insurer information that is necessary to carry out the insured's representation.[243] The lawyer should further explain the insured's duty to cooperate in the defense of the lawsuit and the effect a failure to cooperate may have on coverage or on the insurer's defense obligation. The insured needs all this information regardless of whether the insurer is a co-client of the defense lawyer, or the insured is the defense lawyer's sole client.

Where the lawyer is asked to represent co-defendants in a case, the lawyer must further explain her duty of confidentiality to each co-defendant and obtain their consent to the mutual sharing of information that is material to the defense. If the defendants do not agree to share such information with one another, this is a sign that there perhaps is a conflict of interest that requires the defendants to have separate counsel.

It is generally accepted that because the scope of the defense lawyer's representation is limited to defending the insured in the third-party action, the lawyer has no obligation to disclose to the insurer any information that bears on coverage.[244] This is true even where the insurer is also a client of the defense

243. *See* Model Rules of Pro. Conduct r. 1.6(a) (Am. Bar Ass'n 2023).

244. *See* ABA Comm. on Ethics & Pro. Resp., Formal Op. 08-450, at 6–7 (2008) [hereinafter ABA Formal Op. 08-450]. In fact, the defense lawyer has no duty or right to share with the insurer any information of the insured's that is unrelated to the defense of the lawsuit.

lawyer.[245] For example, section 11(2) of the Restatement of the Law of Liability Insurance states that an insurer "does not have the right to receive any information of the insured that is protected by . . . a defense lawyer's duty of confidentiality under rules of professional conduct, if that information could be used to benefit the insurer at the expense of the insured."[246] A comment to section 134 of the Restatement (Third) of the Law Governing Lawyers similarly provides:

> When there is a question whether a claim against the insured is within the coverage of the policy, a lawyer designated to defend the insured may not reveal adverse confidential client information of the insured to the insurer concerning that question . . . without explicit informed consent of the insured. . . . That follows whether or not the lawyer also represents the insurer as a co-client and whether or not the insurer has asserted a "reservation of rights" with respect to its defense of the insured. . . .[247]

The lawyer needs to advise both the insured and the insurer of this limitation on the lawyer's duty to communicate early on.

An insurer that is a client of the defense lawyer under the dual client doctrine is not entitled to obtain from the lawyer information relevant to coverage on the rationale that such disclosure is impliedly authorized to carry out the insurer's representation. Implied authority applies only when the lawyer reasonably believes that disclosure is necessary to protect the interests of the client whose information will be disclosed.[248] In other words, it is the insured's implied authority that counts here, not the insurer's. It is not logical to believe that an insured would authorize the defense lawyer to disclose to the insurer information that might deprive the insured of coverage. To the same point, a client may never be presumed to have impliedly authorized the disclosure of information adverse to its interests.[249]

Where the insured's confidential information relates solely to the defense of the case, the insured should be understood to have impliedly authorized the lawyer's disclosure to the insurer even if the insured did not expressly authorize

245. *See* Cal. Eth. Op. 1995-139, 1995 WL 255397, at *3 (Cal. State Bar, Comm. on Pro. Resp. & Conduct 1995) ("[E]ven where the attorney . . . considers insurer an important 'client,' . . . it is the obligation to protect the insured's confidences and secrets which is paramount. Thus, if, for example, the attorney gains information during the course of representation which the attorney believes demonstrates that the insured is actually not entitled to coverage, the attorney nevertheless owes a duty to the insured/client not to reveal this information to the insurer."); Barker & Silver, *supra* note 11, § 10.03[1], at 10-9 to -10 (offering examples of information bearing on coverage that need not be disclosed to the insurer because it is irrelevant to liability or damages in the third-party action).

246. Restatement of the L. of Liab. Ins. § 11(2) (Am. L. Inst. 2019).

247. Restatement (Third) of the L. Governing Laws. § 134 cmt. f (Am. L. Inst. 2000) (citations to other Restatement sections omitted).

248. ABA Formal Op. 08-450, *supra* note 244, at 6.

249. *Id.*

it. The insured will surely be agreeable to the defense lawyer's disclosure to the insurer in any event. An insured may not welcome disclosure, however, where the lawyer is representing the insured and another co-defendant and the co-defendant will also receive the information the lawyer plans to disclose to the insurer.

Assume, for example, that a company and its employee are sued in connection with a serious accident and the employee is an insured as defined in the company's CGL policy. The company's insurer appoints a lawyer to jointly defend the company and the employee. The case proceeds smoothly until the employee confides in the lawyer that unbeknownst to everyone—including the company and, so far, the plaintiff, because the employee has yet to be deposed—he was intoxicated when he allegedly caused the accident. The insurer needs to know this information because it may prompt the insurer to settle the case before the employee's impairment is revealed and inflates the case's value. The employee is fine with the lawyer's disclosure of his impairment to the insurer, but he does not want the information revealed to the company because he anticipates that the company will fire him for violating its substance-free workplace policy. Yet, the company needs to know the information because it potentially affects the plaintiff's case against it. Where does that leave the lawyer?

The lawyer should remind the employee that he consented to the lawyer's disclosure of any information material to the case to the company at the outset of the representation. The lawyer should also advise the employee that the information will likely come out at his deposition, which a company representative may attend, and that the employee cannot lie under oath to conceal his impairment. The lawyer further needs to inform the employee that disclosure of his impairment to the insurer may not end there because the insurer might reveal the information to the company. If the lawyer did not previously obtain the employee's consent to the disclosure of information related to the joint representation, however, she will be hard-pressed to seek consent now because the information is adverse to the employee's interests; indeed, the lawyer may well decide that she cannot seek the employee's consent given the downside. Even knowing that his intoxication may come out at his deposition, the employee will likely refuse to consent to any disclosure absent assurance that the company will not fire him for violating its substance-free workplace policy. Unfortunately, the lawyer cannot realistically seek that assurance from the company without revealing the employee's violation. No exception to confidentiality listed in Model Rule 1.6(b) permits the lawyer to reveal the employee's intoxication to the company without the employee's consent.[250]

250. *See* Model Rules of Pro. Conduct r. 1.6(b) (Am. Bar Ass'n 2023).

If the employee consented to the lawyer's disclosure of case-related information to the company at the start of the representation, he could revoke his consent. If the employee did not consent in advance to the disclosure of his confidential information to the company and now refuses to permit disclosure or, alternatively, revokes any consent previously given, the lawyer has a conflict of interest that requires her to withdraw from the case.[251] The same result follows where the lawyer did not obtain the employee's consent to disclosure at the outset of the representation and decides that she cannot later seek consent. In any event, the lawyer cannot tell the company why she must withdraw beyond saying that ethical considerations mandate her withdrawal even though her reticence may frustrate the company. The lawyer cannot say more than that to the insurer, either, lest she make a disclosure that is harmful to the employee. Finally, the lawyer cannot give the court any reason for her withdrawal beyond (1) citing the governing ethics rule (Model Rule 1.16(a)(1));[252] or (2) reporting that professional or ethical considerations necessitate her withdrawal, or that there has been an irreconcilable breakdown in the attorney-client relationship with the employee that prevents her continued participation in the case.[253] The solution for the insurer after this episode is to appoint separate counsel for the employee and the company.

Next, consider the disclosure of information to the insurer in a case where the defense lawyer has a dual client relationship with the insured and the insurer. Assume that the insured's corporate representative is being deposed regarding an accident on the insured's property and, during the deposition, he or she discusses prior accidents.[254] If the insured was asked about prior accidents on the application for the policy under which coverage is being provided and did not disclose them, the insurer may be able to rescind the policy based

251. *See* ABA Formal Op. 08-450, *supra* note 244, at 5 (discussing a conflict of interest caused by a lawyer's inability to share information between co-clients and referring to Model Rule 1.4(b)). It might have been possible for the lawyer to structure the joint representation to allow her the option of continuing to represent either the company or the employee instead of having to withdraw from the matter entirely by including a provision to that effect in her engagement letter or in a separate consent form. To do so, the lawyer would have had to disclose all the reasonably foreseeable practical aspects and consequences of that arrangement to the company and the employee. *See, e.g.*, *In re* Rite Aid Corp. Sec. Litig., 139 F. Supp. 2d 649, 655–60 (E.D. Pa. 2001) (denying a disqualification motion where a law firm defending a corporation and its CEO in securities litigation withdrew from the CEO's representation and continued to represent the corporation as contemplated by the engagement letter); Zador Corp. v. Kwan, 37 Cal. Rptr. 2d 754, 759–63 (Ct. App. 1995) (permitting a law firm to continue representing companies in litigation adverse to an agent where the agent agreed not to seek the law firm's disqualification in a detailed consent form).

252. *See* Model Rules of Pro. Conduct r. 1.16(a)(1) (Am. Bar Ass'n 2023) (mandating withdrawal where "the representation will result in violation of the Rules of Professional Conduct or other law," in this instance a violation of Rule 1.7).

253. *See* Cal. Eth. Op. 2015-192, 2015 WL 1308145, at *8 (Cal. State Bar, Comm. on Pro. Resp. & Conduct 2015); N.Y. Eth. Op. 1057, 2015 WL 4592234, at *3 (N.Y. State Bar Ass'n, Comm. on Pro. Ethics 2015).

254. *See* Barker & Silver, *supra* note 11, § 10.02, at 10-9 (providing this example).

on the insured's misrepresentation. In all probability, the defense lawyer will not know the contents of the insured's application and therefore would have no reason to withhold this information when reporting on the deposition to the insurer.[255] In addition, the prior accidents may be relevant to the insured's defense, so sharing this portion of the corporate representative's testimony with the insurer seems natural.

If, however, the defense lawyer has reviewed a copy of the application or otherwise recognizes the threat to coverage that the corporate representative's testimony potentially poses, trouble is percolating. If the prior accidents are not relevant to the insured's liability—they might be dissimilar to the accident at issue or occurred on distant areas of the property—the defense lawyer can avoid reporting the corporate representative's testimony to the insurer because coverage issues are outside the scope of the defense lawyer's representation. But if the prior accidents *are* relevant to the insured's liability, they are precisely the sort of information the insurer expects to receive from the defense lawyer. And because of the coverage implications, the lawyer cannot assume that the insured has impliedly authorized the lawyer to disclose the prior accidents to the insurer. It is no answer to say that the lawyer can report the testimony to the insurer without the insured's consent because the accidents became "public knowledge" through the deposition. Lawyers' duty of confidentiality under Model Rule 1.6(a) encompasses information that may be considered a public record or that is thought to be in the public domain.[256]

---

255. *Id.*

256. *See* People v. Braham, 470 P.3d 1031, 1044 (Colo. 2017) (stating that Rule 1.6 "contains no exception permitting the disclosure of previously disclosed or publicly available information"); *In re* Anonymous, 654 N.E.2d 1128, 1129–30 (Ind. 1995) (holding that the lawyer violated Rule 1.6(a) by revealing information "readily available from public sources"); Iowa Sup. Ct. Att'y Disciplinary Bd. v. Marzen, 779 N.W.2d 757, 766 (Iowa 2010) (holding that "confidentiality is breached when an attorney discloses information learned through the attorney-client relationship even if that information is otherwise publicly available"); *In re* Bryan, 61 P.3d 641, 656 (Kan. 2003) (explaining that a former client's alleged "history of making false claims" had been publicly disclosed in court pleadings did not mean that the lawyer's disclosure regarding the same to a store manager and a loss prevention manager was not the disclosure of information protected as confidential by Rule 1.6); Sullivan Cnty. Reg'l Refuse Disposal Dist. v. Town of Acworth, 686 A.2d 755, 758 (N.H. 1996) ("[A]n attorney's duty to protect confidential information gleaned from a client does not disappear simply because portions of that information have been included in public documents or discussed in public forums."); Law. Disciplinary Bd. v. McGraw, 461 S.E.2d 850, 861–62 (W. Va. 1995) ("The ethical duty of confidentiality is not nullified by the fact that the information is part of a public record or by the fact that someone else is privy to it."); ABA Comm. on Ethics & Pro. Resp., Formal Op. 480, at 4 (2018) (footnote omitted) ("Rule 1.6 does not provide an exception for information that is 'generally known' or contained in a 'public record.'"). *But see In re* Lim, 210 S.W.3d 199, 201–02 (Mo. 2007) (reasoning that the lawyer's letter to the INS saying that his former clients "lack[ed] the good moral character needed to obtain immigration benefits" because they had "lied and deceived" him and owed him more than $7,000 did not violate Rule 1.6(a) in part because "the outstanding debt was a matter of public record by virtue of the [lawyer's] collection action"); Hunter v. Va. State Bar *ex rel.* Third Dist. Comm., 744 S.E.2d 611, 620 (Va. 2013) (concluding that the lawyer had a First Amendment right to blog about his criminal defense clients' court cases without the clients' consent and that doing so did not violate the lawyer's duty of confidentiality under Rule 1.6).

Assuming that the prior accidents are relevant to the defense of the current case, the lawyer should explain the situation to the insured, inform the insured of the conflict, and encourage the insured to consult with a coverage lawyer. Unless the insured agrees that the defense lawyer may reveal the prior accidents to the insurer or the insured's coverage counsel does so (perhaps having concluded that rescission is not available to the insurer), the lawyer's inability to disclose the corporate representative's testimony to the insurer creates a conflict of interest that requires the lawyer to withdraw from the representation.

Of course, any replacement lawyer will face the same conflict as the first lawyer unless the second lawyer treats the insured as the lawyer's sole client. If the second lawyer solely represents the insured and does not report the testimony about the prior accidents to the insurer, that omission may implicate the insured's duty to cooperate in the defense, but the lawyer will not be laboring under a conflict of interest.

3. *An Illustrative Case:* Cosgrove v. National Fire & Marine Insurance Co.

Cosgrove v. National Fire & Marine Insurance Co.[257] illustrates the challenges that a defense lawyer's duty of confidentiality can present for both the lawyer and the insurer. In that case, Karen Cosgrove hired WTM Construction (WTM), which was owned by William and Lana Mitzel, to remodel her house. Believing that WTM did a poor job, Cosgrove sued WTM and the Mitzels in Arizona state court. WTM was insured by National Fire & Marine Insurance Co. (National), which hired lawyer Richard Righi to defend WTM under a reservation of rights. National reserved its rights based on a "Subcontractors Exclusion" in its policy, which provided in relevant part:

> This insurance does not apply to "bodily injury," "property damage," or "personal or advertising injury" arising out of operations performed for you by independent contractors or subcontractors unless:
>
> (1) Such independent contractors or sub-contractors agree in writing to defend, indemnify, and hold harmless you and your affiliates, subsidiaries, directors, officers, employees, agents, and their representatives from and against all claims, damages, losses, and expenses attributable to, resulting from, or arising out of the independent contractor's or sub-contractor's operations performed for you, caused in whole or in part by any act or omission of the independent contractor or sub-contractor or any one directly or indirectly employed by any of them or anyone for whose acts any of them may be liable, regardless of whether or not it is caused in part by you. . . .[258]

257. No. 2:14-cv-2229-HRH, 2017 WL 11437374 (D. Ariz. Apr. 10, 2017), *vacated*, No. 2:14-cv-2229-HRH, 2017 WL 11490239 (D. Ariz. May 5, 2017) (approving the parties' stipulation to vacate the April 10, 2017, order because the case settled).

258. *Id.* at *1.

On June 2, 2009, Righi wrote to Anne Rohling, the National adjuster handling the case, to report that he had met with Mr. Mitzel to prepare the defense of Cosgrove's lawsuit and that he would try to gather as much information as possible regarding Cosgrove's claims and the nature of WTM work at her home. Righi promised Rohling that he would provide her with an initial case analysis as soon as he had this information.

On June 30, 2009, Righi gave Rohling his initial evaluation. Righi advised Rohling that he had learned that all work on Cosgrove's home other than framing was performed by subcontractors and that he was unable to locate any subcontracts.[259] Righi would later testify that he thought he learned this information both from Mr. Mitzel and from reading the job file.[260] Although the job file was eventually produced in discovery in the state court suit, the file had not been produced at the time of Righi's initial evaluation.[261]

A few weeks later, Righi informed Rohling that, in fact, even the framing of Cosgrove's home was performed by a subcontractor. Righi further advised Rohling that "[w]e have been unable to locate written contracts between WTM and th[e] subcontractors who performed work on the project. At this point, we are doubtful any such contracts exist."[262] When he was later questioned about how he reported developments in the case to Rohling, Righi testified:

> "We provide information that is out there in the public domain . . . Certainly nothing secretive, nothing privileged in the sense that it could harm the client." . . . "[W]e report all the facts, all the developments, everything that happens, because what we're reporting is . . . in the record. It's in a deposition or disclosure or it's in a depository. It's out there for public consumption. So if that's the case, we report it." But, . . . "if a client tells me something privileged, tells me something important, I'm not going to report that."[263]

Righi did not consider the information about the subcontracts to be confidential or privileged because it "was very clear in the documents. It was published to everyone."[264]

In April 2010, Righi filed a third-party complaint against seven subcontractors who worked on Cosgrove's home. In the third-party complaint, WTM asserted common law implied indemnity claims against the subcontractors. Righi obviously pleaded common law implied indemnity claims as opposed

259. *Id.* at *2.
260. *Id.*
261. *Id.*
262. *Id.* (quoting Righi).
263. *Id.* at *3 (quoting Righi).
264. *Id.* (quoting Righi).

to contractual indemnity claims because there were no written subcontracts indemnifying WTM.[265]

At some point, Rohling calculated that National had an 80 percent chance of defeating coverage based on the Subcontractors Exclusion.[266] In reaching this conclusion, she relied on Righi's reports that subcontractors had done all or most of the work on Cosgrove's home and that WTM had no contracts with any of them.[267]

Rohling's determination that there was an 80 percent chance of National prevailing on coverage affected settlement negotiations in the state court suit. For instance, when Righi recommended settling the suit for $110,000, Rohling would not offer more than $23,000 based on her coverage analysis. Likewise, when Cosgrove later made a $109,000 offer of judgment, Rohling refused Righi's request for up to $109,000 in authority to attempt to negotiate a lower settlement and rejected the offer of judgment.

Cosgrove, WTM, and the Mitzels finally settled their dispute through a nonexecution agreement and stipulated judgment for over $443,000.[268] The state court held a reasonableness hearing and reduced the judgment to around $304,000. Cosgrove then sued National in an Arizona state court for breach of contract and bad faith. National removed the case to federal court, where the parties filed competing motions for partial summary judgment.

Cosgrove's motion was based on the Arizona Supreme Court's decision in *Parsons v. Continental National American Group*,[269] where the supreme court held:

> When an attorney who is an insurance company's agent uses the confidential relationship between attorney and a client to gather information so as to deny the insured coverage under the policy . . . such conduct constitutes a waiver of any policy defense, and is so contrary to public policy that the insurance company is estopped as a matter of law from disclaiming liability under an exclusionary clause in the policy.[270]

The *Parsons* court also held that a reservation of rights is immaterial when the same lawyer represents "conflicting clients."[271] Furthermore, the Arizona Supreme Court explained that an insurer does not have "the right to engage an

265. *Id.*
266. *Id.* at *4.
267. *See id.*
268. Nonexecution agreements and stipulated judgments (also known as consent judgments) are discussed in Chapter 11.
269. 550 P.2d 94 (Ariz. 1976).
270. *Id.* at 99.
271. *Id.*

attorney to act on behalf of the insured to defend a claim against the insured while at the same time build a defense against the insured on behalf of the insurer."[272]

Cosgrove contended that National violated *Parsons* by denying coverage based on information that Righi learned from Mr. Mitzel (acting as WTM's agent) during the attorney-client relationship.[273] National countered that *Parsons* only applies where the defense lawyer discloses the insured's confidential or privileged information, which the missing subcontracts were not.[274] National specifically argued that:

> [A]ll Mr. Righi learned was the identity of who had performed the work on the project and that WTM had no written agreements with its subcontractors. Defendant argues that there is no evidence that suggests that WTM intended to keep this information confidential or that Mr. Mitzel relayed this information to Mr. Righi in confidence. In short, . . . the information about the subcontractors was simply routine information and that this information in a construction defect case is almost always a known fact based on the insured's job file. Defendant reminds the court that Mr. Righi testified that he thought he learned this information both from Mr. Mitzel and from a "review of the job file." Thus, . . . it [was] not even clear that Mr. Righi learned the information about the subcontractors from Mr. Mitzel. Defendant suggests that it could have learned this information if it had . . . completed its own investigation rather than relying on the information it received from Mr. Righi. If it could have learned this information on its own, then . . . this information cannot possibly be considered confidential information.[275]

The court, however, believed that National was reading *Parsons* too narrowly. Here, Righi used his attorney-client relationship with WTM to collect information that he passed on to National, which National then used to WTM's detriment.[276] When Righi disclosed the subcontractor information to Rohling, he either knew or reasonably should have known that WTM's policy contained the Subcontractors Exclusion and that National might attempt to deny coverage on that basis.[277] Nonetheless, Righi provided Rohling the very information that National would need to deny coverage based on the Subcontractors Exclusion. Indeed, in his June 2, 2009, report to Rohling, Righi expressly said that he would try to gather information concerning WTM's use of subcontractors on Cosgrove's project. As the *Cosgrove* court saw things,

272. *Id.*
273. Cosgrove v. Nat'l Fire & Marine Ins. Co., No. 2:14-cv-2229-HRH, 2017 WL 11437374, at *6 (D. Ariz. Apr. 10, 2017), *vacated*, No. 2:14-cv-2229-HRH, 2017 WL 11490239 (D. Ariz. May 5, 2017) (approving the parties' stipulation to vacate the April 10, 2017, order because the case settled).
274. *Id.*
275. *Id.* at *7 (footnote omitted).
276. *Id.*
277. *Id.*

Righi owed his full loyalty to WTM, but his loyalty to WTM was diluted by his allegiance to National.[278] This was a clear *Parsons* violation.[279]

The court further explained that *Parsons* does not require the information at issue to be independently confidential. Liability under *Parsons* only requires that the insurer obtain the information through the defense lawyer's attorney-client relationship with the insured and that the disclosure of the information be detrimental to the insured.[280]

The court recognized that the subcontractor information formed the basis for WTM's third-party complaint, which then made the information freely available.[281] By the time Righi filed WTM's third-party complaint, however, he had already crossed the *Parsons* line. Righi disclosed the information about the subcontractors to Rohling in 2009, long before he filed the third-party complaint in April 2010. The court rejected National's argument that finding a *Parsons* violation would mean that Righi could not have filed a third-party complaint. As the court explained, "[a] lawyer must obtain his client's consent to disclose information in pleadings."[282] Disclosing the subcontractor information by filing a third-party complaint with WTM's consent would not have violated *Parsons*.[283]

The court acknowledged that precluding National from invoking the Subcontractors Exclusion might seem punitive. But, if National had done its own investigation of WTM's situation rather than relying on the information disclosed by Righi, it could have safely denied coverage based on the Subcontractors Exclusion.[284] Instead, because National learned the subcontractor information from Righi and then used it to WTM's detriment before it was publicized, National was estopped from relying on the information to deny coverage.[285]

In conclusion, the court awarded Cosgrove partial summary judgment. In granting her motion, the court allowed National to argue against coverage for any reason other than the Subcontractors Exclusion.

Looking back on *Cosgrove*, Righi was in a difficult position. If he received a copy of National's reservation of rights letter or was familiar with subcontractor exclusions by virtue of his practice, he should have recognized the challenges posed by Mr. Mitzel's revelation that WTM had no written subcontracts

---

278. *Id.* (quoting Lake Havasu Cmty. Hosp., Inc. v. Ariz. Title Ins. & Tr. Co., 687 P.2d 371, 384 (Ariz. Ct. App. 1984), *disapproved on other grounds by* Barmat v. John & Jane Doe Partners A–D, 747 P.2d 1218, 1223 (Ariz. 1987)).

279. *Id.* (quoting *Lake Havasu*, 687 P.2d at 384).

280. *Id.*

281. *Id.* at *8.

282. *Id.*

283. *Id.*

284. *Id.*

285. *Id.*

with the subcontractors who worked on Cosgrove's home. Although the lack of subcontracts likely would have emerged in discovery because Cosgrove would have sought production of WTM's job file to pursue her own claims against the subcontractors or for other purposes, that prospect did not empower Righi to reveal the subcontractor information to National without WTM's express consent. In addition, Righi could not file a third-party action against the subcontractors alleging common law implied indemnity claims without WTM's express consent because filing that action would highlight the missing subcontracts. At the same time, *not* filing a third-party action seeking contractual indemnity would have equally alerted National to the lack of subcontracts.

National could have avoided estoppel if Rohling had asked WTM for copies of the subcontracts rather than relying on Righi to provide the information. If Mr. Mitzel would have asked Righi how to respond to such a request, Righi should have advised him that he could not give coverage advice and urged Mr. Mitzel to obtain coverage counsel.

4. *Summary*

Cosgrove aside, conflicts of interest attributable to an insured's confidential information are rare. A defense lawyer can avoid or mitigate many such conflicts through appropriate disclosures at the outset of the representation. When they do surface, conflicts and other problems related to an insured's confidential information can be incredibly nuanced and require significant care to navigate.

F. Disagreements over Litigation Strategy as Conflicts of Interest

An insurer's right to control its insured's defense naturally encompasses the right to control litigation strategy in conjunction with the appointed defense lawyer. As long as the insurer conducts the defense reasonably,[286] the insured cannot rightly insist on representation by independent counsel based on its dissatisfaction with the direction of the defense. The insured's disagreement with

---

286. *See* Harvey v. GEICO Gen. Ins. Co., 259 So. 3d 1, 6 (Fla. 2018) (explaining that when handling an insured's defense, an insurer must use the same degree of care and diligence that a person of ordinary care and prudence should exercise in managing his or her own business (quoting Boston Old Colony Ins. Co. v. Gutierrez, 386 So. 2d 783, 785 (Fla. 1980))); Gruber v. Est. of Marshall, 482 P.3d 612, 618 (Kan. Ct. App. 2021) (stating that defending claims against its insureds, an insurer "must conduct itself with that degree of care which would be used by an ordinarily prudent person in the handling of his or her own business"); Hartford Cas. Ins. Co. v. N.H. Ins. Co., 628 N.E.2d 14, 16 (Mass. 1994) ("The general rule . . . is that an insurer is held to a standard of reasonable conduct in its defense of its insured."); Cleaver–Brooks, Inc. v. Twin City Fire Ins. Co., 865 N.W.2d 105, 116 (Neb. 2015) (footnote omitted) ("When a claim arises, an insurer generally owes a duty to the insured to exercise reasonable care in defending the suit."); Nautilus Ins. Co. v. Access Med., Inc., 482 P.3d 683, 687 n.3 (Nev. 2021) ("When an insurer has a contractual duty to defend, the law implies a duty to do so in a reasonable manner.").

the insurer's or defense lawyer's litigation strategy does not create a conflict of interest.[287] *Roussos v. Allstate Insurance Co.*[288] is a representative case.

In that case, Robert Baxley sued Shirley Roussos for injuries he suffered in a car wreck with Roussos, who was insured by Allstate. Allstate notified Roussos that it would defend her in connection with Baxley's suit, but she disagreed with Allstate's plan to either settle the case or stipulate to damages and try the case on liability alone. She vehemently denied liability and did not want Allstate to pay Baxley a dime. She therefore rejected the lawyer Allstate hired to defend her on the basis that the lawyer had a conflict of interest and asked Allstate to pay for a lawyer of her choice or let her control her defense. Allstate declined and repeatedly tried to persuade her to let it defend her. Roussos steadfastly refused and represented herself pro se. Allstate filed a declaratory judgment action seeking to avoid its duty to indemnify her if she lost Baxley's case. Allstate subsequently moved for summary judgment, which the trial granted on the basis that Roussos's breach of her duty to cooperate relieved Allstate of its contractual obligations. Roussos appealed.

On appeal, Roussos alleged several conflicts of interest that she claimed excused her failure to cooperate. The conflict she principally focused on was Allstate's planned defense of Baxley's lawsuit. Briefly, while Allstate believed that Roussos was potentially liable for the accident and wanted to consider settling, Roussos aspired to maintain her clean driving record and thus did not want Allstate to pay Baxley anything.[289]

The *Roussos* court reasoned that Roussos's disagreement with Allstate over the manner in which she was to be defended did not present the type of conflict of interest that required Allstate to provide her with independent counsel.[290] Although Roussos's and Allstate's goals were not identical—Roussos believed that she had been unjustly sued and wanted vindication while Allstate was willing to minimize her liability and expedite the litigation—they were simply not adverse.[291] Roussos and Allstate both would have benefited greatly if, at trial, Roussos were found not to have been negligent.[292]

The court observed that an insurer's right to control an insured's defense is essential to protect the insurer's financial interest in the outcome of the lawsuit.[293] Accordingly, it was unwilling to extend an insurer's duty to provide independent counsel to a case "where the insured merely disagrees with the

287. *See* Nede Mgmt., Inc. v. Aspen Am. Ins. Co., 282 Cal. Rptr. 3d 122, 131 (Ct. App. 2021); OneBeacon Am. Ins. Co. v. Celanese Corp., 84 N.E.3d 867, 873 (Mass. App. Ct. 2017); Steinman v. Silbowitz, 714 N.Y.S.2d 209, 210 (App. Div. 2000).

288. 655 A.2d 40 (Md. Ct. Spec. App. 1995).

289. *Id.* at 43.

290. *Id.* at 44.

291. *Id.*

292. *Id.*

293. *Id.*

manner in which she is to be defended."[294] After resolving one more issue, the *Roussos* court affirmed the trial court judgment for Allstate.

OneBeacon America Insurance Co. v. Celanese Corp.[295] arose out of numerous asbestos and chemical injury lawsuits against Celanese. OneBeacon agreed to take over Celanese's defense in these cases rather than just sharing the defense costs as it had for years, and further agreed to indemnify Celanese up to the liability limits of its policy. But in taking control of Celanese's defense, OneBeacon insisted on replacing the law firm that had been defending Celanese in the litigation for 14 years. Celanese refused to cede control of its defense or to allow OneBeacon to appoint new counsel based on a supposed conflict of interest.

In the declaratory judgment action that followed, the *OneBeacon* court explained that because OneBeacon had agreed to defend Celanese without a reservation of rights, it had the right to control the defense.[296] OneBeacon's right to control Celanese's defense included the authority to choose defense counsel and to make other defense-related decisions that would traditionally be vested in Celanese as the named party in the case.[297]

Boxed in by OneBeacon's unconditional promise to indemnify it up to its policy limits and by the court's firm view of the scope of OneBeacon's right to control the defense, Celanese argued that a conflict of interest existed by virtue of its disagreement with OneBeacon over the appropriate way to defend the underlying tort litigation.[298] The trial court had summarized the parties' competing positions as follows:

> Celanese understandably places a high priority on its reputation, and seeks publicly to defend and to rebut any and all claims that its products or premises contain carcinogenic or other poisonous material. OneBeacon's business view is, equally unsurprisingly, a more pragmatic one. OneBeacon's focus is on reducing the volume and cost of pending cases wherever possible, by seeking out reasonable settlements and thus incurring and applying indemnity payments towards the policy limits, not solely defense payments.[299]

The *OneBeacon* court easily rejected Celanese's position. Under its policy, OneBeacon agreed to defend and indemnify Celanese with respect to claims of bodily injury or property damage and nothing more. Celanese's reputation "was not something that OneBeacon was required to insure or defend."[300]

294. *Id.* (citing Cardin v. Pac. Emps. Ins. Co., 745 F. Supp. 330, 336–38 (D. Md. 1990)).
295. 84 N.E.3d 867 (Mass. App. Ct. 2017).
296. *Id.* at 872.
297. *Id.*
298. *Id.* at 875.
299. *Id.* (footnote omitted) (quoting the trial court).
300. *Id.*

Bottom line, Celanese declined OneBeacon's offer to defend and conducted its own defense because it believed that its lawyers would defend it better than might any lawyer OneBeacon selected. Celanese had that right. But because there was no conflict of interest, Celanese was not entitled to recover its defense costs after it rejected OneBeacon's offer of a defense without a reservation of rights.[301]

Northern County Mutual Insurance Co. v. Davalos[302] is yet another case where the court held that the insured's disagreement with the insurer over litigation strategy was not a conflict that entitled the insured to independent counsel. The insured there, Timoteo Davalos, was injured in a car accident in Dallas County, Texas. He lived in Matagorda County, Texas. He sued the driver of the other car in Matagorda County. The other driver and his wife then sued Davalos and another party in Dallas County. Although Davalos had insurance with Northern County Mutual Insurance Co. (Northern), he turned over the Dallas County litigation to his lawyers in the Matagorda County case, who answered the suit and moved to transfer it to Matagorda County. Davalos's lawyers then notified Northern of the Dallas County suit. In response, Northern informed Davalos that it would defend him without a reservation of rights, that it would not hire his lawyers to defend the Dallas County case, that it opposed transfer of the Dallas County case to Matagorda County, and that it had retained another lawyer to defend him in the Dallas County action.[303] Northern also warned Davalos that his coverage might be jeopardized if his personal counsel did not drop their motion to transfer venue and withdraw.[304] Lastly, Northern told Davalos that he was free to retain his personal counsel at his own expense to consult on the Dallas County case, and that Northern's chosen lawyer would cooperate with Davalos's personal lawyer so long as their collaboration did not jeopardize the defense.[305] Northern reasonably believed Dallas County to be the proper venue for both actions arising out of the accident.

Davalos's lawyers rejected Northern's offered defense. They asserted that Northern's offered defense was qualified and thus breached the duty to defend, and that Northern could not select defense counsel because its dispute with Davalos over the venue motion created a conflict of interest.[306] The Matagorda County action ultimately was transferred to Dallas County on another party's motion. Northern settled the original Dallas County case against Davalos. Meanwhile, Davalos sued Northern in Matagorda County, claiming that

301. *Id.* at 876–77.
302. 140 S.W.3d 685 (Tex. 2004).
303. *Id.* at 687.
304. *Id.*
305. *Id.*
306. *Id.*

Northern had breached its duty to defend him in the Dallas County action, that Northern was guilty of bad faith, and that it had violated the Texas Insurance Code.[307]

Both the trial court and a lower appellate court concluded that Northern had breached its duty to defend by insisting that Davalos withdraw his venue motion and violated the Texas Insurance Code by neither accepting nor rejecting his defense within the statutorily-mandated time. Northern successfully sought review by the Texas Supreme Court, which reversed the lower appellate court.

The Texas Supreme Court rejected Davalos's argument that Northern had improperly conditioned his defense. An insurer's right to defend an insured includes the authority to select defense counsel and make other decisions that would normally be entrusted to the insured as the named party in the case.[308] Moreover, not every disagreement between an insurer and an insured about the conduct of a defense creates a conflict of interest; were the rule otherwise, the insured could commandeer the defense merely by disagreeing with the insurer's tactics.[309] Instead, an insured may "rightfully refuse an inadequate defense and may also refuse any defense conditioned on an unreasonable, extra-contractual demand that threatens the insured's independent legal rights."[310] Thus, and by way of example, Northern could not have conditioned Davalos's defense on his promise to dismiss his Matagorda County action.[311] Here, however, the disagreement centered on the appropriate venue for the defense of the Dallas County action, not Davalos's right to pursue his own remedy.

Northern never deprived Davalos of a defense. It was difficult for the *Northern County* court to imagine a situation in which a choice of venue might spawn a disqualifying conflict of interest.[312] Choosing venue is a strategic litigation decision entrusted to the insurer or to defense counsel.[313] According to the court, the selection of venue "should ordinarily have no impact on the insured's legitimate interests under the policy."[314]

The *Northern County* court concluded that Northern did not breach its duty to defend. Its offer to defend Davalos in the Dallas County action satisfied its contractual obligations. The court also found that Northern did not violate the Texas Insurance Code. Northern's disagreement with Davalos over venue did not render its offer to defend him equivocal.

307. *Id.* at 688.
308. *Id.*
309. *Id.* at 689.
310. *Id.*
311. *Id.*
312. *Id.* at 690.
313. *See id.*
314. *Id.*

The *Northern County* court reached the correct decision given its focus on Northern's alleged breach of its duty to defend but Davalos's venue stance arguably had some merit. The court ruled against Davalos in part by reasoning that venue is a logistical issue. But Davalos's lawyers surely believed that venue is more than that. They probably believed based on their experience that Matagorda County was a favorable plaintiffs' venue or was at least better than Dallas County. Consolidating the cases in Dallas County therefore reduced the chances of winning Davalos's case against the other driver or diminished its settlement or verdict value. From Davalos's perspective, then, Northern's insistence on keeping venue in Dallas County was an unreasonable demand that threatened his independent rights.

On the other hand, the Dallas County and Matagorda County actions were going to be consolidated in one county or the other. Assuming that Matagorda County was a favorable plaintiffs' venue, consolidation of the cases there would have enhanced the value of the other driver's lawsuit against Davalos. Northern was only obligated to give Davalos's interests consideration equal to its own; it was not required to subordinate its own interests. Northern was therefore within its rights to demand that Davalos maintain venue in Dallas County.

G. The Insured's Pursuit of Affirmative Claims for Relief

In *Northern County*, Davalos and Northern got crosswise because Davalos prioritized his claim against the other driver over Northern's defense of the other driver's lawsuit against him. In fact, an insurer generally has no duty to fund an insured's prosecution of affirmative claims—such a counterclaims, crossclaims, third-party claims, or even separate actions—as part of its duty to defend the insured.[315] An insurer may not, however, prevent an insured from prosecuting an affirmative claim. The insurer has no authority to do so under its policy, which grants it control only over the insured's defense. Moreover,

315. Aldous v. Darwin Nat'l Assur. Co., 851 F.3d 473, 483 (5th Cir. 2017) (applying Texas law), *vacated in part on other grounds on reh'g*, 889 F.3d 798 (5th Cir. 2018); Spada v. Unigard Ins. Co., 80 F. App'x 27, 29–30 (9th Cir. 2003) (applying Oregon law); Morgan, Lewis & Bockius LLP v. Hanover Ins. Co., 929 F. Supp. 764, 773 (D.N.J. 1996) (applying New Jersey law); Emerald Bay Cmty. Ass'n v. Golden Eagle Ins. Corp., 31 Cal. Rptr. 3d 43, 57 (Ct. App. 2005); Int'l Ins. Co. v. Rollprint Packaging Prods., Inc., 728 N.E.2d 680, 694 (Ill. App. Ct. 2000); Ramsey v. Lee Builders, Inc., 95 P.3d 1033, 1040 (Kan. Ct. App. 2004); Mount Vernon Fire Ins. Co. v. Visionaid, Inc., 76 N.E.3d 204, 213 (Mass. 2017); St. Paul Fire & Marine Ins. Co. v. Nat'l Comput. Sys., Inc., 490 N.W.2d 626, 632 (Minn. Ct. App. 1992); Goldberg v. Am. Home Assur. Co., 439 N.Y.S.2d 2, 4, (App. Div. 1981); Red Head Brass, Inc. v. Buckeye Union Ins. Co., 735 N.E.2d 48, 56 (Ohio Ct. App. 1999); Towne Realty, Inc. v. Zurich Ins. Co., 548 N.W.2d 64, 68–69 (Wis. 1996); Shoshone First Bank v. Pac. Emps. Ins. Co., 2 P.3d 510, 516–17 (Wyo. 2000). As discussed in Chapter 4, however, some courts recognize exceptions to this general rule, such as where an insured's counterclaim, crossclaim, or third-party claim is inextricably intertwined with the defense of the action against the insured or the insured's affirmative claim is defensive in nature. See Chapter 4 for a discussion of these issues.

the insurer's right to control the defense does not broadly permit the insurer to impair the insured's rights in the process of defending the case. Thus, if asked by a defense lawyer or the insured about the insured's prosecution of a counterclaim, for example, the insurer should inform the lawyer and the insured that it will not pay for the insured's pursuit of the counterclaim, but nor will it stop the defense lawyer from advising the insured with respect to the claim or prosecuting it at the insured's expense.

A defense lawyer appointed by an insurer may, if she chooses, prosecute an insured's affirmative claim. In that case, and as indicated earlier, the insured must pay the lawyer to do so. After all, litigation of the insured's affirmative claim is outside the scope of the defense lawyer's representation arranged with the insurer. The lawyer's unwillingness to represent the insured in prosecuting its affirmative claim unless the insured agrees to pay the lawyer for those services on terms acceptable to the lawyer does not pose a conflict of interest that requires the lawyer's replacement by independent counsel.[316] Of course, a defense lawyer may not want to represent an insured in its planned prosecution of an affirmative claim. The defense lawyer's refusal to represent the insured in connection with its affirmative claim is not a conflict of interest, either.[317]

Although a defense lawyer's unwillingness to prosecute an insured's affirmative claims does not constitute a conflict of interest, that does not necessarily mean that a defense lawyer never has any obligations with respect to an insured's affirmative claims. For instance, the insured may not have identified a compulsory counterclaim that it might wish to pursue but the defense lawyer has spotted the issue. In that scenario, the lawyer should alert the insured to the compulsory counterclaim, inform the insured that the lawyer is not willing to prosecute the counterclaim on the insured's behalf, and encourage the insured to promptly seek separate counsel to advise it regarding the claim because the statute of limitations is running.[318] As a legal malpractice treatise explains:

> A lawyer may be obligated to advise the client regarding collateral matters or, at least, alert the client to the need for legal representation. This concept of a "peripheral" duty concerns those legal needs that should be reasonably apparent to a lawyer, even if neither the lawyer nor the client intended the matter to be within the scope of the representation. The controlling standard is whether the remedy or liability should have been apparent to the ordinary lawyer under the circumstances.[319]

316. Flexi-Van Leasing, Inc. v. Travelers Indem. Co., 837 F. App'x 141, 147 (4th Cir. 2020).
317. Simonyan v. Nationwide Ins. Co. of Am., 293 Cal. Rptr. 3d 555, 564 (Ct. App. 2022).
318. *See* Prevratil v. Mohr, 678 A.2d 243, 250 (N.J. 1996) (stating that insurance defense lawyers should advise insureds of the need to seek the advice of personal counsel regarding affirmative claims).
319. Ronald E. Mallen, Legal Malpractice § 8.8, at 1017 (2024) (footnote omitted).

A California court took a similar stance in the workers' compensation insurance context:

> One of an attorney's basic functions is to advise. Liability can exist because the attorney failed to provide advice. Not only should an attorney furnish advice when requested, but he or she should also volunteer opinions when necessary to further the client's objectives. The attorney need not advise and caution of every possible alternative, but only of those that may result in adverse consequences if not considered. . . . [E]ven when a retention is expressly limited, the attorney may still have a duty to alert the client to legal problems which are reasonably apparent, even though they fall outside the scope of the retention. The rationale is that, as between the lay client and the attorney, the latter is more qualified to recognize and analyze the client's legal needs. The attorney need not represent the client on such matters. Nevertheless, the attorney should inform the client of the limitations of the attorney's representation and of the possible need for other counsel.[320]

The lawyer has no duty, however, to ascertain the length of the applicable limitations period or to so inform the insured. Such advice is, again, outside the scope of the lawyer's representation and it is not necessary to fulfill any peripheral duty the lawyer allegedly may owe the insured. If the lawyer reasonably believes that the limitation period will soon expire, however, the lawyer should alert the insured so that the insured appreciates the need to promptly consult another lawyer.[321]

H. The Defense Lawyer or Other Lawyers in the Law Firm Represent the Insurer in Unrelated Coverage Matters

It is common for a lawyer to defend an insurance company's policyholders in litigation and to also represent the insurer in coverage matters. Even if a lawyer who defends an insurer's policyholders in litigation does not represent the insurer in coverage matters, other lawyers in her firm may. Do these separate representations create a conflict of interest for the defense lawyer and entitle the insured to representation by independent counsel? The short answer to this question is "no."[322] The answer is the same regardless of whether the case being defended is a full coverage case or is being defended under a reservation

320. Nichols v. Keller, 19 Cal. Rptr. 2d 601, 608 (Ct. App. 1993).

321. Barker & Silver, *supra* note 11, § 9.02[5], at 9-22.

322. *See, e.g.*, Arden v. Forsberg & Umlauf, P.S., 402 P.3d 245, 251 (Wash. 2017) ("We reject the suggestion advanced that wherever a previous relationship between the insurer and retained counsel exists, a per se disqualification rule is supported."); *see also* Red Head Brass, Inc. v. Buckeye Union Ins. Co., 735 N.E.2d 48, 60 (Ohio Ct. App. 1999) (rejecting the insured's claim that the defense lawyers should have advised it about the other defense work their firm did for Buckeye and finding no conflict of interest to support a breach of fiduciary duty claim).

of rights.[323] Now, if a lawyer hired by an insurer to defend its insured or other members of the lawyer's firm also represent the insurer in unrelated coverage matters, must the lawyer disclose that fact to the insured? The answer to this question is more complex.

A lawyer has no duty to advise the insured that either she or her colleagues represent the insurer in unrelated coverage matters in a full coverage case. When an insurer accepts coverage, the insurer's commitment to indemnify the insured up to the policy limits means that there is no divergence of interests between the insurer and the insured regarding the conduct of the defense. Indeed, their interests are fully aligned. Accordingly, the lawyer's or her colleagues' unrelated representations of the insurer in coverage matters are immaterial to the insured. A lawyer has no duty to convey immaterial information to a client.[324] Nor does a lawyer have a duty to share with the client information that is unrelated to the client's representation,[325] which in this instance the lawyer's or her firm's representation of the insurer in unrelated coverage matters plainly is.

The lawyer also has no duty to disclose unrelated coverage representations where the insurer reserves its right to disclaim coverage on grounds that do not entitle the insured to representation by independent counsel. Here, again, the defense lawyer's or her colleagues' representation of the insurance company in unrelated coverage matters is immaterial to the insured.

On the other hand, the lawyer may have to disclose her or her firm's representation of the insurer in unrelated coverage matters where there *is* a conflict of interest that entitles the insured to independent counsel. In such a case—assuming the insured is willing to consider representation by the lawyer appointed by the insurer despite the conflict—the insured's consent to the representation must be informed. In this situation, the defense lawyer's, or her firm's representation of the insurer in unrelated coverage matters may influence the insured's decision. Rightly or wrongly, the insured may question whether the lawyer's or law firm's coverage work for the insurer will prompt the lawyer to act to the insured's detriment when conducting the defense. The insured

323. As the context suggests, a "full coverage" case as described here is one in which the insurer's duty to indemnify the insured up to the liability limits of its policy is unquestioned.

324. Douglas R. Richmond et al., Professional Responsibility in Litigation 453 (3d ed. 2021); *see also* Tracy W. McCormack & Christopher J. Bodnar, *Honesty Is the Best Policy: It's Time to Disclose Lack of Jury Trial Experience*, 23 Geo. J. Legal Ethics 155, 189 (2010) (stating that a lawyer's fiduciary duties do not include a duty to disclose information that is immaterial, unreliable, or already known to the client).

325. *See, e.g.*, L.A. Cnty. Bar Ass'n, Pro. Resp. & Ethics Comm., Formal Op. No. 506, at 5 (2001) (opining that under California Rule of Professional Conduct 3-500, a lawyer has no duty to disclose information to a client that is unrelated to the client's representation).

cannot evaluate this risk unless he or she is aware of it. The defense lawyer is the natural source of information for the insured.[326]

Similarly, the lawyer may have a duty to disclose her or her firm's representation of the insurer in unrelated coverage matters in a jurisdiction that allows an insured to reject a defense under reservation of rights. In theory, the lawyer's or her law firm's relationship with the insurer could influence the insured's decision whether to accept or reject a defense by appointed counsel in a case defended under a reservation of rights.

Finally, even without a duty to do so, a defense lawyer might disclose her or her law firm's representation of the insurer in unrelated coverage matters even in a full coverage case because she believes it to be important in establishing a relationship with the insured or because she considers it to be prudent risk management. For instance, a lawyer might include a statement along these lines in her engagement letter to the insured:

> The firm and I represent [the insurer] in coverage matters adverse to other insureds in cases unrelated to yours. Neither I nor any other lawyer in the firm will advise [the insurer] regarding any duties or obligations that it may owe to you in this case. We will not discuss your insurance coverage with [the insurer]. I do not believe that my representation of [the insurer] in unrelated matters or my colleagues' representation of [the insurer] in unrelated matters will affect our ability to defend you competently and diligently. Even so, I wanted to make you aware of our unrelated representations of [the insurer] so that you may give our relationship with [the insurer] whatever consideration you wish.

Alternatively, a lawyer might discuss her relationship with the insurer in her initial meeting with the insured and then send a confirming letter. If a lawyer opts to make such a disclosure, written confirmation is a good practice.

V. Representing Insureds under Defense-within-Limits Policies

Standard liability insurance policies include a supplementary payments provision that states that the insurer will pay all defense expenses incurred in litigation against the insured in addition to the policy limits. Accordingly, no matter how costly the litigation, the full policy limits are always available to indemnify the insured or to pay a settlement. Some liability insurance policies,

326. *See generally* Model Rules of Pro. Conduct r. 1.4 (Am. Bar Ass'n 2023) (governing lawyers' duty to communicate with clients).

however, provide that the policy limits are reduced by defense expenses, including defense counsel's fees, rather than the insurer paying those expenses outside the policy limits as supplementary payments.[327] These policies are variously described as "burning limits," "cannibalizing," "defense-within-limits," "depleting" or "depleting limits," "eroding limits," "wasting," "spend down," "self-consuming," or "self-liquidating" policies because the liability limits are reduced by defense expenses. Every dollar spent on the insured's defense correspondingly reduces the amount of money available to settle the case or indemnify the insured. Defense-within-limits policies are common in directors and officers (D&O) liability insurance, employment practices liability (EPL) insurance, and errors and omissions (E&O) insurance, including lawyers' professional liability (LPL) insurance.

To understand how coverage under defense-within-limits policies operates, consider this hypothetical case. Lawyer *L* is insured under a defense-within-limits LPL policy with liability limits of $1 million per claim. Client *C* sues *L* for professional negligence and breach of fiduciary duty. The case goes to trial and defense expenses through trial are $250,000. If *C* wins a $500,000 judgment against *L*, the insurer will fully indemnify *L* because it has $750,000 available under the policy after paying the defense expenses. If, however, *C* obtains a $1 million judgment, the insurer will pay $750,000 (its available policy limits) and *L* will have to pay the remaining $250,000 unless *L* has excess insurance.

Alternatively, consider the following settlement scenario. Client *C* sues Lawyer *L* for professional negligence and breach of fiduciary duty. *L*'s defense-within-limits LPL policy provides $1 million in coverage. *L* and *C* fiercely litigate their dispute but, as trial nears, they participate in court-ordered mediation. By the end of the mediation, *L*'s defense costs will have reached $300,000. If *C* is willing to settle for $700,000 or less and the proposed settlement is reasonable from the defense perspective, the case will resolve at no cost to *L*. On the other hand, if *C* refuses to settle for less than $900,000, the case will either go to trial or *L* will have to contribute $200,000 to achieve a settlement.

Most defense-within-limits policies are defense-cost-indemnification policies. This means that the insured controls the defense—including selecting defense counsel—and the insurance company either advances or reimburses the insured's "defense expenses," including defense counsel's legal fees, or advances or reimburses the insured's "claim expenses," which include defense costs.[328]

327. *See* Fed. Ins. Co. v. Singing River Health Sys. Found., 850 F.3d 187, 198 (5th Cir. 2017) (rejecting the insured's claim that an insurer that issued a defense-within-limits policy was required to pay defense costs in addition to the policy limits on the basis that the policy should be enforced as written).

328. Defense-cost-indemnification policies are discussed in Chapter 10.

Under other defense-within-limits policies, however, the insurer retains the duty and right to defend the insured.

Defense-within-limits policies pose few problems for defense lawyers or insurers where the insured controls the defense and the insurer simply pays the expenses. Nonetheless, some commentators and courts have diagnosed defense-within-limits policies as being infused with conflicts of interest.[329] This prognosis is most acute where the insurer controls the defense.[330] One scholar has characterized the problem where the insurer controls the defense as follows:

> Under the [defense-within-limits] policy, there is an inherent conflict between the insured and the insurer in every case where payment of loss plus payment of defense costs could exceed the limits of liability, since every dollar spent on defense of the claim is a dollar that will not be available for settlement or satisfaction of judgment. This is no problem as long as the insured and insurer are fully agreed (and continue to agree) on the merits of settling versus defending including issues of timing and resources invested in the process.
>
> The problem is that the insured has a direct interest in assuring that the limit of liability is available for settlement or payment of judgment, while the insurer may seek to defend on the merits. It may be in the financial interest of a risk averse insured to offer the entire limits even in a case of poor liability rather than run the risk that a hard fought defense will deplete the limits and block settlement later or leave an unsatisfied judgment. On the other hand, it may be in the insurer's interest to establish through a hard fought defense that "nuisance" claims will not invoke any settlement offers from this insurance company. Hence, a conflict is born.[331]

Despite these concerns, conflicts of interest linked to defense-within-limits policies are an exaggerated threat, as perhaps best evidenced by the lack of reported cases on the subject. An insurer that has the right to control the insured's defense under a defense-within-limits policy has no incentive to spend wastefully in the process. In fact, in most cases, the insured's interests and the insurer's interests will be aligned. Where the insured has a defense-cost-indemnification policy, the insured controls its own defense and can balance

329. *See, e.g.*, Edwards v. Daugherty, 883 So. 2d 932, 942 (La. 2004) ("The cause for concern [with a defense-within-limits policy] is the interest conflict that arises in every case between the insured and the insurer when dollars spent on defending claims result in fewer dollars being available for settlement of the claims or satisfaction of judgments.").

330. *See* Shaun M. Baldwin, *Legal and Ethical Considerations for "Defense within Limits" Policies*, 61 Def. Couns. J. 89, 89 (1994) ("DWL policies can present practical and ethical dilemmas for both plaintiffs' attorneys and defense counsel because every dollar spent on defense reduces the amount available to satisfy potential judgments. When the insurer attempts to control the defense under a DWL policy, defense counsel also can be placed in a conflict of interest position.").

331. Gregory S. Munro, *Defense within Limits: The Conflicts of "Wasting" or "Cannibalizing" Insurance Policies*, 62 Mont. L. Rev. 131, 148–49 (2001).

its interests in defeating the plaintiff's claims versus settling within available policy limits.

Nevertheless, to protect its insured and itself, an insurer that controls the defense under a defense-within-limits policy should remind the insured at the outset of the case that the policy limits are eroded by defense expenses. Thereafter, the insurer should keep the insured reasonably informed about defense costs and the remaining policy limits.[332] In managing the defense, the insurer should also confirm that the defense expenses are reasonable.[333] Insurers are generally sensitive to defense expenses, but the need for attention is greater where they are controlling the litigation against the insured under a defense-within-limits policy.

For lawyers who are either appointed to defend an insured under a defense-within-limits policy or hired by the insured directly, communication is essential. At the outset of the representation, the lawyer should remind the insured that the policy will be eroded by defense expenses. The lawyer should engage both the insured and the insurer in developing the litigation strategy and then provide them both with a projected litigation budget. To the extent reasonably possible, the lawyer should evaluate the insured's potential liability and the verdict value of the case at the first opportunity and share those evaluations with the insured and the insurer. As the case progresses, the lawyer should either copy the insured on invoices the lawyer sends to the insurer or timely inform the insured of the amounts billed. If the insurer is controlling the defense, the lawyer should copy the insured on all status reports to the insurer. Consistent with a lawyer's duties generally, the lawyer should promptly inform the insured and the insurer of all settlement offers or demands from the plaintiff. Finally, when producing a copy of the insured's policy in discovery, the defense lawyer may want to consider highlighting for the plaintiff's lawyer the fact that the defendant is insured under a defense-within-limits policy. Depending on the facts, this information may cause the plaintiff to moderate its settlement demands to avoid reducing its potential source of recovery through continued or aggressive litigation.

VI. Insurance Company Outside Counsel Guidelines

Insurers have long required the lawyers they engage to defend their insureds to comply with outside counsel guidelines (sometimes described as litigation management guidelines) prepared by the insurer. Insurers' insistence on defense lawyers' adherence to outside counsel guidelines became predominant

332. *See* Ross v. Frank B. Hall & Co. of Wash., 870 P.2d 1007, 1011 (Wash. Ct. App. 1994).
333. *Id.*

in the 1990s and continues today. For example, an insurance company's outside counsel guidelines might specify intervals for reporting on cases; prohibit the attendance of more than one lawyer at a deposition, trial, or hearing without the insurer's prior permission; require prior approval for certain activities, such as filing a dispositive motion or hiring an expert witness; and list tasks or services for which the insurer will not pay, such as secretarial overtime, summer associate or law clerk time, intraoffice conferences, creating files or other supposedly clerical projects, summarizing depositions, legal research in excess of some specified time limit, computerized legal research, and local travel. In imposing such requirements, insurers do not intend to hamstring the defense lawyers they appoint to defend their insureds or to compromise the quality of their insureds' defenses. Rather, they are trying to manage their defense costs. To the extent they impose pre-approval requirements for some activities, such as filing dispositive motions or hiring expert witnesses, insurers aim to force strategic consultation between the lawyer and the claims professional responsible for the case. Among other things, such exchanges may cause either the claims adjuster or the lawyer to reasonably alter their approaches to the defense or potentially to settlement.

However benign an insurer's motives for requiring the lawyers it appoints to defend its insureds to adhere to outside counsel guidelines may be, insisting on compliance with them could in some situations create a conflict of interest for the defense lawyer. Conflict concerns spring first from Model Rule 1.8(f), which prohibits a lawyer from accepting compensation for representing a client from a third party unless "there is no interference with the lawyer's independence of professional judgment or with the client-lawyer relationship."[334] Similarly, Model Rule 5.4(c) states that a lawyer cannot "permit a person who recommends, employs, or pays the lawyer to render legal services for another to direct or regulate the lawyer's professional judgment in rendering such legal services."[335] And if an insurer's outside counsel guidelines were to materially limit a lawyer's reasonable defense of an insured, they might also create a conflict for the lawyer under Model Rule 1.7(a)(2).[336]

In response to requests for guidance from lawyers with insurance defense practices, a number of state ethics committees have opined that lawyers cannot permit insurers to interfere with their professional judgment in defending insureds by mandating compliance with restrictive outside counsel guidelines.[337]

334. Model Rules of Pro. Conduct r. 1.8(f) (Am. Bar Ass'n 2023).

335. *Id.* r. 5.4(c).

336. *See id.* r. 1.7(a)(2) (providing that a lawyer has a conflict of interest where there is a significant risk that the lawyer's representation of a client will be materially limited by the lawyer's responsibilities to another client, a former client, or a third person or by the lawyer's personal interests).

337. *See, e.g.*, 1998 NC Eth. Op. 17, 1999 WL 33262174, at *1 (N.C. State Bar 1998) (citation omitted) ("If the . . . guidelines will restrain a lawyer's professional judgment in representing a particular insured, the lawyer is ethically prohibited from complying with the guidelines. . . . However,

In 2001, the ABA's Standing Committee on Ethics and Professional Responsibility weighed in on the propriety of lawyers complying with insurers' outside counsel guidelines. In Formal Opinion 01-421, the committee observed that while defense lawyers "must be sensitive to the economic interests of the insurance companies that employ them," they could not meet insurers' economic expectations by sacrificing their professional judgment or the quality of their legal services when defending insureds.[338] Consistent with that observation, the committee concluded that lawyers representing insureds must not permit the insurance company to require compliance with outside counsel guidelines that they reasonably believe will materially compromise their professional judgment or impair their ability to competently represent the insured.[339]

Courts have reached similar conclusions.[340] *In re Rules of Professional Conduct and Insurer Imposed Billing Rules and Procedures*[341] is the leading case on insurers' use of outside counsel guidelines. The *In re Rules* court concluded that the insurers' outside counsel guidelines that required defense lawyers to obtain prior approval to schedule depositions, conduct research, employ experts, or prepare motions fundamentally interfered with the lawyers' exercise of their independent professional judgment in violation of Rule 1.8(f).[342] The court was not moved by the insurers' argument that they enforced their preapproval requirements only rarely because that stance begged the question

a lawyer may comply with billing restrictions and guidelines if the insured consents . . . after full disclosure of the benefits and risks involved."); OH Adv. Op. 2000-3, 2000 WL 1005223, at *6 (Sup. Ct. of Ohio, Bd. of Comm'rs on Grievances & Discipline 2000) ("[I]t is improper . . . for an insurance defense attorney to abide by an insurance company's litigation management guidelines in the representation of an insured when the guidelines interfere with the professional judgment of the attorney. Attorneys must not yield professional control of their legal work to an insurer."); OR Eth. Op. 2005-166, 2005 WL 5679592, at *1 (Or. State Bar Ass'n, Bd. of Governors 2005) ("Lawyer may comply with the Guidelines only if Lawyer has an opportunity to review and evaluate the Guidelines with respect to each case and, based on that review, Lawyer reasonably concludes that compliance with the Guidelines will not materially compromise Lawyer's professional, independent judgment or Lawyer's ability to provide competent representation to Insured. . . . Moreover, throughout the case, Lawyer has an ongoing ethical obligation to reevaluate whether his or her continued compliance with the Guidelines impedes his or her ability to exercise independent judgment."); TX Eth. Op. 533, 2000 WL 987291, at *3 (Sup. Ct. of Tex., Pro. Ethics Comm. 2000) ("It's impermissible . . . for a lawyer to agree with an insurance company to restrictions which interfere with the lawyer's exercise of his or her independent professional judgment in rendering such legal services to the insured/client."); UT Eth. Op. 02-03, 2002 WL 340262, at *8 (Utah State Bar, Ethics Advisory Op. Comm. 2002) ("If compliance with the guidelines will be inconsistent with the lawyer's professional obligations, and if the insurer is unwilling to modify the guidelines, the lawyer must not undertake the representation.").

338. ABA Comm. on Ethics & Pro. Resp., Formal Op. 01-421, at 4 (2001) [hereinafter ABA Formal Op. 01-421].

339. *Id.* at 1.

340. *See, e.g.*, *In re* Youngblood, 895 S.W.2d 322, 328 (Tenn. 1995) ("Any policy, arrangement or device which effectively limits, by design or operation, the attorney's professional judgment on behalf of or loyalty to the client is prohibited by the Code, and, undoubtedly, would not be consistent with public policy.").

341. 2 P.3d 806 (Mont. 2000).

342. *Id.* at 815.

of whether the prior approval requirement violated Montana's rules of professional conduct.[343] Nor was the court persuaded by the insurers' argument that their preapproval requirements did not impair defense lawyers' independent judgment because "when an insurer denies approval for particular actions that defense counsel propose, nothing prevents defense counsel from exercising their independent judgment and doing the very thing for which the insurer has denied approval."[344] The *In re Rules* court rejected the insurers' "dubious premise" that the threat to withhold payment for litigation activities would not interfere with defense lawyers' independent judgment, pointing out that the defense firms' conduct in petitioning the court for relief plainly indicated that the threat of nonpayment impaired their exercise of professional judgment.[345]

In fact, insurers' outside counsel guidelines rarely interfere with lawyers' independent professional judgment in representing insureds.[346] Most defense lawyers effectively represent insureds while complying with insurers' outside counsel guidelines. In the unusual case where a defense lawyer believes that an insurer's unwillingness to approve a task or project or pay for an activity impairs her ability to effectively represent the insured, the lawyer should ask the responsible claims professional to waive the guideline and explain the reasoning for the request. Presumably, the claims professional will agree with the defense lawyer's rationale and excuse compliance with the guideline. After all, the insurer has no interest in providing the insured with an inadequate defense. Nor does the insurer generally have reason to doubt the professional judgment of the lawyer to whom it has entrusted the insured's defense.

If the insurer will not waive the guideline and the lawyer still believes that compliance with the guideline will materially limit the insured's representation, the lawyer should consult with the insured. The lawyer should explain the need for the task or activity, the effect on the insured's defense if the work goes undone, and the insurer's right under the policy to control the insured's defense. If the lawyer is unwilling to perform the task or undertake the activity without being paid and the insured will not consent to the limitation on its representation or agree to pay the lawyer for the work in lieu of the insurer doing so, the lawyer has a conflict of interest that requires her withdrawal from the insured's representation.

At this point, the defense lawyer should again try to persuade the insurer to change its position and lift the restriction imposed by the guideline. A prudent

343. *Id.* at 814.

344. *Id.* at 815.

345. *Id.*

346. *See generally* PA Eth. Op. 01-200, 2001 WL 1744775, at *4 (Pa. Bar Ass'n, Comm. on Legal Ethics & Pro. Resp. 2001) ("In the insurance defense context, undivided loyalty to the insured is usually fully consistent with loyalty to the insurance company and its directives because the insurer is usually in the best position to manage the litigation to the advantage of both the insured and itself in a cost-effective fashion.").

insurer should relent because of the complications the lawyer's withdrawal will pose for the defense, not to mention the risk that the insured will claim that the insurer has breached its duty to defend or has acted in bad faith by creating the conflict. But if the insurer will not change its position, the lawyer must seek to withdraw from the insured's representation in accordance with the jurisdiction's version of Model Rule 1.16 and applicable court rules governing withdrawal.[347] Fortunately, very few (if any) disagreements between insurers and the lawyers they appoint to defend their insureds ever reach this stage.

Insurers may attempt to head off any confusion or controversy by including in outside counsel guidelines instructions to defense lawyers to exercise their independent professional judgment in defending insureds even if it runs afoul of a guideline. For example, an insurer might include language like the following in an introduction or preamble to its outside counsel guidelines, with "you" and "your" being defined to refer to appointed defense lawyers:

> These guidelines are not intended to interfere with your exercise of independent professional judgment or compliance with rules of professional conduct in representing an insured. If you ever conclude that adherence to these guidelines would hinder or impair your representation of the insured, would interfere with your exercise of independent professional judgment in representing the insured, or would conflict with your duties to the insured, you must prioritize the insured's interests and take such action as is necessary to represent the insured competently and diligently.

The insurer might further add that the defense lawyer's performance of a task that is otherwise impermissible under the outside counsel guidelines will not result in a reduction in, or nonpayment of, the lawyer's associated fees, although that assurance should be unnecessary because it is implicit in the proposed text.

347. *See* ABA Formal Op. 01-421, *supra* note 338, at 6.

CHAPTER 4
Insurers' Duty to Defend Offensively

Seth Lamden

I. Introduction

This chapter discusses whether a liability insurer's defense obligation includes the prosecution of, or reimbursement for the prosecution of, affirmative claims such as counterclaims, crossclaims, third-party claims for contribution or indemnity, and parallel lawsuits. Standard commercial general liability (CGL) policies confer upon the insurer the "right and duty" to defend lawsuits seeking potentially covered damages.[1] Absent a conflict of interest between the insurer and insured, the insurer also has the right to control the defense.[2] When an insurer defends a lawsuit without reserving its rights to deny coverage, its right to control the defense usually means that it has the right to make strategy decisions regarding whether to pursue affirmative claims as part of the defense. Things get more complicated, however, if the insurer has lost the right to control the defense and the insured has selected independent defense counsel. In that instance, the insurer discharges its duty to defend by funding the cost of the defense. Disputes between an insurer and its insured can arise if the insured asks its insurer to reimburse it for the cost of prosecuting a claim seeking affirmative relief in connection with the defense of a potentially covered lawsuit and the insurer contends that its defense obligation does not extend to funding affirmative claims.[3] An insurer's contractual duty to defend only requires it to pay for reasonable defense activities. But what does it mean to defend a lawsuit?

1. Ins. Servs. Off., Inc., Commercial General Liability Coverage Form (CG 00 01 04 13), at 1 (2012).

2. An insurer's right to control the insured's defense and conflicts of interest that may divest the insurer of that right are discussed in Chapter 3.

3. These disputes also may arise where the insurer controls the defense.

A review of the case law reveals that courts across the country are divided on whether a liability insurer's duty to defend can require it to pursue or fund an insured's affirmative claims. Many courts appear to follow a bright line rule that the duty to defend never requires an insurer to pursue an insured's affirmative claim.[4] A close review of the case law, however, reveals that many other courts addressing this issue eschew a bright line rule. These courts base their decisions on whether the affirmative claim is part of a reasonable defense strategy, the context of the specific facts, and the procedural posture of the underlying case. They approach the question pragmatically, rooting their decisions in the purpose of the duty to defend, which is to reduce or eliminate the insured's liability to the underlying claimant.

Courts holding that an insurer must fund the insured's pursuit of affirmative claims typically do so where the insurer has lost the right to control the

4. *See, e.g.*, Aldous v. Darwin Nat'l Assur. Co., 851 F.3d 473, 483 (5th Cir. 2017) ("The duty to *defend* the entire suit does not give rise [under Texas law] to a duty to prosecute claims helpful to or even inextricably intertwined with that defense, however."), *vacated in part on other grounds on reh'g*, 889 F.3d 798 (5th Cir. 2018); Barletta Heavy Div., Inc. v. Travelers Ins. Co., No. 12-11193-DPW, 2013 WL 5797612, at *14–15 (D. Mass. Oct. 25, 2013) (applying Massachusetts law); Hester v. Navigators Ins. Co., 917 F. Supp. 2d 290, 298 (S.D.N.Y. 2013) (rejecting the insured's argument that his "proactive 'defensive' lawsuit" triggered his insurer's duty to defend); Morgan, Lewis & Bockius LLP v. Hanover Ins. Co., 929 F. Supp. 764, 773 (D.N.J. 1996) (applying New Jersey law); James 3 Corp. v. Truck Ins. Exch., 111 Cal. Rptr. 2d 181, 188 (Ct. App. 2001) ("[T]here is nothing in the policy that contractually obligates [the insurer] to fund and prosecute an insured's affirmative relief counterclaims or cross-complaints."); Ramsey v. Lee Builders, Inc., 95 P.3d 1033, 1040 (Kan. Ct. App. 2004) ("[The insured] does not direct us to any provision in the policy which obligated Farm Bureau to engage counsel for its insured to do anything other than defend an action for which coverage might be invoked under the policy. Simply put, Farm Bureau's defense obligation was limited to the claims asserted against its insured. . . ."); Mt. Vernon Fire Ins. Co. v. VisionAid, Inc., 76 N.E.3d 204, 210–11 (Mass. 2017) (requiring an insurer "to defend claims brought against its insured, but not to require an insurer to assert affirmative claims on behalf of that insured"); Goldberg v. Am. Home Assur. Co., 439 N.Y.S.2d 2, 4 (App. Div. 1981) ("It was clear that [the insurer] was under no obligation to represent [the insured] in his counterclaim against the client and his cross-claim against his former associates."); Duke Univ. v. St. Paul Mercury Ins. Co., 384 S.E.2d 36, 46 (N.C. Ct. App. 1989) ("We believe the trial court correctly disallowed [the insured's] legal expenses incurred in connection with the prosecution of its counterclaims."); Red Head Brass, Inc. v. Buckeye Union Ins. Co., 735 N.E.2d 48, 57 (Ohio Ct. App. 1999) ("The contract does not define 'defend' or 'defense.' For these terms, we will apply their plain and ordinary meaning. . . . Neither [dictionary] definition [reviewed] includes the prosecution of one's legal claim against another. Thus, giving the plain meaning to the words of the contract, we find that the contract did not require Buckeye to pay for the prosecution of [the insured's] counterclaim."); Berlant v. McAllister, 480 P.2d 126, 127 (Utah 1971) ("The insurance contract provides that the insurer will . . . investigate, defend or settle any claims against the insured. It does not provide for any representation of its insured in an action against another party. Separate counsel always represents an insured plaintiff when he sues or an insured defendant when he counterclaims."); Towne Realty, Inc. v. Zurich Ins. Co., 548 N.W.2d 64, 68–69 (Wis. 1996) (denying coverage because "[a]t the risk of stating the obvious, a countersuit initiated by the insured cannot logically be a suit seeking damages from the insured"); Shoshone First Bank v. Pac. Emps. Ins. Co., 2 P.3d 510, 517 (Wyo. 2000) ("With respect to the costs of prosecuting a counterclaim, unless the policy specifically provides coverage for those expenses, we will not amend the contract. Because there was no coverage for prosecuting the counterclaim in this case, [the insurer] is not required to assume the expense of [the insured's] counterclaims. . . .").

insured's defense due to a coverage denial or reservation of rights, and such affirmative claims are either (1) inextricably intertwined with potentially covered underlying claims against the insured or (2) defensive in nature. Courts holding that an insurer is not required to fund the insured's pursuit of affirmative claims typically do so where the insurer has retained the right to control the defense, or where the affirmative claims are neither defensive nor inextricably intertwined with a potentially covered suit against the insured.[5]

II. What Does It Mean to Defend?

The evaluation of whether a legal expense incurred to prosecute an affirmative claim falls within the scope of a liability insurer's duty to defend should begin with an examination of what it means to "defend" a claim or suit and how to properly define a "defense expense." One court found the answer in a dictionary, which defined "defense" as "the method and collected facts adopted by a defendant to protect himself against a plaintiff's action."[6] According to an oft-cited decision by the Supreme Court of California, an expense can constitute a covered defense expense if it is for an activity that is a "reasonable and necessary effort to avoid or at least minimize liability."[7] The court in *Aerojet-General Corp. v. Transportation Indemnity Co.*[8] was asked to determine whether a liability insurer was required to pay, as covered defense expenses, site investigation expenses that the insured incurred pursuant to a CERCLA consent decree. Holding that the CERCLA site investigation expenses were covered defense expenses, the *Aerojet-General* court explained that "[w]hat matters here is whether the site investigation would be conducted against liability by a reasonable insured under the same circumstances."[9]

Under the *Aerojet-General* definition of "defense expense," reasonable activities undertaken to avoid or minimize the insured's liability are covered defense expenses, regardless of whether the activities also serve another purpose. *Aerojet-General* provides a reasonable framework for evaluating whether

5. *See, e.g.*, Spada v. Unigard Ins. Co., 80 F. App'x 27, 29 (9th Cir. 2003) (declining to decide whether an insurer generally must reimburse an insured for prosecuting counterclaims and cross-claims because in this case, the insured's affirmative claims were not offered as a reason in law or fact for defeating or minimizing the underlying plaintiff's claims).

6. Acradyne, Inc. v. Travelers Cas. & Sur. Co. of Am., No. Civ. CV 04-362-AS, 2005 WL 1839042, at *4 (D. Or. July 29, 2005) (quoting Webster's dictionary), *aff'd in part, rev'd in part*, 263 F. App'x 594, 598 (9th Cir. 2008).

7. Aerojet-General Corp. v. Transp. Indem. Co., 948 P.2d 909, 922 (Cal. 1997); *see also* Am. Bumper & Mfg. Co. v. Hartford Fire Ins. Co., 550 N.W.2d 475, 486 (Mich. 1996) (stating that defense costs include costs incurred to "disprove or limit the scope of liability").

8. 948 P.2d 909 (Cal. 1997).

9. *Id.* at 923.

an insurer's defense obligation extends to affirmative claims. If a counterclaim, crossclaim, or third-party claim would be conducted by a reasonable insured in similar circumstances to avoid or minimize its potentially covered liability, that claim should be part of an insurer's defense obligation.[10]

III. Third-Party Claims

A. Indemnity or Contribution

Claims for contribution and indemnification are the most common types of affirmative claims that courts have held fall within the scope of the duty to defend.[11] One of the leading cases on this issue is *Great West Casualty Co. v. Marathon Oil Co.*[12] In *Great West*, Paul Howe, an employee of Heidenreich Trucking Co. (Heidenreich) was killed while loading his truck with gasoline at a Marathon Oil Co. (Marathon) facility with gasoline purchased by or for Krystal Gas Marketing Co. (Krystal). After Howe's estate sued Marathon for Howe's wrongful death, Marathon brought third-party claims against Heidenreich and Krystal for contribution and indemnity. Marathon was an additional insured on a liability insurance policy issued by Great West Casualty Co. (Great West), which filed a declaratory judgment action seeking a ruling that it had no duty to defend or indemnify Marathon. The court in the declaratory judgment action held that Great West was required to defend Marathon, but it was premature to rule on Great West's duty to indemnify. After the declaratory judgment ruling, a dispute arose between Great West and Marathon over whether Great West was required to pay for Marathon's contribution and indemnity claims against Heidenreich and Krystal.

Holding that Great West's defense obligation required it to pay for the contribution and indemnity claims, the *Great West* court noted that the law was "virtually uniform in holding that there is a class of affirmative claims which, if successful, have the effect of reducing or eliminating the insured's liability and that the costs and fees incurred in prosecuting such 'defensive' claims are

10. *See, e.g.*, KLA-Tencor Corp. v. Travelers Indem. Co. of Ill., No. C-02-05641, 2004 WL 1737297, at *4–7 (N.D. Cal. Aug. 4, 2004) (citing *Aerojet-General* and finding the insurer liable for some costs incurred by insured to prosecute patent infringement claims because they were reasonable and necessary for the insured's defense of a potentially covered claim).

11. *See, e.g.*, Nationwide Mut. Fire Ins. Co. v. D.R. Horton, Inc.-Birmingham, No. 15-351, 2016 WL 6828206, at *9 (S.D. Ala. Nov. 18, 2016) (finding that the insured's "fees and expenses relating . . . efforts to demand indemnification from third parties and other third-party settlements are appropriately categorized as 'defense costs' . . . ."); D.R. Horton, Inc.-Denver v. Mountain States Mut. Cas. Co., 69 F. Supp. 3d 1179, 1200 (D. Colo. 2014) (holding that if the insured's "pursuit of third-party claims against the subcontractors was a reasonable defense strategy . . . those costs are part of the defense costs").

12. 315 F. Supp. 2d 879 (N.D. Ill. 2003).

encompassed in an insurer's duty to defend."[13] The *Great West* court explained that "'defense' is about shifting liability," and "third-party claims for contribution and indemnity are a means of avoiding liability just as clearly as is disputing the claims alleged to give rise to liability."[14] As the court continued, the duty to defend "would be nothing but a form of words if it did not encompass all litigation by the insured which could defeat its liability, including claims and actions for contribution and indemnification."[15]

Selective Insurance Co. of the Southeast v. Creation Supply, Inc.[16] is another leading case discussing whether an insurer's duty to defend extends to indemnity claims. In that case, the insured, Creation Supply, Inc. (Creation Supply), imported and sold "MEPXY" colored art markers. Creation Supply was sued in an Oregon federal court for trademark infringement, violation of trade dress, and unfair competition by Too Marker Products and Imagination International, Inc. (collectively, Too Marker), who sought to protect their line of "COPIC" art markers. As part of its defense strategy, Creation Supply sued Alpha Art Materials Co., Ltd. (Alpha), the manufacturer of the markers, for breach of warranty and implied indemnity in federal court in Illinois. Creation Supply also asserted the same claims in a third-party complaint against Alpha in the Oregon lawsuit. The Oregon and Illinois actions were eventually consolidated into the Oregon action.

Creation Supply tendered its defense to its CGL insurer, Selective Insurance Co. of the Southeast (Selective), which declined to defend and filed a declaratory judgment action against Creation Supply.[17] The court in the declaratory judgment action found that Selective had a duty to defend, but a dispute arose between Selective and Creation Supply over whether Selective had a duty to pay for the breach of warranty and indemnity claims against Alpha.

Creation Supply argued that the claims against Alpha were part of Selective's defense obligation because the claims "were part of the same dispute as that of the underlying lawsuit and were brought to offset or defeat any liability that [Creation Supply] would have owed to plaintiffs in the underlying lawsuit."[18] In response, Selective argued that the affirmative claims were unrelated to the defense of the suit against Creation Supply and, in any event, the fees in the suit against Alpha were incurred after the Too Marker action was dismissed.[19] The court in the coverage action held that Selective was required to pay for the claims against Alpha because, among other things, the third-

13. *Id.* at 881.
14. *Id.*
15. *Id.* at 882–83.
16. No. 1-16-1899, 2017 WL 2855984 (Ill. App. Ct. June 30, 2017).
17. *Id.* at *1.
18. *Id.* at *2 (internal quotation marks omitted).
19. *Id.* at *3.

party complaint "was aimed at shifting the liability for the underlying intellectual property infringement claims."[20] Put differently, the third-party complaint was "an attempt to limit [Creation Supply's] potential liability in the underlying lawsuit."[21] The court agreed with Selective that its duty to fund the third-party claim against Alpha ended when the underlying lawsuit against Creation Supply was dismissed because the duty to defend ends "when the uncontroverted facts preclude the possibility of a duty to indemnify."[22]

The *Great West* and *Creation Supply* holdings make good sense. In both cases, the insurer was disputing its duty to indemnify, which means that the insured potentially would be liable for damages if the defense effort were unsuccessful. The reason the insureds in *Great West* and *Creation Supply* brought contribution or indemnity claims was to avoid or minimize liability. If the insurer has accepted coverage, it is reasonable for the insurer to be entitled to decide whether to try to minimize its own liability by bringing third-party claims. Likewise, if the insurer has declined coverage, it is reasonable for the insurer to be required to reimburse the insured for asserting third-party claims that may avoid or minimize liability.

B. Counterclaims and Crossclaims

An insurer's duty to pay defense expenses can encompass counterclaims and crossclaims asserted in a potentially covered lawsuit if such claims are "defensive in nature," at least where the insurer is contesting coverage. For example, the court in *Oscar W. Larson Co. v. United Capitol Insurance Co.*[23] held that an insurer with a contractual defense obligation was required to reimburse its insured for the cost of pursuing a counterclaim and crossclaims because such claims were defensive in nature. After the insured, Oscar W. Larson Co. (Larson), was sued in a multiparty environmental pollution action, it brought a counterclaim and crossclaims against other parties that allegedly contributed to the pollution.[24] Larson sought a defense and indemnity from its CGL insurer, which denied coverage. In coverage litigation, the court found that the CGL insurer's duty to defend extended to the cost of the counterclaim and crossclaims because such claims "are actually defensive in nature and prosecuted to limit or defeat [the insured's] liability in the [underlying] action."[25] Other courts have applied the rationale of the *Oscar W. Larson* decision to

20. *Id.* at *7.
21. *Id.* at *8.
22. *Id.* at *9.
23. 845 F. Supp. 458 (E.D. Pa. 1993).
24. *Id.* at 460.
25. *Id.* at 461.

find that the cost of pursuing potentially responsible parties in environmental pollution cases are covered defense expenses.[26]

An insurer's duty to defend can also encompass counterclaims and cross-claims that are "inextricably intertwined" with the defense of a potentially covered claim,[27] at least if such claims are "necessary to the defense of the litigation as a strategic matter."[28] In one such case, *Safeguard Scientifics, Inc. v. Liberty Mutual Insurance Co.*,[29] Liberty Mutual Insurance Co. (Liberty Mutual) refused to defend its insured against an underlying defamation lawsuit. In coverage litigation that followed, the court found that Liberty Mutual had breached its duty to defend. In assessing damages for the insurer's breach of its duty to defend, the court found that Liberty Mutual was responsible for paying for the insured's counterclaims for breach of contract, fraud, breach of fiduciary duty, breach of contract as an assignee, and breach of duties of good faith and fair dealing.[30] In support of this holding, the *Safeguard Scientifics* court observed that "Liberty Mutual has pointed to no case law suggesting that an insurance company's obligation does not extend to the litigation of counterclaims raised in the same lawsuit," and "the pursuit of the counterclaims was inextricably intertwined with the defense of [the underlying] claims and was necessary to the defense of the litigation as a strategic matter."[31]

The court in *Ultra Coachbuilders, Inc. v. General Security Insurance Co.*[32] reached a similar result. *Ultra Coachbuilders* arose out of a trademark dispute in which Ford Motor Co. (Ford) sued Ultra Coachbuilders for infringement. Ford sought a preliminary injunction that would have put Ultra Coachbuilders out of business. In opposing Ford's application for injunctive relief, Ultra Coachbuilders filed counterclaims for unfair competition and interference with competitive advantage to support its argument that the requested injunction

26. *See, e.g.*, Emhart Indus. Inc. v. Home Ins. Co., No. 02-53S, 2006 WL 2460908, at *2 (D.R.I. Aug. 2, 2006) ("In view of CERCLA's statutory liability/contribution scheme, this Court concludes that [the insured's] pursuit of other PRPs is defensive in nature and the costs of such pursuit are recoverable if a duty to defend is established.").

27. *See, e.g.*, TIG Ins. Co. v. Nobel Learning Cmtys., No. Civ. A. 01-4708, 2002 WL 1340332, at *14–15 (E.D. Pa. June 18, 2002); Ford Motor Co. v. Ultra Coachbuilders, Inc., 57 U.S.P.Q.2d 1356, 2000 WL 33256536, at *10 (C.D. Cal. July 11, 2000); Aerosafe Int'l, Inc. v. ITT Hartford of the Midwest, No. C-92-1532 MHP, 1993 WL 299372, at *5 (N.D. Cal. July 23, 1993); *see also* Post v. St. Paul Travelers Ins. Co., 691 F.3d 500, 521 (3d Cir. 2012) ("Had [the insured] asserted counterclaims in [the] suit against him, no doubt the expenses incurred by him to prosecute the counterclaims would have been covered by the Policy.").

28. Safeguard Scientifics, Inc. v. Liberty Mut. Ins. Co., 766 F. Supp. 324, 334 (E.D. Pa. 1991), *rev'd in part on other grounds*, Nos. 91-1480, 91-1527, 1992 WL 12915247 (3d Cir. Mar. 19, 1992).

29. *Id.* at 327.

30. *Id.*

31. *Id.* at 334; *see also Safeguard Scientifics*, 1992 WL 12915247, at *5 (affirming the portion of the district court decision regarding Liberty Mutual's obligation to pay for prosecuting the counterclaims because "the counterclaims were strategic and were utilized in defense of the [underlying] action. . . .").

32. 229 F. Supp. 2d 284 (S.D.N.Y. 2002).

was barred by the doctrine of unclean hands.[33] The counterclaims were unsuccessful; Ultra Coachbuilders instead defeated Ford's request for an injunction on the basis that Ford was not likely to succeed on the merits.[34] Nevertheless, because the counterclaims were used to argue (albeit unsuccessfully) that Ford was not entitled to injunctive relief, the court concluded that they were inextricably intertwined with Ultra Coachbuilder's defense and were strategically necessary to the defense of the litigation.[35] As a result, Ultra Coachbuilders' insurer, General Security Insurance Co., had to pay as defense costs the attorney's fees and costs incurred in prosecuting the counterclaims.[36]

Another case in this line of authority, *TIG Insurance Co. v. Nobel Learning Communities, Inc.*,[37] was rooted in a copyright dispute. Nobel Learning Communities, Inc. (Nobel) sued Dr. Deborah Levy, a former employee, seeking a declaratory judgment concerning the ownership of several copyrights. Dr. Levy counterclaimed for copyright infringement. Nobel tendered the matter to its insurer, TIG Insurance Co. (TIG), which declined to defend Nobel in connection with the counterclaim.[38]

Nobel and Dr. Levy soon began settlement negotiations. Nobel informed TIG of the settlement discussions, but TIG again refused to provide a defense. Nobel settled with Dr. Levy and thereafter demanded that TIG reimburse it for the $315,000 in attorney's fees it incurred in the copyright litigation. TIG refused and filed a declaratory judgment action in a Pennsylvania federal court.[39]

The *Nobel* court concluded that TIG breached its duty to defend Nobel against Dr. Levy's counterclaim in the copyright litigation. One of the issues then became TIG's obligation to pay Nobel's defense costs. Nobel argued that TIG was required to pay its attorney's fees incurred in prosecuting its declaratory judgment case against Dr. Levy as well as its fees incurred in defending Dr. Levy's counterclaim. Nobel contended that its affirmative claims and Dr. Levy's counterclaim "were 'inextricably intertwined,' and the pursuit of the affirmative claims was 'necessary to the defense of the litigation as a strategic matter.'"[40] Therefore, Nobel argued, TIG was responsible for paying both. The *Nobel* court mostly agreed.[41] As the court explained:

---

33. *Id.* at 289.
34. *Id.* at 287, 289.
35. *Id.* at 289 (quoting Safeguard Scientifics, Inc. v. Liberty Mut. Ins. Co., 766 F. Supp. 324, 334 (E.D. Pa. 1991), *aff'd in part, rev'd in part*, 961 F.2d 209 (3d Cir. 1992)).
36. *Id.*
37. No. CIV.A. 01-4708, 2002 WL 1340332 (E.D. Pa. June 18, 2002).
38. *Id.* at *1.
39. *Id.*
40. *Id.* at *14.
41. *Id.*

> Although prior to the filing of the counterclaim TIG had no duty to defend, once copyright infringement was alleged against Nobel . . . Nobel's affirmative claims became critical to and "inextricably intertwined" with the defense of the copyright infringement claim. As the prosecution of the affirmative claims was essential to the defense against the counterclaim, it was logically encompassed by TIG's duty to defend Nobel.[42]

In a small victory for TIG, the court held that the insurer was only obligated to pay Nobel's attorney's fees incurred after Dr. Levy filed her counterclaim; that is, after the time at which TIG's duty to defend arose.[43] TIG was also entitled to offset its obligation to Nobel by the $175,000 that Dr. Levy paid to Nobel as part of their settlement.[44]

Although courts frequently are willing to require an insurer to prosecute an insured's counterclaims that are inextricably intertwined with the insured's defense, they draw the line at obligating the insurer to fund a separate lawsuit by the insured asserting the same claims or causes of action.[45] *Post v. St. Paul Travelers Insurance Co. (Post II)*[46] is illustrative.

In *Post II*, Mercy Hospital and an affiliate (collectively, Mercy) accused lawyer Benjamin Post of committing legal malpractice in defending a medical malpractice case against Mercy known as *Bobbett*. The medical malpractice case was litigated in Luzerne County, Pennsylvania. After all sorts of procedural wrangling and a sanctions action initiated by the *Bobbett* plaintiffs in which Mercy intervened, Mercy sued Post for legal malpractice in Luzerne County.[47] Post responded by suing Mercy in Philadelphia County for wrongful use of civil proceedings, breach of contract, fraud and misrepresentation, and civil conspiracy.[48] Post sued Mercy in Philadelphia County rather than Luzerne County because he believed that he could not get a fair trial in Luzerne County.[49]

Post's professional liability insurer, St. Paul Travelers (Travelers), declined to defend or indemnify him in connection with the sanctions action in which Mercy had intervened and in which it effectively alleged Post's legal malpractice, and he thus sued the company for breach of contract and bad faith in a Pennsylvania federal court. In finding that Travelers breached its duty to

42. *Id.* at *15 (footnote omitted).

43. *Id.* at *14.

44. *Id.* at *15.

45. *See, e.g.*, Amquip Corp. v. Admiral Ins. Co., No. 03-4411, 2005 WL 742457, at *7 (E.D. Pa. Mar. 31, 2005) ("If courts were to consider the costs an insured incurred by instituting its own action for the purpose of bringing pressure on the other party under the guise of a litigation defense, it would encourage and endorse multiplicity of litigation.").

46. 691 F.3d 500 (3d Cir. 2012).

47. Post v. St Paul Travelers Ins. Co. (*Post I*), 752 F. Supp. 2d 499, 506 (E.D. Pa. 2010), *vacated in part by* 691 F.3d 500 (3d Cir. 2012) (*Post II*).

48. *Id.* at 507.

49. *Id.*

defend Post, the district court in *Post I* concluded that Post's lawsuit against Travelers was inextricably intertwined with the defense of Mercy's legal malpractice action, so St. Paul had to pay Post's attorney's fees associated with the prosecution of his affirmative claims against Mercy.[50] In *Post II*, the Third Circuit agreed that Travelers had a duty to defend Post in connection with Mercy's legal malpractice allegations but rejected the district court's conclusion that Travelers' duty extended to the prosecution of Post's lawsuit against Mercy.[51]

The *Post II* court began its analysis by acknowledging that if Post had asserted counterclaims in Mercy's suit against him rather than suing Mercy separately, Travelers would have had to pay his fees and expenses incurred in prosecuting the counterclaims.[52] But he instead filed a separate lawsuit. Although Post's Philadelphia County suit was tied to Mercy's lawsuit against him in Luzerne County, "to hold that Post's separate action was covered by the [Travelers policy] simply because it related to Mercy's suit would condone, and perhaps even encourage, the multiplicity of litigation."[53] In addition, a holding to that effect "would place insurers in the difficult and unenviable situation of having to determine whether related cases are related enough—i.e., 'inextricably intertwined'—to trigger coverage for the insured's counterclaims."[54] The *Post II* court considered both these possibilities to be "highly undesirable" and therefore declined to adopt the district court's approach.[55]

Rather than requiring insurers to decide whether they have a duty to fund an insured's separate action based on an intensely contextual and subjective inquiry into its relation to the action against the insured, the *Post II* court favored a bright line rule that an insurer must fund an insured's pursuit of inextricably intertwined counterclaims, but has "no duty to cover the expenses incurred by an insured in prosecuting an entirely new and separate action (even if that action is related to the underlying case)."[56] The *Post II* court reasoned that although there may be strategic or tactical reasons for an insured to file a related lawsuit in a different venue, it is more important to discourage overlapping litigation and provide clear coverage guidelines for insurers.[57] A bright-line rule provides clarity to insurers and insureds, avoids unnecessary

50. *Id.* at 515–16.
51. *Post II*, 691 F.3d at 522.
52. *Id.* at 521.
53. *Id.* at 522.
54. *Id.*
55. *Id.*
56. *Id.*
57. *Id.* (citing Amquip Corp. v. Admiral Ins. Co., No. 03-4411, 2005 WL 742457, at *7 (E.D. Pa. Mar. 31, 2005)).

legal costs and expenses, and conserves judicial resources, and consequently best serves insurance coverage litigants.[58]

C. Offensive Litigation Is the Only Practical Alternative to a Defense

There occasionally are cases in which the insured prosecutes affirmative claims to head off litigation in which it will be sued as a defendant or to preempt certain claims that might be brought against it, or in which the pursuit of affirmative claims is the only practical alternative to defending litigation brought by an adversary. In such cases, the insurer's duty to defend should expand to include the duty to fund litigation initiated by the insured. In some instances, a declaratory judgment action aimed at defeating or minimizing the insured's liability may fit this description. Another example of this approach is a case where a government agency withholds funds due an insured under a contract to compensate for alleged negligence by the insured in performing the agreed work, which forces the insured to sue the government to absolve itself of liability and recover the funds it is owed.

Simon v. Maryland Casualty Co.[59] leads the second line of cases outlined earlier. In May 1953, Douglas Brothers, Inc. (Douglas), contracted with the United States (the Government) to convert the voltage of an electrical system at an Air Force base. The contract stated that Douglas would be responsible for any property damage attributable to its negligence. In June, Douglas subcontracted part of the Air Force project to Simon Electric Co. (Simon). Simon was insured by Maryland Casualty Co. (Maryland Casualty). Simon employees working on the voltage conversion allegedly started a fire that damaged two buildings on the base. The Government withheld from Douglas slightly more than $32,000 from the amount due on the contract as damages caused by the alleged negligence of its employees and Simon's employees. Douglas, in turn, withheld from the Simon just under $8,000 from the amount otherwise due Simon under the subcontract.

Although the Government could initially withhold the contract funds as a matter of administrative procedure, it could lawfully retain them only if the related damages actually were caused by Douglas's and Simon's negligence. Here the trouble started, because if Douglas or Simon disputed the Government's position, federal procedure required them to sue the Government in the U.S. Court of Claims to defeat their presumed negligence and recoup the funds withheld.[60] Simon was prepared to fight for its money, and it asked Maryland

58. *Id.* (referring to *Amquip*).
59. 353 F.2d 608 (5th Cir. 1965).
60. *Id.* at 610.

Casualty to fund a planned effort with Douglas to challenge the Government's action. Maryland Casualty refused to do so because the Government had not sued Simon,[61] and Maryland Casualty's only contractual duty was to defend Simon against covered suits.[62]

Frustrated by the Government's "permissible self-help" and with Maryland Casualty staying on the sidelines, Simon resorted to "self-help as would a prudent uninsured person."[63] Simon authorized Douglas to pursue recovery from the Government on its behalf and agreed to share costs and attorneys' fees. The Court of Claims ultimately determined that Simon's employees caused the fire.[64]

Around the same time that it authorized Douglas to sue the Government, Simon filed a declaratory judgment action against Maryland Casualty seeking an order that Maryland Casualty had to fund Simon's share of the action against the Government. The declaratory judgment action was stayed until the Court of Claims found in the Government's favor. When the declaratory action was finally tried, the district court held for Maryland Casualty.[65] Simon appealed the judgment to the Fifth Circuit.

The Fifth Circuit concluded that Maryland Casualty had to pay Simon's legal fees and expenses to the extent they were "incurred in the resistance—i.e., 'defense'—of the contention of liability for damage."[66] As the *Simon* court explained:

> Both from the standpoint of the risks for which [Simon] needed coverage and which [Maryland Casualty] obviously meant to cover, there is a complete parallel between the policy and the result we ordain. [Simon] . . . obviously had need of insurance against damage to persons and property occasioned by negligence of its servants. This is precisely what [Maryland Casualty] undertook to sell. . . . [Simon's] employees were negligent. That negligence caused substantial damage. The property owner (the Government) asserted a claim and had on its side the greatest sanction of all—possession of the money. . . . On the other side . . . [Maryland Casualty] got every protection it would have obtained had the litigation followed the traditional, orthodox pattern of a suit and judgment against [Simon].
>
> And this all becomes doubly clear when approached in terms of what practical steps could have been taken and what practical significance any such

61. *Id.*

62. *Id.* at 611 & n.9.

63. *Id.* at 610–11.

64. In 1982, Congress abolished the Court of Claims and transferred its trial jurisdiction to a new court, the U.S. Claims Court, which is now known as the U.S. Court of Federal Claims. The Court of Federal Claims hears primarily monetary claims based on the Constitution, federal statutes and regulations, and contracts with the United States. The Court of Appeals for the Federal Circuit now holds the appellate jurisdiction formerly vested in the Court of Claims.

65. *Simon*, 353 F.2d at 611 & n.6.

66. *Id.* at 613.

> steps would have had to put this . . . claim of negligent damage in the mold of the traditional third-party damage suit which would have satisfied every requirement and theory asserted now by [Maryland Casualty]. There was, first, no way to force the . . . Government to sue either [Doulas] or [Simon]. Nor was anything to be gained by requiring that [Douglas] sue [Simon]. That suit would have been a conditional, protective one at best. It would have asserted only that the damage had been done and that the Government . . . was taking the position that the damage was caused by negligence of [Douglas] and [Simon]. Since the only way to test this issue was to file suit in the Court of Claims for recovery of sums otherwise due . . . the prayer could then have been for nothing more than either a declaration or a judgment for damages if and when, but not before, the Court of Claims would sustain the contention of the Government.[67]

As the *Simon* court saw matters, Maryland Casualty was taking the position that despite owing coverage given Simon's negligence, it had no duty to protect Simon "because the form of the litigation was unorthodox."[68] The court reasoned that the duty to defend language in the Maryland Casualty policy was not intended to produce "such an artificial windfall."[69] The court accordingly reversed the district court judgment and remanded the case for further proceedings.

Although it did not arise out of a government contracting dispute, *Busch v. Fidelity National Title Insurance Co.*[70] is another case where a court held that an insurer's duty to defend included a duty to fund litigation necessarily initiated by the insured. The plaintiff in *Busch*, Donald Busch (Busch), owned property that was covered by a title insurance policy issued by a Fidelity predecessor. In 2003, his neighbors claimed that an easement granted them the right to build a road over his property. To halt the road's imminent construction, Busch hired a lawyer to file a quiet title action. Fidelity approved Busch's strategy and agreed to pay his legal fees.[71] After the trial court denied Busch's request for a preliminary injunction, Fidelity wrote to Busch's lawyer purporting to settle Busch's title insurance claim—not the underlying action—for $5,000. The parties disputed whether the claim was settled. The underlying litigation nonetheless continued, and Busch ran through four law firms before prevailing. In the meantime, he sued Fidelity for breach of contract and for a declaration that Fidelity was obligated to pay all his legal fees in the quiet title

67. *Id.*
68. *Id.* at 614.
69. *Id.*
70. 923 N.Y.S.2d 280 (App. Div. 2011).
71. *Id.* at 281.

action—not just those charged by his first lawyer.[72] Busch moved for partial summary judgment in his suit against Fidelity and lost. He then appealed.

On appeal, Fidelity argued that it had no duty to pay for Busch's pursuit of his quiet title action because he was a plaintiff rather than a defendant.[73] The court disagreed. Busch filed suit in response to his neighbors' claims against his title and the looming threat that they would begin carving a road across his property.[74] Recognizing the need for an immediate response to his neighbors' plans, he hired a lawyer who obtained a temporary restraining order and sought a preliminary injunction, and quickly informed Fidelity of the action. Fidelity then agreed to provide counsel to protect his title. The court therefore rejected Fidelity's argument that it never had a duty to fund the quiet title action.[75] Additionally, Busch's neighbors brought counterclaims attacking his title, so Fidelity was obligated to defend him against those counterclaims.[76]

IV. Cases Finding That an Insurer Has No Duty to Pay for Affirmative Claims

Insurers contend that there are good reasons for courts' refusal to recognize a duty on insurers' part to fund insureds' offensive litigation, starting with the plain language of standard liability insurance policies. It is well-established that courts must enforce clear and unambiguous policy language as written,[77] and "defend" means to "deny, contest, or oppose" an allegation or claim.[78] Thus, insurers argue, a court must effectively rewrite the duty to defend language in the policy at issue if it is to require the insurer to prosecute the insured's affirmative claims or to reimburse the insured's associated attorney's fees.[79]

Some decisions finding that an insurer has no duty to prosecute affirmative claims are based, in part, on the fact that the insurer has retained the right

72. *Id.*
73. *See id.* (framing the court's disagreement with Fidelity's position).
74. *Id.*
75. *Id.*
76. *Id.* at 281–82.
77. *See, e.g.*, Dua v. Stillwater Ins. Co., 308 Cal. Rptr. 3d 110, 117 (Ct. App. 2023) ("If the language of the policy is clear and explicit, then it governs."); Great Divide Ins. Co. v. Lexington Ins. Co., 84 N.E.3d 844, 848 (Mass. 2017) ("If the language [of the insurance policy] is clear and unambiguous, we must give effect to that language, without considering the underlying intent of the parties."); Garner v. AMCO Ins. Co., 670 S.W.3d 172, 177 (Mo. Ct. App. 2023) ("If an insurance policy is unambiguous, it must be enforced according to its terms.").
78. *Defend*, Black's Law Dictionary (9th ed. 2009).
79. *See* Cherokee Nation v. Lexington Ins. Co., 521 P.3d 1261, 1266 (Okla. 2022) ("The Court will not undertake to rewrite the terms of an insurance contract or make a better contract than the one which the parties executed."); Shugarts v. Mohr, 909 N.W.2d 402, 407 (Wis. 2018) ("When the language of an insurance policy is unambiguous, a court will not rewrite the policy by interpretation or impose obligations the parties did not undertake.").

to control the defense and is not contesting coverage.[80] In one such case, the Massachusetts Supreme Judicial Court concluded in *Mount Vernon Fire Insurance Co. v. VisionAid, Inc.*[81] that the word "defend," as used in a liability policy, unambiguously requires a defending "insurer to work to defeat a claim brought against the insured, but not to prosecute an affirmative claim against the plaintiff in the underlying suit, no matter how advantageous that claim would be to the insured."[82] The *VisionAid* court held that an insurer defending an underlying employment discrimination lawsuit was not required to prosecute a compulsory counterclaim against the terminated employee for misappropriation of company funds.[83]

The insured in *VisionAid* argued "that the duty to 'defend' under its insurance policy may be understood as meaning anything a reasonable defense attorney would do to reduce the liability of the insured."[84] The *VisionAid* court disagreed, holding that the insurer's defense obligation did not extend to an affirmative counterclaim because the policy language was "clear" that "the essence of what it means to defend is to work to defeat a claim that could create liability against the individual being defended."[85] The *VisionAid* court gave an unusual explanation for its holding that an insurer was not required to fund a compulsory counterclaim that is intertwined with the defense of a covered claim: "it would result in extensive preliminary litigation to determine what claims are sufficiently intertwined, litigation that would be brought by 'any reasonable attorney.'"[86] This explanation is unusual because disputes regarding the reasonableness of defense expenses are common in litigation regarding an insurer's breach of its duty to defend. A more reasonable explanation would have been that the insurer was not contesting coverage and, therefore, had the right to make strategic defense decisions.

The dissenting justices in *VisionAid* stated that the duty to defend includes the duty to prosecute a compulsory counterclaim that is intertwined with the defense of the suit against the insured.[87] As they explained, prosecuting a compulsory counterclaim for employee theft against a terminated employee "would be entirely consistent with the defense,"[88] and noted that "[w]here the insured

80. *See, e.g.*, James 3 Corp. v. Truck Ins. Exch., 111 Cal. Rptr. 2d 181, 189–90 (Ct. App. 2001) (stating that the insurer had no obligation to file counterclaim where it "has not breached its duty to defend and therefore has not given up its right to control the litigation").

81. 76 N.E.3d 204 (Mass. 2017).

82. *Id.* at 209 (first citing Morgan, Lewis & Bockius LLP v. Hanover Ins. Co., 929 F. Supp. 764, 771 (D.N.J. 1996); then citing Shoshone First Bank v. Pac. Emps. Ins. Co., 2 P.3d 510, 516 (Wyo. 2000); and then citing Aldous v. Darwin Nat'l Assur. Co., 851 F.3d 473, 483 (5th Cir. 2017)).

83. *Id.* at 209–10.

84. *Id.* at 210.

85. *Id.* at 208–09.

86. *Id.* at 210.

87. *Id.* at 213 (Gants, C.J. & Lenk, J., dissenting).

88. *Id.* at 215 (Gants, C.J. & Lenk, J., dissenting).

agrees that any award of damages arising from the compulsory counterclaim would offset any such award arising from the complaint that the insurer would be obligated to indemnify, a successful compulsory counterclaim would benefit both the insured and the insurer."[89]

The decisions on which the *Visionaid* majority relied provide little explanation of why prosecuting a counterclaim that is inextricably intertwined with the defense should not be part of an insurer's duty to defend. In one decision, *Goldberg v. American Home Assurance Co.*,[90] the entirety of the court's discussion on the issue was the statement that "[i]t was clear that defendant was under no obligation to represent plaintiff in his counterclaim against the client and his cross-claim against his former associates."[91] In another, *Shoshone First Bank v. Pacific Employers Co.*,[92] the court rejected the insured's argument that the insurer was required to prosecute a counterclaim that was "inextricably intertwined with the facts and circumstances" of conduct in the underlying action, but also noted that "[a] major difficulty with this contention is that the stipulation between [the insured and the insurer] forecloses the position that the counterclaims were 'inextricably intertwined' with the allegations of the complaint, thus permitting the allocation of costs."[93]

In another such case, the court in *Bennett v. St. Paul Fire & Marine Insurance Co.*[94] held that an insurer was not obligated to cover the cost of pursuing a counterclaim brought by an insured attorney against a former client because the counterclaim was not "sufficiently related" to the potentially covered claim against the insured. Notably, the insurer in *Bennett* did not contest coverage and, therefore, had the right to control defense strategy.

In *Bennett*, an attorney was sued for defamation and malicious prosecution by his client's former spouse. The attorney submitted the claim to his professional liability insurer, which agreed to defend him. However, the insurer refused to cover the expense to bring a counterclaim alleging that the plaintiff had committed various torts against him, including intentional infliction of emotional distress, assault, defamation, and civil conspiracy.[95] The attorney contended that the insurer breached its duty to defend when it refused to cover the expense of the counterclaim because the counterclaim arose from the "same core of operative facts" as the underlying lawsuit and is, therefore, "inextricably intertwined" with his defense.[96] The attorney further argued that the counterclaim and a related third-party claim seeking damages for unpaid legal fees

89. *Id.* at 216 (Gants, C.J. & Lenk, J., dissenting).
90. 439 N.Y.S.2d 2 (App. Div. 1981).
91. *Id.* at 4.
92. 2 P.3d 510 (Wyo. 2000).
93. *Id.* at 517.
94. No. ME CIV. 04-CV-212, 2006 WL 1313059 (D. Me. May 12, 2006)
95. *Id.* at *3.
96. *Id.*

and harassment were "essential to his defense because they could reduce or offset his liability and will put pressure on [the underlying plaintiff] to dismiss or settle his claims."[97] The court rejected the attorney's argument, explaining that generalized allegations of defamation in the counterclaim were not sufficiently related to the underlying complaint to require the insurer to fund the counterclaim. The court also found that the third-party claim, at most, shifted the burden of proof to a third party, but when the insurer agreed to defend it "retained the right to control the defense strategy."[98]

Other courts finding that an insurer has no duty to fund the pursuit of affirmative claims do so after finding that prosecution of the affirmative claim at issue was not reasonable or necessary to limit the insured's liability. The court in *International Insurance Co. v. Rollprint Packaging Products, Inc.*,[99] for example, held that an insurer defending a federal employment discrimination lawsuit was not obligated to prosecute a counterclaim seeking to enjoin the underlying plaintiff from using the insured's trade secrets because the counterclaim was not "defensive in nature," meaning that it was not "prosecuted to limit or defeat [the insured's] liability [to a third party]."[100] Instead, the court explained, the counterclaim "was comparable to any action [the insured] might have had to take to enjoin [the underlying plaintiff] from using his trade secrets after his termination."[101]

V. Settlements Involving Insureds' Affirmative Claims

Finally, it is necessary to consider settlement in cases where the insured is both a defendant and a counterclaim, crossclaim, or third-party plaintiff. After all, most civil litigation settles.[102] An obviously complicating factor in this situation is the insurer's right to control settlement. For example, a standard CGL policy provides: "We will have the right and duty to defend the insured against any 'suit' seeking [covered] damages. . . . We may, at our discretion, investigate any 'occurrence' and settle any claim or 'suit' that may result."[103] Similarly, a standard personal auto policy states: "We will settle or defend, as we consider

97. *Id.*
98. *Id.* at *5.
99. 728 N.E.2d 680 (Ill. App. Ct. 2000).
100. *Id.* at 694.
101. *Id.*
102. *See* Douglas R. Richmond, *Liability Insurance and Contractual Aspects of Settlement*, 87 Mo. L. Rev. 195, 197 (2022) (footnotes omitted) ("In federal courts, only around two percent of cases go to trial. In state courts, only about three percent of civil cases go to trial. As these statistics indicate, most civil litigation settles. Certainly, most tort cases settle.").
103. Ins. Servs. Off., Inc., Commercial General Liability Coverage Form (CG 00 01 04 13), at 1 (2012).

appropriate, any claim or suit asking for these damages."[104] Such language is not necessarily as broad as it appears, however. An insurer's contractual right to settle a lawsuit against its insured is limited to the insurer's own resources.[105] An insurer does not have the authority without the insured's consent to commit the insured's resources to a settlement—including causes of action belonging to the insured.[106] Accordingly, even where a policy provides that the insurer may settle a claim or suit against the insured as the insurer deems appropriate, the insurer is not empowered to release the insured's affirmative claims unless the insured consents.[107]

An insurer that preserves an insured's affirmative claims in a settlement may still encounter resistance from the insured. *Elworthy v. Hawkeye-Security Insurance Co.*[108] is exemplifying.

Bruce Elworthy and his wife owned a home in Wyoming. They were sued in a Wyoming state court by Cosner Construction Co. (Cosner) for breach of contract and unjust enrichment for failing to pay Cosner for more than $132,000 in remodeling services and materials. The Elworthys counterclaimed against Cosner and alleged third-party claims against subcontractors for construction defects, breaches of contract and warranties, and fraudulent billings related to Cosner's remodeling job. Cosner responded by amending its complaint to include RICO claims against the Elworthys, alleging that they had engaged in extortion. The Elworthys tendered the defense of Cosner's amended complaint to some of their insurers, described collectively as CGU, which defended them under a reservation of rights.[109]

The parties soon began negotiating a "global" settlement under which Cosner and the Elworthys would each receive $100,000 and sign mutual releases.[110] CGU would have been responsible to pay all the money owed to Cosner, plus almost half the money owed to the Elworthys; the balance would be paid by other insurers that were involved in the litigation. When those negotiations failed, CGU approached Cosner about settling its claims against the Elworthys.[111] Cosner was agreeable to a global settlement for $100,000 or, if the settlement did not include the Elworthys' counterclaims, to settle its claims against them for $120,000. In the latter scenario, Cosner wanted the additional $20,000 to fund its continued defense of the Elworthys' counterclaims.

104. Ins. Servs. Off., Inc., Personal Auto Policy (PP 00 01 09 18), at 2 (2017).

105. Birkholz v. Cheese Makers Mut. Cas. Co., 79 N.W.2d 665, 666 (Wis. 1956).

106. Bratton v. Speaks, 286 S.W.2d 526, 528 (Ky. Ct. App. 1956); *Birkholz*, 79 N.W.2d at 666. The precedential or persuasive value of *Bratton* and *Birkholz* is not lessened by their age. *See* Consol. Rail Corp. v. Metro-N. R.R. Co., 638 F. Supp. 350, 356 (Reg'l Rail Reorg. Ct. 1986) ("The patina of old cases does not affect their quality.").

107. Landin v. Yates, 651 P.2d 1026, 1027 (N.M. 1982).

108. 166 F. App'x 363 (10th Cir. 2006).

109. *Id.* at 354–55.

110. *Id.* at 355.

111. *Id.*

One day later, Cosner and CGU agreed to a settlement that required Cosner to dismiss its claims against the Elworthys in return for $120,000. The settlement agreement expressly stated that it would not affect the Elworthys' affirmative claims.[112] The Elworthys did not consent to the settlement.[113]

The Elworthys later sued CGU for breach of contract and bad faith in federal court based in part on the Cosner settlement. The district court granted summary judgment for CGU and the Elworthys appealed to the Tenth Circuit.

The Elworthys acknowledged that CGU had the right to settle Cosner's lawsuit against them. They nevertheless argued that in settling with Cosner, CGU impaired their ability to recover on their counterclaims and consequently violated the duty of good faith and fair dealing.[114] They specifically contended that CGU (1) deprived them of $100,000 they would have received in the failed global settlement; (2) aided Cosner's defense of their counterclaims by paying Cosner $20,000 more than it would have received under the proposed global settlement; and (3) breached its assumed duty to represent them in their counterclaims against Cosner.[115]

The Tenth Circuit concluded that there was no genuine factual dispute as to whether CGU breached its implied duty of good faith and fair dealing. CGU's policy granted it the right to settle a suit against its insured as it deemed appropriate.[116] The policy did not obligate CGU to negotiate a global settlement that included the Elworthys' claims against Cosner, to represent the Elworthys in their counterclaims against Cosner, or to seek the Elworthys' consent to settle Cosner's claims against them.[117] Given the policy's clear language, the *Elworthy* court saw no basis to infer a duty on CGU's part to do any of these things.[118]

Moreover, the settlement did not hinder the Elworthys' ability to recover on their counterclaims against Cosner. Indeed, the settlement agreement expressly preserved the Elworthys' claims against Cosner and the third parties.[119]

Persisting, the Elworthys argued that CGU's settlement with Cosner on their behalf *did* impair their right to recover on their counterclaims because the lawyers CGU hired for them withdrew from their representation after the settlement.[120] The Tenth Circuit succinctly rejected that argument because the Elworthys' personal lawyer was continuously involved in the underlying case

112. *Id.*
113. *Id.*
114. *Id.* at 355–56.
115. *Id.* at 356.
116. *Id.*
117. *Id.* at 356–57.
118. *Id.* at 357 (quoting Whitlock Constr., Inc. v. S. Big Horn Cnty. Water Supply Joint Powers Bd., 41 P.3d 1261, 1268 (Wyo. 2002)).
119. *Id.*
120. *Id.* (reporting that the lawyers withdrew shortly before the scheduled trial of the counterclaims and third-party claims).

and the Elworthys never tried to retain the defense lawyers to prosecute their affirmative claims.[121] Plus, the state court had dismissed the Elworthys' counterclaims as a sanction for discovery violations due solely to their misconduct, such that it was impossible to attribute any blame for their state court loss to CGU.[122]

In summary, CGU met the language of its policy and in so doing did not impair the Elworthys' ability to prosecute their counterclaims.[123] CGU satisfied its implied duty of good faith and fair dealing because it did not injure the Elworthys' right to receive the benefits of their agreement.[124] After rejecting the Elworthys' remaining claims, the *Elworthy* court affirmed the judgment for CGU.

The Tenth Circuit reached the correct result. In settling with Cosner, CGU effectively accepted coverage for Cosner's claims against the Elworthys, thereby contractually entitling CGU to settle those claims as it deemed expedient. The fact that the settlement may have had some negative ramifications for the Elworthys did not mean that CGU breached its duty of good faith and fair dealing by settling with Cosner as it did.[125]

VI. Conclusion

The outcomes of most of the cases cited in this chapter can be explained in one of the following ways: (1) the insurer was entitled to control the defense of the insured and elected not to bring a third-party claim; (2) the insured's assets were exposed due to a coverage denial or reservation of rights, and the affirmative claim was a reasonable measure to avoid or minimize potentially covered liability; or (3) the affirmative claim was inextricably intertwined with the defense of the underlying lawsuit and was part of a reasonable defense strategy. These cases illustrate that courts have not necessarily split into two camps regarding whether the duty to defend extends to affirmatively covered claims, as some commentators suggest. Rather, most courts have focused on whether the insurer or the insured is entitled to decide whether to bring third party claims, and whether the third-party claim was part of a reasonable defense strategy.

121. *Id.* (citing Shoshone First Bank v. Pac. Emps. Ins. Co., 2 P.3d 510, 517 (Wyo. 2000)).
122. *Id.*
123. *Id.*
124. *Id.* (citing Scherer Constr., LLC v. Hedquist Constr., Inc., 18 P.3d 645, 653 (Wyo. 2001)).
125. *See* Sec. Plans, Inc. v. CUNA Mut. Ins. Soc'y, 769 F.3d 807, 817 (2d Cir. 2014) ("The implied covenant [of good faith and fair dealing] does not 'undermine a party's general right to act on its own interests in a way that may incidentally lessen' the other party's expected benefit." (quoting M/A-COM Sec. Corp. v. Galesi, 904 F.2d 134, 136 (2d Cir. 1990))).

CHAPTER 5
The Duty to Appeal or Pursue Post-Judgment Relief

Patrick J. Kenny

I. Introduction

As explained in Chapter 1, the rules governing an insurer's defense obligations leading up to trial are well established. But an insurer's duty to defend its insured does not necessarily end when a jury returns a verdict or a trial court enters judgment.[1] As the Fifth Circuit reasoned in *Gibbons-Markey v. Texas Medical Liability Trust*,[2] "[e]ven if the language of a policy requiring an insurer 'to defend any lawsuit' against the insured does not explicitly require an insurer to seek post-judgment relief, it is illogical to suppose that the word 'defense' relates only to the trial of the action and does not embrace such relief."[3] Alternatively, as the Sixth Circuit explained in *Ziebart International Corp. v. CNA Insurance Cos.*[4] when applying Michigan law:

> [A]n insured whose policy includes a "duty to defend" clause is entitled to a defense from its insurer at both the trial and the appellate levels, unless the insurance contract specifically provides otherwise. . . . This is so because (1) insurance companies can limit their duties when they draft insurance contracts, (2) ambiguous language in insurance contracts is construed against the

1. *See* Reichert v. Cont'l Ins. Co., 290 So. 2d 730, 734 (La. Ct. App. 1974) ("[T]he insurer must provide a meaningful defense. Mere resistance of claims against the insured at trial level may not be sufficient in all instances."); Bruce v. Junghun, 912 N.E.2d 1144, 1148 (Ohio Ct. App. 2009) ("The duty to defend does not automatically cease when the trial court enters judgment.").
2. 163 F. App'x 342 (5th Cir. 2006).
3. *Id.* at 346.
4. 78 F.3d 245 (6th Cir. 1996).

> drafting insurance company, and (3) an insured could reasonably expect the insurance company to appeal an adverse judgment.[5]

What then is the nature and scope of an insurer's duty to defend after trial?

Analyzing an insurer's post-trial duty to defend begins with the language in the insurance policy.[6] Barring contrary language, the policy provisions creating the insurer's right and duty to defend also can give rise to duties to (1) defend the insured in an opponent's appeal of potentially covered claims;[7] (2) appeal on behalf of the insured in certain circumstances;[8] (3) file post-trial pleadings;[9] and (4) participate in funding a bond to stay execution pending appeal.[10]

II. The Insurer's Duty to Defend an Appeal

If the insured prevails at trial and the unsuccessful plaintiff appeals, the insurer generally must defend the appeal absent contrary policy language.[11] The

5. *Id.* at 248–49 (citations omitted).

6. *See, e.g.*, Burford Equip. Co. v. Centennial Ins. Co., 857 F. Supp. 1499, 1501–02, 1504 (M.D. Ala. 1994) (applying Alabama law and discussing the insurer's duty to defend the insured on appeal and pay the premium for an appeal bond); Mortensen v. Stewart Title Guar. Co., 235 P.3d 387, 392–93 (Idaho 2010) (discussing the insurer's contractual right to abandon the insured's appeal and to instead tender full payment of the policy limits to the insured); City of Hartsville v. S.C. Mun. Ins. & Risk Fin. Fund, 677 S.E.2d 574, 582 (S.C. 2009) ("[T]he liability policy provided for the Insurer 'to indemnify [the City] all costs and expenses incurred in the investigation, adjustment, settlement, defense *and appeal* of any claim or suit for which coverage is afforded by this Section III (General Liability) of this Contract.' . . . Therefore, the Insurer was responsible for the costs and expenses incurred by the City through the appeal of Byrd's lawsuit.").

7. See *infra* Part II.

8. *See, e.g.*, Associated Auto. Inc. v. Acceptance Indem. Ins. Co., 705 F. Supp. 2d 714, 724 (S.D. Tex. 2010) ("[C]ourts in jurisdictions across the country have held that, absent an express provision in the policy to the contrary, an insurer's duty to defend encompasses a duty to appeal an adverse judgment against the insured as long as there are reasonable grounds to believe that the insured's interest would be furthered by the appeal."); Crist v. Ins. Co. of N. Am., 529 F. Supp. 601, 606 (D. Utah 1982) ("It is clear that a duty to defend encompasses, at least in certain circumstances, a duty to appeal an adverse judgment."); Reichert v. Cont'l Ins. Co., 290 So. 2d 730, 734 (La. Ct. App. 1974) ("Having undertaken, for a price, to defend the insured, the insurer must provide a meaningful defense. Mere resistance of claims against the insured at trial level may not be sufficient in all instances. Where there appears [to be] reasonable grounds that a substantial interest of the insured may be served or protected by appeal, insurer owe[s] the duty to appeal.").

9. *See, e.g.*, Cathay Mortuary (Wah Sang) Inc. v. United Pac. Ins. Co., 582 F. Supp. 650, 656 n.1 (N.D. Cal. 1984) ("[T]he reasoning of the cases on the duty to appeal applies with equal force to the duty to pursue other post-trial remedies. For this reason, the Court will treat the duty to appeal and the duty to pursue post-trial remedies as synonymous.").

10. *See, e.g.*, Franklin v. Nat'l Gen. Assur. Co., No. 2:13-CV-103-WKW, 2013 WL 3854486, at *2 (M.D. Ala. July 25, 2013) ("Defendant's contractual obligations involving the posting of an appeal bond fall within Defendant's duty to defend its insured.").

11. *See, e.g.*, City of W. Haven v. Com. Union Ins. Co., 894 F.2d 540, 546 (2d Cir. 1990) ("As long as an appeal is pending that possibly raises issues invoking liability under an insurance policy, an insurance company bound by a general duty-to-defend clause remains under a duty to defend so long as it might be held liable."); Commerce & Indus. Ins. Co. v. Bank of Haw., 832 P.2d 733, 737 (Haw. 1992) (stating that the duty to defend "continues until the potential for liability is finally resolved");

insurer likewise must defend against any post-trial motions an unsuccessful plaintiff files, such as a motion for new trial or a motion for judgment as a matter of law.[12] In short, "unless the action is settled or the insurer prevails in a declaratory-judgment action establishing that the action is not covered by the liability insurance[,]"[13] an insurer's duty to defend continues until the plaintiff has exhausted all post-trial avenues of relief and the case finally concludes.[14]

Even so, an insurer does not have a duty to defend post-trial motions or an appeal where no covered claims or causes of action remain in the case and there is no reasonable basis to conclude that the plaintiff's motions or appeal will restore one.[15] In comparison, if there is a dispute as to whether certain claims are covered, the insurer's duty to defend continues through appeal.[16]

III. The Insurer's Duty to Prosecute an Appeal

Post-trial defense controversies typically involve an insurer's duty, or the absence of any duty, to prosecute an appeal on the insured's behalf. These

Restatement of the L. of Liab. Ins. § 18(2) & reporters' note c (Am. L. Inst. 2019) (explaining that, although dependent upon the law of the relevant jurisdiction, termination of the duty to defend through "[f]inal adjudication of the action" generally requires "the entry of judgment and the expiration of all appeal rights").

12. Millennium Labs., Inc. v. Darwin Select Ins. Co., 676 F. App'x 734, 737 (9th Cir. 2017) (applying California law); Truck Ins. Exch. v. Century Indem. Co., 887 P.2d 455, 459 (Wash. Ct. App. 1995); *see also* Restatement of the L. of Liab. Ins. § 13(3) (Am. L. Inst. 2019) (stating that, subject to several listed exceptions, "An insurer that has the duty to defend under subsections (1) and (2) must defend until its duty to defend is terminated under § 18 by declaratory judgment or otherwise . . .").

13. Restatement of the L. of Liab. Ins. § 13(3) cmt. a (Am. L. Inst. 2019).

14. *Commerce & Indus. Ins. Co.*, 832 P.2d at 737; *see also* Meadowbrook, Inc. v. Tower Ins. Co., 559 N.W.2d 411, 416 (Minn. 1997) (citation omitted) ("An insurer's duty to defend claims arguably within the policy's coverage extends until it can be concluded as a matter of law that there is no basis on which the insurer may be obligated to indemnify the insured. . . . As a result, the duty to defend extends through the appellate process.").

15. Westminster Am. Ins. Co. v. Spruce 1530, LLC, 853 F. App'x 793, 797 (3d Cir. 2021) (holding that under Pennsylvania law the insurer owed no duty to appeal "[b]ecause it is 'clear and free from doubt' that no covered claim could lead to recovery in this case. . . ."); *Millennium Labs.*, 676 F. App'x at 737 (applying California law); First Advantage Litig. Consulting, LLC v. Am. Int'l Specialty Lines Ins. Co., 525 F. App'x 60, 62 (2d Cir. 2013) (citing cases applying New York and California law); Hackman v. W. Agric. Ins. Co., No. 103,967, 2011 WL 1878135, at *7 (Kan. Ct. App. May 6, 2011); Jacobs v. Aetna Cas. & Sur. Co., 628 N.Y.S.2d 894, 895 (App. Div. 1995); *see also City of W. Haven*, 894 F.2d at 546 (emphasis added) ("As long as an appeal is pending that possibly raises issues invoking liability under an insurance policy, an insurance company . . . remains under a duty to defend so long as it might be held liable. On the other hand, *the duty to defend is not the duty to commit hari kari*. Once the insured exhausts an appeal from the original award in question, the insurer is under no duty to defend subsequent collateral attacks on the judgment that might render it newly liable on the policy."); Restatement of the L. of Liab. Ins. § 18(3) (Am. L. Inst. 2019) (stating that an insurer's duty to defend may terminate upon a "[f]inal adjudication or dismissal of parts of the action that eliminates any basis for coverage of any remaining parts of the action"); *id.* § 18(5) (stating that an insurer's duty to defend may terminate upon a "[p]artial settlement of the action, entered into with the consent of the insured, that eliminates any basis for coverage of any remaining parts of the action").

16. Valley Forge Ins. Co. v. Swiderski Elecs., Inc., 834 N.E.2d 562, 577 (Ill. App. Ct. 2005).

disputes can arise in numerous circumstances. Where an underlying judgment against the insured on covered claims is within the insurance policy limits, the insured might want to appeal for reputational or other reasons whereas the insurer might prefer to settle or pay the judgment for business reasons. When the judgment against the insured includes amounts that are not covered or potentially are not covered by, or are in excess of, the indemnity afforded by the insurance policy, the controversy is more pronounced. Adding another layer of complexity are the underlying merits of any potential appeal. An insured facing a significant uncovered judgment likely would favor an appeal even where the chances of success on appeal are slim whereas an insurer in such a setting likely would prefer to pay the covered portion of the claim or otherwise resolve the matter. How, then, are courts and litigants to resolve the question of whether an insurer should prosecute an appeal on behalf of its insured?

A. Policy Language and the Duty to Appeal

It bears remembering that insurance policies are contracts and the obligations under an insurance policy are, in the first instance, governed by the terms of the policy. Consequently, language in an insurance policy that addresses the insurer's obligations related to appeals generally will be enforced.[17]

A good illustration of this proposition can be found in *Mortensen v. Stewart Title Guaranty Co.*[18] The question there was whether a title insurance company had breached its duties under the insurance policy by tendering to the insured the limit of the title insurance policy and then refusing to appeal on the insured's behalf from a judgment adverse to the insured's property interests.[19] The insured had purchased real estate that was connected to a county highway via a primitive access road that ran across other properties owned by the insured's neighbors.[20] When the insured acquired his property, part but not all of the access road was subject to an express easement in the insured's favor.[21] Later the neighbors improved the road across their property, still permitting the insured's access to his property, but the improvements would not permit the insured to subdivide and sell a portion of his property as he then was planning without widening the road.[22]

17. *See, e.g.*, Mortensen v. Stewart Title Guar. Co., 235 P.3d 387, 392 (Idaho 2010) ("The generally accepted rule is that express terms in the policy can specifically enable the insurer to abandon an appeal.").
18. 235 P.3d 387 (Idaho 2010).
19. *Id.* at 391.
20. *Id.* at 390.
21. *Id.*
22. *Id.*

The insured nevertheless proceeded with work to expand the road, bulldozing portions of the neighbors' improvements in the process. The neighbors sued and obtained a judgment that exceeded the limits of the insured's title insurance.[23] The title insurer defended the insured through the underlying proceeding and told the insured that it would pursue an appeal. The insurer changed course, however, after the insured's motion to reconsider was denied, and instead tendered its full policy limit and ended its representation of the insured.[24] The insured then sued the insurer for fraud, breach of contract, and emotional distress, among other claims.[25]

The trial court awarded the insurer summary judgment and the Idaho Supreme Court affirmed. In so doing, the supreme court reasoned in part that:

> the plain text of the insurance policy also permitted Stewart Title to pay the limit of the policy instead of pursuing Mortensen's appeal. Insurance policies are a contract between the insurer and the insured. . . . The generally accepted rule is that express terms in the policy can specifically enable the insurer to abandon an appeal.[26]

As to that generally accepted rule, after observing that the policy conferred upon the insurer "the right, in its sole discretion, to appeal from any adverse judgment or order[,]"[27] the *Mortensen* court held that the following additional policy language unambiguously enabled the insurer to abandon the insured after tendering to the insured the full policy limit:

> In case of a claim under this policy, the Company shall have the following additional options:
>
> * * *
>
> To pay or tender payment of the amount of insurance under this policy together with any costs, attorneys' fees and expenses incurred by the insured claimant, which were authorized by the Company, up to the time of payment or tender of payment and which the Company is obligated to pay.
>
> Upon the exercise by the Company of this option, all liability and obligations to the insured under this policy, other than to make the payment required, shall terminate, including any liability or obligation to defend, prosecute, or continue any litigation, and the policy shall be surrendered to the Company for cancellation.[28]

23. *Id.*
24. *Id.* at 391.
25. *Id.*
26. *Id.* at 392.
27. *Id.*
28. *Id.* at 393.

Other courts similarly have recognized that any duty on the part of an insurer to appeal is subject, in the first instance, to the language of the insurance policy.[29] Indeed, in those decisions discussed later in the chapter in which courts analyze the circumstances under which an insurer has a duty to appeal on behalf of its insured, the analysis generally begins with the insurer's then-present contractual duty to defend.[30]

B. A Duty to Defend Does Not Always Lead to a Duty to Appeal

An insurer is not required to pursue an objectively futile or meritless appeal.[31] This is explained well by the court in *P. Gioioso & Sons, Inc. v. Liberty Mutual Insurance Co.*:[32]

> The court disagrees that a duty to appeal arises if there is only a 5% to 10% chance of success. Those minimal chances of success on appeal could be assigned to any case tried to completion. At a minimum, the insured must point to a particular appellate issue and explain why the trial court committed error and why this error was sufficiently prejudicial that judgment for the plaintiff might be reversed. The issue cannot be decided based on a percentage likelihood of success on appeal in the absence of some mathematically valid means of assigning such a percentage, and none was suggested in this case. Rather, a breach of the duty to defend could be established by identifying a material, prejudicial ruling and explaining the basis for arguing that it

29. *See, e.g.*, Associated Auto. Inc. v. Acceptance Indem. Ins. Co., 705 F. Supp. 2d 714, 724 (S.D. Tex. 2010) ("It is perhaps for this reason that courts in jurisdictions across the country have held that, absent an express provision in the policy to the contrary, an insurer's duty to defend encompasses a duty to appeal an adverse judgment against the insured as long as there are reasonable grounds to believe that the insured's interest would be furthered by the appeal."); Sanchez *ex rel.* Sanchez v. Kirby, 40 P.3d 1009, 1011–12 (N.M. Ct. App. 2001) ("The general rule appears to be that an insurer has a fiduciary duty to file and prosecute an appeal, absent a policy provision to the contrary, where there are reasonable grounds to believe substantial interests of the insured may be served or protected thereby."); City of Hartsville v. S.C. Mun. Ins. & Risk Fin. Fund, 677 S.E.2d 574, 582 (S.C. 2009) ("[T]he liability policy provided for the Insurer 'to indemnify [the City] all costs and expenses incurred in the investigation, adjustment, settlement, defense *and appeal* of any claim or suit for which coverage is afforded by this Section III (General Liability) of this Contract.' . . . Therefore, the Insurer was responsible for the costs and expenses incurred by the City through the appeal of Byrd's lawsuit.").

30. *See, e.g.*, Chrestman v. U. S. Fid. & Guar. Co., 511 F.2d 129, 130 (5th Cir. 1975) (beginning its analysis as to whether the insurer had breached its duty to appeal with the observation that "U.S.F.&G. was obligated to defend [the insured] and did so through the trial").

31. *See, e.g.*, Ill. Founders Ins. Co. v. Guidish, 618 N.E.2d 436, 441 (Ill. App. Ct. 1993) ("We reject [the insured's] invitation to adopt an absolute rule that an insurer is always obligated to prosecute an appeal. When taken to the extreme, such a rule could place an insurer in the untenable position of being obligated to pursue a totally groundless appeal simply to avoid a charge that it breached its duty to defend.").

32. No. 123738BLS1, 2016 WL 5372570 (Mass. Super. Ct. Aug. 27, 2016).

> was erroneous. The record in this case contains nothing of that nature. To the contrary neither trial counsel nor secondary counsel retained to review the trial record suggested the existence of a potentially meritorious ground[ ] for appeal. Summary judgment [for the insurer on the insured's contract claim for breach of the duty to defend] cannot be avoided by simply arguing that "any likelihood whatsoever" of success requires that an appeal be pursued.[33]

Furthermore, an insurer retains any right it might have to satisfy the judgment against the insured rather than continuing to litigate.[34] That certainly is the case where the adverse judgment is wholly within the insurer's policy limits.[35] Even where an adverse judgment exceeds the liability limits of the insured's policy, the insurance company may properly decide to negotiate a settlement with the plaintiff rather than appealing, as *Johnson v. Proselect Insurance Co.*[36] illustrates.

In that case, Dr. Ellen Johnson, a radiologist, sued her professional liability insurer, Proselect Insurance Co. (Proselect), for bad faith after it settled without her consent an underlying medical malpractice suit against her. The trial in the medical malpractice case resulted in a $5 million judgment against Johnson. Proselect chose to forgo post-trial motions and an appeal and, over Johnson's objection, settled the case for $3.75 million, which was within its $4 million policy limits. The settlement released Johnson from all liability and spared her a $1 million personal financial hit. Johnson nonetheless claimed that the settlement harmed her by bruising her professional reputation, impairing her career prospects, and causing her emotional distress.[37]

---

33. *Id.* at *8; *see also* Issa v. Allstate Ins., No. 1-21-0343, 2022 WL 17730851, at *3 (Ill. App. Ct. Dec. 16, 2022) ("Although the duty to defend does not automatically encompass a duty to appeal an adverse judgment, such a duty can arise 'in the context of the duty of good faith and fair dealing owed by the insurer to its insured' where 'reasonable grounds are present' for bringing an appeal." (quoting *Ill. Founders*, 618 N.E.2d at 441)); Getchell & Martin Lumber & Mfg. Co. v. Emps. Liab. Assur. Corp., 90 N.W. 616, 617 (Iowa 1902) ("It is upon this failure to have the appeal heard upon its merits that the claim of liability is founded. We very much doubt whether defendant, under the clause of the contract we have set out, would be liable for failing to take an appeal if it thought it inadvisable, or in any event be under obligation to do more than employ a competent attorney. . . .").

34. *See, e.g.*, Restatement of the L. of Liab. Ins. § 18(4) (Am. L. Inst. 2019) (noting that an insurer's duty to defend may terminate with a "[s]ettlement of the action that fully and finally resolves the entire action"); *id.* at 18(5) (stating that the duty to defend may terminate upon "[p]artial settlement of the entire action, entered into with the consent of the insured, that eliminates any basis for coverage of any remaining parts of the action"); *cf.* Mortensen v. Stewart Title Guar. Co., 235 P.3d 387, 392–93 (Idaho 2010) (upholding a clause in a title insurance policy that allowed the insurer to tender its policy limits to the insured and abandon the insured's appeal).

35. Robert H. Jerry II & Douglas R. Richmond, Understanding Insurance Law 750 (6th ed. 2018).

36. No. 17-P-109, 2017 WL 6327844 (Mass. App. Ct. Dec. 12, 2017).

37. *Id.* at *1.

Proselect's policy gave it the right to settle the lawsuit, but Johnson contended that Proselect's contractual right to settle was not absolute. She argued that Proselect had a duty to pursue her allegedly meritorious post-trial motions and an appeal despite the contrary policy language because those efforts would have served her "substantial and compelling" interests.[38] The trial court disagreed and, applying controlling New Hampshire law, awarded Proselect summary judgment. Johnson then appealed.

The appellate court made short work of Johnson's arguments. First, while New Hampshire recognizes an insurer's implied duty of good faith and fair dealing, it does not recognize a breach of the that duty "where a party merely exercises a right expressly granted under an enforceable contract."[39] Second, the duty of good faith and fair dealing does not require an insurer to pursue an appeal of an excess verdict rather than settling within its policy limits.[40] Certainly, New Hampshire courts had never recognized a breach of the duty of good faith and fair dealing in the absence of conduct exposing the insured to personal liability for a verdict in excess of the policy limits.[41] Accordingly, the *Johnson* court affirmed the trial court judgment for Proselect.

C. Circumstances in Which an Insurer Has a Duty to Appeal

Nevertheless, absent policy language to the contrary, an insurer should be expected to pursue an appeal on behalf of its insured in at least some cases. The question, therefore, is identifying the circumstances in which an insurer should be so required.

1. *Duty to Appeal Where There Is a Reasonable Basis to Believe That an Appeal Would Benefit the Insured*

The answer, in most courts, is that an insurer is obligated to appeal an adverse judgment against its insured when there are reasonable grounds to believe that

38. *Id.* (internal quotation marks omitted).

39. *Id.* at *2 (first citing Milford-Bennington R.R. Co. v. Pan Am Rys., Inc., 695 F.3d 175, 179 (1st Cir. 2012) (applying New Hampshire law); then citing Centronics Corp. v. Genicom Corp., 562 A.2d 187, 193–94 (N.H. 1989)).

40. *Id.*

41. *Id.*

an appeal would serve the insured's interests.[42] *Associated Automotive Inc. v. Acceptance Indemnity Insurance Co.*[43] illustrates this approach.

The issue in *Associated Automotive* arose from an underlying lawsuit filed by a worker against Associated Automotive, Inc. (AAI) and others for injuries the worker suffered on a premises shared by AAI and another entity,

42. *See, e.g.*, Millennium Labs., Inc. v. Darwin Select Ins. Co., 676 F. App'x 734, 737 (9th Cir. 2017) (applying California law); Chrestman v. U.S. Fid. & Guar. Co., 511 F.2d 129, 130 (5th Cir. 1975) (predicting that under Mississippi law there would be no claim against the insurer for failing to appeal unless the insured showed "reasonable grounds for taking an appeal"); Associated Auto. Inc. v. Acceptance Indem. Ins. Co., 705 F. Supp. 2d 714, 724 (S.D. Tex. 2010) (predicting Texas law and agreeing that "absent an express provision in the policy to the contrary, an insurer's duty to defend encompasses a duty to appeal an adverse judgment against the insured as long as there are reasonable grounds to believe that the insured's interest would be furthered by the appeal"); Cathay Mortuary (Wah Sang) Inc. v. United Pac. Ins. Co., 582 F. Supp. 650, 657 (N.D. Cal. 1984) (applying California law and recognizing "a general consensus that an insurer is obliged to pursue an appeal on behalf of its insured where there are reasonable grounds for appeal"); MedMarc Cas. Ins. Co. v. Forest Healthcare, Inc., 199 S.W.3d 58, 62 (Ark. 2004) (stating that an insurer is obligated to appeal a judgment against its insured only when there are reasonable grounds to believe that the insured's interest would be furthered by the appeal); Jenkins v. Ins. Co. of N. Am., 272 Cal. Rptr. 7, 12 (Ct. App. 1990) (concluding that the duty to defend may include a duty to appeal "where reasonable grounds for an appeal exist"); Delmonte v. State Farm Fire & Cas. Co., 975 P.2d 1159, 1168–69 (Haw. 1999) (explaining that the duty to defend includes a duty to appeal where there are reasonable grounds for the appeal unless the insurance policy expressly provides to the contrary, but concluding that the insurer did not have a duty to appeal in this case); Koppie v. Allied Mut. Ins. Co., 210 N.W.2d 844, 847 (Iowa 1973) ("We are not now inclined to encourage expansion of our appellate case backlog with utterly hopeless appeals brought to gain negotiating time. We hold Allied's failure to appeal the judgment constitutes no evidence of bad faith, in the absence of proof of any ground for appeal."); Ursprung v. Safeco Ins. Co. of Am., 497 S.W.2d 726, 730–31 (Ky. 1973) ("After reviewing the rules of other jurisdictions, we have concluded that the contractual obligation to defend carries with it an obligation to prosecute an appeal from a judgment against an insured where there are reasonable grounds for appeal."); Chatoney v. Safeway Ins. Co., 801 So. 2d 448, 450–51 (La. Ct. App. 2001) ("'[An] insurer's obligation to defend includes the duty to appeal judgment adverse to the insured where there appears reasonable grounds for taking an appeal.'" (quoting Reichert v. Cont'l Ins. Co., 290 So. 2d 730, 733 (La. Ct. App. 1974))); Davis v. Allstate Ins. Co., 747 N.E.2d 141, 146 (Mass. 2001) (noting "the established rule that an insurer's duty to defend generally encompasses an obligation to appeal from an adverse judgment against its insured, but only if reasonable grounds exist to believe that the insured's interest might be served by the appeal"); Sanchez *ex rel.* Sanchez v. Kirby, 40 P.3d 1009, 1011–12 (N.M. Ct. App. 2001) ("The general rule appears to be that an insurer has a fiduciary duty to file and prosecute an appeal, absent a policy provision to the contrary, where there are reasonable grounds to believe substantial interests of the insured may be served or protected thereby."); Schneider v. Commonwealth Land Title Ins. Co., 844 N.Y.S.2d 657, 661 (Sup. Ct. 2007) (concluding that "absent an express provision defining or limiting the same, the duty to defend includes the duty to appeal where there are reasonable grounds to do so"); Pharmacists Mut. Ins. Co. v. Myer, 993 A.2d 413, 421 (Vt. 2010) (quoting a treatise) ("[T]he general rule is that an insurer under a general duty to defend is required to bring an appeal on its insured's behalf 'when there are reasonable grounds to believe that the insured's interests might be served by an appeal.'"); Truck Ins. Exch. v. Century Indem. Co., 887 P.2d 455, 459 (Wash. Ct. App. 1995) (adopting "the rule that where there are reasonable grounds to believe a substantial interest of the insured may be served or protected thereby, absent an express provision to the contrary, the insurer's duty to defend includes the duty to seek postjudgment relief").

43. 705 F. Supp. 2d 714 (S.D. Tex. 2010).

AAI Automated Salvage (Salvage).[44] There was a dispute as to whether AAI employed the worker (which would give rise to certain defenses), and AAI's insurer, Acceptance Indemnity (Acceptance), filed a coverage suit seeking a declaration that it had no duty to defend AAI in the worker's suit.[45] Ultimately the worker prevailed in his suit and was found to be an employee of Salvage and not AAI, but judgment nevertheless was entered against both AAI and Salvage, jointly and severally, based on the "single business enterprise theory."[46] Though not known at the time of the judgment against AAI, the Texas Supreme Court soon would invalidate the single business enterprise theory.[47]

AAI asked that Acceptance file an appeal on AAI's behalf.[48] Acceptance declined to appeal and the judgment against AAI became final.[49] Later, AAI sued Acceptance, claiming that Acceptance had "breached its insurance contract by failing to appeal" the judgment against AAI in the worker's suit.[50] It was that breach of contract suit that led to the *Associated Automotive* opinion. Both sides moved for summary judgment.[51]

After disposing of an array of procedural and estoppel questions, the court addressed the merits of "AAI's breach of contract claim based on Acceptance's decision to not appeal the [worker's] Judgment."[52] On that point, Acceptance defended its decision not to appeal on behalf of AAI by arguing that "because the insurance policy in issue does not specifically contain any language that Acceptance must appeal a judgment against the insured, Acceptance had no duty to do so."[53] The court rejected that argument, first noting that it "is at odds with the general cannon of insurance contract construction that when the policy is capable of more than one interpretation, it must be construed in favor of the insured."[54]

Next, based on a review of extensive case law from across the country, the court observed that:

> It is perhaps for this reason that courts in jurisdictions across the country have held that, absent an express provision in the policy to the contrary, an insurer's duty to defend encompasses a duty to appeal an adverse judgment against the

44. *Id.*
45. *Id.*
46. *Id.*
47. *Id.* at 718.
48. *Id.* at 717–18.
49. *Id.*
50. *Id.* at 718.
51. *Id.* at 716.
52. *Id.* at 723.
53. *Id.*
54. *Id.* at 724.

insured as long as there are reasonable grounds to believe that the insured's interest would be furthered by the appeal.[55]

Indeed, because it viewed its task as making an "*Erie* guess" as to how the Texas Supreme Court would address the question, the *Associated Automotive* court also analyzed a number of decisions addressing the "good faith" standard,[56] discussed later,[57] after which it held:

> [I]t appears that the majority rule is that an insurer has a duty to appeal an adverse judgment against an insured, in the absence of an express policy provision to the contrary, where there are reasonable grounds for appeal. The Court finds this formulation to strike the best balance between the competing interests implicated by a decision to lodge or forego an appeal of an adverse judgment, and predicts that the Texas Supreme Court would adopt it.[58]

In light of the preceding, there are at least two instances in which an insurer likely would have a duty to appeal under the reasonable basis test. The first would be when there are reasonable grounds to believe that a judgment in excess of the policy limits might be reversed or reduced. In such a case the potential benefit to the insured is clear. The second situation would be where there are reasonable grounds to believe that a judgment on uncovered claims might be reduced or reversed.[59]

2. *Duty to Appeal Only Where Required by the Implied Duty of Good Faith and Fair Dealing*

The minority approach to the question borrows from the law of third-party bad faith, holding that an insurer is obligated to appeal only where the failure to appeal would breach the insurer's implied duty of good faith and fair

55. *Id.*
56. *See id.* at 725.
57. See *infra* Part II.C.2.
58. *Associated Auto.*, 705 F. Supp. 2d at 725–26.
59. Allan D. Windt, 1 Insurance Claims and Disputes § 4:17, at 181–82 (6th ed. 2013 & Supp. 2023); *cf.* Restatement of the L. of Liab. Ins. § 18(3) & reporters note c (Am. L. Inst. 2019) (noting that a "[f]inal adjudication or dismissal of parts of the action that eliminates any basis for coverage of any remaining parts of the action" only terminates the duty to defend where the right to appeal as to potentially covered claims has expired). *But cf.* Reller, Inc. v. Hartford Ins. Co. of the Se., 765 So. 2d 87, 88 (Fla. Dist. Ct. App. 2000) (indicating that in a mixed action an insurer can satisfy a judgment on a covered cause of action and leave it to the insured to appeal the remaining uncovered cause of action at its own expense).

dealing.[60] A good example of this approach can be found in *Hawkeye-Security Insurance Co. v. Indemnity Insurance Co. of North America*.[61]

The issue in *Hawkeye-Security* arose from a fire at a business.[62] That company sued Northern Utilities Co. (Northern) for its negligence in causing the fire.[63] Northern was insured by Hawkeye-Security Insurance Co. (Hawkeye), which investigated the claim and defended Northern in the lawsuit.[64] Eventually a judgment was entered against Northern in excess of the Hawkeye policy limits.[65] Hawkeye ultimately refused to appeal because, though the opinion is less than clear on the point, Hawkeye insisted on a proration with Northern of the costs on appeal, presumably between covered and uncovered damages, and Northern refused.[66]

Because Hawkeye refused to appeal, Northern's excess insurer, Indemnity Insurance Co. (Indemnity) prosecuted the appeal on Northern's behalf.[67] The judgment was affirmed, Indemnity paid the portion of the judgment that exceeded Hawkeye's policy limit, and Indemnity then sued Hawkeye to recover the costs of the appeal and reasonable attorney's fees.[68]

The trial court held that "Hawkeye was guilty of a breach of duty it owed its insured in refusing to take its counsel's advice that an appeal should be taken and that this subjected it to liability for the costs of the appeal[,]" and

60. *See, e.g.*, Hawkeye-Sec. Ins. Co. v. Indem. Ins. Co. of N. Am., 260 F.2d 361, 363 (10th Cir. 1958) ("Of course, when rights of others for which the insurer is responsible are involved in the litigation, it must take those rights as well as its own into consideration in determining whether an appeal shall be taken. The insurer will become liable to such parties only if acts fraudulently or in bad faith in refusing to take an appeal. The failure to take the advice of counsel employed to try a case, that an appeal should be taken, in itself, and without more, is insufficient to sustain a finding of bad faith."); Aetna Ins. Co. v. Borrell-Bigby Elec. Co., 541 So. 2d 139, 141 (Fla. Dist. Ct. App. 1989) ("Where good faith grounds exist, the insurer is obligated to appeal from an adverse judgment."); Ill. Founders Ins. Co. v. Guidish, 618 N.E.2d 436, 441 (Ill. App. Ct. 1993) (concluding that "the question of whether the insurer is obligated to prosecute an appeal from a judgment adverse to an insured must be resolved in the context of the duty of good faith and fair dealing owed by the insurer to its insured"); Guarantee Abstract & Title Co. v. Interstate Fire & Cas. Co., 618 P.2d 1195, 1200 (Kan. 1980) (calling the good faith approach "the majority view"), *abrogated on other grounds by statute as stated in* Hartford Accident & Indem. Co. v. Am. Red Ball Transit Co., 938 P.2d 1281 (Kan. 1997); Goddard *ex rel.* Est. of Goddard v. Farmers Ins. Co., 22 P.3d 1224, 1229 (Or. Ct. App. 2001) ("[T]he duty to defend includes the duty to appeal in an appropriate case"; further stating that after entry of an excess judgment, "an insurer must continue to give equal consideration to the interests of its insured. The insurer must act as if it alone were liable for . . . the entire judgment, and the reasonableness of the insurer's actions after judgment should be viewed in this context.").

61. 260 F.2d 361 (10th Cir. 1958).

62. *Id.* at 362.

63. *Id.*

64. *Id.*

65. *Id.*

66. *Id.* at 363 ("Hawkeye refused to take an appeal unless the costs thereof were prorated by the insured in accordance with the exposure of the parties, and that when the insured refused to do this, Hawkeye refused to appeal, although requested to do so, and withdrew from the case.").

67. *Id.*

68. *Id.*

the Tenth Circuit reversed.[69] After noting that defense counsel was not able to take the appeal without instruction from the principal, the *Hawkeye-Security* court observed that:

> The insurer will become liable to such parties [who have an interest in the appeal] only if acts fraudulently or in bad faith in refusing to take an appeal. The failure to take the advice of counsel employed to try a case, that an appeal should be taken, in itself, and without more, is insufficient to sustain a finding of bad faith.[70]

Notably, the court apparently did review the law as it existed at that time, and concluded that there was "no well settled line of decisions respecting the duty of an indemnitor to take an appeal where a judgment in excess of the maximum amount of coverage has been entered against its insured."[71] Ultimately the *Hawkeye-Security* court reversed the district court because it did not believe that Hawkeye's refusal to follow the defense lawyer's advice was "sufficient to sustain a finding of bad faith and the record [was] devoid of any other fact or circumstances which would tend to support such a finding."[72]

3. *Practical Differences between the Two Approaches*

In truth, the differences between the "reasonable grounds to believe" and "good faith" approaches likely are primarily semantic.[73] As one commentator has explained:

> The good faith test . . . should amount to the same thing as the reasonable grounds test; if there are reasonable grounds for prosecuting an appeal, but the insurer fails to finance one, it will have acted unreasonably, sacrificed the insured's interests in favor of its own, and, therefore, breached its duty of good faith and fair dealing.[74]

However:

> Whether [the reasonable grounds] test necessarily leads to different results from the good faith and fair dealing standard is not obvious. If the finding of

---

69. *Id.*

70. *Id.*

71. *Id.*

72. *Id.* at 364.

73. Windt, *supra* note 59, § 4:17, at 182 n.3; *see also* Associated Auto. Inc. v. Acceptance Indem. Ins. Co., 705 F. Supp. 2d 714, 725 (S.D. Tex. 2010) ("It is not clear that this good faith standard differs from the 'reasonable grounds standard' enunciated above."); Cathay Mortuary (Wah Sang) Inc. v. United Pac. Ins. Co., 582 F. Supp. 650, 656 (N.D. Cal. 1984) (quoting from a treatise for the proposition that there are "essentially two distinct lines of authority with respect to this issue [whether an insurer is obligated to prosecute an appeal from an adverse judgment against its insured]. However, close examination of the cases demonstrates that the lines of authority are not as disparate as they might first appear.").

74. Windt, *supra* note 59, § 4:17, at 182 n.3.

reasonable grounds presupposes a good faith inquiry, the tests are probably the same. Yet if one views "reasonable grounds" as something equivalent to a basis for bringing an appeal that is not frivolous, it would seem that one could almost always find a "reasonable ground" for appeal, even though it is clearly futile and an exercise of poor judgment to pursue it.[75]

4. *The Michigan Rule*

Only one court appears to have granted the insured sole discretion in deciding whether to pursue an appeal. *Palmer v. Pacific Indemnity Co.*[76] arose out of a medical malpractice case against Dr. Benjamin Palmer. The jury awarded the plaintiff $82,000, which far exceeded the $10,000 liability limit of Palmer's insurance policy with Pacific Indemnity. Palmer claimed that his defense lawyer, who Pacific Indemnity appointed, promised him that the insurer would appeal the verdict. When Pacific Indemnity did not do so, he hired independent counsel to handle the appeal. The Michigan Court of Appeals and the Michigan Supreme Court rejected his appeal. He then sued Pacific Indemnity to recover his attorneys' fees and costs incurred in his failed appeal.[77]

The Pacific Indemnity policy included a duty to defend.[78] The trial court, based on Pacific Indemnity's assertion that there were no reasonable grounds to appeal the malpractice verdict, instructed the jury in a fashion that effectively assured a verdict for the insurer.[79] Palmer appealed to the Michigan Court of Appeals. The appellate court framed the issue as "whether the trial court erred in concluding that the promise to defend provision of the insurance policy did not include the duty to appeal from an adverse decision, where the verdict exceed[ed] the limit of the policy and the insurer believe[d] that there [were] no reasonable grounds upon which to base an appeal."[80]

Pacific Indemnity argued that its duty to pursue an appeal should be conditioned upon whether it reasonably believed there were grounds for an appeal.[81] The *Palmer* court reasoned that this approach was fundamentally flawed because "only if the insurance company declines to appeal, the insured seeks its own counsel and appeals alone, and wins, will it be absolutely determined that the insurance company erred and that reasonable grounds existed."[82] This approach severely burdens the insured, particularly where the judgment far

75. Jerry & Richmond, *supra* note 35, at 749 (footnote omitted).
76. 254 N.W.2d 52 (Mich. Ct. App. 1977).
77. Palmer also sued the insurance broker who placed his malpractice coverage for procuring a policy with inadequate liability limits. *Id.* at 54.
78. *Id.*
79. *Id.*
80. *Id.*
81. *Id.* at 55.
82. *Id.*

exceeds the policy limits.[83] Furthermore, the mere fact that an appeal fails "does not necessarily imply that the grounds for appeal were not reasonable."[84]

The *Palmer* court observed that in contractually promising a defense, Pacific Indemnity did not limit its duty to trials, such that Palmer could reasonably have expected the insurer to appeal the judgment against him.[85] The court thus held that an insurance company must prosecute an appeal "if requested by an insured, if it writes a broad 'duty to defend' clause into its [policies]."[86] The court reasoned that to hold otherwise would allow an insurer in an excess verdict case to pay its policy limits into court and leave its insured helpless with respect to any potential appeal.[87] The court therefore reiterated that the "insured is entitled to be defended by the insurer at both the trial level as well as the appellate level unless otherwise specifically set forth in the contract of insurance."[88] As a result, the trial court erred in instructing the jury as it did, and the *Palmer* court reversed the judgment for Pacific Indemnity.

The different outcomes in the trial and appellate courts can be traced to the courts' differing views of what it means for there to be reasonable grounds to appeal. The trial court obviously believed (with Pacific Indemnity's encouragement) that the phrase "reasonable grounds to appeal" must be interpreted to require a factual or legal basis for an appeal that is not frivolous. In contrast, the appellate court reasoned that "reasonable grounds to appeal" means that there are reasonable grounds to believe that an appeal would further the insured's interests.

Unfortunately, the *Palmer* court's holding that an insurer must prosecute an appeal upon the insured's request rather than just when there are reasonable grounds to believe that an appeal will further the insured's interests potentially encourages wasteful and unnecessary litigation. Because the court never quoted the policy, it is impossible to know from the opinion whether Pacific Indemnity's insuring agreement granted it discretion to settle litigation against the insured. If it did not, then where policy language does provide the insurer that discretion, *Palmer* would not bar an insurer from settling a case or satisfying the judgment against the insured so as to avoid an unnecessary appeal.[89] If Pacific Indemnity *did* enjoy such discretion under its policy and the court either disregarded or overlooked the relevant language, then courts should treat the

83. *Id.*
84. *Id.*
85. *Id.*
86. *Id.*
87. *Id.*
88. *Id.*
89. *See, e.g.*, Ins. Servs. Off., Inc., Commercial General Liability Coverage Form (CG 00 01 04 13), at 1 (2012) (granting the insurer the discretion to settle any claim or suit against an insured).

Palmer approach as being incorrect and reject it.[90] It is perhaps noteworthy that the *Palmer* approach has not gained traction outside of Michigan.

IV. No Duty to Prosecute an Offensive Appeal

Because an insurer's duty to appeal is an aspect of its duty to defend, it follows that an insurer should not have to prosecute an appeal where the appellate issue is not intertwined with the claim or suit the insurer is required to defend. In other words, an insurer should have no duty to prosecute an "offensive" appeal. *WGF National Title Insurance Co. v. Pinnacle Premier Properties, Inc.*[91] is a representative case.

Pinnacle Premier Properties, Inc. (Pinnacle Premier) bought a Houston residential property. WFG National Title Insurance Co. (WFG) issued Pinnacle Premier a title insurance policy covering the property.

Pinnacle Premier moved to evict the residents of the homes on the property. The residents—known as the "Breton Plaintiffs"—then sued Pinnacle Premier and its sister company Pinnacle Realty in Texas state court to enjoin the eviction proceedings and challenge a preceding foreclosure on the property. That lawsuit became known as the "Breton Action." The state court granted the Breton Plaintiffs a temporary injunction that barred Pinnacle Premier from evicting them pending trial. Pinnacle Premier and Pinnacle Realty filed an interlocutory appeal to overturn the temporary injunction in order to proceed with the evictions.

Pinnacle Premier demanded that WFG defend and indemnify it in the Breton Action. It also requested that WFG prosecute its interlocutory appeal of the state court's order entering the temporary injunction.[92] WFG agreed to defend Pinnacle Premier in the Breton Action under a reservation of rights. It also filed a declaratory judgment action in federal court.

In the declaratory judgment action, WFG moved for summary judgment on its alleged duty to prosecute the interlocutory appeal. The court acknowledged that an insurer's duty to defend "'encompasses a duty to appeal an adverse judgment against the insured as long as there are reasonable grounds to believe that the insured's interest would be furthered by the appeal.'"[93] Yet, Pinnacle

90. *See* Bruce v. Junghun, 912 N.E.2d 1144, 1148 (Ohio Ct. App. 2009) ("We do not read the contract as saying that Allstate must pursue an appeal if the insured wishes to do so. (It retains the right to settle.)").

91. No. H-14-0842, 2014 WL 12537168 (S.D. Tex. July 18, 2014).

92. *Id.* at *2.

93. *Id.* at *7 (quoting Associated Auto. Inc. v. Acceptance Indem. Ins. Co., 705 F. Supp. 2d 714, 724 (S.D. Tex. 2010)).

Premier's interlocutory appeal did not fall within WFG's duty to defend.[94] As the court explained:

> WFG is liable to defend Pinnacle Premier against claims of loss or damage resulting from title in the [p]roperty being vested in an entity other than Pinnacle Premier, and WFG thus must defend Pinnacle Premier against all of the Breton Plaintiffs' claims. . . . However, the interlocutory appeal . . . in the Breton Action is a request for affirmative relief not encompassed within the duty to defend. . . . Appellants seek to overturn the state court's injunction barring them from applying to an appropriate court to evict the Breton Plaintiffs. . . . An eviction is affirmative relief seeking possession of property, not a defense to an adverse claim. Thus . . . Pinnacle Premier and Pinnacle Realty's interlocutory appeal is not defensive in nature, and that appeal does not fall within WFG's duty to defend.[95]

In granting WFG summary judgment, the *WFG National* court emphasized that its ruling was "specific to the facts presented."[96] The court declined to address WFG's duty to defend "regarding any other potential appeal in this case or any other case."[97]

Although its ruling was case- and fact-specific, *WFG National* clearly reflects the correct approach. Just as an insurer generally has no duty to prosecute an insured's affirmative claims at the trial court level as part of its duty to defend,[98] an insurer similarly should have no duty to prosecute such claims at the appellate level.

V. The Insurer's Duty to Seek Post-Judgment Relief

Though under the Restatement an insurer's duty to defend generally would include the duty to file post-trial motions,[99] few jurisdictions have addressed the question directly. In one such case, *Cathay Mortuary (Wah Sang) Inc. v.*

94. *Id.*
95. *Id.*
96. *Id.*
97. *Id.*
98. *See, e.g.*, Aldous v. Darwin Nat'l Assur. Co., 851 F.3d 473, 483 (5th Cir. 2017) ("No Texas court has ever held that the duty to defend includes the duty to pay legal fees incurred in the course of prosecuting affirmative claims that are inextricably intertwined with the defense"), *vacated in part on other grounds*, 889 F.3d 798 (5th Cir. 2018); Morgan, Lewis & Bockius LLP v. Hanover Ins. Co., 929 F. Supp. 764, 771 (D.N.J. 1996) (applying New Jersey law); Ramsey v. Lee Builders, Inc., 95 P.3d 1033, 1040 (Kan. Ct. App. 2004); Mt. Vernon Fire Ins. Co. v. Visionaid, Inc., 76 N.E.3d 204, 209–12 (Mass. 2017); Shoshone First Bank v. Pac. Emps. Ins. Co., 2 P.3d 510, 516–17 (Wyo. 2000).
99. Restatement of the L. of Liab. Ins. § 13(3) (Am. L. Inst. 2019) (stating that, subject to several listed exceptions, "[a]n insurer that has the duty to defend under subsections (1) and (2) must defend until its duty to defend is terminated under § 18 by declaratory judgment or otherwise. . . .").

United Pac. Ins. Co.,[100] the court resolved the question by treating the duty to file post-trial motions as synonymous with the duty to appeal.[101]

Cathay Mortuary arose from a coverage action filed by the insureds after suffering a jury verdict in an underlying lawsuit which included $15,000 in potentially insured damages and $45,000 in damages based on uncovered intentional acts.[102] The insureds believed they had meritorious grounds for an appeal and brought them to the insurers' attention.[103]

The insurers declined to pursue any post-trial remedies on the insureds' behalf.[104] The insureds filed their own post-trial motions and, after those motions were denied, opted not to appeal.[105] Instead, they filed the subject coverage action, charging:

> their insurers with breach of the insurance contract, bad faith breach of the covenant of good faith and fair dealing, breach of fiduciary duty, violation of the insurance code, and negligence. All of plaintiffs' causes of action arise from the insurers' refusal to pursue post-trial remedies in the state courts.[106]

In particular, the insureds argued that the insurers' post-judgment conduct had breached the insurers' duty to defend.[107] According to the court:

> The insurers instructed trial counsel . . . not to file a motion for new trial. The insurers also directed counsel not to file a notice of appeal, and refused to post an appeal bond [and,] while [the insured's] own motion for new trial was pending, the insurers tendered $15,000 to plaintiffs to cover the jury award for negligent acts.[108]

To analyze the issues raised by the insureds, the court first confirmed that the insurers' did have a duty to defend under the policy in question, noting that the duty will include a duty to appeal unless the policy "specifically exempts the insurer from the duty[.]"[109] Because the policy at issue did not explicitly exclude post-trial remedies from the duty to defend,[110] the court examined "what the law requires of an insurer with respect to pursuing post-trial remedies on behalf of an insured."[111]

100. 582 F. Supp. 650 (N.D. Cal. 1984).
101. *See id.* at 656 n.1.
102. *Id.* at 653.
103. *Id.*
104. *Id.*
105. *Id.*
106. *Id.*
107. *Id.* at 652–53.
108. *Id.*
109. *Id.* at 655.
110. *Id.* at 656.
111. *Id.*

Finding no case law addressing insurers' duties with respect to post-trial remedies, the court treated "the duty to appeal and the duty to pursue post-trial remedies as synonymous obligations."[112] Then, after extensive analysis regarding the duty to appeal, the court held:

> [T]here is a general consensus that an insurer is obliged to pursue an appeal on behalf of its insured where there are reasonable grounds for appeal. In the case at bar, the insurer plainly had very strong grounds for appeal.[113]

That led the court to conclude that the insurers had a duty to appeal and, for that reason, they also "had the obligation to pursue other post-trial remedies" on the insured's behalf.[114] Consequently, the *Cathay Mortuary* court held that the insurers had breached their duty to defend, exposing them under California law to the liability established by the insured's settlement.[115] Other courts addressing similar questions agree.[116]

VI. Insurer's Duties Related to Appeal Bonds

Apart from the initial question of whether to appeal, an appealing insured often must secure a bond to prevent execution while the matter is on appeal. The need for such a bond raises several questions for insurers, such as whether a carrier that insures the appellant must participate in posting, funding, or securing an appeal bond and, in the case of a judgment in excess of an insurer's limit, whether an insurer's duties regarding the bond on appeal stop with it limit or extend to the full amount of the judgment. The answers to these questions largely are governed by the language of the insurance policy at issue.[117]

112. *Id.* at 656 n.1.
113. *Id.* at 657.
114. *Id.* at 657–58.
115. *Id.* at 659–60.
116. *See, e.g.*, Gibbons-Markey v. Texas Med. Liab. Tr., 163 F. App'x 342, 346 (5th Cir. 2006) (holding that the insurer had a duty to seek review of a default against its insured reasoning that "[e]ven if the language of a policy requiring an insurer 'to defend any lawsuit' against the insured does not explicitly require an insurer to seek post-judgment relief, it is illogical to suppose that the word 'defense' relates only to the trial of the action and does not embrace such relief"); Truck Ins. Exch. of Farmers Ins. Grp. v. Century Indem. Co., 887 P.2d 455, 459 (Wash. Ct. App. 1995) (adopting "the rule that where there are reasonable grounds to believe a substantial interest of the insured may be served or protected thereby, absent an express provision to the contrary, the insurer's duty to defend includes the duty to seek postjudgment relief").
117. *See, e.g.*, United Fire & Cas. Co. v. Shelly Funeral Home, Inc., 642 N.W.2d 648, 658 & n.4 (Iowa 2002) (noting that the policy gave the insurer discretion regarding bonds).

A. Policy Language as the Source of Duties Regarding Appeal Bonds

As an initial matter, in that policy language plainly can affect rulings regarding an insurer's obligations with respect to appeal bonds, it is worth keeping in mind that insurance policy forms changed significantly in 1973:

> The 1973 ISO primary policy form expressly required that the insurer pay for appeal bonds as a part of the Supplementary Payments. When amended in 1985, standard ISO CGL policies removed that express requirement; but many excess policies include a provision in the Supplementary Payments section of their policy form obligating the insurer to pay the premium on an appeal bond, but the provision will not require that the insurer actually furnish the bond.[118]

The current version of the standard commercial general liability (CGL) policy does not obligate the insurer to furnish appeal bonds.[119] In comparison, the current standard auto policy does provide that the insurer will pay premiums on appeal bonds.[120]

1. *Language Requiring Insurer to Pay the Premiums on Appeal Bonds Required in Any Such Suit*

It hardly is surprising that courts will require insurers to comply with provisions in their insurance policies bearing on the question of appeal bonds. A particularly good illustration of this proposition can be found in *Burford Equipment Co. v. Centennial Insurance Co.*[121]

Burford was a declaratory action brought by Burford Equipment Co. (Burford), against its two insurance companies, Centennial Insurance Co. (Centennial) and International Insurance Co. (International). Centennial had issued Burford primary CGL coverage with a $1 million limit.[122] International had issued Burford umbrella coverage with a $5 million limit.[123] In the declaratory action Burford sought an order requiring, as to Burford's underlying appeal:

> Centennial, International, or both to pay the premiums on a bond in the amount of the judgment in the underlying action, not in the amount of the policy limits.[124]

118. Susan Knell Bumbalo, *Duty to Appeal: Examining Insurers' Obligations to Their Insureds Post-Verdict*, For the Def., Oct. 2017, at 46 (pinpoint citation unavailable).
119. Ins. Servs. Off., Inc., Commercial General Liability Coverage Form (CG 00 01 04 13), at 8–9 (2012).
120. Ins. Servs. Off., Inc., Personal Auto Policy (PP 00 01 09 18), at 3 (2017).
121. 857 F. Supp. 1499 (M.D. Ala. 1994).
122. *Id.* at 1501.
123. *Id.*
124. *Id.* at 1502.

With respect to the Centennial policy, the court resolved the bond question based on the policy language, noting that it provided:

> The Company will pay, in addition to the applicable limits of liability:
>
> > A. all expenses incurred by the Company, all costs taxed against the insured in any suit defended by the Company . . . ;
> >
> > B. premiums on appeal bonds required in any such suit, premiums on bonds to release attachments in any such suit for an amount not in excess of the applicable limit of liability, and cost of bail bonds required of the insured. . . .[125]

After first observing that "[t]he language of the policy should be given its clear meaning, and if that is uncertain, the policy should be construed favorably to the insured[,]"[126] the court concluded that:

> The express terms of the underlying insurance policy issued by Centennial provide that in addition to the liability limits of the policy, where Centennial has a duty to defend the insured, it must "pay the premiums on appeal bonds required in any such suit." The court finds that the language of the policy is clear.[127]

Notably, because the policy language did not limit Centennial's obligation to pay the bond premium to that portion of the judgment within its limit ("[t]he Company will pay . . . premiums on appeal bonds required in any such suit"), the court reasoned that:

> Centennial, unless it no longer has a duty to defend the suit on the plaintiffs' behalf, has a clear duty to pay the premiums on the appeal bond *regardless of whether the amount of the bond exceeds the policy's limits* because the language of the policy couches the duty to post bond as one "in addition to the applicable limits of the policy."[128]

The *Burford* court therefore held that "Centennial, if it has a duty to defend, should be required to pay the premiums on an appeal bond in the amount of the judgment in the underlying action."[129] The court rejected Centennial's further arguments that its duty to defend had ended, and held that "Centennial must pay the premiums on an appeal bond in the underlying action in the amount of the judgment."[130]

125. *Id.* at 1501.
126. *Id.* at 1504.
127. *Id.* at 1504 (footnote omitted).
128. *Id.* (emphasis added).
129. *Id.*
130. *Id.* at 1505.

The court's similar analysis regarding International's bonding obligations led to a different outcome because the defense provision in the International policy had not yet been triggered and thus International currently had no duty to defend. The umbrella policy plainly required exhaustion of the Centennial policy before a defense would be required from International:

> J. Underlying Insurance. If the underlying insurance is exhausted by any occurrence the company shall be obliged to assume charge of the settlement or defense of any claim or proceeding against the insured resulting from the same occurrence. . . .[131]

Although the umbrella policy did include bond obligations, those only arose when the underlying insurance was exhausted and International was obligated to defend, providing in that case that International would:

> (b) pay all premiums on bonds to release attachments for an amount not in excess of the applicable limit of liability of this policy, all premiums on appeal bonds required in any such defended suit, but without any obligation to apply for or furnish any such bonds;
>
> (c) pay all expenses incurred by the company, all costs taxed against the insured in such suit . . . ;[132]

Because the court already had held that Centennial's defense obligation was ongoing, the court had no difficulty concluding that International had no then-present duty to defend and thus no bonding obligations.[133] At least one other court, considering comparable policy language in the context of appeal bond obligations, reached results similar to those in *Burford*.[134]

It is worth noting that *Burford* also included a further opinion that if Centennial paid the limits of its policy and complied with the mandates of the Alabama Supreme Court's decision *Samply v. Integrity Insurance Co.*,[135] International was required under its policy to pay the premiums on an appeal bond.[136] Although the court did not elaborate, it appears from the reference to *Samply* that the insured or the insured's primary carrier might be able to trigger the defense obligations in an excess policy, including any bonding

131. *Id.* at 1502.
132. *Id.*
133. *Id.* at 1505.
134. *See, e.g.*, Fletcher v. Ratcliffe, No. CIV. A. 89C06160SCD, 1995 WL 790992, at *3 (Del. Super. Ct. Dec. 7, 1995) (holding that insurer may post bond less than judgment amount but also must pay the bond premium for the entire judgment, if procured by the insured, where the policy provided the insurer would pay "[p]remiums on appeal bonds and bonds to release attachments in any suit we defend").
135. Samply v. Integrity Ins. Co., 476 So. 2d 79, 83 (Ala. 1985) (holding that an insurer may end its defense obligation by "exhaustion of its policy limits by settlement or judgment").
136. *Burford Equip.*, 857 F. Supp. at 1505.

obligations, by settling or otherwise resolving with the tort plaintiff the claims to be appealed in such a manner as to exhaust the primary layer of coverage.

2. *Language Requiring the Insurer to Pay the Cost of Appeal Bonds, but Not to Apply for or Furnish Appeal Bonds*

James River Insurance Co. v. Interlachen Propertyowners Ass'n[137] is another opinion enforcing policy language. The underlying suit in *James River* involved allegations of negligent construction and professional design defects by Kuepers Construction, Inc. (Kuepers).[138] Kuepers tendered the negligent construction claims to State Auto Insurance Co. (State Auto) and the professional design defect claims to James River Insurance Co. (James River).[139] The James River policy provided claims made and reported coverage with limits reduced by payment of "claim expenses."[140] With respect to "claim expenses," the policy provided that James River would pay:

> reasonable and necessary fees, costs and expenses resulting from the investigation, adjustment, defense and appeal of a "Claim", including the cost of appeal bonds, however, we shall not be obligated to apply for or furnish appeal bonds on your behalf.[141]

The court in the underlying action entered summary judgment on the professional construction defect claims that Kuepers had tendered to James River.[142] James River advised Kuepers that it nevertheless would continue to defend under a reservation of rights. [143] The trial on the remaining claims resulted in a $2,147,000 verdict against Kuepers and Kuepers appealed.[144]

After State Auto refused to post an appeal bond, Kuepers demanded that James River post the bond, arguing that the underlying plaintiff planned to appeal from the dismissal of the professional design defect claims.[145] James River refused but agreed that, if Kuepers posted a bond, James River would reimburse Kuepers for the reasonable bond premium upon request.[146]

Kuepers eventually entered an agreement with the underlying plaintiff in which Kuepers stipulated to a $2 million judgment on the design defect claims in exchange for the plaintiff's promise to seek recovery of the judgment solely against James River and other professional liability insurers and not against

137. No. CV 14-3434 ADM/LIB, 2016 WL 3093383, at *7 (D. Minn. June 1, 2016).
138. *Id.* at *1.
139. *Id.*
140. *Id.*
141. *Id.*
142. *Id.* at *2.
143. *Id.*
144. *Id.*
145. *Id.*
146. *Id.*

Kuepers.[147] Kuepers then withdrew its notice of appeal in the underlying lawsuit and, two days later, James River filed the declaratory action giving rise to the opinion.[148]

In the declaratory action, James River argued that Kuepers had breached the policy's cooperation clause by entering the agreement with the underlying plaintiffs. Kuepers counterclaimed, arguing that James River had breached its duty to defend by refusing to post the appeal bond.[149] The parties then filed cross-motions for summary judgment. Thus, the question before the court "turn[ed] on whether the [p]olicy obligated James River to post the supersedeas bond on Kuepers' behalf."[150]

Citing the policy's definition of "Claims Expenses," the court concluded that James River was not obligated to post the appeal bond.[151] Noting that the policy obligated James River only to pay the "cost of appeal bonds," the court reasoned that the policy language did not require James River to post the bond itself.[152]

3. *Language Requiring the Insurer to Pay the Cost of Appeal Bonds, but Only for Bond Amounts within Limits*

Where policies provide that the insurer will pay the "cost of bonds to release attachments, but only for bond amounts within the applicable limit of insurance," which also state that the insurer does not "have to furnish these bonds[,]" courts generally hold that the insurer need not pay for a bond amount beyond the policy limit.[153] Although seemingly contrary decisions can be found, the

147. *Id.* at *3.
148. *Id.*
149. *Id.* at *4.
150. *Id.*
151. *Id.* at *5.
152. *Id.* at *5–6.
153. *See, e.g.*, Graf v. Hosp. Mut. Ins. Co., 956 F. Supp. 2d 337, 342–43 (D. Mass. 2013); St. Paul Fire & Marine Ins. Co. v. Nolen Grp., Inc., No. CIV.A. 02-8601, 2007 WL 4245740, at *3 (E.D. Pa. Nov. 30, 2007); Fitzgerald v. Addison, 287 So. 2d 151, 153 (Fla. Dist. Ct. App. 1973) (stating that "it appears that an insurance carrier should now be permitted to supersede the judgment against itself pending appeal without having to supersede the balance of the judgment against its insured"); Cansler v. Harrington, 643 P.2d 110, 114 (Kan. 1982) (permitting insurer to bond up to its limit, notwithstanding contrary statutory language, because "[i]t is inequitable to require an insurance company to post a $25,000 supersedeas bond to stay a garnishment when its policy limits are only $15,000"); Wilcox v. Bd. of Educ. of Warren Cnty., 779 S.W.2d 221, 223 (Ky. Ct. App. 1989) ("Since a supersedeas guarantees satisfaction of a judgment, however, the glitch in this problem is that the insurance carrier need not commit to satisfying more than the amount it is obligated to pay."); Bowen v. Gov't Emps. Ins. Co., 451 So. 2d 1196, 1198 (La. Ct. App. 1984); O'Donnell v. McGann, 529 A.2d 372, 377 (Md. 1987) (holding that the trial court could enter a limited stay because it "was justified in finding that the face amount of the Medical Mutual policy was $1 million and that Medical Mutual could not be expected to post a bond in excess of the face amount of its policy plus interest on the judgment and costs"); State *ex rel.* Brickner v. Saitz, 664 S.W.2d 209, 214 (Mo. 1984) (holding that the bond posted by the insurer in the amount of its limit "is adequate to support a stay of proceedings in execution and

rulings in those cases do not address the language in the applicable insurance policies.[154]

4. *Alleged Bad Faith by the Insurer Generally Does Not Affect Duties Regarding the Appeal Bond*

An issue that sometimes arises is whether allegations of insurer bad faith with respect to the matter being appealed should affect the insurer's obligations with respect to the appeal bond. Most courts addressing the question hold that such unresolved allegations of bad faith do not affect the insurer's obligations with respect to the appeal bond.[155] Some courts, however, suggest that "in the proper case" an insurer's obligations regarding appeal bonds "might be affected by bad faith dealing or a failure to properly settle within the limits of the insurance policy."[156]

B. Implied Duty of Good Faith and Fair Dealing as the Source of Duties Regarding Appeal Bonds

As might be expected, in many cases the applicable insurance policy is silent with respect to the insurer's possible roles with respect to the appeal bond. Courts in those cases often address questions concerning appeal bonds in the context of the implied duty of good faith and fair dealing. For instance, in *Merritt v. J. A. Stafford Co.*,[157] the California Supreme Court reasoned:

> In every contract, including policies of insurance, there is an implied covenant of good faith and fair dealing that neither party will do anything which will injure the right of the other party to receive the benefits of the agreement. Failure of the insurer to file any bond may result in the insured losing large amounts of property due to execution sales during the appeal and thus losing in large part, if not entirely, the benefits of the insurance. On the other hand,

---

garnishment directed against the insurance company"); Courvoisier v. Harley Davidson of Trenton, Inc., 742 A.2d 542, 548 (N.J. 1999) (ruling similarly without discussing the policy language).

154. *See, e.g.*, Wentzel v. Huebner, 104 N.W.2d 476, 477 (S.D. 1960) (reasoning, without reference to policy language, that: "No provision is made in our law for superseding a judgment for the payment of money by a bond in an amount less than the judgment. It is a statutory right which is available only on compliance with the terms and conditions prescribed by the statute. Since the undertaking here did not satisfy the requirements of our statute it did not prevent plaintiff from attempting to enforce his judgment.").

155. *See, e.g.*, *Fitzgerald*, 287 So. 2d at 154 (noting that alleged bad faith is not "present in the instant case"); State *ex rel.* Kissell v. Clark, 848 S.W.2d 44, 45 (Mo. Ct. App. 1993) (refusing to consider alleged bad faith in bond determination because "that remains to be established in another proceeding"); *Courvoisier*, 742 A.2d at 549 (refusing to factor alleged insurer bad faith into bond ruling, though stating that the court was "still troubled . . . by the possibility of pre-appeal execution against a judgment debtor whose insurer is later found liable for the excess on a breach of good faith theory").

156. Wilcox v. Bd. of Educ. of Warren Cnty., 779 S.W.2d 221, 223 (Ky. Ct. App. 1989).

157. 440 P.2d 927 (Cal. 1968).

> the insurer cannot be required to post a bond for the entire judgment when its liability does not extend to the entire judgment. Fairness to the insurer and the insured requires that the insurer be permitted to fulfill its covenant of good faith and fair dealing by filing an appeal bond in an amount sufficient to cover the part of the judgment for which it is liable and that the respondent be denied his right to seek execution with regard to such part of the judgment. Such a rule does no harm to the respondent. As to the excess part of the judgment he may seek execution or enter into an agreement to stay execution with the insured, and as to the part of the judgment within the policy limits he will be protected by the bond.[158]

Another example can be found in *Bowen v. Government Employees Insurance Co.*[159] There, the insured, John Bowen (Bowen), appealed from a $23,557.76 judgment, which exceeded the $5,000 coverage limit of his insurance policy. The insurer, GEICO, posted "an appeal bond only in the amount of its policy limits, i.e., $5,000.00."[160] Bowen was unable to bond the excess portion of the judgment and ultimately settled for $17,000, after which the appellate court reversed the judgment against him.[161] Thus, Bowen was bound by a $17,000 settlement in a suit in which he was held not liable. He thereafter sued GEICO for failing to "provide a bond sufficient to suspensively appeal the entire judgment."[162]

Bowen argued that GEICO's duty to defend included a duty to provide a bond sufficient to prevent execution as to the entire amount of the judgment. Hence, GEICO's failure to do so breached its duty to defend.[163]

After recognizing that an insurer's duty to defend includes a duty to appeal a judgment in excess of the policy limits, the appellate court quoted with approval the Appleman treatise in support of the proposition that "[i]n the vast majority of states, there is no such duty imposed on the insured."[164] The court reasoned that:

> If the insurer were to post a bond on the entire amount of the judgment and the case was affirmed on appeal, the insurer would be liable on the bond for the entire amount of the judgment. This would in effect rewrite the policy to provide coverage beyond the contractual policy limits.[165]

158. *Id.* at 931.
159. 451 So. 2d 1196 (La. Ct. App. 1984).
160. *Id.* at 1197.
161. *Id.*
162. *Id.*
163. *Id.*
164. *Id.* (quoting a treatise).
165. *Id.* at 1198 (internal citation omitted).

But the court also made the important observation that, even where the insurer is not required to arrange an appeal bond for its insured, the insurer's duty of good faith nevertheless "requires it to assist the insured in attempting to arrange bond for the amount of the judgment in excess of the policy limits."[166] By virtue of "its duty to defend in good faith, the insurer cannot merely abandon the insured's interest on appeal. The insurer should make a reasonable effort to help the insured protect his property pending the outcome of the appeal."[167] Thus, although the *Bowen* court affirmed the trial court's judgment for GEICO on the question of whether GEICO had breached its duty to defend Bowen on appeal, it also made clear its ruling was based on the factual "circumstances of this case[,]"[168] rather than some fixed rule of law.

C. Duties Regarding Appeal Bonds Where the Insurer Has No Duty to Defend

As reflected earlier, an insurer's duties with respect to appeal bonds arise from the insurer's duty to appeal, if any, and an insurer's duty to appeal arises from the insurer's duty to defend. Thus, it follows that an insurer's obligations regarding appeal bonds should be tied to the insurer's duty to defend, or lack thereof.[169]

Decisions that explicitly consider putative bond obligations on the part of an insurer with no duty to defend the insured are scarce. However, to the extent an insurer's obligations with respect to appeal bonds is tied to its obligation to defend the insured, where the insurer's duty to defend has not arisen, it follows that the insurer's duties with respect to any appeal bond also have not arisen.[170]

166. *Id.*

167. *Id.* (internal citation omitted).

168. *Id.*

169. *See, e.g.*, James River Ins. Co. v. Interlachen Propertyowners Ass'n, No. CV 14-3434 ADM/LIB, 2016 WL 3093383, at *6 (D. Minn. June 1, 2016) ("Because James River was not obligated to post the supersedeas bond, it did not breach its duty to defend under the Policy."); Franklin v. Nat'l Gen. Assur. Co., No. 2:13-CV-103-WKW, 2013 WL 3854486, at *2 (M.D. Ala. July 25, 2013) ("As an initial matter, Defendant's contractual obligations involving the posting of an appeal bond fall within Defendant's duty to defend its insured."); Hyundai Motor Am. v. Nat'l Union Fire Ins. Co., No. SACV080020JVSRNBX, 2011 WL 13134897, at *2 (C.D. Cal. Sept. 1, 2011) ("It is clear that when a defending insurer elects to appeal a judgment against the insured, the insurer has a duty to furnish the appeal bond."); Burford Equip. Co. v. Centennial Ins. Co., 857 F. Supp. 1499, 1504–05 (M.D. Ala. 1994) (applying Alabama law).

170. *See, e.g.*, *Burford Equip. Co.*, 857 F. Supp. at 1502, 1505 (explaining that International Insurance Co. had no duties with respect to the appeal bond because its duty to defend had yet to arise at the time of the insured's appeal).

D. Duties That Exist Even When the Insurer Is Not Required to Fund an Appeal Bond

With respect to appeal bonds, insurers should be cautious even when they do not have a present duty to defend (and thus no duty to appeal). There is sparse authority, in the context of an insurer with a duty to appeal but which is not obliged to pay for the full appeal bond, that the "duty to act in good faith requires it to assist the insured in attempting to arrange a bond for the amount of judgment in excess of the policy limits, and the insurer cannot merely abandon the insured's interest on appeal."[171]

Precisely what actions might satisfy that obligation is unclear. One decision that addressed the aforementioned proposition affirmed the factual finding from the trial court that an insurer had satisfied that obligation where:

> throughout the settlement negotiations and litigation, the attorneys for the insured [sic] kept the insured informed of developments in the case. The insured was in full agreement with the defense urged by the insurer. Moreover, they communicated with the insured's attorney concerning the status of the appeal and the issue of execution of judgment. [The insured] elected to settle rather than furnish an appeal bond for the excess judgment. Under the circumstances of this case, the insurance company was not obligated to furnish a suspensive appeal bond for the amount of the judgment in excess of its in solido liability with its insured. Hence, we cannot say the trial court erred in finding that the insurer did not breach its duty toward the insured.[172]

VII. Conclusion

As a general rule, a liability insurer's duty to defend its insured does not end when a jury returns a verdict, or a trial court enters judgment. Absent a final declaration of noncoverage or the elimination of all possible covered claims through settlement or otherwise, the duty to defend continues following entry of judgment against the insured.

That said, the continuing duty to defend does not impose upon insurers a duty to appeal from every judgment against the insured. Insurers can resolve claims by paying of the amount of the judgment or some reduced amount established through settlement. Absent payment, in a majority of jurisdictions an insurer's post-judgment duty to defend only requires the insurer to appeal where there are reasonable grounds to believe that an appeal would serve the insured's interests. In a minority of jurisdictions an insurer's potential duty to

171. Steven Plitt et al., 14A Couch on Insurance § 205:44 (3d ed. 2005 & Supp. 2023).
172. Bowen v. Gov't Emps. Ins. Co., 451 So. 2d 1196, 1198 (La. Ct. App. 1984).

prosecute an appeal of an adverse judgment is governed by its implied duty of good faith and fair dealing. An insurer does not have a duty to prosecute an appeal for an insured where the issue on appeal is distinct from the claim or suit as to which the insurer's duty to defend pertains.

Where an insurer's ongoing duty to defend does require the insurer to appeal on the insured's behalf, the insurer also will a duty to file post-trial pleadings on behalf of the insured. An insurer with a duty to appeal also might have obligations with respect to securing a bond to prevent execution during appeal, though any such obligation depends heavily on the language of the insurance policy.

CHAPTER 6
Terminating the Duty to Defend

Robert H. Jerry, II

I. Introduction

Nothing lasts forever, and contractual duties are no exception. Once created, duties have a lifespan that eventually terminates in some manner. Insurance policies are contracts,[1] and the insurer's duty to defend contained in liability insurance policies is a contractual duty.[2] This chapter discusses how the duty to defend terminates and the situations that produce this result.

This chapter proceeds as follows. Part II discusses termination of the duty to defend by final adjudication or a full and final settlement of an action in which the duty to defend is owed. Part III examines termination by final adjudication, dismissal, or settlement of parts of an action that eliminates any basis for coverage in the remaining parts of the action. Part IV discusses termination by exhaustion of the policy limits under a policy's indemnity provisions. Part V discusses termination by exhaustion of the policy limits under a policy's defense provisions. Part VI explores termination through the proof of undisputed extrinsic facts not at issue in the underlying litigation that demonstrate that the alleged claims brought against the insured are not within coverage. Part VII analyzes termination pursuant to the insured's waiver of its right to a defense. Part VIII discusses termination through a final adjudication in which a court determines that an insurer does not have a duty to defend (in situations other than those already discussed). Part IX concludes the chapter with a summary of key principles.

---

1. Perkins v. King, 358 So. 3d 538, 543 (La. Ct. App. 2023); Blazek v. Ohio Bar Liab. Ins. Co., 215 N.E.3d 592, 597 (Ohio Ct. App. 2023); Cherokee Nation v. Lexington Ins. Co., 521 P.3d 1261, 1266 (Okla. 2022).

2. Robert H. Jerry, II & Douglas R. Richmond, Understanding Insurance Law 691 (6th ed. 2018).

II. Final Adjudication or Settlement Resolving the Entire Action

Contractual duties are the obligations a promisor owes the promisee under a validly formed and enforceable contract. Such duties are either unconditional or conditional. If it is unconditional, the promisor's duty is either immediately due and owing—meaning that it is due as soon as the contract is formed—or it will become due and owing at a future time the parties specify in the contract.[3] If conditional, the promisor's duty exists as soon as the contract is formed but it does not become due and owing until all the conditions to the duty are satisfied; if the conditions are not satisfied, the duty will not become due and will never be owed. Thus, in the classic example often used to illustrate conditional duties, assume that a buyer contracts with a seller to purchase real estate, but the buyer's promise to purchase is conditioned on the buyer successfully obtaining a loan to make the purchase. As soon as the contract is formed, the buyer is obligated to purchase the real estate, but this duty to purchase will not become due and owing unless and until the condition to the buyer's duty—successfully securing a loan to make the purchase—is met. If after a reasonable time (or, more likely, after a deadline specified in the contract for securing the loan) the buyer is unable despite reasonable and good faith efforts to obtain the loan, the nonsatisfaction of the condition (that is, the buyer's inability to obtain the loan) will have the effect of *discharging* the buyer's duty and thereby terminating all the buyer's obligations under the contract.[4]

The concept of *discharge* is fundamental to the law of contract performance. When a contractual duty is fully performed (or satisfied, completed, or finished, which means the same thing), it is discharged. Full performance by the promisor is the most common method of discharging contractual duties; this is because most of the time duties are performed to the parties' satisfaction.

3. The passage of time, in and of itself, cannot be a contractual condition because the passage of time is certain to occur. Conditions are events that are uncertain to occur (including events that may be certain, such as death, but the timing of which is uncertain). *See* Restatement (Second) of Contracts § 224 cmt. b (Am. L. Inst. 1981). If the parties form a valid contract but do not specify a future time for performance, it is clear from the circumstances that the duty is not immediately due and owing, and the parties do not subsequently fill the gap in their contract with an agreed term, a court hearing a later dispute will fill the gap with an implied term that requires performance at a reasonable time.

4. Conditions are powerful risk-shifting devices. As the real estate purchase example shows, the condition allocates the risk of the buyer being unable to secure a loan; when the buyer's duty to buy is conditioned, the risk of not being able to buy is allocated to the seller, who will lose the sale if the buyer cannot secure the loan and will have recourse against the buyer. If the duty is unconditional, however, the buyer will be obligated to buy the real estate regardless of whether a loan is secured, which puts the risk of being unable to secure the loan on the buyer; that is, the buyer who cannot proceed with the sale breaches the contract and becomes vulnerable to remedies the seller may pursue against the buyer for breach of contract.

But other ways of discharging contractual duties without full performance also exist, such as nonoccurrence of a condition to a duty,[5] unilateral and bilateral mistake,[6] impracticability,[7] frustration,[8] the statutory law of bankruptcy,[9] and res judicata,[10] to name a few. Upon discharge by whatever means, the promisor is no longer obligated under the duty, and nothing remains of the duty that the promisee can enforce. As a result, the promisee has no claim against the promisor for breach of the duty nor does the promisee have any remedy for breach.

As explained in more detail in Chapter 1, liability insurance policies contain two primary insurer duties—the duty to indemnify and the duty to defend. Both duties come into existence when the insurance contract is formed, which is ordinarily when the insurer accepts the policyholder's application.[11] Also, both duties are *conditional*, which means that the duties, although presently existing, do not become due and owing until the conditions to their performance occur. The duty to defend is conditioned on a suit potentially within coverage being brought against the insured, and the duty to indemnify is conditioned on a claim within coverage resulting in a judgment or settlement for which the insured is responsible. If no event covered by the policy occurs during the policy's term, neither duty will become due and owing. Courts and commentators often say that the duty to defend is *triggered* by a claim potentially within coverage being brought against the insured; a statement that "the duty to defend was triggered" is simply another way of saying that the condition to the duty occurred.

Once the duty to defend is triggered, the insurer is bound to defend until a final judgment or settlement is entered against the insured in the plaintiff's

5. *See* Restatement (Second) of Contracts § 225 (Am. L. Inst. 1981) ("Unless it has been excused, the non-occurrence of a condition discharges the duty when the condition can no longer occur.").

6. *See id.* §§ 153 & 154 (specifying circumstances under which a mistake in a basic assumption of the contract by one party and by both parties makes the contract voidable).

7. *See id.* § 261 ("Where, after a contract is made, a party's performance is made impracticable without his fault by the occurrence of an event the non-occurrence of which was a basic assumption on which the contract was made, his duty to render that performance is discharged, unless the language or circumstances indicate the contrary.").

8. *See id.* § 265 ("Where, after a contract is made, a party's performance is substantially frustrated without his fault by the occurrence of an event the non-occurrence of which was a basic assumption on which the contract was made, his remaining duties to render performance are discharged, unless the language or circumstances indicate the contrary.").

9. Bankruptcy discharges debts created by contracts and leases, which means that the duties giving rise to the debts cannot be enforced (and are, hence, discharged). In some circumstances, however, the reaffirmation of a debt discharged in bankruptcy can be enforced. *See id.* § 83.

10. *See* Restatement (Second) of Judgments §§ 18 & 19 (Am. L. Inst. 1982).

11. The insurer creates the forms through which contracting occurs; thus, the insurer organizes the offer and acceptance mechanics so that the applicant makes an offer to the insurer that the insurer has the power to accept or reject. Under the rules of contract law, an offeror can designate what must happen for an acceptance to be effective and when the moment of acceptance occurs. Accordingly, some insurers organize the mechanics so that acceptance occurs when the policy is issued by the insurer or delivered to the applicant, or at some other time. *See* Jerry & Richmond, *supra* note 2, at 167–70.

action, unless special circumstances exist (as discussed later in this chapter) that allow the duty to defend to be terminated earlier. Thus, in most situations where the duty to defend is triggered, insurers respond by undertaking the duty when the action against the insured is filed and then continuing to defend until the action is concluded. A California appeals court explained it this way:

> Normally, the insurer must defend until the underlying action is resolved by settlement or judgment. However, circumstances may change such that there is no longer a potential for coverage by, for example, (1) the discovery of new or additional evidence, (2) a narrowing or partial resolution of claims in the underlying action, or (3) the exhaustion of the policy. When any such circumstances exist, an insurer may bring a declaratory judgment action, in order to conclusively establish that there is no longer a duty to defend.[12]

When the insurer defends an action until a complete and final adjudication occurs or until a full settlement is reached, the insurer fully performs its defense obligation and nothing is left to be defended, which has the effect of discharging the insurer's duty. Because the duty to defend (like contractual duties generally) is normally fulfilled by full performance, it is common for courts to state that "[n]ormally, the insurer must defend until the underlying action is resolved by settlement or judgment."[13]

Numerous courts have held that a final adjudication requires resolving the entire action.[14] What constitutes a "final adjudication" depends on the law of the jurisdiction, but typically it occurs whenever a judgment has been entered and all appeal rights have expired or have been resolved.[15] As discussed in

12. Great Am. Ins. Co. v. Super. Ct., 100 Cal. Rptr. 3d 258, 269 (Ct. App. 2009). The *Great American* court explained the insurer's burden in the declaratory judgment action as follows: "To prevail in a declaratory relief action regarding the duty to defend (where the issue cannot be resolved as a matter of law), 'the insured must prove the existence of *a potential for coverage*, while the insurer must establish *the absence of any such potential*. In other words, the insured need only show that the underlying claim *may* fall with policy coverage; the insurer must prove it *cannot*.'" *Id.* (quoting Montrose Chem. Corp. v. Super. Ct., 861 P.2d 1153, 1161 (Cal. 1993)).

13. *Id.*

14. *See, e.g.*, Burka v. Garrison Prop. & Cas. Ins. Co., 521 F. Supp. 3d 97, 104 (D. Me. 2021) (holding that while the insurer's duty to defend ended when the plaintiff, former spouse, and parents of the former spouse entered into settlement agreement, a sealed docket cannot be the basis of determining whether the defendant was absolved of its duty to defend and explaining that generally an insurer's duty to defend ends upon adjudication or settlement of the underlying action and when the claimant relinquished his or her appeal rights); San Diego Hous. Comm'n v. Indus. Indem. Co., 116 Cal. Rptr. 2d 103, 115 (Ct. App. 2002) ("The duty to defend runs directly to the insured, and is discharged when the action against the insured is concluded."); Atkinson v. Atkinson, 326 S.E.2d 206, 213 (Ga. 1985) (holding that the divorcing father's wrongful death claim arising out of his daughter's fatal auto accident was not settled via the mother's consent judgment and settlement agreement, and the insurer continued to owe a duty to defend, which was not discharged by its payment of the policy limits under the settlement agreement, which "did not resolve the one wrongful death claim in its entirety"; also holding that "[a]n insurer's duty to defend its insured is not satisfied when the insurer settles by paying its policy limits to the wrong party").

15. *See, e.g.*, Stein v. Axis Ins. Co., 216 Cal. Rptr. 3d 804, 810–13 (Ct. App. 2017) (explaining that the insurer declined to defend the insured's criminal appeal because the insurer considered the

Chapter 5, the requirement that appeals be fully resolved may require the insurer to represent the insured in post-trial proceedings. The duty to appeal is properly understood as being subsumed within and constituting part of the insurer's duty to defend, which means that if a plaintiff appeals a judgment in favor of the insured, the insurer must continue to defend the insured on appeal. If, however, the result in the trial court is a judgment against the insured, the question sometimes arises as to the insurer's obligation, if any, to bring an appeal. Again, as discussed more fully in Chapter 5, when the insured suffers an adverse judgment in the trial court, the insurer must sometimes pursue an appeal on the insured's behalf. If instead of appealing, however, the insurer chooses to satisfy the judgment and thereby resolve all claims against the insured, the duty to defend is terminated, because this fully and finally resolves the action.

Similarly, the insurer can terminate the duty to defend, and by extension the duty to appeal, by settling with the plaintiff (and securing a complete release of the insured) and thereby resolving the action. This is because a settlement that finally and permanently resolves all claims in the action functions as the equivalent of a final adjudication.[16]

III. Final Adjudication, Dismissal, or Settlement of Parts of Action Eliminating Any Basis for Coverage of the Remaining Parts of the Action

Sometimes part of an action may reach final adjudication before the entire action is resolved. This can occur after a full trial when only part of the action is appealed, when partial summary judgment is granted and the associated order is final, or when part of the action is dismissed with prejudice. If an action is a combination of covered and noncovered claims and the final adjudication removes all covered claims from the litigation and leaves only noncovered claims for further proceedings, this partial final adjudication terminates

conviction to be a final adjudication, but holding that because all appeals had not been exhausted, the action was pending until its final determination upon direct appeal, and the insurer was liable for the insured's litigation expenses); Meadowbrook, Inc. v. Tower Ins. Co., 559 N.W.2d 411, 416–17 (Minn. 1997) (stating that the duty to defend did not terminate until the plaintiffs had no further right to appeal); Bruce v. Jong-un, 912 N.E.2d 1144, 1148 (Ohio Ct. App. 2009) ("The duty to defend does not automatically cease when the trial court enters judgment."); Klamath Pac. Corp. v. Reliance Ins. Co., 950 P.2d 909, 916 (Or. Ct. App. 1997) (concluding that an intermediate order from a trial court dismissing a claim does not relieve an insurer of its duty to defend because such an order is not a final resolution of the claim).

16. *See* Kocse v. Liberty Mut. Ins. Co., 387 A.2d 1259, 1262 (N.J. Super. Ct. Law Div. 1978) ("Certainly, if [the insurer] could have effected settlement of the claim and it saw fit to dispose of it in this fashion, there would be no duty to defend the action.").

the duty to defend, given that nothing remains within coverage that the insurer is required to defend.[17] Conversely, if what remains after the final disposition of part of the action contains a covered claim, the insurer must continue to defend the entire action. The general principle is straightforward, but its application in some situations is nuanced.

First, consistent with the rule regarding the disposition of all claims in an action discussed earlier, the partial disposition must be final. Thus, when a partial summary judgment is entered on all the covered claims, but the court's judgment is not final, the insurer cannot terminate the duty to defend. For example, in *City of Sandusky, Ohio v. Coregis Insurance Co.*,[18] a Sixth Circuit case applying Ohio law, several people with disabilities and the Ability Center of Greater Toledo filed a class action against the city for its alleged failure to install and create a schedule for installing curb ramps, which prevented the class members' safe travel on city streets. On cross-motions for summary judgment, the district court granted portions of the city's and the plaintiffs'

---

17. *See, e.g.*, Westminster Am. Ins. Co. v. Spruce 1530, LLC, 853 F. App'x 793, 797–98 (3d Cir. 2021) (applying Pennsylvania law and concluding that the insurer could refuse defend where only the covered claim was dismissed with prejudice and only uncovered claims remained); Cincinnati Ins. Co. v. AMSCO Windows, 921 F. Supp. 2d 1226, 1235–36 (D. Utah 2013) (applying Utah law and stating that "[i]f one claim or allegation triggers the duty to defend, the insurer must defend all claims (that is, covered and non-covered claims), at least until the suit is limited to the non-covered claims"); Britamco Underwriters, Inc. v. C.J.H., Inc., 845 F. Supp. 1090, 1093 (E.D. Pa. 1994) (applying Pennsylvania law and explaining that "if coverage depends upon the existence of facts yet to be determined, the insurer is obliged to provide a defense until such time as those facts are determined, and the claim is narrowed to one patently outside the scope of the coverage"); C.A. Fielland, Inc. v. Fid. & Cas. Co. of N.Y., 297 So. 2d 122, 127 (Fla. Dist. Ct. App. 1974) ("An insurer has a duty to proceed in defense of a suit to the point of establishing that liability upon which the plaintiff is relying is in fact not covered by the policy, and not merely that it might not be. The duty to defend continues until the potential for liability is finally resolved."); Preferred Mut. Ins. Co. v. Vt. Mut. Ins. Co., 32 N.E.3d 336, 342 (Mass. App. Ct. 2015) ("If the claimant's factual allegations are susceptible of an interpretation that leaves room for coverage, or are insufficiently developed, the insurer must defend unless and until it demonstrates with conclusive effect on the third party [i.e., the claimant] that as matter of fact—as distinguished from the appearances of the complaint and policy—the third party cannot establish a claim within the insurance."); Frankenmuth Mut. Ins. Co. v. Beyer, 395 N.W.2d 36, 38 (Mich. Ct. App. 1986) (holding that the insurer was not required to defend the insured after the negligence count against the insured was dismissed with prejudice, and all that remained was an assault-and-battery count for which no coverage was provided); Franklin v. W. Nat'l Mut. Ins. Co., 558 N.W.2d 277, 281 (Minn. Ct. App. 1997) (applying the rule that insurer may terminate its defense of an insured when all arguably covered claims have been resolved), *rev'd on other grounds*, 574 N.W.2d 405 (Minn. 1998); City of Niagara Falls v. Merch. Ins. Grp., 824 N.Y.S.2d 841, 843 (App. Div. 2006) (stating that an insurer that initially "failed to establish . . . that it had no duty to defend" the insured because one of the allegations fell within the scope of the policy could later terminate its defense when the insured was absolved of liability for that claim); Pa. Mfrs. Ass'n Ins. Co. v. Johnson Matthey, Inc., 160 A.3d 285, 290 (Pa. Commw. Ct. 2017) ("If a complaint against the insured pleads facts that are potentially within the scope of the policy's coverage, the insurer has a duty to defend the action until all covered claims are removed from the action."); Benjamin v. Amica Mut. Ins. Co., 140 P.3d 1210, 1215 (Utah 2006) ("Where an insurance policy obligates an insurer to defend claims of unintentional injury, the insurer is obligated to do so until those claims are either dismissed or otherwise resolved in a manner inconsistent with coverage.").

18. 192 F. App'x 355 (6th Cir. 2006).

motions and denied other parts. The district court's orders removed all the plaintiffs' covered claims from the litigation, but several claims for equitable relief remained as did a claim for attorney fees, which meant the order dismissing the covered claims was not immediately appealable.[19] The insurer, believing it had a right to terminate the defense, withdrew from the defense, which forced the city to hire a new lawyer to defend the remaining claims. Before that litigation was resolved, the city filed a declaratory judgment action in which it alleged that the insurer breached the duty to defend.

Affirming the district court's decision that the insurer breached the duty, the *City of Sandusky* court explained that "[a]n insurer's duty to defend continues until no remaining claims against an insured are covered by the subject policy"[20] and that "the duty to defend continues until there is a final judgment on the covered claims."[21] The court stated that the insurer "could have provided that it had the right to withdraw its defense before a final judgment was entered or an appeal pursued," but it did not do this, and "in the absence of such language it was the reasonable expectation of the insured that [the insurer] would maintain its defense at least through a final judgment."[22] Thus, the insurer's duty to defend remained because the covered claims were dismissed in a nonfinal order.[23]

Second, dismissals without prejudice, whether full or partial, that remove all covered claims from an action do not automatically terminate the duty to defend. A court-ordered dismissal without prejudice is not a final adjudication because the plaintiff has the right to refile the action. Voluntary dismissals, whether full or partial, are ordinarily without prejudice as well.[24] The duty to defend ceases to exist when the dismissal removes all covered claims from the action, but the duty may spring back into existence if a new action is filed that alleges covered claims. Moreover, if the partial nonfinal dismissal removes all covered claims, what remains of the complaint must be analyzed under the rules for whether a duty to defend would have existed if this remaining complaint were the complaint originally filed. These rules are discussed in detail

19. *Id.* at 357.
20. *Id.* at 361.
21. *Id.* at 362.
22. *Id.*
23. *Id.*; *see also* Wells Dairy, Inc. v. Travelers Indem. Co. of Ill., 336 F. Supp. 2d 906, 911–12 (N.D. Iowa 2004) (applying Iowa law, under which a summary judgment ruling is not final when the court intends to act further on case before signifying its final adjudication, and holding that the insurer's duty to defend continued to exist, despite summary judgment removing all covered claims from the case, because the plaintiff's right to appeal that decision continued to exist); Com. & Indus. Ins. Co. v. Bank of Haw., 832 P.2d 733, 737 (Haw. 1992) (holding that the insurer could not withdraw its defense after a partial summary judgment until either a "Rule 54(b) certification was granted and the appeal period had expired or a final judgment had disposed of the entire case").
24. *See, e.g.*, Fed. R. Civ. P. 41(a)(1) (stating that a plaintiff's voluntary dismissal "[u]nless the notice or stipulation states otherwise, . . . is without prejudice").

in Chapter 1, but in brief, in jurisdictions following a strict eight-corners rule, the absence of a covered claim in the complaint means that the insurer can terminate its duty to defend (realizing that the duty may be triggered again if an amended complaint with covered claims is filed). In jurisdictions following the potentiality rule, however, if the dismissed claims can be refiled and they contain a potential for coverage, the insurer must continue to defend, at least until the insurer through a declaratory judgment action establishes that no duty to defend exists.[25]

The plaintiff's filing of an amended complaint that deletes claims from the original complaint is the functional equivalent of a voluntary dismissal of the removed claims and should be analyzed in accordance with the rules described earlier. In cases where the plaintiff filed an amended complaint that removed all the covered claims, courts have held that the insurer's duty to defend was terminated.[26]

Third, the partial disposition of claims after trial and before appeal can raise the question of whether the disposition is final. If an action includes both covered and noncovered claims, the insurer fully satisfies the judgment against the insured on the covered claims, and the only claims to be appealed pertain to the noncovered claims, the insurer, as a Florida court put it, "[h]aving paid the insured claim . . . ha[s] no further obligation because 'the claims giving rise to coverage have been eliminated from the suit.'"[27] Likewise, in a Montana case where the action included both covered and noncovered claims, the

25. *See, e.g.*, Scottsdale Ins. Co. v. MV Transp., 115 P.3d 460, 468 (Cal. 2005) (stating that an insurer's duty to defend continues until litigation ends "unless the insurer sooner proves, by facts subsequently developed, that the potential for coverage which previously appeared cannot possibly materialize, or no longer exists"). For an argument that the insurer's defense obligations should end when a nonfinal judgment removes all covered claims, see Frank R. Malpigli, *Does the Duty Ever End? An Insurer's Continued Duty to Defend After All Covered Claims Are Dismissed*, For the Def., Oct. 2017, at 71, 71 ("Many jurisdictions hold an insurer has a continuing duty to defend the noncovered claims until there is no possible legal scenario under which the covered claims would be reactivated. Some jurisdictions go even further and hold an insurer's duty to defend essentially never ends as due to the possibility the dismissed, covered claims could be reactivated during trial if a court allows a plaintiff to amend their complaint. These holdings stray from the principles governing contracts as well as the reasonable expectations of an insured doctrine.").

26. *See, e.g.*, Baron Oil Co. v. Nationwide Mut. Fire Ins. Co., 470 So. 2d 810, 815 (Fla. Dist. Ct. App. 1985) (citation omitted) ("[W]hen an original complaint has been superseded by an amended complaint, the original complaint can no longer furnish a basis for determining the insurer's duty to defend. . . . It follows, therefore, that where an amended complaint alleges facts that clearly bring the entire cause of action within a policy exclusion, and the amended complaint contains no additional counts or causes of action which show coverage, the allegations in the amended complaint control and the insurer's duty to defend comes to an end."); Herbert A. Sullivan, Inc. v. Utica Mut. Ins. Co., 788 N.E.2d 522, 531 (Mass. 2003) (involving an original complaint that stated a covered claim where the insurer undertook the defense but explaining that the lack of covered claims in an amended complaint meant that the insurer no longer had a duty to defend); Nat'l Union Fire Ins. Co. v. Starplex Corp., 188 P.3d 332, 336 n.1 (Or. Ct. App. 2008) (holding that once the duty to defend "has arisen, it may be extinguished by the filing of a subsequent amended complaint").

27. Reller, Inc. v. Hartford Ins. Co. of the Se., 765 So. 2d 87, 88 (Fla. Dist. Ct. App. 2000) (quoting *Baron Oil Co.*, 470 So. 2d at 815).

insured prevailed on the covered claims but lost on the noncovered claims, and neither the plaintiff nor the insured appealed the jury's verdict on the covered claims, the Montana Supreme Court concluded that the insurer had no duty to represent the insured on appeal.[28] As the court put it, "there were no issues on appeal relating to claims covered by the terms of [the insurer's] policy with the [insured]."[29]

If the insurer has a duty to appeal an adverse judgment against the insured and pays the policy limits in *partial* satisfaction of a judgment instead of appealing (as could happen if the trial court judgment against the insured is an amount exceeding the policy limits), the analysis is more complicated. Whether tender of the policy limits by depositing them with the court or payment of the policy limits terminates the duty to defend in this situation depends on how the rules on exhaustion, discussed in Part IV, apply. As explained in more detail there, the language of the policy is pivotal. Insurers have been allowed in many cases to terminate the duty to defend under policy language, known as "pay and walk" provisions, which permits the insurer "to tender or offer" the policy limits and decline to defend. This right to terminate is qualified by the insurer's obligation to treat its insureds in good faith. Moreover, the lawyers appointed by the insurer to represent the insured are subject to the fiduciary responsibilities that attach to the attorney-client relationship and ethical obligations under rules of professional conduct. These responsibilities and obligations can prevent insurers (and appointed counsel) from withdrawing from the defense in the middle of a case or trial if prejudice to the insured is likely.[30] This analysis applies with equal force to situations where the insurer has a duty to appeal an adverse verdict, which means that the insurer may not be able to utilize a "pay and walk" provision to avoid the obligation to appeal.[31]

Most policies provide that the payment of proceeds must be pursuant to a "judgment or settlement." Courts consistently apply this language to prevent insurers from tendering proceeds and declining to defend an action in the trial court.[32] When the duty to appeal an adverse judgment is in question, however, a tender of the policy limits in partial satisfaction of the judgment

28. City of Bozeman v. AIU Ins. Co., 865 P.2d 268, 273 (Mont. 1993).

29. *Id.*

30. *See, e.g.*, Zurich Ins. Co. v. Raymark Indus. Inc., 514 N.E.2d 150, 163–64 (Ill. 1987) (holding that pre-1967 policies do not oblige insurers to defend after their duty to indemnify has been exhausted "by the payments of judgments or settlements *and they have made an orderly withdrawal* from the [insured's] defense") (emphasis added)); *see generally* RONALD D. ROTUNDA & JOHN S. DZIENKOWSKI, LEGAL ETHICS: THE LAWYER'S DESKBOOK ON PROFESSIONAL RESPONSIBILITY § 1.16-2, at 713 (2021–2022) (stating that "if a matter is before a tribunal, the lawyer must follow the tribunal's rules, which typically require securing the tribunal's permission before withdrawing"); MODEL RULES OF PRO. CONDUCT r. 1.16 (AM. BAR ASS'N 2023) (governing lawyers' ability to withdraw from representations).

31. See *infra* Part IV.B.

32. See *infra* Part IV.B.

would appear to meet the policy language; however, the same insurer good faith obligations and lawyer fiduciary duties and ethical obligations mentioned earlier also apply in this situation. These responsibilities may constrain an insurer's attempt to terminate its defense prior to filing an appeal. This was the situation in *Aetna Insurance Co. v. Borrell-Bigby Electric Co.*,[33] where the insured and the insurer's counsel both urged an appeal of an adverse judgment against the insured, but the insurer paid the policy limits and declined to pursue the appeal.[34] The policy in question provided that the insurer was not obligated "to defend any suit after the applicable limit of the Company's liability has been exhausted by payment of judgments or settlements."[35] The insurer interpleaded its policy limits into the court registry, refused to appeal, and refused to defend the insured on other claims arising out of the fire that spawned the litigation. The court explained:

> Florida recognizes that the duty to defend an insured is broader than the duty to indemnify. We find this duty precludes an insurer from interpleading its policy limits and walking away from the defense of its insured, at either the trial or appellate level. Where good faith grounds exist, the insurer is obligated to appeal from an adverse judgment. In this case, [the insurer] acted based on its own best interests, disregarding the advice of its own counsel and the interests of its insured. . . . As to actions instituted after its policy limits have been exhausted through payment of a valid judgment or settlement it may decline to defend. However, the insurer cannot truncate its defense obligations by leaping to pay a questionable judgment or claim, as [the insurer] attempted to do here; it must first in good faith establish the validity of such a judgment before paying out its limits and ceasing to defend.[36]

The court concluded as follows:

> In summary, we hold that an insurer cannot truncate its duty to defend by interpleading the policy limits. It must continue its defense until the policy limits have been expended in satisfaction of a valid judgment or settlement, and must test the validity of judgments, by appeal, if good faith grounds exist for doing so.[37]

Thus, the insurer's effort to terminate the duty to defend (and to appeal) by paying the policy limits failed.

Just as a partial adjudication may fully resolve all the covered claims in an action, a partial settlement can have the same effect. A partial settlement that resolves all covered claims and leaves only noncovered claims for further

33. 541 So. 2d 139 (Fla. Dist. Ct. App. 1989).
34. *Id.* at 140.
35. *Id.*
36. *Id.* at 141.
37. *Id.*

proceedings also terminates the duty to defend under the same analysis applying to final adjudications or dismissals that dispose of parts of an action.[38] Conversely, a partial settlement that does not release the insured does not terminate the duty to defend, even though the policy limits were paid in full.[39] The insurer's ability to terminate the defense upon a partial settlement of all covered claims is subject to an important qualification, however, because a partial settlement of an action differs from a full settlement in an important respect. A full settlement relieves the insured from any potential liability for any claim, but a partial settlement leaves the insured vulnerable to liability on noncovered claims. Because the insurer has a duty to defend an action that combines covered and noncovered claims, often described as a "mixed action,"[40] a rule that allowed the insurer to settle covered claims without the insured's involvement and relieve itself of its responsibility to defend noncovered claims would encourage insurers to avoid their obligations to defend the entire action by settling only the covered portions. Thus, a partial settlement of an action requires the insured's consent after informing the insured of the consequences of the partial settlement.[41] For example, in *Levenfeld v. Clinton*,[42] the insurer attempted to settle only the covered claims in an effort to avoid the cost of defending the remaining noncovered claims. The court held that the settlement was unenforceable because the insurer had acted in bad faith, stating:

> There is no question that the settlement proposed by [the insurers] harms [the insureds] severely. While [insureds] insist they do not fear the outcome of the malicious prosecution suit, they rightly fear the cost of litigating those issues.

---

38. *See, e.g.*, United Fire & Cas. Co. v. Prate Roofing & Installations, LLC, 7 F.4th 573, 585 (7th Cir. 2021) (holding that where the insurer only owed a duty to defend the insured for potential vicarious liability and the insurer settled this claim to eliminate any potential for the insured's future vicarious liability, the duty to defend terminated even though the insured remained a defendant in the action); Meadowbrook, Inc. v. Tower Ins. Co., 559 N.W.2d 411, 417 (Minn. 1997) ("Even though the insurer agreed to defend the entire claim against the insured, its duty extended only to those claims arguably covered by the policy. Once the insurer settled and paid those claims, it had completely performed its contractual duty. . . . Regardless of the insurer's motivation in settling the defamation claims, the fact remains that the insurer's action relieved the insured of any liability resulting from those arguably coverable claims.").

39. *See, e.g.*, Cal. Cas. Ins. Co. v. State Farm Mut. Auto. Ins. Co., 913 P.2d 505, 510 (Ariz. Ct. App. 1996) (holding that the primary insurer, which paid policy limits to settle in partial satisfaction of auto accident victim's claim, had "a continuing contractual duty to defend" until the insured received a "Release and Covenant Not to Execute").

40. *See, e.g.*, Gonzalez v. Fire Ins. Exch., 184 Cal. Rptr. 3d 394, 403 (Ct. App. 2015) ("When a complaint states multiple claims, some of which are potentially covered by the insurance policy and some of which are not, it is a mixed action."); Fire Ins. Exch. v. Weitzel, 371 P.3d 457, 461 (Mont. 2016) ("If a complaint states multiple claims, some of which are covered by the insurance policy and some of which are not, it is a mixed action.").

41. *See* 1 Steven Plitt & Jordan R. Plitt, Practical Tools for Handling Insurance Cases § 2:19 (2017); Seth D. Lamden, *Duty to Defend*, *in* 3 New Appleman on Insurance Library Edition § 17.06[2][a], at 17-48 (Jeffrey E. Thomas & Francis J. Mootz, III eds., 2017 & Supp. 2019).

42. 674 F. Supp. 255 (N.D. Ill. 1987) (applying Illinois law).

> . . . [The insurers] freely concede that they are offering [the plaintiff] $500,000 rather than facing the expense of seeing this case through.[43]

In short, a partial settlement of an action that removes all covered claims can terminate the duty to defend if the insured's interests are protected, which presumably occurs if the insured consents to the settlement.

IV. Exhaustion of the Policy Limits under the Indemnity Obligation

A. Policy Language and General Principles

In addition to discharges of contractual duties through full performance and by operation of a legal rule when not fully performed, it is possible for the parties to specify in the language of the contract itself the circumstances in which a duty is discharged. Functionally, this is no different from parties placing conditions on their duties that result in discharge when the conditions to the duties do not occur. In commercial contracts, the most common example of parties specifying the circumstances of discharge are provisions allowing one (or both) of the parties to cancel or terminate the contract upon notice. Assuming the provision does not render the duty illusory (in which case the underlying promise lacks value and cannot serve as the consideration needed to make the contract enforceable), termination clauses are valid and provide the party possessing a right to terminate with a way to discharge a duty simply by giving notice to the other party.

Also under general contract law principles, when a promisor agrees to perform multiple duties for a promisee, the parties can agree that the promisor's performance of one or a subset of the duties constitutes full performance. For example, if the parties agree that multiple duties are in the alternative and the promisor fulfills the contract by performing any one of them, this agreement controls, and all the promisor's duties under the contract are discharged when the promisor performs a single duty.[44] Similarly, if the contract specifies that the all the promisor's duties under the contract end if one particular duty is fully performed, the promisor can discharge all its duties by performing that one obligation.[45]

43. *Id.* at 258.

44. The common law of contract is clear that when a contract allows a promisor to choose among alternative performances, the existence of this choice does not render the contract illusory. *See* Restatement (Second) of Contracts § 77 (Am. L. Inst. 1981).

45. This structure is highly unusual in contracts; it is rare to give the promisor the power to pretermit all its duties by performing one of them. In the liability insurance context, this is what insurers

Today, most liability policies contain language providing that the duty to defend is dependent on the continued existence of a duty to indemnify. Courts, consistent with the rules of general contract law discussed previously, look to the policy language to determine whether payment of proceeds pursuant to judgment or settlement, and sometimes pursuant to a tender of proceeds or offer to pay prior to judgment or a settlement, terminates the duty to defend. Where the policy language is clear and the insurer has satisfied the exhaustion language, courts usually allow insurers to terminate the duty to defend. Where termination of the duty to defend has been disallowed, the results usually involve variations in standard policy language, a court giving an alternative interpretation to standard policy language, or a court giving significance to facts that distinguish the case at hand. The common theme in all the cases, however, is that policy language controls and that if the language is explicit enough and the insurer complies with it, insurers can terminate the duty to defend through exhaustion of the policy limits pursuant to the duty to indemnify.[46] In addition, if a dispute arises about whether an insurer has exhausted the policy limits, the insurer has a continuing duty to defend until a court determines that the insurer has exhausted the policy limits.[47]

The policy language used by insurers to terminate the duty to defend through exhaustion of policy limits has varied over time. Before 1966, standard liability insurance forms did not contain language explicitly linking the insurer's defense obligation to performance of the indemnity obligation.[48] In this era, policies typically stated that the insurer agreed to defend any suit alleging bodily injury or property damage and seeking damages "payable under the terms of the policy," or words to that effect. Insurers argued that damages could not be "payable under the terms of the policy" if the policy limits had previously been fully expended to satisfy covered claims. In essence, the insurers' argument was that if no *further* duty to indemnify existed because the duty to indemnify was already discharged due to prior payment of the policy limits, no duty to defend could exist. Some courts agreed with this reasoning.[49]

---

seek to accomplish with provisions stating that the duty to defend is discharged when policy limits are paid through judgment or settlement—and sometimes by tender.

46. For a compilation of cases on this issue, *see* T. Scott Belden, *Liability Insurer's Duty to Defend Action Against Insured After Insurer's Full Performance of Its Payment Obligations Under Policy Expressly Providing that Duty to Defend Ends on Payment of Policy Limits*, 16 A.L.R.6th 603 (2006).

47. *See* Hartford Accident & Indem. Co. v. Super. Ct., 29 Cal. Rptr. 2d 32, 36 (Ct. App. 1994) ("When a dispute arises over exhaustion of policy limits, a primary insurer must defend until it obtains a declaratory judgment or summary judgment that it has exhausted its policy limits.").

48. *See* Belden, *supra* note 46, at § 2.

49. *See, e.g.*, Com. Union Ins. Co. v. Pittsburgh Corning Corp., 789 F.2d 214, 219–20 (3d Cir. 1986) ("The pre-1966 Travelers policies do not oblige Travelers to assume the costs of defending actions against its insured after its duty to indemnify has terminated by the payment of judgments or settlements and it has made an orderly withdrawal from the insured's defense."); Zurich Ins. Co. v. Raymark Indus., Inc., 514 N.E.2d 150, 163 (Ill. 1987) (stating that under pre-1967 CGL policies, "[w]here the insurer has exhausted its indemnity limits, . . . the insurer cannot ultimately be obligated

In this era, the provisions setting forth the insurer's duty to defend were typically located in a section of the policy separate from the section where the duty to indemnify appeared. This permitted insureds to argue that the duty to defend was independent from the duty to indemnify, and that as long as a claim against the insured within the coverage (that is, within the events or occurrences covered by the policy as distinct from being within the amount of unpaid policy limits), the insurer was obligated to defend regardless of whether the policy limits had been paid. Insureds also sometimes argued that the language was ambiguous, making an interpretation against the drafter and in favor of the insured the outcome. Some courts followed this reasoning and embraced the insureds' analysis of these provisions.[50] In sum, courts disagreed about how pre-1966 provisions applied when insureds tendered defenses and insurers claimed the duty to defend was extinguished by prior payment of the policy limits.[51]

In 1966, insurers attempted to clarify this issue by changing standard liability policy forms to expressly link the indemnity and defense duties.[52] As this

to indemnify the insured"); Zurich Ins. Co. v. Northbrook Excess & Surplus Ins. Co., 494 N.E.2d 634, 645 (Ill. App. Ct. 1986) (concluding that pre-1966 policy language limiting the insurer's duty to defend to the limits of liability clearly evinced the parties' intent to extinguish the insurer's duty to defend upon exhaustion by judgment or settlement, and stating that the court would "not stretch to find ambiguity where none [was] present").

50. *See, e.g.*, Am. Cas. Co. v. Howard, 187 F.2d 322, 327 (4th Cir. 1951) ("The obligation to defend suits is entirely independent of the obligation to pay for bodily injuries and property damage. The two obligations are assumed in different paragraphs of the contract and under distinctive sub-heads."); Nat'l Cas. Co. v. Ins. Co. of N. Am., 230 F. Supp. 617, 622 (N.D. Ohio 1964) (citations omitted) ("Under the law of Ohio, if the petition states a claim which is within the ambit of the policy, the insurer is required to make defense regardless of the outcome of the action or the liability to the insured. . . . We are cited to no Ohio case where the insurer has tendered its policy limits into court and then sought to be relieved of its duty to defend, but other Courts have generally denied such a request."); St. Paul Fire & Marine Ins. Co. v. Thompson, 433 P.2d 795, 798–99 (Mont. 1967) ("[T]he payment of policy limits is clearly distinct and separate from the duty to defend. . . . Under the facts of the instant case, [the insurer's] duty to defend continued even though it had paid the policy limits."); Kocse v. Liberty Mut. Ins. Co., 387 A.2d 1259, 1262 (N.J. Super. Ct. Law Div. 1978) ("Certainly the language in question does not clearly and plainly indicate that the insurer may withdraw from defense of the insured upon paying the policy limits. Considerations of fairness lead to the conclusion that the obligation to defend should be considered an independent obligation.").

51. *See* Aetna Cas. & Sur. Co. v. Sullivan, 597 N.E.2d 62, 65 (Mass. App. Ct. 1992) ("Cases raising the issue [of whether payment of policy limits terminated the duty to defend] first began to arise under the pre-1966 version of the standard automobile liability insurance contract. With some variation in exact terms, those contracts set forth the insurer's duty to defend or to settle claims against the insured without mention of the consequences of the full coverage by tender or otherwise. The cases in which the issue was the effect of such exhaustion on the insurer's duty to defend were sharply divided."); Robert E. Keeton, *Ancillary Rights of the Insured Against His Liability Insurer*, 13 Vand. L. Rev. 837, 853–56 (1960) ("One of the sharply disputed problems concerning the duty of defense is the question whether the insurer may discharge its entire duty to paying out the limit in settlement, or else tendering the policy limit for application to settlements at the discretion of the policyholder. The few decisions in point are not in harmony.").

52. *See* Gross v. Lloyds of London Ins. Co., 358 N.W.2d 266, 270 (Wis. 1984) ("The 1966 revisions were meant to clarify when the insurer's duty to defend the insured has been satisfied by providing

language commonly appeared in the 1966 modifications and continues to exist in many modern forms, the insurer's duty to defend terminates once the insurer pays the policy limits pursuant to judgments or settlements. The most common forms used today in the homeowners, auto, and commercial liability insurance markets contain language making explicit this connection between the duties to defend and indemnify. For example, the most widely used standard homeowners policy provides: "Our duty to settle or defend ends when our limit of liability for the 'occurrence' has been exhausted by payment of a judgment or settlement."[53] The standard personal auto provides: "Our duty to settle or defend ends when our limit of liability for this coverage has been exhausted by payment of judgments or settlements."[54] Similarly, the current standard commercial general liability (CGL) coverage form states: "Our right and duty to defend ends when we have used up the applicable limit of insurance in the payment of judgments or settlements under Coverages A [Bodily Injury and Property Damage Liability] or B [Personal and Advertising Injury Liability] or medical expenses under Coverage C [Medical Payments]."[55]

More recently, some insurers have introduced language that expands the "pursuant to judgments or settlements" provision to also include situations where the insurer tenders the proceeds or offers payment, without regard to whether the tender, offer, or payment is made pursuant to a judgment or settlement. Although some courts have been unreceptive to this more restrictive language and have found ways to disallow insurers from withdrawing from defenses absent a final judgment or settlement, most courts have enforced the plain language and allowed insurers to terminate defenses upon the tender of proceeds, an offer to pay, or payment in the absence of a judgment or settlement, provided the withdrawal or termination of a defense occurs in good faith and without prejudice to the insured in pending litigation.

---

that the duty to defend ceases after the policy limits are exhausted either by payment of judgments or settlements."); Belden, *supra* note 46, at § 2.

53. Ins. Servs. Off., Inc., Homeowners 3 – Special Form (HO 00 03 05 11), at 17 (2010). According to the National Association of Insurance Commissioners, the HO-3 policy form accounts for 77.7 percent of owner-occupied exposures and 55.4 percent of all policy exposures, making it the most common homeowners policy sold. NAIC Newsroom, *NAIC's Homeowners Insurance Data Shows 2.2% Premium Increase for 2018–19*, Nat'l Ass'n of Ins. Comm'rs (Mar. 10, 2022), https://content.naic.org/article/naics-homeowners-insurance-data-shows-22-premium-increase-2018-2019.

54. Ins. Servs. Off., Inc., Personal Auto Policy (PP 00 01 09 18), at 2 (2017). The personal auto policy is one of the most widely used, and may be the most widely used, standard auto form. *See* Joseph D. Zavaglia, *The Risk of Financial Irresponsibility under New York C.P.L.R. 1602(6): Call for Reform*, 69 Brook. L. Rev. 727, 737 (2004) ("The most widely-used automobile policy throughout the United States is the Personal Auto Policy (PAP).").

55. Ins. Servs. Off., Inc., Commercial General Liability Coverage Form (CG 00 01 04 13), at 1 (2012).

B. Representative Cases

When a policy contains language that the duty to defend ends when the policy limits are exhausted through the payment of "judgments or settlements" against the insured, courts generally hold that the policy means what the plain language says and that payment of policy limits in judgment or settlement terminates the insurer's duty to defend.[56] For example, *Zurich Insurance Co. v. Raymark Industries, Inc.*,[57] a 1987 Illinois Supreme Court decision, involved CGL policies issued by two insurers both before and after 1967. The post-1967 policies contained the following language:

> The company shall have the right and duty to defend any suit against the insured seeking damages on account of such bodily injury . . . but the company shall not be obligated . . . to defend any suit after the applicable limit of the company's liability has been exhausted by payment of judgments or settlements.[58]

The court reasoned that this language was "plain and unambiguous" and that the insurer's duty to defend "all actions, including pending actions" was limited

56. *See, e.g.*, Aggreko, L.L.C. v. Chartis Specialty Ins. Co., 942 F.3d 682, 696–97 (5th Cir. 2019) (concluding that under the law of both Louisiana and Texas, the insurer's payment of its CGL policy limits after entering into covenant with plaintiff not to execute against the insured's assets constituted a "settlement" that relieved the insurer of its duty to defend); U.S. Fire Ins. Co. v. Mother Earth Sch., 423 F. Supp. 3d 1048, 1054–55 (D. Or. 2019) (applying Oregon law and determining that where the policy provided that the "duty to defend ends when we have used up the applicable limit of insurance in the payment of judgments or settlements," the insurer's payment of limits into the court's registry did not extinguish the insurer's duty to defend); Siltronic Corp. v. Emps. Ins. Co. of Wausau, 921 F. Supp. 2d 1099, 1107, 1110 (D. Or. 2013) (applying Oregon law and concluding that the insurer's payment of its policy limits to satisfy insured's remediation obligations in state and federal government cleanup actions was "equivalent to the 'payment of judgments or settlements' for the purposes of exhausting the liability limits" and explaining that when its policy limits are exhausted, an insurer "has no continuing duty to defend"); *In re* Caceres, No. 18-80776, 2023 WL 2543713, at *26 (Bankr. M.D.N.C. Feb. 27, 2023) ("[A]ll claims against Caceres had resulted in settlement or judgment no later than January 2017, and the [insurer] had compensated all claimants up to policy limits. Accordingly, the [insurer's] contractual duty to defend Caceres expired by January 2017."); Johnson v. Cont'l Ins. Cos., 248 Cal. Rptr. 412, 416–18 (Ct. App. 1988) (finding that where the insurer expended the policy limits to settle claims against the insured pre-suit, the insurer had no duty to defend crossclaims filed against the insured in a subsequent product liability action by the plaintiff); Conway v. Country Cas. Ins. Co., 442 N.E.2d 245, 247 (Ill. 1982) (involving a policy that provided that the insurer would not be obligated to defend any suit or prosecute any appeal "after the applicable limits of the Company's liability have been exhausted by payment of any judgments or settlements," and determining that the insurer was not discharged from its duty to defend by the payment of the policy limits pursuant to advanced payment program to a third-party victim before she sued the insured); Nat'l Beef Packing Co. v. Zurich Am. Ins. Co., 336 S.W.3d 181, 187 (Mo. Ct. App. 2011) (holding that the insurer exhausted its coverage "by payment of judgments or settlements" when it settled claims of some plaintiffs in good faith, and thereby terminated its duty to defend); Millers Mut. Ins. Ass'n of Ill. v. Shell Oil Co., 959 S.W.2d 864, 869–72 (Mo. Ct. App. 1997) (concluding that the insurer's duty to defend an additional insured terminated when the insurer in good faith paid its policy limits to settle the claims against the named insured).

57. 514 N.E.2d 150 (Ill. 1987).

58. *Id.* at 164.

"to the period of time prior to the time when its obligation to indemnify [was] discharged by the payment of judgments or settlements."[59] Thus, the insurer was not obligated to continue to defend actions pending against the insured after the limits of its policies were exhausted by the payment of judgments or settlements.[60]

Where the policy language specifies that the insurer's duty to defend is terminated after the insurer pays the policy limits pursuant to judgments or settlements, it is well settled that merely tendering the proceeds is insufficient to terminate the duty to defend.[61] For example, in *First Mercury Insurance Co. v. Cincinnati Insurance Co.*,[62] First Mercury Insurance Co. (First Mercury) insured a subcontractor in connection with a wrongful death action brought by a subcontractor's employee's personal representative. First Mercury argued that its duty to defend the suit terminated when it offered to pay its policy limits, and that it was therefore entitled to reimbursement from the excess insurer, Cincinnati Insurance Co. (Cincinnati), for defense costs incurred after that offer. First Mercury's policy language, however, stated that the "duty to defend ends when [the insurer has] used up the applicable limit of insurance in the payments of judgments or settlements."[63] The court agreed with Cincinnati that First Mercury's "duty to defend ceases when it has 'used up' its limit; its duty is not extinguished merely by *offering* to pay its policy limit toward a settlement," and thus First Mercury had no right to reimbursement of its defense costs.[64]

---

59. *Id.* at 165.
60. *Id.*
61. *See, e.g.*, Cont'l Cas. Co. v. N. Am. Capacity Ins. Co., 683 F.3d 79, 89–90 (5th Cir. 2012) (applying Texas law); Bhd. Mut. Ins. Co. v. M.M., 292 F. Supp. 3d 1195, 1209 (D. Kan. 2017) (applying Kansas law); BBL-McCarthy, LLC v. Baldwin Paving Co., 646 S.E.2d 682, 686–87 (Ga. Ct. App. 2007) (explaining that "'exhaust' as it applies to policy limits means the payment either of a settlement or of a judgment, which wholly depletes the policy amount," such that the primary insurer's "tender of the remaining liability to [the excess insurer] did not extinguish its duty to defend"); Am. Std. Ins. Co. v. Basbagill, 775 N.E.2d 255, 259–62 (Ill. App. Ct. 2002) (holding that interpleading the policy limits does not constitute payment, and thus the duty to defend is not terminated, while declining to decide whether the insurer had "offered" the limits on procedural grounds); Douglas v. Allied Am. Ins., 727 N.E.2d 376, 382–83 (Ill. App. Ct. 2000) (holding that interpleading the policy proceeds did not terminate the duty to defend); Perez Trucking, Inc. v. Ryder Truck Rental, Inc., 886 P.2d 196, 201 (Wash. Ct. App. 1994) (stating that an "insurer may not abandon its defense of a claim prior to settlement or judgment simply by paying its limits to the insured"). *But see* Davis v. Counts, 880 So. 2d 968, 970–71 (La. Ct. App. 2004) (determining that an insurer that deposited its policy limits with the court, after which the court allowed the plaintiff to withdraw them, had no duty to defend the insured in a subsequent suit by the plaintiff); IMO Indus., Inc. v. Transamerica Corp., 101 A.3d 1085, 1105 (N.J. Super. Ct. App. Div. 2014) (holding that an allocation model for long-tail environmental claims covered by multiple insurers displaces a CGL provision on exhaustion of policy limits by payment of judgments or settlements, and thus the insurer was entitled to terminate its duty to defend having paid the policy limits under the allocation model).
62. 882 F.3d 1289 (10th Cir. 2018) (applying New Mexico law).
63. *Id.* at 1304.
64. *Id.* at 1304–05.

Consistent with the results in these cases, courts have also held that paying the "maximum potential liability" to a plaintiff is not the same as paying the policy limits. Thus, when an insurer pays proceeds equivalent to an amount that represents the plaintiff's maximum potential recovery, but which is an amount less than the policy limits, this payment does not discharge the insurer's duty to defend.[65]

When the policy language gives the insurer the right to terminate the duty to defend upon exhaustion of the policy's liability limits and does not mention payment pursuant to judgments or settlements, courts have reached varied results depending on the circumstances. For example, in *American States Insurance Co. of Texas v. Arnold*,[66] payment of the policy limits to settle claims against the named insured without securing a release of all covered claims against an additional insured, terminated the insurer's duty to defend the additional insured.

Bessie Mayes (Mayes) was a passenger in her vehicle while it was being driven by Eoline Arnold (Arnold). Mayes was insured by American States Insurance Co. of Texas (American States). Arnold was insured by American Fire & Indemnity Insurance Co. (American Fire) but also was insured under Mayes's policy as a permissive driver of her car. Arnold struck another car, injuring the passenger in that vehicle, Michael Cassady (Cassady). Mayes died in the wreck and Arnold was injured. American States paid the policy limits to secure a release of Mayes's estate from Cassady's personal injury claims. American States paid an additional sum to settle Cassady's property damage claim, securing a release for both Mayes's estate and Arnold in exchange. When American Fire (Arnold's insurer) refused to settle Cassady's personal injury claim against Arnold, Cassady sued her. Arnold and American Fire then demanded that American States defend the action. American States refused based on policy language which stated: "Our duty to settle or defend ends when our limit of liability for this coverage has been exhausted."[67] The court said that this language could "be characterized only as precise, plain, and clear" and lacking any ambiguity, and that "the defense obligation will terminate if and when

65. *See, e.g.*, Burgraff v. Menard, Inc., 875 N.W.2d 596, 605–09 (Wis. 2016) (holding that insurer breached the duty to defend when it withdrew its defense of a permissive user after settling with the insured for less than the policy limits, even though the settlement might have represented the insurer's maximum potential liability when the permissive user's CGL was considered); St. John's Home of Milwaukee v. Cont'l Cas. Co., 434 N.W.2d 112, 121–22 (Wis. Ct. App. 1988) (involving policy language which provided that the insurer "shall not be obligated . . . to defend any suit after the applicable limit of the company's liability has been exhausted by payment of judgments or settlements," and stating that "'maximum potential liability' cannot be equated with 'maximum policy limits', and therefore a duty to defend exists even though an insurer tenders its 'maximum potential liability' as [the insurer] did here").

66. 930 S.W.2d 196 (Tex. App. 1996).

67. *Id.* at 201 (internal quotation marks omitted).

the insurer's policy limits are exhausted."[68] Thus, the court held that American States, when it paid the policy limits to settle Cassady's personal injury claim against Mayes's estate, terminated any obligation it had to defend Arnold in Cassady's lawsuit against her.[69]

Pareti v. Sentry Indemnity Co.,[70] decided by the Louisiana Supreme Court in 1988, followed the same reasoning when applying identical policy language in a different fact pattern. In *Pareti*, the insured-tortfeasor's liability insurer paid its $50,000 policy limits to settle the plaintiffs' claims arising out of an accident in which the insured rear-ended the plaintiffs' vehicle. In the settlement agreement, the plaintiffs reserved their rights against their own underinsured motorist (UIM) carrier. When the UIM carrier filed a crossclaim against the insured-tortfeasor seeking indemnity for all amounts it might be required to pay the plaintiffs under the UIM coverage, the insured-tortfeasor's liability insurer declined to defend the crossclaim because it had exhausted its policy limits in settling the plaintiffs' liability claims. The court observed that the policy did not contain the "by judgments or settlements" language, but this omission did not matter because "[i]t is self-evident that an insurer which has settled for its policy limits (or paid its full limits responsive to a judgment) has 'exhausted' its limit of liability under the policy."[71] The *Pareti* court distinguished cases holding that the duty to defend was not terminated under language in the pre-1966 policy forms, stating that "[t]hese policies did not specify that the duty to defend would terminate upon exhaustion of the insurer's policy limits."[72]

The North Carolina Supreme Court took a different approach in a 1990 case involving policy language identical to that in *Arnold* and *Pareti*, with the key distinction being that the insurer did not obtain a full release of the insured. In *Brown v. Lumbermens Mutual Casualty Co.*,[73] the insurer paid the proceeds to the injured plaintiff under an "Advance Payment Agreement" authorized by state statute,[74] which released the insurer but did not release the insured, who remained subject to the plaintiff's continuing action. The insurer then stopped defending the insured, and the insured continued its defense without retaining counsel. When a judgment exceeding the policy limits was entered against the insured, the insured sued the insurer for breaching the duty to defend. The trial court entered summary judgment for the insurer, reasoning that the insurer had

---

68. *Id.*
69. *Id.* at 203.
70. 536 So. 2d 417 (La. 1988).
71. *Id.* at 421.
72. *Id.* at 422.
73. 390 S.E.2d 150 (N.C. 1990).
74. *See* N.C. Gen. Stat. § 1-540 (allowing insurers to make advance payments to persons making claims against their insureds prior to a final settlement without admitting liability on the part of the insured or the insurer).

paid the policy limits to the claimant and thereby met the exhaustion language that allowed the insurer to terminate the defense.[75] The North Carolina Court of Appeals reversed and remanded, holding that the word "exhaust" in the policy was ambiguous and that the insurer was required to continue defending the insureds until a settlement or judgment was reached, even though it had already paid the full policy limits.[76]

The North Carolina Supreme Court affirmed but relied on different reasoning. The *Brown* court parsed the paragraph in which the exhaustion provision resided, which read as follows:

> We will pay damages for bodily injury or property damage for which any **covered person** becomes legally responsible because of an auto accident. *We will settle or defend, as we consider appropriate, any claim or suit asking for these damages. In addition to our limit of liability, we will pay all defense costs we incur. Our duty to settle or defend ends when our limit of liability for this coverage has been exhausted.*[77]

The court observed that the second sentence created the duty to defend, and that the third sentence required the insurer to pay defense costs in addition to the limit for the indemnity obligation (in the first sentence).[78] The fourth sentence, which limited the defense obligation, stated that the duty to defend ended when "liability for this coverage has been exhausted," but did not specify how that exhaustion must occur.[79] The *Brown* court explained that an ambiguity did not arise from the use of the word "exhausted," but instead arose from the fact that multiple ways exist for an insurer "to exhaust" the limit of liability for the coverage—paying proceeds into court and interpleading conflicting claimants in a declaratory judgment action; paying proceeds to one of several claimants and obtaining a release from that claimant; paying proceeds in full or partial satisfaction of a judgment against its insured; advancing the proceeds to the insured in lieu of investigating available defenses; or, as was done in this case, paying proceeds to the injured party in exchange for a release of the insurer but not the insured.[80] The insured argued that the payment must be pursuant to settlement or judgment; the insurer argued that any manner of exhaustion terminates the duty to defend. The court explained that both arguments being reasonable, the policy language was ambiguous, and ambiguities are interpreted in favor of the insured.[81]

75. *Brown*, 390 S.E.2d at 152.
76. *Id.*
77. *Id.* at 153 (italicized emphasis added by the court).
78. *Id.* at 154.
79. *Id.*
80. *Id.*
81. *Id.*

Thus, the court in *Brown* held that the insurer did not terminate the duty to defend when it paid proceeds to the plaintiff without securing a release for the insured: "[The insurer's] unilateral tender to, and [the plaintiff's] acceptance of, the policy limit without effecting settlement of [the plaintiff's] claim against the [insureds] did not relieve [the insurer] of its duty to defend against this claim."[82] This aligned the *Brown* court with those courts holding that an insurer could not pay its policy proceeds into court and wait for a determination of liability. As the court explained, whether the proceeds were tendered to the court or paid to the claimant without a release to the insured, "[t]he claim against the insured remains outstanding, because there has been neither a judgment nor settlement disposing of that claim."[83] Other courts, in line with *Brown*, have held that when policy language terminates the duty to defend when policy limits are "exhausted," the payment, if it is to terminate the duty to defend, must be made pursuant to a judgment or settlement, and must not be a tender, offer, or other kind of payment.[84]

82. *Id.* at 155–56.

83. *Id.* at 155. The Nevada Supreme Court followed *Brown* in a case with the same policy language where the insurer sought to terminate the duty to defend by depositing the policy limits in court. *See* Benchmark Ins. Co. v. Sparks, 254 P.3d 617, 621–23 (Nev. 2011) (holding that tender of policy limits did not "exhaust" the policy limits and thereby terminate the duty to defend).

84. *See, e.g.*, Stanley v. Cobb, 624 F. Supp. 536, 537–38 (E.D. Tenn. 1986) (tendering the policy limits into court does not terminate the duty to defend under a policy that provides that duty to defend "ends when our limit of liability for this coverage has been exhausted"); Samply v. Integrity Ins. Co., 476 So. 2d 79, 83–84 (Ala. 1985) (construing policy language stating that the duty to defend ends "when our limit of liability for this coverage has been exhausted," and holding that the insurer could not avoid its duty to defend by tendering its policy limits into court without achieving a settlement or obtaining the insured's consent); Cal. Cas. Ins. Co. v. State Farm Mut. Auto. Ins. Co., 913 P.2d 505, 510 (Ariz. Ct. App. 1996) (reasoning that when the plaintiff signed a "Release and Covenant to Execute" against the insured's assets, the document terminated the insurer's duty to defend as of the date of the release where the insurer had previously paid the policy limits to the plaintiff); Cont'l Cas. Co. v. Farmers Ins. Co. of Ariz., 883 P.2d 473, 476 (Ariz. Ct. App. 1994) (holding that the policy—which read in relevant part: "[w]e will not defend any suit or make additional payments after we have paid the limit of liability for the coverage"—terminated the insurer's duty to defend once the insurer paid its policy limits and obtained a covenant not to execute against the insured); Cont'l Ins. Co. v. Burr, 706 A.2d 499, 502 (Del. 1998) (interpreting policy language allowing the insurer to terminate its duty to defend "when our payments have reached your Limit of Coverage," and reasoning that "a reasonable policy holder would expect to be defended until claims arising under the policy are resolved," such that paying the policy limits to the court or the claimants does not extinguish the duty to defend); Anderson v. U.S. Fid. & Guar. Co., 339 S.E.2d 660, 661 (Ga. Ct. App. 1986) ("There is no intimation in the policy that its duty to defend may be satisfied by merely paying into court the applicable policy limits. To read the policy otherwise would render a near nullity a most significant protection afforded by the policy—that of defense. We do not agree with appellee that the term 'exhaust' encompasses the paying into court of the policy limits, but interpret that term to mean the payment either of a settlement or of a judgment wholly depleting the policy amount."); Lafauci v. Jenkins, 844 So. 2d 19, 27 (La. Ct. App. 2003) (holding that under an auto policy providing that "[o]ur duty to settle or defend ends when our limit of liability for this coverage has been exhausted," the insurer's deposit of funds into the court registry with conditions, in circumstances where the plaintiff had to litigate to recover the proceeds, did not conform to a Louisiana statute and therefore did not constitute exhaustion of the policy limits that terminated the duty to defend); Aetna Cas. & Sur. Co. v. Sullivan, 597 N.E.2d 154, 157–60 (Mass. App. Ct. 1992) (stating that when an auto policy provided

The *Brown* court and numerous other courts in a wide variety of cases have routinely interpreted ambiguities in policy language in favor of insureds and against insurers.[85] Thus, an insurer's failure to draft policy language clearly and explicitly can result in a court interpreting language intended by the insurer to terminate its defense obligation upon payment of proceeds as failing to accomplish this purpose. This is a risk that insurers face when they employ customized language that varies from standard forms with well-settled meanings from frequent litigation.

To illustrate, in *Chicago Title Insurance Co. v. Kent School Corp.*,[86] a title insurance policy with limits of $100,000 contained the following provision: "In every case where claim is made for loss or damages this company . . . (2) may terminate its liability hereunder by paying or tendering the full amount of this policy. . . ."[87] The insurer argued that this language, which appeared later in the policy and did not appear on the cover sheet where the duties to indemnify and defend were stated, allowed it to tender the policy limits to the insured and not defend a second lawsuit brought by a plaintiff that claimed an interest in the insured property.[88] The parties did not dispute that the policy created a duty to defend. The cover sheet stated that the insurer "insures [the school]

that "[o]ur duty to settle or defend ends when we have paid the maximum limits of coverage under this policy," tendering the proceeds without a judgment or settlement that releases the insured does not terminate the duty to defend, and reasoning that no significant difference exists between policies using the word "exhausted" instead of "paid"); Exch. Mut. Ins. Co. v. Geiser, 498 N.Y.S.2d 291, 292 (Sup. Ct. 1986) (applying policy language stating that the insurer's duty to defend ended when "limit of liability under the policy has been exhausted" and that the insurer could not pay policy limits into court and be relieved of its defense obligation); Nationwide Mut. Ins. Co. v. Simmonds, 434 S.E.2d 277, 278 (S.C. 1993) (concluding that under a policy providing that no duty to defend exists where the policy limits were "exhausted by payment," the insurer's tender of its policy limits into court did not terminate duty to defend); Farmers Ins. Co. of Wash. v. Romas, 947 P.2d 754, 756 (Wash. Ct. App. 1997) (finding that under an auto policy stating that insurer would "not defend any suit . . . after we have paid the limit of liability for coverage," depositing proceeds into court did not terminate duty to defend where the insurer procured a release for the named insured but not for all its insureds); *see also* Cnty. of Santa Clara v. U.S. Fid. & Guar. Co., 868 F. Supp. 274, 278–80 (N.D. Cal. 1994) (applying California law and holding that a primary insurer could not extinguish its duty to defend by tendering its $500,000 policy limits to the County; the policy could not be exhausted until a remediation plan was approved "that clearly establishe[d] that the costs of remediation [would] exceed the primary liability limits," at which point the insurer could tender its policy limits to the County and thereby extinguish its duty to defend).

85. *See, e.g.*, Cadwallader v. Allstate Ins. Co., 848 So. 2d 577, 580 (La. 2003) ("Ambiguous policy provisions are generally construed against the insurer and in favor of coverage."); Crown Energy Co. v. Mid-Continent Cas. Co., 511 P.3d 1064, 1070 (Okla. 2022) ("We construe ambiguities against the insurer and in favor of the insured."); Hill & Stout, PLLC v. Mut. of Enumclaw Ins. Co., 515 P.3d 525, 531 (Wash. 2022) ("Any ambiguity in an insurance policy is construed in favor of the insured."); Acuity v. Est. of Shimeta, 987 N.W.2d 689, 737 (Wis. 2023) ("We interpret the policy language as a reasonable insured would understand it, and if the language is ambiguous, we construe it in favor of the insured.").

86. 361 F. Supp. 2d 4 (D. Conn. 2005).

87. *Id.* at 8.

88. In 1975, the insurer had paid $695,844 in legal fees to successfully defend the school's title; the district court dismissed that case because the Tribal Nation bringing the action had not been granted

against all loss or damage not exceeding the amount of insurance stated herein and in addition the costs and expenses of defending the title, estate, or interest insured . . . excepting all loss and damage . . . by the conditions of this policy hereby incorporated into this contract . . . ."[89] Section Two(a) also stated separately that the insurer would "defend the insured in all actions or proceedings found on a claim of title . . . ."[90] The insurer contended that the language in Paragraph Five(b) constituted "conditions" that could "except" loss from the coverage, and thus gave the insured the option to pay policy limits in lieu of defending the insured.[91]

The court rejected the insurer's analysis, denied the insurer's summary judgment motion, and granted the policyholder's summary judgment motion. The court, after parsing the policy language, concluded that "liability" did not refer to the insurer's liability for judgments and defense expenses, but instead only referred to the insurer's monetary liability under the indemnity obligation.[92] The court noted that this policy's language was not as explicit as that used by other insurers to reserve the right to terminate the defense by paying the policy limits.[93] Thus, in *Kent School*, the insurer lost because it did not draft the relevant policy language in a manner that would cause a policyholder to understand that the duties to indemnify and defend were interdependent and that the insurer could discharge the defense obligation by paying the policy limits.

In contrast, the title insurer in *Batdorf v. Transamerica Title Insurance Co.*[94] avoided the insurer's fate in *Kent School* through more precise drafting. That more precise policy language enabled the insurer to tender the policy limits to the insured whose title had been challenged and thereby to fulfill all its obligations under the policy. Paragraph 1 of the *Batdorf* policy stated that the insurer "shall have the right to, and will, at its own expense, defend the insured with respect to all demands and legal proceedings founded upon a claim of title, . . . reserving however, the option at any time of settling the claim or *paying the amount of this policy in full*."[95] In addition, Paragraph 3 of the policy provided that "[t]he Company may at any time pay this policy in full, *whereupon all liability of the Company shall terminate*."[96] The insurer initially accepted the tender of the defense by the insured when the quiet title action was filed, but

tribal status by the Bureau of Indian Affairs. In 1998, the Tribal Nation reinstated its suit, and the insurer sought to avoid the obligation to defend this action by tendering the policy limits. *Id.* at 5–6.

89. *Id.* at 8.

90. *Id.* at 9.

91. *Id.* at 8–9.

92. *Id.* at 9. The court stated that "[n]o layman, when reading this policy, would understand 'full amount of this policy' to mean anything other than the $100,000 indemnity portion of the policy." *Id.*

93. *Id.* at 11.

94. 702 P.2d 1211 (Wash. Ct. App. 1985).

95. *Id.* at 1212 (emphasis added).

96. *Id.* at 1213 (emphasis added).

the court held that when the insurer subsequently tendered the policy limits to the insured and withdrew from the defense, the insurer validly exercised its option to terminate the duty to defend.[97]

When insurers insert language in a policy's termination provision that allows them to end the duty to defend by tendering the policy limits, courts generally enforce this language.[98] These provisions are commonly referred to as "pay and walk" clauses, meaning that if the insurer offers to pay or pays the policy limits, the insurer can "walk away" and leave the insured responsible for defending itself in any continuing litigation.[99]

In *Gross v. Lloyds of London Insurance Co.*,[100] the policy provided that "the Company shall not be obligated to pay any claim or judgment or to defend any suit after the applicable limit of the Company's liability has been exhausted by payment of judgments or settlements or after such limit of the Company's liability *has been tendered for settlements*."[101] The insurer filed suit and the trial court granted a motion seeking permission to pay its policy limit into court and to be relieved of any further duty to defend the insured, and the court's order was affirmed on appeal.

The Wisconsin Supreme Court, in discussing the history of the evolution of the termination by payment of policy limits language in standard forms, explained that the "tendered for settlements" phrase was added to the "judgments or settlements" language in order to reduce the scope of the insurer's defense obligation and that this constituted a significant change from the earlier standard language.[102] But the court was concerned that the insured had no notice of the change, in that the new language was first included in a renewal policy which did not reach the insured until after the accident occurred.[103]

97. *Id.*

98. *See, e.g.*, Mt. Hawley Ins. Co. v. Mesa Med. Grp., PLLC, 267 F. Supp. 3d 955, 959–60 (E.D. Ky. 2017) (applying Kentucky law and holding that a policy that provided that the insurer "shall not be obligated . . . to defend or to continue to defend any suit or Claim after the applicable limit of the Company's liability has been tendered to the insured or the claimant or exhausted by the payment of judgments, settlements, or by Claims Expenses," allowed the insurer to withdraw from the defense upon tender of the policy limits); Farmers Ins. Co. v. Pers. Representative of Mitchell, 755 F. Supp. 255, 256–57 (W.D. Ark. 1989) (holding that where the policy provided that the insurer "will not defend any suit or make any additional payments after we paid the limit of liability for coverage," the insurer had no duty to defend after it interpleaded its policy limits).

99. Some commentators have given the label "pay and walk" to clauses that refer to paying the limits of liability (i.e., "exhausting") pursuant to judgments and settlements. *See, e.g.*, Michael D. Wade & Tara L. Velting, *Validity of the "Pay and Walk" Provision of a Liability Insurance Policy*, MICH. B. J., Mar. 2020, at 24, 24. More commonly, however, "pay and walk" describes provisions that allow the insurer to terminate the defense by tendering or paying policy limits in the absence of a final judgment or full settlement. *See, e.g.*, Kontowicz v. Am. Std Ins. Co. of Wis., 714 N.W.2d 105, 108 n.2 (Wis. 2006) (stating that the policy "contained a pay-and-walk provision," which provided that the insurer would "not defend any suit after our limit of liability has been offered or paid").

100. 358 N.W.2d 266 (Wis. 1984).

101. *Id.* at 269 (emphasis added).

102. *Id.* at 269–70.

103. *Id.* at 271.

Thus, the court held "that [the insurer's] tender of the policy limits into court does not relieve it of its duty to defend [the insured]," and stated that this was "[b]ecause the 'tendered for settlements' language was a substantial change from past industry practice and because [the insured] had received no notice at the time of the accident that [the insurer] could terminate its defense efforts upon tender of the policy limits."[104] The court observed that in future cases, the "tendered for settlements" language "must be highlighted in the policy and binder by means of conspicuous print, such as bold, italicized, or colored type, which gives clear notice to the insured" of the provision—so that with notice of the limited coverage, insureds "may choose to afford themselves greater protection of the defense of claims by increasing the amount of their policy limits or seek a policy which provides for unlimited defense."[105] Thus, the *Gross* court announced that it would enforce the tender of limits clause in future cases "but . . . only . . . if the insureds receive adequate notice as outlined in this opinion."[106]

Subsequently, a case did reach the Wisconsin court of appeals where the insurer included conspicuous, highlighted "tender for settlements" language in the policy. In *Novak v. American Family Mutual Insurance Co.*,[107] the insured struck and killed a bicyclist while driving her covered vehicle. Her policy provided: "We will defend any suit or settle any claim for damages payable under this policy as we think proper. HOWEVER, WE WILL NOT DEFEND ANY SUIT AFTER OUR LIMIT OF LIABILITY HAS BEEN OFFERED OR PAID."[108] The insurer advised the insured that it would not defend the victim's claim in excess of policy limits, and when the victim rejected the insurer's policy-limits settlement offer, the insurer secured a settlement which, upon the insurer's payment of the policy limits, released the insurer and the insured to the extent of policy limits. The insured hired her own lawyer to defend the excess claim and, after reaching a settlement with the plaintiff, sued the insurer for breaching the duty to defend. The court affirmed the trial court's summary judgment for the insurer, holding that under the reasoning of *Gross*, the policy language was enforceable and did not violate public policy. The court also held that the insurer fulfilled its contractual obligations by paying the policy limits

104. *Id.*

105. *Id.* at 271–72. These statements by the court were at the least dicta, and it is arguable that they constitute judicial overreach because the court announced rules that could have been made, and presumably should have been made, in insurance department rulemaking or in statutes promulgated by the legislature. In defense of the court, however, one could argue that the court was simply explaining the common law of contract with respect to how terms enter contracts when standardized forms are involved.

106. *Id.* at 272.

107. 515 N.W.2d 504 (Wis. Ct. App. 1994).

108. *Id.* at 505.

without securing a settlement of all claims against its insured and a final disposition of the victim's action.[109]

An important caveat is that the insurer may not exhaust the policy limits simply to avoid its duty to defend an action or to continue to defend another action. This caveat arises out of the insurer's duty to exercise good faith and fair dealing in the performance of the contract.[110] The contract law principle which gives rise to this caveat is *prevention*, which provides that a party to a contract (in this situation, the insurer) may not act in a manner that prevents its counterpart (here, the insured) from receiving the benefits of the contract. Behaviors that deliberately undercut the purpose of the contract and thereby prevent the other side from obtaining the contract's expected benefits have the effect of excusing conditions to the promisor's duty (in this case, the insurer's duty to defend), which leaves the promisor with an unconditional duty to the promisee (in this case, a continuing obligation by the insurer to defend the insured against covered claims despite having exhausted the policy limits).[111] A Washington court stated the idea succinctly as follows: "Thus, while the policy may specifically provide for termination of the duty to defend upon payment of the policy limits, public policy requires the insurer to act in good faith in the interest of the insured."[112]

To illustrate how the good faith principle serves as a limiting doctrine, consider *Lockwood International, B.V. v. Volm Bag Co.*,[113] a 2001 Seventh Circuit case applying Wisconsin law. The *Lockwood* plaintiff's suit alleged covered and noncovered claims under the insured's CGL policy. Four years

109. *Id.* at 506–08; *see also* Young v. Welytok, 798 N.W.2d 881, 886–89 (Wis. Ct. App. 2011) (enforcing a "pay and walk" provision after the insurer paid its policy limits to the third-party victim); Rubrich v. Piotruszewicz, 655 N.W.2d 546 (Wis. Ct. App. 2002) (holding that the insurer's "pay and walk" provision in an auto policy was enforceable and the insurer was entitled to terminate its duty to defend); Woodson v. Kreutzer, 526 N.W.2d 788, 790–91 (Wis. Ct. App. 1994) (holding that a "tendered for settlements" provision was sufficiently conspicuous and enforceable). In *Hoffman v. Economy Preferred Insurance Co.*, 606 N.W.2d 590 (Wis. Ct. App. 1999), the court held that the conspicuousness requirement announced in *Gross* did not apply to a permissive user covered under an auto liability policy. Consequently, even though the "pay and walk" provision was inconspicuous, the insurer was allowed to withdraw from the defense after tendering the policy limits. *See id.* at 592–93.

110. *See* Maguire v. Ohio Cas. Ins. Co., 602 A.2d 893, 896 (Pa. Super. Ct. 1992) (involving an auto policy providing that the duty to defend ended when "our limit of liability for this coverage has been exhausted," and explaining that the insurer's payment of its policy limits in settlement and securing of releases for insured pre-suit occurred in good faith, thereby relieving the insurer of the duty to defend subsequent actions against the insured).

111. To amplify, in policies that allow termination upon tender of the policy limits, the insurer's duty to defend is conditioned upon the policy limits not previously being tendered or paid pursuant to judgments or settlements. If the insurer makes such payments solely to protect its own interests and to escape its obligation to continue to defend an insured, the analysis is that the insurer's prevention of the insured receiving the benefits of the contract has the effect of excusing the condition, which leaves the insurer with an unconditional duty to defend.

112. Viking Ins. Co. of Wis. v. Hill, 787 P.2d 1385, 1390 (Wash. Ct. App. 1990); *see also* Singh v. Zurich Am. Ins. Co., 428 P.3d 1237, 1244–45 (Wash. Ct. App. 2018).

113. 273 F.3d 741 (7th Cir. 2001).

after the complaint was filed, the insurer paid the plaintiff $1.5 million, which was more than the $1 million policy limits, without consulting the insured or obtaining the insured's agreement, to file an amended complaint that deleted the covered claims. The plaintiff agreed to credit that amount against any judgment plaintiff might obtain against the insured. Thus, the insurer's agreement with the plaintiff served to protect the insured from financial responsibility for the covered claims.

After the amended complaint was filed, the insured asked the insurer to continue to defend, but the insurer claimed that the payment of the policy limits terminated its duty to defend. The court recognized the rule that "if in the course of litigation the covered claims fall out of the case through settlement or otherwise, the insurer's duty to defend ceases."[114] But the court also observed: "We have difficulty imagining a more conspicuous betrayal of the insurer's fiduciary duty to its insured than for its lawyers to plot with the insured's adversary a repleading that will enable the adversary to maximize his recovery of uninsured damages from the insured while stripping the insured of its right to a defense by the insurance company."[115] Thus, the fact that the insurer paid the policy limits did not relieve it of the duty to defend, notwithstanding language in the policy purporting to give it this right.[116]

This limiting principle is particularly important where multiple claims, often exceeding the policy limits, are brought against the insured, and the insurer seeks to terminate its duty to defend after exhausting the policy limits by settling one of the claims. Multiple-claim cases are complicated, and courts vary in the rules they apply for how insurers should proceed when settling such cases.[117] Numerous courts have held that policy language that terminates the duty to defend when the policy limits are exhausted is valid and enforceable where the policy limits were exhausted by settling one or more, but not all, of the multiple claims against the insured.[118] The insurer, however, must act

---

114. *Id.* at 744.

115. *Id.*

116. *Id.* at 746–47.

117. *See generally* Douglas R. Richmond, *Too Many Claimants or Insureds and Too Little Money: Insurers' Good Faith Dilemmas* 44 Tort Trial & Ins. Prac. L. J. 871 (2009).

118. *See, e.g.*, Johnson v. Cont'l Ins. Co., 248 Cal. Rptr. 412, 415–18 (Ct. App. 1988) (concluding that where the insurer settled four claims at the insured's request and thereby exhausted its policy limits, the insurer was not obligated to defend additional complaints brought against insured thereafter); Underwriters Guarantee Ins. Co. v. Nationwide Mut. Fire Ins. Co., 578 So. 2d 34, 35–36 (Fla. Dist. Ct. App. 1991) (determining that the insurer had no duty to defend an additional insured after paying its policy limits to obtain its named insured's release); Champagne v. USAA Cas. Ins. Co., 290 So. 3d 664, 667–69 (La. Ct. App. 2019) (holding that where the driver's insurer paid or tendered its policy limits when its checks for policy limits were given as part of settlement to the occupants of car rear-ended by the driver while on the job, the insurer's duty to defend terminated, and the insurer had no duty to defend the employer, even though the settlement checks were not yet deposited in court registry, because the insurer had no ability to settle claims against the employer after issuing checks for policy limits); Maguire v. Ohio Cas. Ins. Co., 602 A.2d 893, 896 (Pa. Super. Ct. 1992) (finding that

reasonably and in good faith in settling the claims and cannot abandon the insured in the midst of a defense in a manner that prejudices the insured.[119]

C. Statutory or Administrative Override

To summarize the forgoing discussion, whether an insurer can terminate the duty to defend by paying the policy limits depends on the policy language and how courts construe such language in the jurisdiction whose law applies. Yet, on this question as well as all others involving insurance policy language, if a state statute or administrative regulation mandates particular content in an insurance policy, the statute or regulation controls regardless the policy's terms.[120] Legislatures and insurance departments have not specifically addressed under what circumstances paying the policy limits under a liability policy terminates the duty to defend, but New York courts have interpreted a New York administrative regulation as applying to the exhaustion question and as superseding inconsistent policy language. New York Insurance Department Regulation (11 NYCRR) § 60–1.1, which dates to the 1990s, prescribes a number of provisions that must be included as minimum content in an automobile owner's policy of liability insurance.[121] Section 60-1.1(b) states as follows:

> With respect to such insurance as is afforded, the insurer, subject to the policy terms shall: defend any suit, with the right to make such investigation, negotiation and settlement as it deems expedient. . . . The amounts so incurred under the subdivision, except settlement of claims and suits, shall be payable by the company in addition to the applicable policy limits.[122]

---

the insurer had no duty to defend when the insured was joined as an additional defendant after the insurer had already paid policy limits in a direct action); Mid-Century Ins. Co. v. Childs, 15 S.W.3d 187, 189–90 (Tex. App. 2000) (declaring that the insurer owed no duty to defend the insured against a claim by one victim after the insurer paid the policy limits to other victims).

119. *See, e.g.*, Pareti v. Sentry Indem. Co., 536 So. 2d 417, 423 (La. 1988) ("[T]he insurer must make every effort to avoid prejudicing the insured by the timing of its withdrawal from the litigation. The insurer should make allowances for the time that insured will need to retain new counsel, and should continue to represent the insured after the settlement, if necessary, until new counsel can be retained."); *Maguire*, 602 A.2d at 895 (involving the exhaustion of policy limits by settling one of multiple claims and explaining that "[b]efore an insurer will be excused from defending an action against an insured on whose behalf the insurer has already paid policy limits, the insurer must have acted in good faith," and "[t]he exercise of good faith prevents an insurer from entering into a dubious release in order to quickly exhaust the limit of its liability to the insured").

120. *See* Shepard v. Farmers Ins. Co., 678 P.2d 250, 251 (Okla.1983) ("Under Oklahoma law, insurance policies are issued pursuant to statutes, and the provisions of those statutes are given force and effect as if written into the policy."); 45 C.J.S. Insurance § 609 (2023) ("A contract of insurance must conform to valid conditions imposed by a state statute, and a statute applicable to a contract of insurance and in force at the time of the making of the contract enters into and forms a part thereof in the same manner as if it had actually been written or copied therein.").

121. *See* N.Y. Comp. Codes R. & Regs. tit. 11, § 60-1.1 (2023).

122. *Id.* § 60-1.1(b).

New York courts have interpreted this regulation as requiring an automobile liability insurer to pay all defense costs until a case ends and as prohibiting an insurer from terminating the defense after paying the policy limits to resolve claims. Thus, in *Liberty Mutual Fire Insurance Co. v. National Casualty Co.*,[123] when the insurer paid the policy limits to settle some of the claims arising out of insured's operation of a motor vehicle, the court held that the policy language providing that the insurer's duty to defend or settle ends when the limits have been exhausted by payment of judgments or settlements conflicted with the regulation and was unenforceable. Thus, the insurer's "duty to defend and pay defense costs continued until all of the underlying personal injury actions are fully resolved."[124] Other New York decisions align with this result.[125]

V. Exhaustion of the Policy Limits under the Defense Obligation

In most liability insurance policies, the policy limits attach to the duty to indemnify, and the duty to defend is not subject to a separate policy limit. In other words, no limits exist on the amount of defense expenditures the insurer must pay in fulfilling the duty to defend in typical liability policies. Some policies, however, provide that the costs of defense reduce the limits of liability available for indemnification. These policies are typically labeled "defense-within-limits" (sometimes shortened to DWL) policies, but they are also referred to as "burning limits," "cannibalizing," "defense-within-limits," "depleting" or "depleting limits," "eroding limits," "wasting," "spend down," "self-consuming," or "self-liquidating" policies.[126] With these policies, the liability limits are reduced dollar for dollar by defense costs until the limits reach zero, at which point both

123. 935 N.Y.S.2d 319 (App. Div. 2011).

124. *Id.* at 321.

125. *See, e.g.*, People v. ELRAC, Inc., 745 N.Y.S. 2d 671, 674–75 (Sup. Ct. 2002) (explaining the applicability of the regulation to a rental car company operating as a self-insurer); Delaney v. Vardine Paratransit, Inc., 504 N.Y.S.2d 70, 71 (Sup. Ct. 1986) (stating that the regulation "clearly anticipates that the insurer may not unilaterally avoid payment of defense costs and related expenses by the ex parte payment of the limits of its policy"); *see also In re* E. 51st St. Crane Collapse Litig., 923 N.Y.S.2d 64, 66 (App. Div. 2011) (allowing the insurer to terminate its duty to defend under a CGL policy after expending policy limits to settle claims and, in the process, noting that no similar regulation applies to CGL policies).

126. For additional discussions of these policies, see Mitchell A. Orpett & Kevin J. Grigsby, *Eroding Limits Policies: One Bad Case Away from Disaster?*, The Brief, Spring 2020, at 36; Michael A. Hamilton & Thomas J. Seery, *Avoiding Bad Faith, and Other Emerging Issues Involving Eroding Limits Policies*, IADC Comm. Newsletter, Ins. & Reinsurance Pro. Liab. Subcomm. (Int'l Ass'n of Def. Couns., Chicago, Ill.), Oct. 2017, https://www.iadclaw.org.

the duty to indemnify and the duty to defend are terminated.[127] Thus, when defense costs equal or exceed the policy's liability limits, nothing is left in the policy to indemnify the insured if the insured is found liable to the plaintiff. On the other hand, because defense-within-limits provide less coverage, they should have lower premiums and therefore be more affordable, which potentially increases the availability of some coverage. The key point, however, is that under defense-within-limits policies, when defense costs exhaust the policy limits, the insurer can terminate the duty to defend, subject to any limitations imposed by defense counsel's fiduciary duties and professional obligations and the insurer's duty of good faith owed to the insured.

Policies that deduct defense costs from the coverage available for indemnity have existed for many years in professional liability insurance, directors and officers liability insurance, and other niche markets. An effort by the ISO in 1986 to add the clause to claims-made CGL policies did not take hold.[128] Indeed, regulators and commentators have raised numerous concerns about the clauses outside the specialty markets where they are now used, and statutes and regulations in many states restrict their use.[129] Notably, every state requires motor vehicle owners to carry minimum amounts of insurance for bodily injury liability to further the public policy of compensating auto accident victims. Where insurers have sought to insert defense-within-limits provisions in auto liability policies, courts have struck down these provisions as conflicting with minimum liability coverage mandates in state law.[130]

---

127. *See* Aerojet-General Corp. v. Transp. Indem. Co., 948 P.2d 909, 932 n.29 (Cal. 1997) (explaining how the insurer could have limited its liability for defense costs by issuing a defense-within-limits policy).

128. *See* Orpett & Grigsby, *supra* note 126, at 37.

129. *See* Hamilton & Seery, *supra* note 126, at 2–3 (listing and describing statutes in various states restricting use of defense-within-limits policies). In 2023, the Nevada legislature enacted a statute that prohibits defense-within-limits provisions in all insurance policies. The statute prohibits insurers from issuing or renewing a liability insurance policy containing a provision that "[r]educes the limit of liability stated in the policy by the costs of defense, legal costs and fees and other expenses for claims; or . . . [o]therwise limits the availability of coverage for the costs of defense, legal costs and fees and other expenses for claims." Nev. Rev. Stat. § 679A (Eff. Oct. 1, 2023). It will be interesting to see whether this statute becomes the subject of industry efforts to amend it in the future. Although the available legislative history on this statute is sparse and there is no clear indication of how far its proponents wanted it to reach, the "otherwise" clause is arguably broad enough to invalidate common provisions that allow insurers to terminate the duty to defend through exhaustion of policy limits. Whether courts will interpret it this way when the argument is eventually made remains to be seen.

130. *See, e.g.*, Gibson v. Northfield Ins. Co., 631 S.E.2d 598, 606 (W. Va. 2005) (stating that "in the typical motor vehicle insurance policy, it would violate W. Va. Code 33-6-31(a) to include a defense within limits provision that 'erodes,' 'exhausts,' 'wastes,' and 'cannibalizes' the death, bodily injury, loss or damage liability coverage of the policy" and holding that on remand that the policy had to be reformed to comply with statutory motor vehicle insurance requirements); *cf.* Donaldson Bros., Ready Mix, Inc. v. Phila. Ins. Cos., No. CV 06-139-M-DWM, 2008 WL 11349981, at *6 (D. Mont. May 14, 2008) (noting the parties' agreement that the defense-within-limits provision in a D&O policy was void and unenforceable because it apparently was never submitted to the Montana Insurance Commissioner for approval).

In the absence of statutory or administrative restrictions, courts have generally enforced unambiguous defense-within-limits provisions according to their terms.[131] *Amerisure Mutual Insurance Co. v. Arch Specialty Insurance Co.*,[132] a 2015 Fifth Circuit decision applying Texas law, is illustrative.

In *Amerisure*, Amerisure Mutual Insurance Co. (Amerisure) issued a commercial package policy to Admiral Glass & Mirror Co. (Admiral), which was a subcontractor on a construction project. Arch Specialty Insurance Co. (Arch) issued a liability policy to the project's owner and its contractors and subcontractors (one of which was Admiral). The Arch policy included an endorsement that provided that "[supplementary payments] will reduce the limits of insurance" and that Arch's duty to defend ended "when we have used up the applicable limits of insurance in the payment of judgments or settlements."[133] When the owner sued Admiral and others for faulty work, Amerisure tendered the lawsuit to Arch as the primary insurer. Thereafter, Arch withdrew from the defense, claiming that its settlements of prior claims and defense costs exhausted the policy limits, thereby entitling it to terminate its defense. Amerisure sued Arch for breach of the duty to defend. In reversing the district court on the duty to defend issue, the Fifth Circuit, applying Texas law, reasoned that the endorsement converted the Arch policy into a defense-within-limits policy, which meant that Arch's "payments to defense counsel to defend the liability

131. *See, e.g.*, Fed. Ins. Co. v. Singing River Health Sys., 850 F.3d 187, 194–98 (5th Cir. 2017) (applying Texas law and holding that eroding limits provisions contained in policies covering a health care system's fiduciary and employment practices liabilities were enforceable and did not violate public policy); Gabarick v. Laurin Mar. (Am.), Inc., 650 F.3d 545, 553–54 (5th Cir. 2011) (applying Louisiana law to a protection and indemnity policy commonly used in the maritime industry and holding that the eroding limits provision was unambiguous and that defense costs counted against policy limits); Essex Ins. Co. v. Doe, 511 F.3d 198, 202 (D.C. Cir. 2008) (stating that the "defense-within-limits provision means that [insurer] may reduce its coverage by the amount [it] spent on investigation and defense"); Zurn Indus., LLC v. Allstate Ins. Co., No. 1:18-cv-299-SPB, 2021 WL 4502726, at *2–8 (W.D. Pa. Oct. 1, 2021) (interpreting various insurance policies as either eroding or non-eroding and treating eroding provisions as enforceable); Westport Ins. Co. v. Mylonas, No. 14-5760, 2015 WL 4273311, at *2–3 (E.D. Pa. July 15, 2015) (holding that a lawyer's professional liability insurance policy with eroding limits provision does not violate Pennsylvania public policy and that the insurer was entitled to enforce the provision); W. Va. Mut. Ins. Co. v. Vargas, 933 F. Supp. 2d 847, 854–58 (N.D. W. Va. 2013) (determining that an eroding limits provision in medical malpractice policy did not violate West Virginia public policy and was enforceable); Bateman v. Fed. Ins. Co., No. CV 08-96-M-DWM-JCL, 2009 WL 10678815, at *5–6 (D. Mont. Nov. 9, 2009) (holding that a defense-within-limits policy did not violate Montana public policy), *aff'd in part, rev'd in part, and remanded on other grounds*, 432 F. App'x 763 (9th Cir. 2011); Edwards v. Daugherty, 883 So. 2d 932, 943–47 (La. 2004) (discussing the history of defense-within-limits policies and regulation by other states and concluding that such policies do not violate Louisiana public policy, but holding that policy did not allow insurer to deduct attorney's fees assessed by insurer's separate counsel). *But see* Flowers v. Max Specialty Ins. Co., 761 S.E.2d 787, 792–96 (W. Va. 2014) (finding a CGL policy issued to a bar to be ambiguous and rejecting the insurer's argument that it could deduct defense costs from the policy limits and terminate the defense; the insurer could not include defense costs in "supplementary payments" that the policy allowed to be set off from indemnity limits).

132. 784 F.3d 270 (5th Cir. 2015).

133. *Id.* at 271–72.

suit count[ed] against the policy limits."[134] Because the previously paid settlements plus the defense costs exceeded the liability limits, Arch had no duty to defend.[135]

Espinosa v. Accor North America, Inc.,[136] a 2014 Louisiana court of appeals decision, is also instructive. In that case, Jorge Espinosa was robbed and shot in the parking lot of a Motel 6 owned by Bayou Hospitality, LLC (Bayou). Espinosa later sued several defendants, including Bayou. Bayou was insured under a CGL policy issued by Century Indemnity Co. (Century) that included an assault and battery endorsement. The endorsement contained an eroding limits provision that stated that Century "will pay, with respect to . . . any 'suit' against an insured we defend, the expenses we incur associated with the coverage provided by this form. These expense payments will reduce the limits of insurance available and provided by this form."[137] The court applied the provision to reduce the indemnity limit based on the costs incurred in defending Espinosa's lawsuit. The court then observed that the "policy limits have been exhausted by the payments of attorney's fees incurred in the defense of this suit," which led the court to hold that the Century's "duty to defend ended when its policy limits were exhausted."[138]

VI. Extrinsic Facts Showing That the Alleged Claims Are Not within Coverage

A. Overview: A General Rule Subject to Exceptions

As a general rule, an insurer cannot use facts outside the complaint to demonstrate the absence of a duty to defend.[139] As the Restatement of the Law of Liability Insurance explains:

134. *Id.* at 274.
135. *Id.* at 275.
136. 148 So. 3d 244 (La. Ct. App. 2014).
137. *Id.* at 250.
138. *Id.* at 259.
139. *See, e.g.*, Selective Ins. Co. of S.C. v. Target Corp., 845 F.3d 263, 269 (7th Cir. 2016) ("When an insurer tries to deny coverage without seeking a declaratory judgment or defending under a reservation of rights, our inquiry [under Illinois law] is necessarily limited to the allegations in the underlying complaint."); EMD Millipore Corp. v. HDI-Gerling Am. Ins. Co., 511 F. Supp. 3d 41, 47 (D. Mass. 2021) (quoting Essex Ins. Co. v. BloomSouth Flooring Corp., 562 F.3d 399, 403–04 (1st Cir. 2009)); Atl. Cas. Ins. Co. v. Innovative Roofing Sys., Inc., 411 F. Supp. 3d 1287, 1291 (M.D. Fla. 2019) ("In determining whether an obligation to defend exists [under Florida law], a court may not consider any evidence or testimony outside the four corners of the complaint against the insured."); ACE Am. Ins. Co. v. Ascend One Corp., 570 F. Supp. 2d 789, 795 (D. Md. 2008) (applying Maryland law); Cap. Env't Servs., Inc. v. N. River Ins. Co., 536 F. Supp. 2d 633, 642 (E.D. Va. 2008) (interpreting Virginia law); Nortek, Inc. v. Liberty Mut. Ins. Co., 858 F. Supp. 1231, 1236 (D.R.I. 1994) (applying Rhode Island law); Devine v. Great Divide Ins. Co., 350 P.3d 782, 788 (Alaska 2015) (quoting Afcan v. Mut.

> [E]ven an insurer with a strong factual basis for contesting coverage must defend under a reservation of rights and then file a declaratory-judgment action to terminate the duty to defend. Only in a declaratory-judgment action filed while the insurer is defending, or in a coverage action that takes place after the insurer has fulfilled the duty to defend, may the insurer use facts outside the complaint as the basis for avoiding coverage.[140]

This general rule, however, is subject to exceptions. In a variety of situations, courts have held that the duty to defend does not exist where undisputed extrinsic facts not at issue in the underlying action establish that the claims

Fire, Marine & Inland Ins. Co., 595 P.2d 638, 645 (Alaska 1979)); Kolbek v. Truck Ins. Exch., 431 S.W.3d 900, 907–08 (Ark. 2014) ("Generally, insurers are not allowed to refuse to defend on the grounds that they are in possession of information establishing that the allegations in the complaint giving rise to coverage are untrue."); Cotter Corp. v. Am. Empire Surplus Lines Ins. Co., 90 P.3d 814, 829 (Colo. 2004) ("[W]e base the determination of an insurer's duty to defend on the allegations contained in the underlying complaint when such insurer refuses to defend his insured."); New London Cnty. Mut. Ins. Co. v. Sielski, 123 A.3d 925, 936 (Conn. App. Ct. 2015) ("Although there are circumstances where facts beyond those alleged in the underlying complaint and which are known to the insurer can require the insurer to provide a defense, an insurer cannot rely on extrinsic facts to refuse to provide a defense."); Penn-Am. Ins. Co. v. Disabled Am. Veterans, Inc., 481 S.E.2d 850, 852 (Ga. Ct. App. 1997) (rejecting the insurer's argument that the court should excuse its duty to defend based on extrinsic evidence); Dairy Rd. Partners v. Island Ins. Co., Ltd., 992 P.2d 93, 117 (Haw. 2000) (adopting the general rule that an insurer may not use extrinsic evidence to defeat the duty to defend while, at the same time, recognizing a limited exception); Alombro v. Salman, 536 So. 2d 764, 767 (La. Ct. App. 1988) ("The insurer's duty to defend is measured by the allegations of the petition even though the insurer may have determined there was no coverage on the basis of known or ascertainable fact."); Penney v. Capitol City Transfer, Inc., 707 A.2d 387, 389 (Me. 1998) ("Even though evidence beyond the pleadings may later establish the absence of a duty to indemnify, that evidence is not properly considered in determining the duty to defend."); Aetna Cas. & Sur. Co. v. Cochran, 651 A.2d 859, 863 (Md. 1995) (noting the court's prior holding that "an *insurer* may not use extrinsic evidence to contest coverage under an insurance policy if the tort suit complaint establishes a potentiality of coverage"); Century Sur. Co. v. Andrew, 432 P.3d 180, 184 n.4 (Nev. 2018) ("[A]s a general rule, facts outside of the complaint cannot justify an insurer's refusal to defend its insured."); W9/PHC Real Est. LP v. Farm Fam. Cas. Ins. Co., 970 A.2d 382, 391 (N.J. Super. Ct. App. Div. 2009) ("[A]n insurer must defend if the complaint states a cause of action covered by the policy even if the insurer knows of extrinsic facts which would put the claim outside of the insurance coverage."); Found. Reserve Ins. Co. v. Mullenix, 642 P.2d 604, 606 (N.M. 1982) ("[T]he complaint filed in this case alleges facts within the coverage of the policy, and it is the duty of the insurer to undertake the defense even though its own investigation has revealed that the claim sued upon is not in fact covered."); Fitzpatrick v. Am. Honda Motor Co., 575 N.E.2d 90, 92 (N.Y. 1991) ("[T]he courts of this State have refused to permit insurers to look beyond the complaint's allegations to avoid their obligation to defend."); De Smet Farm Mut. Ins. Co. v. Gulbranson Dev. Co., 779 N.W.2d 148, 155–56 (S.D. 2010) ("Even when extraneous facts available in depositions and other record evidence outside the pleadings show the claim as pleaded in the underlying action is false, groundless, or even fraudulent, the duty to defend cannot be defeated if on the face of the pleadings it indicates the claim falls within the policy coverage."); Webb v. USAA Cas. Ins. Co., 457 P.3d 1258, 1265 (Wash. Ct. App. 2020) ("An insurer can consider facts outside of the complaint only to find a duty to defend, not to deny a duty to defend."); *see generally* Douglas R. Richmond, *Using Extrinsic Evidence to Excuse a Liability Insurer's Duty to Defend*, 74 SMU L. Rev. 119 (2021). Numerous commentators have also discussed this issue and described this as the general rule. *See, e.g.*, Jerry & Richmond, *supra* note 2, at 700 ("Insurers are not allowed to refuse to defend when the complaint makes allegations within coverage simply because the insurer has knowledge of extrinsic evidence showing that the complaint's allegations are incorrect or untrue.").

140. Restatement of the L. of Liab. Ins. § 13 cmt. c (Am. L. Inst. 2019).

alleged against the insured in the plaintiff's action are not covered.[141] It is critical that the extrinsic facts be ***undisputed***; if they are disputed, an insurer is not entitled to avoid its duty to defend because the insurer seeking declaratory relief based on facts in dispute in the underlying action could prejudice the insured in that action.[142] As one court put it, "[o]nce it attaches, the duty to defend continues until the conclusion of the underlying action, 'unless the insurer sooner proves, by facts subsequently developed, that the potential for coverage which previously appeared cannot possibly materialize, or no longer exists.'"[143] The Restatement of the Law of Liability Insurance agrees. After describing the general rule, it states that "[c]ourts that follow this general rule have identified . . . five specific exceptions . . . [where] courts have allowed insurers to refuse to defend even when the elements of the complaint-allegation rule are otherwise met."[144] Moreover, the case law is evolving with respect to the possibility of additional exceptions to the general rule. As discussed in more detail later, numerous courts have already recognized other exceptions in a variety of situations.

B. Two Scenarios: Refusing to Defend and Terminating a Defense Already Undertaken

The insurer's argument that undisputed extrinsic facts not in dispute in the underlying litigation negate the duty to defend might be raised either before

141. *See, e.g.*, Riddell, Inc. v. Super. Ct., 222 Cal. Rptr. 3d 384, 391 (Ct. App. 2017) ("Extrinsic facts can also negate the duty to defend, but only if the facts are undisputed and conclusively eliminate the potential for coverage."). As discussed later, section 13 of the Restatement of the Law of Liability Insurance recognizes and approves several exceptions to the general rule. *See* Restatement of the L. of Liab. Ins. § 13(3) (2019). Insurers sometimes seek to use extrinsic evidence to justify a decision not to undertake a defense. The same considerations apply when an insurer undertakes a defense but then seeks to terminate the defense (and withdraw from the representation) based on extrinsic evidence.

142. As the California Supreme Court explained in *Scottsdale Ins. Co. v. MV Transportation*, 115 P.3d 460 (Cal. 2005), "'[w]hen an insured calls upon a liability insurer to defend a third party action, the insurer as a general rule may not escape the burden of defense by obtaining a declaratory judgment that it has no duty to defend.'" *Id.* at 471 (quoting Montrose Chem. Corp. v. Super. Ct., 861 P.2d 1153, 1164 (Cal. 1993) (Kennard, J., concurring)). Otherwise, "'the insured would be forced to defend simultaneously against both the insurer's declaratory relief action and the third party's liability action. Because the duty to defend turns on the potential for coverage, and because coverage frequently turns on factual issues to be litigated in the third party liability action, litigating the duty to defend in the declaratory relief action may prejudice the insured in the liability action.'" *Id.* (quoting *Montrose*, 861 P.2d at 1164 (Kennard, J., concurring)). The solution thus becomes either a stay or dismissal of the declaratory judgment action. Indeed, "'*only* where there is no potential conflict between the trial of the coverage dispute and the underlying action that an insurer can obtain an early trial date and resolution of its claim that coverage does not exist.'" *Id.* (quoting Haskel, Inc. v. Super. Ct., 39 Cal. Rptr. 2d 520, 529 (Ct. App. 1995)).

143. Fed. Ins. Co. v. MBL, Inc., 160 Cal. Rptr. 3d 910, 926 (Ct. App. 2013) (quoting *Scottsdale Ins. Co.*, 115 P.3d at 468); *see also* Md. Cas. Co. v. Nat'l Am. Ins. Co., 56 Cal. Rptr. 2d 498, 504 (Ct. App. 1996) (concluding that the defending insurer was entitled to equitable contribution until the nondefending insurer successfully proved its defense against insured).

144. Restatement of the L. of Liab. Ins. § 13 cmt. c (Am. L. Inst. 2019).

or after the insurer undertakes the defense. If an insurer undertakes a defense and later determines based on extrinsic evidence that the claims fall within one of these exceptional situations, the insurer at that point, assuming it can withdraw from the defense without violating its duty of good faith or causing appointed counsel to violate their professional responsibilities, may terminate the defense. But unlike the other bases for terminating a defense discussed in this chapter, the extrinsic facts argument is derived from the boundaries of the duty to defend itself. In other words, if extrinsic facts negate the duty to defend, the duty to defend is not owed, and an insurer that correctly refuses to undertake a defense for this reason does not breach the duty to defend.[145]

The Restatement of the Law of Liability Insurance provisions on the scope of the duty to defend (section 13) and the insurer's ability to terminate a defense (section 18) recognize the coextensive nature of the undisputed extrinsic evidence analysis. Section 13 outlines the "Conditions Under Which the Insurer Must Defend" in subsections (1) and (2), but then states in subsection (3):

> An insurer that has the duty to defend under subsections (1) and (2) must defend until its duty to defend is terminated under § 18 by declaratory judgment or otherwise, unless facts not at issue in the legal action for which coverage is sought and as to which there is no genuine dispute establish that [any one of six situations, as described in the subsection, exist].[146]

Thus, the duty to defend exists until one of the bases for terminating the duty under section 18 is presented. Section 18 states that "[a]n insurer's duty to defend a legal action terminates only upon the occurrence of one or more of the following events," eight of which are listed.[147] The seventh listed event is "[a] correct determination by the insurer that it does not have a duty to defend the legal action under the rules stated in § 13."[148] So, the same exceptional circumstances identified in section 13 that justify an insurer refusing to defend

145. Refusing to defend or withdrawing from a defense already undertaken without seeking approval from the court is a risky proposition, however. If the insurer is incorrect, it breaches the duty to defend and is liable for the full range of damages resulting from the breach. As the court in *Ringler Associates, Inc. v. Maryland Cas. Co.*, 96 Cal. Rptr. 2d 136 (Ct. App. 2000) explained, "there is no particular requirement that an insurer ask the permission of a trial court before withdrawing from a defense, once the insurer has determined that no potential for indemnification liability exists. Although—in order to avoid any possibility of liability for bad faith—it may be *prudent* for an insurer to obtain a declaratory judgment that it has no defense duty before unilaterally withdrawing from a defense, it is not required to do so." *Id.* at 157. In arguing that the insurer should not be allowed to withdraw its defense, Ringler cited cases supporting the proposition that where a duty to defend appears from the face of a complaint, "it may only be terminated *prospectively,* and not *retrospectively.*" *Id.* The court was unpersuaded, explaining that Ringler apparently had "confuse[d] this principle—which was clearly not violated in this case—with an imagined duty to obtain a declaratory judgment in all cases before withdrawing a defense. No such obligation exists." *Id.*

146. Restatement of the L. of Liab. Ins. § 13 cmt. c (Am. L. Inst. 2019).

147. *Id.* § 18.

148. *Id.*

also serve as the basis for the insurer terminating a defense already undertaken. A comment to section 18 explains this interrelationship between the rule on whether a duty to defend exists and the rule for terminating the duty to defend:

> *Subsection (7) clarifies that an insurer has a continuing opportunity to reevaluate whether it has a duty to defend under the rules in § 13. An insurer that starts to defend an action is permitted to withdraw from the defense if it subsequently determines, correctly, that it does not have a duty to defend under the rules in § 13*, for example because (a) the insurer has learned of facts to which there is no genuine dispute establishing that one of the § 13(3) exceptions to the complaint-allegation rule applies, (b) there has been a legal development in the jurisdiction resolving a previously undecided question of law, (c) the insurer determines for some other reason that it incorrectly applied the complaint-allegation rule in the first instance, or (d) the circumstances have clarified that there is no obligation to defend under the potentiality rule.[149]

Accordingly, if the law in a particular jurisdiction allows an insurer to use extrinsic evidence to negate the duty to defend in a particular situation, an insurer wishing to withdraw from a defense already undertaken for the same reasons should be allowed to do so.

C. Determining the Boundary between the General Rule and the Exceptions

Understanding the circumstances in which an insurer has a right to terminate a defense based on the discovery of undisputed extrinsic evidence that negates coverage requires understanding the boundaries of the duty to defend itself. As discussed in Chapter 1, two approaches exist in the decided cases for determining whether allegations against an insured trigger the insurer's duty to defend. Under the "eight corners" rule (sometimes called "four corners" or "complaint allegation" rule), extrinsic facts (that is, facts outside the complaint) cannot be used to refute the allegations of the complaint, and under the "potentiality" rule, extrinsic facts work in one direction only—to demonstrate the existence of a duty to defend notwithstanding the absence of an allegation within coverage, and not to justify a refusal or failure to defend. Thus, the usual procedure when the insurer believes it has a basis for denying coverage based on extrinsic evidence is for the insurer to defend under a reservation of rights and file a declaratory judgment action seeking a court order terminating the duty to defend.[150] Under the general rule, an insurer that disclaims coverage and

149. *Id.* cmt. i (emphasis added).

150. *See, e.g.*, Maneikis v. St. Paul Ins. Co., 655 F.2d 818, 821 (7th Cir. 1981) ("Under well-settled Illinois law, only three options are available to a liability insurer requested to defend an insured against claims which the insurer believes exceed policy coverage. The insurer can (1) seek a declaratory judgment regarding its obligations before or pending trial of the underlying action, (2) defend the insured under a reservation of rights, or (3) refuse either to defend or to seek a declaratory judgment at the

declines to defend based on extrinsic facts in the face of allegations in the complaint either within or potentially within coverage breaches the duty to defend and is subject to the remedies available for breach as discussed in Chapter 9.

The rationale for the general rule disallowing insurers to use extrinsic facts to negate the duty to defend is derived from the importance of preserving the security insureds seek by purchasing liability insurance. Defending lawsuits is expensive, and insureds want security from these expenses. Insureds receive substantial benefits from their insurers' promises to defend them against covered claims, regardless of whether the claims are meritorious or groundless. If the contours of the duty to defend were delineated to allow insurers to respond to insureds' requests for defenses of complaints containing allegations within coverage by arguing that the "true facts" do not support coverage and therefore no duty to defend exists, insureds would never be certain whenever they are sued that they will receive a defense from the insurer. In such a world, insureds would invariably be required to contemplate hiring counsel at their own expense as they await their insurer's decision about whether to disclaim coverage and not defend (or, alternatively, choosing to defend or to defend under a reservation of rights). In such a world, it would be no comfort to insureds to tell them that if the insurer erroneously disclaims coverage and refuses to defend, the insured can sue the insurer for breach of contract—because in the meantime the insured would have been forced to finance its own defense, which is exactly what the insured sought to avoid when it purchased liability coverage. This uncertainty would vitiate the security insureds seek when they purchase liability insurance. The way to preserve this security is to require insurers to defend under a reservation of rights if they wish to contest coverage, which they can do in a separate declaratory judgment action.

Insurers, however, sometimes offer an alternative perspective on the scope of their duties. From this perspective, the insurer promises *to defend covered claims*. As is often said in explanations of an insurer's duties under liability insurance policies, the duty to defend is broader than the duty to indemnify, which is correct because not all covered claims have merit. Claims without merit will presumably be successfully defended and no duty to indemnify will ever arise.[151] But the insurer's promise, by its terms, is to defend *covered claims*, and if the true, undisputed facts conclusively demonstrate that the plaintiff's

---

insurer's peril that it might later be found to have breached its duty to defend."); Tidyman's Mgmt. Serv. Inc. v. Davis, 330 P.3d 1139, 1151 (Mont. 2014) (stating that "where the insurer believes a policy exclusion applies, it should defend under a reservation of rights and seek a determination of coverage through a declaratory judgment action"); Century Sur. Co. v. Andrew, 432 P.3d 180, 186 (Nev. 2018) (holding that insurer that refused to defend insured could be liable for all consequential damages arising from the insurer's refusal to defend and explaining that although an insurer generally cannot use facts outside the complaint as a basis for refusing to defend, it could use such facts after defending the insured to establish lack of coverage).

151. *See* Jerry & Richmond, *supra* note 2, at 691–93.

claim is outside the coverage and that the insurer could never have a duty to indemnify these claims, the insurer, by this analysis, should not be obligated to defend the noncovered claim simply because the plaintiff's lawyer crafted a complaint alleging or suggesting claims within coverage. Furthermore, in jurisdictions where extrinsic evidence can be used to *establish* the existence of the duty to defend when the complaint does not clearly allege a claim within coverage, insurers offering this different perspective argue that they should be allowed to use extrinsic evidence to *refute* the existence of a duty to defend. In other words, the argument is that fairness requires the use of evidence of extrinsic facts to be a two-way street; if insureds can use extrinsic evidence to *establish* a duty to defend, insurers should be able to use such evidence to *refute* the existence of a duty to defend.[152]

The general rule, however, reasons that the balance of interests should favor insureds and that the use of extrinsic evidence to establish the contours of the duty to defend is a one-way street.[153] Thus, as the general rule states, insurers must defend any suit where the complaint's allegations, if proved to be true, fall within coverage.[154] Even when the insurer "has a solid factual defense to coverage, . . . [it] generally must defend the insured under a reservation of rights and file a separate declaratory judgment action to establish that it will have no duty to indemnify the insured and can therefore terminate its duty to defend."[155] Not surprisingly, the general rule is not fully satisfying to insurers; in most situations under the general rule, the insurer inevitably ends up incurring the expenses of defending a lawsuit alleging claims outside the coverage.[156] But the well-settled general rule favors the insured's interests and expects that "[t]he insurer's exclusive concern when analyzing its duty to defend should be 'whether the judgment that may ultimately be entered against the insured might, either in whole or in part, be encompassed by the policy[,]'"[157] and not whether the underlying claim is meritorious or beyond the coverage, or whether the policy is invalid or unenforceable.[158] Nevertheless, the logic of the

---

152. For a detailed argument that insurers should be allowed to use extrinsic facts and circumstances to justify refusals to defend when coverage issues do not overlap with the facts in the underlying action, *see* Ellen S. Pryor, *The Tort Liability Regime and the Duty to Defend*, 58 MD. L. REV. 1 (1999). Her position is that "[o]n balance, the actual facts approach seems preferable. It delivers the appropriate level of defense insurance in theory, and the usual breach of contract and extracontractual remedies would be available for mistakes or abuses in the application of the approach." *Id.* at 52.

153. Douglas R. Richmond, *Another Texas Twist in Insurers' Use of Extrinsic Evidence to Avoid a Duty to Defend*, 57 TORT TRIAL & INS. PRAC. L.J. 743, 746–47 (2022).

154. *See* Richmond, *supra* note 139, at 122–24.

155. *Id.* at 126.

156. *See id.*

157. *Id.* at 124 (quoting ALLAN D. WINDT, 1 INSURANCE CLAIMS AND DISPUTES § 4:3 (6th ed. 2013 & Supp. 2023)).

158. To be clear, this does not mean that the insurer should disregard the scope of coverage or the validity or enforceability of the policy. Rather, when determining whether to defend, the insurer should focus on the complaint's allegations; if it also and separately concludes that coverage, validity,

insurers' analysis has not been dismissed entirely, and in today's case law, the general rule is subject to exceptions, which are discussed in the next subsection.

D. The Exceptions: Settled Categories and Evolving Extensions

Insurers have frequently tested the limits of the general rule; indeed, in the drafting process for the Restatement of the Law of Liability Insurance, the extrinsic-evidence exceptions included in subsection 13(3) were advocated by and added at the request of the insurance industry.[159] The position that insureds are not entitled to receive defenses for indisputably uncovered claims has received support from many courts.[160] Thus, the general principle that forbids insurers from using extrinsic facts to terminate the duty to defend is subject to several exceptions. The overarching rationale for these exceptions is that the plaintiff controls the allegations of the complaint and should not be able to control the scope of the insurer's contractual obligations to its insured simply by inserting allegations into a complaint that suggest coverage where none, in fact, exists. In the same vein, if a policy is invalid or unenforceable for reasons unrelated to the issues in the underlying litigation, insurers should not be required to provide defenses when it is undisputed that they have no contractual obligations to do so. Some of these exceptions fall into straightforward and well-recognized categories, while others have some support but have not been tested in most jurisdictions.

First, courts have routinely held that when extrinsic facts establish that the defendant in the action is not an insured under the policy pursuant to which the duty to defend is asserted, the insurer need not defend, and if the defense is already underway when these facts are discovered, the insurer may terminate

or enforceability of the policy is in doubt, ordinarily the proper response is to undertake the defense under a reservation of rights and separately seek a declaratory judgment establishing the lack of coverage, validity, or enforceability.

159. Lorelie S. Masters & Geoffrey B. Fehling, *The American Law Institute's Restatement of the Law, Liability Insurance: Scholarship and Controversy*, 27 Conn. Ins. L.J. 116, 176–77 (2020).

160. *See, e.g.*, United Specialty Ins. Co. v. Cole's Place, Inc., 936 F.3d 386, 403 (6th Cir. 2019) (applying Kentucky law and stating that when "[t]here is no possibility of coverage, there is no duty to defend"); Dua v. Stillwater Ins. Co., 308 Cal. Rptr. 3d 110, 118 (Ct. App. 2023) (explaining that an insurer has no duty to defend where there is no possibility of coverage under its policy (quoting Waller v. Truck Ins. Exch., Inc., 900 P.2d 619, 627 (Cal. 1995))); Colony Ins. Co. v. First Specialty Ins. Corp., 262 So. 3d 1128, 1135 (Miss. 2019) (stating that no duty to defend arises when the plaintiff's claims fall outside the policy's coverage (quoting Minn. Life Ins. Co. v. Columbia Cas. Co., 164 So. 3d 954, 970 (Miss. 2014))); Merrick v. Fischer, Rounds & Assocs., Inc., 939 N.W.2d 795, 807 (Neb. 2020) (footnote omitted) ("[A]n insurer is not bound to defend a suit if the pleadings and facts ascertained by the insurer show the insurer has no potential liability."); Acuity v. Masters Pharm., Inc., 205 N.E.3d 460, 465 (Ohio 2022) ("[A]n insurer need not defend an action when all the claims are clearly and indisputably outside the policy coverage.").

it.[161] The Arizona Court of Appeals explained the reasoning supporting this exception in *Navajo Freight Lines, Inc. v. Liberty Mutual Insurance Co.*:[162]

> The rationale of the rule recognizes the obligation of the insurer to defend the insured against even a groundless claim, but before the rule may be applied it must be shown the defendant is in fact an insured, named or omnibus, under the policy. This must be so because the insurer is not obligated to provide a defense for a stranger merely because the plaintiff alleges the defendant is an insured or alleges facts, which, if true, would make defendant an insured.[163]

Thus, "[a] *sine qua non* to the existence of any obligation to defend, or pay, whether the suit be groundless or otherwise, is the pre-existing relationship of insurer and insured. The creation of this basic relationship cannot be left to the imagination of the drafter of a complaint."[164]

Second, courts have routinely held that when extrinsic facts establish that a vehicle or other property involved in an accident is not covered property under the liability insurance policy pursuant to which the duty to defend is asserted, the insurer may terminate the defense (assuming the defendant is not entitled to a defense for some other reason).[165] In *Rowell v. Hodges*,[166] for example, the insured owned a 1958 Cadillac that he insured. At the time of the accident that gave rise to the claims against him, however, he was driving his 1955 Cadillac.[167] A minor passenger in the other vehicle and her father sued the

161. *See, e.g.*, Cohne v. Navigators Specialty Ins. Co., 361 F. Supp. 3d 132, 146–48 (D. Mass. 2019) (holding that extrinsic facts established that the defendant-bouncer was not an insured under a night club's CGL policy and therefore the insurer had no duty to defend him); Texaco, Inc. v. Hartford Accident & Indem., 453 F. Supp. 1109, 1112–13 (E.D. Okla. 1978) (concluding that the insurer had no duty to defend when extrinsic evidence established the lack of an agency relationship with the insured); Nateman v. Hartford Cas. Ins. Co., 544 So. 2d 1026, 1027 (Fla. Dist. Ct. App. 1989) ("The insurer is not obligated to provide a defense for a stranger merely because the plaintiff alleges that the defendant is an insured or alleges facts which, if true, would make the defendant an insured. The mere allegations of the plaintiff's petition may not create an obligation on the part of the insurer to defend where no such obligation previously existed."); Weingarten Realty Mgmt. Co. v. Liberty Mut. Fire Ins. Co., 343 S.W.3d 859, 865 (Tex. App. 2011) (permitting the insurer to refuse to defend based on incontestable extrinsic evidence that the defendant was not an insured under the policy).

162. 471 P.2d 309 (Ariz. Ct. App. 1970).

163. *Id.* at 315–16 (quoting Smith v. Ins. Co. of the State of Pa., 161 So. 2d 903, 919 (La. Ct. App. 1964)).

164. *Id.* at 315.

165. *See, e.g.*, Harco Nat'l Ins. Co. v. Bobac Trucking Inc., 107 F.3d 733, 735–36 (9th Cir. 1997) (holding that the insurer had no duty to defend the insured in the underlying tort action where the vehicle was not covered under the policy); Superior Fuels, Inc. v. Nationwide Agribusiness Ins. Co., No. 14-cv-1420-SMY-PMF, 2016 WL 4366468, at *3 (S.D. Ill. Aug. 16, 2016) (holding that the insurer had no duty to defend the insured under a CGL policy because "Renewable Identification Numbers" which attach to biodiesel fuel did not constitute covered property). *But see* Chandler v. Doherty, 702 N.E.2d 634, 637–40 (Ill. App. Ct. 1998) (arguing that there was no coverage and thus no duty to defend because the insured was driving his "replicar" at time of accident rather than his insured Chevrolet, but the plaintiff's complaint alleging that the insured was driving "his motor vehicle" created a duty to defend).

166. 434 F.2d 926 (5th Cir. 1970) (applying Florida law).

167. *Id.* at 928.

insured but pleaded only that the insured was "operating 'an automobile'" at the time of the accident.[168] The insurer declined to defend because the insured was not driving the insured vehicle at the time of the accident.[169] In upholding the insurer's refusal to defend, the court stated:

> In a sense, to say here that the [insurer] must gauge its obligation strictly by the . . . Complaint, and put blinders on, so to speak, to what it actually knows and has definitely ascertained, is somewhat archaic, considering the nature of our present system of notice pleading. The Court simply cannot find any just or logical reason why it should be held that the mere allegation by the Plaintiffs that [the insured] was operating 'an automobile' thereby invokes a contractual obligation to defend the suit brought by the Plaintiffs, when reality, i.e., the actual identity of the vehicle involved in the accident, told everybody that there was not and never had been any insurance coverage for the [the insured], in the first place.[170]

As a result, the plaintiffs were not allowed to collect their judgments from the insurer.[171]

Third, some courts have recognized exceptions when undisputed extrinsic facts not at issue in the underlying litigation establish lack of coverage under claims-made policies. The court in *Biochemics, Inc. v. Axis Reinsurance Co.*[172] explained the rationale for these exceptions as follows:

> An insurer may not use extrinsic evidence to avoid its duty to defend by challenging the allegations in the complaint; instead, the insurer must defend if the allegations in the complaint are reasonably susceptible to an interpretation that states a claim within the scope of the policy. . . . But an insurer *may* use extrinsic evidence to deny a duty to defend based on facts irrelevant to the merits of the underlying litigation, such as whether the claim was first made during the policy period, whether the insured party reported the claim to the insurer as required by the policy, or whether the underlying wrongful acts were related to prior wrongful acts.[173]

Under the logic of this reasoning, when extrinsic facts establish that a claim was reported late under a claims-made policy and the circumstances are such that the insurer's performance is excused under the rules for late notice, the insurer may terminate the defense.[174] Courts have also held that when extrin-

168. *Id.* at 929.
169. *Id.* at 928.
170. *Id.* at 930.
171. *Id.*
172. 963 F. Supp. 2d 64 (D. Mass. 2013) (applying Massachusetts law).
173. *Id.* at 69–70.
174. *See, e.g.*, Edwards v. Lexington Ins. Co., 507 F.3d 35, 40–41 (1st Cir. 2007) (applying Maine law and permitting the insurer to refuse to defend based on incontestable extrinsic evidence regarding late reporting of a claim under a claims-made policy); Nat'l Union Fire Ins. Co. v. Est. of Calendine,

sic facts establish that an action is subject to a prior and pending litigation exclusion or a related claim exclusion in a claims-made policy, the insurer may terminate the defense.[175] Section 13(3) of Restatement of the Law of Liability Insurance recognizes both of these exceptions.[176]

Fourth, courts have consistently held that when extrinsic facts establish that the insurance policy under which the duty to defend is asserted was properly cancelled, the insurer need not provide a defense.[177] The logic of this exception is straightforward: if no contract exists between the purported insured and insurer, the insured has no contractual rights, including the right to receive a defense.

To recapitulate, the forgoing list of five exceptional situations where undisputed extrinsic facts not at issue in the action under which the duty to defend is asserted was endorsed by the American Law Institute in section 13(3) of the Restatement of the Law of Liability Insurance.[178] Significantly, section 13(3) goes on to state that this list is not static and that other situations may exist where courts recognize (or will recognize in the future) additional exceptions. Thus, section 13(3) adds a sixth exception in the black letter as section 13(3)(f)):

No. 21-cv-01541-NYW-MDB, 2022 WL 3446023, at *6–9 (D. Colo. Aug. 17, 2022) (applying Colorado law and holding that where the insured gave late notice under claims-made policy, the insurer had no duty to defend); Am. Guar. & Liab. Ins. Co. v. Law Off. of Richard C. Weisberg, 524 F. Supp. 3d 430, 454–55 (E.D. Pa. 2021) (holding that late notice of claim arising out of a testamentary trust action entitled the insurer to refuse to defend the insured under a claims-made lawyers' professional liability policy).

175. *See, e.g.*, HR Acquisition I Corp. v. Twin City Fire Ins. Co., 547 F.3d 1309, 1315 (11th Cir. 2008) (permitting consideration of extrinsic evidence regarding the application of the pending-litigation exclusion in a claims-made policy under Alabama law); Worthington Fed. Bank v. Everest Nat'l Ins. Co., 110 F. Supp. 3d 1211, 1235 (N.D. Ala. 2015) (applying Alabama law and allowing consideration of extrinsic evidence regarding the relationship between the current action and a prior action for purposes of determining coverage under a claims-made policy); Biochemics, Inc. v. Axis Reinsurance Co., 963 F. Supp. 2d 64, 68–70 (D. Mass. 2013) (applying Massachusetts law and holding that extrinsic evidence may be considered to determine that the insurer has no duty to defend under a claims-made policy due to interrelated wrongful acts provision, and that the insurer has no interim duty to defend); Acosta, Inc. v. Nat'l Union Fire Ins. Co., 39 So. 3d 565, 573–77 (Fla. Dist. Ct. App. 2010) (examining the complaint in a prior case to evaluate whether a prior-litigation exclusion applied); *see also* RLI Ins. Co., Inc. v. Carr, No. 8:14-CV-2246-T-35-MAP, 2016 WL 7320911, at *6–8 (M.D. Fla. Jan. 22, 2016) (applying Pennsylvania law and allowing consideration of extrinsic evidence to determine the applicability of a related claims exclusion, but holding that there was a possibility of coverage and the insurer thus had a duty to defend).

176. Restatement of the L. of Liab. Ins. § 13(3)(c) & (d) (Am. L. Inst. 2019).

177. *See, e.g.*, Maxum Indem. Co. v. Cadillac Joe Promotions, LLC, No. 4:16-cv-275-MW/CAS, 2017 WL 10527430, at *3 (N.D. Fla. Sept. 1, 2017) (concluding that the insurer owed no duty to defend or indemnify the insured because the insured admitted (by default) that the policy was not in effect during the relevant time period); Scottsdale Ins. Co. v. Bounds, No. TJS-11-2912, 2013 WL 937905, at *4 (D. Md. Mar. 8, 2013) ("Because the policies were cancelled prior to the Accident, [the insurers] are not obligated to defend or indemnify any party with respect to the Accident under the terms of the Policies."); Hunt v. State Farm Mut. Auto. Ins. Co., 994 N.E.2d 561, 569 (Ill. App. Ct. 2013) (holding that "State Farm had no duty to defend Smith if there was no insurance policy in existence at the time of the accident").

178. *See* Restatement of the L. of Liab. Ins. § 13(3) (Am. L. Inst. 2019).

"There is no duty to defend under a similar, narrowly defined exception to the complaint-allegation rule recognized by courts in the applicable jurisdiction."[179] This final exception is appropriate because numerous examples exist in the case law where courts have permitted an inquiry into facts and circumstances beyond the allegations of the complaint to determine whether a duty to defend exists.[180] These include situations where the undisputed facts show that (1) the harm or loss did not occur during the policy period; (2) the insured fraudulently colluded with the plaintiff to create false allegations within coverage;[181] (3) the insured's conviction of a crime triggered a policy's criminal act, illegal act, or criminal conviction exclusion;[182] (4) the insured was convicted of a crime where intent was an element thereby triggering the policy's intentional act exclusion;[183] (5) the insured conceded a fact that had the effect of eliminating the possibility of coverage;[184] and (6) undisputed extrinsic facts in a potpourri

---

179. *Id.* § 13(3)(f).

180. Although the black letter of section 13 allows that the case law may evolve and additional exceptions may be recognized in the future, the section's commentary does not approve exceptions beyond the five specifically recognized in the black letter.

Courts in a few states have recognized a broader, general exception to the complaint-allegation rule that allows insurers to refuse to defend based on their unilateral assessment of any facts that are not at issue in the legal action for which coverage is sought. Although this Section does not recognize this broader exception, a court following this Section could recognize other narrow exceptions on a case-by-case basis, reasoning by analogy to the exceptions stated in subsection (3). Each such case requires striking a balance between the benefits of judicial supervision of the decision to refuse to provide a defense and the benefits of avoiding the need for declaratory-judgment actions in cases in which undisputed facts, not at issue in the liability action for which coverage is sought, establish that a legal action is not covered.

Id. § 13 cmt. c.

181. *See, e.g.*, Loya Ins. Co. v. Avalos, 610 S.W.3d 878, 884 (Tex. 2020).

182. *See, e.g.*, Pompa v. Am. Fam. Mut. Ins. Co., 520 F.3d 1139, 1147–49 (10th Cir. 2008) (applying Colorado law).

183. *See, e.g.*, W. Nat'l Assur. Co. v. Wipf, 702 F. App'x 542, 544 (9th Cir. 2017) (applying Washington law); Am. Fam. Mut. Ins. Co. v. Savickas, 739 N.E.2d 445, 453–54 (Ill. 2000) (concluding that the insured's criminal conviction for first-degree murder collaterally estopped the administrator of the victim's estate from contending that the victim's injury was not expected or intended); State Mut. Ins. Co. v. Bragg, 589 A.2d 35, 38 (Me. 1991) ("[M]urder, attempted murder and sexual abuse of a child convictions are narrow exceptions to the general rule that determines a duty to defend solely from the insurance contract and the allegations of the complaint."); Aetna Cas. & Sur. Co. v. Sprague, 415 N.W.2d 230, 232 (Mich. Ct. App. 1987) ("The trial court did not err in concluding, based on the conviction and on the deposition evidence presented, that there was no genuine issue of material fact as to whether [the insured] expected or intended to kill [the victim]. Therefore, there was no duty to defend or provide coverage."); Burns v. Underwriters Adjusting Co., 765 P.2d 712, 712–13 (Mont. 1988) (explaining that the insured pled guilty to felony aggravated assault and that the allegations of negligence in the plaintiff's complaint did not determine the insurers' duty to defend); Home Mut. Ins. Co. v. Lapi, 596 N.Y.S.2d 885, 887 (App. Div. 1993) (reasoning that the insured's guilty plea trumped his incredible claim that he did not mean to injure the plaintiff and rejecting the insured's transparent attempt to manufacture coverage); Cummings v. Lyles, 27 N.E.3d 985, 991 (Ohio Ct. App. 2015) (stating that the insured's plea to felonious assault created a rebuttable presumption of intent to harm); Peerless Ins. Co. v. Viegas, 667 A.2d 785, 788–89 (R.I. 1995) (involving the sexual molestation of a minor and inferring the intent to harm as a matter of law).

184. *See, e.g.*, Nationwide Mut. Fire Ins. Co. v. Keen, 658 So. 2d 1101, 1102–03 (Fla. Dist. Ct. App. 1995).

of other situations demonstrated the absence of coverage despite the complaint-allegation rule.[185]

These additional exceptions follow the same rationale as the previously discussed exceptions; if no possibility of coverage exists based on extrinsic facts not at issue in the underlying litigation, the insurer should not be required to defend—and should be allowed to terminate a defense already undertaken once these facts become clear. First, in circumstances where undisputed evidence demonstrates that the event allegedly triggering coverage did not occur during the policy period, numerous courts have held that the insurer need not defend despite the presence of covered allegations in the petition or complaint.[186] This exception closely follows the logic of the policy cancellation exception, which reasons that if the policy term is pretermitted before the event allegedly triggering coverage occurs, the nonexistence of a policy necessarily means that the insurer owes no obligation to the insured with respect to that event. Likewise, if undisputed extrinsic facts not at issue in the underlying litigation show that the event allegedly triggering liability is outside the policy term, no contractual obligations exist between insurer and insured with respect to the event in question, and thus the insurer has no duty to defend. Many liability insurance policies require that the bodily injury or property damage that is the subject of the plaintiff's claim must occur within the policy period; the standard CGL policy is a common example.[187] A number of courts have held that when the extrinsic facts establish that the alleged harm did not occur within the policy period of the CGL under which the duty to defend is asserted, no duty to defend exists and the insurer may terminate the defense.[188]

---

185. *See, e.g.*, ChemTreat, Inc. v. Certain Underwriters at Lloyd's of London, 488 F. Supp. 3d 343, 370–71 (E.D. Va. 2020) ("'New York State law recognizes a narrow exception to the duty to defend, which permits a disclaimer of defense prior to litigation or a withdrawal during the course of litigation, if extrinsic evidence . . . is unrelated to the merits of the plaintiff's action [and] plainly take[s] the case outside the policy coverage.'" (quoting Striker Sheet Metal II Corp. v. Harleysville Ins. Co. of N.Y., No. 2:16cv05916, 2018 WL 654445, at *9 (E.D.N.Y. Jan. 31, 2018))) (internal quotation marks omitted); Farm Fam. Mut. Ins. Co. v. Whelpley, 767 N.E.2d 1101, 1104 (Mass. App. Ct. 2002) (recognizing an exception where an undisputed extrinsic fact that will not be litigated in the underlying case takes the underlying case outside coverage); Blake v. Nationwide Ins. Co., 904 A.2d 1071, 1077 (Vt. 2006) (holding that the insurer could rely on undisputed extrinsic evidence that would not be at issue in the underlying litigation to avoid its duty to defend).

186. *See, e.g.*, Bilyeu v. Nat'l Union Fire Ins. Co., 184 So. 3d 69, 72–73, 78–79 (La. Ct. App. 2015) (permitting the insurer to consider extrinsic evidence regarding the date of the wrongful act for purposes of applying a prior-act exclusion in a claims-made D&O policy and upholding its denial of coverage); Fireman's Fund Ins. Co. v. Hyster-Yale Grp., Inc., 135 N.E.3d 499, 507 (Ohio Ct. App. 2019) (holding that the insurer had no duty to defend asbestos personal injury cases where it could establish that the plaintiff's injury occurred outside the effective dates of the policy).

187. *See* Ins. Servs. Off., Inc., Commercial General Liability Coverage Form (CG 00 01 04 13), at 1 (2012) (setting forth the insuring agreement for bodily injury and property damage liability). For a discussion of "occurrence" policies, *see* Jerry & Richmond, *supra* note 2, at 431–44.

188. *See, e.g.*, Liberty Mut. Fire Ins. Co. v. Ferrara Candy Co., No. 1-18-1385, 2019 WL 6830764, at *6–7 (Ill. App. Ct. Dec. 11, 2019) (concluding that the insurer had the right to terminate the defense when extrinsic evidence established that "none of the allegations in the second amended complaint

Second, courts have held that the insured's collusion with the victim allows the insurer to terminate the duty to defend. The Texas Supreme Court's 2020 decision in *Loya Insurance Co. v. Avalos*[189] is illustrative. The insured's auto policy expressly excluded coverage for her husband, who drove the insured's car anyway and was involved in an accident with another vehicle. The occupants of the other vehicle agreed with the insured and her husband that they would tell the insurer that the insured was driving the car at the time of the accident instead of the husband.[190] The insurer undertook the defense, but before the insured was deposed, she told her defense lawyer about the parties' scheme and confessed that her husband drove the car at the time of the accident.[191] The insurer then withdrew its defense and denied coverage.[192] After the insured assigned her rights against the insurer to the plaintiffs, the plaintiffs sued the insurer on various theories for denying the insured a defense and indemnity.[193] The trial court granted the insurer summary judgment on the basis that it owed no duty to defend, but an appellate court reversed.[194] The Texas Supreme Court reinstated the trial court's judgment, holding that the complaint-allegation rule "does not bar courts from considering such extrinsic evidence regarding collusive fraud by the insured in determining the insurer's duty to defend."[195] The court explained:

> [T]he duty to defend in liability insurance policies applies to fraudulent allegations against the insured *by third parties*. The insurer has not agreed to undertake, and the insured has not paid for, a duty to defend the insured against fraudulent allegations brought about *by the insured* itself. Thus, an insurer owes no duty to defend when there is conclusive evidence that groundless, false, or fraudulent claims against the insured have been manipulated by the insured's own hands in order to secure a defense and coverage where they would not otherwise exist.[196]

The *Avalos* court also held that "an insurer faced with undisputed evidence of collusive fraud should not be required to pursue a declaratory judgment action before withdrawing its defense."[197] Under the same logic, a court might

occurred during the policy period"); Polarome Int'l, Inc. v. Greenwich Ins. Co., 961 A.2d 29, 50 (N.J. Super. Ct. App. Div. 2008) (holding that where the plaintiffs' complaints were ambiguous, two CGL insurers could rely on extrinsic evidence to establish that the plaintiffs' chemical exposure had ceased, and their injuries were diagnosed before the policies took effect).

189. 610 S.W.3d 878 (Tex. 2020).
190. *Id.* at 880.
191. *Id.*
192. *Id.*
193. *Id.*
194. *Id.*
195. *Id.* at 882.
196. *Id.*
197. *Id.* at 883.

be persuaded to hold that when the insured's prejudicial noncooperation is established by undisputed extrinsic evidence, the insurer should be entitled to terminate the defense notwithstanding covered allegations in the complaint.[198]

The law is less clear, however, on whether other kinds of misconduct or deception by an insured justify terminating the duty to defend in the face of allegations within coverage in the complaint. For example, the insured's misrepresentation on the application may unequivocally establish that the policy was void or voidable, and thus was not in effect at the time of the event creating liability. The Restatement of the Law of Liability Insurance takes the position that in this situation, the insurer should defend under a reservation of rights and bring a declaratory judgment action for rescission of the policy and that failing to do so is a breach of the duty to defend. The Restatement addresses this question in two illustrations in a comment to section 13:

> 4. Homeowner is sued by Guest alleging injuries from a slip and fall. Homeowner's liability insurer refuses to defend on the ground that it has the right to rescind the policy because the Homeowner falsely answered "no" to a question regarding prior convictions on the application for the applicable insurance policy. The insurer has breached the duty to defend because the complaint alleges a covered cause of action and a misrepresentation defense is not one of the exceptions to the complaint-allegation rule listed in subsection (3).
>
> 5. Same facts as Illustration 4, except the insurer defends under a reservation of rights and files a declaratory-judgment action seeking to terminate the duty to defend. In that declaratory-judgment action, the insurer's duty to defend is determined based upon all the facts and circumstances including any information not included in the complaint that might show that the insurer is entitled to rescind the policy for misrepresentation.[199]

Consistent with the Restatement commentary, examples can be found of cases of insurers contesting in a declaratory judgment action the validity of a policy based on the insured's alleged misrepresentation while or after undertaking the defense under a reservation of rights.[200] Yet, in other cases where the insurer has sought a rescission based on misrepresentation, the facts indicate that either the insurer rescinded unilaterally and was sued by the insured or

198. *See, e.g.*, Hall v. Travelers Ins. Co. 93 Cal. Rptr. 159, 161–62 (Ct. App. 1971) (holding that insurer was allowed to withdraw its defense for the insured's failure to cooperate in the defense of the lawsuit); Patrons Oxford Mut. Ins. Co. v. Garcia, 707 A.2d 384, 386 (Me. 1998) (mentioning the insured's failure to cooperate as one of the narrow exceptions where an insurer can dispute its duty to defend).

199. Restatement of the L. of Liab. Ins § 13 cmt. c., illus. 4 & 5 (Am. L. Inst. 2019).

200. *See, e.g.*, LA Sound USA, Inc. v. St. Paul Fire & Marine Ins. Co., 67 Cal. Rptr. 3d 917, 922–25 (Ct. App. 2007) (rescinding a personal and advertising injury liability policy after defending the insured under reservation); DeMarco v. Stoddard, 125 A.3d 367, 379 (N.J. 2015) (upholding the insurer's rescission of a professional liability policy for the insured's misrepresentation in declaratory judgment action filed after defending under reservation).

the insurer brought the declaratory judgment without undertaking the defense under reservation, and no objection was made to the insurer's approach.[201]

Allowing the insurer to terminate the defense on account of the insured's fraud, collusion, materially prejudicial noncooperation, or other material breach of the insured's duties under the policy is consistent with well-settled principles of contract law. Contract law allows aggrieved parties to respond in two ways to counterparts' breaches. Pursuing a remedy for nonperformance of the promisor's duty is the most obvious, but contract law also allows an aggrieved promisee in some situations to suspend performance of its duties—and if during the period of suspension the promisor's cure of the breach is not forthcoming, the promisee is eventually entitled to treat the promisee's duties as discharged. The rationale for this result is that a party should not be able to materially breach its contractual duties while insisting upon the other side's performance of its duties. In contract law vocabulary, the shorthand explanation of this framework is that each party's duty to perform its duties is *constructively conditioned* on the absence of a prior material breach by the other side of its duties. This means that small, immaterial breaches will not give rise to a right to suspend performance, because this would risk forfeiture to the promisor who committed an immaterial, insubstantial breach. Notice that the concept of suspension is linked to discharge, in that when the promisor commits a material breach and after a reasonable time fails to correct it, the aggrieved promisee, once it becomes clear that the breach cannot and will not be cured, is entitled to go beyond suspension of its performance and treat its own duties as discharged. Often the aggrieved promisee will also seek a remedy for the breaching promisor's nonperformance, but this is not required, and in some situations the aggrieved promisee may decide that the right to suspend its duties is adequate to protect its interests. Thus, it is consistent with contract law to allow a liability insurer to terminate the defense on account of behaviors by the insured that materially breach the insured's obligations to the insurer, such as the duty to cooperate.

Third, courts have allowed insurers to use extrinsic evidence to disclaim the duty to defend where the insured's conviction of a crime triggers a criminal act, criminal conviction, or illegal act exclusion in the policy. For example, in *Pompa v. American Family Mutual Insurance Co.*,[202] a 2008 Tenth Circuit case applying Colorado law, the insured, who had pled guilty to criminally

---

201. *See, e.g.*, Falls Lake Nat'l Ins. Co. v. Oziel Constr. LLC, No. 21-3162, 2022 WL 523600, at *5 (E.D. Pa. Feb. 22, 2022) (holding in declaratory judgment action brought by the insurer that the insurer was entitled to rescind the policy and was relieved of its duty to defend in circumstances where it did not undertake to defend); Essex Ins. Co. v. Galilee Med. Ctr. SC, 988 F. Supp. 2d 866, 872–73 (N.D. Ill. 2013) (granting the insurer summary judgment on its claim that it was entitled to rescind a professional liability policy for misrepresentation and had no duty to defend a malpractice action).

202. 520 F.3d 1139 (10th Cir. 2008).

negligent homicide, sued his homeowners liability insurer for breach of the duty to defend a civil action brought by his victim's heirs. The insurer declined to defend based on a criminal-conviction exclusion in the policy. The district court entered a summary judgment for the insurer, which the Tenth Circuit affirmed. Noting that other courts have recognized exceptions to the complaint-allegation rule and that no Colorado court had decided the question before it,[203] the *Pompa* court reasoned that "[the insured's] conviction is an indisputable fact that is not an element of either the cause of action or a defense in the underlying litigation (the wrongful-death case). Recognizing an exception in this circumstance would not undercut the policies supporting the complaint rule."[204] The court observed that no reasonable expectation of receiving a defense was defeated when "an indisputable fact, known to all parties, removes the act in question from coverage."[205] In addition, the court cited the "beneficial purpose" of "freeing an insurer from having to defend an action that from the outset clearly falls outside the policy's coverage, particularly when, as here, the insurer has no realistic hope of recovering the costs of the defense from its insured."[206]

Fourth, a related situation involves courts allowing insurers to use extrinsic evidence to disclaim the duty to defend where the insured has been convicted of a crime that establishes the intent to harm the plaintiff or the victim, thereby triggering the "intended or expected injury" exclusion, commonly known as the intentional act exclusion.[207] As Douglas Richmond has explained, standard liability policies do not insure against an insured's intentional injury of a third party for two reasons. First, occurrence-based policies define the term "occurrence" as an accident, and necessarily someone intentionally inflicting injury or damage on another is not an accident.[208] Second, liability policies contain intentional act exclusions that typically excludes coverage for bodily injury or property damage "expected or intended by an 'insured,'" with an exception for the use of reasonable force to protect persons or property.[209] Accordingly:

> [A]n insured's criminal act that includes intent as an element cannot be considered an occurrence and should operate to excuse the insurer's duty to defend because there is no possibility of coverage under the policy. Relatedly, an insurer should be able to offer evidence of an insured's criminal conviction to

203. *Id.* at 1147.
204. *Id.*
205. *Id.* at 1148.
206. *Id.*
207. Richmond, *supra* note 139, at 156–58 (discussing representative cases).
208. *Id.* at 156.
209. *See id.*

excuse its duty to defend under an intentional acts exclusion even if the plaintiff alleges that the insured negligently caused the subject harm.[210]

American Family Mutual Insurance Co. v. Savickas,[211] a 2000 Illinois Supreme Court decision, illustrates this exception. In *Savickas*, the insured under a homeowners policy shot and killed the decedent and was convicted of first degree murder.[212] The administrator of the decedent's estate sued the insured in four counts, two of which alleged an intentional tort and the other two of which alleged that the insured either negligently shot the decedent or negligently assessed his need to defend himself against the decedent.[213] The insured tendered the defense to his insurer, which agreed to defend him but promptly filed a declaratory judgment action seeking to establish that it had no duty to either defend or indemnify him.[214] The trial court granted the insurer's motion for summary judgment, but an appellate court reversed on the ground that the negligence allegations in the complaint triggered the duty to defend.[215] The Illinois Supreme Court reinstated the trial court's order, holding that the insured's murder conviction collaterally estopped him from denying that he intentionally shot the decedent.[216] The *Savickas* court explained that the jury, when it found the insured guilty of first degree murder, "necessarily found him either to have intended to kill the victim, or at least to have known that his acts created a strong probability of death or great bodily harm."[217] That finding caused the insured's conduct to fall squarely with the "intended or expected" exclusion,[218] which eliminated the insurer's duties to defend and indemnify.[219]

Fifth, at least one court has recognized an exception when the insured conceded against his own interest a material extrinsic fact that indisputably put the plaintiff's claim outside the policy's coverage. In *Nationwide Mutual Fire Insurance Co. v. Keen*,[220] a 1995 Florida case, the court held that the insurer had no duty to defend in those circumstances. In *Keen*, the plaintiff sued the insured for injuries suffered while the insured was operating a boat, but the policy's coverage was limited to boats with engines whose horsepower fit within a specified range. The plaintiff did not allege the boat engine's horsepower, but

210. *Id.*
211. 739 N.E.2d 445 (Ill. 2000).
212. *Id.* at 447.
213. *Id.*
214. *Id.* at 448.
215. *Id.*
216. *Id.* at 451.
217. *Id.*
218. *Id.* at 452.
219. *Id.* at 453. Because the estate's rights were derivative of the decedent's, the plaintiff could have no greater rights under the policy than the decedent. Thus, the estoppel was equally effective against the estate. *Id.*
220. 658 So. 2d 1101 (Fla. Dist. Ct. App. 1995).

the insured conceded against his own interest that he operated the boat with a 40-horsepower engine, which indisputably was outside the coverage. The question presented was "whether there is any reason why a carrier must defend an insured who concedes a critical fact against his monetary interest that places a claim beyond the carrier's obligation to pay."[221] The court distinguished cases where honest disputes existed about the facts on which coverage turned, noting that in those cases the insurer should defend under a reservation of rights and seek a declaratory judgment determining the parties' rights and liabilities, and held that in the circumstances presented the insurer did not owe its insured a duty to defend.[222] The court explained that "if uncontroverted evidence places the claim outside of coverage, and the claimant makes no attempt to plead the fact creating coverage or suggest the existence of evidence establishing coverage, we think the carrier is relieved of defending."[223]

Lastly, in a smattering of other cases, courts have allowed insurers to refuse to defend complaints containing covered allegations when the insurer's assessment of facts not at issue in the legal action for which a defense is sought indisputably demonstrates that the plaintiff's claim is outside the coverage. For example, in *Farm Family Mutual Insurance Co. v. Whelpley*,[224] a 2002 Massachusetts case, the court agreed with the insurer's position that an accident involving the insured's ATV, when being operated by the insured's 12-year-old guest, was excluded from coverage as a "recreational motor vehicle" being operated away from the insured's premises, and thus the insurer had no duty to defend claims brought by the guest and his mother.[225] The court also held that the plaintiffs' negligent supervision claims were derivative of the accident and thus also within the exclusion, and as such did not trigger the duty to defend.[226] The court explained: "[T]his case falls within one of the rare exceptions to the rule that an insurer has a duty to defend as long as the complaint states or adumbrates a claim within the coverage, . . . that exception being the existence of an undisputed extrinsic fact that takes the case outside the coverage and that will not be litigated at the trial of the underlying action."[227]

The same analysis was applied in *Arch Specialty Insurance Co. v. Colony Insurance Co.*,[228] where a CGL insurer defending a condominium trust's board of governors sought a declaratory judgment against a prior insurer seeking to establish that the prior insurer was required to share in the board's defense. The court explained that "Massachusetts courts generally use extrinsic facts . . . to

221. *Id.* at 1102.
222. *Id.* at 1103.
223. *Id.*
224. 767 N.E.2d 1101 (Mass. App. Ct. 2002).
225. *Id.* at 1103–04.
226. *Id.* at 1104.
227. *Id.*
228. 590 F. Supp. 3d 395 (D. Mass. 2022).

aid interpretation of the complaint, and not as independent factual predicates for a duty to defend."[229] But the court added that "[t]here are two types of extrinsic evidence that can be used to demonstrate the duty to defend does not apply: (1) 'undisputed, readily knowable, and publicly available information' in court records and (2) 'undisputed extrinsic facts that take the case outside the coverage and that will not be litigated at trial of the underlying action.'"[230] The court's examination of undisputed extrinsic evidence in the court records indicated that the board had prior knowledge of roof leaks before the policy's coverage period, and this prior awareness was "sufficient to destroy coverage"[231] under the policy and eliminate the defendant insurer's duty to defend.[232]

Similarly, in *Blake v. Nationwide Insurance Co.*,[233] a 2006 Vermont Supreme Court case, the injuries sustained by an employee, who was a passenger in a truck owned by his employer, were deemed to fall under the employment-related exclusion in the employer's policy, which excluded coverage for liability for injury to an employee "while engaged in activities of employment."[234] The *Blake* court held that the insurer could rely on undisputed extrinsic evidence concerning "factual questions not covered in the complaint, namely, whether the accident occurred in the scope of employment," which were not at issue in the underlying litigation.[235] Thus, the insurer was entitled to refuse to defend and was not required to seek a declaratory judgment that no coverage existed.[236]

E. Summary

The precise contours of the law on whether an insurer can rely on extrinsic facts not at issue in the legal action against the insured as the basis for terminating the duty to defend (or not defending at all) notwithstanding the presence of covered allegations in the complaint, is not fully and precisely settled. Three propositions are correct and exist in tension with each other. First, the general rule is that insurers may not use facts outside the complaint as a basis for refusing to defend; the insurer that wishes to claim that extrinsic evidence negates the duty to defend should defend under a reservation of rights and then file a declaratory judgment action to terminate the duty to defend. Second, the general rule is subject to some well-recognized exceptions where the

229. *Id.* at 412 (quoting Open Software Found., Inc. v. U.S. Fid. & Guar. Co., 307 F.3d 11, 15 (1st Cir. 2002)).
230. *Id.*
231. *Id.* at 422.
232. *Id.* at 424–25.
233. 904 A.2d 1071 (Vt. 2006).
234. *Id.* at 1076–77.
235. *Id.* at 1076.
236. *Id.* at 1077.

insurer does not have a duty to defend based on extrinsic facts despite the presence of covered allegations in the complaint. Third, some courts have pushed beyond the well-recognized exceptions to allow insurers to negate the duty to defend. These courts' decisions reflect that the list of exceptions is evolving and the precise boundaries of the general rule are unsettled.[237] For the foreseeable future, the insurer's ability to terminate the duty to defend (or refuse to defend at all) based on extrinsic facts outside the complaint will remain among the most contentious issues involving the duty to defend.

VII. Insured's Waiver of the Right to a Defense

Although, as many commentators have observed, the rules of waiver in contract law are murky,[238] some generalizations are possible. Waiver occurs when a party surrenders or gives up a right under a contract. When waiver exists, it essentially functions as a modification of a contract's terms. What is special about waiver, however, and what gives it particular power as an argument or as a rationale for a judicial decision, is that waiver does not require the existence of an agreement, consideration, or detrimental reliance to modify a contractual relationship. To amplify, contracting parties can modify or rescind their contract by agreement, but because a modification or rescission is itself a contract, generally such an alteration must satisfy the rules for contract formation. In the usual case, this requires a consideration, meaning a bargained-for exchange for value. Thus, one party can give its counterpart something of value

237. To illustrate the tension at the boundary between the general rule and the exceptions, consider the following hypothetical. Vehicle owner (VO) parks her car in her driveway. A car owned by the insured is negligently driven in a manner that it strikes VO's car and causes it damage. VO believes that the insured was driving the insured's auto at the time of the accident and makes these allegations in a complaint filed against the insured, who tenders the defense to his insurer. But the undisputed facts show that at the time of the accident, the insured's brother, who is an excluded driver under the insured's policy, was driving the vehicle, which means the policy provides no coverage to the insured. The insurer asserts that it should not be required to defend a claim that undisputed extrinsic facts show is outside the coverage—and the insurer's argument would seem to be strong. Yet these facts do not fall within the recognized exception where the defendant in the action is not an insured; instead, the defendant in the hypothetical is an insured, and what has happened is that the plaintiff has inaccurately pleaded the driver's identity. The insured would argue that the insurer must defend—and if it wishes to contest coverage, it must do so under reservation and then bring a declaratory judgment action to establish the facts of who was driving. The Restatement of the Law of Liability Insurance resolves this hypothetical by straddling the fence—stating that the majority rule applies and the insurer that refuses to defend breaches the duty to defend "unless a court subsequently determines that this defense should be recognized as a new narrowly defined exception to the complaint-allegation rule." RESTATEMENT OF THE L. OF LIAB. INS. § 13 cmt. c, illus. 7 (AM. L. INST. 2019).

238. As one prominent observer put it, one of contract law's challenges "is the use of the nebulous term 'waiver.' For many years, writers have criticized the use of the term as one of imprecise and indefinite connotation. . . . Notwithstanding the pervasive confusion in the use of the term, courts continue its use. It also appears in statutes, including the UCC, without definition." JOHN EDWARD MURRAY, JR., MURRAY ON CONTRACTS 700 (5th ed. 2011).

in exchange for the counterpart giving up a right. Likewise, to rescind a contract in its entirety, the parties can agree to give up all their remaining rights to performance, which involves an exchange of value through the mutual forbearances to assert all remaining contractual rights.[239] As an alternative to consideration, some promises are enforced if they justifiably and reasonably induce detrimental reliance;[240] thus, a promise to modify a contract can be enforced without consideration if the promise to modify reasonably induces detrimental reliance.[241] In contrast to contract modifications or rescissions through agreement or detrimental reliance, waiver involves a knowing, intentional, explicit, and voluntary surrender of a right. Waivers are ordinarily revocable, but if the recipient of the waiver relies on it, this reliance can cause the waiver to become irrevocable.

Although uncommon, situations have arisen where a court has concluded that the insured waived its right to receive the insurer's defense, which allowed the insurer to terminate its defense of the insured. When the duty to defend is triggered, it is possible—although rare—that an insured may demand that the insurer withdraw from the defense under the reasoning that a party to litigation has a right to choose its own counsel. If the insured makes such a demand upon the insurer, it has been held that the insured waives its right to receive a defense from the insurer.[242] Moreover, when the insured demands

239. To elaborate on how the consideration doctrine operates, when a contract is not fully performed on each side, each party's surrender of its remaining rights to the other as part of an exchange satisfies the consideration requirement and results in rescission. If the contract is fully performed on one side and the party who has fully performed wishes to give up one of its rights to a return performance, the obligor on that performance must give something of value to the obligee to be freed of the obligation to perform. Similarly, when a contract is not fully performed on either side, neither party can unilaterally give up a right without receiving something of value in a bargained-for exchange. When the consideration doctrine is not met, the modification is not enforceable, and the party who purported to give up a right without receiving something of value is not bound by the attempted modification.

240. This is known as promissory estoppel. *See* Restatement (Second) of Contracts § 90 (Am. L. Inst. 1981).

241. *See* Richard A. Lord, Williston on Contracts § 39:29, at 687–88 (4th ed. 2019 & Supp. 2023) (footnote omitted) ("Under the doctrine of implied waiver, a waiver of contractual rights may be found . . . when there is . . . conduct by one party which misleads the other into a reasonable belief that a provision of the contract has been waived, or that the first party will not insist on compliance with it. A condition precedent to performance may be said to be waived by estoppel when a promisor's words or conduct justify the promisee in believing that a conditional promise will be performed despite the failure of the condition to occur or be performed, and the promisee relies on the promisor's manifestations to its substantial detriment.").

242. *See, e.g.*, Cincinnati Cos. v. W. Am. Ins. Co., 701 N.E.2d 499, 503–04 (Ill. 1998) ("[A]n insured may knowingly forgo the insurer's assistance by instructing the insurer not to involve itself in the litigation. The insurer would then be relieved of its obligation to the insured with regard to that claim."); Richard Marker Assocs. v. Pekin Ins. Co., 743 N.E.2d 1078, 1082–83 (Ill. App. Ct. 2001) (holding that the "right to forgo coverage" with insurer "included an ability to deactivate the coverage" even after settlement of the underlying dispute); Garcia v. Underwriters at Lloyd's London, 156 P.3d 712, 722 (N.M. Ct. App. 2007) ("If the insured indicates that it does not want the insurer's assistance [in defense of a claim], or is unresponsive or uncooperative, the insurer is relieved of its duty to defend."), *aff'd*, 182 P.3d 113 (N.M. 2008); 1 Allan D. Windt, Insurance Claims & Disputes

that the insurer withdraw from the defense, the insured also waives its right to receive indemnification for any judgment or settlement within coverage. This is because, as discussed in Chapters 1 and 3, the insurance contract gives the insurer the right to control the defense; if the insured denies the insurer its contractual right to control the defense, the insured is preventing the insurer from securing the benefits that come from exercising such control. Under general contract law principles, when a party materially prevents the other party from securing the substantial benefits of the contract,[243] this prevention, which amounts to noncompliance with contractual obligations, discharges the other party's obligation to give a return performance. In the liability insurance context, this means that once the insured waives its right to a defense, the insurer need not defend or indemnify the insured.

In short, waiver constitutes the insured's disavowal of its rights under the policy. As the Illinois Supreme Court once explained, "an insured may knowingly forgo the insurer's assistance by instructing the insurer not to involve itself in the litigation. The insurer would then be relieved of its obligation to the insured with respect to that claim."[244]

VIII. Judicial Determination That the Insurer Does Not Have a Duty to Defend

Whenever a court determines that an insurer does not have a duty to defend, the insurer may terminate the defense. This principle states the obvious; if a court enters a final judgment authorizing a party to do an act, that party is permitted to do the act without incurring liability. Although this principle is broad enough to encompass all the specific situations discussed earlier in this chapter where case law allows the insurer to withdraw a defense, it also encompasses the common situation where the insured tenders a defense to the insurer, the insurer concludes it has no obligations under the policy, and the insurer opts to defend under a reservation of rights while pursuing a declaratory judgment action to contest coverage or challenge the policy's validity or enforceability.[245]

§ 2:17, at 2-75 (6th ed. 2013 & Supp. 2023) (stating that "an insured is always presented with the following choice when the proffered defense satisfies the carrier's contractual obligations: the insured can either accept the defense offer, or reject it and forfeit insurance coverage").

243. Another way to describe substantiality is by reference to materiality. A party that substantially performs only commits an immaterial breach. A party that has received everything in return except for some immaterial shortfalls has received substantial performance. When material shortfalls occur in performance, the obligee has not received substantial performance.

244. *Cincinnati Cos.*, 701 N.E.2d at 503–04.

245. *See, e.g.*, Freeman v. Leader Nat'l Ins. Co., 58 S.W.3d 590, 593 (Mo. Ct. App. 2001) (holding that an auto liability insurer had no duty to defend actions after it paid its policy limits into court and obtained a declaratory judgment that it had no further duty to defend, notwithstanding

The principle also encompasses situations where an insurer defends an action against its insured and brings a declaratory judgment against other insurers to establish their obligations to assume or contribute to the defense.[246] The Restatement of the Law, Liability Insurance describes this rule in comment j to section 18 as follows:

> An insurer that is providing a defense after adequately reserving the right to contest coverage may avoid the continued duty to defend through a declaratory-judgment action seeking to prove that the action is not covered, subject to any applicable rules of the jurisdiction regarding the scope and timing of declaratory-judgment actions. (For example, in some jurisdictions courts stay a coverage proceeding when it involves the determination of facts that are also at issue in the underlying action.) In the declaratory-judgment action, the insurer's continuing duty to defend is adjudicated on the basis of all the relevant facts and circumstances, without a presumption that the facts set forth in the complaint or comparable document that concern coverage are true.[247]

In a declaratory judgment action, the insurer may assert any plausible argument that a policy does not provide coverage, is invalid, or is unenforceable—in short, any reason that the insured lacks rights under the policy. These possibilities include the successful assertion of an exclusion, the successful assertion of a defense that demonstrates the policy's invalidity (such as misrepresentation, fraud, or the insured's collusion with the plaintiff), or the successful demonstration that the insured did not satisfy a condition to coverage that causes substantial prejudice to the insurer (under the relevant state rule), or any other valid and complete defense to coverage. Importantly, the lack of merit or invalidity of one or more causes of action in the complaint in not a basis for refusing to defend, because, as discussed in Chapter 1, the insurer is obligated to defend a covered action even when the claim is groundless, meritless, or invalid.

This principle was affirmed in *Fireman's Fund Insurance Cos. v. Ex-Cell-O Corp.*,[248] where the insured made the interesting argument that an insurer

---

the assignment of insured's causes of action by his trustee in bankruptcy); Am. & Foreign Ins. Co. v. Jerry's Sport Ctr., Inc., 2 A.3d 526, 542 (Pa. 2010) (deciding that an insurer is relieved of the duty to defend if it is successful in a declaratory judgment action); Baumann v. Elliott, 704 N.W.2d 361, 366 (Wis. Ct. App. 2005) ("The insurer breaches its duty to defend if it refuses to provide a defense before the court decides the issue of coverage, but the duty to defend ends once the court resolves the coverage issue in favor of the insurer.").

246. *See, e.g.*, Hartford Acc. & Indem. Co. v. Super. Ct., 29 Cal. Rptr. 2d 32, 35 (Ct. App. 1994) (explaining that the insurer was obligated to defend until it obtained a judicial declaration relieving it of its defense obligation; "the duty to defend begins when a potential for coverage arises, and the duty continues until the insurer proves otherwise"); Md. Cas. Co. v. Nat'l Am. Ins. Co., 56 Cal. Rptr. 2d 498, 504 (Ct. App. 1996) (stating that a defending insurer was entitled to equitable contribution until a nondefending insurer successfully proves its defense against the insured).

247. Restatement of the L. of Liab. Ins § 18 cmt. j (Am. L. Inst. 2019).

248. 752 F. Supp. 812 (E.D. Mich. 1990).

could not obtain a declaratory judgment authorizing it to withdraw from the defense unless the policy contained an explicit provision authorizing declaratory judgments actions as a manner of terminating the duty to defend. Not surprisingly, the court rejected the contention that its own judgment would be ineffective unless the policy contained language expressly authorizing this manner of terminating the duty to defend.

In *Ex-Cell-O Corp.*, the court had held in an earlier declaratory judgment proceeding that the insurer had no duty to indemnify an environmental enforcement action because the policy did not provide coverage, but the court's prior ruling did not address the insurer's duty to defend.[249] In a second proceeding, the insureds argued that the insurer had a continuing duty to defend, which the insurer contested. The insureds, referring to language in the policy stating that the duty to defend terminates after the applicable limits are exhausted by payment of judgments or settlements, argued that the insurer "could have included a provision in the policy language stating that the duty to defend terminates upon resolution of a declaratory judgment in its favor," but "[b]ecause it did not, [the insurer's] duty to defend continues."[250] The court rejected the insured's argument, stating that "the duty to defend does not exist when it has been judicially determined that there is no indemnity coverage based on a policy exception to coverage."[251]

IX. Conclusion

As with contract duties generally, the insurer's duty to defend is ordinarily discharged—and no longer ceases to exist—when the insurer fully performs it, which means defending until final adjudication of the action. The duty is also fully performed, and thereby discharged, when parts of the action (1) are fully adjudicated or are dismissed with prejudice, and (2) no basis for coverage of any remaining parts of the action exists. Dismissals without prejudice where no basis for coverage of any remaining parts of the action exists justify termination of the duty to defend (unless the cases is in a potentiality jurisdiction where the insurer is aware of facts outside the pleadings that, if alleged, would create coverage), but the duty to defend may spring back into existence if an amended complaint with covered allegations is filed. As with final adjudications, a settlement that fully and finally resolves the entire action terminates the duty to defend, and a partial settlement of the action with the insured's consent that eliminates any basis for coverage also terminates the duty to defend.

249. *Id.* at 184.
250. *Id.*
251. *Id.*

Under the general contract rule that allows the parties to state in the contract circumstances short of full performance that discharge a duty, a policy provision that allows the insurer to terminate the duty to defend upon exhaustion of the policy limits (i.e., fulfilling the duty to indemnify) is enforceable, and this manner of discharging the duty to indemnify also terminates the duty to defend.

If the insured explicitly and validly waives its right to receive a defense, this waiver enables the insurer to terminate the defense.

Generally, an insurer may not rely on facts extrinsic to the complaint to negate the duty to defend. Under certain exceptional circumstances, however, an insurer has no duty to defend when undisputed extrinsic facts not at issue in the underlying litigation establish that no coverage exists under the policy. In these exceptional circumstances, the insurer need not defend when the defense is tendered; there is no requirement in such circumstances that the insurer defend under reservation of rights or contest coverage in a separate action. In addition, if these exceptional circumstances are found to exist after the insurer has already undertaken the defense, the insurer can terminate the defense.

Whenever a court rules in a final adjudication that the insurer does not have a duty to defend (which ruling will typically occur in a declaratory judgment action), the insurer may terminate the defense.

Each of these valid grounds for terminating the defense presumes that the withdrawal of the defense by the insurer and defense counsel can be accomplished in an orderly manner that fulfills the insurer's good faith obligations to the insured and does not violate defense counsel's professional responsibilities to the insured client.

CHAPTER 7
Insurers' Right to Recover Defense Costs for Uncovered Claims or Causes of Action

Laura A. Foggan and Stephanie V. Corrao

I. Introduction

The duty to defend under a liability insurance policy exists when the underlying claimant seeks to obtain a judgment against an insured that is potentially covered by the policy.[1] Because the duty to defend attaches where there is merely the potential for coverage, an insurer may have a duty to defend an insured even though it ultimately has no duty to indemnify the insured.[2] On the other hand, when a policy clearly does not provide coverage for a lawsuit, the insurer has no duty to defend the insured.[3] What does an insurer do when it has a good faith belief that it will never be obligated to indemnify the insured and thus that it owes no defense, but the insured disputes the insurer's coverage analysis? What are the parties' rights and obligations when such a dispute cannot be resolved by the courts before the underlying case must be defended as is so often the situation? Must the insurer choose between denying coverage outright at the risk of breaching the policy if its coverage position is later determined to be wrong, or assuming the defense under a reservation of rights with the risk that it will bear the costs of a defense it does not owe with no

1. Essential aspects of the duty to defend are extensively discussed in Chapter 1.

2. Greene v. Westfield Ins. Co., 963 F.3d 619, 628 (7th Cir. 2020) (applying Indiana law); U-Haul Co. of Mo. v. Carter, 567 S.W.3d 680, 685 (Mo. Ct. App. 2019) (quoting Arch Ins. Co. v. Sunset Fin. Servs., Inc., 475 S.W.3d 730, 733 (Mo. Ct. App. 2015)); Zurich Am. Ins. Co. v. Nokia, Inc., 268 S.W.3d 487, 490–91 (Tex. 2008); Fire Ins. Exch. v. Est. of Therkelsen, 27 P.3d 555, 560 (Utah 2001).

3. CeFO, Inc. v. Navigators Specialty Ins. Co., 646 F. Supp. 3d 1362, 1367 (D. Colo. 2022) (applying Colorado law); Dua v. Stillwater Ins. Co., 308 Cal. Rptr. 3d 110, 118 (Ct. App. 2023) (quoting Waller v. Truck Ins. Exch., Inc., 900 P.2d 619, 627 (Cal. 1995)); Travelers Cas. Ins. Co. of Am. v. Bozovich, 888 S.E.2d 656, 660 (Ga. Ct. App. 2023).

means of recovering the amounts expended on the insured's behalf? And what of a so-called "mixed action," where some of the claims against the insured are covered and others clearly are not?[4] Must the insurer be forced to shoulder the cost of defending those claims that are outside the scope of the policy's insuring agreement?

The dilemma facing insurers in this circumstance is not a new one, and it has generated a fair amount of case law addressing whether, and under what circumstances, an insurer that incurs or advances disputed costs of defense may recoup those costs from the policyholder.[5] Insurers and policyholders agree on very little with respect to this dilemma and, to shed light on the recurring issue of recoupment, this chapter will set out the legal and policy points on which they disagree. This chapter also discusses how courts analyze an insurer's ability to recoup uncovered costs and address the public policy considerations.

II. The Right to Reimbursement or Recoupment of Costs Advanced for Uncovered Claims or Causes of Action

A. Policyholders' and Insurers' Competing Positions

Policyholders often contend that insurers have no right to the recoupment or reimbursement of defense costs—the terms "reimbursement" and "recoupment" are used interchangeably in this context—because standard liability

4. *See* Gonzalez v. Fire Ins. Exch., 184 Cal. Rptr. 3d 394, 403 (Ct. App. 2015) ("When a complaint states multiple claims, some of which are potentially covered by the insurance policy and some of which are not, it is a mixed action."); Fire Ins. Exch. v. Weitzel, 371 P.3d 457, 461 (Mont. 2016) ("If a complaint states multiple claims, some of which are covered by the insurance policy and some of which are not, it is a mixed action.").

5. The subject has also attracted a fair amount of scholarly discussion over the years. *See, e.g.*, William G. Passannante & Jessica Goldberg, *Why Insurance Companies Should Lose the Battle over Recoupment of Defense Costs*, For the Def., Nov./Dec. 2023, at 18; Jeffrey W. Stempel, *A Deeper Dive into* Nautilus: *Differentiating Insurer Efforts to Recover Defense Costs and Assessing Recoupment in the Wake of the ALI Restatement*, 57 Tort Trial & Ins. Prac. L.J. 57 (2022); Bryana L. Blessinger, *Courts Split:* Nautilus *and the Right to Reimbursement of Defense Costs*, The Brief, Fall 2021, at 8; Johnny C. Parker & Tim J. Schaefer, *The Legal Implications of a Reservation of Rights Defense Examined in the Context of Recoupment of Defense Costs and Tripartite Conflicts of Interest*, 90 UMKC L. Rev. 37 (2021); Kristen Matteoni, Note, *The Right to Reimbursement: Nevada Courts Should Follow the Trend and Forbid Insurers from Seeking Recoupment of Defense Costs*, 17 Nev. L.J. 263 (2016); Laura A. Foggan, *Insurer Recoupment of Defense Costs: Why the Restatement Adopts the Wrong Approach*, 68 Rutgers U. L. Rev. 193 (2015); Joseph N. Cunningham & James N. Markels, *Attorneys' Fees Incurred in Defending Insurance Policy Non-Covered Claims: Who Pays?*, 2 Brook. J. Corp., Fin. & Com. L. 69 (2007); Angela R. Elbert & Stanley C. Nardoni, Buss *Stop: A Policy Language Based Analysis*, 13 Conn. Ins. L.J. 61 (2006); Stephen G. Massiochi, *Rights in Flux: The Insurer's "Right to Recoup Defense Costs and the Insured's "Right" to Independent Counsel*, The Brief, Winter 2003, at 30; Robert H. Jerry, II, *The Insurer's Right to Reimbursement of Defense Costs*, 42 Ariz. L. Rev. 13 (2000); Melinda L. Kirk, Comment, *Will the* Buss *Stop in Oklahoma?*, 35 Tulsa L.J. 599 (2000); Douglas R. Richmond, *Reimbursing Insurers' Defense Costs: Restitution and Mixed Actions*, 35 San Diego L. Rev. 457 (1998).

insurance policy language is silent on whether the insurer is entitled to recover costs incurred for what is ultimately found to be an uncovered defense.[6] Insurers point out that, far from being silent on the parties' obligations with respect to defense costs, the policy terms speak directly to when the insurer must pay for the defense and to the fact that anything other than a covered defense cost is and remains the policyholder's responsibility.

Liability insurance policies define the scope of the duty to defend, and an insurer has no duty to incur costs to defend or indemnify the policyholder in any suit not meeting those criteria. After all, while an insurer's duty to defend may be broad, it is not limitless.[7] In fact, most standard liability insurance policy insuring agreements expressly set out not only when the duty to defend attaches, but also the absence of any insurer duty to defend uncovered claims. For instance, the standard commercial general liability (CGL) policy states: "However, [the insurer] will have no duty to defend the insured against any 'suit' seeking damages for 'bodily injury' or 'property damage' to which this insurance does not apply."[8] Similarly, the current version of the standard personal auto policy provides: "We have no duty to defend any suit or settle any claim for 'bodily injury' or 'property damage' not covered under this Policy."[9]

Insurers do not agree that a standard liability insurance policy can fairly be described as "silent" on the question of recoupment. Rather, they argue the policy makes clear that an insurer has not agreed to accept the costs of non-covered risks and, at a minimum, implies a right to recover amounts that it expressly states are not the insurer's obligation. Policyholders argue that that rights derive from the policy's words alone and, if the policy does not provide for recoupment, there is no recoupment. According to insurer advocates, the policy terms unmistakably state where the insurer's obligations under the

6. *See, e.g.*, Hayes v. Wis. & S. R.R., LLC, 514 F. Supp. 3d 1055, 1062 (E.D. Wis. 2021) (applying Wisconsin law) ("If an insurer wishes to obtain reimbursement of costs expended defending uncovered claims, then it must include such a provision in the policy."); Gen. Agents Ins. Co. of Am., Inc. v. Midwest Sporting Goods Co., 828 N.E.2d 1092, 1103 (Ill. 2005) ("Certainly, if an insurer wishes to retain its right to seek reimbursement of defense costs in the event it later is determined that the underlying claim is not covered by the policy, the insurer is free to include such a term in its insurance contract. Absent such a provision in the policy, however, an insurer cannot later attempt to amend the policy by including the right to reimbursement in its reservation of rights letter."); Am. & Foreign Ins. Co. v. Jerry's Sport Ctr., Inc., 2 A.3d 526, 544 (Pa. 2010) ("Where the insurance contract is silent about the insurer's right to reimbursement of defense costs, permitting reimbursement for costs the insurer spent exercising its right and duty to defend potentially covered claims prior to a court's determination of coverage would be inconsistent with Pennsylvania law.");

7. Westfield Ins. Co. v. Nat'l Decorating Serv., Inc., 863 F.3d 690, 695 (7th Cir. 2017) ("[W]hile under Illinois law the duty to defend is broad, the duty is not limitless."); Prime Tanning Co. v. Liberty Mut. Ins. Co., 750 F. Supp. 2d 198, 208 (D. Me. 2010) ("Although the duty to defend is broad, it is not limitless."); McMillin Homes Constr., Inc. v. Nat'l Fire & Marine Ins. Co., 247 Cal. Rptr. 3d 825, 830 (Ct. App. 2019) ("Although broad, the duty to defend is not limitless and is measured by the nature and kinds of risks covered by the policy.").

8. Ins. Servs. Off., Inc., Commercial General Liability Coverage Form (CG 00 01 04 13), at 1 (2012).

9. Ins. Servs. Off., Inc., Personal Auto Policy (PP 00 01 09 18), at 2 (2017).

policy end. There is no need for the policy to go further to describe the insurer's rights with respect to recouping any costs advanced for uncovered claims, insurers say. When the policy expressly limits the insurer's duty to defend to matters "to which the insurance applies," the right to be reimbursed for costs advanced to defend an uncovered claim is fully supported by the policy terms, insurers contend.[10] Moreover:

> It is unrealistic to expect liability insurance policies to explicitly discuss every possible situation that could occur, and all issues relating to the rights and obligations of the parties where the policy coverage is inapplicable. The suggestion that a right of reimbursement should not exist ignores the facts that the policy unmistakably provides that the duty to defend does not apply to uncovered claims, and that the right to recoup costs advanced by the insurer is based on longstanding unjust enrichment principles that are part of the fabric of settled law over which the insurance contract is written.[11]

A majority of courts hold that insurers have a right to seek reimbursement of expenses incurred in the defense of uncovered claims,[12] although case law is

10. *See, e.g.*, Amici Curiae Brief of Complex Ins. Claims Litig. Ass'n & Am. Prop. Cas. Ins. Ass'n at 8, Nautilus Ins. Co. v. Access Med., LLC, 482 P.3d 683 (Nev. 2021) (No. 79130), 2019 WL 6841106, at *8.

11. *Id.*

12. *See, e.g.*, Cont'l Cas. Co. v. Indian Head Indus., Inc., 666 F. App'x 456, 467–69 (6th Cir. 2016) (applying Michigan law); Valley Forge Ins. Co. v. Health Care Mgmt. Partners, LLC, 616 F.3d 1086, 1090–94 (10th Cir. 2010) (discussing Colorado law); Great Am. Fid. Ins. Co. v. Stout Risius Ross, Inc., 638 F. Supp. 3d 763, 767–69 (E.D. Mich. 2022) (applying Michigan law); Starr Indem. & Liab. Co. v. Rodriguez, 495 F. Supp. 3d 1279, 1288 (S.D. Fla. 2020) ("Under Florida law, a liability insurer that has reserved the right to seek reimbursement is entitled to recover fees and costs once it is determined that the insurer has no duty to defend." (quoting Certain Interested Underwriters at Lloyd's, London v. Halikoytakis, 556 F. App'x 932, 933 (11th Cir. 2014))); Cincinnati Ins. Co. v. Grand Pointe, LLC, 501 F. Supp. 2d 1145, 1168 (E.D. Tenn. 2007) (predicting that Tennessee law would permit the reimbursement of defense costs if the insurer reserved its right to recoupment and it was later determined that the insurer had no duty to defend); Buss v. Super. Ct., 939 P.2d 766, 776 (Cal. 1997) ("The insurer therefore has a right of reimbursement that is implied in law as quasi-contractual, whether or not it has one that is implied in fact in the policy as contractual."); Hecla Mining Co. v. N.H. Ins. Co., 811 P.2d 1083, 1089 (Colo. 1991) (footnote omitted) ("The appropriate course of action for an insurer who believes that it is under no obligation to defend, is to provide a defense to the insured under a reservation of its rights to seek reimbursement should the facts at trial prove that the incident resulting in liability was not covered by the policy, or to file a declaratory judgment action after the underlying case has been adjudicated."); Sec. Ins. Co. of Hartford v. Lumbermens Mut. Cas. Co., 826 A.2d 107, 125 (Conn. 2003) ("A cause of action for reimbursement is cognizable to the extent required to ensure that the insured not reap a benefit for which it has not paid and thus be unjustly enriched. Where the insurer defends the insured against an action that includes claims not even potentially covered by the insurance policy, a court will order reimbursement for the cost of defending the uncovered claims in order to prevent the insured from receiving a windfall."); Catlin Specialty Ins. Co. v. CBL & Assocs. Props., No. N16C-07-166 PRW CCLD, 2018 WL 3805868, at *5 (Del. Super. Ct. Aug. 9, 2018) (allowing reimbursement under Tennessee law); Nationwide Mut. Ins. Co. v. Flagg, 789 A.2d 586, 597 (Del. 1991) (footnote omitted) ("Nationwide has as a duty to defend on all claims, but it may seek reimbursement from Flagg of those expenses, costs or fees incurred by providing his defense on those claims which may be proven later to fall outside the policy coverage."); Allianz Ins. Co. v. Guidant Corp., 884 N.E.2d 405, 419 (Ind. Ct. App. 2008) ("[I]n the event that the insurer secures a declaratory judgment that, as a matter of law, coverage does not exist, it is free to disassociate itself

split, and there is a significant minority of courts that reject insurers' claimed right to recoupment—at least in the absence of a policy provision granting the insurer that right.[13] Courts following the majority rule typically reason that

from the case and seek reimbursement for its expenses incurred up to that point in time."); Travelers Cas. & Sur. Co. v. Ribi ImmunoChem Rsch., Inc., 108 P.3d 469, 480 (Mont. 2005) (concluding that the insurer was entitled to the reimbursement of costs paid do defend claims that were ultimately found to be outside the scope of coverage where it expressly reserved the right to do so); Nautilus Ins. Co. v. Access Med., LLC, 482 P.3d 683, 690 (Nev. 2021) ("When a court determines that an insurer never owed a duty to defend, the insurer expressly reserved its right to seek reimbursement in writing after defense was tendered, and the policyholder accepted the defense from the insurer, then the insurer is entitled to that reimbursement."); Hebela v. Healthcare Ins. Co., 851 A.2d 75, 86 (N.J. App. Div. 2004) ("[T]he right of reimbursement exists because the insured would be unjustly enriched in benefiting by, without paying for, the defense of a non-covered claim."); Dupree v. Scottsdale Ins. Co., 947 N.Y.S.2d 428, 429 (App. Div. 2012) (citing Fed. Ins. Co. v. Kozlowski, 792 N.Y.S.2d 397 (App. Div. 2005)) (acknowledging an insurer's right to recoupment in the event that a later determination of no coverage is made); Chiquita Brands Int'l, Inc. v. Nat'l Union Fire Ins. Co., 57 N.E.3d 97, 104 (Ohio Ct. App. 2015) ("[W]here (1) an insurer does not provide a defense until after a court has entered judgment declaring that the insurer has a duty to defend, (2) the insured demands that the insurer provide a defense, (3) the insurer provides the defense under a reservation-of-rights stating that it may seek to be reimbursed, and later (4) an appellate court determines that a duty-to-defend never existed, then (5) the insurer is entitled to be reimbursed for its defense-cost expenditures under a theory of restitution.").

13. *See, e.g.*, Emps. Mut Cas. Co. v. Bartile Roofs, Inc., 618 F.3d 1153, 1175–76 (10th Cir. 2010) (citing and quoting Shoshone First Bank v. Pac. Emps. Ins. Co., 2 P.3d 510, 515–16 (Wyo. 2000))); Perdue Farms, Inc. v. Travelers Cas. & Sur. Co. of Am., 448 F.3d 252, 258–59 (4th Cir. 2006) (predicting that Maryland law would not permit reimbursement of defense costs for noncovered claims); Am. Fam. Ins. Co. v. Almassud, 522 F. Supp. 3d 1263, 1269 (N.D. Ga. 2021) (predicting Georgia law and stating that "absent a provision in the insurance policy—or some other express agreement—an insurer who issued an otherwise valid, unilateral reservation of rights cannot recoup its costs of defense"); Hayes v. Wis. & S. R.R., LLC, 514 F. Supp. 3d 1055, 1062 (E.D. Wis. 2021) (applying Wisconsin law) ("If an insurer wishes to obtain reimbursement of costs expended defending uncovered claims, then it must include such a provision in the policy."); Blue Cross of Idaho Health Serv., Inc. v. Atl. Mut. Ins. Co., 734 F. Supp. 2d 1107, 1113–17 (D. Idaho 2010) (predicting Idaho law); Att'ys Liab. Prot. Soc'y, Inc. v. Ingaldson Fitzgerald, P.C., 370 P.3d 1101, 1112 (Alaska 2016) (rejecting insurers' right to reimbursement of defense costs); Med. Liab. Mut. Ins. Co. v. Alan Curtis Enters., Inc., 285 S.W.3d 233, 237 (Ark. 2008) (holding that in the absence of statutory authority, an insurer may not recoup defense fees under a unilateral reservation of rights); St. Paul Fire & Marine Ins. Co. v. Bodell Constr. Co., 538 P.3d 1049, 1053 (Haw. 2023) ("An insurer may not seek reimbursement from an insured for defending claims when an insurance policy contains no express provision for reimbursement."); Gen. Agents Ins. Co. of Am., Inc. v. Midwest Sporting Goods Co., 828 N.E.2d 1092, 1103 (Ill. 2005) ("Certainly, if an insurer wishes to retain its right to seek reimbursement of defense costs in the event it later is determined that the underlying claim is not covered by the policy, the insurer is free to include such a term in its insurance contract. Absent such a provision in the policy, however, an insurer cannot later attempt to amend the policy by including the right to reimbursement in its reservation of rights letter."); Am. W. Home Ins. Co. v. Gjonaj Realty & Mgmt. Co., 138 N.Y.S.3d 626, 630–36 (App. Div. 2020) (rejecting the insurer's claimed right to reimbursement of defense costs); Am. & Foreign Ins. Co. v. Jerry's Sport Ctr., Inc., 2 A.3d 526, 544 (Pa. 2010) ("Where the insurance contract is silent about the insurer's right to reimbursement of defense costs, permitting reimbursement for costs the insurer spent exercising its right and duty to defend potentially covered claims prior to a court's determination of coverage would be inconsistent with Pennsylvania law."); U.S. Fid. & Guar. Co. v. U.S. Sports Specialty Ass'n, 270 P.3d 464, 468 (Utah 2012) ("Because an insurer's right to reimbursement from an insured substantially affects the relative levels of risk assumed by each, Utah law does not allow an insurer to seek reimbursement or restitution through an extracontractual claim of unjust enrichment. Instead, we hold that an insurer's right to reimbursement from an insured must be expressly provided in an insurance policy before it can be enforced."); Nat'l Sur. Co. v. Immunex Corp., 297 P.3d 688,

insurance policies afford coverage only for certain defined risks, and make clear than an insurer has not agreed to accept noncovered risks. Under general liability insurance policies, an insurer with a duty to defend is typically required to defend "if, but only if, any of the allegations against the insured could result in a judgment that the insurer would be obligated to pay."[14] Rights and obligations not addressed by the insurance policy, such as the terms of a defense offered for claims not covered by the policy, are not controlled by the insurance policy.[15]

Courts recognizing insurers' right to reimbursement have agreed with insurers that, because there is no contractual duty to defend claims that are not potentially covered, an insurer's right to seek reimbursement is not expressly addressed, but is implied by the basic insuring agreement of the policy.[16] In other words, where the insurance policy expressly limits the insurer's duty to defend or indemnify to matters "to which the insurance applies," the right to reimbursement of defense costs advanced for an uncovered claim is fully supported by the policy terms. Courts adopting the majority view hold that the policy need not expressly set out a right to recoupment of costs advanced for the defense of noncovered claims because there is no coverage to begin with and no expectation that such costs would be incurred.[17]

Buss v. Superior Court[18] is often considered the seminal case supporting reimbursement. In *Buss,* the California Supreme Court explained:

> Under the policy, the insurer does not have a duty to defend the insured as to claims that are not even potentially covered. With regard to defense costs for these claims, the insurer has not been paid premiums by insured. It did not bargain to bear these costs. . . . The insurer therefore has a right of reimbursement that is implied in law as quasi-contractual, whether or not it has one that is implied in fact in the policy as contractual. [19]

695 (Wash. 2013) (citation omitted) ("Disallowing recoupment in this instance does not leave insurers without options to protect their interests. An insurer is not forced to undertake a defense if it believes the claims asserted against the insured are not covered at all. . . . Here, however, National Surety did choose to defend Immunex, following the reservation of rights approach our precedent allows. It cannot claim the benefits of doing so and simultaneously avoid the costs.").

14. Allan D. Windt, Insurance Claims and Disputes § 4:1, at 4-17 (6th ed. 2013 & Supp. 2023).

15. *See, e.g.*, Cont'l Cas. Co. v. Indian Head Indus., Inc., 666 F. App'x 456, 468 (6th Cir. 2016) (applying Michigan law); Scottsdale Ins. Co. v. MV Transp., 115 P.3d 460, 469 (Cal. 2005); Nautilus Ins. Co. v. Access Med., LLC, 482 P.3d 683, 690 (Nev. 2021).

16. *See, e.g.*, United Nat'l Ins. Co. v. SST Fitness Corp., 309 F.3d 914, 921 (6th Cir. 2002) (applying Ohio law).

17. *See, e.g.*, *Nautilus*, 482 P.3d at 690–91.

18. 939 P.2d 766 (Cal. 1997).

19. *Id.* at 775–76; *see also* Travelers Cas. & Sur. Co. v. Ribi ImmunoChem Rsch., Inc., 108 P.3d 469, 480 (Mont. 2005) (concluding that the insurer was entitled to the reimbursement of costs paid do defend claims that were ultimately found to be outside the scope of coverage where it expressly reserved the right to do so); Century Sur. Co. v. Andrew, 432 P.3d 180, 184–86 (Nev. 2018) ("The

The *Buss* court grounded its holding on the contractual nature of the duty to defend, recognizing that while the duty to defend is broader than the duty to indemnity, it is not unlimited.[20] The duty to defend "extends beyond claims that are actually covered to those that are merely potentially so—but no further."[21] This is because the insurer did not contract to pay defense costs for claims that are not even potentially covered under its policy, and has not received premiums from the insured for such coverage.[22]

The court in *Buss* addressed the conundrum of forcing the insurer to provide a defense for noncovered claims in mixed actions, explaining:

> We cannot justify the insurer's duty to defend the entire "mixed" action contractually, as an obligation arising out of the policy, and have never even attempted to do so. To purport to make such a justification would be to hold what we cannot—that the duty to defend exists, as it were, in the air, without regard to whether or not the claims are at least potentially covered. . . . That being said, we can, and do, justify the insurer's duty to defend the entire "mixed" action prophylactically, as an obligation imposed by law in support of the policy. To defend meaningfully, the insurer must defend immediately. To defend immediately, it must defend entirely. It cannot parse the claims, dividing those that are at least potentially covered from those that are not.[23]

Given the duty imposed beyond the contractual limits of the insurer's defense obligation, the court reasoned, "the insurer may give, and the insured may get, more than they agreed."[24]

In a later case, where the insurer was determined to owe no duty to defend, the California Supreme Court further explained that "the duty to defend, and the extent of that duty, are rooted in basic contract principles. The insured pays for, and can reasonably expect, a defense against third party claims that are potentially covered by its policy, but no more."[25] In addressing the right to reimbursement, the court emphasized that the insurer "does not bargain to assume the cost of defense of claims that are not even potentially covered."[26] The court held:

> To shift these costs to the insured does not upset the contractual arrangement between the parties. Thus, where the insurer, acting under a reservation of rights, has prophylactically financed the defense of claims as to which it owed

insured pays a premium for the expectation that the insurer will abide by its duty to defend when such a duty arises. . . . The obligation of the insurer to defend its insured is purely contractual. . . .").

20. *Buss*, 939 P.2d at 773.
21. *Id.*
22. *Id.* at 774.
23. *Id.* at 775 (internal citation omitted).
24. *Id.*
25. Scottsdale Ins. Co. v. MV Transp., 115 P.3d 460, 469 (Cal. 2005).
26. *Id.*

> no duty of defense, it is entitled to restitution. Otherwise, the insured, who did not bargain for a defense of noncovered claims, would receive a windfall and would be unjustly enriched.[27]

Policyholders have a different view. Policyholder advocates, and the courts that disallow an insurer's claim for recoupment, emphasize the broad nature of the duty to defend.[28] They reason that permitting insurers to recoup defense costs for uncovered claims would erode the distinction between the duty to defend and the duty to indemnify.[29] Specifically, they contend that a retroactive determination of whether the insurer owed a duty to defend together with a right to reimbursement for uncovered costs ignores the insurer's obligation to defend where there is the *potential* for a claim to be covered.[30] After all, the duty to defend attaches for any claim potentially covered by the policy, not solely to covered claims. For instance, the Pennsylvania Supreme Court opined:

> [P]ermitting reimbursement . . . would amount to a retroactive erosion of the broad duty to defend in Pennsylvania by making the right and duty to defend contingent upon a court's determination that a complaint alleged covered claims, and would therefore narrow Pennsylvania's long-standing view that the duty to defend is broader than the duty to indemnify.[31]

The Eleventh Circuit, applying Georgia law, articulated the same concern:

> If we were to adopt a rule allowing for broadscale reimbursement without any contractual provision securing that right, the duty to defend would collapse into the duty to indemnify. That is, if the duty to defend required insurers to mount a defense but the defense was widely reimbursable upon a court's determination that no ongoing duty to defend exists, the duty to defend would simply become the duty to indemnify. Simply put, wide-ranging reimbursement is necessarily inappropriate in a system—like Georgia's—that is predicated on a broad duty to defend and a more limited duty to indemnify.[32]

In a split decision, the Washington Supreme Court also held that insurers may not seek to recoup defense costs incurred under a reservation of rights defense while the insurer's duty to defend is uncertain, justifying its holding on

27. *Id.*

28. *See* Cont'l Cas. Co. v. Winder Labs., LLC, 73 F.4th 934, 949 (11th Cir. 2023); Am. & Foreign Ins. Co. v. Jerry's Sport Ctr., Inc., 2 A.3d 526, 544 (Pa. 2010).

29. Am. W. Home Ins. Co. v. Gjonaj Realty & Mgmt. Co., 138 N.Y.S.3d 626, 631 (App. Div. 2020); *Jerry's Sport Ctr.*, 2 A.3d at 544.

30. St. Paul Fire & Marine Ins. Co. v. Bodell, 538 P.3d 1049, 1052 (Haw. 2023).

31. *Jerry's Sport Ctr.*, 2 A.3d at 544.

32. *Winder Labs.*, 73 F.4th at 949.

the premise that "an insurer's duty to defend is broader than the terms of the policy."[33] The court explained that:

> The duty to indemnify applies to claims that are *actually* covered, while the duty to defend "arises when a complaint against the insured, construed liberally, alleges facts which could, if proven, impose liability upon the insured within the policy's coverage."[34]

Courts that allow recoupment also recognize the broad scope of an insurer's duty to defend, including that the duty attaches to claims that are potentially within the policy coverage and exceeds contractual requirements in the case of mixed actions, but emphasize that the duty is not unlimited.[35] The difference is that courts applying a no-recoupment rule suggest that the retroactive determination of whether a defense duty attached would result in excusing the insurer from the costs of defense for potentially covered claims, whereas insurers argue that correct duty to defend test can be applied by courts prospectively or retroactively and that allowing reimbursement needn't alter the standards for deciding whether a defense obligation existed at all.[36]

In fact, much of the debate over the insurer's right to recoup defense costs centers on whether allowing reimbursement for noncovered costs is tantamount to allowing the insurer to unilaterally amend the insurance contract. Policyholders, and courts rejecting recoupment, have often claimed that because the insurance policy doesn't expressly provide for reimbursement of uncovered costs, recoupment is not allowed—and permitting an insurer to

33. Nat'l Sur. Corp. v. Immunex Corp., 297 P.3d 688, 691 (Wash. 2013).

34. *Id.* (internal quotation marks omitted) (quoting Truck Ins. Exch. v. Vanport Homes, Inc., 58 P.3d 276, 281–82 (Wash. 2002)); *see also Bodell*, 538 P.3d at 1052 ("Reimbursement for defense costs undercuts the duty to defend.").

35. Buss v. Super. Ct., 939 P.2d 766, 773 (Cal. 1997); Nautilus Ins. Co. v. Access Med., LLC, 482 P.3d 683, 688–91 (Nev. 2021).

36. Scottsdale Ins. Co. v. M.V. Transp., 115 P.3d 460, 468 (Cal. 2005) ("By law applied in hindsight, courts can determine that no potential for coverage, and thus no duty to defend, ever existed. If that conclusion is reached, the insurer, having reserved its right, may recover from its insured the costs it expended to provide a defense which, under its contract of insurance, it was never obliged to furnish."). Most states impose a duty to defend based on the potential for coverage if the allegations of the underlying complaint create factual uncertainty. Steven Plitt et al., 14 Couch on Insurance § 200:11 (3d ed. 2017) ("When coverage under the duty to defend depends on an outstanding factual dispute, the disputes must be resolved in favor of coverage until the insurer conclusively establishes that there is no potential for coverage."). But most states also agree, for instance, that legal uncertainty caused by the absence of controlling authority does not give rise to a duty to defend. Allowing recoupment in such circumstances, assuming a court later agrees there was never any coverage—and thus there was never any potential for a duty to defend from the outset—does not undermine the standard for a duty to defend. *M.V. Transp.*, 115 P.3d at 470–71.

recover costs advanced for defense of uncovered claims amounts to a retroactive change in the insurance policy terms.[37]

Adopting the pro-recoupment view in *Nautilus Insurance Co. v. Access Medical, LLC*,[38] the Nevada Supreme Court explained that where a court determines that the insurer never owed a duty to defend, then the insurance contract does not apply to the insurer's recoupment claim.[39] If the insurer reserved its right to seek reimbursement when it undertook the defense that it did not owe, "*[n]o* contract governed its defense."[40] Consequently, there is no reason that the insurer cannot reserve the right it has—not pursuant to the policy—but pursuant to the law of restitution.[41]

Further rejecting the notion that the insurance policy must include an express right to recoupment, the court stated:

> Nautilus did not have any contractual duty to defend respondents, so it could properly condition its provision of a defense on a reservation of rights. In short, Nautilus agreed to defend against certain kinds of allegations, and not others. Allowing reimbursement does not modify the policy, but rather gives effect to the parties' agreement.[42]

Insurers forcefully reject any suggestion that allowing recoupment somehow requires changing the policy terms. They point out that a right to recoup costs an insurer advanced to defend uncovered claims is found in longstanding unjust enrichment principles that are part of the fabric of settled law over which the insurance contract is written.[43] As in all contractual relationships, if the insurance contract is silent on the parties' rights with respect to a particular issue, the question is governed by other existing law on point—in this case, the law of equity. When it turns out that an insurer provided a defense that was

37. *See, e.g.*, Gen. Agents Ins. Co. of Am. v. Midwest Sporting Goods Co., 828 N.E.2d 1092, 1102 (Ill. 2005) ("As a matter of public policy, we cannot condone an arrangement where an insurer can unilaterally modify its contract, through a reservation of rights, to allow for reimbursement of defense costs in the event a court later finds that the insurer owes no duty to defend."); Shoshone First Bank v. Pac. Emps. Ins. Co., 2 P.3d 510, 515–16 (Wyo. 2000) (citations omitted) ("The insurer is not permitted to unilaterally modify and change policy coverage. The [p]olicy issued to Shoshone by Pacific states a duty to defend, and allocation is not mentioned. In light of the failure of the policy language to provide for allocation, we will not permit the contract to be amended or altered by a reservation of rights letter.").

38. 482 P.3d 683 (Nev. 2021).

39. *Id.* at 688.

40. *Id.* at 690.

41. *Id.*

42. *Id.*

43. *Id.* at 689 (citing Restatement (Third) of Restitution and Unjust Enrichment § 35 (Am. L. Inst. 2011)).

never owed, the insured may be unjustly enriched at the insurer's expense.[44] Insurers believe this situation is addressed by settled, equitable theories of implied contract, unjust enrichment, and restitution.[45]

The general rule of unjust enrichment is that, when an obligor acting in good faith with regard to a legally uncertain obligation renders the performance demanded under a unilateral reservation of rights, that party has a right to seek restitution.[46] The Restatement of the Law (Third) of Restitution and Unjust Enrichment expresses this general rule and specifically treats recoupment of liability insurance defense costs as an instance to which the general rule of restitution applies.[47] This engrained law of restitution is the backdrop for any contractual agreement, including insurance policies entered by insurers and policyholders.[48]

Courts that recognize an insurer's right to recoupment base their holdings on the equitable doctrines of implied-in-fact contract, quantum meruit, and

44. Scottsdale Ins. Co. v. MV Transp., 115 P.3d 460, 469 (Cal. 2005); *Access Med.*, 482 P.3d at 688–90. *But see* Jerry, *supra* note 5, at 36 (discussing the Terra Nova Ins. Co. v. 900 Bar, Inc., 887 F.2d 1213, 1219–20 (3d Cir. 1989) (framing the contrary argument that while the insured receives a benefit in this situation, the benefit is not received at the insurer's expense because the insurer is defending the action under a reservation of rights to avoid later estoppel or waiver claims and to avid an inadequate defense by the insured; thus, any benefit the insured received is not unjust, and no principle of fairness requires the insured to return this benefit to the insurer). The contrary argument that Professor Jerry outlines and that the *Terra Nova* court originally framed, however, is not altogether correct. As a California federal court explained:

> A reservation of rights is made by an insurer to protect that insurer's rights to later seek reimbursement for payments made under the reservation of rights if it is shown that the insured was not entitled to such payments. A reservation of rights protects an insurer from potential liability for bad faith if it were to withhold payments, and it also provides the insured with the use of the payments until the determination is made. Thus, the use of a reservation of rights protects both parties.

Mass. Cas. Ins Co. v. Rossen, 953 F. Supp. 311, 315 (C.D. Cal. 1996) (applying California law).

45. *See* Restatement of the L. (Third) of Restitution and Unjust Enrichment § 35 (Am. L. Inst. 2011).

46. *See, e.g.*, Ill. Union Ins. Co. v. NRI Constr., Inc., 846 F. Supp. 2d 1366, 1377 (N.D. Ga. 2012) (applying Georgia law); Catlin Specialty Ins. Co. v. CBL & Assocs. Props., No. N16C-07-166 PRW CCLD, 2018 WL 3805868, at *5 (Del. Super. Ct. Aug. 9, 2018) (allowing reimbursement under Tennessee law).

47. Restatement of the L. (Third) of Restitution and Unjust Enrichment § 35 cmt. c (Am. L. Inst. 2011).

48. *But see* U.S. Fid. & Guar. Co. v. U.S. Sports Specialty Ass'n, 270 P.3d 464, 471 (Utah 2012) ("Under Utah law, an insurer may not seek restitution based on the extracontractual theory of unjust enrichment where there is an express contract governing the 'subject matter' of the dispute. An insurance policy is a contract that defines the risk relationship of the insurer and the insured. The right to reimbursement would alter this risk relationship, and therefore the right falls squarely within the "subject matter" of the policy. As a result, there can be no extracontractual right to restitution between the insurer and its insured, and only the express terms of a policy create an enforceable right to reimbursement.").

unjust enrichment.[49] As a matter of general contract law, where one party to a contract demands performance from the other that is not owed under the contract, the other party is entitled to render such performance under a reservation of rights "preserving a claim in restitution to recover the value of the benefit conferred" outside its contractual obligations.[50]

In *Buss*,[51] the California Supreme Court reasoned that because an insurer owes no duty to defend claims that are not even potentially covered, an insurer that advances such costs for noncovered claims is entitled to reimbursement based on a quasi-contractual right implied in law.[52] As the court explained:

> The insurer therefore has a right of reimbursement that is implied in law as quasi-contractual, whether or not it has one that is implied in fact in the policy as contractual. As stated, under the law of restitution such a right runs against

49. *See, e.g.*, United Nat'l Ins. Co. v. SST Fitness Corp., 309 F.3d 914, 921 (6th Cir. 2002) (applying Ohio law) ("Because [the policyholder] entered into an implied in fact contract by accepting the defense costs subject to a reservation of right to recoupment if a court determined that [the insurer] had no duty to defend [the policyholder] and a court found [the insurer] had no duty to defend, [the insurer] is entitled to reimbursement of its defense costs and prejudgment interest."); Cincinnati Ins. Co. v. Grand Pointe, LLC, 501 F. Supp. 2d 1145, 1169 (E.D. Tenn. 2007) (applying Tennessee law) (ruling that it would be inequitable for the insureds to retain the benefits of the defense without repaying defense costs because they "received the benefit of a defense they were not paying for, [] knew they were receiving a defense they were not funding, and [] were aware from [the insurer's] reservation-of-rights letter that [the insurer] claimed a right to reimbursement" upon a determination of no duty to defend); Resure, Inc. v. Chem. Distribs., Inc., 927 F. Supp. 190, 194 (M.D. La. 1996) (applying New Mexico law) (holding that the insurer was entitled to reimbursement where the "reservation [of rights] specifically referred to the possibility that [the insurer] might seek reimbursement for any and all costs of defense" and where "[t]here [was] nothing in the record to suggest [the policyholder] objected to the reservation"); Knapp v. Commonwealth Land Title Ins. Co., 932 F. Supp. 1169, 1172 (D. Minn. 1996) (applying Minnesota law) (stating that where an insurer properly meets its duty to defend "and subsequently successfully challenges policy coverage, it should be entitled to the full benefit of such a challenge and be reimbursed for the benefits it bestowed, in good faith, to its insured"); Sec. Ins. Co. of Hartford v. Lumbermens Mut. Cas. Co., 826 A.2d 107, 125 (Conn. 2003) ("Where the insurer defends the insured against an action that includes claims not even potentially covered by the insurance policy, a court will order reimbursement for the cost of defending the uncovered claims in order to prevent the insured from receiving a windfall."); G & E Tires & Serv., Inc., 777 So. 2d 1034, 1039 (Fla. Dist. Ct. App. 2000) (holding that the insurer's unilateral reservation of rights preserved its right to seek reimbursement of defense costs incurred to defend noncovered claims); Nautilus Ins. Co. v. Access Med., LLC, 482 P.3d 683, 692 (Nev. 2021) (permitting reimbursement under principles of unjust enrichment "gives effect to the parties' agreement" that the insurer is liable only for covered claims).

50. Metro. Life Ins. Co. v. Cotter, 984 N.E.2d 835, 850 (Mass. 2013) (quoting Salamon v. Terra, 477 N.E.2d 1029, 1031 (Mass. 1985) (noting that "quasi contract or contract implied in law" are obligations created by law "without any expression of assent, and sometimes even against a clear expression of dissent"); *see also* Keller v. O'Brien, 683 N.E.2d 1026, 1029 (Mass. 1997) ("Restitution is an equitable remedy by which a person who has been unjustly enriched at the expense of another is required to repay the injured party.").

51. Buss v. Super. Ct., 939 P.2d 766 (Cal. 1997).

52. *Id.* at 776.

> the person who benefits from "unjust enrichment" and in favor of the person who suffers loss thereby. The "enrichment" of the insured by the insurer through the insurer's bearing of unbargained-for defense costs is inconsistent with the insurer's freedom under the policy and therefore must be deemed "unjust."[53]

As in California, the rule that insurers are entitled to reimbursement has been applied in Colorado,[54] Connecticut,[55] Delaware,[56] Florida,[57] Indiana,[58]

---

53. *Id.* at 776–77.

54. Valley Forge Ins. Co. v. Health Care Mgmt. Partners, Ltd., 616 F.3d 1086, 1094 (10th Cir. 2010) (allowing recoupment under Colorado law); Cotter Corp. v. Am. Empire Surplus Lines Ins. Co., 90 P.3d 814, 828 (Colo. 2004) (citation omitted) ([P]ermitting reimbursement balances "the interests of both the insurers and the insureds by ensuring that the broad rule basing the duty to defend on the complaint will not require insurers to pay defense costs if coverage ultimately does not exist under the policies" while creating "an incentive for insurers to defend by allowing them to subsequently seek reimbursement."); Hecla Mining Co. v. N.H. Ins. Co., 811 P.2d 1083, 1089 (Colo. 1991) (footnote omitted) ("The appropriate course of action for an insurer who believes that it is under no obligation to defend, is to provide a defense to the insured under a reservation of its rights to seek reimbursement should the facts at trial prove that the incident resulting in liability was not covered by the policy, or to file a declaratory judgment action after the underlying case has been adjudicated.").

55. Sec. Ins. Co. of Hartford v. Lumbermens Mut. Cas. Co., 826 A.2d 107, 125 (Conn. 2003) ("Where the insurer defends the insured against an action that includes claims not even potentially covered by the insurance policy, a court will order reimbursement for the cost of defending the uncovered claims in order to prevent the insured from receiving a windfall.").

56. Nationwide Mut. Ins. Co. v. Flagg, 789 A.2d 586, 597 (Del. 1991) (footnote omitted) ("Nationwide has as a duty to defend on all claims, but it may seek reimbursement from Flagg of those expenses, costs or fees incurred by providing his defense on those claims which may be proven later to fall outside the policy coverage.").

57. Jim Black Assocs., Inc. v. Transcon. Ins. Co., 932 So. 2d 516, 518 (Fla. Dist. Ct. App. 2006) ("Transcontinental provided a defense for claims that were clearly not covered by its policy with Jim Black. Transcontinental did not bargain for these costs and has not been paid premiums to defend uncovered claims. . . . Now that it has been determined that Transcontinental never had a duty to defend, Transcontinental is entitled to reimbursement."); Colony Ins. Co. v. G & E Tires & Serv., Inc., 777 So. 2d 1034, 1039 (Fla. Dist. Ct. App. 2000) ("Colony timely and expressly reserved the right to seek reimbursement of the costs of defending clearly uncovered claims, which it consistently identified as such. Having accepted Colony's offer of a defense with a reservation of the right to seek reimbursement, G E ought in fairness make Colony whole, now that it has been judicially determined that no duty to defend ever existed."); *see also* Travelers Indem. Co. v. Figg Bridge Eng'g, Inc., 389 F. Supp. 3d 1060, 1081 (S.D. Fla. 2019) ("Florida law requires nothing more from Plaintiffs to be reimbursed for defense-related payments determined to be outside the scope of Plaintiffs' duty to defend.").

58. Allianz Ins. Co. v. Guidant Corp., 884 N.E.2d 405, 419 (Ind. Ct. App. 2008) ("[I]n the event that the insurer secures a declaratory judgment that, as a matter of law, coverage does not exist, it is free to disassociate itself from the case and seek reimbursement for its expenses incurred up to that point in time.").

Kentucky,[59] Michigan,[60] Montana,[61] Nevada,[62] New Jersey,[63] Ohio,[64] and Tennessee.[65] One recent state supreme court decision on-point is *Nautilus Insurance Co. v. Access Medical, LLC*,[66] where, as a matter of first impression, the Nevada Supreme Court applied settled principles of unjust enrichment applicable to contracts generally to the insurance policy at issue. In doing so, the *Nautilus* was persuaded by the Restatement (Third) of Restitution and Unjust Enrichment, which provides:

> If one party to a contract demands from the other a performance that is not in fact due by the terms of their agreement, under circumstances making it reasonable to accede to the demand rather than to insist on an immediate test of the disputed obligation, the party on whom the demand is made may render such performance under protest or with reservation of rights, preserving a claim in restitution to recover the value of the benefit conferred in excess of the recipient's contractual entitlement.[67]

---

59. *See* Travelers Prop. Cas. Co. of Am. v. Hillerich & Bradsby Co., 598 F.3d 257, 268 (6th Cir. 2010) (predicting Kentucky law and discussing settlement costs).

60. Cont'l Cas. Co. v. Indian Head Indus., Inc., 666 F. App'x 456, 467–69 (6th Cir. 2016) (applying Michigan law); NCMIC Ins. Co. v. Dailey, No. 267801, 2006 WL 2035597, at *6 (Mich. Ct. App. July 20, 2006) ("A contract will be implied in law where it would be inequitable for a defendant to retain a benefit received from a plaintiff, absent reasonable consideration.").

61. Nat'l Indem. Co. v. State of Mont., 499 P.3d 516, 534 (Mont. 2021) (stating that an insurer's right to recoupment is enforceable even absent an express agreement by the insured if the insurer satisfies the requirements of explicit reservation and timely notice to the insured); Travelers Cas. & Sur. Co. v. Ribi Immunochem Rsch., Inc., 108 P.3d 469, 480 (Mont. 2005) (permitting the insurer to recoup its defense costs expended on claims outside the CGL policy's coverage).

62. Nautilus Ins. Co. v. Access Med., LLC, 482 P.3d 683, 691 (Nev. 2021) ("When a party to a contract performs a disputed obligation under protest and a court later determines that the contract did not require performance, the party may ordinarily recover in restitution. This rule gives effect to the terms of the parties' bargain. It applies to an insurance policy as it would to any other contract.").

63. Hebela v. Healthcare Ins. Co., 85 A.2d 75, 86 (N.J. Super. Ct. App. Div. 2004) (noting that "the right of reimbursement exists because the insured would be unjustly enriched in benefiting by, without paying for, the defense of a non-covered claim").

64. United Nat'l Ins. Co. v. SST Fitness Corp., 309 F.3d 914, 921 (6th Cir. 2002) (applying Ohio law) ("We agree that allowing an insurer to recover under an implied in fact contract theory so long as the insurer timely and explicitly reserved its right to recoup the costs and provided specific and adequate notice of the possibility of reimbursement promotes the policy of ensuring defenses are afforded even in questionable cases."); Chiquita Brands Int'l, Inc. v. Nat'l Union Fire Ins. Co., 57 N.E.3d 97, 104 (Ohio Ct. App. 2015) ("[W]here (1) an insurer does not provide a defense until after a court has entered judgment declaring that the insurer has a duty to defend, (2) the insured demands that the insurer provide a defense, (3) the insurer provides the defense under a reservation-of-rights stating that it may seek to be reimbursed, and later (4) an appellate court determines that a duty-to-defend never existed, then (5) the insurer is entitled to be reimbursed for its defense-cost expenditures under a theory of restitution.").

65. Cincinnati Ins. Co. v. Grand Pointe, LLC, 501 F. Supp. 2d 1145, 1168 (E.D. Tenn. 2007) (predicting that "the Supreme Court of Tennessee would follow the majority position and recognize reimbursement is available to an insurer when an adequate reservation of rights has been made even if the policy contains no express reimbursement provision").

66. 482 P.3d 683 (Nev. 2021).

67. *Id.* at 689 (quoting Restatement (Third) of Restitution and Unjust Enrichment § 35 (Am. L. Inst. 2011)).

The *Nautilus* court recognized that reasonable parties may disagree as to their rights and obligations under any contract, and ultimately, a court may have to resolve the dispute.[68] In applying long-standing principles of unjust enrichment to recoupment, the court emphasized the timing exigencies, particularly in the insurance context, where it may be impractical to require that the dispute be litigated before performance of the contract begins.[69] The court explained:

> We are persuaded by the Restatement's reasoning. When time is precious, it makes sense for the parties to decide quickly *what to do*, and to litigate later *who must pay*. Because an insurer risks unbounded liability if it loses the coverage dispute after refusing to defend a suit, it is generally "reasonable [for the insurer] to accede to the demand rather than to insist on an immediate test of the disputed obligation." Under these circumstances we conclude that when a court determines that the insurer never had a duty to defend, and the insurer clearly and expressly reserved its right to seek reimbursement, it is equitable to require the policyholder to pay.[70]

Other courts similarly view the need for immediate action in defending the underlying suit against the policyholder, before the coverage dispute can be resolved, as an important factor supporting the insurer's right to recoupment.[71]

On the other hand, some courts have contended that the insured is not enriched, or that the insurer receives equal or greater benefits by defending uncovered claims for which coverage is disputed under a reservation of rights.[72] Advancing this view, the Washington Supreme Court explained that "[u]njust enrichment is simply irrelevant because any 'enrichment' of [the policyholder] was more than matched by benefit to [the insurer]."[73] Several other courts have agreed.[74] As one court stated:

---

68. *Id.*

69. *Id.*

70. *Id.* at 689 (footnote omitted).

71. *See, e.g.*, Probuilders Specialty Ins. Co. v. Double M Constr., 116 F. Supp. 3d 1173, 1182 (D. Nev. 2015) (applying Nevada law); Helca Mining Co. v. N.H. Ins. Co., 811 P.2d 1083, 1089 (Colo. 1991) ("[T]he appropriate course of action for an insurer who believes that it is under no obligation to defend, is to provide a defense to the insured under a reservation of rights to seek reimbursement should the facts at trial prove that the incident resulting in liability was not covered by the policy."); Dupree v. Scottsdale Ins. Co., 947 N.Y.S.2d 428, 429 (App. Div. 2012) (citing Fed. Ins. Co. v. Kozlowski, 792 N.Y.S.2d 397 (App. Div. 2005)) (acknowledging an insurer's right to recoupment when a later determination of no coverage is made).

72. *See, e.g.*, Cont'l Cas. Co. v. Winder Labs., LLC, 73 F.4th 934, 947 n.17 (11th Cir. 2023) ("There is no one-sided enrichment here. The insurers benefit from fulfilling their contractual obligations and following Georgia insurance law to avoid a lawsuit and maintain their reputation, among other things.").

73. Nat'l Sur. Co. v. Immunex Corp., 297 P.3d 688, 691 (Wash. 2013).

74. *See, e.g.*, *Winder Labs.*, 73 F.4th at 947 n.17 ("There is no one-sided enrichment here. The insurers benefit from fulfilling their contractual obligations and following Georgia insurance law to avoid a lawsuit and maintain their reputation, among other things."); Terra Nova Ins. Co., Ltd. v. 900

> Faced with uncertainty as to its duty to indemnify, an insurer offers a defense under reservation of rights to avoid the risks that an inept or lackadaisical defense of the underlying action may expose it to if it turns out there is a duty to indemnify. At the same time, the insurer wishes to preserve its right to contest the duty to indemnify if the defense is unsuccessful. Thus, such an offer is made at least as much for the insurer's own benefit as for the insured's.[75]

While insurers argue that courts permitting recoupment allocate responsibility for defense costs based on the terms of the insurance contract, courts rejecting reimbursement assign the cost of disputed defense fees to insurers, whom they believe benefit at least equally to the policyholder when costs are advanced on an interim basis until guidance can be obtained from the courts.[76] In gauging the extent of the benefit, however, insurers would say that courts denying recoupment have lost sight of the key cost and benefit at the center of the dispute—the expense of the costs of defense of uncovered claims borne by the insurer and the benefit of a free defense enjoyed by the policyholder. That unjust enrichment, insurers say, is not offset by the alleged "benefit" of protecting the insurer from bad faith where there can be no bad faith (and thus no benefit to the insurer) in the absence of coverage. After all, recoupment is only sought by an insurer with respect to costs advanced for uncovered claims.[77]

Apart from the equitable doctrine of unjust enrichment, courts have allowed reimbursement based on implied contract principles or quantum meruit, focusing on an insured's acceptance of the insurer's payments subject to a reservation of rights as constituting "an implied agreement to the reservation of the insurer's right to seek reimbursement for claims outside of the policy's coverage."[78] For instance, in *Probuilders Specialty Insurance Co. v. Double M. Construction*,[79] the insurer was entitled to reimbursement of defense costs where the policyholder "implicitly agreed to the reservation of

Bar, Inc., 887 F.2d 1213, 1219 (3d Cir. 1989); Gen. Agents Ins. Co. of Am., Inc. v. Midwest Sporting Goods Co., 828 N.E.2d 1092, 1103 (Ill. 2005) ("[W]e cannot say that an insured is unjustly enriched when its insurer tenders a defense in order to protect its own interests, even if it is later determined that the insurer did not owe a defense.").

75. *Terra Nova*, 887 F.2d at 1219.

76. Courts that reject an insurer's right to recoupment generally don't discard the equitable principles of unjust enrichment or contend they are inapplicable to insurers. Rather, they commonly hold that a policyholder is not unjustly enriched by an insurer's provision of a defense under a reservation of rights because the insurer is also acting to protect its own interest. *See, e.g.*, *Winder Labs.*, 73 F.4th at 947 n.17; *Terra Nova*, 887 F.2d at 1219–20; *Gen. Agents*, 828 N.E.2d at 1103. The right to defend may allow the insurer to select defense counsel or to oversee the defense, and it obligates the insured to cooperate with their insurer. Further, defending when coverage is disputed protects the insurer against the consequences of breaching its duty to defend if coverage turns out to be owed, which could result in even greater expense to the insurer.

77. *See* Buss v. Super. Ct., 939 P.2d 766, 775 (Cal. 1997) ("As to the claims that are at least potentially covered, the insurer may not seek reimbursement for defense costs.").

78. Walbrook Ins. Co. Ltd. v. Goshgarian & Goshgarian, 726 F. Supp. 777, 784 (C.D. Cal. 1989).

79. 116 F. Supp. 3d 1173 (D. Nev. 2015).

rights by accepting [the insurer's] defense and passing litigation costs to it for two years."[80] Similarly, in *Certain Interested Underwriters at Lloyd's, London v. Halikoytakis*,[81] the insurer was entitled to reimbursement of defense costs where the policyholder accepted the defense subject to a reservation of rights, including right to recoup defense costs, and allowed the insurer to defend for over two years.[82]

Some of these courts have focused on an insurer's reservation of the right to reimbursement provided to the insured as the grounding on which a disputed coverage defense was afforded. The court in *American Economy Insurance Co. v. Hartford Fire Insurance Co.*[83] found that the insurer was entitled to the reimbursement of its defense costs "because [the policyholder] 'implicitly accepted' their defenses under a reservation of rights."[84] And in *United National Insurance Co. v. SST Fitness Corp.*,[85] the court held that the policyholder's acceptance of a defense subject to the insurer's reservation of a right to recoupment created an implied in fact contract under Ohio law.[86] Following similar reasoning but reaching the opposite result, in *Westchester Fire Insurance Co. v. Wallerich*,[87] the Eighth Circuit concluded there was no right to reimbursement on an implied contract theory where insured accepted a defense, but objected to the terms of the insurer's reservation of rights.[88] The *Wallerich* court was predicting Minnesota law.[89]

B. The Restatement of the Law of Liability Insurance

In 2010, the American Law Institute (ALI) began work on the Principles of the Law of Liability Insurance.[90] In 2014, the ALI Council recharacterized the Principles project to become a Restatement and, in 2019, the ALI published the Restatement of the Law of Liability Insurance (RLLI).[91] The RLLI proved

80. *Id.* at 1182.
81. 556 F. App'x 932 (11th Cir. 2014).
82. *Id.* at 933.
83. 695 F. App'x 194 (9th Cir. 2017).
84. *Id.* at 196.
85. 309 F.3d 914 (6th Cir. 2002).
86. *Id.* at 921.
87. 563 F.3d 707 (3d Cir. 2009).
88. *Id.* at 719.
89. *See id.* (noting that Minnesota courts had not announced whether they would support reimbursement).
90. "A Principles project is distinguished from a Restatement in that the former is less tethered to existing law and has greater freedom to adopt an approach regarded as superior even if it lacks support in existing law or has even been rejected by courts. However, a Restatement need not adopt as a rule only positions embraced by the majority of courts." Jeffrey W. Stempel, *Hard Battles over Soft Law: The Troubling Implications of Insurance Industry Attacks on the American Law Institute Restatement of the Law of Liability Insurance*, 69 CLEVE. ST. L. REV. 605, 619–20 (2021).
91. RESTATEMENT OF THE L. OF LIAB. INS. (AM. L. INST. 2019).

to be extremely controversial.[92] The controversy surrounding the RLLI principally stemmed from critics' charge that the reporters' work product did not faithfully "restate" prevailing liability insurance rules, but instead reflected an effort to reshape liability insurance law by establishing novel recommended rules for courts to adopt.[93] Among the provisions attracting such criticism was section 21,[94] which states: "Unless otherwise stated in the insurance policy or otherwise agreed to by the insured, an insurer may not obtain recoupment of defense costs from the insured, even when it is subsequently determined that the insurer did not have a duty to defend or pay defense costs."[95] In rejecting the law permitting equitable restitution to liability insurers, the RLLI contended that a special exception should be made to deny restitution to insurers unless a right to recoupment was stated in the insurance policy or otherwise agreed by the policyholder. In doing so, the RLLI departed from the position taken in section 35 of the Restatement (Third) of Restitution and Unjust Enrichment.[96] The RLLI soft-pedaled its departure from existing case law, which it noted generally favored recoupment,[97] and from the competing Restatement (Third) of Restitution and Unjust Enrichment, by noting that section 21 is "merely a default" rule and that insurers could incorporate an express right to recoupment in their policies.[98] It further explained that an express provision sets out the scope and conditions for recovery in advance and puts the basis for

92. *See, e.g.*, Victor E. Schwartz & Christopher E. Appel, *Restating or Reshaping the Law? A Critical Analysis of the Restatement of the Law, Liability Insurance*, 22 U. Pa. J. Bus. L. 718, 719 (2020) (describing the RLLI as "one of the most controversial work products in the [ALI's] nearly 100-year history").

93. *Id.*

94. *See, e.g.*, Foggan, *supra* note 5, at 193 (footnote omitted) ("In adopting the minority view in a sweeping rule that would prohibit recoupment in all circumstances where there is no explicit contractual agreement permitting it, this section of the draft turns too far away from articulating black letter law as it stands. To the extent this section is seeking 'to ascertain the relative desirability of competing rules,' a Restatement provision reversing the majority common law approach to recoupment is unsound because it is not a subtle change in the law, but a major one—and this change is not supported by reliable empirical analysis or (as shown below) a clear trend in the direction of the law.").

95. Restatement of the L. of Liab. Ins. § 21 (Am. L. Inst. 2019).

96. Restatement (Third) of Restitution and Unjust Enrichment § 35 (Am. L. Inst. 2011); *see* Restatement of the L. of Liab. Ins. § 21 cmt. b (Am. L. Inst. 2019) ("This Restatement does not question the R3RUE's analysis of a general pattern of unjust enrichment outside of the liability insurance context, but there are substantial reasons to conclude that recognition of such a claim by a liability insurer is inappropriate because of special considerations of insurance law."); *see also* John Moriarty & Assocs., Inc. v. Zurich Am. Ins. Co., 207 N.E.3d 542, 553 n.11 (Mass. App. Ct. 2023) (citations omitted) ("The position of the Restatement of the Law of Liability Insurance contrasts with that in the Restatement (Third) of Restitution & Unjust Enrichment § 35 (2011). The latter suggests recoupment may be appropriate in certain circumstances and provides specific examples of when an insurer may recover for unjust enrichment. . . . The Restatement of the Law of Liability Insurance expressly rejects that position. . . .").

97. *See* Restatement of the L. of Liab. Ins. § 21 cmt. a (Am. L. Inst. 2019) (recognizing that a slight majority of state courts permit recoupment).

98. *Id.*

recovery of uncovered costs beyond dispute.[99] Finally, the RLLI stated that its proposed rule would place the burden of contracting around the denial of restitution on "the party best able to do so."[100]

Unlike the RLLI arguments, most courts precluding recoupment agree that equitable principles of unjust enrichment apply to insurers, just as they apply to everyone else, and that the policyholder was enriched (defense of uncovered claims) at the insurer's expense, but they differ on whether that enrichment was unjust or unfair on the grounds that the insurer allegedly benefited as well.[101] They then conclude that the insurer's recovery of defense costs will not be allowed unless there was an express agreement that an insurer would be entitled to recoup the costs of defending uncovered claims.[102]

By contrast, courts allowing recoupment conclude that once the no-coverage determination is made, unjust enrichment is shown when the insurer paid, and the policyholder received, amounts not owed under the contractual parameters of duty to defend.[103] Given the split in authority, why do insurers resist the RLLI suggestion that courts should adopt a new rule allowing recoupment only when that right is laid out in the policy terms or other agreement with the policyholder? After all, the RLLI approach would appear to end disputes over whether the insurer has a right to reimbursement.

While heading off disputes in advance is laudable, it is unrealistic to expect liability insurance policies to explicitly address every possible situation that could occur, and all issues relating to the parties' rights and obligations. Moreover, since standard liability insurance policies unmistakably provide that the insurer's duty to defend does not apply to uncovered claims, and equity supplies the remedy of unjust enrichment, an express term allowing recoupment seems unnecessary.

A rule requiring the insurance policy to expressly provide for recoupment might eliminate policyholder contentions that they did not expect to be required to reimburse the insurer for amounts it paid but did not owe. But requiring an insurer to expressly reserve the right to reimbursement before assuming the defense already serves that purpose because no costs for allegedly uncovered claims are incurred before the policyholder is advised through the reservation of rights that the insurer will seek to recover defense costs advanced for suits where coverage is disputed, if a court later agrees no coverage was owed. Further, as a practical matter, the policyholder who may be called upon to reimburse the insurer for the cost of defending uncovered claims is generally a Fortune 100 or Fortune 500 company, which is sophisticated about the

99. *Id.*
100. *Id.*
101. *See, e.g.*, Am. & Foreign Ins. Co. v. Jerry's Sport Ctr., Inc., 2 A.3d 526, 545–46 (Pa. 2010).
102. *See, e.g.*, Cont'l Cas. Co. v. Winder Labs., LLC, 73 F.4th 934, 949 (11th Cir. 2023).
103. *See, e.g.*, Nautilus Ins. Co. v. Access Med., LLC, 482 P.3d 683, 691–92 (Nev. 2021).

issues posed by coverage disputes. Moreover, courts can and do confirm that appropriate notice of a claimed right to recoup costs, that is, notice that can be read, understood, and acted upon, has been given to the policyholder as a prerequisite for enforcing an insurer's right to reimbursement.[104]

According to insurers, the unfairness of a new rule requiring an express policy term or policyholder agreement to allow recoupment, and the reasons why this issue is so hotly debated, can be seen clearly in the context of occurrence-based liability policies involving long-tail claims. To adopt a new, no-recoupment default rule—whether supported by recent court rulings or not, would be a significant change to the parties' rights. When policies called upon to respond to long-tail claims today were entered into decades ago, there was no rule requiring an express recoupment provision. To the contrary, through years of settled law when older occurrence policies were priced and issued, courts overwhelmingly agreed that the recoupment of defense costs advanced insurers for uncovered claims was permissible under equitable principles. The parties understood that, as with any contract, principles of equity provided the backdrop for any matters not expressly addressed by the insurance policy.

Insurers contend that changing the rules of the game after the fact would set off an unjustified and unfair transfer of millions of dollars from insurers that, by definition, owed no duty to defend, to policyholders that were never entitled to a defense of uncovered claims. Retroactively applying a new rule making an express contract provision a prerequisite for recoupment would dramatically alter the financial consequences of existing insuring agreements whose terms cannot now be amended and for which no new premium can be charged. At stake is the massive burden of the costs of defending disputed coverage matters involving decades of long-tail claims such as asbestos, environmental, and sexual abuse suits brought against policyholders today for conduct over many past years. Insurers warn that, if insurers who wrote those policies are held to different rules than those governing the insurance agreements when they were entered, this would fundamentally upset expectations and unduly burden the insurance market.

Even in cases that do not involve long-tail claims under older policies, case law on both sides of the recoupment question recognizes that important public policy considerations are implicated by whether an insurer has a right to seek reimbursement from the policyholder for noncovered claims. Courts allowing recoupment reason that, when coverage is disputed and the insurer lacks the opportunity to resolve the coverage dispute before undertaking a defense, a rule permitting recoupment encourages insurers that in good faith believe they owe no coverage at all to nevertheless defend the policyholder while concurrently

---

104. *See, e.g.*, Travelers Cas. & Sur. Co. v. Ribi ImmunoChem Rsch., Inc., 108 P.3d 469, 480 (Mont. 2005).

seeking a judicial determination of coverage.[105] Such a rule protects policyholders' interests, while balancing insurers' interests by permitting recoupment if it is determined that the insurer was correct and no coverage was owed. Courts identify several public policy reasons supporting recoupment.

First, permitting recoupment is fundamentally fair. A recoupment claim is premised on the determination in a coverage action that there was in fact no coverage to begin with.[106] In a case where there was no coverage at all, the policyholder was never entitled to any assistance from its insurer regarding the claims asserted against it.[107] As already discussed, if the insurer defends or pays to settle, the policyholder will have received a substantial benefit it was never due under the insurance contract. A right to reimbursement protects the insurer against the risk of having to defend claims for which it had no obligation without recourse. It thus supports the important public policy of encouraging insurers to fully defend even when there is a good faith belief that there is no potential for coverage or where there are uncovered claims in a mixed action.

Second, prohibiting recoupment could eliminate the benefit to policyholders of the insurer defending in the first instance, subject to the right to recoup amounts it pays.[108] For example, if an insurer that believes it owes no coverage is precluded from recoupment, the consequences of denying coverage outright may be viewed as a lesser risk than having to forgo any amounts advanced for defense or indemnity under a reservation of rights. This is because any rational insurer would be forced to weigh the risk of an adverse coverage determination (however unlikely or unreasonable such a determination might be) or a finding of bad faith against the potentially long-term obligation to pay defense costs for an uncovered claim.[109]

---

105. *See, e.g.*, Knapp v. Commonwealth Land Title Ins. Co., 932 F. Supp. 1169, 1172 (D. Minn. 1996) (applying Minnesota law); Buss v. Super. Ct., 939 P.2d 766, 775–77 (Cal. 1997).

106. *See also* Travelers Prop. & Cas. In. Co. v. Hillerich & Bradsby Co., 598 F.3d 257, 269 (6th Cir. 2010) (predicting Kentucky law) ("It would seem an unjust outcome for the insurer if this Court were to sanction [the] position that . . . [the] insured would be both getting the settlement at the time it preferred and having that settlement funded by the insurer when no coverage was afforded under the policy.").

107. *See, e.g.*, Nautilus Ins. Co. v. Access Med., LLC, 482 P.3d 683, 686 (Nev. 2021) ("This rule gives effect to the terms of the parties' bargain.").

108. *See* Scottsdale Ins. Co. v. MV Transp., 115 P.3d 460, 470 (Cal. 2005).

109. One court aptly described the dilemma faced by the insurer deciding whether to indemnify a settlement without an established right to recoup amounts advanced for an uncovered claim:

> If an insurer waived its coverage position simply by settling a claim for the insured, the insurer would be forced either to refuse to settle and face a bad faith claim, or to settle the lawsuit and lose its coverage defenses. . . . The "resulting Catch-22" would force insurers to indemnify non-covered claims, violating "basic notions of fairness."

Phillips & Assocs., PC v. Navigators Ins. Co., 764 F. Supp. 2d 1174, 1176 (D. Ariz. 2011) (citations omitted) (quoting Blue Ridge Ins. Co. v. Jacobsen, 22 P.3d 313, 321 (Cal. 2001)).

Third, courts have recognized that an insurer's savings from the reimbursement of defense costs where the insurer never had a duty to defend under the insurance policy will translate into lower premiums for all policyholders.[110] Conversely, a per se rule banning recoupment would raise prices on all policyholders. Courts have thus noted that any defense provided to an insured for which it paid no premium is not "free," and is borne in the end by other policyholders in the form of higher premiums. The effect of denying recoupment for uncovered costs is that a policyholder who does not pay a premium for certain coverage receives coverage, while the other policyholders are left holding the bag. By contrast, allowing an insurer to recoup the costs of defending uncovered claims ameliorates costs the insurer would otherwise have to pass on to all policyholders in the form of increased premiums.[111]

Fourth, allowing reimbursement of defense costs paid under a reservation of rights promotes judicial economy. Absent an obligation to reimburse insurers for defense costs paid under a reservation of rights, policyholders who are receiving such a defense while a declaratory judgment action is pending would have no incentive to seek a swift determination of coverage.[112] Instead, policyholders would be motivated to draw out the coverage litigation as long as possible while the underlying litigation proceeds. A policyholder that successfully delayed any coverage ruling might, in effect, unfairly create de facto defense and indemnity coverage.

Fifth, a no-recoupment rule could reduce the opportunity for reasonable settlements in the underlying litigation.[113] The better approach is to encourage insurer participation in settlements even when coverage is uncertain by allowing for recoupment if an insurer pays under a reservation of rights before a judicial determination of coverage can be obtained.

In sum, courts that recognize a right to recoup defense costs paid under a reservation of rights for claims that are not covered will encourage insurers to accept the defense of their policyholders and advance settlement funds in cases involving coverage disputes. Allowing recoupment permits insurers to advance

110. *See* Excess Underwriters at Lloyd's London v. Frank's Casing Crew & Rental Tools, Inc., 246 S.W.3d 42, 54 (Tex. 2008) (J. Hecht, dissenting) ("Worst of all, the burden of the windfalls in this and many other cases will most likely fall on other policyholders who have never tried to get away with demanding more coverage than they bought, so that insureds who stick to their policies will have the privilege of paying extra to satisfy the claims of those who do not.").

111. *Id.*

112. Buss v. Super. Ct., 939 P.2d 766, 778 (Cal. 1997).

113. *Phillips & Assocs.*, 764 F. Supp. 2d at 1176 (permitting the insurer to defend and reserve the right to recoup costs "provides for the settlement of cases when coverage is uncertain, and thus ensures compensation of the injured party by placing 'the risk that the insured may not be financially able to pay the injured party's damages' on the insurer" (quoting Blue Ridge Ins. Co. v. Jacobsen, 22 P.3d 313, 321 (Cal. 2001))).

costs of defense and indemnity while preserving their coverage defenses. This benefits policyholders by providing the initial resource of the insurer for the defense, and also may more expeditiously move the case toward resolution.

On the other hand, courts that deny recoupment deem reimbursement of an insurer's costs incurred to defend noncovered claims to be inconsistent with the insurer's duty to defend. Their public policy rationales tend to center on that premise. First, these courts believe that recognizing a right outside the insurance contract "based solely on a unilateral reservation of rights letter" would create obligations beyond the parties' agreement.[114]

Second, these courts believe a reservation of rights letter "offering" to defend subject to a right to recoupment protects the insurer's own interest from claims of breach "while placing the full risk of a determination of non-coverage on its insured."[115] Moreover, they claim the insurer is not faced with a "Hobson's choice" because it is free to decline a defense if it believes the claims asserted against the insured are not covered.[116]

Third, policyholders claim that allowing an insurer to settle claims and then seek recoupment from the policyholder could undermine trust in the relationship between an insurer and its insured, create a conflict in the defense, and risk weakening the insurer's incentive to negotiate a settlement most favorable to its insured.[117]

Fourth, policyholders say a no-recoupment rule makes sense because insurers are "in a superior position to evaluate the risks stemming from a coverage dispute."[118] And, relatedly, the RLLI has posited that a default rule prohibiting recoupment in the absence of an explicit provision in the insurance policy is the most functional, because insurers, as the drafting party, are free to address the issue (at least prospectively) in future contracts.[119]

114. Am. & Foreign Ins. Co. v. Jerry's Sport Ctr., Inc., 2 A.3d 526, 544 n.17 (Pa. 2010); *see also* Gen. Agents Ins. Co. of Am. v. Midwest Sporting Goods Co., 828 N.E.2d 1092, 1102 (Ill. 2005) ("As a matter of public policy, we cannot condone an arrangement where an insurer can unilaterally modify its contract, through a reservation of rights, to allow for reimbursement of defense costs in the event a court later finds that the insurer owes no duty to defend."); Shoshone First Bank v. Pac. Emps. Ins. Co., 2 P.3d 510, 516 (Wyo. 2000) (refusing to permit a unilateral modification of insurance contract via a reservation of rights letter).

115. Nat'l Sur. Corp. v. Immunex Corp., 297 P.3d 688, 694 (Wash. 2013).

116. *Id.* at 695.

117. Excess Underwriters at Lloyd's London v. Frank's Casing Crew & Rental Tools, Inc., 246 S.W.3d 42, 46–47 (Tex. 2008) ("Knowing that the insured will likely bear the ultimate payment obligation could incentivize the insurer to curtail attorney's fees and litigation expenses early in the proceedings by negotiating a quick settlement, with the added benefit of extinguishing any risk of *Stowers* liability.").

118. *Id.* at 51.

119. Bush v. Metro. Life Ins. Co., 656 F.2d 231, 233 (6th Cir. 1981) (involving a recoupment provision in a disability insurance policy).

III. Conclusion

The insurer's right to reimbursement of costs for uncovered claims paid under a reservation of rights is a hotly contested issue. While the case law is split, and legal and public policy rationales have been advanced for each side's position, the better view leaves the existing law in place: when an insurer has agreed to undertake a defense that it did not owe, the insurer can reserve the right to recoup costs advanced for uncovered claims under the law of restitution.

CHAPTER 8
Allocating Defense Costs

Scott M. Seaman, Maida Chinosi, and Madeline Cook

I. Introduction

Over the past four decades, courts have been called upon to determine how to allocate insurance coverage under different types of policies for a wide range of claims. Allocation involves apportioning defense and indemnity costs associated with claims between and among triggered insurance policies and the policyholder (reflecting self-insured periods, insufficient limits, insolvent insurers, and where insurance was unavailable for purchase in the marketplace). The starting point for most courts is the language in the insurance contract. It is important to recognize, however, that policy language varies and policy forms have evolved as allocation decisions have been rendered. In addition, courts sometimes are guided by equitable considerations and the underlying facts in allocating defense costs. Simply stated, there is not a universal rule or a "one size fits all" approach to allocating defense costs.

Although this chapter focuses on allocating defense costs, some courts apply the same allocation method to defense costs that they apply to the allocation of indemnity payments.[1] Other courts have held that allocation of defense costs is distinct from allocation of indemnity payments and should be governed by different principles, most notably the broader scope of the duty to

1. For a comprehensive examination of the allocation of defense and indemnity costs, including the various issues in the allocation mix, see SCOTT M. SEAMAN & JASON R. SCHULZE, ALLOCATION OF LOSSES IN COMPLEX INSURANCE COVERAGE CLAIMS (11th ed. 2023). Proper characterization of costs as defense costs or indemnity payments generally is straightforward. Indemnity payments are those sums paid to settle a claim or satisfy a judgment. Defense costs, in contrast, generally are paid to resist, oppose, or minimize a claim, most notably including defense counsel's fees. In some instances, such as when determining whether environmental remedial investigation and feasibility study costs are indemnity payments or defense costs, analysis of the particular costs at issue and applicable law may be required.

defend (potential for coverage) as compared to the duty to indemnify (actual coverage). In other jurisdictions, the method used for allocating defense costs may depend upon the type of claim and the type of policy at issue[2]—sometimes creating confusion or inconsistency on how the principles are applied. Finally, there are some jurisdictions that either have not yet ruled on these issues or are subject to conflicting decisions creating an unsettled landscape in that jurisdiction as to the method for allocating defense costs.

There is now a body of case law that addresses the ways in which courts have allocated a policyholder's defense costs not only among multiple insurers but also to the policyholder. The result of the evolution in the allocation case law is two general allocation methods: (1) the "all sums" method, also known as the "joint and several liability" or "pick and choose" method; and (2) the pro rata method.

Because policyholders' goal is to maximize their insurance recovery, they generally argue for an "all sums" allocation method so that they may "pick and choose" the insurance policies to which defense costs are allocated. Under the "all sums" approach, each of the triggered insurance policies is liable for the entire loss, up to the applicable policy limit. Utilizing this method, the policyholder can collect the full amount of its claim from any triggered policy it chooses subject to the policy's liability limits and thereby best avoid multiple deductibles or self-insured retentions (SIRs), insolvent insurers, or some policy exclusions.

Where the extent of damages or injuries that takes place in the various periods cannot be determined, insurers generally advocate for an allocation on a pro rata basis, such as "time-on-the-risk," or "time-on-the-risk and by policy limits." Under a pro rata allocation method, the costs are spread proportionately across all triggered policy years. In equitable contribution actions between and among insurers, apportionment by "equal shares" may sometimes be used.

As discussed later, a significant difference between the "all sums" and the pro rata approaches is that courts in "all sums" jurisdictions generally do not allocate any sums to the policyholders except for deductibles and SIRs in the policy year selected. In practice, this means that, under an "all sums" approach, one insurer (or more) may pay more than its pro rata share of the defense costs. In contrast, under a pro rata methodology, the policyholder may also be responsible to bear a share of the defense costs and be included in the allocation for uninsured periods, lost policies, policies with exclusions, and

2. This chapter focuses on general liability policies. Other types of policies, such as directors and officers liability policies or worker's compensation policies address allocation or trigger of coverage with more specificity.

periods of insurer insolvency. Although most states permit equitable contribution among primary insurers for defense costs, a minority of states do not.

This chapter provides a general overview of the issues involving the allocation of defense costs across multiple policy periods. It focuses on long-tail claims—that is, claims involving continuing injury or damage or claims otherwise potentially impacting multiple policy periods—and allocating defense costs among successive policies. Traditional claims—claims that are limited in time—often do not present defense cost allocation issues. Many times, only a single insurer is involved. Although not the focus of this chapter, when concurrent policies are involved, resolution of priority of coverage and sharing of defense costs generally is through application of the "other insurance" clauses in the policies.[3]

II. Trigger of Coverage

Prior to any determination of the allocation method to apply to defense costs, there must be a determination regarding which policies will respond to the loss in the first instance. This aspect of allocation is described as the "trigger of coverage." Whether insurance coverage is triggered refers to the question of "what events, from the point of exposure to the point of manifestation, trigger coverage."[4] Standard commercial general liability (CGL) policies cover "bodily injury" and "property damage" that occurs during the policy period and that are caused by an "occurrence."[5] In a standard CGL policy, this "during the policy period" language is contained in the insuring agreement, but in other policies it may be found in the definitions of "occurrence," "bodily injury," or "property damage." The word "trigger" or phrase "trigger of coverage" is not found in the insurance policy but refers to which insurance policy or policies are required to respond to a covered claim for property damage or bodily injury that may take place in one or more policy periods. The trigger theory does not determine whether there is coverage, but rather which claims fall within particular periods of time and under particular insurance policies.[6]

---

3. *See generally* Seaman & Schulze, *supra* note 1, ch. 5 (Reallocation Among Insurers Through "Other Insurance").

4. Ins. Co. of the State of Pa. v. Equitas Ins. Ltd., 68 F.4th 774, 782 (2d Cir. 2023) (citing Keene Corp. v. Ins. Co. of N. Am., 667 F.2d 1034, 1042 (D.C. Cir. 1981)).

5. Ins. Servs. Off., Inc., Commercial General Liability Coverage Form (CG 00 01 014 13), at 1 (2012).

6. *See generally* Mangerchine v. Reaves, 63 So. 3d 1049, 1054–56 (La. Ct. App. 2011) (explaining trigger of coverage and courts' various approaches); Quincy Mut. Fire Ins. Co. v. Borough of Bellmawr, 799 A.2d 499, 502–03 (N.J. 2002) (explaining trigger of coverage); *see also* Gregory A. Goodman, Note, *Insurance Triggers as Judicial Gatekeepers in Toxic Mold Litigation*, 57 Vand. L. Rev. 241, 259–60 (2004) (referring to trigger of coverage theories as "judicial gatekeepers" because they identify which insurance policies may have to respond to the claims brought).

In the context of long-tail claims, courts generally apply one of four trigger theories: (1) exposure, (2) manifestation, (3) injury-in-fact, or (4) continuous. Because these triggers of coverage principles focus on different timing aspects of a loss, the trigger of coverage that a court applies may have a significant impact on which policies are eligible to have sums allocated to them.

A. Exposure Trigger

Under the exposure trigger, policies on the risk when a person or property is exposed to the harmful act or condition are triggered, regardless of whether the person or property is actually injured at the time of exposure. Accordingly, courts applying an exposure trigger find that the policies on the risk during the time when either the environment was exposed to pollutants (in the context of environmental property claims) or when the person was exposed to harmful substances (in the bodily injury claim context) are triggered.[7] The time relevant for this trigger is not when the injured party discovered their damage or injury, but rather when they were exposed to the damage or injury causing act or condition.[8] Courts adopted the exposure theory to establish the trigger of coverage in cases involving diseases when there is a "lengthy temporal separation between the alleged tortious conduct and the appearance of injury."[9] This

7. *See, e.g.*, Briggs & Stratton Corp. v. Royal Globe Ins. Co., 64 F. Supp. 2d 1346, 1350 (M.D. Ga. 1999) (applying Georgia law); Cole v. Celotex Corp., 599 So. 2d 1058, 1076 (La. 1992) ("[W]e find that the exposure theory is a sound one and adopt that theory as a precept of this court."); Lloyd E. Mitchell, Inc. v. Md. Cas. Co., 595 A.2d 469, 478 (Md. 1991) ("[A]t a minimum, coverage under the policy to provide a defense and indemnification of the insured is triggered upon exposure to the insured's asbestos products during the policy period by a person who suffers bodily injury as a result of that exposure."); A.W. Chesterton Co. v. Mass. Insurers Insolvency Fund, 838 N.E.2d 1237, 1251–52 (Mass. 2005) (concluding that the exposure trigger applied to asbestos bodily injury claims); Radiator Specialty Co. v. Arrowood Indem. Co., 881 S.E.2d 597, 609–10 (N.C. 2022) (adopting the exposure trigger for bodily injury claims resulting from benzene exposure).

8. *See, e.g.*, Hancock Labs., Inc. v. Admiral Ins. Co., 777 F.2d 520, 524 (9th Cir. 1985) (applying California law and ruling that the implantation of a heart valve, not the subsequent discovery of the valve's contamination, was the occurrence that triggered coverage under an exposure theory); Com. Union Ins. Co. v. Sepco Corp., 765 F.2d 1543, 1545–46 (11th Cir. 1985) (applying Alabama law and ruling that undisputed medical evidence supported the exposure theory because asbestos-related injury results from the inhalation of asbestos fibers); Mapco Alaska Petroleum, Inc. v. Cent. Nat'l Ins. Co. of Omaha, 795 F. Supp. 941, 948 (D. Alaska 1991) (predicting that the Alaska Supreme Court would find that "coverage should be triggered by exposure to contaminants rather than by manifestation of the damage"); Chantel Assoc. v. Mount Vernon Fire Ins. Co., 656 A.2d 779, 786 (Md. 1995) (ruling under Maryland law, that in the context of lead paint bodily injury claims, coverage was triggered from the time claimants began residing at the property and being exposed to the lead paint chips, including through *in utero* exposure prior to the expiration of the insurance policy); Kremers-Urban Co. v. Am. Emps. Ins. Co., 351 N.W. 2d 156, 167 (Wis. 1984) (adopting the exposure theory in the context of DES bodily injury claims and holding that ingesting the drug during the policy period triggered coverage).

9. Arceneaux v. Amstar Corp., 200 So. 3d 277, 282 (La. 2016).

trigger theory is based on "the concept that insurers may limit their liability to discrete and finite periods."[10]

B. Manifestation Theory

Under a manifestation theory, policies in effect when damage or injury is discovered, or manifests, are triggered.[11] The practical effect of this theory is to place the bulk of responsibility on the insurers with the most recent policies. This theory focuses on the time when an injury or damage manifests, is discovered, or is reasonably discoverable, and not when the tortious act was committed.[12] Under a manifestation trigger, often only one policy period may be implicated.

---

10. *Id.*

11. *See, e.g.*, Zurich Am. Ins. Co. v. Arch Ins. Co., 20 F.4th 250, 255–57 (5th Cir. 2021) (applying Illinois law) (applying the manifestation trigger based on policy language providing that property damage occurred when damage first began to manifest); Mraz v. Canadian Universal Ins. Co., Ltd., 804 F.2d 1325, 1328 (4th Cir. 1986); Arch Specialty Ins. Co. v. Colony Ins. Co., 590 F. Supp. 3d 395, 417–19 (D. Mass. 2022) (applying a manifestation trigger to construction defect claims); Century Sur. Co. v. S & R Dev. Inc., 483 F. Supp. 3d 400, 403–05 (S.D. Miss. 2020) (applying Mississippi law); Chi. Ins. Co. v. City of Council Bluffs, Iowa, 859 F. Supp. 2d 967, 984–84 (S.D. Iowa 2012) (applying Iowa law), *aff'd in part, rev'd in part on other grounds*, 713 F.3d 963 (8th Cir. 2013); Cincinnati Ins. Co. v. Amerisure Ins. Co., No. 11-0271-WS-M, 2012 WL 4033724, at *9 (S.D. Ala. Sept. 12, 2012) (applying Alabama law); Travelers Cas. & Sur. Co. v. Providence Wash. Ins. Co., 809 F. Supp. 2d 7, 10 (D.R.I. 2011), *rev'd and vacated*, 685 F.3d 22 (1st Cir. 2012) (applying Rhode Island law); Langan Eng'g & Envtl. Servs., Inc. v. Greenwich Ins. Co., No. 07-2983 (JAG), 2008 WL 5146538, at *9 (D.N.J. Dec. 8, 2008), as amended, (Dec. 9, 2008) (internal citations omitted) (applying New Jersey law) (adopting the manifestation trigger in the context of a property damage claim and refusing to extend the continuous trigger theory "beyond its application to asbestos, toxic tort, environmental spills, and related cases"); Mathews Heating & Air Conditioning LLC v. Liberty Mut. Ins. Co., 384 F. Supp. 2d 988, 994 (N.D. Tex. 2004) (applying Texas law); Pa. Nat'l Mut. Cas. Ins. Co. v. St. John, 106 A.3d 1, 21 (Pa. 2014) (applying the manifestation trigger to construction defect claims); Fletcher v. Pa. Prop. & Cas. Ins. Guar. Ass'n, 27 A.3d 299, 304 (Pa. Commw. Ct. 2011) (applying the manifestation trigger to a medical malpractice claim).

12. *See, e.g.*, Am. Home Assur. Co. v. Libbey-Owens-Ford Co., 786 F.2d 22, 30 (1st Cir. 1986) (applying Massachusetts law) (adopting manifestation trigger and concluding that an occurrence takes place when "a reasonable person would be aware that a defect exists that may give rise to a cause of action"); Eagle-Picher Indus., Inc. v. Liberty Mut. Ins. Co, 682 F.2d 12, 15 (1st Cir. 1982) (applying Ohio law) (holding that coverage is triggered when disease becomes reasonably apparent of medical diagnosis); CPC Int'l v. Northbrook Excess & Surplus Ins. Co., 668 A.2d 647, 648 (R.I. 1995) (concluding that "coverage under a general liability policy is triggered by an occurrence that takes place when property damage, which includes property loss, manifests itself or is discovered or in the exercise of reasonable diligence is discoverable"); Tacker v. Am. Fam. Mut. Ins. Co., 530 N.W.2d 674, 676 (Iowa 1995) (concluding that under occurrence-based policies, coverage is triggered when a claimant sustains damages within the contract period and not when the act or omissions causing damage takes place); Mann v. Tim Clark Constr., LLC, 273 So. 3d 397, 402 (La. Ct. App. 2019) (holding that property damage occurred under general liability policy when "it became manifest, regardless of when the act which it resulted occurred"); Allstate Ins. Co. v. Hunter, 242 S.W.3d 137, 142 (Tex. App. 2007) (concluding that the policy language supported the parties' agreement that the manifestation trigger applied); Pa. Nat'l Mut. Cas. Ins. Co. v. St. John, 106 A.3d 1 (Pa. 2014) (adopting the manifestation trigger in a construction defect property damage case and holding that coverage was triggered under the policy in effect when the property damage became reasonably apparent).

C. Injury-in-Fact

Courts applying an injury-in-fact trigger require the policyholder to demonstrate actual damage or injury during the policy period to be entitled to coverage.[13] Some jurisdictions conclude that the general liability policy language requires an injury-in-fact trigger.[14] Here, coverage is triggered under the policies in effect when the actual damage or injury occurs, regardless of when the person or property was exposed to the harmful act or condition or whether the harm manifests itself.[15]

13. *See, e.g.*, Stonewall Ins. Co. v. Asbestos Claims Mgmt. Corp., 73 F.3d 1178, 1195 (2d Cir. 1995), *modified on other grounds*, 85 F.3d 49 (2d Cir. 1996) (applying New York law, finding that injury-in-fact applied to both asbestos property damage and bodily injury claims, and holding that property damage occurred when asbestos-containing materials were installed); Trizec Props., Inc. v. Biltmore Constr. Co., 767 F.2d 810, 813 (11th Cir. 1985) (applying Florida law and holding that the actual injury rule applies); Aetna Cas. & Sur. Co. v. Abbott Labs, Inc., 636 F. Supp. 546, 549–50 (D. Conn. 1986) (finding that that coverage for DES bodily injury claims are triggered upon "injury-in-fact" during the policy period); U.S. Fid. & Guar. Co. v. Warick Dev. Co., Inc. 446 So. 2d 1021, 1024 (Ala.1984) (applying injury-in-fact and holding that the time the property damage was actually damaged was the triggering event and not the time when the work was performed); PSI Energy, Inc. v. Home Ins. Co., 801 N.E.2d 705, 733 (Ind. Ct. App. 2004) ("We agree with the Insurers that our courts are required to apply the 'injury-in-fact' trigger of coverage approach."); Don's Bldg. Supply, Inc. v. OneBeacon Ins. Co., 267 S.W.3d 20, 25 (Tex. 2008) (adopting the injury-in-fact approach in the context of property damage claims); Transcon. Ins. Co. v. Wash. Pub. Util. Dist. Util. Sys., 760 P.2d 337, 345 (Wash. 1988) ("Washington case law hold[s] that the time of an occurrence for insurance coverage purposes is determined by when damages or injuries took place.").

14. *See, e.g.*, Am. Home Prods. Corp. v. Liberty Mut. Ins. Co., 748 F.2d 760, 764 (2d Cir. 1984) (applying New York law) (holding that "the trigger-of-coverage clause unambiguously provides for coverage based upon the occurrence during the policy period of an injury in fact"); Cessna Aircraft Co. v. Hartford Accident & Indem. Co., 900 F. Supp. 1489, 1503 (D. Kan. 1995) ("[A]pplication of the 'injury-in-fact' trigger is more consistent with the language of the . . . policies, especially where, as here, the contamination is alleged to have occurred in particular policy periods and to have continued through many policy periods."); Gary G. Day Constr. Co., Inc. v. Clarendon Am. Ins. Co., 459 F. Supp. 2d 1039, 1046 (D. Nev. 2006) (noting the insurance policy specifically provided that the injury-in-fact trigger applied because it required "both the 'property damage' and an 'occurrence' resulting in property damage to occur within the Policy period"); Sentinel Ins. Co. v. First Ins. Co. of Haw., Ltd., 875 P.2d 894, 915 (Haw. 1994) (holding that injury-in-fact trigger was compelled by the plain language of the policies); Traveler's Ins. Co. v. Eljer Mfg., Inc., 757 N.E.2d 481, 502–03 (Ill. 2001) (holding, under CGL policies covering "physical injury to tangible property," that claims the insured manufactured defective plumbing system were covered if buildings suffered water damage due to leaks during the policy period, regardless of when the plumbing systems were installed, because the policies stated "that the insurable event which gives rise to the insurers' obligation to provide coverage is the physical damage to tangible property"); Gelman Sci., Inc. v. Fid. & Cas. Co. of N.Y., 572 N.W.2d 617, 623 (Mich. 1998), *overruled on other grounds by* Wilkie v. Auto-Owners Ins. Co., 664 N.W.2d 776, 786 (Mich. 2003) ("[A]ccording to the policies' explicit terms, actual injury must occur during the time the policy is in effect in order to be indemnifiable, i.e., the policies dictate an injury-in-fact approach. The manifestation trigger simply is not supported by the policy language.").

15. *See, e.g.*, Transcon. Ins. Co. v. W.G. Samuels Co., 370 F.3d 755, 758 (8th Cir. 2004) ("The Kansas Supreme Court has adopted an injury-in-fact rule for purposes of determining when coverage is triggered under a CGL policy. Under this rule, insurance coverage is triggered on the date when an actual injury and damage occurs, even if the injury has not yet been discovered or become manifest."); *In re* Silicone Breast Implant Ins. Coverage Litig., 667 N.W.2d 405, 415–17 (Minn. 2003) (finding that the injury occurred when the plaintiff received the silicone breast implants and not when symptoms manifested themselves); Kief Farmers Coop. Elevator Co. v. Farmland Mut. Ins. Co., 534

D. Continuous Trigger

The continuous trigger theory of liability requires courts to allocate costs among the policies in effect from the date of initial exposure to the harmful act or condition through the date of first manifestation.[16] As a result, under the continuous trigger theory—as with exposure or injury-in-fact triggers—multiple policies may be triggered.[17] The continuous trigger theory is commonly applied to claims of continuous or progressively deteriorating damage or injury made under CGL policies.[18] Notably, application of the continuous theory across multiple policy periods implicates distinct allocation issues because under certain circumstances an insurer may be liable "even though that insurer provided coverage during only a short part of the period of exposure to the risk that later evolved into harm."[19]

N.W.2d 28, 35–36 (N.D. 1995) (rejecting the manifestation rule in a first-party insurance case and holding that "a real but undiscovered loss or damage, proved in retrospect to have commenced during the policy period, triggers coverage, irrespective of the time the loss or damage became manifest").

16. *See, e.g.*, Flintkote Co. v. Gen. Accident Assur. Co. of Canada, 480 F. Supp. 2d 1167, 1173–74 (N.D. Cal. 2007) (applying California law); Young Women's Christian Ass'n of the Nat'l Cap. Area, Inc. v. Allstate Ins. Co. of Canada, 275 F.3d 1145, 1150 (D.C. Cir. 2002) (applying continuous trigger "where the damage can be characterized as being continuous or progressive"); Harleysville Mut. Ins. Co. v. Hartford Cas. Ins. Co., 90 F. Supp. 3d 526, 548 (E.D.N.C. 2015) (applying North Carolina law); Travelers Cas. & Sur. Co. of Am. v. Netherlands Ins. Co., 95 A.3d 1031, 1052–53 (Conn. 2014) (applying the continuous trigger to claims involving water intrusion); R.T. Vanderbilt Co., Inc. v. Hartford Accident & Indem. Co., 156 A.3d 539, 571 (Conn. App. Ct. 2017) (adopting a continuous trigger theory as a matter of law for asbestos bodily injury cases); Riley v. United Servs. Auto. Ass'n, 871 A.2d 599, 609 (Md. Ct. Spec. App. 2005), *aff'd*, 899 A.2d 819 (Md. 2006) (finding that continuous injury, not solely manifestation, was the appropriate trigger in lead paint poisoning cases); Spaulding Composites Co. v. Aetna Cas. & Sur. Co., 819 A.2d 410, 420–22 (N.J. 2003) (declining to enforce a noncumulation clause); Owens-Illinois, Inc. v. United Ins. Co., 650 A.2d 974, 995 (N.J. 1994) (adopting the continuous trigger in the context of asbestos-related injury or damage); Air Master & Cooling, Inc. v. Selective Ins. Co. of Am., 171 A.3d 214, 221 (N.J. Super. Ct. App. Div. 2017) (applying continuous trigger to progressive water infiltration); Aetna Cas. & Sur. Co. v. Ply Gem Indus., Inc., 778 A.2d 1132, 1146 (N.J. Super. Ct. App. Div. 2001) (applying the continuous trigger theory to claims caused by incorporation of defective fire retardant plywood into roofing systems); *In re* Ambassador Ins. Co., 275 A.3d 122, 127 (Vt. 2022) (applying a continuous trigger theory to asbestos bodily injury claims).

17. Some courts in Illinois have applied a "triple trigger," finding coverage triggered when the claimant suffered "bodily injury," "sickness," or "disease" during the policy period. *See, e.g.*, Zurich Ins. Co. v. Raymark Indus., Inc., 514 N.E.2d 150, 159 (Ill. 1987).

18. Montrose Chem. Corp. v. Admiral Ins. Co., 913 P.2d 878, 880 (Cal. 1995); *see, e.g.*, Keene Corp. v. Ins. Co. of N. Am., 667 F.2d 1034, 1045–46 (D.C. Cir. 1981) (holding that because asbestos-related disease develops slowly, the date of occurrence should be a continuous period from exposure to manifestation); Harleysville Mut. Ins. Co. v. Sussex Cnty., Del., 831 F. Supp. 1111, 1124 (D. Del. 1993) (applying Delaware law and finding that the slow leaching of pollutants from a landfill to adjacent property was a progressive injury requiring the use of the continuous trigger theory); Spaulding Composites Co. v. Aetna Cas. & Sur. Co., 819 A.2d 410, 415 (N.J. 2003); Arrow Exterminators, Inc. v. Zurich Am. Ins. Co., 136 F. Supp. 2d 1340, 1349 (N.D. Ga. 2001) (concluding that where a policy defines an "occurrence" as including "continuous or repeated exposure," the appropriate trigger is continuous).

19. Ins. Co. of the State of Pa. v. Equitas Ins. Ltd., 68 F.4th 774, 782 (2d Cir. 2023).

E. Summary

Insurance law varies from state to state and, therefore, the trigger theories courts will apply may also vary from state to state. Most jurisdictions apply an injury-in-fact trigger or continuous trigger. The greatest difference between the continuous and injury-in-fact triggers is that the injury-in-fact trigger requires the policyholder to prove discrete injury or damage during the effective periods of the insurance contract. What that exactly that proof is, and who carries the burden of proof, varies by jurisdiction.[20] Depending on the facts, the same policies may be triggered under different trigger theories. A smaller number of jurisdictions apply a manifestation trigger, particularly in the context of property damage claims. It is important to understand the trigger theory adopted by the court or advanced by the parties because the trigger of coverage will define the policies and periods of time under which losses may be allocated. Logic and fairness appear to dictate consistency between the trigger theory and allocation method so, for example, a loss should not be viewed expansively to implicate multiple policies for purposes of applying a continuous or injury-in-fact trigger and then artificially truncated into a single policy period under an "all sums" allocation approach. In some jurisdictions applying the "all sums" approach, however, the opposite actually takes place. In those jurisdictions, after adopting an expansive injury-in-fact or continuous trigger, courts truncate the allocation to the policies to a single year.

III. Differing Jurisdictional Approaches to Allocation of Defense Costs

With the universe of policy periods potentially available to respond, the proper allocation methodology must be decided. The approach applicable to how defense costs will be allocated varies from state to state. As an initial matter, we examine whether there is symmetry in the approach a given state takes in allocating defense and indemnity costs.

---

20. *See, e.g.*, D.R. Sherry Constr., Ltd. v. Am. Fam. Mut. Ins. Co., 316 S.W.3d 899, 905–06 (Mo. 2010) (ruling that the contractor carried its burden of proving that unanticipated soil conditions caused property damage and that actual property damage occurred during the policy period); Cont'l Cas. Co. v. Emps. Ins. Co. of Wausau, 871 N.Y.S.2d 48, 54 (App. Div. 2008) (ruling that the burden was on the claimants to prove injury during operations and not on the insurer to establish that the injury occurred after operations were completed).

A. Some Courts Apply Different Allocation Methods for Defense Costs and Indemnity Payments

Some courts have drawn a distinction between the allocation of indemnity payments and the allocation of defense costs.[21] These courts tend to distinguish between the scope of the duty to defend and the duty to indemnify.

In *Pella Corp. v. Liberty Mutual Insurance Co.*,[22] the U.S. District Court for the Southern District of Iowa considered this divergence. Pella Corporation (Pella), a window manufacturer, was faced with hundreds of claims arising from water damage caused by alleged defects in its windows.[23] Based on these allegations, Pella made a claim to its insurer, Liberty Mutual Insurance Co., which issued eight CGL policies with aggregate self-insured retentions covering an eight-year period.[24] The parties filed a variety of motions for summary judgment, including motions to determine the policy periods triggered and the method of allocation for defense costs and indemnity payments.[25] With respect to the allocation of defense costs and indemnity payments, the court concluded different approaches applied based on the difference between the insurers' duties to defend and indemnify under the policies.[26]

The *Pella* court held that, although indemnity payments would be allocated across all triggered policy periods on a pro rata basis,[27] the defense costs would be allocated on an "all sums" basis.[28] In reaching its decision, the court found that there was no language in the policies that limited coverage of defense costs to those incurred during the policy period. The court noted that although the "CGL Policies treat defense costs and indemnity payments identically in many ways—in particular, they essentially work in tandem to erode the SIR applying for a given occurrence—they are not treated identically in this one respect

21. *See* Narragansett Elec. Co. v. Am. Home Assur. Co., 999 F. Supp. 2d 511, 518–24 (S.D.N.Y. 2014) (predicting that the Massachusetts Supreme Judicial Court would allocate defense costs jointly and severally despite the fact that the pro rata method would apply to indemnity payments); Cincinnati Ins. Co. v. Crossman Cmtys. of N.C. Inc., No. 4-09-1379, 2013 WL 1283381, at *6 (D.S.C. Mar. 27, 2013) (explaining that although South Carolina recognizes pro rata allocation of indemnity costs, there is no state authority supporting such allocation of defense costs); Peerless Ins. v. Vt. Mut. Ins. Co., 849 A.2d 100, 103 (N.H. 2004); Consol. Edison Co. of N.Y., Inc. v. Allstate Ins. Co., 774 N.E.2d 687, 694–95 (N.Y. 2002) (holding that indemnity should be allocated pro rata despite the court allowing joint and several allocation of defense costs); Cont'l Cas. Co. v. Rapid-Am. Corp., 609 N.E.2d 506, 509–10 (N.Y. 1993) (finding that the duty to defend is broader than the duty to indemnify in allowing joint and several liability for defense costs).

22. 244 F. Supp. 3d 931 (S.D. Iowa 2017).

23. *Id.* at 935.

24. *Id.* at 937–38.

25. *Id.* at 935.

26. *Id.* at 948–50.

27. *Id.* at 948–49.

28. *Id.* at 949–50.

most relevant to allocation."[29] Further, the *Pella* court noted that "the duty to defend is broader than the duty to indemnify and generally covers an insured's whole defense for a given claim."[30] Given the policy language and the principles governing the duty to defend versus the duty to indemnify, the court applied an "all sums" approach to allocating defense costs among the insurers.

In *Crosby Valve LLC v. OneBeacon America Insurance Co.*,[31] a Massachusetts business court addressed whether defense costs in a long-tail claim involving asbestos bodily injuries were subject to the same pro rata allocation methodology the Massachusetts Supreme Judicial Court (SJC) adopted to govern successively triggered insurers' indemnity obligations in *Boston Gas Co. v. Century Indemnity Co.*[32] The *Crosby Valve* court declined to follow *Boston Gas* with respect to allocation of defense costs, and found that the SJC's holding in that case was limited to insurers' *indemnity* obligations.[33]

Notably with respect to the allocation of defense costs, the *Crosby Valve* court did not rely on the insurance policy language. Rather, the court switched its focus to judicial decisions outside the long-tail context, which hold that "Massachusetts follows the 'in for one, in for all' rule, under which an insurer that has a duty to defend its insured on just one claim must provide a complete defense to the entire action."[34] On that basis, the court determined "if multiple CGL policies give rise to a duty to provide a complete defense to the entire action, then the insurer that issued each policy must be jointly and severally liable to pay for the full cost of the defense, subject to any policy limits (such as . . . provisions . . . that terminate defense obligations if any when the maximum indemnity limit has been paid out)."[35]

As *Pella* and *Crosby Valve* illustrate, it is important to recognize that the methods courts use to allocate defense costs and indemnity payments vary by jurisdiction and, in any given jurisdiction, courts may apply different methods to allocate defense costs and indemnity payments.

29. *Id.* at 949.
30. *Id.*
31. No. 1284CV02705-BLS2, 2022 WL 16855608, at *1 (Mass. Super. Ct. Feb. 22, 2022), *vacated by, in part, superseded by, on different grounds by* Crosby Valve, LLC v. OneBeacon Am. Ins. Co., No. 1284CV02705-BLS2, 2022 WL 16855611, at *1 (Mass. Super. Ct. July 19, 2022).
32. 910 N.E.2d 290, 315 (Mass. 2009).
33. *Crosby Valve*, 2022 WL 16855608, at *5–6.
34. *Id.* at *5.
35. *Id.*

B. Many Courts Apply the Same Allocation Methods to Defense Costs and Indemnity Payments

Many jurisdictions that follow a pro rata method for allocating indemnity payments apply the same approach for allocating defense costs.[36] Recently, the North Carolina Supreme Court, in a case of first impression under North Carolina law, decided that a pro rata by time-on-the-risk allocation applies to both defense costs and indemnity payments in long-tail personal injury claims. In *Radiator Specialty Co. v. Arrowood Indem. Co.*,[37] the North Carolina high court reversed a lower court decision allowing the policyholder to take "all sums" from any insurer of its choosing, and instead spread the loss over periods of years or decades.[38] In reaching its decision, the court explained that "[a]s the insurers argue, the modern trend is to apply pro rata allocation when limiting language like 'during the policy period' exists, even when the policy contains a reference to paying 'all sums' arising out of certain liabilities."[39] The court then concluded that "using Fireman's Fund's policies as an example, the insurer agreed to pay for all of the sums (1) arising from bodily injuries; (2) resulting from occurrences; and (3) that took place during the policy periods."[40] It found that "the language 'during the policy period' therefore cabins the phrase 'all

36. *See, e.g.*, Cont'l Cas. Co. v. Indian Head Indus., 666 F. App'x 456, 467 (6th Cir. 2016) (applying Michigan law); Pa. Nat'l Mut. Cas. Ins. Co. v. Roberts, 668 F.3d 106, 119 (4th Cir. 2012) (applying pro rata time-on-the-risk allocation to both defense and indemnity in lead poisoning bodily injury claims under Maryland law); Ins. Co. of N. Am. v. Forty-Eight Insulations, Inc., 633 F.2d 1212, 1225 (6th Cir. 1980), *clarified*, 657 F.2d 814 (6th Cir. 1981) (applying Illinois and New Jersey law and holding that "indemnity costs can be allocated by the number of years [of exposure, and] . . . [t]here is no reason why this same theory should not apply to defense costs"); Liberty Mut. Fire Ins. Co. v. Harper Indus., No. 5:05-cv-243-R, 2007 WL 528523, at *14 (W.D. Ky. Feb. 12, 2007) (applying Kentucky law to a property damage claim and holding that defense costs, like indemnity payments, are to be allocated among multiple insurers pro rata); St. Paul Mercury Ins. Co. v. Mountain W. Farm Bureau Mut. Ins. Co., 148 Cal. Rptr. 3d 625, 640–41 (Ct. App. 2012) (ruling in connection with a construction defect property damage claim that defense and indemnity to be allocated pro rata by time-on-the-risk); R.T. Vanderbilt Co. Inc. v. Hartford Accident & Indem. Co., 156 A.3d 539, 563 (Conn. App. Ct. 2017) (re-affirming the application of the pro rata time-on-the-risk allocation method for defense and indemnity costs associated with long latency personal injury claims); Shook v. Fletcher Asbestos Settlement Tr. v. Safety Nat'l Cas. Corp., No. 04C-02-087 MMJ, 2005 WL 2436193, at *24 (Del. Super. Ct. 2005) (applying Alabama law and determining that defense and indemnity costs should be allocated pro rata by limits in asbestos bodily injury cases); Arceneaux v. Amstar Corp., 200 So. 3d 277, 289 (La. 2016) (reasoning that applying a pro rata allocation to both defense and indemnity costs was more consistent with the policy language and reflected the reasonable expectations of the insurer and the policyholder); Cont'l Ins. Co. v. Honeywell Int'l, Inc., 188 A.3d 297, 307 (N.J. 2018); Potomac Ins. Co. of Ill. v. Pa. Mfrs. Ass'n Ins. Co., 73 A.3d 465, 474–75 (N.J. 2013) (holding that the "allocation of defense costs comports with *Owens-Illinois* and its progeny"); Towns v. N. Sec. Ins. Co., 964 A.2d 1150, 1167 (Vt. 2008) (allocating defense and indemnity costs based on time on the risk).

37. 881 S.E.2d 597 (N.C. 2022).

38. *Id.* at 620–21.

39. *Id.* at 615.

40. *Id.*

sums' to a finite period of time."[41] Based on its review of the policy language, the court decided that "the insurers did not agree to cover all sums arising out of benzene exposure without regard to the policy periods during which incidents of exposure took place. Instead, '[c]onsistent with the policy language limiting coverage to that which occurs "during the policy period," the timing of the [occurrence/injury] dictates . . . the portion of damages for which each policy is responsible.'"[42]

A smaller number of jurisdictions that have adopted the "all sums" allocation for indemnity payments have also adopted the same allocation for defense costs.[43] In some instances, the courts come to this conclusion based on the policy language. For example, some courts focus on the policy language that provides for defense of the insured for "all sums" up to the policy limit.[44] Other courts look at whether the policy contains a noncumulation clause.[45]

IV. Allocation Methodologies

Like the "trigger of coverage" analysis, jurisdictions take differing approaches in how to allocate liability payments and which allocation method to apply to defense costs. There are two main approaches: (1) the "all sums," also known as the "joint and several" or "pick-and-choose" approach and (2) a pro rata approach.

Policyholders generally advocate for an "all sums" approach to maximize their recovery under the policies and limit their exposure to share in the defense costs and liability loss. In contrast, insurers generally advocate for a pro rata

41. *Id.*

42. *Id.* (citations omitted).

43. *See, e.g.*, Keene Corp. v. Ins. Co. of Am., 667 F.2d 1034, 1050–51 (D.C. Cir. 1981) (determining that defense and indemnity costs are to be allocated jointly and severally in asbestos bodily injury claims); Zurich Ins. Co. v. Raymark Indus. Inc., 514 N.E. 2d 150, 165 (Ill. 1987) (applying "all sums" allocation to defense and indemnity costs related to asbestos bodily injury claims); J.H. France Refractories Co. v. Allstate Ins. Co., 626 A.2d 502, 507 (Pa. 1993) (holding that each insurer is jointly and severally liable for the full amount of defense costs and indemnity costs, subject only to its limit of liability).

44. *See, e.g.*, Monsanto Co. v. C.E. Heath Comp. & Liab. Ins. Co., 652 A.2d 30, 34–35 (Del. 1994) (finding that policy language that provides that the insurer will indemnify "the Assured" for all sums defines the insurer's duty under its policies as the obligation to pay "all sums" for which Monsanto becomes liable—not a proportionate share); Nooter Corp. v. Allianz Underwriters Ins. Co., 536 S.W.3d 251, 271–72 (Mo. Ct. App. 2017) (concluding that "all sums" language is not limited by the "during the policy" language); Plastics Eng'g Co. v. Liberty Mut. Ins. Co., 759 N.W.2d 613, 627 (Wis. 2009).

45. *See, e.g.*, Danaher Corp. v. Travelers Indem. Co., 414 F. Supp. 3d 436, 452 (S.D.N.Y. 2019) (applying joint and several allocation to defense costs for policies that contain noncumulation provisions); Liberty Mut. Ins. Co. v. Fairbanks Co., 170 F. Supp. 3d 634, 645–46 (S.D.N.Y. 2016), *rev'd in part on reconsideration*, 2016 WL 4203543, at *1 (S.D.N.Y. 2016) (applying New York and Georgia law); *In re* Viking Pump Inc, 52 N.E.3d 1144, 1156 (N.Y. 2016) (holding that "all sums" allocation is appropriate in policies containing noncumulation and noncumulation/prior insurance provisions).

allocation to minimize their exposure under their respective policy period(s) and to spread the loss across multiple policies and insurers. A major distinction between the "joint and several liability" fiction[46] and the pro rata approaches is that courts adhering to the former method generally are averse to allocating sums to the policyholder other than self-insured retentions or deductibles in the year or years selected by the insured.[47] Allocation to triggered periods in which there is no insurance or insufficient limits is the natural and appropriate consequence of a pro rata approach.

Fundamentally, the pro rata approach comports with the insurance contract language. Most general liability policies expressly provide coverage only for injuries or damages that take place "during the policy period." There also are many equitable and jurisprudential reasons supporting a pro rata allocation, including that the pro rata approach is consistent with the continuous trigger and the injury-in-fact trigger, the unfairness of burdening insurers with damages outside the policy period, unjust enrichment to policyholders in receiving more coverage than the policy provides, and avoidance of the inefficiencies to insurers and courts associated with reallocation of defense costs through contribution claims.[48]

The policyholders that advocate that the courts adopt an "all sums" approach to allocation generally view the "all sums" language in isolation. Properly viewed, however, the express "during the policy period" requirement applies with full force to the issue of allocation as well as to the issue of trigger and evinces a clear intent to not cover damages happening before a policy incepts or after a policy period ends. The "all sums" language was removed from the CGL form decades ago and replaced with "those sums," in response to the inappropriate treatment of the language afforded by court's adopting an "all sums" allocation approach.[49]

---

46. "Joint and several liability" may be defined as "[l]iability that may be apportioned either among two or more parties or to only one or a few select members of the group, *at the adversary's discretion*." *Joint and Several Liability*, BLACK'S LAW DICTIONARY (11th ed. 2019) (emphasis added). But while an insurer's duty to defend may be a joint and several obligation, an insurer's right to equitable contribution is not. *See* Travelers Indem. Co. of Am. v. AAA Waterproofing, Inc., No. 10-CV-02826-WJM-KMT, 2014 WL 201726, at *3 n.3 (D. Colo. Jan. 17, 2014) (distinguishing an insurer's contractual duty to defend, which is a joint and several legal obligation, from its noncontractual obligation to contribute its share of an insured's defense costs, which is a pro rata equitable obligation, and explaining that an insurer's right to seek equitable contribution therefore does not allow an insurer to "shift[] completely" its monetary contribution "onto any other co-insurer, as that would inevitably result in a nearly interminable string of actions for equitable contribution").

47. *See generally* SEAMAN & SCHULZE, *supra* note 1, ch. 4 (Allocation Methodologies); *see, e.g.*, Keene Corp. v. Ins. Co. of N. Am., 667 F.2d 1034, 1047–48 (D.C. Cir. 1981) (applying D.C. law, the court adopted the joint and several liability approach, in part on the basis of the "all sums" language and in part to avoid an allocation of liability to the insured).

48. *See generally* SEAMAN & SCHULZE, *supra* note 1, ch. 4 (Allocation Methodologies).

49. *Id.*; *see also* Thomson Inc. v. Ins. Co. of N. Am., 11 N.E.3d 982, 1020–21 (Ind. Ct. App. 2014) (affirming the trial court's holding that a pro rata allocation method, rather than "all sums," applied

As in other areas of insurance law, the method of allocating defense costs is not settled in many jurisdictions. In those jurisdictions that have addressed the issue, there sometimes is inconsistency within the jurisdiction on how the methods are applied depending upon the injury or damage at issue in the underlying action. For example, one court may apply a pro rata method of allocation for bodily injury claims and the same court may adopt an "all sums" approach to an environmental property damage claim.[50] Alternatively, as already discussed, some courts may apply an "all sums" method to the allocation of defense costs and pro rata method to indemnity payments.[51] Because of the differing approaches, it is important to review the controlling case law and determine the particular allocation method that may apply to your facts.[52]

A. Pro Rata Allocation: The Majority Rule for Allocation of Defense Costs

A pro rata allocation is the preferred method of insurers apportioning defense costs and indemnity payments over multiple policy periods. An early leading decision advancing pro rata allocation is *Insurance Co. of North America v. Forty-Eight Insulations, Inc.*[53] Under this approach, "[e]ach insurer is liable for its pro rata share. The insurer's liability is not 'joint and several,' it is 'individual and proportionate.'"[54] The Sixth Circuit allocated the costs of defense among the triggered contracts based on the number of years of exposure to the insured's asbestos-containing products. Thus, if an insurer provided coverage during three of a total of nine years of exposure, that insurer would be responsible for one-third of the total defense costs, subject to its limits of liability.[55]

Unlike courts that adhere to the "all sums" approach to allocation, *Forty-Eight Insulations* did not exclude the policyholder's participation in the allocation. The district court determined that the policyholder was responsible for

to allocating liability, given that the subject policy language was "those sums" as opposed to "all sums" and expressly limited coverage for damages during the policy period).

50. *See, e.g.*, New England Insulation Co., Inc. v. Liberty Mut. Ins. Co., 988 N.E.2d 450, 454–55 (Mass. App. Ct. 2013) (adopting pro rata time on the risk allocation for defense costs and indemnity payments for asbestos bodily injury claims); Rubenstein v. Royal Ins. Co. of Am., 694 N.E.2d 381, 388 (Mass. App. Ct. 1998) (adopting joint and several liability to both defense costs and indemnity payments for environmental property damage claims).

51. *See, e.g.*, Narragansett Elec. Co. v. Am. Home Assur. Co., 999 F. Supp. 2d 511, 518–19 (S.D.N.Y. 2014) (predicting that Massachusetts Supreme Judicial Court would allocate defense costs jointly and severally despite the fact that the pro rata method would apply to indemnity payments); Consol. Edison Co. of N.Y., Inc. v. Allstate Ins. Co., 774 N.E.2d 687, 694–95 (N.Y. 2002) (holding that indemnity should be allocated pro rata despite the court allowing for joint and several allocation of defense costs).

52. For 50-state surveys of trigger of coverage and allocation decisions, see SEAMAN & SCHULZE, *supra* note 1, apps. A & C.

53. 633 F.2d 1212 (6th Cir. 1980), *clarified on reh'g*, 657 F.2d 814 (6th Cir. 1981).

54. *Id.* at 1225.

55. *Id.*

its pro rata share of the costs of defense and indemnification based upon the number of years of exposure it was uninsured.[56] On appeal, the policyholder challenged the district court's determination only with respect to the allocation of defense costs. The Sixth Circuit upheld the district court's ruling, finding that the costs of defense could be "readily apportioned." As stated by the Sixth Circuit:

> An insurer contracts to pay the entire cost of defending a claim which has arisen within the policy period. The insurer has not contracted to pay defense costs for occurrences which took place outside the policy period. Where the distinction can be readily made, the insured must pay its fair share for the defense of the non-covered risk.[57]

The pro rata approach is the majority rule for the allocation of defense costs.[58] Within this majority rule, are a couple of approaches used in allocation disputes involving policyholders and insurers. The most common approach utilized by courts is pro rata based on "time-on-the-risk." A limited number of states pro rate defense costs based on "time-on-the-risk" and policy limits. These approaches are explained in further detail later in the chapter. Some courts have utilized the "equal shares" method wherein there is an equal

---

56. *Id.* at 1224.

57. *Id.* at 1224–25.

58. *See, e.g., In re* Wallace & Gale Co., 385 F.3d 820, 835–36 (4th Cir. 2004) (applying Maryland law); Stonewall Ins. Co. v. Asbestos Claims Mgmt. Corp., 73 F.3d 1178, 1194 (2d Cir. 1995), *opinion modified on denial of reh'g*, 85 F.3d 49 (2d Cir. 1996) (applying Texas and New York law); Gulf Chem. & Metallurgical Corp. v. Associated Metals & Mins. Corp., 1 F.3d 365, 372 (5th Cir. 1993) (applying Texas law and holding that defense costs are to be apportioned on a pro rata basis); Com. Union Ins. Co. v. Sepco Corp., 918 F.2d 920, 924 (11th Cir. 1990) (applying Alabama law and allocating defense costs for asbestos bodily injury claims pro rata by time-on-the risk); Ins. Co. of N. Am. v. Forty-Eight Insulations Inc., 633 F.2d 1212, 1224 (6th Cir. 1980) (adopting the pro rata method); Fireman's Fund Ins. Cos. v. Ex-Cell-O Corp., 662 F. Supp. 71, 76 (E.D. Mich. 1987); Uniroyal, Inc. v. Home Ins. Co., 707 F. Supp. 1368, 1394 (E.D.N.Y. 1988); Stonewall Ins. Co. v. City of Palos Verdes Estates, 54 Cal. Rptr. 2d 176, 207 (Ct. App. 1996); Pub. Serv. Co. of Colo. v. Wallis & Cos., 986 P.2d 924, 940–41 (Colo. 1999); Sec. Ins. Co. of Hartford v. Lumbermens Mut. Cas. Co., 826 A.2d 107, 110 (Conn. 2003); Maremont Corp. v. Cont'l Cas. Co., 760 N.E.2d 550, 556 (Ill. App. Ct. 2001); Outboard Marine Corp. v. Liberty Mut. Ins. Co., 670 N.E.2d 740, 750 (Ill. App. Ct. 1996); Mayor & City Council of Balt. v. Utica Mut. Ins. Co., 802 A.2d 1070 (Md. Ct. Spec. App. 2002); Bos. Gas Co. v. Century Indem. Co., 910 N.E.2d 290, 311 (Mass. 2009); Arco Indus. Corp. v. Am. Motorists Ins. Co., 594 N.W.2d 61, 69 (Mich. Ct. App. 1998); Wooddale Builders, Inc. v. Md. Cas. Co., 722 N.W.2d 283, 297 (Minn. 2006); Muralo Co. v. Emps. Ins. of Wausau, 759 A.2d 348, 354–55 (N.J. Super. Ct. App. Div. 2000) (stating that under the continuous-trigger theory, defense and indemnification cost are allocated among all insurers on the risk in accordance with their respective exposure based on time-on-the-risk and degree of risk); Owens-Illinois, Inc. v. United Ins. Co., 650 A.2d 974, 993–94 (N.J. 1994) (holding that indemnity costs should be allocated pro rata time on the risk by policy limits); Consol. Edison Co. of N.Y., Inc. v. Allstate Ins. Co., 774 N.E.2d 687 (N.Y. 2002); Nat'l Hockey League v. TIG Ins. Co., 172 N.Y.S.3d 342, 347 (Sup. Ct. 2022) (stating that defense costs are allocated among insurers and the policyholder, for self-insured periods, commensurate with their proportionate time-on-the-risk); Crossmann Cmtys. of N.C., Inc. v. Harleysville Mut. Ins. Co., 717 S.E.2d 589, 601 (S.C. 2011).

apportionment among insurers in the context of equitable contribution claims among insurers.[59]

1. *"Time-on-the-Risk"*

Most courts that apply a pro rata allocation of defense costs prorate based on a time-on-the-risk analysis.[60] Under this approach, defense costs are allocated based on the amount of time each insurer was on the risk during the period in which defense obligations are triggered.[61] In essence, this is "apportionment based upon the relative duration of each primary policy as compared with the overall period of coverage during which the 'occurrences' 'occurred.'"[62] The time-on-the-risk method is based on the principle that the policy language limits its coverage to liability incurred "within the policy period."[63]

2. *Pro Rata Based on Time-on-the-Risk and Policy Limits*

Courts in a few jurisdictions, most notably New Jersey, apply a pro rata allocation based on time-on-the-risk and policy limits. This approach is different than a straight pro rata time-on-the-risk method where it is presumed that the amount of damage during each annual period is the same during the

59. *See, e.g.*, Taco Bell Corp. v. Cont'l Cas. Co., 388 F.3d 1069, 1079 (7th Cir. 2004) (applying Illinois law) (affirming the lower court's 50–50 division of defense costs); N.Y. v. Blank, 27 F.3d 783, 788–89 (2d Cir. 1994) (finding that policies' "other insurance" and contribution clauses required contribution to defense costs by equal shares); U.S. Fid. & Guar. Co. v. Exec. Ins. Co., 893 F.2d 517, 520 (2d Cir. 1990) (finding that the policy's language legally obligated the insurers to "contribute in equal shares to defense"); Atl. Mut. Ins. Co. v. Truck Ins. Exch., 797 F.2d 1288, 1296 n.6 (5th Cir. 1986) (affirming the district court's decision applying equal shares allocation of defense costs); Reliance Ins. Co. v. St. Paul Surplus Lines Ins. Co., 753 F.2d 1288 (4th Cir. 1985) (applying California law and applying equal shares method of allocating costs in homeowner's liability insurer's action against commercial general liability insurer); Century Indem. Co. v. Liberty Mut. Ins. Co., 815 F. Supp. 2d 508, 517 (D.R.I. 2011).

60. Another approach is the pro rata apportionment among primary insurers in proportion to policy limits. This method also is generally limited to cases of concurrent coverage among insurers. *See, e.g.*, Cont'l Ins. Co. v. U.S. Fid. & Guar. Co., 528 P.2d 430, 435–36 (Alaska 1974); Emps. Reinsurance Corp. v. Phoenix Ins. Co., 230 Cal. Rptr. 792, 798–800 (Ct. App. 1986); Shook & Fletcher Asbestos Settlement Tr. v. Safety Nat'l Cas. Corp., No. 04C-02-087 MMJ, 2005 WL 2436193, at *25 (Del. Super. Ct. Sep. 29, 2005) (applying Alabama law).

61. *See, e.g.*, Clarendon Nat'l Ins. Co. v. Nat'l Fire & Marine Ins. Co., 512 F. App'x 671, 673 (9th Cir. 2013); Century Indem. Co. v. Marine Grp., LLC, No. 3:08-CV-1375-AC, 2016 WL 2606989, at *43 (D. Or. May 6, 2016); Ky. League of Cities Ins. Servs. Ass'n v. Argonaut Great Cent. Ins. Co., No. 5:11-CV-00187, 2013 WL 120013, at *11 (W.D. Ky. Jan. 7, 2013); Alticor, Inc. v. Nat'l Union Fire Ins. Co., 916 F. Supp. 2d 813, 832–33 (W.D. Mich. 2013); Liberty Mut. Ins. Co. v. U.S. Fid. & Guar. Co., 232 F. Supp. 76, 84 (D. Mont. 1964); Centennial Ins. Co. v. U.S. Fire Ins. Co., 105 Cal. Rptr. 2d 559, 562–64 (Ct. App. 2001) (upholding the time-on-the-risk method of allocating defense costs as more equitable than the equal shares approach).

62. Crusader Ins. Co. v. USF&G Ins. Co., No. B188516, 2007 WL 1140417, at *15 (Cal. Ct. App. Apr. 18, 2007).

63. Wolverine World Wide, Inc. v. Liberty Mut. Ins. Co., No. 260330, 2007 WL 705981, at *3 (Mich. Ct. App. Mar. 8, 2007) (quoting Arco Indus. Corp. v. Am. Motorists Inc. Co., 594 N.W.2d 61 (Mich. Ct. App. 1998)).

entire trigger period. Rather, under the pro rata time-on-the-risk and policy limits methodology, the court presumes that the amount of damage ordinarily increases over time as the insured purchases higher limits of liability in the later years. This legal fiction often results in insurers in later periods, when higher limits were purchased, bearing a larger share of the loss than the insurers in the earlier periods, when the amount of limits purchased were small by comparison. This is the approach the Supreme Court of New Jersey enunciated in the seminal case of *Owens-Illinois v. United Ins. Co.*[64]

In *Owens-Illinois*, the court adopted the pro rata, by limits and years, method of allocation in the context of claims for bodily injury and property damage from exposure to asbestos. In rejecting the "all sums" approach, the court concluded that "to convert the 'all sums' or 'ultimate net loss' language into the answer to apportionment when injury occurs over a period of years is like trying to place one's hat on a rack that was never designed to hold it. It does not work. The language was never intended to cover apportionment when continuous injury occurs over multiple years."[65]

To spread the risk, the *Owens-Illinois* court followed the California Court of Appeals decision in *Armstrong World Industries, Inc. v. Aetna Casualty & Surety Co.*[66] In *Armstrong*, the losses were allocated among the insurers based on the extent of the risk assumed, "proration on the basis of policy limits, multiplied by years of coverage."[67] The *Owens-Illinois* court held that courts may treat progressive indivisible injury or damage from exposure to injurious conditions as an occurrence within each year of a CGL policy. "That is the continuous-trigger theory for activating the insurers' obligation to respond under the policies."[68] Under this approach, the "allocation [is made] in proportion to the degree of the risks transferred or retained during the years of exposure."[69]

New Jersey state and federal courts' addressing the *Owens-Illinois* approach have observed that "[t]he *Owens-Illinois* method intentionally assigns a greater portion of indemnity costs to years in which greater amounts of insurance were purchased, based on the view that this measure of allocation is more consistent with the economic realities of risk retention and risk

64. 650 A.2d 974 (N.J. 1994); *see also* EnergyNorth Natural Gas, Inc. v. Certain Underwriters at Lloyd's, 934 A.2d 517, 527 (N.H. 2007) (stating that "in future cases, trial courts should, where practicable, apply the pro ration by years and limits method described in *Owens-Illinois* for the reasons set forth in that case"); Carter-Wallace, Inc. v. Admiral Ins. Co., 712 A.2d 1116, 1123 (N.J. 1998).

65. *Owens-Illinois*, 650 A. 2d at 989.

66. *Id.* (citing Armstrong World Indus., Inc. v. Aetna Cas. & Sur. Co., 26 Cal. Rptr. 2d 35 (Ct. App. 1993)).

67. *Id.* at 993.

68. *Id.* at 995.

69. *Id.* at 993.

transfer."[70] The higher policy limits over time reflects an increase in the risks being transferred. The "apportionment of damages among policy years [should be done] without reference to the layering of policies in the triggered years."[71]

Although *Owens-Illinois* only considered indemnity cost obligations, defense costs are allocated in the same manner under New Jersey law.[72] Once the allocation is determined for each year, the costs are allocated vertically beginning with the primary policy until its applicable limits are depleted and then proceeding upward through the excess coverage. Rather than require "each layer of insurance [to] be exhausted across all of the triggered policy years before the next layer would be allocated[.] . . . apportionment of damages among policy years [is done] without reference to the layering of policies in the triggered years."[73] The allocation for both defense and indemnity costs, therefore, is based on the degree of risk transferred as reflected by the purchase of insurance, regardless of the likelihood that the policy will answer a claim.

B. "All Sums" or "Joint and Several" Allocation of Defense Costs

A minority of courts have rejected the use of a pro rata approach to allocate defense costs and instead have required a single insurer to fund the entire defense.[74] In most coverage disputes, the policyholder will advocate for the

70. Carter-Wallace, Inc. v. Admiral Ins. Co., 712 A.2d 1116, 1123 (N.J. 1998) (citing Chem. Leaman Tank Lines, Inc. v. Aetna Cas. & Sur. Co., 978 F. Supp. 589 (D.N.J. 1997)).

71. *Id.*; *see also* Travelers Indem. Co. v. Thomas & Betts Corp., No. 13-6187 (MAS) (LHG), 2017 WL 3187217, at *7 (D.N.J. July 26, 2017) ("The allocation for both defense and indemnity costs . . . are based on the degree of risk transferred as reflected by the purchase of insurance, regardless of the likelihood that the policy will answer a claim."); Potomac Ins. Co. of Ill. v. Pa. Mfrs. Ass'n Ins. Co., 73 A.3d 465, 477 (N.J. 2013) (reiterating the *Owens-Illinois* and *Carter-Wallace* holdings in determining that non-settling insurer could seek contribution towards insured's defense from settling insurer); Quincy Mut. Fire Ins. v. Borough of Bellmawr, 799 A.2d 499, 515–16 (N.J. 2002) (holding that allocation must be reflected by actual days on the risk rather than rounding up by the year); *Carter-Wallace*, 712 A.2d at 1123 (adopting a pro rata method of allocation, accounting for the time-on-the-risk and the degree of the risk assumed in connection with property damage caused by environmental contamination).

72. *See Potomac Ins. Co. of Ill.*, 73 A.3d at 474 (stating that the "allocation of defense costs comports with *Owens-Illinois* and its progeny"); Universal-Rundle Corp. v. Com. Union Ins. Co., 725 A.2d 76, 87 (N.J. Super. Ct. App. Div. 1999).

73. *Carter-Wallace*, 712 A.2d at 1123.

74. *See* Peabody Essex Museum, Inc. v. U.S. Fire Ins. Co., 802 F.3d 39, 52–53 (1st Cir. 2015) (declining to extend Massachusetts' pro rata allocation rule for indemnity costs to defense costs); Emhart Indus., Inc. v. Century Indem. Co., 559 F.3d 57, 70–74 (1st Cir. 2009) (applying Rhode Island law and ruling that "all sums" policy language guides the allocation of defense costs); Narragansett Elec. Co. v. Am. Home Assur. Co., 999 F. Supp. 2d 511, 518–19 (S.D.N.Y. 2014) (predicting that the Massachusetts Supreme Judicial Court would allocate defense costs jointly and severally); *see also* Montrose Chem. Corp. v. Super. Ct., 460 P.3d 1201, 1209 (Cal. 2020) (noting that under the "all sums" rule, an insurer is responsible for defending the insured for all claims triggering damage in a continuous injury case, so long as the insurer provides coverage at some point during the continuous damage period); FMC Corp. v. Plaisted & Cos., 72 Cal. Rptr. 2d 467, 497–98 (Ct. App. 1998)

application of an "all sums" or joint and several liability allocation. Under the "all sums" allocation method, each insurer that issued a policy that covers a loss may bear full responsibility for the loss up to the monetary limit of each policy.[75]

A policyholder following an "all sums" approach chooses one insurer that is on the risk and holds it liable for the entire loss up to the policy limits. In certain jurisdictions, the insurer may then seek contribution from the other insurers who also covered the loss. Under this method, defense costs are divided only among the insurance carriers, even for periods during which there was no coverage in place.[76]

The most significant difference between joint and several allocation and pro rata allocation is the treatment of uninsured periods. Jurisdictions following the "all sums" approach do not allocate any costs to the insured for periods during the continuing loss when the insured was self-insured or uninsured.[77] For this reason, policyholders prefer this method because it gives them control to pick and choose the policy period that offers them the maximum amount of recovery while avoiding policy periods containing policies with exclusions, conditions, and especially deductibles that could limit or bar their recovery.

Although the "all sums" approach affords a policyholder greater flexibility, it does not mean that it will fully recover its defense costs. Some courts applying an "all sums" allocation limit the insured to selecting a single year of coverage for an occurrence.[78] Other courts allow the insured to select additional triggered policy years and "stack" years of coverage.[79]

(applying the "all sums" approach to environmental property damage claims at multiple sites); Armstrong World Indus., Inc. v. Aetna Cas. & Sur. Co., 52 Cal. Rptr. 2d 690, 705–06 (Ct. App. 1996) (affirming the trial court's approach); Am. Nat'l Fire Ins. Co. v. B&L Trucking & Constr. Co., 951 P.2d 250, 256–57 (Wash. 1998) (relying on the "all sums" language to apply joint and several liability); Plastics Eng'g Co. v. Liberty Mut. Ins. Co., 759 N.W.2d 613, 627 (Wis. 2009) (applying the "all sums" allocation approach based on the express policy language).

75. *See, e.g.*, Keene Corp. v. Ins. Co. of N. Am., 667 F.2d 1034, 1050–51 (D.C. Cir. 1981) (applying D.C. law and holding that each insurer is jointly and severally liable for the full amount of the loss, subject to its limits of liability); *Montrose Chem. Corp.*, 460 P.3d at 1209.

76. *See, e.g.*, Goodyear Tire & Rubber Co. v. Aetna Cas. & Sur. Co., 769 N.E.2d 835, 841 (Ohio 2002) (adopting the "all sums" approach for environmental property damage claims and holding that an insured can chose which policy will respond and the selected insurer can obtain contribution from the other triggered policies); J.H. France Refractories Co. v. Allstate Ins. Co., 626 A.2d 502, 509 (Pa. 1993) (holding that there is no bar to an insurer obtaining a share of indemnification or defense costs from other insurers under "other insurance" clauses or under equitable doctrine of contribution).

77. *See, e.g.*, *Keene Corp.*, 667 F.2d at 1050–51; *Armstrong World Indus.*, 52 Cal. Rptr. 2d at 705–10, 741–43.

78. *See, e.g.*, *Keene Corp.*, 667 F.2d at 1050; *FMC Corp.*, 72 Cal. Rptr. 2d at 497–98.

79. *See, e.g.*, Ins. Co. of the State of Pa. v. Cnty. of San Bernardino, No. CV 16-0128 PSG (SSx), 2017 WL 2903259, at *2 (C.D. Cal. Mar. 7, 2017); State of Cal. v. Cont'l Ins. Co., 281 P.3d 1000, 1008–09 (Cal. 2012) (allowing stacking in an "all sums" allocation in the absence of contrary policy language); Cole v. Celotex Corp., 599 So. 2d 1058, 1075–75 (La. 1992) (allowing horizontal stacking of coverages).

V. Allocation of Defense Costs to the Insured

The most significant difference between joint-and-several and pro rata allocation approaches is the treatment of uninsured periods. This includes years where the insured did not purchase insurance coverage (i.e., the insured chose to "go bare"), years where insurance was not available, years where exclusions bar coverage, and years where policies have been lost or insurers are now insolvent. Under an "all sums" allocation, the insured can select a year to minimize its exposure for uninsured periods, insolvencies, and exclusions.

A. "Unavailability" of Insurance

In more recent years, one topic that has garnered significant attention in the context of pro rata allocation is whether the insured should be included in the allocation scheme where insurance coverage was not available in the marketplace for a particular loss. Almost all courts that apply a pro rata allocation require the insured to bear responsibility for no insurance or insufficient insurance regardless of the reason and regardless of whether insurance was available in the marketplace.[80]

---

80. *See, e.g.*, Pa. Nat'l Mut. Cas. Ins. Co. v. Roberts, 668 F.3d 106, 119 (4th Cir. 2012) (applying Maryland law and explaining that an insurer need pay no more than its pro rata share of a judgment because "[t]o place the entire judgment on the insurer would be chaotic, rewarding those who decline to purchase adequate coverage and ultimately punishing those who do"); *In re* Wallace & Gale Co., 385 F.3d 820, 833, 834 (4th Cir. 2004) (applying Maryland law and holding that "it is neither equitable nor fair to require an insurance company to pay for coverage during a period for which no effective coverage is in force"); Com. Union Ins. Co. v. Sepco Corp., 918 F.2d 920, 924 (11th Cir. 1990) (applying Alabama law and finding that the policyholder must share defense costs allocated to years when it lacked coverage); Ins. Co. of N. Am. v. Forty-Eight Insulations, Inc., 633 F.2d 1212, 1224 (6th Cir. 1980), *clarified on reh'g*, 657 F.2d 814 (6th Cir. 1981) (holding that the policyholder "must bear its share of the liability risk for those years in which it had no insurance"); Uniroyal, Inc. v. Home Ins. Co., 707 F. Supp. 1368, 1392 (E.D.N.Y. 1988) ("A firm that fails to purchase insurance for a period . . . is self-insuring for all the risk incurred in that period; otherwise it would be receiving coverage for a period for which it paid no premium. Self-insurance is called 'going bare' for a reason."); Sec. Ins. Co. of Hartford v. Lumbermens Mut. Cas. Co., 826 A.2d 107, 127 (Conn. 2003) (ruling that, for "long latency loss claims that implicate multiple insurance policies, the pro rata method of allocating defense costs applies for purposes of allocating costs to the insured for periods during which it was uninsured or has 'lost or destroyed its policies'"); AAA Disposal Sys., Inc. v. Aetna Cas. & Sur. Co., 821 N.E.2d 1278, 1290 (Ill. App. Ct. 2005) (holding that "it would be unfair to allocate the damages occurring during the uninsured period to an insurer that did not agree to provide coverage during that time"); Norfolk S. Corp. v. Cal. Union Ins. Co., 859 So. 2d 167, 198 (La. Ct. App. 2003) (requiring the policyholder to contribute to the pro rata allocation for any "period in which no insurer is on the risk"); Bos. Gas Co. v. Century Indem. Co., 910 N.E.2d 290, 315–16 (Mass. 2009) (stating that "the policyholder is responsible for any periods that it went without insurance"); Wooddale Builders, Inc. v. Md. Cas. Co., 722 N.W.2d 283, 297–98 (Minn. 2006) ("We therefore conclude that the total period over which liability is allocated must include any times during which damages occurred but Wooddale was voluntarily self- insured."); Owens-Illinois, Inc. v. United Ins. Co., 650 A.2d 974, 995 (N.J. 1994) ("When periods of no insurance reflect a

The vast majority of courts applying a pro rata allocation have ruled the insured should be included in an allocation during periods where insurance was not available.[81] In *Boston Gas Co. v. Century Indem. Co.*,[82] for instance, the Massachusetts Supreme Judicial Court declined to adopt the "unavailability" exception because to do so would contravene the limitations in the subject policies to liability attributable to property damage during the policy periods. The *Boston Gas* court reasoned that:

> The unavailability exception effectively provides insurance where insurers made the calculated decision not to assume risk and not to accept premiums. In effect, because the policyholder could not buy insurance, it is treated as though it did by passing those uninsurable losses to insured periods. This would not be equitable to insurers if the insured purchased coverage for only a few years where there was protracted damage.[83]

In 2018, the New York Court of Appeals issued a landmark decision in *KeySpan Gas East Corp. v. Munich Reinsurance America, Inc.*[84] In *KeySpan*, the court held that that an insured can be held responsible for indemnification of claims occurring during periods when it was uninsured, even when relevant insurance was not available on the market during those time periods.[85] In rejecting the "unavailability rule" used in several other jurisdictions, the court made clear that, where insurance policies provide for pro rata risk allocation, an insured will bear the risk for policy periods in which it did not have coverage, regardless of the reason for the lack of coverage.[86]

---

decision by an actor to assume or retain a risk, as opposed to periods when coverage for a risk is not available, to expect the risk bearer to share in the allocation is reasonable.").

81. *See* Sybron Transition Corp. v. Sec. Ins. of Hartford, 258 F.3d 595, 598–600 (7th Cir. 2001) (applying New York law); Allstate Ins. Co. v. Rochkind, 381 F. Supp. 3d 488, 511–12 (D. Md. 2019) (rejecting the "unavailability" exception, finding "no authority for the existence of such a rule in Maryland," and requiring the policyholder to contribute to the pro rata allocation for years where lead paint exclusions precluded coverage); H.B. Fuller Co. v. U.S. Fire Ins. Co., No. 09-2827(JRT/JJG), 2011 WL 2884711, at *23 (D. Minn. July 18, 2011) (rejecting the policyholder's argument that insurance was "unavailable" to it because the contracts it bought that would have provided coverage for the asbestos); *AAA Disposal Sys.*, 821 N.E.2d at 1290 ("Because the policy periods contained in the American Employers insurance policies do not include the years plaintiffs went uninsured, we fail to understand why American Employers should have to bear the costs from that period. . . . We understand that insurance coverage was not available for the period at issue, but intervenors cannot shift responsibility for the uninsured years to American Employers."); Crossmann Cmtys. of N.C., Inc. v. Harleysville Mut. Ins. Co., 717 S.E.2d 589, 602 (S.C. 2011) (relying on *Boston Gas* and holding that employing an "unavailability" exception would "exceed the trial court's authority, as the effect is to shift losses from one policy period to another in order to create coverage where none was purchased"); Bradford Oil Co., Inc. v. Stonington Ins. Co., 54 A.3d 983, 991 (Vt. 2011) (rejecting the unavailability exception, the court held that "the reason for the absence of effective insurance is not determinative" and that such an exception "is not consistent with a pure time-on-the-rise methodology").

82. 910 N.E.2d 290 (Mass. 2009).

83. *Id.* at 315 (citations omitted).

84. 96 N.E.3d 209 (N.Y. 2018).

85. *Id.* at 214–16.

86. *Id.* at 216.

The underlying claims in *KeySpan* arose from environmental contamination caused by coal tar constituents from three manufactured gas plants owned and operated by the predecessor of KeySpan Gas East Corporation, Long Island Lighting Co., dating back to the late 1800s. In rejecting the "unavailability exception," the *KeySpan* court relied on the policy language.[87] The court agreed with the arguments advanced by one of the insurers that the unavailability rule is inconsistent with the policy language that mandates pro rata allocation and that the imposition of liability on an insurer for damages resulting from occurrences outside the policy period would contravene the very premises underlying pro rata allocation.[88] The court also relied on its previous holdings in *Consolidated Edison* that, although the insurance policies do not speak directly to allocation in the context of long-tail claims, each of the policies contains language limiting the insurer's liability to losses and occurrences happening "during the policy period" and that pro rata allocation—rather than "all sums" allocation—was more consistent with such policy language because "the policies provide indemnification for liability incurred as a result of an accident or occurrence during the policy period, not outside that period."[89]

Notably, *Keyspan* only addressed the allocation of indemnification costs and did not tackle the question of whether or how defense costs should be divided among insurers and insured. The issue of how defense costs would be allocated in connection with long-tail bodily injury claims was addressed squarely in *Danaher Corp. v. Travelers Indemnity Co.*[90]

In *Danaher*, the court had to decide various insurance coverage issues involving underlying silica and asbestos-related bodily injury claims asserted against Chicago Pneumatic Tool Co. (Chicago Pneumatic), which Danaher Corp. (Danaher) acquired in 1986.[91] In 1987, Danaher sold Chicago Pneumatic to Atlas Copco.[92] Danaher filed the declaratory judgment action to resolve disputes over insurance coverage among Chicago Pneumatic's insurers, including Travelers Indemnity Co. and Travelers Casualty & Surety Company (collectively, Travelers), which issued various primary insurance policies to Chicago Pneumatic prior to 1987, excess insurers, and the insured companies themselves, which did not have insurance policies for the entire period which gave rise to the bodily injury claims.[93]

87. *Id.* at 213.
88. *Id.* at 211.
89. *Id.*
90. 414 F. Supp. 3d 436 (S.D.N.Y. 2019).
91. *Id.* at 445.
92. *Id.*
93. *Id.* at 443.

In 2019, after the *Keyspan* decision was rendered, Travelers filed a summary judgment motion seeking a declaration that the liabilities at issue should be subject to pro rata allocation among the parties, relative to their "time on the risk," and that it could seek contribution for both indemnity and defense costs from the other parties consistent with their pro rata obligations.[94] The court agreed with Travelers that many of the relevant policies contained provisions that necessitated a pro rata allocation of indemnity costs.[95] Following *KeySpan*'s dictate that the unavailability exception did not apply, the court found that other insurers also were responsible for certain policy periods, and that the insureds themselves would be liable for periods where there was no coverage.[96] The court further found that Travelers' right to contribution "may be applied in the context of an insurer's overpayment of *both* indemnification *and* defense costs."[97] Based on the *Danaher* court's determination that the insureds were "among the parties responsible for indemnifying" the claims, it concluded that there was "no compelling basis for excusing [the insureds] from contributing to defense costs for those periods as well."[98]

A small and distinct number of jurisdictions that apply a pro rata approach to allocation recognize an exception, albeit limited, in the context of asbestos and environmental claims to periods of time where insurance coverage is not available in the marketplace for a loss.[99] These jurisdictions exclude policyholders from participating in the allocation in years where insurance was unavailable for such risk in the marketplace.

This "unavailability" argument was first addressed by the New Jersey Supreme court in the seminal case of *Owens-Illinois, Inc. v. United Insurance Co.*[100] In *Owens-Illinois*, New Jersey's highest court adopted a pro rata allocation scheme when addressing losses triggering multiple policy periods. In doing so, the court recognized that "when periods of no insurance reflect a decision by an actor to assume or retain a risk, as opposed to periods where coverage for a risk is not available, to expect the risk-bearer to share in the allocation is reasonable."[101]

94. *Id.* at 451.
95. *Id.*
96. *Id.* at 450.
97. *Id.* at 452.
98. *Id.* at 454.
99. *See, e.g.*, R.T. Vanderbilt Co. v. Hartford Accident & Indem. Co., 56 A.3d 539, 584 (Conn. App. Ct. 2017) (affirming the lower court's decision that a policyholder does not have to share in costs related to the asbestos personal injury claims for years it was unable to purchase insurance coverage); Wooddale Builders, Inc. v. Md. Cas. Co., 722 N.W.2d 283, 297–98 (Minn. 2006) (applying the "unavailability" exception to pro rata allocation).
100. 650 A.2d 974 (N.J. 1994).
101. *Id.* at 995.

In *Continental Insurance Co. v. Honeywell International, Inc.*,[102] the New Jersey Supreme Court addressed whether there should be an equitable exception to the unavailability rule under New Jersey's *Owens-Illinois* and *Carter-Wallace* long-tail allocation approach if an insured continues to manufacture and sell asbestos products after insurance for asbestos bodily injury claims became unavailable. The *Honeywell* court declined to adopt an equitable exception to Owens-Illinois' unavailability rule.[103]

The insurers in *Honeywell* argued that Honeywell International, Inc. (Honeywell) should be treated as self-insured from 1987, when excess insurance for its asbestos products became unavailable, through 2001, because Honeywell continued to manufacture asbestos-containing friction products from 1987 to 2001.[104] The court rejected that argument.[105] The court stressed that Honeywell was not asking the insurers to provide coverage for claims where the first exposure was after 1987.[106] The court characterized the insurers' proposal to extend the allocation block as "a novel equitable exception . . . that would retroactively deprive parties of paid-for insurance coverage due to their post-coverage-period conduct," and held that the insurers did "not present a proper factual basis to revisit the unavailability rule that is part of the coherent principles that comprise [New Jersey's] allocation methodology."[107] The court's reasoning is closely tied to the policies and principles behind New Jersey's unique allocation approach, rather than the language of the insurance policies. The unavailability exception has not been widely applied outside of New Jersey.

In sum, most jurisdictions addressing the unavailability argument in the context of pro rata allocation require the policyholder to bear the consequence of being uninsured no matter the reason. Although policyholders who have chosen to not purchase insurance or who are otherwise uninsured during policy periods advocate for the unavailability exception, only a limited number of courts recognize the exception.

B. Period of Self-Insurance

In cases in which it is determined that the insured is self-insured for part of the coverage period because the insured chose not to purchase insurance that otherwise would have been available to provide coverage, the weight of authority holds that the insured must bear a pro rata share of the defense costs.[108] The

102. 188 A.3d 297 (N.J. 2018).
103. *Id.* at 324.
104. *Id.* at 308.
105. *Id.*
106. *Id.*
107. *Id.* at 324.
108. *See, e.g.*, Gulf Chem. & Metallurgical Corp. v. Associated Metals & Mins. Corp., 1 F.3d 365, 372 (5th Cir. 1993); Com. Union Ins. Co. v. Sepco Corp., 918 F.2d 920, 924 (11th Cir. 1990); Budd

rationale for these decisions that allocate a portion of the defense costs to the insured is that the insured chose to bear the risk for those years it was self-insured. Based on this rationale, courts have ruled that the insured is responsible for the periods of time it choose not to have insurance.[109]

In *Security Ins. Co. of Hartford v. Lumbermens Mutual Casualty Co.*,[110] the Connecticut Supreme Court held that "the *pro rata* method of allocating defense costs applies for purposes of allocating costs to the insured for periods during which it was uninsured or has 'lost or destroyed its policies' . . . ."[111] In affirming the trial court's decision, the court held that the insured should be forced to pay a share of defense costs prorated for the years in which no insurer was identified or for which the policyholder lost or destroyed its policies and the alleged insurer refused coverage.[112] The court also affirmed the trial court's allocation of defense costs to the insured for a period where the insured had coverage, but had subsequently entered into an agreement with the insurer releasing it of any obligation under the policies in exchange for a cash payment.[113]

Recently, New York addressed the allocation of defense costs with respect to insurance coverage claims by the National Hockey League (NHL) arising from the concussion claims asserted against the league. In *NHL v. TIG Insurance Co.*,[114] the court was presented with a motion for summary judgment to determine if it was appropriate to allocate defense costs to the NHL for periods when it was self-insured.[115] The court found that allocating defense costs to the NHL for the periods that it was self-insured was appropriate.[116] In reaching its decision, the court relied on the specific policy language addressing the indemnity and defense obligations under the policy.[117] The insuring agreement language relied upon by the court stated that the defendants would "pay

Co. v. Travelers Indem. Co., 820 F.2d 787, 790–91 (6th Cir. 1987); Fireman's Fund Ins. Co. v. Ex-Cell-O Corp., 662 F. Supp. 71, 76 (E.D. Mich. 1987); Ins. Co. of N. Am. v. Forty-Eight Insulations, Inc., 633 F.2d 1212, 1224 (6th Cir. 1980), *clarified on reh'g*, 657 F.2d 814 (6th Cir. 1981) (holding that the policyholder "must bear its share of the liability risk for those years in which it had no insurance"); Uniroyal, Inc. v. Home Ins. Co., 707 F. Supp. 1368, 1392 (E.D.N.Y. 1988) ("A firm that fails to purchase insurance for a period . . . is self-insuring for all the risk incurred in that period; otherwise it would be receiving coverage for a period for which it paid no premium. Self-insurance is called 'going bare' for a reason."); Sec. Ins. Co. v. Lumbermens Mut. Cas. Co., 826 A.2d 107, 110 (Conn. 2003); Bos. Gas Co. v. Century Indem. Co., 910 N.E.2d 290, 301 (Mass. 2009); N. States Power Co. v. Fid. & Cas. Co. of N.Y., 523 N.W.2d 657, 664 (Minn. 1994).

109. *See, e.g.*, *Uniroyal*, 707 F. Supp. at 1392; *Lumbermens Mut. Cas. Co.*, 826 A.2d at 107; *Bos. Gas Co.*, 910 N.E.2d at 315.

110. 826 A.2d 107 (Conn. 2003).

111. *Id.* at 123–24.

112. *Id.* at 110.

113. *Id.* at 115.

114. 172 N.Y.S.3d 342 (Sup. Ct. 2022).

115. *Id.* at 345–46.

116. *Id.* at 348.

117. *Id.* at 347–48.

damages the insured becomes legally obligated to pay . . . because of . . . bodily injury . . . caused by an occurrence . . . to which this insurance applies."[118] The policy also contained language that "the insurance applies to bodily injury that 'occurs during the policy period' only."[119]

With respect to the provisions addressing defense costs, the court found that allocating defense costs to the NHL was appropriate, again based on the language in the policies at issue. The court noted that the defense costs portions of the policies provided that the insurer would "defend claims or suits against the insured seeking damages to which this insurance applies even if the allegations of the suit are groundless, false or fraudulent. . . . SUIT means a civil proceeding in which damages because of bodily injury . . . to which this insurance applies are alleged."[120] The court further noted that the policy "language 'to which this insurance applies' plainly limits the scope of both the defendants' indemnification and defense obligations to bodily injury caused by an occurrence during the applicable policy periods."[121]

The court determined that each of the policies was limited to the amount of time that it covered.[122] The court further ruled that the defense costs must be allocated among the insurers and the insured (for the insured's self-insured periods) in alignment with their proportionate time-on-the-risk.[123] Here, the court noted that the NHL did not carry insurance for approximately 57 of the 97 years that the underlying concussion litigation addressed.[124] As such, the court held that the "NHL must pay its fair share for the defense of the non-covered risk."[125]

In reaching its decision, the *NHL* court also relied on two decisions previously issued by courts applying New York law: *Danaher Corp. v. Travelers Indemnity Co.*[126] and *Generali-U.S. Branch v. Caribe Realty Corp.*[127] The courts in both *Danaher* and *Generali* determined that in the context of long-tail claims, once it is determined that at least one occurrence happened during the self-insured period, there is a basis for apportioning defense costs between the insurer and policyholder.[128] In *NHL*, there was evidence that some, if not many, of the proposed class members' alleged injuries occurred during the

118. *Id.* at 345.
119. *Id.*
120. *Id.*
121. *Id.* at 348.
122. *Id.*
123. *Id.*
124. *Id.*
125. *Id.*
126. 414 F. Supp 3d 436 (S.D.N.Y. 2019).
127. Generali-U.S. Branch v. Caribe Realty Corp., No. 25499/91, 1994 WL 903279 (N.Y. Sup. Ct. Dec. 5, 1994).
128. *Danaher*, 414 F. Supp. 3d at 460; *Generali*, 1994 WL 903279, at *5–6.

years that the NHL failed to obtain insurance. Therefore, the *NHL* court held that "[t]o the extent that the defense of the Concussion Litigation encompassed claims of bodily injury that arose prior to NHL's insured years, NHL should be required to pay its own reasonable costs for that defense. In the policies, defendants agreed to cover the defense for only suits alleging bodily injury that occurred during the policy periods ('to which this insurance applies')."[129]

C. Other Issues Regarding Allocation

It is important to be aware of other issues that may need to be addressed when allocating defense costs across multiple policy periods. These issues include how courts address the issue of policy periods with exclusions or insolvent policies and are commonly seen in long-tail claims where coverage blocks can go back for decades and involve numerous insurers on the risk for one single policyholder.

1. Exclusions

An often-disputed issue in coverage litigation is whether defense and indemnity costs should be allocated to the insured for periods in which the insured purchased insurance policies containing an exclusion that bars coverage.

The issue of whether a policy period with a policy exclusion should be allocated to the insured was first addressed by the Sixth Circuit in *Insurance Co. of North America v. Forty-Eight Insulations, Inc.*[130] In adopting a pro rata time-on-the-risk method for apportioning defense and indemnity costs for asbestos bodily injury claims, the court ruled that the insured should be treated as an insurer for periods when it had no insurance coverage.[131] The court held that, while an insurer must bear the entire cost of the defense when it is impossible to prorate costs between covered and not-covered claims, the same is not true when it is possible to apportion defense costs.[132] Under the insurance policy at issue, the insurer had agreed to pay only the cost of defending a claim that arose during the policy period, not for any claim outside the policy period.[133] "Where the distinction can be readily made, the insured must pay its fair share for the defense of the non-covered risk."[134]

---

129. *NHL*, 172 N.Y.S.3d at 348.
130. 633 F.2d 1212 (6th Cir. 1980), *clarified*, 657 F.2d 814 (6th Cir. 1981), *cert. denied*, 454 U.S. 1109 (1981).
131. *Id.* at 1225.
132. *Id.* at 1224.
133. *Id.* at 1224–25.
134. *Id.* at 1225.

In *Sybron Transition Corp. v. Security Insurance of Hartford*,[135] the Seventh Circuit addressed the allocation of losses during periods where the policies contained exclusions that barred coverage.[136] The *Sybron* court specifically allocated indemnity costs to the policyholder for periods in which it purchased insurance with an applicable exclusion and declined to require that insurance have been "available."[137] The court stated that to require the insurer to pay extra because the policyholder did not find it cost-effective to purchase coverage during the relevant period "would be the economic equivalent of requiring Security to furnish free coverage" during that period.[138]

Similarly, in *Arceneaux v. Amstar Corp.*,[139] the Louisiana Supreme Court found the insured responsible for a portion of defense costs for a suit brought by individuals claiming noise-induced hearing loss as a result of working at the insured's sugar refinery for 60 years.[140] In *Arceneaux*, the insured had 26 months of primary general liability coverage with no exclusion for employment-related claims; however, the remainder of the policies in the allocation block contained an exclusion precluding coverage for employment-related claims.[141] The court held that that the insurer's defense obligation should be prorated such that the insured should be obligated to pay for the defense of the remainder of the 60-year exposure period during which coverage for the employee noise-induced hearing loss claims was excluded.[142]

2. *Insolvent Insurers*

One issue that is raised in many long-tail claim allocation disputes is whether liability should be allocated to the insured for years where the insurers that issued the policies have since been declared insolvent. This often requires the court to address whether the umbrella or excess policies should be required to "drop down" in place of the insolvent insurer to fill any gaps. Most courts to address this issue have refused to require umbrella or excess insurers to drop down to cover losses that should have been covered under insurance policies issued by insolvent insurers.[143] When an umbrella or excess insurer is not

135. 258 F.3d 595 (7th Cir. 2001).
136. *Id.* at 598–99.
137. *Id.* at 599.
138. *Id.* at 600.
139. 200 So. 3d 277 (La. 2016).
140. *Id.* at 280.
141. *Id.*
142. *Id.* at 289; *see also* Allstate Ins. Co. v. Rochkind, 381 F. Supp. 3d 488, 511–12 (D. Md. 2019) (requiring the policyholder to contribute to the pro rata allocation for policy years in which lead paint exclusions precluded coverage).
143. Canal Ins. Co. v. Montello, Inc., 632 F. App'x 448, 450 (10th Cir. 2015) (affirming the district court's ruling that an excess insurer had no duty to defend a manufacturer after the primary insurer became insolvent); Highlands Ins. Co. v. Gerber Prods. Co., 702 F. Supp. 109, 112 (D. Md. 1988) (stating that excess insurers ordinarily are not required to provide "drop down" coverage in the event

required to drop down, then the insured is required to bear the loss allocable to the insolvent policies.[144]

In *AAA Disposal Systems, Inc. v. Aetna Casualty & Surety Co.*,[145] an Illinois appellate court held that the risk of an insurer's insolvency is on the insured rather than on another insurer that was a stranger to the insurer "selection process."[146] Thus, a successor excess insurer's insolvency should not increase its predecessor's liability. Based on this reasoning, the court found that "it would be unfair to allocate the damages occurring during the uninsured [due to insurer insolvency] period to an insurer that did not agree to provide coverage during that time."[147]

In *Benjamin Moore & Co. v. Aetna Casualty & Surety Co.*,[148] the New Jersey Supreme Court explained that, under its pro rata by years and limits method of allocation, "insurers are allocated losses based on their undertakings, the insured is required to pay its 'aliquot' share of both defense and indemnification on account of years in which it is uninsured or self-insured, and the insured is also responsible for years in which coverage is exhausted or its insurer bankrupt."[149] Indeed, the court went so far as to state "policyholders are required to underwrite the risk of insurer insolvency or bankruptcy."[150]

of underlying insurers' insolvency); Revco D.S., Inc. v. Gov't Emps. Ins. Co., 791 F. Supp. 1254, 1268 (N.D. Ohio 1991) (holding that excess insurers do not have a duty to "drop down" absent express policy language to that effect); S. Silica of La., Inc. v. La. Ins. Guar. Ass'n, 979 So. 2d 460, 466 (La. 2008) (holding that solvent insurers were not required to fill the gap created by an insurer's insolvency and pay more than their prorated share of defense and indemnity for Silica claims); Wurth v. Ideal Mut. Ins. Co., 518 N.E.2d 607, 610 (Ohio Ct. App. 1987) (holding that an excess insurer does not "drop down" where a primary insurer is insolvent, because to hold otherwise would "place the risk of loss for securing an insolvent insurer not on the insurance purchaser, who purchased the policy, but on the excess coverage provider, who never contracted to cover such a contingency"). *But see* O'Reilly Auto Enters., LLC v. U.S. Fire Ins. Co., No. 6:17-03007-CV-RK, 2020 WL 520129, at *9 (W.D. Mo. Jan. 31, 2020) (applying California law and finding that excess insurers had to drop down to provide coverage in place of an insolvent primary insurer where the controlling limits of liability provision stated that insurers would do so "if the applicable limit of liability of the underlying insurance is less than as stated in the schedule of underlying insurance because the aggregate limit of liability of the underlying insurance has been reduced" and the policy did not further define how those limits may be "reduced").

144. H.B. Fuller Co. v. U.S. Fire Ins. Co., No. 09-2827(JRT/JJG), 2011 WL 2884711, at *22 (D. Minn. July 18, 2011) (holding that the policyholder must bear its share of losses for to periods in which policies are unable to respond because they were issued by insurers that are now insolvent).

145. 821 N.E.2d 1278 (Ill. App. Ct. 2005).

146. *Id.* at 1290.

147. *Id.*

148. 843 A.2d 1094 (N.J. 2004).

149. *Id.* at 1102.

150. *Id.* at 1103. In contrast, in *Farmers Mutual Fire Insurance Co. v. New Jersey Property-Liability Insurance Guaranty Ass'n*, 74 A.3d 860 (N.J. 2013), the court held that, in long-tail, continuous-trigger cases, when an insolvent carrier was on the risk along with solvent carriers, the exhaustion provision of the New Jersey Property-Liability Insurance Guaranty Association Act (PLIGA) mandated that an insured first exhaust the policy limits of the solvent carriers prior to seeking statutory benefits from the Association. The "exhaustion" definition did not unconstitutionally impair the insurer's contract rights, as the Act was motivated by public policy and imposed reasonable conditions related to proper

In more recent years, in response to insurer insolvency and courts rulings on these so-called "drop down" issues, excess insurers have added an insolvency clause to their policies that expressly provides that the insolvency of an underlying insurer does not result in any "drop down" obligation.[151]

3. *Paying Insurer's Ability to Obtain Contribution*

In most jurisdictions, an insurer that defends an insured or that pays defense costs may seek contribution for defense costs from other insurers who also had a duty to defend through the assertion of equitable contribution claims and via application of "other insurance" clauses or other equitable principles applied in the subject jurisdiction.[152] Equitable contribution applies to insurers that share the same type of obligation on the same risk with respect to the same insured. An insurer may not be able to obtain contribution for the amount it paid in excess of its equitable share.[153]

Even where contribution is permitted, an insurer that has been selected by the policyholder under an "all sums" allocation approach may end up paying more than its pro rata share of liability. This can be the case where insurers against whom contribution claims otherwise would be asserted are insolvent or where the other insurers have substantive defenses to contribution claims.[154]

government objectives. Thus, when a solvent insurer paid property-damage claims due to environmental contamination, it was not entitled to reimbursement from the New Jersey Property-Liability Insurance Guaranty Ass'n under the *Owens-Illinois* methodology. *Id.* at 863. This decision superseded an earlier appellate court decision, *Farmers Mutual Fire Insurance Co. of Salem v. N.J. Property-Liability Insurance Guaranty Ass'n*, 74 A.3d 860 (N.J. 2013), which held that the New Jersey Surplus Lines Guaranty Fund was required to pay the share that would have been allocated to the insolvent carrier's policy and was based on amendments to both the PLIGA and the Surplus Lines Guaranty Fund.

151. *See generally* SEAMAN & SCHULZE, *supra* note 1, Ch. 9 (Insolvency of Underlying Insurers).

152. *See generally* SEAMAN & SCHULZE, *supra* note 1, Ch. 9 (Reallocation among Insurers Through "Other Insurance Clauses"); *see, e.g.*, Clarendon Nat. Ins. Co. v. Nat'l Fire & Marine Ins. Co., 512 F. App'x 671, 673 (9th Cir. 2013); Forum Ins. Co. v. Allied Sec., Inc., 866 F.2d 80, 84–85 (3d Cir. 1989) (applying Pennsylvania law); Home Ins. Co. v. Certain Underwriters at Lloyd's, London, 729 F.2d 1132, 1134–35 (7th Cir. 1984) (applying Illinois law); Keene Corp. v. Ins. Co. of N. Am., 667 F.2d 1034, 1050 (D.C. Cir. 1981); Cont'l W. Ins. Co. v. Colony Ins. Co., 69 F. Supp. 3d 1075, 1088 (D. Colo. 2014) (applying Colorado law and holding that a participating insurer with a duty to defend is entitled to equitable contribution from a nonparticipating insurer with a duty to defend, when the former provides a complete defense to an insured against a common risk arising throughout the successive coverage periods of both insurers); Cargill, Inc. v. Ace Am. Ins. Co., 784 N.W.2d 341, 353 (Minn. 2010); J.H. France Refractories Co. v. Allstate Ins. Co., 626 A.2d 502, 509 (Pa. 1993) (permitting an insurer that is liable to collect from any other insurer whose contract was triggered); Polygon Nw. Co. v. Am. Nat'l Fire Ins. Co., 189 P.3d 777, 799 (Wash. Ct. App. 2008) (allowing insurers that paid all indemnity and defense costs to seek contribution from another co-insurer and holding that "liability for purposes of contribution was defined by both [the] 'other insurance' clause . . . as well as other applicable provisions" of the triggered policies).

153. *See, e.g.*, Steadfast Ins. Co. v. Greenwich Ins. Co., 922 N.W.2d 71, 84–85 (Wis. 2019) (ruling that an insurer that breached its duty to defend did not have to pay the full amount another insurer incurred defending the claim but rather the "proper approach was to allocate a proportional share of defense costs to each insurer based on the limits of liability of each policy").

154. *See, e.g.*, Cont'l Cas. Co. v. Nat'l Union Fire Ins. Co., No. 09-287 (JRT/JJG), 2014 WL 4546039, at *8 (D. Minn. Sept. 12, 2014); Nucor Corp. v. Emps. Ins. Co., 296 P.3d 74, 87 (Ariz. Ct.

The costs of pursuing contribution and the prospect of having to potentially take pro-policyholder positions in prosecuting a contribution claim may, in some instances, cause an insurer to forgo pursuing contribution.

In a minority of jurisdictions contribution may not be available.[155] Until relatively recently, Florida was one of the few states that did not permit equitable contribution among primary insurers for defense costs. The law was changed by statute in 2020. Section 624.1055 of the Florida statutes now provides liability insurers a statutory right to seek contribution for defense costs under many circumstances.[156]

VI. Conclusion

Allocation of defense costs requires ascertaining the controlling law and trigger and allocation methodology rules and an application of those rules to the policy language, facts, and costs at issue. The focus of this chapter has been on the rules applicable to allocation of defense costs and decisional authority in the context of long-tail claims. In some instances, the disputes regarding allocation of defense costs may be significant and require resolution through litigation. In many instances, the policyholder and the insurers potentially implicated may be able to reach agreement on payment of defense costs or at least agree upon arrangements under an interim defense funding agreement or coverage-in-place agreement.

App. 2012).

155. *See, e.g.*, Cincinnati Ins. Co. v. Crossmann Cmtys. of N.C., Inc., No. 4-09-1379-RBH, 2013 WL 1283381, at *21 (D.S.C. Mar. 27, 2013) (finding no right of pro rata contribution toward defense costs); Barton & Ludwig, Inc. v. Fid. & Deposit Co. of Md., 570 F. Supp. 1470, 1472 (N.D. Ga. 1983) (finding that there could be no contribution of defense costs arising from a collapsed deck because the insurer did no more than it was obligated to do)..

156. FLA. STAT. § 624.1055 (2023). For a discussion of equitable contribution claims, "other insurance" clauses and resolving conflicts in "other insurance" clauses, self-insurance and guarantee funds, and apportionment of defense costs, see SEAMAN & SCHULZE, *supra* note 1, ch. 5 (Reallocation Among Insurers Through "Other Insurance" Clauses). In some instances, there are disputes regarding attorney fees and rates, the reasonableness of defense costs, and compliance with insurer litigation management and legal auditing requirements. SEAMAN & SCHULZE, *supra* note 1, ch. 12 (Defense Costs, Attorney's Fees, and Legal Audits).

CHAPTER 9

Consequences of Breaching the Duty to Defend

Lorelie S. Masters and Rachel E. Hudgins

I. Introduction

If an insurer refuses to defend its insured because it believes the policy does not provide coverage for the claims in the underlying action or withdraws from the defense before its duty to defend is terminated, it does so "at its own peril."[1] If

1. Ayers v. C & D Gen. Contractors, 269 F. Supp. 2d 911, 914 (W.D. Ky. 2003); *see also* Nielsen v. TIG Ins. Co., 442 F. Supp. 2d 972, 981 (D. Mont. 2006) ("The bottom line is when TIG neglected to assume its duty it assumed a risk. It is too late to cry foul now."); Erie Ins. Exch. v. V.I. Enters. Inc., 264 F. Supp. 2d 261, 263–64 (D.V.I. 2003) ("Once this obligation is triggered, the insurer can (1) seek a declaratory judgment that it owes no duty to defend the insured, (2) defend the insured under a reservation of rights, or (3) refuse to either defend or seek a declaratory judgment action at its own peril that it might later be found to have breached the duty to defend."); Quihuis v. State Farm Mut. Auto. Ins. Co., 334 P.3d 719, 730 (Ariz. 2014) (citation omitted) ("[W]hen an insurer refuses to defend, as State Farm did here, it does so 'at its peril,' . . . and if a court later finds coverage, the insurer must pay the damages awarded in the default judgment (at least up to the policy limits) unless it can prove fraud or collusion."); Capstone Bldg. Corp. v. Am. Motorists Ins. Co., 67 A.3d 961, 993 (Conn. 2013) ("If the insurer declines to provide its insured with a defense and is subsequently found to have breached its duty to do so, it bears the consequences of its decision, including the payment of any reasonable settlement agreed to by the plaintiff and the insured, and the costs incurred effectuating the settlement up to the limits of the policy."); S. Guar. Ins. Co. v. Dowse, 605 S.E.2d 27, 29 (Ga. 2004) (footnote omitted) ("In Georgia, an insurer that denies coverage and refuses to defend an action against its insured, when it could have done so with a reservation of its rights as to coverage, 'waives the provisions of the policy against a settlement by the insured and becomes bound to pay the amount of any settlement [within a policy's limits] made in good faith[,] plus expenses and attorneys' fees.'"); Tidyman's Mgmt. Servs. Inc. v. Davis, 330 P.3d 1139, 1149 (Mont. 2014) ("[W]here an insurer refuses to defend its insured, it does so at its peril."); Dove v. State Farm Fire & Cas. Co., 399 P.3d 400, 405 (N.M. 2017) (citations omitted) ("[A]n insurer who refuses to defend a covered insured without seeking a judicial determination that the alleged insured is not covered under the policy, . . . or without a voluntary waiver from the insured, . . . does so at its peril."); Builders Mut. Ins. Co. v. Mitchell, 709 S.E.2d 528, 535 (N.C. Ct. App. 2011) (observing that an insurer fails to defend at its own peril if coverage is later found to exist); Water Well Sols. Serv. Grp., Inc. v. Consol. Ins. Co., 881 N.W.2d 285, 297 (Wis. 2016) (explaining that an insurer has the option to deny a defense and state the grounds for deciding that the complaint does not trigger any obligation to defend under the policy, but an insurer that selects this option does so at its own peril).

the insurer's decision is wrong, meaning it failed to provide a defense when it had a duty to do so, the insurer has breached its duty and "open[ed] itself up to a myriad of adverse consequences."[2] The U.S. Court of Appeals for the Seventh Circuit has explained the reason for such "grave" consequences to the insurer is based on the "grave" effects of the insurer's failure to defend on the insured:

> The consequences to an insurer of a mistaken refusal to defend can be very grave because the consequences for the insured of such a refusal can be very grave. The insured will have to go and find himself a lawyer. He [or she] may not find one, or he may have only enough information about the legal services market, and money to spend on the lawsuit, to be able to hire a weak lawyer. So he [or she] may lose (or lose worse) a case that a lawyer hired by the insurance company would have won—and the facts determined in that case may make it impossible for him [or her] to establish coverage; for example, the court may have found deliberate wrongdoing on his [or her] part, taking him [or her] out of the policy's coverage.[3]

An insurer's unjustified failure to defend, even if based on an honest mistake by the insurer, exposes the insurer to damages for breach of contract.[4] That failure also may expose the insurer to consequences and damages "it did not insure against."[5] For instance, an insurer may be requested to reimburse an insured for the amounts the insured paid to pursue the declaratory judgment action that establishes coverage.[6] In some jurisdictions, an insurer may be responsible for indemnification even if the eventual settlement or judgment is above policy limits or the insurer has other coverage defenses.[7] An insurer may also waive certain policy conditions and terms, particularly the condition that an insured not enter a settlement agreement without the insurer's approval.[8]

The safer course for an insurer that doubts that it has a duty to defend is to (1) provide a defense under a reservation of rights and (2) seek a declaratory

---

2. *Water Well Sols. Serv. Grp.*, 881 N.W.2d at 297.

3. Guar. Bank v. Chubb Corp., 538 F.3d 587, 592 (7th Cir. 2008) (applying Wisconsin law).

4. *See, e.g.*, Peterson Tractor Co. v. Travelers Indem. Co. of Ill., 156 F. App'x 21, 23 (9th Cir. 2005) (applying California law) ("When an insurer breaches its duty to defend, the insured may recover as contract damages the funds it expended defending itself, and also any damages that proximately resulted from the insurer's breach of the insurance contract."); Bucci v. Essex Ins. Co., 323 F. Supp. 2d 84, 92 (D. Me. 2004) (applying Maine law and stating that "normal contract damage principles apply to a breach of the duty to defend").

5. Century Sur. Co. v. Andrew, 432 P.3d 180, 186 (Nev. 2018).

6. See *infra* Part II.C (discussing an insured's ability to recover fees incurred in pursuing coverage).

7. See *infra* Part II.B (discussing insurer's indemnification obligations for settlements and judgments, including whether insurer's indemnification obligation is subject to policy limits).

8. See *infra* Part III (discussing nonmonetary consequences of an insurer's breach of it duty to defend, including estoppel and forfeiture of coverage defenses, waiver of right to contest insured's liability in underlying action, and waiver of right to control the defense of and settle the underlying action).

judgment regarding its coverage defenses.[9] For an insured whose insurer does not take this approach, the availability of remedies beyond breach of contract damages recognizes the unique harm of a wrongful failure to defend.[10] Courts apply a broad "potential for coverage" standard to the insurer's defense obligation to preserve the value of the defense promised when policyholders buy this "litigation insurance." As the Washington Supreme Court put it, "[t]he insurer's duty to defend is one of the main benefits of the liability insurance contract."[11] Policyholders—both individuals and businesses—buy insurance to protect their assets and livelihoods, and, with regard to defense coverage in particular, to get the benefit of an immediate and experienced defense if they are sued.[12] This is the "litigation insurance" policyholders seek when they purchase a liability insurance policy that includes a duty to defend.[13] Unlike with many other contracts, typical contract damages cannot make an insured

---

9. *See* Std. Mut. Ins. Co. v. Lay, 989 N.E.2d 591 (Ill. 2013); Ass'n of Trial Lawyers Assur. v. Tsai, 879 So. 2d 1024, 1030 (Miss. 2004).

10. *See, e.g.*, Clarendon Nat'l Ins. Co. v. Am. States Ins. Co., 688 F. Supp. 2d 1186, 1192 (D. Or. 2010) (stating that the insurer could not rely on the "No Action" clause in its policy because its duty to defend was disputed); King Cnty. v. Travelers Indem. Co., No. C14-1957 MJP, 2016 WL 362249, at *4 (W.D. Wash. Jan. 29, 2016) (applying Washington law and stating that "the failure to defend can result in bad faith liability even if it is ultimately determined that there is no coverage); Black v. Goodwin, Loomis & Britton, Inc., 681 A.2d 293, 299 (Conn. 1996) (reasoning that a breach of the duty to defend operates as a waiver of policy's requirement that the insurer consent to settlement); L.C.S., Inc. v. Lexington Ins. Co., 853 A.2d 974, 985 (N.J. Super. Ct. App. Div. 2004) ("While Lexington obviously disputes the issue, we state once again that it had its opportunity to participate in the defense of the action under reservation of rights but chose instead to disclaim and leave its insured to fend for itself. Accordingly, Lexington is not entitled to a hearing to re-litigate on the issue of whether Cosgrove's injuries were the proximate result of a negligent or intentional act.").

11. Safeco Ins. Co. of Am. v. Butler, 823 P.2d 499, 504 (Wash. 1992) (citing R. Long, 1A The Law of Liability Insurance § 5B.15 (1990)); *see also* Avondale Indus., Inc. v. Travelers Indem. Co., 887 F.2d 1146, 1148 (2d Cir. 1989) (applying New York law); Brohawn v. Transamerica Ins. Co., 347 A.2d 842, 851 (Md. 1975); Seth D. Lamden, *Scope of Duty to Defend*, *in* 3 New Appleman on Insurance Law Library Edition § 17.01[1][a], at 17-4 (Jeffrey E. Thomas & Francis J. Mootz III eds., 2009 & Supp. 2023) ("Many insureds purchase liability insurance for the peace of mind that comes with knowing that their insurer will defend them if they are sued in an action that comes within the scope of protection provided by their policy.").

12. *See, e.g.*, Montrose Chem. Corp. v. Super. Ct., 861 P.2d 1153, 1157 (Cal. 1993) ("The insured's desire to secure the right to call on the insurer's superior resources for the defense of third-party claims is, in all likelihood, as significant a motive for purchase of insurance as is the wish to obtain indemnification for possible liability."); *see also* William T. Barker, *Insurer Control of Defense, Reservation of Rights and Right to Independent Counsel*, 71 Def. Couns. J. 16, 16 (2004) ("Insurers have more expertise than most insureds in managing litigation."); Restatement of the L. of Liab. Ins. § 10 cmt. b (Am. L. Inst. 2019) (stating that "insurers have greater capacity to direct the defense of a legal action than all but the most sophisticated insureds").

13. *See, e.g.*, Avondale Indus., Inc. v. Travelers Indem. Co., 887 F.2d 1200, 1204 (2d Cir. 1989) (applying New York law); Indep. Petrochem. Corp. v. Aetna Cas. & Sur. Co., 654 F. Supp. 1334, 1346 (D.D.C. 1986), *aff'd in part and rev'd in part on other grounds*, 944 F.2d 940 (D.C. Cir. 1991); Brohawn v. Transamerica Ins. Co., 347 A.2d 842, 851 (Md. 1975) (stating that liability insurance provides "litigation insurance" to cover the expense of defense). As the Idaho Supreme Court explained, "[t]o allow the insurer to avoid providing defense on questionable claims would frustrate one of the insured's basic purposes in procuring insurance coverage—protection from the expenses of litigation." Black v. Fireman's Fund Am. Ins. Co., 767 P.2d 824, 830 (Idaho 1989).

whole when the insurer fails to perform its defense obligations. As the Delaware Supreme Court noted:

> In a typical contract, the non-breaching party can replace the performance of the breaching party by paying the then-prevailing market price for the counter-performance. With insurance this is simply not possible. This feature of insurance contracts distinguishes them from other contracts. . . . [14]

Thus, courts often conclude that key protections policyholders seek when they purchase liability insurance are lost when insurers do not perform their defense obligations as expected.[15] Insureds purchase insurance policies not to "obtain a commercial advantage, but to protect [themselves] against the risk of accidental losses."[16] Liability insurance provides insured "peace of mind and security."[17] If a claim is made against an insured that potentially falls within the scope of its insurance policy's coverage,

> the insured would reasonably expect that he [or she] would stand a better chance of vindication if supported by the resources and expertise of his [or her] insurer than if compelled to handle and finance the presentation of his [or her] case. He [or she] would, moreover, expect to be able to avoid the time, uncertainty and capital outlay in finding and retaining an attorney of his [or her] own.[18]

Where the insurer breaches its duty to defend its insured, the undefended insured loses the benefit of the litigation insurance and must fend for itself. Such consequences

> may include default judgment, judgment in excess of policy limits, and attorneys' fees incurred for defense of the case. The insured may suffer financial straits, distress concerning the lawsuit and the financial strain of defending and paying any judgment, and deterioration of mental and physical health. The insured may also have to pay attorneys' fees to defend or prosecute a declaratory judgment action to determine the insurer's obligation to defend.[19]

---

14. E.I. du Pont de Nemours & Co. v. Pressman, 679 A.2d 436, 447 (Del. 1996). The Delaware Supreme Court in *Pressman* noted that these differences justified "the availability of punitive damages for breach in limited circumstances." *Id.* As a claims-handling textbook explains, "contractual damages are inadequate" when an insurer fails to perform. James J. Markham et al., The Claims Environment 274 (1993).

15. *See generally* Richard E. Stewart & Barbara D. Stewart, *The Loss of the Certainty Effect*, 4 Risk Mgmt. & Ins. Rev. 29, 29–30 (2001).

16. Crisci v. Sec. Ins. Co. of New Haven, Conn., 426 P.2d 173, 179 (Cal. 1967).

17. *Id.*

18. Gray v. Zurich Ins. Co., 419 P.2d 168, 178 (Cal. 1966). For a critique of *Gray*, see James M. Fischer, *Broadening the Insurer's Duty to Defend: How* Gray v. Zurich Insurance Co. *Transformed Liability Insurance into Litigation Insurance*, 25 U.C. Davis L. Rev. 141, 181 (1991).

19. Karon O. Bowdre, *"Litigation Insurance": Consequences of an Insurance Company's Wrongful Refusal to Defend*, 44 Drake L. Rev. 743, 746–47 (1996) (collecting examples of the effects of insurers' failure to defend on insured individuals and companies).

For these reasons, some jurisdictions recognize damages beyond breach of contract remedies.

II. Monetary Damages

Monetary damages may be awarded for a breach of the duty to defend or pay defense costs. First, compensatory damages cover the loss the insured directly experienced because of the breach. The amount awarded is intended to make the insured whole.[20] The most obvious direct losses for an insurer's failure to defend are the reasonable attorney's fees and costs the insured incurred in mounting its own defense.[21] From a traditional contract law perspective:

> Hiring defense counsel is tantamount to 'covering': the insurer promises to provide a service, but when the insurer fails to do so, the insured is free to purchase a substitute service. Having already paid for the insurer's service with the insurance premium, the insured is entitled to have the costs of cover fully reimbursed by the insurer. The substitute purchase must be reasonable; thus, the insured is entitled to recover the reasonable attorney's fees incurred in defending the lawsuit. The insured can also recover other costs incidental to the defense, such as witness fees, court costs, investigation costs, and the like.[22]

Second, consequential damages may be recoverable for the breach of the duty to defend. Consequential damages are losses that do not directly flow from the breach of contract.[23] These are actual losses caused by the breach, but perhaps not in an immediate or obvious way. To recover for this type of loss, consequential damages "cannot be reasonably prevented and arise naturally from the breach, or which are reasonably contemplated by the parties."[24] These

---

20. Bucci v. Essex Ins. Co., 323 F. Supp. 2d 84, 94 (D. Me. 2004) ("When it is an insurer's clear duty to defend and the insurer wrongfully refuses to do so on the ground that the claim upon which the action against the insured is based is not within the coverage of the policy, the insurer is guilty of a breach of contract that renders it liable to pay such damages as will place the insured in a position equally good as the insured would have occupied had the insurance contract been fully and properly performed from the beginning."); Newhouse v. Citizens Sec. Mut. Ins. Co., 501 N.W.2d 1, 7 (Wis. 1993) ("The insurance company must pay damages necessary to put the insured in the same position he would have been in had the insurance company fulfilled the insurance contract.").

21. Selective Way Ins. Co. of Am. v. Fireman's Fund Ins. Co., 289 A.3d 719, 726 n.3 (Md. App. Ct. 2023); T.A. Schifsky & Sons, Inc. v. Bahr Constr., LLC, 773 N.W.2d 783, 789 (Minn. 2009).

22. Robert H. Jerry, II & Douglas R. Richmond, Understanding Insurance Law 716–17 (6th ed. 2018) (footnotes omitted).

23. *See, e.g.*, Goodstein v. Cont'l Cas. Co., 509 F.3d 1042, 1058 (9th Cir. 2007) (applying Washington law) (finding that the measure of damages for a good faith, but unjustified, breach of the duty to defend is the costs and reasonable attorneys' fees incurred by the insured in defending itself plus consequential damages that the insured incurred as a result of the breach).

24. Innovative Mold Sols., Inc. v. Cent. Mut. Ins. Co., 277 F. Supp. 3d 222, 224 (D. Mass. 2017); *see also* Bainbridge, Inc. v. Travelers Cas. Co. of Conn., 159 P.3d 748, 756 (Colo. App. 2006) ("[T]he insured may recover consequential damages for the breach which, if based on contract principles, include those damages that arose naturally from the breach and were reasonably foreseeable at the

may include indemnity payments for any settlement by or judgment against the insured within policy limits.[25]

Differences arise between jurisdictions regarding recovery for costs and damages outside of basic contract damages. These can include attorneys' fees the insured incurred in the coverage action; judgments against the insured that exceed policy limits; monetary recovery for mental anguish; and bad faith damages.[26] The difference is usually attributable to whether states view the breach of the duty to defend as a "pure" breach of contract, giving rise only to contract damages, or whether the breach may give rise to a tort for bad faith, which, if proven, may give rise to extracontractual damages.[27]

Even with this explanation, the simplicity of these categories—compensatory or consequential; breach of contract or extra-contractual—can be deceiving. What one court labels compensatory damages, another might label as consequential. And what one court labels as consequential damages, another might consider punitive or bad-faith tort damages.[28] Across the laws of the 50 states, damage categories, and the labels used by the courts to describe those categories, may overlap significantly.

A. Defense Costs Incurred in the Underlying Claim

An insurer that breaches its duty to defend generally is liable for the reasonable attorney's fees and costs the insured incurred in defending the underlying claim.[29] This liability is based on traditional breach of contract principles

---

time of contract. . . . If the circumstances are sufficiently egregious to constitute a tort, then the consequential damages include all damages that were proximately caused by the breach, regardless of foreseeability."); A.B.C. Builders, Inc. v. Am. Mut. Ins. Co., 661 A.2d 1187, 1192 (N.H. 1995) ("[B]ecause an insurance policy is a contract, its breach may result in an award of consequential damages if they were foreseeable and can be proved.").

25. *See, e.g.*, Gibson v. First Mercury Ins. Co., 633 F. Supp. 3d 627, 647 (D. Conn. 2022) (stating that the consequences for the insurer breaching its duty to defend included paying for a reasonable settlement); UMIA Ins., Inc. v. Arguelles, 591 F. Supp. 3d 876, 882 (D. Mont. 2022) (applying Montana law) ("When an insurer unjustifiably refuses to defend, it is estopped from denying coverage and is liable for defense costs and any judgment against the insured."); Choinsky v. Germantown Sch. Dist. Bd. of Educ., 926 N.W.2d 196, 203 (Wis. Ct. App. 2019) (including settlement and judgment amounts as damages that flow naturally from an insurer's breach of its duty to defend).

26. Bowdre, *supra* note 19, at 760.

27. *Id.* at 761; *see also* Nautilus Ins. Co. v. Blagrave, No. CV 05-00662 SOM/LEK, 2006 WL 8436302, at *4 (D. Haw. Mar. 29, 2006) ("[I]n bad faith tort claims, insureds may recover compensatory or punitive damages if properly pled and proved.").

28. *Compare* Bryant v. Gen. Cas. Co. of Wis., No. 1:18-CV-562, 2019 WL 367292, at *3 (N.D.N.Y. Jan. 30, 2019) (equating consequential and bad-faith damages), *with* My Left Foot Children's Therapy, LLC v. Certain Underwriters at Lloyd's, London, No. 215CV01746MMDVCF, 2021 WL 1093094, at *6 (D. Nev. Mar. 22, 2021) (distinguishing extracontractual and consequential damages).

29. Tibbs v. Great Am. Ins. Co., 755 F.2d 1370, 1373–74 (9th Cir. 1985) (applying California law); Liberty Mut. Ins. Co. v. Jotun Paints, Inc., 555 F. Supp. 2d 686, 709–10 (E.D. La. 2008) (applying Louisiana law); C. Raymond Davis & Sons, Inc. v. Liberty Mut. Ins. Co., 467 F. Supp. 17, 19 (E.D. Pa.

recognizing compensatory damages. This may be true even if the insurance policy does not cover all the alleged claims in the third-party action.[30] Insurers may dispute whether the insured's defense costs were reasonable.[31] Unlike other attorney's fee disputes where the party seeking its fees must prove their reasonableness, however, some courts presume that the insured's attorney's fees claimed as damages are reasonable and shift to the insurer the burden to prove that the fees are unreasonable.[32]

B. Indemnification of Settlements and Judgments

Practically all liability insurance policies contain clauses that provide that the insured cannot, except at its own cost, voluntarily assume any liability or settle claims without the insurer's consent.[33] Even so, an insurer's unjustified refusal to defend relieves the insured of its obligation to comply with such provisions,[34] and the insurer may also have to indemnify the insured for a settlement that the insured reaches on its own. Decisions splinter based on whether an insurer's indemnification obligations are subject to the policy limits.

1979) (applying Pennsylvania law); Ala. Farm Bureau Mut. Cas. Ins. Co. v. Moore, 349 So. 2d 1113, 1116–17 (Ala. 1977); Campbell v. Gov't Emps. Ins. Co., 306 So. 2d 525, 532 (Fla. 1974); Kistler v. N.J. Mfrs. Ins. Co., 411 A.2d 1175 (N.J. Super. Ct. App. Div. 1980); U.S. Fid. & Guar. Co. v. Copfer, 400 N.E.2d 298, 298–99 (N.Y. 1979).

30. Emhart Indus., Inc. v. Century Indem. Co., 559 F.3d 57, 74–75 (1st Cir. 2009) (applying Rhode Island law) (explaining that the insurer liable for defense costs as the measure of damages for breach of duty to defend); Mesa Underwriters Specialty Ins. Co. v. First Mercury Ins. Co., 411 F. Supp. 3d 607, 612 (N.D. Cal. 2019) (quoting Md. Cas. Co. v. Nat'l Am. Ins. Co., 56 Cal. Rptr. 2d 498, 501 (Ct. App. 1996)); Crist v. Ins. Co. of N. Am., 529 F. Supp. 601, 604 (D. Utah 1982); Deluna v. State Farm Fire & Cas. Co., 233 P.3d 12, 17 (Idaho 2008) (stating that the proper measure of damages for a breach of the duty to defend is attorney's fees and costs of defending the claim, together with any other damages resulting from the breach).

31. *See, e.g.*, U.S. Sugar Corp. v. Com. & Indus. Ins. Co., No. 22-21737-CIV, 2023 WL 4953191, at *3 (S.D. Fla. Aug. 3, 2023); *see also* KB Home Orlando LLC v. Mid-Continent Cas. Co., No. 19-1573-CIV, 2022 WL 4354845, at *1 (M.D. Fla. Sept. 20, 2022) ("Only reasonable attorney's fees are recoverable as damages when an insurer breaches its duty to defend.").

32. *See, e.g.*, E. Ramapo Cent. Sch. Dist. v. N.Y. Schs. Ins. Reciprocal, 158 N.Y.S.3d 173, 179 (App. Div. 2021).

33. *See, e.g.*, INS. SERVS. OFF., INC., COMMERCIAL GENERAL LIABILITY FORM (CG 00 01 04 13), at 11 (2012) ("No insured will, except at that insured's own cost, voluntarily make a payment, assume any obligation, or incur any expense, other than for first aid, without our consent.").

34. Sacred Heart Health Servs. v. MMIC Ins., Inc., 575 F. Supp. 3d 1137, 1165 (D.S.D. 2021) ("[C]ourts almost universally allow an insured to voluntarily settle with a third party despite a 'no action' or 'no voluntary payment' provision in an insurance contract when an insurer has breached its contractual duty to defend. The general idea is that by committing a prior material breach of the contract, the insured has waived any of the insured's preconditions to performance."); Nautilus Ins. Co. v. Concierge Care Nursing Ctrs., Inc., 804 F. Supp. 2d 557, 560 (S.D. Tex. 2011) (applying Texas law); Weber v. Indem. Ins. Co. of N. Am., 345 F. Supp. 2d 1139, 1145 (D. Haw. 2004) (applying Hawaii law); Risely v. Interinsurance Exch. of the Auto. Club, 107 Cal. Rptr. 3d 343, 352 (Ct. App. 2010). This result flows from the general principle that a party cannot seek to enforce a contract when it has breached the contract. RESTATEMENT (SECOND) OF CONTRACTS § 347 (AM. L. INST. 1981).

The majority view holds that, absent bad faith, consequential damages for breach of the duty defend are capped at the policy limits.[35] This principle

35. *See, e.g.*, Nalder v. United Auto. Ins. Co., 824 F.3d 854, 857 (9th Cir. 2016) (quoting Comunale v. Traders & Gen. Ins. Co., 328 P.2d 198, 201 (Cal. 1958)); Quorum Health Res., L.L.C. v. Maverick Cnty. Hosp. Dist., 308 F.3d 451, 468 (5th Cir. 2002) (applying Texas law and stating that damages for an insurer's breach of the duty to defend are capped at policy limits); Liberty Mut. Fire Ins. Co. v. Canal Ins. Co., 177 F.3d 326, 336 (5th Cir. 1999) (footnotes omitted) (Under Mississippi law, "if the insurer has acted in good faith, it is not liable for any amount beyond the stated policy limit. With respect to excess judgments, an insurer is not liable for the amount in excess of the policy limit so long as the insurer has not acted in bad faith and has not wrongfully refused to settle the claim within its policy limits."); Am. Safety Cas. Ins. Co. v. City of Waukegan, 776 F. Supp. 2d 670, 702 (N.D. Ill. 2011) ("Under Illinois law, . . . 'the mere failure to defend does not, in the absence of bad faith, render the insurer liable for that amount of the judgment in excess of the policy limits.'" (quoting Conway v. Country Cas. Ins. Co., 442 N.E.2d 245, 249 (Ill. 1982))); Cincinnati Ins. Co. v. Grand Pointe, LLC, 501 F. Supp. 2d 1145, 1174 (E.D. Tenn. 2007) ("Under Tennessee law an insurer which breaches its duty to defend is liable for the amount of the policy plus the reasonable costs incurred in providing a defense for its insured."); Spence-Parker v. Md. Ins. Grp., 937 F. Supp. 551, 557–58 (E.D. Va. 1996) (applying Virginia law and requiring bad faith to impose extracontractual liability for breach of the duty to defend); Quihuis v. State Farm Mut. Auto. Ins. Co., 334 P.3d 719, 730 (Ariz. 2014) (stating that if an insurer breaches its duty to defend and "a court later finds coverage, the insurer must pay the damages awarded in the default judgment (at least up to the policy limits) unless it can prove fraud or collusion"); Desert Mountain Props. Ltd. P'ship v. Liberty Mut. Fire Ins. Co., 236 P.3d 421, 444 (Ariz. Ct. App. 2010) ("An insurer's wrongful failure to indemnify or defend its insured 'does not expose the insurance carrier to greater liability than that contractually provided in the policy.'" (quoting State Farm Mut. Auto. Ins. Co. v. Paynter, 593 P.2d 948, 954 (Ariz. Ct. App. 1979))); Capstone Bldg. Corp. v. Am. Motorists Ins. Co., 67 A.3d 961, 993 (Conn. 2013) ("If the insurer declines to provide its insured with a defense and is subsequently found to have breached its duty to do so, it bears the consequences of its decision, including the payment of any reasonable settlement agreed to by the plaintiff and the insured, and the costs incurred effectuating the settlement up to the limits of the policy."); State Farm Mut. Auto. Ins. Co. v. Horkheimer, 814 So. 2d 1069, 1071 (Fla. Dist. Ct. App. 2001) ("Absent a showing of bad faith, a judgment cannot be entered against an insurer in excess of its policy limits."); Colonial Oil Indus. Inc. v. Underwriters Subscribing to Policy Nos. TO31504670 & TO31504671, 491 S.E.2d 337, 339 (Ga. 1997) ("[W]hen the insurer breaches the contract by wrongfully refusing to provide a defense, the insured is entitled to receive only what it is owed under the contract—the cost of defense. The breach of the duty to defend, however, should not enlarge indemnity coverage beyond the parties' contract."); Johnson v. Westhoff Sand Co., 62 P.3d 685, 699 (Kan. Ct. App. 2003) ("[A]n insurer who wrongfully refuses to defend an action against its insured is not liable for the amount of a judgment in excess of policy limits, absent a showing by the insured that the excess judgment is traceable to the refusal to defend."); Arceneaux v. Amstar Corp., 66 So. 3d 438, 452 (La. 2011) ("The duty to defend is provided in the insurance contract; therefore, its breach is determined by ordinary contract law principles and the insurer is liable for the insured's reasonable defense costs."); Mesmer v. Md. Auto. Ins. Fund, 725 A.2d 1053, 1064 (Md. 1999) ("[T]he damages for breach of the contractual duty to defend are limited to the insured's expenses, including attorney fees, in defending the underlying tort action, as well as the insured's expenses and attorney fees in a separate contract or declaratory judgment action if such action is filed to establish that there exists a duty to defend."); Engeldinger v. State Auto. & Cas. Underwriters, 236 N.W.2d 596, 602 (Minn. 1975) (reaffirming the rule announced in a 1921 case); Allen v. Bryers, 512 S.W.3d 17, 38 (Mo. 2016) (quoting Landie v. Century Indem. Co., 390 S.W.2d 558, 562 (Mo. Ct. App. 1965)); Gedeon v. State Farm Mut. Auto. Ins. Co., 188 A.2d 320, 322 (Pa. 1963) ("[T]he amount of [the] recovery for breach of the [duty to defend] is the cost of hiring substitute counsel and other costs of the defense, and not the judgment obtained against the insured."); Waite v. Aetna Cas. & Sur. Co., 467 P.2d 847, 851 (Wash. 1970) (stating that where an insurer wrongfully refuses to defend, it must pay the judgment or settlement to the extent of its policy limits and also to reimburse the insured for its reasonable defense costs).

reflects the view that the breach of the duty to defend should not enlarge indemnity coverage beyond the terms of the parties' contract.[36]

Additional arguments support the majority rule. First, any defense lawyer the insured hires will presumably provide the same quality of representation as the lawyer the insurer would have appointed to defend the insured had the insurer properly accepted the defense.[37] Consequently, the amount of any judgment against the insured should be the same or roughly equivalent, regardless of who provided the insured's defense.[38] Alternatively, the plaintiff's case against the insured may be so strong that even the best defense provided by the insurer would not have defeated liability or confined the insured's damages to the policy limits.[39] Of course, if the insurer's provision of a defense would not have altered the outcome, its breach of the duty to defend could not have caused any excess judgment. In other words, any excess judgment did not naturally flow from the breach.[40]

The same is true if the insured settles the case for an amount exceeding the policy limits after the insurer breaches the duty to defend. The settlement should reflect the reasonable value of the plaintiff's claim; the settlement value should not depend upon or be increased by the insurer's breach of its duty to defend.[41]

---

36. McGregor v. Columbia Nat'l Ins. Co., 680 S.E.2d 559, 562 (Ga. Ct. App. 2009).

37. *See, e.g.*, Brockmann v. Bd. of Cnty. Comm'rs, 404 F. App'x 271, 286 (10th Cir. 2010) (observing that because the county was represented by competent counsel—an assistant county attorney—in lieu of a defense lawyer appointed by the insurer, the insurer's refusal to defend was not a factor in the excess judgment); Snodgrass v. State Farm Mut. Auto. Ins. Co., 804 P.2d 1012, 1022 (Kan. Ct. App. 1991) ("Although State Farm refused to represent [its insured] Owen, he was represented by competent counsel in a case in which Owen's liability was clear and [the underlying plaintiff's] injuries were extensive, and there was no offer to settle within State Farm's policy limits. . . . [T]here is no basis to conclude that judgment would have been for a lesser sum if State Farm had defended Owen."); Burgraff v. Menard, Inc., 875 N.W.2d 596, 609 (Wis. 2016) ("Menard cannot demonstrate that the amount of the jury verdict was a result of the breach. Menard chose its own counsel and there is no assertion that it would have achieved a better result at trial had [the insurer] chosen Menard's counsel.").

38. *Snodgrass*, 804 P.2d at 1022.

39. *See, e.g.*, Hyland v. Liberty Mut. Fire Ins. Co., 885 F.3d 482, 487 (7th Cir. 2018) ("[The insured's liability was too clear for argument; counsel could not have hoped to defeat [the plaintiff's] suit. There was no difference between what counsel could have achieved and what actually happened (a default judgment when [the insured] did not defend herself).").

40. Douglas R. Richmond, *A Liability Insurer's Breach of the Duty to Defend and the Often Erroneous Consequence of Extracontractual Liability*, 122 W. Va. L. Rev. 211, 218 (2019).

41. *See, e.g.*, Hamlin v. Hartford Accident & Indem. Co., 86 F.3d 93, 95 (7th Cir. 1996) (involving a case in which the insurer refused to pay for counsel for the insured, the insured hired its own counsel, and the case settled; there was no evidence that a better settlement might have been achieved with insurer-provided counsel, especially since the plaintiff's claims against the insured appeared to be "entirely valid"); Conway v. Country Cas. Ins. Co., 442 N.E.2d 245, 249 (Ill. 1982) ("The $10,000 paid by Conway to [the plaintiff] cannot be said to have been proximately caused by Country Casualty's breach [of the duty to defend] absent a showing that there could have been a settlement for a lesser amount if Country Casualty had defended the action. . . . There was no such showing . . . and it will be assumed that Conway would have been required to pay . . . $10,000 even had Country Casualty defended the . . . action against him.").

Finally, an insurer's breach of the duty to defend cannot be said to have proximately caused an insured's excess liability in a case where the plaintiff was unwilling to settle within policy limits,[42] or in which the plaintiff never offered to settle within policy limits.[43] In those situations, the plaintiff cannot establish that the insurer's defense of the insured would have prevented an excess judgment.[44]

On the other hand, some courts, applying a minority view,[45] hold that damages in excess of policy limits are recoverable if the insured can prove that the insurer's breach caused the excess judgment.[46] If the breach did not cause the excess judgment, on the other hand, damages are capped at the policy limits.[47]

In *Century Surety Company v. Andrew*,[48] the Nevada Supreme Court acknowledged the majority rule that, where there is no bad faith, damages are typically limited to policy limits.[49] The court determined, however, that damages arising from a breach of the duty to defend are not automatically capped

---

42. *See, e.g.*, Liberty Mut. Fire Ins. Co. v. Canal Ins. Co., 177 F.3d 326, 336–38 (5th Cir. 1999) (applying Mississippi law).

43. George R. Winchell, Inc. v. Norris, 633 P.2d 1174, 1177 (Kan. Ct. App. 1981).

44. Richmond, *supra* note 40, at 220.

45. *See, e.g.*, Atlanta Cas. Ins. Co. v. Gardenhire, 545 S.E.2d 182, 184 (Ga. Ct. App. 2001) ("[W]here an insurance company fails to offer a defense, it may be liable to its insured beyond the policy limits to the full amount of the judgment."); Tidyman's Mgmt. Servs. Inc. v. Davis, 330 P.3d 1139, 1149 (Mont. 2014) ("[A]n insurer who breaches the duty to defend is liable for the full amount of the judgment, including amounts in excess of policy limits."); Water Wells Sols. Serv. Grp., Inc. v. Consol. Ins. Co., 881 N.W.2d 285, 297 (Wis. 2016) (explaining that an insurer that wrongly fails to defend its insured opens itself up to a myriad of adverse consequences, including liability in excess of the policy limits).

46. *See, e.g.*, Race City Fasteners, Inc. v. Selective Ins. Co. of S.C., No. 505-CV-9-V, 2007 WL 1340404, at *8 (W.D.N.C. May 3, 2007) (applying Rhode Island law); Delatorre v. Safeway Ins. Co., 989 N.E.2d 268, 274–76 (Ill. App. Ct. 2013) (reasoning that the insurer was liable for the portion of a default judgment that exceeded the policy limits because it "could have been averted altogether had [the insurer] seen to it that its insured was actually defended as contractually required"); Aselco, Inc. v. Hartford Ins. Grp., 21 P.3d 1011, 1019 (Kan. Ct. App. 2001); Century Sur. Co. v. Andrew, 432 P.3d 180, 186 (Nev. 2018); Conanicut Marine Servs., Inc. v. Ins. Co. of N. Am., 511 A.2d 967, 971 (R.I. 1986) ("An insurer who denies coverage does so at its own risk, and, although its position may not have been entirely groundless, if the denial is found to be wrongful it is liable for the full amount which will compensate the insured for all the detriment caused by the insurer's breach of the express and implied obligations of the contract.").

47. *See, e.g.*, Hamlin Inc. v. Hartford Accident & Indem. Co., 86 F.3d 93, 95 (7th Cir. 1996) (observing that the insurer "did not pay the entire bill for [the insured's] defense. But neither is [the insured] some hapless individual who could not afford a good defense unless his insurer or insurers picked up the full tab."); *Century Sur. Co.*, 432 P.3d at 186 ("However, we are not saying that an entire judgment is automatically a consequence of an insurer's breach of its duty to defend; rather, the insured is tasked with showing that the breach caused the excess judgment and 'is obligated to take all reasonable means to protect himself and mitigate his damages.'" (quoting Thomas v. W. World Ins. Co., 343 So.2d 1298, 1303 (Fla. Dist. Ct. App. 1977))); Burgraff v. Menard, Inc., 875 N.W.2d 596, 609 (Wis. 2016) (explaining that the insured could not show that the amount of the jury verdict resulted from the breach where the insured chose its own counsel and did not argue that it would have achieved a better result at trial had its insurer selected defense counsel).

48. 432 P.3d 180 (Nev. 2018).

49. *Id.* at 184.

at policy limits.[50] If harmed by the insurer's denial of a defense, the insured may recover all consequential damages resulting from that breach, including any underlying judgment, plus interest.[51] The Nevada Supreme Court adopted the minority rule after concluding that the majority rule improperly equated damages for breach of the duty to defend with the remedy available for breach of the duty to indemnify:

> We conclude that the minority view is the better approach. Unlike the minority view, the majority view places an artificial limit to the insurer's liability within the policy limits for a breach of its duty to defend. That limit is based on the insurer's duty to indemnify but "[a] duty to defend limited to and coextensive with the duty to indemnify would be essentially meaningless; insureds pay a premium for what is partly litigation insurance designed to protect . . . the insured from the expense of defending suits brought against him." . . . Indeed, the insurance policy limits "only the amount the insurer may have to pay in the performance of the contract as compensation to a third person for personal injuries caused by the insured; they do not restrict the damages recoverable by the insured for a breach of contract by the insurer."[52]

The court also pointed out that the minority rule enforced the general rule of contract law on damages awarded for breach of contract. The obligation of the insurer to defend its insured is purely contractual and a refusal to defend is considered a breach of contract.[53] The court cited the rationale for the minority rule set forth in the penultimate draft of the Restatement of the Law of Liability Insurance: "Consistent with general contract principles, the minority view provides that the insured may be entitled to consequential damages resulting from the insurer's breach of its contractual duty to defend."[54] The court further explained that "[c]onsequential damages 'should be such as may fairly and reasonably be considered as arising naturally, or were reasonably contemplated by both parties at the time they made the contract.'"[55] The determination of the insurer's liability depends on the unique facts of each case and is left to the jury's determination.[56]

Some courts that apply the majority rule—which holds that consequential damages are capped at the policy limits—switch to the minority rule if the insurer rejected its duty to defend in bad faith. "When an insurer denies its

50. *Id.* at 185.
51. *Id.* at 186.
52. *Id.* at 185–86 (citations omitted).
53. *Id.* at 186.
54. *Id.* (citing Restatement of the L. of Liab. Ins. § 48 (Am. L. Inst., Proposed Final Draft No. 2, 2018)).
55. *Id.* (quoting Hornwood v. Smith's Food King No. 1, 772 P.2d 1284, 1286 (Nev. 1989)).
56. *Id.* (citing Khan v. Landmark Am. Ins. Co., 757 S.E.2d 151, 155 (Ga. Ct. App. 2014)); *see also* Restatement (Second) of Contracts § 347 (Am. L. Inst. 1981). For a critique of *Century Surety Co.*, see Richmond, *supra* note 40, at 229–31.

insured a defense, and does so in bad faith, it becomes automatically liable for all of the consequences of that decision, including but not limited to, the amount of the underlying judgment, regardless of foreseeability, and regardless of whether the theory of damages was actually covered by the policy."[57]

Regardless of whether the insured's recovery of indemnity is capped at policy limits, in some jurisdictions, the insured must prove that its settlement is reasonable to recover such costs as consequential damages for breach of the duty to defend. For example, in *Capstone Building Corp. v. American Motorists Insurance Co.*,[58] the Connecticut Supreme Court held that the insured has the burden to prove reasonableness of the settlement "in proportion to the insurer's liability under its duty to defend."[59] If some claims at issue would "not independently trigger the insurer's duty to defend,"[60] then the breaching insurer's liability is "limited to the portion of the settlement corresponding to claims for which the insurer had a duty to defend."[61] On that basis, the insurer may assert that the settlement amount is too high.[62] To determine whether a settlement amount was unreasonable, a court may consider "whether there is a significant prospect of an adverse judgment, whether settlement is generally advisable, whether the action is taken in good faith, and whether it is not excessive in amount."[63] Other jurisdictions do not allow an insurer to question reasonableness of a settlement amount.[64]

An insurer can challenge a settlement that follows a breach of the duty to defend on the basis that it is the product of fraud or collusion between the insured and the underlying plaintiff. Such settlements may be unenforceable against the insurer.[65]

57. Anderson v. Nationwide Mut. Ins. Co., 339 F. Supp. 3d 933, 943 (E.D. Cal. 2018); *see also id.* ("Where, as here, there is at least a possibility of coverage, an unreasonable failure to defend renders the insurer liable for extracontractual damages, including any judgment against the insured.").

58. 67 A.3d 961 (Conn. 2013).

59. *Id.* at 969.

60. *Id.* at 996.

61. *Id.* at 998.

62. *Id.* at 999.

63. Fortin v. Hartford Underwriters Ins. Co., 59 A.3d 247, 256–57 (Conn. App. Ct. 2013).

64. *See, e.g.*, Evanston Ins. Co. v. ATOFINA Petrochemicals, Inc., 256 S.W.3d 660, 671 (Tex. 2008) ("[I]f an insurer wrongfully denies coverage and its insured then enters into an agreed judgment, the insurer is barred from challenging the reasonableness of the settlement amount.").

65. *See* Capitol Specialty Ins. Corp. v. Higgins, 953 F.3d 95, 106–08 (1st Cir. 2020) (discussing the concern that consent judgments and settlement agreements formed without an insurer's participation pose a risk of collusion and have limited application); Salvati v. Am. Ins. Co., 855 F.3d 40, 52 n.14 (1st Cir. 2017) (stating that "the dangers of possible collusion between the insured, the primary insurance carrier, and the plaintiff means that courts must always take steps to ensure that settlements are reached in good faith"); Bucci v. Essex Ins. Co., 393 F.3d 285, 295–96 (1st Cir. 2005) (reasoning that, although the Maine Supreme Judicial Court had not yet decided the question, settlements procured through collusion were likely unenforceable against an insurer because "Maine would not want to encourage collusion or fraud"); Ayers v. C & D Gen. Contractors, 269 F. Supp. 2d 911, 914 (W.D. Ky. 2003) ("[I]n spite of the insured's authority to settle a claim after an insurer has refused a defense, a plaintiff may not collect any amount desirable if it appears 'that the plaintiff and the insured are

C. Fees Incurred in Pursuing Coverage

Jurisdictions are split as to whether, and under what circumstances, a policyholder is entitled to recover attorney's fees it incurs when it must sue to enforce in a declaratory relief action an insurer's duty to defend.[66] A handful of courts deny policyholders the right to recover attorney's fees, strictly applying the "American Rule," which holds that, absent any contractual provision, statute,[67] or a recognized equitable ground, a prevailing party's attorney's fees are not recoverable.[68]

On the other hand, many jurisdictions allow insureds who prevail in coverage litigation against their insurers to recover attorney's fees incurred in coverage litigation.[69] An initial distinction arises between actions alleging that the insurer breached the insurance contract in bad faith and those not including claims for bad-faith breach. As stated in the Restatement of the Law of Liability Insurance, "[c]ourts in all but a very few states award attorney's fees to a prevailing insured when the insurer breaches in bad faith."[70] With regard to coverage actions not involving bad faith, about half of U.S. jurisdictions allow insureds to receive attorney's fees incurred in cases addressing applicability of insurance in the absence of bad faith.[71] In allowing for such recovery, courts frequently point to the often significant expense associated with such litigation. As one court stated, "[w]hen in insured purchases a contract of insurance,

cooperating together to create an inflated collusive judgment.'"); Cont'l Ins. Co. v. McAuliffe, No. FSTCV054006778S, 2007 WL 127315, at *1 (Conn. Super. Ct. Jan. 3, 2007) (leaving the door open for the insurer to challenge the stipulated judgment based on fraud or collusion).

66. ACMAT Corp. v. Greater N.Y. Mut. Ins. Co., 923 A.2d 697, 703–07 (Conn. 2007) (surveying states with differing rules on awarding attorney's fees incurred by insureds in pursuing declaratory judgment actions).

67. *See, e.g.*, Me. Rev. Stat. tit. 24-A, § 2436-B (2023) ("In an action . . . to determine an insurer's contractual duty to defend an insured under an insurance policy, if the insured prevails in such action, the insurer shall pay court costs and reasonable attorney's fees.").

68. Asher v. Unarco Material Handling, Inc., 862 F. Supp. 2d 551, 558 (E.D. Ky. 2012) (applying Kentucky law); Forrest Constr., Inc. v. Cincinnati Ins. Co., 728 F. Supp. 2d 955, 967 (M.D. Tenn. 2010) (making an *Erie* guess that Tennessee courts would not award attorney's fees for costs incurred in bringing an action to establish the insurer's duty to defend); *ACMAT*, 923 A.2d at 703 ("Presently, seven states, specifically, Alabama, California, Kentucky, Louisiana, Michigan, New Mexico and Tennessee, follow the American rule strictly, and have not yet adopted any common-law exceptions allowing for the payment of attorney's fees to policyholders that are successful in coverage actions against their insurance companies.").

69. It can be hard to determine the law in a particular jurisdiction on this point; results can depend on facts of a case or a court's predilections. As one treatise notes, "[w]hile an unsuccessful insurer in coverage litigation likely faces an exception to the American Rule, requiring it to pay for its insured's attorney's fees, the specific approaches vary widely and can have a significant impact on the likelihood of the insurer in fact incurring such obligation." Randy Maniloff et al., General Liability Insurance Coverage 341 (5th ed. 2021).

70. Restatement of the L. of Liab. Ins. § 47 cmt. c. (Am. L. Inst. 2019); *see also* Maniloff et al., *supra* note 69, Ch. 8 (including a 50-state survey of the prevailing insurer's right to recover attorney's fees in coverage litigation).

71. *See* Restatement of the L. of Liab. Ins. § 47 cmt. c (Am. L. Inst. 2019); *see also* Maniloff et al., *supra* note 69, Ch. 8.

it seeks protection from expenses arising from litigation, not vexatious, time consuming, expensive litigation with its insurer."[72]

Indeed, many jurisdictions, whether by rule or statute[73] or by common law,[74] allow prevailing insureds to recover their coverage-counsel fees. Those provisions or decisions allow for such recovery either generally or specifically for violation of the duty to defend. These rules help to ensure that insureds receive the benefit of the bargain from their liability insurance policies.

Courts split on whether a policyholder must make a showing of bad faith by the insurer before obtaining an award of coverage-counsel fees. The Massachusetts Supreme Judicial Court, in explaining the Massachusetts common-law rule allowing such fee-shifting, stated that it was "immaterial" whether the insurer had acted in good faith or bad faith in avoiding its duty to defend:

> The existence of a breach of the terms of the policy is irrelevant because "a special relationship exists between the insured and the insurer under a liability insurance policy, [wherein] . . . insureds obtain liability insurance to avoid the prospect of being burdened by significant legal expenses." "The intent of an insured in acquiring liability insurance is to transfer to the insurer the responsibility for defending the insured against any claim which may fall within the coverage of the policy." In this respect, liability insurance is "'litigation insurance' as well." Thus, . . . "[i]t should not matter whether (as in *Gamache*) the insurer announces withdrawal from the third-party action and sues for a declaration, or . . . brings a declaratory action and provisionally maintains

72. Olympic S.S. Co. v. Centennial Ins. Co., 811 P.2d 673, 681 (Wash. 1991); *see also* Mountain W. Farm Bureau Mut. Ins. Co., v. Brewer, 69 P.3d 652, 657–58 (Mont. 2003) (citing 7C John A. Appleman et al., Insurance Law and Practice § 4691 (1979)).

73. Those fee-shifting statutes may specifically allow prevailing insureds to recover their coverage counsel fees. *See, e.g.*, Ark. Code § 23-79-209 (2023); Fla. Stat. § 627.428 (2023); Haw. Stat. § 431:10-242 (2016); Me. Rev. Stat. tit. 24-A, § 2436-B (2023); Neb. Rev. Stat. § 44-359 (2023); N.H. Rev. Stat. Ann. § 491:22-b (2023). Some states allow this recovery specifically regarding liability insurance, allowing prevailing insureds to recover fees when their liability insurer forces litigation to enforce coverage. *See, e.g.*, N.J. Ct. R. Ann. § 4:42-9. Other states allow such recovery under statutes that allow prevailing parties generally to recover their attorney's fees. *See, e.g.*, Alaska R. Civ. P. 82; Okla. Stat. tit. 36, § 3629 (2023).

74. *See, e.g.*, D.C. Hartford Mut. Ins. Co. v. New LeDroit Park Bldg. Co., 313 F. Supp. 3d 40, 49 (D.D.C. 2018) (citing Hundley v. Johnston, 18 A.3d 802, 806 (D.C. 2011)); Nugent v. Unum Life Ins. Co., 752 F. Supp. 2d 46, 57 (D.D.C. 2010) (relying on an exception to the American Rule which allows awards of attorney's fees for "oppressive or vexatious conduct"); Brandt v. Super. Ct., 693 P.2d 796, 798 (Cal. 1985); Learman v. Auto-Owners Ins. Co., 769 N.E.2d 1171, 1178 (Ind. Ct. App 2002) (insured entitled to recover fees when insurer acts in bad faith); Bausch & Lomb, Inc. v. Utica Mut. Ins. Co., 735 A.2d 1081, 1094–95 (Md. 1999); Mighty Midgets, Inc. v. Centennial Ins. Co., 389 N.E.2d 1080, 1085 (N.Y. 1989); Hegler v. Gulf Ins. Co., 243 S.E.2d 443, 444–45 (S.C. 1978). *But see* ACMAT Corp. v. Greater N.Y. Mut. Ins. Co., 923 A.2d 697, 708 (Conn. 2007); (allowing fees only if the insurer is guilty of bad faith); AIK Selective Self-Ins. Fund v. Minton, 192 S.W.3d 415, 420 (Ky. 2006) (identifying Kentucky as one of seven states that apply the American Rule "strictly"); Steptore v. Masco Constr. Co., 643 So. 2d 1213, 1218 (La. 1994); Shepard Marine Constr. Co. v. Md. Cas. Co., 250 N.W.2d 541, 543 (Mich. Ct. App. 1976); D.J. Painting Co. v. Baraw Enters. 776 A.2d 413, 419 (Vt. 2001) (recognizing there may be an exception that allows an insured to recover coverage-counsel fees when the court finds bad faith by the insurer).

defense of the third-party action pending instruction by the declaration. In either case the insured deserves reimbursement for his reasonable outlay "in successfully establishing the insurer's duty to defend under the policy."[75]

Courts awarding such fees to insureds reason that, when an insurer breaches its duty to defend, the insured should be compensated for all expenses it incurs as a result of that breach, including the fees expended in connection with enforcing that contractual right.[76] Otherwise, "the insured [would be left] footing the bill for two litigations they should not have been required to defend or initiate."[77] This rule enforces the policyholder's expectation of the protection afforded by "litigation insurance."[78] Courts also award insureds such attorney's fees based on the "quasi-fiduciary" relationship between insurers and their insureds.[79]

Some courts have limited the fee-shifting rule that an insured may recover its attorney's fees expended in a declaratory judgment action to instances in which the insurer acted in bad faith in refusing to provide a defense.[80] And some states have enacted statutes that expressly allow a policyholder to recover

75. Hanover Ins. Co. v. Golden, 766 N.E.2d 838, 840–41 (Mass. 2002) (citations omitted). The Massachusetts high court in 2006 stated that this "*Gamache* exception" was limited to litigation over the insurer's duty to defend and, thus, does not apply to litigation over the insurer's duty to indemnify. Wilkinson v. Citation Ins. Co., 856 N.E.2d 829, 835 (Mass. 2006).

76. Flannery v. Allstate Ins. Co., 49 F. Supp. 2d 1223, 1233 (D. Colo. 1999) (applying Colorado law); New Eng. Env't Techs. Corp. v. Am. Safety Risk Retention Grp., Inc., 810 F. Supp. 2d 390, 396 (D. Mass. 2011) (applying Massachusetts law); Stryker Corp. v. XL Ins. Am. Inc., No. 1:05-CV-51, 2009 WL 3256081, at *4 (W.D. Mich. Oct. 7, 2009) (recognizing an exception to the American Rule where "such fees and costs arise in separate litigation with a third party as a consequence of the defendant's wrongful conduct"); Gorelick v. Star Mkts. Co., 203 N.E.3d 610, 617–18 (Mass. App. Ct. 2023) (recognizing an exception to the traditional rule, thus entitling an insured to recover "reasonable attorney's fees and expenses incurred in successfully establishing the insurer's duty to defend under the policy" and explaining that "[t]he rationale for the exception is that a 'special relationship' exists between an insured and its insurer arising from the policy and 'the assumption of responsibility for the insured's defense in litigation is one of the core purposes for which liability insurance is purchased'"); Mountain W. Farm Bureau Mut. Ins. Co. v. Brewer, 69 P.3d 652, 660 (Mont. 2003) (holding that "an insured is entitled to recover attorney fees, pursuant to the insurance exception to the American Rule, when the insurer forces the insured to assume the burden of legal action to obtain the full benefit of the insurance contract, regardless of whether the insurer's duty to defend is at issue").

77. Innovative Mold Sols., Inc. v. Cent. Mut. Ins. Co., 277 F. Supp. 3d 222, 225 (D. Mass. 2017).

78. Cap. Env't Servs., Inc. v. N. River Ins. Co., 536 F. Supp. 2d 633, 640 (E.D. Va. 2008) (quoting Perdue Farms, Inc. v. Travelers Cas. & Sur. Co. of Am., 448 F.3d 252, 258 (4th Cir. 2006)); RESTATEMENT OF THE L. OF LIAB. INS. § 14 cmt. a (AM. L. INST. 2019).

79. *See, e.g.*, Am. Fam. Ins. Co. v. Dewald, 597 F.2d 1148, 1151 (8th Cir. 1979) (applying North Dakota law and limiting the rule to cases where the insurer wrongly refused to defend the insured); Wheeler v. Reese, 835 P.2d 572, 577 (Colo. App. 1992); Gibson v. Farm Fam. Mut. Ins. Co., 673 A.2d 1350, 1354 (Me. 1996); Olympic S.S. Co. v. Centennial Ins. Co., 811 P.2d 673, 680–81 (Wash. 1991).

80. *See, e.g.*, TIG Ins. Co. v. Nobel Learning Cmtys., Inc., No. CIV.A. 01-4708, 2002 WL 1340332, at *18 (E.D. Pa. June 18, 2002) (recognizing the rule but declining to apply it because the insured had not alleged bad faith); Westfield Cos. v. O.K.L. Can Line, 804 N.E.2d 45, 56 (Ohio Ct. App. 2003) (awarding attorney's fees to the insured in connection with a declaratory judgment action because the insurer acted "with a stubborn propensity for needless litigation"); Ins. Co. of N. Am. v. Kayser-Roth Corp., 770 A.2d 403, 419 (R.I. 2001) (vacating an award of attorney's fees and remanding the matter to the trial court to evaluate the insurer's alleged bad faith); Nationwide Mut. Ins. Co. v. St. John,

attorneys' fees from an insurer which acts in bad faith or is guilty of wanton or oppressive conduct, and requires the insured to sue to enforce its rights.[81]

D. Extracontractual Damages

If the insurer acts egregiously in refusing to provide a defense, the insured may receive damages proximately caused by the breach, regardless of the foreseeability of such damages.[82] Some states, however, do not allow bad faith claims for a breach of contract absent some tort independent of the contract.[83] If the duty to defend was unclear, a court may find that the insurer's breach was not in bad faith and therefore the insured cannot recover extracontractual damages.[84]

E. Mental Anguish

In rare instances, courts allow insureds to recover for mental anguish suffered when they were forced to defend themselves and thereafter pursue recovery from their insurer.[85] Typically, the insured must provide "evidence demonstrating quantifiable effects" to support the claim.[86]

524 S.E.2d 649, 651 (Va. 2000) (finding that an attorney's fee award was justified where the insured established the insurer's bad faith).

81. *See, e.g.*, N.H. Rev. Stat. § 491:22 (2023); *see also* ACMAT Corp. v. Greater N.Y. Mut. Ins. Co., 923 A.2d 697, 705 (Conn. 2007) (stating that Indiana, Iowa, Maine, Mississippi, North Carolina, Pennsylvania, Utah, Vermont, and Wisconsin have created common-law exceptions to the American rule for the situation where the insurance coverage litigation is the product of bad faith conduct on the insurer's part).

82. Mitchell v. State Farm Fire & Cas. Co., 799 F. Supp. 2d 680, 696 (N.D. Miss. 2011) ("Mississippi caselaw provides for 'extra-contractual damages' when an insurance company has tortiously breached its contract. . . . This is because an insurance company's financial default is often less than the cost to the insured of judicially forcing a correct payment.").

83. *See, e.g.*, Lunde v. Cincinnati Ins. Co., No. 18-CV-238 (JNE/HB), 2018 WL 1972475, at *2 (D. Minn. Apr. 26, 2018); *see also* Bryant v. Gen. Cas. Co. of Wis., No. 1:18-CV-562, 2019 WL 367292, at *3 (N.D.N.Y. Jan. 30, 2019) (finding that a breach of the implied covenant of good faith and fair dealing is not a separate cause of action from a breach of contract claim).

84. Dewitt Constr. Inc. v. Charter Oak Fire Ins. Co., 307 F.3d 1127, 1138 (9th Cir. 2002) (applying Washington law) (deciding that a bad-faith claim was properly dismissed because the insurer's duty to defend "was not unambiguous" and "coverage was unclear"); United States v. CNA Fin. Corp., 168 F. Supp. 2d 1109, 1122 (D. Alaska 2001) (stating that "[t]o establish a claim for bad faith denial of coverage, a plaintiff must show that the defendant-insurer lacked a reasonable basis for denying benefits of the policy and that the defendant-insurer had knowledge that no reasonable basis existed to deny the claim or acted in reckless disregard for the lack of a reasonable basis for denying the claim"); MCE Auto., Inc. v. Nat'l Cas. Co., No. 6:11–1245–TMC, 2012 WL 4479163, at *6 (D.S.C. Sept. 28, 2012) (applying South Carolina law).

85. Bucci v. Essex Ins. Co., 323 F. Supp. 2d 84, 92 (D. Me. 2004); Acceptance Ins. Co. v. Brown, 832 So. 2d 1, 22 (Ala. 2001).

86. *Brown*, 832 So. 2d at 23; *see also* Kan. Bankers Sur. Co. v. Lynass, 920 F.2d 546, 549 (8th Cir. 1990) (applying Kansas law) (finding that, despite the policyholder's claim that his insurer's denial of a defense left him "naked in the face of an enormous, multi-million dollar claim" and caused him to suffer "anxiety, uncertainty, inability to sleep, and humiliation," his failure to offer any medical bills or

III. Nonmonetary Consequences

Along with judgments requiring payment of compensatory damages, depending upon the facts and circumstances involved and controlling law, an insurance company that wrongly refuses to defend its policyholder may lose rights under the insurance policy.[87] For instance, an insurer may "be precluded from denying coverage after it has unjustifiably refused to defend."[88] An insurer may also relinquish control over decisions related to the insured's defense or settlement. The insurer may be estopped from asserting certain insurance policy exclusions and provisions as a bar to insurance coverage.[89] This forfeiture is based on the general contract law principle "that a party which has itself breached the terms of a contract may not rely on other terms of the same contract."[90]

A. Estoppel and Waiver of Coverage Defenses

The duty to defend is separate from and broader than the duty to indemnify.[91] While the duty to defend is measured from the complaint, the duty to indemnify is determined by the insured's actual liability.[92] Thus, even if the insured

records to substantiate his claim meant that no reasonable jury could find that his insurer caused him to suffer severe emotional distress).

87. *See, e.g.*, Bainbridge, Inc. v. Travelers Cas. Co. of Conn., 159 P.3d 748, 756 (Colo. App. 2006) ("[T]o the extent that Travelers . . . argue[s] that Bainbridge cannot expand the policy to recover damages awarded to the Rays on their [Colorado Consumer Protection Act] claim, because this is a coverage question, this issue should be addressed by the trial court in the context of indemnification claims, if any, sought by Bainbridge on remand. Bainbridge may, however, otherwise be entitled to such damages if, upon remand, it is determined that Travelers's breach of its duty to defend was tortious and that the tortious conduct proximately caused those damages."); Missionaries of Co. of Mary, Inc. v. Aetna Cas. & Sur. Co., 230 A.2d 21, 26 (Conn. 1967) (citation omitted) ("The defendant having, in effect, waived the opportunity which was open to it to perform its contractual duty to defend under a reservation of its right to contest the obligation to indemnify the plaintiff, reason dictates that the defendant should reimburse the plaintiff for the full amount of the obligation reasonably incurred by it. . . . The defendant, after breaking the contract by its unqualified refusal to defend, should not thereafter be permitted to seek the protection of that contract in avoidance of its indemnity provisions. Nor should the defendant be permitted, by its breach of the contract, to cast upon the plaintiff the difficult burden of proving a causal relation between the defendant's breach of the duty to defend and the results which are claimed to have flowed from it."); Emps. Ins. of Wausau v. Ehlco Liquidating Tr., 708 N.E.2d 1122, 1135 (Ill. 1999) ("Once the insurer breaches its duty to defend, . . . the estoppel doctrine has broad application and operates to bar the insurer from raising policy defenses to coverage, even those defenses that may have been successful had the insurer not breached its duty to defend.").

88. Allan D. Windt, Insurance Claims & Disputes § 4:37 (6th ed. 2013 & Supp. 2023).

89. M/A Com, Inc. v. Perricone, 543 N.E.2d 228, 231 (Ill. App. Ct. 1989), *overruled on other grounds by* Emps. Ins. of Wausau v. Ehlco Liquidating Tr., 708 N.E.2d 1122, 1136 (Ill. 1999).

90. *Id.*

91. *See* Liberty Mut. Fire Ins. Co. v. Copart of Conn., Inc., 75 F.4th 522, 528 (5th Cir. 2023) (applying Texas law) ("These two duties are distinct, and the duty to defend is generally broader than the duty to indemnify."); Eckerd Youth Alternatives, Inc. v. Devereux Found., Inc., 366 So. 3d 1154, 1158 (Fla. Dist. Ct. App. 2023).

92. Servidone Constr. Corp. v. Sec. Ins. Co. of Hartford, 477 N.E.2d 441, 423–24 (N.Y. 1985).

has proven that the insurer breached its duty to defend, the insurer may not have a duty to indemnify if it can establish that the loss was not covered by the policy.[93] According to this majority rule, allowing the breach of the duty to defend to establish a duty to indemnify would "enlarge[] the bargained-for coverage as a penalty for breach of the duty to defend."[94]

The Supreme Court of Hawaii adopted the majority rule, expressing its concern about expanding the duty to indemnify as a penalty:

> [A] blanket application of coverage by waiver or estoppel, based upon the failure to provide a defense, subverts any meaningful distinction between the duty to defend and the separate duty to indemnify and, in many cases, serves no more than to punish the insurer for the breach of a contractual duty.[95]

The court further explained that a breaching insurer still faced other significant consequences by refusing to defend, including forfeiture of the "right to control the defense costs and strategy, including the right to compel the insured's cooperation in the defense of the claims," the obligation to reimburse the insured for its defense fees and costs in the underlying lawsuit, waiver of "its right to approve any settlement," and the insured's ability to use a reasonable and good faith settlement of the underlying claim as "presumptive evidence of the breaching insurer's liability."[96]

Similarly, in *Arceneaux v. Amstar Corp.*,[97] the Supreme Court of Louisiana applied the majority rule holding that an insurer's breach of its duty to defend does not warrant the relinquishment of valid policy defenses. Rather, the appropriate remedy in that context is the reimbursement of the policyholder's reasonable defense costs. The court explained that forfeiture of coverage defenses "judicially imposes a result that would permit insureds to reap a windfall of potentially enormous profits, far beyond the natural consequences of the insurer's bad faith breach of the duty to defend, and far beyond the scope of the insurer's contractual undertaking."[98]

93. *Id.*

94. *Id.* at 424; *see also* Ross v. Home Ins. Co., 773 A.2d 654, 658 (N.H. 2001) (rejecting the insured's argument that the insurer's breach of its duty to defend estopped it from arguing against coverage in a declaratory judgment action); Med. Prot. Co. v. Fragatos, 940 N.E.2d 1011, 1015 (Ohio Ct. App. 2010) ("Generally, the doctrines of waiver and estoppel may not be used to expand . . . coverage.").

95. Sentinel Ins. Co. v. First Ins. Co. of Haw., Ltd., 875 P.2d 894, 912 (Haw. 1994).

96. *Id.* at 913.

97. 66 So. 3d 438 (La. 2011).

98. *Id.* at 452; *see also* Quihuis v. State Farm Mut. Auto. Ins. Co., 334 P.3d 719, 728 (Ariz. 2014) ("[A]pplying issue preclusion to deprive an insurer of its coverage defense because the insurer allegedly breaches its duty to defend 'subverts any meaningful distinction between the duty to defend and the separate duty to indemnify, and, in many cases, serves no more than to punish the insurer for the breach of a contractual duty.'" (quoting Sentinel Ins. Co. v. First Ins. Co. of Haw., Ltd., 875 P.2d 894, 912 (Haw. 1994))); Garamendi v. Golden Eagle Ins. Co., 10 Cal. Rptr. 3d 724, 745–47 (Ct. App. 2004); Nw. Pump & Equip. Co. v. Am. States Ins. Co., 925 P.2d 1241, 1244 (Or. Ct. App.

A minority of courts have held that, as a consequence of the breach of the duty to defend, the insurer forfeits or is estopped from asserting coverage defenses.[99] The principle developed in Illinois and so it sometimes is referred to as the "Illinois estoppel rule."[100] Under this rule, the insurer becomes "automatically" liable for the entire judgment, even where facts may show that no indemnity is due for all or a portion of the claim.[101]

Courts applying the estoppel rule find that contract damages are not an adequate remedy for the breach of the duty to defend. Even though the duty to defend is contractual, the insurance contract is said to also create a fiduciary relationship. Namely, "the insurer controls the disposition of claims against its insured, who relinquishes any right to negotiate on his own behalf," and an insurer's "failure to act in good faith exposes its insured to a judgment and personal liability in excess of the policy limits."[102] Thus, a breach of the duty to defend merits equitable remedies, including the forfeiture of the insurer's coverage defenses.[103]

1996) (finding that the non-estoppel approach "is the only one consistent with the general rule that an insured is entitled to the benefit of its bargain, and no more").

99. Twin City Fire Ins. Co. v. City of Madison, Miss., 309 F.3d 901, 906 (5th Cir. 2002) (applying estoppel under Mississippi law); Valley Improvement Ass'n, Inc. v. U.S. Fid. & Guar. Corp., 129 F.3d 1108, 1125 (10th Cir. 1997) (applying New Mexico law) (holding that an insurer that breaches the duty to defend "will not be heard to complain that the claims might not have been within the coverage"); Santa's Best Craft, LLC v. St. Paul Fire & Marine Ins. Co., 353 F. Supp. 2d 966, 971 (N.D. Ill. 2005); Dove v. State Farm Fire & Cas. Co., 399 P.3d 400, 406 (N.M. 2017) ("[A]n insurer who unilaterally refuses to defend effectively waives its ability to later challenge the underlying merits as to coverage because the ultimate question of coverage is to be properly resolved in the primary action in order to protect the interests of the insured and for judicial efficiency.").

100. Todd J. Weiss, *A Natural Law Approach to Remedies for the Liability Insurer's Breach of the Duty to Defend: Is Estoppel of Coverage Defenses Just?*, 57 Alb. L. Rev. 145, 149–54 (1993) (identifying *Sims v. Illinois National Casualty Co.*, 193 N.E.2d 123 (Ill. App. Ct. 1963) as establishing the "modern estoppel rule"); *see, e.g.*, Title Indus. Assur. Co., R.R.G. v. First Am. Title Ins. Co., 853 F.3d 876, 892 (7th Cir. 2017) ("This Illinois rule of estoppel is strong stuff, but it is intended to protect insureds' reasonable expectations of coverage when they most need it."); Little v. USAA Cas. Ins. Co., No. 09-30948, 2010 WL 4909869, at *4 (5th Cir. Apr. 2, 2010) (applying Arizona law) ("Under the 'Illinois Rule,' if a court determines that an insurer violated its duty to defend, the insurer is estopped from denying coverage.").

101. Dowson v. Scottsdale Ins. Co., 645 F. App'x 532, 533 (9th Cir. 2016) (applying Montana law) ("[B]ecause [the insurer] breached its duty to defend [the insureds], it is liable for 100% of the defense and settlement costs incurred in the third-party lawsuit."); Race City Fasteners, Inc. v. Selective Ins. Co. of S.C., No. 505-CV-9-V, 2007 WL 1340404, at *7 (W.D.N.C. May 3, 2007) (applying Rhode Island law) ("[W]hen an insurer breaches its duty to defend, it waives its right to rely on any coverage defense and is then liable for the full amount of any judgment or settlement against its insured in the action it refused to defend."); Nat'l Indem. Co. v. State, 499 P.3d 516, 536 (Mont. 2021) (finding that the insurer was estopped from asserting coverage defenses and had to pay the full defense costs and indemnity).

102. Beck v. Farmers Ins. Exch., 701 P.2d 795, 799 (Utah 1985).

103. Jeffrey W. Stempel, *Enhancing the Socially Instrumental Role of Insurance: The Opportunity and Challenge Presented by the ALI Restatement Position on Breach of the Duty to Defend*, 5 U.C. Irvine L. Rev. 587, 595–96, 602–14 (2015) (collecting authority and arguing in favor of the minority, automatic loss-of-coverage-defenses rule).

Some courts are not so "automatic" in their application of the minority rule. For instance, in *Pulte Home Corp. v. American Southern Insurance Co.*,[104] the North Carolina Court of Appeals began by recognizing that it was "well established in North Carolina that '[w]hen an insurer without justification refuses to defend its insured, the insurer is estopped from denying coverage and is obligated to pay the amount of any reasonable settlement.'"[105] The *Pulte* court nevertheless allowed the insurer to raise a late notice defense, albeit unsuccessfully.[106]

A more significant carve-out is those courts that only apply the estoppel rule when the insurer's breach of the duty to defend is in bad faith. The Restatement of the Law of Liability Insurance explains that this rule "reinforces the importance" of the "litigation insurance" policyholders seek when buying liability coverage:

> The loss-of-coverage-defense remedy is particularly appropriate when an insurer refuses to defend in bad faith. Requiring the insurer to pay for a judgment or settlement entered in such a case reinforces the importance of the defense coverage provided by traditional liability insurance policies, which promise to pay for the defense of any potentially covered claim and, in most cases, also to select the defense lawyer and manage the defense. An insurer that could abandon the defense whenever it concluded that the coverage-relevant facts were in its favor, without any risk of having to pay a judgment or settlement of the action, would have an incentive to do so.[107]

Nonetheless, the Illinois estoppel rule remains the minority position.[108] In a curious turn of events, the New York Court of Appeals rejected the minority rule in *K2 Investment Group, LLC v. American Guarantee & Liability Insurance Co. (K2–II)*,[109] after the court had initially adopted it less than one year earlier in *K2 Investment Group, LLC v. American Guarantee & Liability*

---

104. 647 S.E.2d 614 (N.C. Ct. App. 2007).

105. *Id.* at 617 (quoting Ames v. Cont'l Cas. Co., 340 S.E.2d 479, 485 (N.C. Ct. App. 1986)).

106. *Id.* at 622.

107. Restatement of the L. of Liab. Ins. § 50 cmt. c (Am. L. Inst. 2019).

108. Flannery v. Allstate Ins. Co., 49 F. Supp. 2d 1223, 1227–28 (D. Colo. 1999) (collecting cases); Quihuis v. State Farm Mut. Auto. Ins. Co., 334 P.3d 719, 728 (Ariz. 2014); S. Guar. Ins. Co. v. Dowse, 605 S.E.2d 27, 29 (Ga. 2004) ("By refusing to defend, however, [the insurer] did not waive its right to contest its insured's assertion that the insurance policy provides coverage for the underlying claim. Obviously, if the underlying claim is outside the policy's scope of coverage, then [the insurer's] refusal to indemnify or defend was justified and it is not liable to make payment within the policy's limits. This question of whether the policy provides coverage for the claim is separate from the legal consequences of an insurer's refusal to indemnify or defend."); Harlor v. Amica Mut. Ins. Co., 150 A.3d 793, 801 (Me. 2016) ("To award to the insured the entire settlement as consequential damages after a breach of the duty to defend, when some claims against the insured were for covered damages and others were for uncovered damages, would improperly enlarge the bargained-for coverage.").

109. 6 N.E.3d 1117 (N.Y. 2014).

Insurance Co. (K2–I).[110] In its decision applying the minority rule in *K2–I*, the court concluded that "an insurance company that has disclaimed its duty to defend 'may litigate only the validity of its disclaimer.' If the disclaimer is found bad, the insurance company must indemnify its insured for the resulting judgment, even if policy exclusions would otherwise have negated the duty to indemnify."[111] The court further explained that the minority rule seeks to encourage insurers to "defend the cases they are bound by law to defend, and thus to give insureds the full benefit of their bargain."[112] In contrast, allowing an insurer that wrongfully denied coverage and refused to defend the insured to then require the insured to litigate the effect of policy exclusions on the insurer's duty to indemnify "would be unfair to insureds, and would promote unnecessary and wasteful litigation."[113]

In *K2–II*, New York's high court reversed course. In vacating its prior decision, the *K2–II* court held that an insurer who wrongfully refused to defend its policyholder *may* deny coverage based on policy exclusions.[114] The court concluded that its original ruling could not be reconciled with its 1985 decision in *Servidone Construction Corp. v. Security Insurance Co. of Hartford*.[115] In *Servidone*, the court held that an insurer that breaches the duty to defend is not automatically liable to indemnify the insured for a reasonable underlying settlement if coverage is disputed.[116] In *K2–II*, the court ultimately concluded that, "to decide this case we must either overrule *Servidone* or follow it. We choose to follow it."[117] In rationalizing its choice, the court observed that the *Servidone* rule—which allows an insurer that breaches its duty to defend to later dispute coverage—apparently had proved workable in practice and had worked no significant injustice or hardship.[118]

B. Waiver of the Right to Contest Insured's Liability in Underlying Action

Courts also apply waiver, precluding insurers from contesting the insured's liability in an underlying action, where the insurer has breached its duty to defend. If a default judgment is entered against an insured, the insurer that failed to defend its insured is bound by the factual allegations about the

110. 993 N.E.2d 1249 (N.Y. 2013), *vacated by* 6 N.E.3d 1117 (N.Y. 2014).
111. *Id.* at 1254.
112. *Id.*
113. *Id.*
114. *K2–II*, 6 N.E.3d at 1120.
115. 477 N.E.2d 441 (N.Y. 1985).
116. *K2–II*, 6 N.E.3d at 1119 (quoting and citing *Servidone*, 477 N.E.2d at 442).
117. *Id.* at 1120.
118. *See id.* ("[W]e see no justification for overruling *Servidone*. Plaintiffs have not presented any indication that the *Servidone* rule has proved unworkable, or caused significant injustice or hardship, since it was adopted in 1985.").

policyholder's negligence in an action to determine whether the insurer has a duty to indemnify.[119]

C. Waiver of the Insurer's Right to Control the Defense and Settle

An unjustified refusal by an insurer to defend an insured may result in the insurer's loss of the ability to control the defense,[120] including the selection of counsel,[121] and the ability to accept, reject, or consent to a settlement.[122] The Restatement of the Law of Liability Insurance states the black-letter rule as follows: "An insurer that breaches the duty to defend a legal action forfeits the right to assert any control over the defense or settlement of the action."[123]

A minority of courts have rejected waiver, finding that an insurer does not forfeit its right to contest coverage when it wrongfully refuses to defend. The basis for this rule is that "when the insurer breaches the contract by wrongfully refusing to provide a defense, the insured is entitled to receive only what it is owed under the contract—the cost of defense. The breach of the duty to defend, however, should not enlarge indemnity coverage beyond the parties' contract."[124]

---

119. Metro. Prop. & Cas. Ins. Co. v. Morrison, 951 N.E.2d 662, 670 (Mass. 2011); L.C.S., Inc. v. Lexington Ins. Co., 853 A.2d 974, 985 (N.J. Super. Ct. App. Div. 2004).

120. *See, e.g.*, Yowell v. Seneca Specialty Ins. Co., 117 F. Supp. 3d 904, 909 (E.D. Tex. 2015) (applying Texas law); Episcopal Church in S.C. v. Church Ins. Co. of Vt., 53 F. Supp. 3d 816, 826 (D.S.C. 2014) (applying South Carolina law); Wells Dairy, Inc. v. Travelers Indem. Co. of Ill., 266 F. Supp. 2d 964, 968 (N.D. Iowa 2003) (predicting Iowa law); Intergulf Dev. LLC v. Super. Ct., 107 Cal. Rptr. 3d 162, 165 (Ct. App. 2010); Sentinel Ins. Co. v. First Ins. Co. of Haw., 875 P.2d 894, 913 (Haw. 1994); Water Well Sols. Serv. Grp., Inc. v. Consol. Ins. Co., 881 N.W.2d 285, 297 (Wis. 2016).

121. *See, e.g.*, *Yowell*, 117 F. Supp. 3d at 909; Sierra Pac. Indus. v. Am. States Ins. Co., 883 F. Supp. 2d 967, 975 (E.D. Cal. 2012) (applying California law).

122. *See, e.g.*, Burgett, Inc. v. Am. Zurich Ins. Co., 830 F. Supp. 2d 953, 965 (E.D. Cal. 2011) (applying California law); Willcox v. Am. Home Assur. Co., 900 F. Supp. 850, 855 (S.D. Tex. 1995) (applying Texas law) ("[O]nce an insurer has breached its duty to defend, as in the instant case, the insured is free to proceed as he sees fit; he may engage his own counsel and either settle or litigate, at his option.").

123. Restatement of the L. of Liab. Ins. § 19 (Am. L. Inst. 2019); *see also* Foti v. United Serv. Auto. Ass'n, No. FSTCV116010120, 2014 WL 3906863, at *12 (Conn. Super. Ct. July 2, 2014) ("Having not fulfilled its initial duty to defend, at least with a reservation of rights to contest coverage, [the insurer's] arguments regarding the scope of coverage offered to [the insured] are no longer at issue."); S. Guar. Ins. Co. v. Dowse, 605 S.E.2d 27, 29 (Ga. 2004) ("In Georgia, an insurer that denies coverage and refuses to defend an action against its insured, when it could have done so with a reservation of its rights as to coverage, waives the provisions of the policy against a settlement by the insured and becomes bound to pay the amount of any settlement within a policy's limits made in good faith, plus expenses and attorney's fees."); Truck Ins. Exch. v. Prairie Framing, LLC, 162 S.W.3d 64, 89–90 (Mo. Ct. App. 2005) ("Having breached the contract, [the insurer] 'is treated as if it waived any control of the defense of the underlying tort action.' . . . [The insurer's] breach also 'relieved [the insured] from the contractual obligation not to settle' so that it was free to go its own way, and 'to make a reasonable settlement or compromise without losing the right to recover on the policy.'").

124. Colonial Oil Indus., Inc. v. Underwriters Subscribing to Policy Nos. T031504670 & T031504671, 491 S.E.2d 337, 339 (Ga. 1997).

D. Waiver of Proof of Cooperation and Timely Notice Requirements

An insurer's breach of the duty to defend may also operate to waive additional duties and obligations by the insured under the policy, including the policyholder's duties to cooperate[125] and to provide timely notice.[126] Courts explain that a denial might "reasonably induce" an insured to believe that notice of additional related claims would be "useless" based on prior denials, thereby waiving further notification duties.[127]

IV. Statute of Limitations

A threshold issue when an insured sues its insurer for breach of the duty to defend is whether the insured's claim is barred by the statute of limitations. To make that determination, one must know when a claim for a breach of duty to defend accrues. There are two possibilities: when the insurer first denies a defense or when the underlying litigation has concluded. Courts are split between the two.

Some courts have ruled that the statute of limitations begins to run when the insurer provides an "unconditional denial of coverage."[128] In some scenarios, a court may equitably toll the statute that accrues upon the insurer's denial until the underlying action reaches final judgment.[129] Other courts have ruled that the statute of limitations on a breach of the duty to defend begins to run on the latter date—when judgment is obtained against the insured.[130]

125. Coffeyville Res. Refin. & Mktg., LLC v. Liberty Surplus Ins. Corp., No. CIV.A. 08-1204-MLB, 2012 WL 4088703, at *6 (D. Kan. Sept. 17, 2012) (stating that a breach of the duty to defend "may estop the insurer from invoking policy defenses such as an insured's failure to cooperate or a failure to obtain the insurer's approval for settlement").

126. Craige v. Gov't Emps. Ins. Co., 503 F. Supp. 3d 365, 377 (M.D.N.C. 2020) ("[E]ven if [the insureds'] late notice may have otherwise excused the duty to defend, the rule in North Carolina is that the denial of liability on another ground operates as a waiver of the notice requirements, being regarded as a statement that payment would not be made even though policy provisions had been complied with."); *Prairie Framing*, 62 S.W.3d at 92.

127. Dutton-Lainson Co. v. Cont'l Ins. Co., 716 N.W.2d 87, 104 (Neb. 2006).

128. *See, e.g.*, Land O' Lakes, Inc. v. Emps. Mut. Liab. Ins. Co. of Wis., 846 F. Supp. 2d 1007, 1043–44 (D. Minn. 2012) (explaining that the six-year statute of limitations for policyholder's duty to defend claims against insurer began to run when the insurers denied a defense, so the policyholder's claims were time barred); Wiseman Oil Co. v. TIG Ins. Co., 878 F. Supp. 2d 597, 605 (W.D. Pa. 2012) ("The statute of limitations period for the alleged breach of duty to defend commences upon a clear or unequivocal denial of coverage by the insurer. . . .").

129. Brannon v. Cont'l Cas. Co., 137 P.3d 280, 284–87 (Alaska 2006) (collecting cases).

130. *See, e.g.*, Narragansett Elec. Co. v. Am. Home Assur. Co., 999 F. Supp. 2d 511, 517 (S.D.N.Y. 2014) (concluding that "the Rhode Island Supreme Court likely would follow the majority view and reasoning of most other state courts and hold that the statute of limitations first begins to run on the date of final judgment and not the date on which the insurer initially refused to defend"); *Dutton-Lainson Co.*, 716 N.W.2d at 100–02 (collecting cases).

CHAPTER 10
Defenses under Defense-Cost-Indemnification Policies

Douglas R. Richmond

I. Introduction

As discussed in Chapter 1, a liability insurer typically has a contractual duty to defend an insured in litigation. Also as explained previously, courts have settled on two approaches for determining an insurer's duty to defend. Under the eight corners rule, the factual allegations in the plaintiff's complaint or petition are compared with the policy, and the insurer owes a defense only if those allegations potentially implicate the policy's coverage. In contrast, courts employing an extrinsic evidence approach hold that an insurer must look beyond the effect of the pleadings and consider any facts brought to its attention or any facts that it reasonably could have discovered in determining whether it has a duty to defend. Courts have additionally developed common law rules regarding the scope of an insurer's duty to defend, such as the requirement that any doubts about the duty to defend be resolved in the insured's favor.

Although most liability insurance policies impose on the insurer a duty to defend, a significant percentage of them do not.[1] Under policies in the second category, which the Restatement of the Law of Liability Insurance aptly labels "defense-cost-indemnification" policies,[2] the insurance company either

1. *See, e.g.*, AIG DIRECTORS & OFFICERS STATEMENT (144302), at 9 (2022) ("The Insureds shall defend any Claim made against them. The Insurer does not assume any duty to defend or investigate."); THE TRAVELERS INDEM. CO., DIRECTORS, OFFICERS, AND ORGANIZATION LIABILITY COVERAGE (PCDO-16001), at 10 (2017) [hereinafter TRAVELERS D&O POLICY] ("The Company has no duty under this Policy to defend any Claim. The Insureds have the duty to defend Claims made against them.").

2. RESTATEMENT OF THE L. OF LIAB. INS. § 22 (AM. L. INST. 2019).

advances or reimburses the insured's "defense expenses," including defense counsel's legal fees,[3] or advances or reimburses the insured's "claim expenses," which are defined to include defense costs.

Defense-cost-indemnification policies originated in the directors and officers (D&O) liability insurance market. Companies that purchased D&O coverage wanted to be able to control the defense and settlement of litigation against their directors and officers, and defense-cost-indemnification policies allowed them that flexibility. D&O policies were introduced by London insurers in the late 1930s in response to the increase in securities regulation, best reflected in the enactment of the Securities Act of 1933 and the Securities and Exchange Act of 1934.[4] Companies' interest in D&O insurance did not gain momentum until the late 1960s, but by the early 1970s, approximately 70 percent of public companies bought D&O coverage.[5] By the 1980s, almost all public companies purchased D&O insurance.[6]

Now, in addition to D&O policies, insurers often issue employment practices liability (EPL) policies, errors and omissions (E&O) policies, fiduciary liability policies, and excess policies on a defense-cost-indemnification basis. A typical D&O policy, for example, states in pertinent part: "The Insureds, and not the Insurer, shall have the duty to defend all claims."[7] With respect to defense costs, the insured is not to incur them without the insurer's prior written consent, which the insurer cannot unreasonably withhold or delay. As for payment, the policy states that the insurer "shall advance such Defense Costs on a current basis but no later than sixty (60) days after the Insurer received itemized invoices for such Defense Costs."[8] The insureds are expressly required to repay the insurer for any defense costs if it is ultimately determined that there is no coverage under the policy. "Defense Costs" are defined in the policy to "mean that part of Loss consisting of . . . reasonable fees, costs and expenses

3. *See, e.g.*, Travelers D&O Policy, *supra* note 1, at 10 ("The Company will advance, on behalf of the Insureds, Defense Expenses . . . that the Company believes to be covered under this Policy and are incurred in connection with a Claim first made against them during the Policy Period, or any applicable Extended Reporting Period. . . . Such Defense Expenses . . . will be advanced within 90 days of the date when the Company's Claims department receives: (i) the invoices documenting that such Defense Expenses . . . have been incurred; and (ii) any additional information or documentation reasonably requested by the Company related to such Defense Expenses. . . ."); *id.* at 2 (defining "Defense Expenses" in part as "the reasonable costs, charges, fees, or expenses . . . incurred: (i) defending, investigating, or appealing a Claim. . . .").

4. *See* Brian Sabia et al., PartnerRe, D&O What to Know: A Guide to the Evolution of Directors and Officers Insurance from 1933 to the Present 8 (2017), https://www.partnerre.com/wp-content/uploads/2017/09/DO_Ebook.pdf.

5. *Id.* at 9.

6. *Id.* at 10.

7. Berkshire Hathaway Specialty Ins., Executive First Directors & Officers Liability Policy (EP-EF-001-02/2014), at 12 (2014) [hereinafter Berkshire Hathaway D&O Policy].

8. *Id.*

incurred by the Insureds in the defense or appeal of any Claim . . . including the costs of an appeal bond, attachment bond or similar bond."[9]

An EPL policy might state: "The Insurer does not assume any duty to defend; provided, however, the Named Entity may at its sole option tender to the Insurer the defense of a Claim for which coverage is provided. . . . Regardless of whether the defense is so tendered, the Insurer shall advance Defense Costs of such Claim, excess of the applicable Retention amount, prior to its final disposition."[10] This EPL policy defines "defense costs" to mean:

> [T]he reasonable and necessary fees, costs and expenses consented to by the Insurer (including premiums for any appeal bond, attachment bond or similar bond arising out of a covered judgment, but without any obligation to apply for or furnish any such bond) resulting solely from the investigation, adjustment, defense and appeal of a Claim against the Insureds, but excluding compensation of any Individual Insured.[11]

Alternatively, a lawyers' professional liability (LPL) insurance policy might provide: "If a Claim will be contested, the defense shall be conducted by or on behalf of any Assured in cooperation with the Insurer and by defense counsel selected by the Assured and approved by the Insurer, such approval not to be unreasonably withheld."[12] Furthermore, the insurer "agrees that subject to all of the terms, conditions, exclusions and limitations of this Policy, it will pay all reasonable costs, charges and expenses incurred in connection with the defense of any Claims covered" under the policy.[13] This LPL policy does not obligate the insurer to advance any defense expenses.

To use a final example, a fiduciary liability policy may provide: "Notwithstanding the [insurer's right and duty to defend], the Insureds shall have the right to assume the defense of any claim made against them. This right shall be exercised in writing . . . within sixty (60) days of reporting the claim to the insurer."[14] Upon receiving such a request, "the Insurer shall tender defense

---

9. *Id.* at 3.

10. Chartis, Inc., Employment Practices Liability Insurance (95728), at 1 (2007) (emphasis omitted).

11. *Id.* at 2 (emphasis omitted).

12. This language is adapted from a proprietary lawyers' professional liability insurance policy on file with the author.

13. *Id.*

14. Chartis Inc., Fiduciary Liability Insurance Edge Employee Benefit Plan Fiduciary Liability Insurance Policy (106075 7/10), at 4 (2010) [hereinafter Chartis Fiduciary Liability Policy]. It is common for fiduciary liability policies to reserve to the insurer the right and duty to defend the insured but offer the insured the option of assuming its own defense with the insurer then being obligated to advance or reimburse defense expenses. *See, e.g.*, Phila. Ins. Cos., Private Company Protection Plus Policy (PI-PRD-2), at 11 (2002) (stating the common policy conditions in a policy providing directors & officers private company liability insurance, employment practices liability insurance, and fiduciary liability insurance). Once the insured assumes control of the defense the insurer cannot regain it, although it may have the right to associate in the defense.

of the claim to the Insureds."[15] If the insureds exercise their right to assume the defense of the claim, then "the Insurer shall advance, excess of any applicable Retention, covered Defense Costs, on a current basis, but no later than ninety (90) days after the Insurer has received itemized bills for those Defense Costs."[16] Again, "[s]uch advance payments by the Insurer shall be repaid . . . by each and every Insured, severally according to their respective interests, in the event and to the extent that any such Insured shall not be entitled [to coverage under the policy]."[17] The policy defines "defense costs" to mean "reasonable and necessary fees, costs and expenses consented to by the Insurer . . . resulting solely from the investigation, adjustment, defense and/or appeal of a Claim against an Insured."[18]

A defense-cost-indemnification policy may require the insurer to pay the insured's defense expenses on an ongoing basis, as is the case with the D&O, EPL, and fiduciary liability policies quoted earlier. An insurer's payment of defense expenses on an ongoing basis is commonly described as "advancing" the insured's defense expenses, as the specimen D&O and fiduciary liability policies expressly state. Alternatively, an insurer may be obligated to reimburse the insured's defense expenses only at the conclusion of a covered action, as the LPL policy quoted earlier suggests. Policies in this latter category are sometimes described as "retroactive defense-cost-indemnification" policies.[19]

An insurer's obligation to pay an insured's defense expenses is not the same as a duty to defend the insured.[20] Policies providing for the payment of defense expenses expressly differentiate that obligation from a duty to defend.[21] It is reasonable, however, to ask whether the two obligations should be evaluated or treated identically. For example, should an insurer have to pay defense expenses when there is merely the potential for coverage? Does an insurer's obligation to pay defense expenses extend to every claim in a complaint or petition that arguably falls within coverage, so that the obligation to fund the defense of one claim obligates the insurer to fund the defense of the entire lawsuit? Must an insurer that promises to pay defense expenses reserve its rights to deny coverage to avoid estoppel or waiver allegations like an insurer with a duty to defend? Might a primary insurer that is obligated only to pay defense

15. CHARTIS FIDUCIARY LIABILITY POLICY, *supra* note 14, at 4.

16. *Id.*

17. *Id.*

18. *Id.* at 14.

19. RESTATEMENT OF THE L. OF LIAB. INS. § 22 cmt. c (AM. L. INST. 2019).

20. *See, e.g.*, Am. Legacy Found., RP v. Nat'l Union Fire Ins. Co., 623 F.3d 135, 141 (3d Cir. 2010) (describing these obligations as "discrete concepts"); Crosby Est. at Rancho Santa Fe Master Ass'n v. Ironshore Specialty Ins. Co., 498 F. Supp. 3d 1242, 1254–55 (S.D. Cal. 2020) ("The duty to defend in an insurance contract is distinct from the duty to . . . advance defense costs.").

21. *See, e.g.*, BERKSHIRE HATHAWAY D&O POLICY, *supra* note 7, at 12 ("The Insureds, and not the Insurer, shall have the duty to defend all Claims.").

expenses be required to share defense costs with a concurrent primary insurer? Must an insurer pay for an insured's prosecution of affirmative claims under a defense-cost-indemnification policy? Courts and lawyers have long lamented that there is little authority to guide them when answering these questions, but that is changing.

II. Defense-Cost Indemnification Policies as Claims-Made Policies

A. Claims-Made Policies in Brief

To start, defense-cost-indemnification policies typically are claims-made policies, meaning that the insured event is the assertion of a claim against the insured.[22] More specifically, claims-made coverage falls into one of two further categories; it may be either "claims-made" or "claims-made-and-reported," with the first form requiring only that the claim against the insured be made during the policy period to trigger coverage and the second requiring both that the claim be made against the insured and reported to the insurer during the policy period to trigger coverage.[23] Today, most policies are claims-made-and-reported forms, even though courts and lawyers often use the shorthand "claims-made" descriptor when analyzing them.[24] We will also employ the

22. The purpose of a claims-made policy is to allow the insurance company to easily identify risks, thereby enabling it to know in advance the extent of its claims exposure and more accurately compute its premiums. Uhlich Children's Advantage Network v. Nat'l Union Fire Ins. Co., 929 N.E.2d 531, 537 (Ill. App. Ct. 2010); *see also* Crowley Mar. Corp. v. Nat'l Union Fire Ins. Co., 931 F.3d 1112, 1121 (11th Cir. 2019) ("Insurance companies favor claims-made policies because they allow for a more precise calculation of risks and premiums."). A claims-made policy theoretically allows the insurer to charge the insured a lower premium for the coverage because, unlike an occurrence-based policy, there is no open-ended "tail" after the policy expires. *Crowley Mar. Corp.*, 931 F.3d at 1121 (quoting Gulf Ins. Co. v. Dolan, Fertig & Curtis, 433 So. 2d 512, 516 (Fla. 1983)). Or, as the Seventh Circuit has explained, because an insurer that issues claims-made policies "has a clearer picture of its risk exposure," it in turn may offer insureds less-expensive coverage. Hanover Ins. Co. v. R.W. Dunteman Co., 51 F.4th 779, 785 (7th Cir. 2022) (quoting Mkt. St. Bancshares, Inc. v. Fed. Ins. Co., 962 F.3d 947, 952 (7th Cir. 2020)).

23. *See* Prodigy Commc'ns Corp. v. Agric. Excess & Surplus Ins. Co., 288 S.W.3d 374, 378–81 (Tex. 2009) (distinguishing these types of policies); *see also* ALPS Prop. & Cas. Ins. Co. v. Keller, Reynolds, Drake, Johnson & Gillespie, P.C., 482 P.3d 638, 645 (Mont. 2021) (citation omitted) ("Claims-made policies are classified as either claims-made or claims-made-and-reported policies. Claims-made-and-reported polices are generally a more restrictive form of coverage as 'notice is the event that actually triggers coverage' and is generally required within the policy period or extended reporting period. . . . Both claims-made and claims-made-and-reported policies, however, were specifically developed to limit the insurer's risk by placing a temporal limitation on coverage.").

24. *See, e.g.*, TRT Dev. Co. v. ACE Am. Ins. Co., 566 F. Supp. 3d 118, 124 (D.N.H. 2021) ("[I]n a claims-made policy, the insured event is a combination of two requirements: (1) the claim must be made against the insured by a third party, or a covered loss must be discovered by the insured, during the policy period, and (2) the claim or loss must be reported to the insurer during that same policy period."); Preferred Contractors Ins. Co. v. Baker & Son Constr. Inc., 514 P.3d 1230, 1232 (Wash.

simpler "claims-made" terminology, although the difference in policy forms may be critical and highlights the need for lawyers to carefully read any policies they are asked to interpret.

B. The "Claim" Requirement under a Claims-Made Policy

Because a "claim" is the critical event under a claims-made policy and thus under a defense-cost-indemnification policy, it is important to determine whether a "claim" has, in fact, been made. Most claims-made policies define the term "claim."[25] For example, a professional liability policy which states that the insurer will pay on the insured's behalf defense expenses for any claim first made during the policy period may define a claim to mean "(1) a demand for money or services; (2) a civil proceeding commenced by service of a complaint or similar pleading; or (3) a written request to toll or waive a statute of limitations relating to a potential civil or administrative proceeding, against any Insured for a Wrongful Act."[26] A public company D&O policy may define a claim as:

1. a written demand, other than a Security Holder Derivative Demand, against an Insured, commenced by such Insured's receipt of such demand for monetary damages or non-monetary relief, including arbitration, mediation, or other formal alternative dispute resolution, injunctive relief, or request to toll or waiver any statute of limitations;
2. a proceeding, other than an administrative or regulatory proceeding or investigation, against an Insured, commenced by: (i) service of a civil complaint or similar proceeding; or (ii) the filing of charges, or the return of an indictment, information, or similar document, solely with respect to a criminal proceeding;
3. an administrative or regulatory proceeding, other than an investigation, against an: (i) Insured Person; or (ii) Insured Organization, provided that such proceeding is initially made and continuously maintained against an Insured Person identified by name, commenced by such Insured's receipt of a notice of filed charges or similar document;

2022) (stating that "liability usually attaches in a claims-made policy when the claim is reported to the insurer within the policy period").

25. *But see* Jordan v. Evanston Ins. Co., 23 F.4th 555, 561–62 (5th Cir. 2022) (involving an excess claims-made policy that did not define the term "claim," explaining that "a 'claim' involves a 'demand' or an 'assertion' made by a claimant against a party who could satisfy it," and concluding that the insured did not timely report a "claim" when it became aware of media reports of a customer's injury and sent the reports to the insurer).

26. The Travelers Cos., Inc., Accountants Professional Liability Coverage (APL-1001), at 2 (2008) (emphasis indicating defined terms omitted).

4. a formal investigation of an Insured Person identified by name, commenced by such Insured Person's receipt of a formal order of investigation or similar document, or written notice identifying such Insured Person as a target of an investigatory authority, including a Wells Notice from the SEC indicating that it may commence an enforcement action against such Insured Person;
5. a request for Extradition, commenced by receipt of such request;
6. a Security Holder Derivative Demand, solely with respect to [a particular insuring agreement], commenced by an Insured's receipt of such demand;
7. a subpoena identifying an Insured Person by name, commenced by service upon such Insured Person pursuant an SEC formal investigative order against an Insured, for a Wrongful Act occurring before or during the Policy Period, including any appeal therefrom; or
8. an Interview Request, solely with respect to [a specified policy section], provided notice has been given to the Company pursuant to [a specified policy section], commenced by receipt of such Interview Request.[27]

As the definitions of "claim" in the preceding quote illustrate, an insurer's obligation to pay an insured's defense expenses under a defense-cost-indemnification policy may attach even where the insured has not been sued, in contrast to a standard liability insurance policy's requirement of a "suit" against the insured for the insurer to owe a duty to defend.[28] In *Guaranteed Rate, Inc. v. ACE American Insurance Co.*,[29] for instance, the court held that ACE had a duty to advance the insured's defense costs in connection with a federal government investigation under the False Claims Act because the government's Civil Investigative Demand constituted a claim under the ACE policy.[30]

III. The Scope and Contours of the Duty to Pay Defense Expenses

A. Competing Views of the Duty to Pay Defense Expenses

Setting aside the specific language of claims-made policies that may differentiate an insurer's duty to pay an insured's defense expenses under a defense-cost indemnification policy from an insurer's defense obligation under a liability insurance policy that imposes a duty to defend, there are credible arguments

27. Travelers D&O Policy, *supra* note 1, at 2 (emphasis indicating defined terms omitted).
28. The "suit" requirement for purposes of an insurer's duty to defend is discussed in Chapter 1.
29. No. N20C-04-268 MMJ CCLD, 2021 WL 3662269 (Del. Super. Ct. Aug. 18, 2021).
30. *Id.* at *1–2.

for and against the construction of the scope of an insurer's obligation to pay defense expenses as being equivalent to the scope of an insurer's duty to defend. An insured would surely argue that the duty to pay defense expenses or claim expenses should be construed consistently with the duty to defend because it promotes the same interests[31] and provides benefits akin to the duty to defend. Both duties encourage the defense of meritless suits.[32] Both duties apply to lawsuits that turn out to be groundless, false, or fraudulent.[33]

Along the same lines, the obligation to pay defense expenses, like the duty to defend, sweeps in expenses attributable to defense decisions made prospectively. Put another way, an insured might say, the obligation to pay defense expenses, like the duty to defend, encompasses expenses incurred because of the possibility that a claim or suit may turn out to be covered under the policy.[34] The insured's obligation under many defense-cost-indemnification policies to repay defense expenses if it is finally determined that the policy does not cover the subject loss does not alter this view. First, there may never be such a determination. In cases in which an insurer reserves its right to disclaim coverage, such a conclusion is seldom reached. Second, even under a duty to defend policy, an insurer could, in most jurisdictions, create an enforceable right to recoup defense costs incurred in connection with uncovered claims or causes of action by including appropriate language in its policy.[35]

Although it is true that defense expenses typically erode the liability limits of a defense-cost-indemnification policy, the insurer's duty to indemnify the insured in the event of a covered judgment nonetheless remains an obligation separate from its obligation to pay the insured's defense expenses. If defense expenses or claim expenses are paid in addition to policy limits, treating the

31. Jeffrey E. Thomas, *The Scope of the Obligation to Pay Claim Expenses*, New Appleman Current Critical Issues in Ins. L., Nov. 2006, at 29, 31; *see also* Restatement of the L. of Liab. Ins. § 22 cmt. a (Am. L. Inst. 2019) ("By contracting to pay defense costs on an ongoing basis, the insurer promises to provide the policyholder access to a timely, insurer-funded defense. This promise implicates the same access-to-justice justifications that undergird the duty-to-defend rules incorporated by reference in this Section.").

32. *See* Hurley v. Columbia Cas. Co., 976 F. Supp. 268, 275 (D. Del. 1997) (saying that "it would be an anomaly to require [the insurer] to advance defense costs only for meritorious claims").

33. *See, e.g.*, Fed. Ins. Co. v. Kozlowski, 792 N.Y.S.2d 397, 402 (App. Div. 2005) (stating that under a defense-cost-indemnification policy, the ultimate validity of the plaintiff's allegations is irrelevant).

34. *But see* U.S. TelePacific Corp. v. U.S. Specialty Ins. Co., 815 F. App'x 155, 156 (9th Cir. 2020) ("The district court did not err in concluding that Specialty's duty to advance defense costs under the Policy extended only to actually covered claims. As the district court correctly explained, Condition (D)(2) of the Policy provides that Specialty must advance defense costs for claims 'for which [the] Policy provides coverage,' not for potentially covered claims.").

35. Robert H. Jerry, II & Douglas R. Richmond, Understanding Insurance Law 831 (6th ed. 2018). *But see* Att'ys Liab. Prot. Soc'y, Inc. v. Ingaldson Fitzgerald, P.C., 370 P.3d 1101, 1111 (Alaska 2016) ("When an insurer has a duty to defend, Alaska law prohibits enforcement of a policy provision entitling that insurer to reimbursement of fees and costs incurred during the defense of claims under a reservation of rights."), *abrogated on other grounds by* Buntin v. Schlumberger Tech. Corp., 487 P.3d 595 (Alaska 2021).

scope of the insurer's duty to pay those expenses the same as a duty to defend is especially apt.[36]

Finally, although the insurer's obligation to pay defense expenses gives it less control over the defense than it would enjoy if it owed a duty to defend—typically because the duty to defend is coupled with a right to defend, which includes the right to select defense counsel—the insurer's review of defense counsel's invoices in the payment process provides some small level of supervision over the defense.[37]

An insurer, on the other hand, might reasonably contend that the obligation to pay defense costs is narrower than a duty to defend.[38] Insurance policies are contracts,[39] after all, and absent some ambiguity, courts must enforce them according to their terms.[40] Additionally, defense-cost-indemnification are defense within limits policies.[41] As a result, the payment of defense costs erodes the policy's limit of liability rather than those costs being paid in addition to the limit of liability, as would be the case under a standard liability insurance policy imposing a duty to defend. The duty to pay defense costs therefore more closely resembles the insurer's duty to indemnify the insured than it does a duty to defend. This is especially true under what is sometimes called an "indemnity only" or retroactive defense-cost-indemnification policy, where the insurer reimburses the insured's defense expenses rather than advancing them.[42] An insurer's duty to indemnify is far narrower than its duty to defend.[43]

In addition, defense-cost-indemnification policies typically obligate the insured to repay defense costs if a court ultimately determines that the policy

---

36. Thomas, *supra* note 31, at 30.

37. *Id.* at 31.

38. *See, e.g.*, Millennium Labs., Inc. v. Allied World Assur. Co. (U.S.), Inc., 726 F. App'x 571, 574 (9th Cir. 2018) (observing that a D&O insurer's duty to reimburse the insured's defense costs "applied only to claims actually covered by the policy and did not extend to claims merely potentially covered," in contrast to a policy that included a duty to defend).

39. Perkins v. King, 358 So. 3d 538, 543 (La. Ct. App. 2023); Loftus v. Three Palms Crocker Park, LLC, 211 N.E.3d 771, 775 (Ohio Ct. App. 2023).

40. *See* Westfield Nat'l Ins. Co. v. Quest Pharms., Inc., 57 F.4th 558, 561 (6th Cir. 2023) (applying Kentucky law); Masonic Temple Ass'n of Quincy, Inc. v. Patel, 185 N.E.3d 888, 894 (Mass. 2022) (quoting multiple Massachusetts cases); N. Star Mut. Ins. Co. v. Miller, 977 N.W.2d 195, 201–02 (Neb. 2022).

41. Defense within limits policies may also be described as "burning limits," "cannibalizing," "depleting" or "depleting limits," "eroding limits," "wasting," "spend down," "self-consuming," or "self-liquidating" policies because the liability limits are reduced by defense expenses. They are so described because every dollar spent on the insured's defense correspondingly reduces the amount of money available to settle the case or indemnify the insured.

42. *See Millennium Labs.*, 726 F. App'x at 574 ("The policy was an indemnity-only policy, however, and therefore did not require the contemporaneous advancement of Millennium's defense costs."); Exec. Risk Indem., Inc., v. Jones, 89 Cal. Rptr. 3d 747, 751 n.4 (Ct. App. 2009) ("D & O policies are indemnity-only policies, whereby the insurer reimburses defense expenditures only after the insured selects counsel, controls the defense, and submits the defense bill.").

43. Md. Cas. Co. v. Dough Mgmt. Co., 36 N.E.3d 953, 960 (Ill. App. Ct. 2015).

does not cover the insured's allegedly wrongful conduct.[44] In contrast, the duty to defend exists when there is a claim potentially within coverage, regardless of whether the law would impose liability in the circumstances.[45] In this respect, as well, the obligation to pay defense expenses more resembles a duty to indemnify than it does a duty to defend.

Finally, from an insurer's perspective, unlike a duty to defend policy that grants the insurer the right to defend, a defense-cost-indemnification policy affords an insurer no meaningful control over the insured's defense. The inability to appoint defense counsel under a defense-cost-indemnification policy hamstrings the insurer's ability to influence the defense. The review of defense counsel's invoices when paying defense expenses is nothing like the ability to participate in strategic decisions that the insurer would enjoy under a duty to defend policy. Even if a defense-cost-indemnification policy requires the insured to obtain the insurer's approval before incurring defense expenses, that provision still does not allow the insurer the control it would enjoy under a duty to defend policy, especially considering that the insurer's ability to withhold consent is quite limited in practice.

In fact, while there is authority for the proposition that an insurer's obligation to pay defense expenses is narrower than the duty to defend,[46] most courts

44. *See, e.g.*, Travelers D&O Policy, *supra* note 1, at 10 ("The Company will advance, on behalf of the Insureds, Defense Expenses . . . that the Company believes to be covered under this Policy and are incurred in connection with a Claim first made against them during the Policy Period, or any applicable Extended Reporting Period; provided, that to the extent it is finally established that any such Defense Expenses . . . are not covered under this Policy, the Insureds, severally according to their interests, agree to repay the Company such Defense Expenses. . . .").

45. *See* United Fire & Cas. Co. v. Prate Roofing & Installations, LLC, 7 F.4th 573, 581 (7th Cir. 2021) (applying Illinois law and stating that "a liability insurer may not deny a defense on the ground that the suit against its insured is hopeless"); Mid-Continent Cas. Co. v. Royal Crane, LLC, 169 So. 3d 174, 181 (Fla. Dist. Ct. App. 2015) ("The merits of the underlying suit are irrelevant."); Selective Way Ins. Co. v. Nationwide Prop. & Cas. Ins. Co., 219 A.3d 20, 33 (Md. Ct. Spec. App. 2019) (quoting Litz v. State Farm Fire & Cas. Co., 695 A.2d 566, 570 (Md. 1997)); Renco Grp., Inc. v. Certain Underwriters at Lloyd's, London, 362 S.W.3d 472, 479 (Mo. Ct. App. 2012) (stating that an insurer has a duty to defend "based on the facts known at the outset of the case, no matter how unlikely it is that the insured will be found liable or whether the insured is ultimately found liable"); Nautilus Ins. Co. v. Access Med., LLC, 482 P.3d 683, 691 (Nev. 2021) (explaining that "an insurer must defend even claims that the third party does not ultimately prove"); Abouzaid v. Mansard Gardens Assocs., LLC, 23 A.3d 338, 347 (N.J. 2011) (noting that when evaluating an insurer's duty to defend, "the potential merit of the claim is immaterial"); Tibert v. Nodak Mut. Ins. Co., 816 N.W.2d 41, 44 (N.D. 2012) (stating that "the ultimate result in the case does not affect the duty to defend"); Pepsi-Cola Metro. Bottling Co. v. Emps. Ins. Co. of Wausau, 979 N.W.2d 627, 640 (Wis. Ct. App. 2022) ("The duty to defend hinges on the nature, not the merits, of the plaintiff's claim.").

46. *See, e.g.*, i-Frontier, Inc. v. Gulf Underwriters Ins. Co., No. Civ.A 04-5797, 2005 WL 1353614, at *3–4 (E.D. Pa. June 3, 2005) (appearing to treat the insurer's duty to pay claim expenses identically with its duty to indemnify); Xebec Dev. Partners, Ltd. v. Nat'l Union Fire Ins. Co., 15 Cal. Rptr. 726, 762 (Ct. App. 1993) (noting "the distinction between the historically broad *duty to defend* embodied in most California liability insurance policies and the considerably narrower *duty to pay defense costs* incorporated in this and similar D & O policies"), *disapproved on other grounds by* Essex Ins. Co. v. Five Star Dye House, Inc., 137 P.3d 192, 197–99 (Cal. 2006).

apply traditional duty to defend analysis when deciding whether insurers must advance or reimburse insureds' defense expenses.[47]

47. *See, e.g.*, W. Holding Co. v. AIG Ins. Co.-P.R., 748 F.3d 377, 384 (1st Cir. 2014) (applying Puerto Rico law); Liberty Mut. Ins. Co. v. Pella Corp., 650 F.3d 1161, 1172 (8th Cir. 2011) (applying Iowa law and reasoning that the duty to reimburse defense costs should be determined by examining the allegations in the complaint to determine if they state a covered claim); Atl. Specialty Ins. Co. v. Blue Cross & Blue Shield of Kan., Inc., No. 18-2371-DDC-ADM, 2023 WL 2648223, at *10 n.5 (D. Kan. Mar. 27, 2023) (predicting Kansas law); Sec. Nat'l Ins. Co. v. H.O.M.E., Inc., 312 F. Supp. 3d 777, 783 (D.N.D. 2018) (applying North Dakota law to a D&O policy that required the insurer to advance defense costs); Beazley Ins. Co. v. Ace Am. Ins. Co., 150 F. Supp. 3d 345, 351 (S.D.N.Y. 2015) (applying New York law); Worthington Fed. Bank v. Everest Nat'l Ins. Co., 110 F. Supp. 3d 1211, 1222 (N.D. Ala. 2015) (citations omitted) ("Courts considering whether an insurer's obligation to advance defense costs is triggered generally do so using standards that are the same or similar to those employed to ascertain whether an insurer has a duty to provide the defense itself. . . . The court will likewise do so here."); MapleWood Partners, L.P. v. Indian Harbor Ins. Co., 295 F.R.D. 550, 601 (S.D. Fla. 2013) (observing that an insurer's duty to advance defense expenses is not materially different from a duty to defend (quoting Julio & Sons Co. v. Travelers Cas. & Sur. Co. of Am., 591 F. Supp. 2d 651, 664 (S.D.N.Y. 2008))); Aspen Ins. UK, Ltd. v. Fiserve, Inc., No. 09-cv-02770-CMA-CBS, 2010 WL 5129529, at *3 (D. Colo. Dec. 9, 2010) (observing that there are no material differences between the duty to advance defense costs and the duty to defend); Great Am. Ins. Co. v. Geostar Corp., Nos. 09-12488–BC, 09-12608–BC, 09-14306-BC, 2010 WL 845953, at *14–17 (E.D. Mich. Mar. 5, 2010) (applying Michigan law and treating the duty to pay defense expenses like the duty to defend); Legacy Partners, Inc. v. Clarendon Am. Ins. Co., No. 08cv920 BTM (CAB), 2010 WL 1495198, at *4–6 (S.D. Cal. Apr. 14, 2010) (applying the potentiality standard to the duty to pay defense expenses); Acacia Rsch. Corp. v. Nat'l Union Fire Ins. Co., No. 05-501, 2008 WL 4179206, at *11 (C.D. Cal. Feb. 8, 2008) ("Given the broad scope of [the insurer's] duty to advance defense costs, [the insurer] was required to advance defense costs for potentially covered claims."); *Julio & Sons Co.*, 591 F. Supp. 2d at 659 (finding that there were no material differences between a duty to defend and a duty to advance defense expenses); G-I Holdings, Inc. v. Reliance Ins. Co., No. 00-CV-6189 (DMC), 2006 WL 776809, at *2 (D.N.J. Mar. 24, 2006) (equating the duty to pay defense costs with the duty to defend in holding that the insurer had to advance defense costs); Lowy v. Travelers Prop. & Cas. Co., No. 99 Civ. 2727(MBM), 2000 WL 526702, at *2 n.1 (S.D.N.Y. May 2, 2000) (stating that "there is no relevant difference between the allegations that trigger an insurer's duty to defend and the allegations that trigger an insurer's obligation to pay defense expenses"); Hurley v. Columbia Cas. Co., 976 F. Supp. 268, 275 (D. Del. 1997) ("[T]here does not exist a significant difference between the duty to defend and the promise to advance defense costs, other than the difference between who will direct the defense."); Liggett Grp. Inc. v. Affiliated FM Ins. Co., No. Civ.A. 00C-01-207 HD, 2001 WL 1456853, at *2 (Del. Super. Ct. Sept. 12, 2001) (discussing the insurer's obligation to pay claim expenses); Mt. Vernon Fire Ins. Co. v. Visionaid, Inc., 76 N.E.3d 204, 212 (Mass. 2017) ("[I]n Massachusetts, where an insurer has both the duty to defend and the duty to pay defense costs, the scope of the duty to defend and the scope of the duty to pay defense costs are identical."); Westchester Fire Ins. Co. v. Schorsch, 129 N.Y.S.3d 67, 79 (App. Div. 2020) ("A carrier's duty to defend and the duty to advance defense costs are triggered by the same allegations. . . . The duty to provide defense costs 'must be construed broadly in favor of the policyholder,' and 'exists whenever a complaint against the insured alleges claims that maybe covered under the insurer's policy'. . . ." (quoting Fed. Ins. Co. v. Kozlowski, 792 N.Y.S.2d 397, 402 (App. Div. 2005))); Port Auth. of N.Y. & N.J. v. Brickman Grp. Ltd., LLC, 115 N.Y.S.3d 246, 260–62 (App. Div. 2019) (concluding that the insurers owed reasonable defense costs); Westpoint Int'l, Inc. v. Am. Int'l S. Ins. Co., 899 N.Y.S.2d 8, 9–10 (App. Div. 2010) ("Having failed to demonstrate that there is no possibility of coverage, defendant cannot avoid its obligation to advance defense costs."); Am. Chem. Soc'y v. Leadscope, Inc., No. 04AP-305, 2005 WL 1220746, at *8 (Ohio Ct. App. May 24, 2005) (concluding that "when a policy imposes a duty to advance defense costs but no duty to defend, the [eight corners or four corners] test and the one claim-all claims principle apply to determine the duty of the insurer to advance defense costs").

B. Equating the Duty to Pay Defense Expenses with the Duty to Defend

American Chemical Society v. Leadscope, Inc.[48] is an illustrative case analogizing an insurer's obligation to advance defense costs to a duty to defend. *American Chemical Society* was a D&O coverage dispute. Paul Blower, Wayne Johnson, and Glenn Myatt worked for the American Chemical Society (ACS). They had employment agreements that prohibited them from disclosing certain protected information and provided that ACS would own the property rights to some of their creations.

While at ACS, Blower and Myatt developed a software program called CAPathfinder. In 1997, Blower, Johnson, and Myatt left ACS and formed a company that merged into Leadscope, Inc. (Leadscope) in 2000. In 1998, Blower, Johnson, and Myatt designed a software program similar to CAPathfinder. They patented the software in 2001. ACS believed that the patent was based on its protected information, and demanded that Leadscope assign it all interest in the patent and compensate it for lost sales opportunities and development costs.[49] Leadscope did not respond and, in 2002, ACS sued the men and Leadscope (collectively Leadscope) in an Ohio state court. ACS alleged multiple causes of action with some variation between defendants, including conversion, misappropriation of trade secrets, unfair competition, implied license under the shop-right doctrine, breach of employment agreement, breach of fiduciary duty, and disloyalty.

Leadscope was insured under a D&O policy issued by National Union Fire Insurance Co. (National Union). Leadscope notified National Union of the lawsuit and requested that the insurer advance its defense costs. National Union denied coverage and declined to advance legal fees to Leadscope, stating that its policy did not cover the causes of action alleged by ACS.[50]

Leadscope filed a third-party complaint against National Union in the ACS action seeking a determination that National Union was required to advance legal fees to defend the case. At summary judgment, the trial court held that because ACS's conversion claim fell within the scope of coverage and was not expressly excluded, National Union had to reimburse Leadscope for defending all of ACS's claims.[51] In doing so, the trial court applied to so-called "pleadings test," which holds that where a plaintiff's complaint states a claim that is potentially within coverage—here the conversion claim—the insurer must accept the defense.[52] The trial court then reasoned that under the "one claim-all claims" principle, National Union owed a "duty to defend" Leadscope against all the

48. No. 04AP-305, 2005 WL 1220746 (Ohio Ct. App. May 24, 2005).
49. *Id.* at *1.
50. *Id.*
51. *Id.*
52. *Id.* at *2.

remaining claims in ACS's complaint, regardless of whether those claims were covered.[53]

National Union appealed. The appellate court agreed with National Union that it had no duty to defend Leadscope, but that determination did not dispose of the defense costs issue.[54] Clause 8 in the National Union policy provided:

> When the Insurer has not assumed the defense of a Claim pursuant to this Clause 8, the Insurer shall advance nevertheless, at the written request of the Insured, Defense Costs prior to the final disposition of a Claim. Such advanced payments by the Insurer shall be repaid to the Insurer by the Insureds or the Company . . . in the event and to the extent that the Insureds or the Company shall not be entitled under the terms and conditions of this policy to payment of such Loss.[55]

Clause 8 further provided when National Union could decline to advance defense costs:

> The Insureds shall not . . . incur any Defense Costs without the prior written consent of the Insurer. Only those . . . Defense Costs which have been consented to by the Insurer shall be recoverable as Loss under the terms of this policy. The Insurer's consent shall not be unreasonably withheld, provided . . . that in all events the Insurer may withhold consent to any . . . Defense Costs, or any portion thereof, to the extent such Loss is not covered under the terms of this policy.[56]

National Union contended that the pleadings test and one claim-all claims principle applied only to the duty to defend and not to a duty to advance defense costs.[57] According to National Union, its duty to advance defense costs turned solely on the language of Clause 8, so that it had no duty to advance defense costs related to any loss that was not covered under its policy.[58] The potential for coverage was immaterial, National Union argued; the proper test was whether the claims in ACS's complaint were actually covered.[59] National Union cited the language in Clause 8 allowing it to withhold consent to defense costs where there was no coverage under the policy. The *American Chemical Society* court thus had to decide whether the pleadings test and one claim-all claims principle applied equally to cases involving the duty to defend and those involving the duty to advance defense costs.

53. *Id.* at *3.
54. *Id.* at *3–4.
55. *Id.* at *4.
56. *Id.*
57. *Id.*
58. *Id.*
59. *Id.*

After locating no apposite Ohio cases and studying cases decided by other courts,[60] the court concluded that when a policy imposes a duty to advance defense costs but no duty to defend, the pleadings test and the one claim-all claims principle apply to an insurer's duty to advance defense costs.[61] The court saw no reason to distinguish duty to defend cases and duty to advance defense costs cases in this context.[62]

Applying the pleadings test and one-claim all claim principle, the court determined that because ACS's conversion claim against Blower, Johnson, and Myatt was potentially covered under the policy, National Union had a duty to advance their defense expenses.[63] In contrast, none of ACS's claims against Leadscope as a company were even arguably or potentially covered under the policy.[64] As a result, even applying the pleadings test and one claim-all claims principle, National Union had no duty to advance Leadscope's corporate defense expenses.[65] The *American Chemical Society* court therefore affirmed the trial court in part and reversed it in part, and remanded the case for further proceedings.

Other courts have similarly applied duty to defend concepts or principles to defense-cost-indemnification policies. *Aspen Insurance UK, Ltd. v. Fiserv, Inc.*[66] was a declaratory judgment action over the insurers' obligations to advance defense costs and to indemnify Fiserv Trust Co. and others under a bankers professional liability policy. The insurers' duties were tested by several class actions and two arbitration proceedings brought against the defendants by holders of self-directed IRAs whose funds the defendants sadly invested with Bernard L. Madoff Investment Securities (BLMIS).[67] The policy's insuring agreement provided:

> This policy shall reimburse . . . the Insured arising from a Claim first made against the Insured and reported in writing to the Underwriter during the Policy Period . . . for any Wrongful Act of the Insured or any other person for whose actions the Insured is legally responsible in rendering or failing to render Professional Services, but only if such Wrongful Act occurs before the end of the Policy Period. The Underwriter may in its absolute discretion pursuant

60. *Id.* at *6–7 (discussing *In re* WorldCom, Inc. Sec. Litig., 354 F. Supp. 2d 455 (S.D.N.Y. 2005), Brown v. Am. Int'l Grp., Inc., 339 F. Supp. 2d 336 (D. Mass. 2004), Nat'l Union Fire Ins. Co. v. Willis, 139 F. Supp. 2d 827 (S.D. Tex. 2001), and Hurley v. Columbia Cas. Co., 976 F. Supp. 268 (D. Del. 1997)).
61. *Id.* at *8.
62. *Id.*
63. *Id.* at *8–13, *15.
64. *Id.* at *14.
65. *Id.* at *15.
66. No. 09-cv-02770-CMA-CBS, 2010 WL 5129529 (D. Colo. Dec. 9, 2010).
67. *Id.* at *1.

> to Clause V(E) first paragraph advance Defense Costs prior to the final disposition of a Claim.[68]

Clause V(E) in the policy provided:

> The Underwriter shall advance, at the written request of the Insured, Defense Costs prior to the final disposition of the Claim. Such advance payment by the Underwriter shall be repaid to the Underwriter by the Insured . . . in the event and to the extent that the Insured shall not be entitled under the terms and conditions of this policy to payment of such Loss.
>
> The Underwriter does not, however . . . assume any duty to defend. The Insureds shall defend and contest any Claim made against them. The Insureds shall not admit or assume any liability, enter into any settlement agreement[,] stipulate to any judgment, or incur any Defense Costs without the prior written consent of the Underwriter. Only those settlements, stipulated judgments and Defense Costs which have been consented to by the Underwriter shall be recoverable as Loss under the terms of this policy. The Underwriter's consent shall not be unreasonably withheld, provided that the Underwriter shall be entitled to effectively associate in the defense and the negotiation of any settlement of any Claim.[69]

The insurers argued that they did not have a duty to advance defense costs because the claims asserted in the underlying actions arose out of BLMIS's bankruptcy or suspension of payment and the underlying actions included unjust enrichment and restitution claims, all of which were explicitly excluded from coverage.[70]

The *Aspen* court began its analysis by declaring that there "'are no material differences between a duty to defend and a duty to advance defense costs.'"[71] The court therefore applied a traditional duty to defend analysis to determine the insurers' duty to advance defense costs.[72] Applying Colorado law, which uses the four corners or eight corners test to determine an insurer's duty to defend, the court held that the insurers had to advance the insureds' defense costs on a contemporaneous, as-incurred basis.[73] This was an easy conclusion for the court because the underlying complaints and arbitration demands never used terms like "insolvency" or "bankruptcy," nor did they allege facts or assert claims directly related to BLMIS's insolvency, bankruptcy, or liquidation.[74]

68. *Id.* at *1.
69. *Id.* at *2–3.
70. *Id.* at *3.
71. *Id.* (quoting Julio & Sons Co. v. Travelers Cas. & Sur. Co. of Am., 591 F. Supp. 2d 651, 660 (S.D.N.Y. 2008)).
72. *Id.*
73. *Id.* at *4–7.
74. *Id.* at *4.

In the process of finding for the insureds, the court rejected the insurers' argument that the advancement of defense costs was within their sole discretion. As previously noted, the policy's insuring agreement stated: "The Underwriter may in its absolute discretion pursuant to Clause V(E) first paragraph advance Defense Costs prior to the final disposition of a Claim."[75] Although this language suggested that the advancement of defense costs was at the insurer's option, the first paragraph of Clause V(E) indicated otherwise. Notably, Clause V(E) stated that the insurer "shall advance, at the written request of the Insured, Defense Costs prior to the final disposition of the Claim."[76] Another clause in the policy stated that "the Underwriter shall advance defense costs to the Insured for all Defense Costs reasonably incurred by the Insured in connection" with certain claims.[77] The policy's use of the term "shall" created an obligation and mandated compliance.[78] As a result, under the plain and ordinary meaning of Clause V(E), the advancement of defense costs was mandatory where the insured submitted a prior written request.[79] The discretionary component of Clause V(E) referred to cases where the insured did not submit a prior written request.[80] It was undisputed that, here, the insureds had made the required request.

The *Aspen* court also rejected the insurers' argument that they need not advance defense costs unless the insureds obtained their consent before incurring them. The court reasoned that this argument contradicted the plain language of Clause V(E), which, again, stated: "Only those settlements, stipulated judgments and Defense Costs which have been consented to by the Underwriter shall be recoverable as Loss under the terms of this policy."[81] By definition, the court explained, "the word 'recoverable' relate[d] to the duty to indemnify, not the duty to advance defense costs."[82] Therefore, to obtain an advance on defense costs, the insureds merely needed to request one in writing.[83]

Liberty Mutual Insurance Co. v. Pella Corp.[84] was another declaratory judgment action. Liberty Mutual sued Pella in an Iowa federal court to determine the scope of its obligation under excess liability policies to reimburse Pella's defense costs in two class actions.[85] The plaintiffs in the class actions alleged that Pella sold them defective windows that allowed water to leak

75. *Id.* at *6 (internal quotation marks omitted).
76. *Id.* (internal quotation marks omitted).
77. *Id.* (internal quotation marks omitted).
78. *Id.* (first citing Magenis v. Bruner, 187 P.3d 1222, 1225 (Colo. App. 2008); then citing People v. Steinbeck, 186 P.3d 54, 57 (Colo. App. 2007)).
79. *Id.*
80. *Id.*
81. *Id.* at *7 (internal quotation marks omitted).
82. *Id.* (citing a dictionary).
83. *Id.*
84. 650 F.3d 1161 (8th Cir. 2011).
85. *Id.* at 1164.

through their aluminum cladding.[86] In the declaratory judgment action, the district court awarded Pella summary judgment, holding that Liberty Mutual had a duty to reimburse Pella's defense costs in the class actions.[87] Liberty Mutual appealed to the Eighth Circuit.

The Liberty Mutual policies, which were in effect for six years beginning on September 1, 2000, provided coverage for excess bodily injury and property damage liability as follows:

> a. We will pay those sums in excess of the "Self-Insured Amount" that the insured becomes legally obligated to pay as damages because of "bodily injury" or "property damage" to which this excess insurance applies. No other obligation or liability . . . is covered unless explicitly provided for in SECTION V—SUPPLEMENTARY PAYMENTS/ALLOCATED LOSS ADJUSTMENT EXPENSE . . . . The "bodily injury" or "property damage" must be caused by an "occurrence". . . . The amount we will pay for damages is limited as described in SECTION IV—LIMITS OF INSURANCE.
>
> b. We WILL NOT have the duty to defend or investigate any claim or "suit" seeking damages to which this policy may apply.[88]

Section V of the policies contained one of two versions of an endorsement governing supplementary payments and allocated loss adjustment expense (the ALAE Endorsement), which provided that Liberty Mutual would reimburse Pella for certain expenses incurred in defending covered lawsuits. The ALAE Endorsement to the 2000–2005 policies stated:

> 1. "Allocated Loss Adjustment Expenses" paid by the insured will reduce the "self-insured amount";
>
> 2. For each "occurrence" we will reimburse the insured for "Allocated Loss Adjustment Expense" paid by or on behalf of the insured in excess of the "self-insured amount." Our obligation to reimburse the insured is limited as set forth in the SECTION II—DEFENSE, SETTLEMENT AND INVESTIGATION OF CLAIMS, paragraphs (5) and (6).[89]

The ALAE Endorsement to the 2005–2006 policy used slightly different language:

> 1. For each "occurrence," "Allocated Loss Adjustment Expenses" paid by the insured will reduce the "self-insured amount."
>
> 2. Where the insured controls the defense, we will reimburse the insured for "Allocated Loss Adjustment Expense" incurred by the insured for any

86. *Id.* at 1164–65.
87. *Id.* at 1164.
88. *Id.* at 1165–66.
89. *Id.* at 1166.

> "occurrence" after the "Self-insured Amount" has been exhausted by the payment of damages and/or "Allocated Loss Adjustment Expense" by the insured for that "occurrence". . . .[90]

Liberty Mutual argued that the district court erred in determining that the policies were triggered if the plaintiffs merely alleged an "occurrence."[91] Liberty Mutual contended that the district court construed the policies so as to impose an unqualified duty to reimburse Pella's defense expenses, which the insurer characterized as "the functional equivalent of a duty to defend."[92] From Liberty Mutual's perspective, so interpreting the policies rendered meaningless its disclaimer of a duty to defend.[93]

The Eighth Circuit expressly stated that this case involved a duty to reimburse defense costs—not a duty to defend.[94] Iowa law, however, was silent on how, or to what extent, an insurer's duty to reimburse defense costs might differ from the duty to defend. In an earlier case interpreting Iowa law, the Eighth Circuit had observed that the duty to reimburse defense costs and the duty to defend, although different, are "similar in result."[95] Moreover, the court noted, other courts "'generally have viewed an insurer's duty to advance defense costs as an obligation congruent to the insurer's duty to defend, concluding that the duty arises if the allegations in the complaint could, if proven, give rise to a duty to indemnify.'"[96] Accordingly, even though the case did not involve a duty to defend, "the parameters of that duty" guided the court's analysis of Liberty Mutual's duty to reimburse Pella's defense expenses.[97]

Liberty Mutual's duty to reimburse defense costs was defined two different ways in the policies. As noted earlier, in the 2000–2005 versions, the duty was expressed as follows: "For each 'occurrence' we will reimburse the insured for 'Allocated Loss Adjustment Expense' paid by or on behalf of the insured in excess of the 'self-insured amount.'"[98] The duty was phrased slightly differently in the 2005–2006 policy: "Where the insured controls the defense, we will reimburse the insured for 'Allocated Loss Adjustment Expense' incurred by the insured for any 'occurrence' after the 'Self-insured Amount' has been exhausted by the payment of damages and/or 'Allocated Loss Adjustment Expense' by the

90. *Id.*
91. *Id.* at 1168.
92. *Id.*
93. *Id.*
94. *Id.* at 1170.
95. *Id.* (quoting McCuen v. Am. Cas. Co., 946 F.2d 1401, 1407 (8th Cir.1991)).
96. *Id.* (quoting Fed. Ins. Co. v. Sammons Fin. Grp., Inc., 595 F. Supp. 2d 962, 976 (S.D. Iowa 2009)).
97. *Id.*
98. *Id.* at 1171.

insured for that 'occurrence.'"[99] Liberty Mutual argued that both policy versions conditioned its duty to pay defense expenses on the established fact of an "occurrence" rather than a mere allegation of one.[100] The court disagreed.

To start, the policies did not condition the reimbursement of defense expenses on proof of an "occurrence." Rather, the policies only conditioned reimbursement on Pella paying or incurring the requisite amount of "Allocated Loss Adjustment Expense."[101] Moreover, the 2005–2006 policies stated that Liberty Mutual would reimburse Pella for its defense costs for any "occurrence" after the "Self-insured Amount" was exhausted.[102] This language indicated that Liberty Mutual would begin to reimburse Pella as soon as it paid defense costs equal to the "Self-insured Amount."[103] Pella could reach this threshold prior to any finding of an "occurrence."[104] Nothing else in the policies suggested that the duty to reimburse would arise at the conclusion of the suit—or at least when the existence of an "occurrence" could be established.[105]

Pella interpreted the policies as obligating Liberty Mutual to reimburse defense costs as soon as the "Self-insured Amount" was satisfied for each alleged occurrence.[106] This was a reasonable alternative. If Liberty Mutual's urged interpretation was also reasonable, there would be an ambiguity that would have to be resolved in Pella's favor.[107] Liberty Mutual argued that Pella's interpretation was unreasonable because it would make the duty to reimburse the functional equivalent of a duty to defend, which the policies explicitly disclaimed.[108] That was not so. The duty to defend necessarily requires the insurer to pay defense costs, but it also requires the insurer to conduct and control the defense.[109] Of course, Liberty Mutual would still have no duty to defend even if it had to reimburse defense costs in a lawsuit where an "occurrence" was alleged.[110] Accordingly, the Eighth Circuit determined that the district court did not err in finding that Liberty Mutual's duty to reimburse Pella's defense costs should be determined by examining the allegations in the complaints to determine whether they stated covered claims.[111]

---

99. *Id.*
100. *Id.*
101. *Id.*
102. *Id.*
103. *Id.*
104. *Id.*
105. *Id.*
106. *Id.*
107. *Id.* at 1171–72.
108. *Id.* at 1172.
109. *Id.* (citing Kooyman v. Farm Bureau Mut. Ins. Co., 315 N.W.2d 30, 32–33 (Iowa 1982)).
110. *Id.*
111. *Id.*

Liberty Mutual ultimately prevailed, however, because when scrutinized, the underlying lawsuits did not allege the existence of an occurrence. Thus, Liberty Mutual was not obligated to reimburse Pella's defense costs in connection with either action.[112]

C. A Narrower Duty to Pay Defense Expenses

Although many courts have equated insurers' duty to pay defense expenses with the duty to defend in key respects,[113] many others have not.[114] Courts in the second camp have been guided by the apparently narrowing language of the insurance policies in dispute. Indeed, the language of the policy in dispute is critical here, as *Pendergest-Holt v. Certain Underwriters at Lloyd's of London*[115] illustrates.

Pendergest-Holt arose out of criminal and civil cases against three executives of companies formerly owned by R. Allen Stanford (Stanford).[116] In June 2009, the executives sought coverage under primary and follow-form excess D&O policies issued to several Stanford companies by certain underwriters at Lloyd's and Arch Specialty Insurance Co.[117] The policies did not provide a duty to defend.[118] Rather, the insurers agreed to pay for "[l]oss resulting from any Claim first made during the Policy Period for a Wrongful Act."[119] The poli-

112. *Id.* at 1176.

113. *See, e.g.*, Legacy Partners, Inc. v. Clarendon Am. Ins. Co., No. 08cv920 BTM (CAB), 2010 WL 1495198, at *4–6 (S.D. Cal. Apr. 14, 2010) (applying the potentiality standard used in duty to defend cases to the insurer's duty to pay defense expenses where the policy referred to alleged damages).

114. *See, e.g.*, UMIA Ins., Inc. v. Arguelles, 591 F. Supp. 3d 876, 888–91 (D. Mont. 2022) (applying Montana law and declining to apply the potential for coverage standard used to determine the duty to defend); Conn. Mun. Elec. Energy Coop. v. Nat'l Union Fire Ins. Co., No. 3:19cv839 (JBA), 2021 WL 4170757, at *8–10 (D. Conn. Sept. 14, 2021) (applying Connecticut law and rejecting the plaintiff's argument that an insurer's duty to advance defense costs is equivalent to the duty to defend); Oceans Healthcare, L.L.C. v. Ill. Union Ins. Co., 379 F. Supp. 3d 554, 565–67 (E.D. Tex. 2019) (applying Texas law and rejecting the insured's argument that the insurer's duty to advance defense costs was akin to a duty to defend and should be subject to the automatic trigger and eight-corners rule); United Farm Workers of Am. v. Hudson Ins. Co., No.: 1:18-cv-0134-JLT, 2019 WL 1517568, at *12–13 (E.D. Cal. Apr. 8, 2019) (declining to apply the potentially covered standard to a professional liability policy that did not impose a duty to defend but instead obligated the insurer to reimburse the insured's covered claim expenses); Millennium Labs., Inc. v. Allied World Ins. Co., No. 12-CV-2280 H (KSC), 2013 WL 12072536, at *4–5 (S.D. Cal. July 22, 2013) (concluding that the potential for coverage standard did not apply to a D&O policy that expressly disclaimed a duty to defend and provided that the insurer would reimburse covered defense costs); Ferrellgas Partners L.P. v. Zurich Am. Ins. Co., No. N19C-075-275 MMJ [CCLD], 2020 WL 363677, at *9 (Del. Super. Ct. Jan. 21, 2020) (footnote omitted) ("While the duty to defend test asks whether the 'factual allegations in the underlying complain [sic] potentially support a covered claim' the proper test for determining duty to advance defense costs is 'whether an action states a *claim covered by the policy*.'").

115. 600 F.3d 562 (5th Cir. 2010).

116. *Id.* at 565–66.

117. *Id.* at 566.

118. *Id.*

119. *Id.* (quoting the policy).

cies defined "Loss" to include necessary legal fees and expenses incurred in defending judicial or administrative proceedings against an insured's director or officer.[120] The underwriters agreed to advance defense costs for the executives pending a final coverage determination, but reserved the right to deny coverage based on the policy's fraud and money laundering exclusions.[121]

The money laundering exclusion barred coverage for loss resulting from any claim "arising directly or indirectly as a result of or in connection with any act or acts (or alleged act or acts) of Money Laundering" subject to the following limitation:

> Notwithstanding the foregoing Exclusion, Underwriters shall pay Costs, Charges and Expenses in the event of an alleged act or alleged acts *until such time that it is determined that the alleged act or alleged acts did in fact occur.* In such event the Directors and Officers and the Company will reimburse Underwriters for such Costs, Charges and Expenses paid on their behalf.[122]

The policies defined "money laundering" broadly, so that the term covered more than a violation of a money laundering statute.[123]

In November 2009, the insurers told the executives that they were withdrawing coverage because they had determined from available evidence that money laundering had, in fact, occurred. The executives then sued the insurers in a Texas federal court. They sought damages, a declaration that the insurers had to reimburse their defense costs, and a preliminary injunction ordering the insurers to pay their defense costs until there was a final judgment on the merits of the coverage dispute. The district court found that the money laundering exclusion likely would not apply and granted the executives their requested injunctive relief.[124] The insurers took an expedited appeal to the Fifth Circuit.

On appeal, the executives argued that under the eight corners rule favored by Texas courts in evaluating liability insurers' duty to defend—Texas law controlled—the insurers could not rely on extrinsic evidence to withdraw coverage.[125] The district court had agreed with the executives on this point, but the Fifth Circuit easily rejected the argument based on the D&O policy's language:

> [T]he D&O Policy's terms plainly state that the underwriters must advance defense costs "until it is determined that the alleged act or alleged acts did in fact occur" and, in so doing, require . . . something more than mere allegations. The terms contemplate the use of extrinsic evidence in making the determination. Thus, we need not and hence do not pause to decide whether

120. *Id.*
121. *Id.*
122. *Id.* at 567 (quoting the policy) (emphasis added).
123. *Id.*
124. *Id.* at 568.
125. *Id.* at 574.

> the eight corners rule applies to the duty to advance costs . . . for Texas prefers freedom of contract and honors the well-worn prerogatives of parties to override judge-made doctrines—like the eight corners rule—by contracting around them. . . . Assuming but not deciding the eight corners rule would have applied, the parties chose . . . to displace it and to provide for the use of extrinsic evidence. We must give effect to those bargained-for choices.[126]

The *Pendergest-Holt* court remanded the case to the district court to determine whether, in fact, the money laundering exclusion applied.[127] Interestingly, because the "in fact" call still had to be made, the *Pendergest-Holt* court further came to the "inescapable conclusion" that the insurers were contractually bound to reimburse the executives' reasonable defense costs until the district court reached a decision on the merits.[128] The practical effect of the court's conclusion was to uphold that portion of the preliminary injunction requiring the insurers to reimburse the executives' reasonable defense costs pending a judicial determination of coverage.[129] The Fifth Circuit therefore affirmed the preliminary injunction as modified while clarifying that this conclusion did not control the ultimate coverage decision.[130]

In *Jeff Tracy, Inc. v. U.S. Specialty Insurance Co.*,[131] the insured, Jeff Tracy, Inc. (Tracy), had been sued in a class action for alleged violations of the California Labor Code, among other claimed offenses, and had been slapped with related assessments by a division of the California Department of Industrial Relations. Tracy's D&O insurer, U.S. Specialty Insurance Co. (USSIC), denied coverage and declined to pay Tracy's defense costs or any of the assessments on the basis that there was no "loss" within the meaning of its policy and because three policy exclusions barred coverage.[132] When Tracy could not persuade USSIC to alter its position, Tracy settled the class action, paid the assessments, and then sued USSIC in a California federal court. Tracy's claimed loss included just under $150,000 in defense costs in the form of attorneys' fees. California law controlled the dispute.

Tracy moved for summary judgment and USSIC moved for judgment on the pleadings. Tracy argued that USSIC had a duty to pay Tracy's defense costs because they were incurred under California's "duty to defend" standard.[133] Unless the terms of the policy provide otherwise, California law imposes on an insurer a duty to defend the insured if the underlying complaint asserts

126. *Id.* (footnotes omitted).
127. *Id.*
128. *Id.* at 576.
129. *Id.*
130. *Id.*
131. 636 F. Supp. 2d 995 (C.D. Cal. 2009).
132. *Id.* at 1000.
133. *Id.* at 1003.

claims for damages that are potentially covered by the policy.[134] If even a single claim in the underlying complaint is covered, the insurer must defend the entire action.[135] Unfortunately for Tracy, the court balked at extending traditional California duty to defend analysis to the facts at hand.

First, the USSIC policy expressly disclaimed a duty to defend.[136] Second, requiring USSIC to pay Tracy's defense costs as they were incurred would contradict the policy terms, as the court explained:

> Under [the policy], the "Insureds," not USSIC, "must defend any Claim against them." . . . Jeff Tracy is barred from admitting liability, stipulating to any judgment, or incurring any Defense Cost without USSIC's prior approval. . . . "Only those settlements, stipulated judgments, and Defense Costs to which the Insurer has consented will be recoverable as Loss under the Policy." . . . The parties also agreed to allocate Loss payments when a Claim involves both covered and uncovered Loss. . . . And if the parties "are unable to agree upon an allocation, then until a final allocation is agreed upon or determined . . . the Insurer will be obligated to make an interim payment of that amount or portion of Loss, including Defense Costs, which the parties agree is not in dispute." . . .[137]

In summary, USSIC's duty to pay Tracy's defense costs was tempered by Tracy's responsibility to provide its own defense, to obtain USSIC's approval before incurring defense costs, and to allocate between covered and uncovered defense costs.[138] These conditions were not consistent with the broader duty to defend standard.[139] In addition, because Tracy had presumably paid less for a policy without a duty to defend, requiring USSIC to advance defense costs on a current basis would grant Tracy a windfall.[140]

The court concluded that the duty to defend standard did not apply.[141] Then, analyzing coverage under a traditional analysis, the court determined that there was none. It therefore sustained USSIC's motion for judgment on the pleadings.

Similarly, in *Petersen v. Columbia Casualty Co.*,[142] lawyer Glenn Petersen received an arbitration demand from his former firm, Jackson, DeMarco, Tidius & Peckenpaugh (JDTP), arising out of what apparently was a messy firm split

---

134. *Id.* (quoting Manzarek v. St. Paul Fire & Marine Ins. Co., 519 F.3d 1025, 1031 (9th Cir. 2008)).
135. *Id.* (quoting *Manzarek*, 519 F.3d at 1031).
136. *Id.*
137. *Id.* (citations omitted).
138. *Id.* at 1004.
139. *Id.*
140. *Id.* (quoting Com. Capital Bankcorp, Inc. v. St. Paul Mercury Ins. Co., 419 F. Supp. 2d 1173, 1182 (C.D. Cal. 2006)).
141. *Id.*
142. No. SACV 12-00183 JVS(ANx), 2012 WL 5316352 (C.D. Cal. Aug. 21, 2012).

and a dispute over fees and responsibility for costs in a prior legal malpractice action. He tendered the matter to his professional liability insurers, which were led by Columbia Casualty Co. (Columbia Casualty).[143] The insurers denied coverage and refused to advance claim expenses for the arbitration.[144] Petersen then sued them, seeking, among other forms of relief, a declaratory judgment that they had an immediate duty to advance claim expenses for the JDTP arbitration.[145] The parties soon filed cross-motions for summary judgment.

The Columbia Casualty policy expressly stated that the insureds had the duty to defend any claims against them.[146] With respect to advancing claim expenses, a quota share endorsement to the Columbia Casualty policy provided:

> Subject to the conditions set forth herein, the COMPANY on behalf of the ASSUREDS, shall Advance CLAIM EXPENSES, on the proportionate basis set forth above, in excess of the applicable RETENTION, if any, before the final disposition of a CLAIM against the ASSUREDS.
>
> The COMPANY, on behalf of the ASSUREDS, shall advance CLAIM EXPENSES on the proportional basis set forth above, no later than ninety (90) days after the receipt by the COMPANY of itemized bills in excess of the applicable RETENTION. However, advancement of CLAIM EXPENSES shall be subject to the following conditions . . . .[147]

As for the conditions attached to the duty to advance claim expenses, (1) the assureds had to consult with the insurers about incurring reasonable defense costs; (2) the assureds had to obtain the insurers' consent to settle; and (3) the parties would allocate defense expenses proportionally to covered and uncovered matters, the insurers would advance expenses only as allocated, and the insurers could unilaterally set an allocation if the parties could not agree on one.[148]

Petersen asserted that he was entitled to summary judgment if there was merely a possibility that JDTP had alleged a covered claim.[149] He argued that an insurer's duty to advance claims expenses is sufficiently analogous to the duty to defend that the same standard should apply.[150] The insurers countered that "the possibility of coverage standard" and other duty to defend principles

143. *Id.* at *1.
144. *Id.*
145. *Id.*
146. *Id.* at *7.
147. *Id.*
148. *Id.* at *10.
149. *Id.* at *8.
150. *Id.*

do not apply to a defense-cost-indemnification policy.[151] They viewed the case as a routine coverage dispute over their duty to indemnify Petersen.

The *Petersen* court agreed with the insurers. Reading the policy conditions attached to the duty to advance claim expenses in combination with the policy's express disclaimer of a duty to defend, the court found that the insurers' obligations were "not consistent with the broader duty to defend."[152] The Columbia Casualty policy did not refer to "alleged" damages in establishing the insurers' obligation to pay claim expenses,[153] and the court was therefore unwilling to apply any rule based on a duty to defend policy to this case.[154] The court further concluded that it was Petersen's burden to establish "that the underlying claims [were] within the basic scope of coverage."[155] Ultimately, the court determined that Petersen had no coverage for the arbitration and that the insurers deserved summary judgment on all his claims.

In *XL Specialty Insurance Co. v. Bollinger Shipyards, Inc.*,[156] the insured, Bollinger Shipyards, Inc. (Bollinger), contended that American International Specialty Lines Insurance Co. (AISLIC) and Illinois National Insurance Co. (Illinois National) owed it coverage for an underlying qui tam action under two claims-made D&O policies.[157] Bollinger further alleged that the insurers were obligated to reimburse it for its costs incurred in defending the underlying action.[158] The insurers successfully argued that Bollinger failed to give them timely notice of any related claims and thus that their policies afforded no coverage.[159]

Bollinger asserted that it was nonetheless owed defense costs based on a provision in the policies stating that the insurers "shall advance . . . at the written request of the Insured, Defense Costs prior to the final disposition of a Claim."[160] The *XL Specialty* court rejected this argument. "Defense Costs" was a defined term in the policies and were thus limited to "reasonable and necessary fees, costs and expenses consented to by the Insurer."[161] Both policies conspicuously stated that "in all events the Insurer may withhold consent to any . . . Defense Costs, or any portion thereof, to the extent such Loss is not

151. *Id.* (internal quotation marks omitted).
152. *Id.* at *10 (quoting Jeff Tracy, Inc. v. U.S. Specialty Ins. Co., 636 F. Supp. 2d 995, 1004 (C.D. Cal. 2009)).
153. *Id.*
154. *Id.*
155. *Id.* (quoting *Jeff Tracy*, 636 F. Supp. 2d at 1004).
156. No. 12-2071, 2015 WL 853993 (E.D. La. Feb. 26, 2015).
157. *See id.* at *1.
158. *Id.* at *2.
159. *Id.* at *4–5.
160. *Id.* at *5 (internal quotation marks and footnote omitted).
161. *Id.* (emphasis and internal quotation marks omitted).

covered under the terms of this policy."[162] Because the underlying suit was not covered by AISLIC's and Illinois National's policies based on Bollinger's failure to timely report the associated claims, it followed that neither insurer had to consent to Bollinger's defense costs.[163]

UMIA Insurance, Inc. v. Arguelles[164] arose out of several medical malpractice and fraud claims against Dr. Enrico Arguelles and his clinic (the Arthritis & Osteoporosis Center, or AOC for short) by former patients, as well subpoenas and requests for information by the U.S. Department of Justice and the Department of Health and Human Services. Arguelles's and AOC's insurer, UMIA, defended and ultimately settled the former patients' cases, but contended that it had no duty to defend Arguelles and AOC in connection with the government inquiries. UMIA rested its refusal to defend on an endorsement to its policy that provided regulatory proceedings coverage and stated:

> We have no duty to defend . . . but only to reimburse covered defense costs, shadow audit expenses, and regulatory fines and penalties incurred by the insured. The insured will have complete freedom of choice with respect to the selection of the licensed attorney who provides legal services in connection with any claim covered under the Coverage Agreement. Attorney rates will be capped at a maximum of $300 per hour. All counsel must comply with our reasonable defense counsel guidelines.[165]

Another section of the endorsement provided:

> No insured will incur any defense costs or other expenses, or settle any claim, assume any contractual obligation, admit liability, voluntarily make any payment, or otherwise consent to any settlement or judgment with respect to any claim without our prior written consent, which will not be unreasonably withheld. We will not be liable for defense costs or other expenses, or settlement or judgment to which we have not consented.[166]

UMIA filed a declaratory judgment action in federal court in Montana regarding its defense and indemnity obligations. As is common in such cases, Arguelles and AOC asserted multiple counterclaims. Arguelles and AOC moved for summary judgment on their claim that UMIA owed them a duty to defend.

In ruling on their summary judgment motions, the court rejected Arguelles's and AOC's argument that an insurer's duty to pay defense costs is functionally equivalent to a duty to defend.[167] The court reasoned that the first quoted

162. *Id.* (emphasis and internal quotation marks omitted).
163. *Id.*
164. 591 F. Supp. 3d 876 (D. Mont. 2022).
165. *Id.* at 887 (emphasis omitted).
166. *Id.* at 888 (emphasis omitted).
167. *Id.*

language clearly limited UMIA's duty to reimbursing an insured for covered defense costs rather than imposing a duty to defend.[168]

After observing that the duty to pay defense costs is "not tantamount to a duty to defend,"[169] the court reached "the more difficult question" of the appropriate standard to apply when deciding whether an insurer has a duty to pay defense costs.[170] Arguelles and AOC argued that the same standard applies to both duties. They contended that just as with the duty to defend, an insurer's duty to pay defense costs arises when there is a potential for coverage under the policy.[171] Following a review of similar cases, the court rejected Arguelles's and AOC's argument that the duty to defend and the duty to pay defense costs should be measured by the same standard.

As the court explained, UMIA's policy did not cover claimed damages; it provided for the payment of the insured's defense costs and for the payment of regulatory fines and penalties assessed against the insured. The policy also limited UMIA's duty to the reimbursement of covered defense costs, rather than obligating it to reimburse potentially covered costs. Additionally, the policy did not obligate UMIA to advance an insured's defense expenses but instead provided that UMIA would reimburse the insured for defense costs incurred and fines and penalties imposed.[172]

The endorsement at issue in *Arguelles* clearly stated that UMIA had no duty to defend.[173] It also included conditions for coverage that were inconsistent with the potential for coverage standard, such as granting the insured complete freedom of choice in selecting defense counsel, subject only to an hourly rate cap, and the defense lawyer's agreement to comply with UMIAs reasonable outside counsel guidelines.[174] Finally, the policy also provided that an insured could not incur any defense costs, settle any claim, assume any contractual obligation, make any payment, or consent to any settlement or judgment without UMIA's prior written consent, and established that UMIA would not be liable for any defense costs to which it had not consented.[175] These requirements also were inconsistent with the potentiality standard that applies when determining an insurer's duty to defend.[176]

The *Arguelles* court concluded that the potential for coverage standard that governs an insurer's duty to defend did not apply to UMIA's obligation

168. *Id.* at 887–88.
169. *Id.* at 889 (citing Gon v. First State Ins. Co., 871 F.2d 863, 867 (9th Cir. 1989)).
170. *Id.*
171. *Id.*
172. *Id.* at 891.
173. *Id.*
174. *Id.*
175. *Id.*
176. *See id.*

to reimburse defense costs as provided in the regulatory proceedings endorsement to its policy.[177] Arguelles and AOC bore the burden of showing that their defense costs were covered under the endorsement. Because they had not attempted to do so, the court denied their summary judgment motion.

Time Inc. v. Mutual Insurance Co. Ltd.[178] is among the most recent cases in this line of authority and it illustrates the importance of carefully reading policy language when analyzing an insurer's obligations under a defense-cost-indemnification policy. There, Time Inc. (Time) litigated, and ultimately settled, two class actions alleging that Time had violated California law by automatically renewing customers' magazine subscriptions without their consent. Time was insured under a Mutual Insurance Co. Ltd. (Mutual) media liability policy. The Mutual policy conspicuously stated that Mutual did not owe Time a duty to defend.[179] The policy instead required Mutual to reimburse Time for expenses incurred to defend and settle certain lawsuits involving Time's media business. Specifically, the policy's indemnity agreement stated that that "Mutual 'shall indemnify [Time] for Loss and Defense Expense'" arising from one of 19 enumerated claims, one of which was "negligence, including any actual or alleged error, omissions, misstatement, or misleading statement."[180]

When Mutual denied coverage for the class actions, Time sued for a declaratory judgment and breach of contract. Subsequently, Time moved for partial summary judgment. In its motion, Time asserted that Mutual was obligated to reimburse Time for all expenses it incurred in defending against the class actions. Mutual filed a cross-motion for summary judgment on the basis that it did not owe coverage under its policy.

Time contended that "New York's exceedingly broad duty to defend" obligated Mutual to reimburse all of Time's defense expenses because allegations in the class action complaints suggested a reasonable possibility of coverage.[181] Time stressed that the class action complaints alleged that it failed to disclose automatic renewal terms clearly and conspicuously and therefore at least arguably implicated the Mutual policy's coverage for negligence. The court disagreed, pointing out that the Mutual policy was "an 'indemnity-only' policy" that did not impose a duty to defend.[182] Consequently, Mutual was required to indemnify Time for defenses expenses only for covered claims.[183] Furthermore,

177. *Id.*
178. 667 F. Supp. 3d 61 (S.D.N.Y. 2023).
179. *Id.* at 64.
180. *Id.* (quoting the policy).
181. *Id.* at 66.
182. *Id.* at 67.
183. *Id.*

while Time was correct that negligence claims triggered Mutual's coverage, the class actions plainly alleged intentional misconduct by Time.

In seeking partial summary judgment, Time argued that the outcome in the case was controlled by traditional duty to defend principles.[184] To the contrary, the first page of the Mutual bore a notice in bold type spelled out in all capital letters the policy was an indemnity policy and that Mutual had no duty to defend any claim against Time.[185] The policy's indemnity agreement then stated that Mutual had to indemnify Time for defense expenses connected to claims arising out of negligence in Time's media business.[186]

Time disregarded the statement at the top of the policy that Mutual owed no duty to defend.[187] Time insisted that Mutual effectively did owe a duty to defend because the policy required Mutual to pay defense expenses at "reasonable intervals."[188] Time then cited authority for the proposition that New York courts equate a duty to advance defense costs with a duty to defend, and require an insurer to pay defense costs if the claims against the insured arguably could support a duty to indemnify.[189] This argument failed, however, because Time misconstrued the relevant policy language. As the *Time* court explained:

> The Policy does not, however, impose a general duty to advance or reimburse defense costs. Time simply mischaracterizes the relevant provision. . . . Time[ ] . . . cites Section VI.A.4.c.v of the Policy, which states that, in certain circumstances in which Mutual and Time are cooperating in the defense, "the Company and Insured shall agree to reasonable intervals for reimbursing Defense Expense[s]." . . . Elsewhere, the Policy provides that any "interim payments" of defense expenses "shall not prejudice . . . the ultimate calculation of the amount of Defenses Expense" Mutual actually owes under the Indemnity Agreement. . . . The Policy also contemplates an alternative scenario in which Mutual does not make any interim payments, and, instead, a bill for all of the insured's defense expenses, "paid in the aggregate," is "tendered" to Mutual "within forty-five (45) days after the final payments are made by the Insured." . . . Thus, read in context, the reference to "reasonable intervals" that Time selectively quotes does not reflect an unequivocal promise by Mutual to reimburse defense expenses in all cases.[190]

184. *Id.* at 68.
185. *Id.*
186. *Id.*
187. *Id.*
188. *Id.*
189. *Id.* (first citing Port Auth. of N.Y. & N.J. v. Brickman Grp. Ltd., LLC, 115 N.Y.S.3d 246, 261 (App. Div. 2019); then citing QBE Americas, Inc. v. ACE Am. Ins. Co., 84 N.Y.S.3d 110, 113 (App. Div. 2018)).
190. *Id.*

The *Time* court enforced the unequivocal policy language stating that Mutual had no duty to defend.[191] Mutual's policy did not obligate the company to reimburse Time's defense costs, either. Time collected no "interim payments" while defending the class actions and the ultimate calculation of the defense expense that Mutual owed Time was zero because, as the court soon explained, the Mutual policy did not cover the claims in the class actions.[192]

Because Mutual's policy did not impose a duty to defend or a general obligation to reimburse all defense costs, Time was forced to seek indemnification under the policy. Time thus sought indemnification for all defense expenses and portions of the settlement it paid. In seeking indemnification, Time bore the burden of establishing coverage under Mutual's policy.[193]

Again, Time's arguments were unavailing. The class action complaints did not allege that Time was negligent; rather, they accused Time of intentional misconduct.[194] Thus, they did not trigger the Mutual policy's coverage for negligence.

Retreating, Time again invoked duty to defend principles to argue that Mutual had to pay its defense expenses despite the intentional misconduct accusations because some of the plaintiffs' allegations suggested a reasonable possibility of coverage.[195] The court acknowledged that there was perhaps one claim in one of the complaints that arguably fell within the scope of coverage because it incorporated an assertion that Time had failed to act with due care, but that was immaterial. The court reiterated that this was "not a duty to defend case" and it was "not enough for Time to point to one alternative claim that arguably might trigger coverage."[196]

Because Time could not establish its entitlement to coverage, the court declined to address the parties' arguments over the application of key exclusions. The *Time* court then awarded Mutual summary judgment.

D. Allocating Defense Expenses in Mixed Actions

In many cases, all causes of action in the plaintiff's complaint or petition allege facts that implicate the insurer's duty to indemnify the insured and thus trigger the insurer's duty to defend. That is also true where the insurer is obligated to pay the insured's covered defense expenses rather than defend the insured.

191. *Id.* (quoting Chen v. Ins. Co. of the State of Pa., 163 N.E.3d 447, 450 (N.Y. 2020)).
192. *Id.*
193. *Id.* at 69 (quoting Consol. Edison Co. v. Allstate Ins. Co., 774 N.E.2d 687, 690 (N.Y. 2002)).
194. *Id.*
195. *Id.* at 70.
196. *Id.*

Some cases, however, are "mixed actions," where the plaintiff pleads multiple claims against the insured but only some of them are covered.[197]

As explained in Chapter 1, when an insurer that owes a duty to defend is presented with a mixed action, the insurer's duty to defend any claim in a complaint or petition that arguably falls within coverage generally creates a duty to defend the entire lawsuit.[198] This is the "entire-suit rule," also known as the "in for one, in for all rule," the "mixed-action rule," and the "complete defense rule." Courts have similarly approached insurers' duty to pay defense expenses,[199] as we saw earlier in *American Chemical Society v. Leadscope, Inc.*[200] Recall that the plaintiff in *American Chemical Society*, ACS, sued the four defendants for breach of fiduciary duty, conversion, disloyalty, unfair competition, misappropriation of trade secrets, implied license under the shop-right doctrine, and breach of employment agreement.[201] The defendants were insured under a D&O policy issued by National Union Fire Insurance Co. (National Union). At summary judgment, the trial court held that because ACS's conversion claim was potentially covered, National Union had to reimburse three of the defendants for defending all of ACS's claims.[202]

National Union appealed, arguing that the trial court wrongly applied duty to defend principles when its policy quite differently required it only to reimburse its insureds' defense expenses.[203] The Ohio Court of Appeals, however, concluded that when a policy imposes a duty to advance defense costs rather than a duty to defend, the so-called one claim-all claims principle still controls the insurer's obligation to advance defense costs.[204] The *American Chemical*

---

197. *See* Gonzalez v. Fire Ins. Exch., 184 Cal. Rptr. 3d 394, 403 (Ct. App. 2015) ("When a complaint states multiple claims, some of which are potentially covered by the insurance policy and some of which are not, it is a mixed action."); Fire Ins. Exch. v. Weitzel, 371 P.3d 457, 461 (Mont. 2016) ("If a complaint states multiple claims, some of which are covered by the insurance policy and some of which are not, it is a mixed action.").

198. BITCO Gen. Ins. Corp. v. Monroe Guar. Ins. Co., 31 F.4th 325, 329 (5th Cir. 2022) (applying Texas law); Hartford Cas. Ins. Co. v. J.R. Mktg., L.L.C., 353 P.3d 319, 325 (Cal. 2015); Certain Underwriters at Lloyd's, London v. Metro. Builders, Inc., 158 N.E.3d 1084, 1100 (Ill. App. Ct. 2019); Mt. Vernon Fire Ins. Co. v. Visionaid, Inc., 76 N.E.3d 204, 210 (Mass. 2017); Fire Ins. Exch. v. Weitzel, 371 P.3d 457, 461 (Mont. 2016); Sammy v. First Am. Title Ins. Co., 168 N.Y.S.3d 519, 524 (App. Div. 2022); N. Star Mut. Ins. Co. v. Korzan, 873 N.W.2d 57, 61 (S.D. 2015); Wilson Mut. Ins. Co. v. Falk, 857 N.W.2d 156, 176 (Wis. 2015).

199. *See, e.g.*, Burke v. Ulico Cas. Co., 165 F. App'x 125, 128 (2d Cir. 2006) (quoting Fed. Ins. Co. v. Tyco Int'l Ltd., No. 600507/03, 2004 WL 583829, at *6 (Sup. Ct. Mar. 5, 2004), *aff'd in part and aff'd as modified in part*, Fed. Ins. Co. v. Kozlowski, 792 N.Y.S.2d 397 (App. Div. 2005)); United W. Grocers, Inc. v. Twin City Fire Ins. Co., 457 F.3d 1106, 1112–14 (9th Cir. 2006) (applying California law).

200. No. 04AP-305, 2005 WL 1220746 (Ohio Ct. App. May 24, 2005).

201. *Id.* at *1.

202. *Id.*

203. *Id.* at *2–3.

204. *Id.* at *8.

Society court saw no reason to distinguish between the duty to defend and the duty to advance defense costs in this situation.[205]

To avoid the one claim-all claims principle, some insurers include allocation provisions in their policies. For example, a policy might provide:

> If in any Claim the Insureds incur both Loss covered by this Policy and other amounts which are not covered by this Policy, the Insureds and the Insurer shall allocate such amounts between covered Loss and uncovered loss based on the relative legal and financial exposures of the parties to covered and uncovered matters. If the Insureds and the Insurer cannot agree on an allocation of Defense Costs, the Insurer shall advance Defense Costs which the Insurer believes to be covered under this Policy until a different allocation is negotiated, arbitrated or judicially determined. In such event, such allocation shall be applied retroactively to all Defense Costs.[206]

The court in *Commercial Capital Bankcorp, Inc. v. St. Paul Mercury Insurance Co.*[207] enforced a similar allocation provision in a D&O policy. The allocation clause there provided:

> If in any Claim the Insureds incur Loss jointly with others, including the Company with respect to any Claim not covered under Insuring Agreement C, or incur an amount consisting of both Loss covered under this Policy and loss not covered by this Policy because the Claim includes both covered and uncovered matters, then the Insureds and the Insurer shall allocate such amount between covered Loss and uncovered loss based upon the relative legal exposures of the parties to covered and uncovered matters.
>
> If there can be an agreement on an allocation of Defense Costs, the Insurer shall advance on a current basis Defense Costs allocated to covered Loss. If there can be no agreement on an allocation of Defense Costs, the Insurer shall advance on a current basis Defense Costs which the Insurer believes to be covered under this Policy until a different allocation is negotiated, arbitrated or judicially determined.[208]

The insured, Commercial Capital Bankcorp, Inc. (Commercial Capital), notified St. Paul Mercury Insurance Co. (St. Paul) of a lawsuit against it and associated defendants by Comerica Bank (Comerica). St. Paul acknowledged that that some defendants in the Comerica suit appeared to be insureds under the D&O policy it issued to Commercial Capital and that some claims in the suit appeared to be covered. St. Paul also noted, however, that some of Comerica's claims did not look to be covered, that the suit appeared to seek damages that were not covered, and that Comerica had alleged some conduct falling

205. *Id.*
206. Berkshire Hathaway D&O Policy, *supra* note 7, at 12–13.
207. 419 F. Supp. 2d 1173 (C.D. Cal. 2006).
208. *Id.* at 1177.

outside the scope of the policy. Invoking the allocation clause in its policy, St. Paul proposed to allocate 50 percent of Commercial Capital's defense costs in the Comerica suit to covered claims and to reimburse Commercial Capital on that basis.[209]

Commercial Capital responded by asking St. Paul to pay all defense costs on a current basis, subject to a deferred resolution of St. Paul's claimed right to allocation.[210] St. Paul refused, and Commercial Capital then filed a declaratory judgment action. Commercial Capital alleged that St. Paul was obligated to pay 100 percent of the reasonable defense costs that Commercial Capital had incurred or would incur going forward, and that the allocation clause in the St. Paul policy was unenforceable to the extent it might allow the insurer to do otherwise.[211]

Commercial Capital moved for summary judgment. In ruling on that motion, the district court found that the allocation clause was valid and enforceable under California law and that St. Paul had no duty to pay 100 percent of Commercial Capital's defense costs incurred in the Comerica suit on a current basis.[212]

Among other things, Commercial Capital argued that the California Supreme Court's decision in *Buss v. Superior Court*[213] compelled the district court to find in its favor. According to Commercial Capital, *Buss* reflected California public policy that the district court was obliged to uphold.[214] In *Buss*, the court held that in a mixed action the insurer had a duty to defend the entire action prophylactically and could not "parse" claims.[215] Even if *Buss* reflected California public policy, however, the district court deemed the case to be inapposite because it involved a CGL policy that expressly obligated the insurer to defend the insured against suits seeking covered damages.[216] In contrast, the St. Paul policy expressly disclaimed a duty to defend. The policy provided in pertinent part:

> [Subject to the policy's allocation provision] it shall be the duty of the Insureds and not the duty of the Insurer to defend any Claim.
>
> * * *
>
> [T]he Insurer shall advance on behalf of the Insureds Defense Costs which the Insured Persons . . . have incurred in connection with Claims made against

209. *Id.* at 1178.
210. *Id.*
211. *Id.*
212. *Id.* at 1179.
213. 939 P.2d 766 (Cal. 1997).
214. *Commercial Capital*, 419 F. Supp. 2d at 1181.
215. *Id.* at 1182.
216. *Id.* at 1181–82.

> them, prior to disposition of such Claims, provided that to the extent it is finally established that any such Defense Costs are not covered under this Policy, the Insureds . . . agree to repay the Insurer such Defense Costs.[217]

Thus, rather than paying premiums for the right to a defense of all potentially covered claims, Commercial Capital "paid (presumably lower) premiums for a lesser right."[218] In fact, all Commercial Capital bargained for was the right to allocate defense costs among covered and uncovered claims, and failing related agreement, to have St. Paul advance defense costs that it believed to be covered subject to a later allocation determination.[219] To require St. Paul to advance all of Commercial Capital's defense costs on a current basis despite the clear policy language reflecting the parties' contrary intent would grant Commercial Capital a windfall for which it never bargained.[220]

Commercial Capital also argued that the allocation provision was ambiguous when read together with the policy's provision concerning defense costs, and that to the extent the allocation clause purported to limit its right to contemporaneous payment of its defense expenses, the court should construe the policy against St. Paul.[221] Commercial Capital reasoned that because the defense costs clause provided for the reimbursement of uncovered costs after final disposition of the subject action, a reasonable insured would understand the allocation provision to mean that defense costs would be allocated only after a final resolution of the underlying lawsuit and a final determination of the insurer's right to allocation.[222] Boiled down, the St. Paul policy's defense costs provision would lead an insured to reasonably expect that St. Paul would advance all defense costs as they were incurred.[223]

The court disagreed. The policy provision governing the advancement of defense costs was clearly qualified by the reference to the allocation provision.[224] Indeed, to read the policy to require anything except the apportionment of defense costs before resolution of the underlying action and before the insurer advanced those costs "would be nonsensical."[225] To hold that St. Paul had a duty to advance all defense costs prior to disposition of the action would nullify the language in the allocation provision that allowed St. Paul to advance less than all defense costs on a current basis.[226] The parties' clear intent, as reflected in the policy's defense costs and allocation provisions, was

217. *Id.* at 1176–77.
218. *Id.* at 1182.
219. *Id.*
220. *Id.*
221. *Id.*
222. *Id.*
223. *Id.*
224. *Id.* at 1183.
225. *Id.*
226. *Id.*

that where a lawsuit asserted both covered and uncovered claims and they disagreed on how to apportion the defense costs, the only defense costs St. Paul had to advance were those it believed to be covered.[227] Any different allocation would have to come through negotiation, or a later arbitration award or judicial decision.

The court in *Federal Insurance Co. v. Kozlowski*[228] reached a different result in a case arising out of a mixed action involving Dennis Kozlowski, the disgraced former CEO of Tyco International. The *Kozlowski* court noted that Federal was entitled under its D&O policy to differentiate between covered and uncovered claims, and that its liability for any defense costs was limited to those incurred in connection with covered claims, but it was also bound to pay Kozlowski's defense costs as they were incurred subject to a right of reimbursement.[229] Unfortunately for Federal, the court found it impossible to make an allocation at the time.[230] So, Federal had to pay all of Kozlowski's defense costs as they were incurred, subject to recoupment when his liabilities, if any, were determined.[231]

The contrasting results in *Commercial Capital* and *Kozlowski* are almost certainly attributable to differing policy language. Because the *Kozlowski* court did not quote the key language in the Federal policy in its opinion, however, it is impossible to compare the defense expenses provisions in the policies. In any event, it is clear that many courts weighing the payment of defense expenses in mixed actions are willing to enforce clear allocation provisions in policies before final disposition of the underlying litigation.[232]

E. Summary

To start, absent contrary policy language, an insurer's duty to pay defense expenses should be evaluated in the first instance by the same rules as the duty to defend. For example, if a jurisdiction applies the eight corners test to determine an insurer's duty to defend, a court should use the same test to determine whether an insurer must pay defense costs. If a jurisdiction employs the extrinsic evidence approach to determine whether an insurer owes a duty to defend, an insurer should look beyond the effect of the pleadings and consider any facts brought to its attention or any facts that it reasonably could

227. *Id.* at 1184–85.
228. 792 N.Y.S.2d 397 (App. Div. 2005).
229. *Id.* at 403–04.
230. *Id.* at 404.
231. *Id.*
232. *See, e.g.*, Brown v. Am. Int'l Grp., Inc., 339 F. Supp. 2d 336, 347 (D. Mass. 2004) (holding that the insurer had a duty to advance defense costs in a mixed action prior to final disposition of the underlying action and stating, consistent with the language of the policy, that "the parties [were] to allocate defense costs to potentially covered claims by negotiation").

discover in determining whether it must pay defense expenses. It should not matter whether the policy refers to "alleged" damages, loss, occurrences, or wrongful acts as compared to more certain language; the potential for coverage ought to trigger the insurer's duty to pay defense expenses regardless. In evaluating whether an insurer owes a duty to pay defense expenses based on the potential for coverage, courts should resolve ambiguities or doubts in favor of the insured.

This approach should be uncontroversial; indeed, insurers have previously accepted it and even advocated it.[233] It is practical, reasonable, and should be readily accepted. Under this approach, an insurer's duty to pay defense expenses is roughly analogous in key respects to a duty to defend. Both duties encourage the defense of meritless suits.[234] The duty to pay defense expenses also provides benefits akin to the duty to defend. An insurer's duty to pay defense expenses applies to lawsuits that turn out to be groundless, false, or fraudulent, as does the duty to defend. Moreover, nothing about this approach impairs the contractual rights of an insurer that includes in its policy language allowing it to allocate defense expenses between or among covered and uncovered claims or causes of action, as will be explained later.

Second, where a petition or complaint alleges facts implicating coverage or extrinsic evidence indicates the potential for coverage and the petition or complaint pleads a single claim or cause of action, the insurer must pay all reasonable defense expenses in accordance with the terms of its policy. If the petition or complaint pleads multiple claims or causes of action, all of which allege facts potentially implicating coverage, the insurer again must pay all reasonable defense expenses in accordance with the terms of its policy.

Third, where the complaint or petition presents a mixed action, the insurer's duty to pay defense expenses should be determined by the language of its policy. If the policy does not include an allocation provision that allows the insurer to allocate defense expenses among or between covered and uncovered claims or causes of action, the insurer should be required to fund the defense of the entire action, subject to any right of reimbursement. If the policy includes an allocation provision, on the other hand, that provision should be enforced according to its plain and unambiguous terms. Where it is impossible to allocate defense costs between potentially covered and uncovered claims or causes of action, the insurer should be required to fund the defense of the entire action subject to its contractual right of recoupment (if any) once the insured's liability is finally determined.

---

233. *See, e.g.*, *id.* at 346 ("The [c]ourt . . . applies the construction suggested by [the insurer]: that it assumes a duty to advance defense costs only if the claim suggests a 'reasonable potential for coverage.'").

234. *See* Hurley v. Columbia Cas. Co., 976 F. Supp. 268, 275 (D. Del. 1997) (stating that it would be anomalous to require the insurer to advance defense costs only for meritorious claims).

Where a policy contains an allocation provision, the approach outlined earlier may invite protest as contradicting the one claim-all claims principle that is an established aspect of duty to defend case law. That may be true, but such criticism would still be misplaced. First, despite their similarities or unity of purpose in some circumstances, the duty to pay defense expenses is not a duty to defend. Second, there is no principled basis to reject unambiguous allocation language in a defense-cost-indemnification policy. Third, while application of the one claim-all claims principle is consistent with the language of a duty to defend policy and is thus supportable on that basis, it is not consistent with the language of a defense-cost-indemnification policy that allocates the payment of defense expenses between or among covered and uncovered claims or causes of action. Finally, a defense requires direction by lead counsel—or, perhaps more colloquially, a defense ship can have but one captain—so fulfillment of its duty to defend necessarily requires the insurer to direct the entire defense. Under a duty to defend policy, the right to direct the defense and the obligation to fund it go together. But under a defense-cost-indemnification policy, the insurer typically does not control the defense, and it need only pay in accordance with its policy's allocation provision.

Fourth, whether negotiating the allocation of defense expenses with an insured or allocating defense expenses unilaterally, an insurer must be reasonable. The insurer's implied duty of good faith and fair dealing requires as much.

IV. Reservations of Rights under Defense-Cost-Indemnification Policies

Comparing the duty to pay defense expenses with the duty to defend and formulating related governing principles raises another important practical question: must an insurer that issues a defense-cost-indemnification policy reserve its rights to disclaim coverage to preserve coverage defenses known to the insurer at the time it agrees to fund the defense or reasonably soon thereafter? At least where the policy requires the insurer to advance defense costs, the short answer is yes.[235]

An insurer's obligation to reserve its rights to disclaim its duty to indemnify is tied to its duty to defend.[236] If an insurer that owes a duty to defend assumes an insured's defense in a case where liability and coverage pivot on the same facts, the insured generally is entitled to independent counsel at the insurer's expense. The insurer informs the insured of this situation by way of a reservation of rights letter. Even where liability and coverage are not so blended,

235. Restatement of the L. of Liab. Ins. § 22(2)(b) (Am. L. Inst. 2019).
236. Reservations of rights are discussed in Chapter 2.

the insured still needs to know of coverage defenses or related rights claimed by the insurer to evaluate possible steps to avoid personal liability. Again, the insurer informs the insured of these coverage defenses or rights through a reservation of rights letter.

Under a defense-cost-indemnification policy an insured typically controls its own defense and selects defense counsel. Thus, the insured does not need to be alerted to a conflict of interest entitling it to independent counsel.[237] This eliminates at least one justification for requiring an insurer that issued a defense-cost-indemnification policy to reserve its rights. Indeed, for courts, lawyers, and scholars who reason that the insurer's obligation to reserve its rights exists solely to ensure that the insured's decision to relinquish control of the defense is fully informed, the *only* reason for requiring a reservation of rights has been eliminated.

But even if an insured does not need to be alerted to its right to independent counsel where its defense is funded on an ongoing basis under a primary defense-cost-indemnification policy, it still needs to know whether it potentially faces uninsured liability. For example, an insured that is concerned about an eventual lack of coverage may approach the resolution of a lawsuit differently than it would if its right to indemnity was secure. Absent a reservation of rights, an insured whose defense is being funded on an ongoing basis under a defense-cost-indemnification policy may believe that because the insurer is paying for the defense it has accepted its duty to indemnify the insured down the road.

In the reservation of rights context, the duty to defend and the duty to pay defense expenses—while certainly not the same—are enough alike to treat the insurer's obligation similarly. Consequently, a primary insurer that issues a defense-cost-indemnification policy should be required to reserve its rights when the insured first requests that the insurer advance or reimburse its defense expenses,[238] or when the insured first indicates its intent to defend the claim or loss being notified. Although there is scant authority on the issue, it follows that a primary insurer that fails to timely reserve its rights under a defense-cost-indemnification policy may potentially lose coverage defenses known to it at the time.[239]

If the policy in question is a retroactive defense-cost-indemnification policy, the insurer's duty to reserve its rights, if any, is less certain. There is authority suggesting that an insurer must reserve its rights under such a policy.[240] The obvious argument for an insurer's duty to reserve its rights in this context

237. Conflicts of interest in insurance defense are discussed in Chapter 3.

238. *See* Haley v. Cont'l Cas. Co., 749 F. Supp. 560, 566–67 (D. Vt. 1990) (discussing waiver under a "duty to reimburse" policy).

239. *Id.* at 566–70 (applying waiver doctrine).

240. *Id.*

is that an insured concerned about a lack of coverage might opt to quickly settle the lawsuit rather than incur significant defense costs fighting it. The insured can make that decision only if it knows that the insurer believes that it may owe no duty to indemnify the insured. On the other hand, so long as the insured was competently defended, the insurer will argue that its failure to reserve its rights could not have harmed the insured.

Under either type of policy, the best course for an insurer is to reserve its rights. This approach will not burden insurers. It is already common practice for insurers that issue defense-cost-indemnification policies on a primary basis to reserve their rights when they are notified of a claim or loss, and to send updated reservation of rights letters as they acquire more information about the matter.[241]

V. The Insurer's Duty to Pay for an Insured's Pursuit of Affirmative Claims

As noted earlier, insuring agreements in most standard liability insurance policies provide that the insurer has a duty to defend the insured. Even so, and as discussed in Chapter 4, insureds occasionally assert that an insurer with a duty to defend is obligated to prosecute their affirmative claims, such as counterclaims, crossclaims, and third-party actions. In other words, in some cases the insured asserts that the insurer's duty to defend includes a duty to litigate offensively on the insured's behalf. Courts generally reject these claims. As a rule, insurers' duty to defend does not include a duty to prosecute insureds' affirmative claims.[242] There are good reasons for courts' refusal to recognize a duty on insurers' part to fund insureds' offensive litigation, the most obvious being the plain language of duty to defend policies. Courts must enforce clear and unambiguous policy language as written.[243] Nothing about the use of

241. *See* Restatement of the L. of Liab. Ins. § 22 cmt. b (Am. L. Inst. 2019) (describing this approach as "the current practice among insurers that issue defense-cost-indemnification policies").

242. Aldous v. Darwin Nat'l Assur. Co., 851 F.3d 473, 483 (5th Cir. 2017) (applying Texas law), *vacated in part on other grounds on reh'g*, 889 F.3d 798 (5th Cir. 2018); Spada v. Unigard Ins. Co., 80 F. App'x 27, 29–30 (9th Cir. 2003) (applying Oregon law); Morgan, Lewis & Bockius LLP v. Hanover Ins. Co., 929 F. Supp. 764, 773 (D.N.J. 1996) (applying New Jersey law); Emerald Bay Cmty. Ass'n v. Golden Eagle Ins. Corp., 31 Cal. Rptr, 3d 43, 57 (Ct. App. 2005); Int'l Ins. Co. v. Rollprint Packaging Prods., Inc., 728 N.E.2d 680, 694 (Ill. App. Ct. 2000); Ramsey v. Lee Builders, Inc., 95 P.3d 1033, 1040 (Kan. Ct. App. 2004); Mount Vernon Fire Ins. Co. v. Visionaid, Inc., 76 N.E.3d 204, 213 (Mass. 2017); St. Paul Fire & Marine Ins. Co. v. Nat'l Comput. Sys., Inc., 490 N.W.2d 626, 632 (Minn. Ct. App. 1992); Goldberg v. Am. Home Assur. Co., 439 N.Y.S.2d 2, 4 (App. Div. 1981); Red Head Brass, Inc. v. Buckeye Union Ins. Co., 735 N.E.2d 48, 56 (Ohio Ct. App. 1999); Towne Realty, Inc. v. Zurich Ins. Co., 548 N.W.2d 64, 68–69 (Wis. 1996); Shoshone First Bank v. Pac. Emps. Ins. Co., 2 P.3d 510, 516–17 (Wyo. 2000).

243. Westfield Nat'l Ins. Co. v. Quest Pharms., Inc., 57 F.4th 558, 561 (6th Cir. 2023) (applying Kentucky law); Wilson v. USI Ins. Serv. LLC, 57 F.4th 131, 140–41 (3d Cir. 2023) (applying

"defend" in a policy's insuring agreement when expressing the duty to defend implies a duty on the insurer's part to prosecute affirmative claims the insured may have against the plaintiff or another party.

Similarly, the use of "defend" in a defense-cost-indemnification policy's promise that the insurer will advance or reimburse the insured's defense expenses does not imply that the insurer must advance the costs of, or reimburse the insured for, prosecuting affirmative claims. Nor should the analysis change where the insurer agrees to advance or reimburse the insured's "claim expenses," because policies generally define claim expenses in a way that links them to the insured's defense.

Turner v. XL Specialty Insurance Co.[244] is a complex but instructive case. In 2013, Aubrey McClendon founded American Energy Partners, LP (AELP). Ryan Turner was an officer of both AELP and an AELP affiliate, American Energy Services, LLC (AEMS), until he was fired in 2016. While Turner was still employed, he, McClendon, AEMS, and two other members of the AELP executive team—Scott Mueller and Thomas Blalock—entered into an Equity and Co-Investment Agreement (ECOIA) that established their rights to share the profits from AELP's businesses, including any new businesses. Under the ECOIA, McClendon owned a 76 percent interest in the profit from new businesses, Turner owned a 12 percent interest, and Mueller and Blalock each owned a 6 percent interest.

Soon after the men signed the ECOIA, two new AELP affiliates known collectively as SCOOP were founded. The men agreed that the ECOIA should apply to the sale of any SCOOP assets, so they planned to amend the ECOIA to include SCOOP. Before they could amend the ECOIA, however, McClendon died. Turner, Mueller, and Blalock nonetheless acknowledged that an enforceable agreement had been reached.

Blalock was named special administrator of McClendon's estate and authorized to continue AELP's business. He filed an application in an Oklahoma state court seeking an order allowing the estate to distribute the proceeds from the sale of the SCOOP assets. Turner subsequently filed a creditor claim against McClendon's estate to enforce the ECOIA to collect his share of the profits from the SCOOP asset sale. Another McClendon creditor, however, opposed Blalock's application. Shortly thereafter, Blalock withdrew the application to distribute the SCOOP asset sale proceeds.

Mueller sued SCOOP, Blalock individually and in his representative capacity, and Turner. Mueller sought (1) a determination that he, Blalock, and Turner were due their respective shares of profits; (2) damages for breach of

Pennsylvania and New Jersey law); Garner v. AMCO Ins. Co., 670 S.W.3d 172, 177 (Mo. Ct. App. 2023).

244. 469 F. Supp. 3d 1197 (W.D. Okla. 2020).

contract by SCOOP and the special administratrix of McClendon's estate for failing to distribute the men's profit shares; (3) recovery of the fair value of his work for SCOOP; (4) the imposition of a resulting trust on the net proceeds of the SCOOP assets sale for his benefit; and (5) judgment against McClendon's estate for his rejected creditor claim.

In his answer in the *Mueller* case, Turner either admitted or did not dispute every allegation in Mueller's petition. He then filed his own counterclaims, crossclaims, and third-party claims seeking identical relief. He also asserted a crossclaim for breach of contract against a SCOOP entity, known as SEC, for unpaid consulting fees.[245]

Around six months later, Heath Hibbard—a non-executive SCOOP employee—intervened in the *Mueller* case. He agreed with Mueller's bonus claims and abstained with respect to the other relief sought by Mueller. Hibbard also filed counterclaims and crossclaims seeking (1) a declaratory judgment against SCOOP, Blalock, Mueller, and Turner, recognizing the right, title and obligations of all parties regarding their interests in the profits from the sale of the SCOOP assets; (2) the imposition of a resulting trust against SCOOP, Blalock, Mueller, and Turner for amounts owed to him and other SCOOP associates from the sale of the SCOOP assets; (3) damages for breach of contract against SCOOP; (4) damages for the breach of a partnership agreement against SCOOP, the Blalock, and the SEC partnership; (5) damages for breach of fiduciary duty against SCOOP, Mueller, and Blalock; (6) unjust enrichment against SCOOP; and (7) action on his rejected claim against the special administrator.[246] In answering Hibbard's crossclaims, Turner denied that Hibbard was entitled to the relief he requested.[247]

Turner tendered the *Mueller* lawsuit to XL Specialty Insurance Co. (XL) under AELP's management liability policy. XL denied coverage and, as relevant here, denied that its policy covered Turner's prosecution of his affirmative claims.[248]

Turner sued XL for breach of contract and breach of its implied duty of good faith and fair dealing in failing to reimburse his legal expenses incurred in connection with the *Mueller* case. Both Turner and XL then moved for summary judgment.

The XL policy stated that "[t]he Insurer shall pay on behalf of the Insured Persons Loss resulting from a Claim first made against the Insured Persons during the Policy Period that, in whole or in part, alleges, is based upon, arises from or is in consequence of any Wrongful Act."[249] The policy defined "Loss"

245. *Id.* at 1201.
246. *Id.*
247. *Id.*
248. *Id.* at 1201–02.
249. *Id.* at 1204 (quoting the XL policy).

to mean "damages, judgments, payments, settlements, relief or other amounts . . . and Defense Expenses. . . ."[250] The policy defined "Defense Expenses" as "reasonable legal fees and expenses incurred in the investigation and defense of any Claim. . . ."[251] The policy nowhere defined the term "defense." Turner argued that his legal expenses were "Loss" in the form of "Defense Expenses" and that his affirmative claims were clearly covered when viewing the policy as a whole.[252] XL countered that Turner incurred no "Loss" under the policy because his legal fees were spent pursuing affirmative relief rather than defending any claim.[253]

Applying the contractual language of "Loss" and "Defense Expenses" to the facts, the *Turner* court found that the legal expenses for which Turner sought reimbursement were not incurred to show why Mueller had no valid case, nor to demonstrate why Mueller should not have been awarded the relief he sought.[254] In his petition, Mueller brought five claims against five named defendants; only one claim involved Turner. In that claim, Mueller sought a declaratory judgment affirming the parties' liabilities and rights, including a determination that each AELP executive team member was entitled to his respective share of profits, and that their bonuses be paid in an amount determined by the court. This claim did not place Turner in a defensive posture; to the contrary, it appeared that Mueller asserted the claim for Turner's benefit as well as his own.[255]

Relatedly, Turner neither disputed any of Mueller's alleged material facts nor opposed any of his desired relief. Rather, Turner asserted seven counterclaims and crossclaims in which he requested the same relief that Mueller sought.[256]

Although Turner was named as a defendant in the *Mueller* lawsuit, the pleadings clearly demonstrated that he shared Mueller's interests in obtaining affirmative relief against SCOOP and the special administratrix of McClendon's estate. In fact, it turned out that Turner's lawyer reviewed Mueller's petition before it was filed and conferred with Turner and Mueller regarding the substance of the petition. Turner's legal expenses were thus not incurred in defending against Mueller's claims.[257] Consequently, Turner's legal expenses were not "Defense Expenses," and by extension were not covered "Loss" under the XL policy.

250. *Id.* (quoting the XL policy).
251. *Id.* (quoting the XL policy).
252. *Id.* at 1203.
253. *Id.*
254. *Id.* at 1207.
255. *Id.*
256. *Id.* at 1207–08.
257. *Id.* at 1208.

Retreating, Turner argued that to the extent a defensive posture was required of him, Hibbard's crossclaims put him in that position. The court disagreed. Hibbard made seven claims, only two of which were asserted against Turner. Those two crossclaims included (1) a request for declaratory judgment recognizing all parties' right, title, and obligations regarding their interests in the profits from the sale of the SCOOP assets; and (2) the imposition of a resulting trust on all profits from the sale of the SCOOP assets for the benefit of Hibbard and certain other non-executive employees. While Turner's answer indicated that he opposed Hibbard's crossclaims, other court documents established that Turner believed Hibbard was entitled to his requested relief.[258]

Turner offered no evidence that his legal expenses were incurred to defeat Hibbard's crossclaims. Instead, he contended that Hibbard's claim to the proceeds of the sale of the SCOOP assets would dilute his own share of the profits, and therefore he was forced to "defend" against Hibbard's crossclaims.[259] But this argument failed because he did not ultimately oppose Hibbard's dilution; he instead admitted that the non-executive employees had a right to share in the profits from the sale of the SCOOP assets.

The court concluded that XL Specialty had no obligation to pay for Turner's legal expenses, which were incurred in pursuit of affirmative relief, rather than in defense of a claim.[260] Accordingly, XL did not breach its policy when it denied coverage.[261] XL was therefore entitled to summary judgment on Turner's breach of contract claim.

The *Turner* court reasoned that its conclusion was supported by federal and state court cases holding that an insurer's duty to defend does not include a duty to prosecute and insured's affirmative claims.[262] Turner responded by arguing that the cases analyzing an insurer's duty to defend were irrelevant because the XL policy did not impose such a duty. The court rejected Turner's argument.

> That the policy here does not include a duty to defend does not invalidate the Courts use of precedent discussing that type of clause. The duty to defend is sufficiently analogous to XL Specialty's duty to pay "Defense Expenses" and the Court is within its purview to use duty-to-defend case law in elucidating the contours of XL Specialty's duty—an issue of first impression under Oklahoma law.
>
> Courts interpreting the duty to defend utilize the basic tools of contract interpretation. . . . Here, the Court has likewise conducted its own contract

258. *Id.*
259. *Id.* at 1208–09.
260. *Id.* at 1209.
261. *Id.*
262. *Id.*

> interpretation, as required under Oklahoma law, and found that XL Specialty's duty to pay "Defense Expenses" does not include the duty to assist Mr. Turner in obtaining the relief he sought in the Mueller lawsuit. That most courts to address the related duty to defend have found the duty doesn't include an obligation to pay the legal expenses associated with claims for affirmative relief serves only to buttress the Court's own contract interpretation.[263]

Turner's argument was further doomed to fail by his own summary judgment briefing, where he equated XL's duty to pay "Defense Expenses" with the duty to defend.

The court also found that Turner was not owed coverage under the policy because he was not involved in the *Mueller* lawsuit by virtue of a "wrongful act" as defined in the policy and because he did not qualify as an "insured person." There being no coverage under the policy, XL could not be liable for bad faith under Oklahoma law.

In the end, the *Turner* court awarded XL summary judgment on both of Turner's claims. Naturally, it denied Turner's summary judgment motion in the process.

The *Turner* court reached the correct result. This was not a case where, for example, Turner's affirmative claims were inextricably intertwined with his defense in the *Mueller* case, or where they could be deemed strategically necessary to the defense of that suit.[264] Nor was this a case where the term "defense" as used in the XL policy could arguably be interpreted to mean anything a reasonable defense lawyer would do to reduce Turner's liability.[265] Rather, Mueller's lawsuit was a "friendly" suit from Turner's perspective. And, while Turner was forced to answer Hibbard's crossclaims when Hibbard intervened in the *Mueller* case, he was not adverse to Hibbard in any material way. In short, Turner's affirmative claims were purely that, such that the legal fees he incurred prosecuting them could never reasonably be considered "Defense Expenses."

---

263. *Id.* (citation omitted).

264. *See, e.g.*, TIG Ins. Co. v. Nobel Learning Cmtys., Inc., No. 01-4708, 2002 WL 1340332, at *15 (E.D. Pa. June 19, 2002) (finding that the insured's affirmative claims were inextricably intertwined with its defense); Safeguard Sci., Inc. v. Liberty Mut. Ins. Co., 766 F. Supp. 324, 334 (E.D. Pa. 1991) (concluding that the insured's counterclaims were "inextricably intertwined with the defense" and "necessary to the defense of the litigation as a strategic matter"), *aff'd in part, rev'd in part*, 961 F.2d 209 (3d Cir. 1992).

265. *See* Douglas R. Richmond, *Liability Insurers' Occasional Duty to Defend Offensively*, New Appleman Current Critical Issues in Ins. L., Summer 2019, at 1, 4 (identifying this as an argument an insured may make when asserting that an insurer's duty to defend includes a duty to prosecute affirmative claims).

VI. Equitable Contribution Claims between Insurers to Recover Defense Expenses

Finally, an insured may be covered under concurrent primary liability insurance policies. In that situation, a lawsuit against the insured may trigger the concurrent insurers' duty to defend or to pay defense expenses. If a concurrent insurer does not participate in the insured's defense and thus forces another insurer to assume sole responsibility for protecting their common insured, the insurer providing or funding the defense understandably may want to recover some portion of its costs from the nonparticipating insurer. But an insurer looking to recover defense costs from a recalcitrant concurrent carrier may have a difficult time. This is because there is no contractual relationship between the insurers that might support such recovery; all contractual duties or obligations flow only to the insured.[266] Each insurer owes the insured a separate defense obligation. Accordingly, a few courts do not allow concurrent primary insurers to recover defense costs from one another.[267] As the Supreme Court of South Carolina explained in *Sloan Construction Co. v. Central National Insurance Co.*:[268]

> [W]here two companies insure the identical risk and both policies provide for furnishing the insured with a defense, neither company, absent a contractual relationship, can require contribution from the other for expenses of the defense where one denies liability and refuses to defend. The duty to defend is personal to both insurers; neither is entitled to divide the duty.[269]

Most jurisdictions, however, hold that an insurer honoring its duty to defend may seek contribution from a concurrent primary insurer that has declined to defend their common insured despite having a duty to do so.[270] The

266. Certain Underwriters at Lloyd's, London v. Arch Specialty Ins. Co., 200 Cal. Rptr. 3d 786, 792 (Ct. App. 2016); Shell Oil Co. v. Winterthur Swiss Ins. Co., 15 Cal. Rptr. 2d 815, 850 (Ct. App. 1993); Church Mut. Ins. Co. v. Smith, 509 N.W.2d 274, 275 (S.D. 1993).

267. *See, e.g.*, Progressive Express Ins. Co. v. Fla. Dep't of Fin. Servs., 125 So. 3d 201, 203 (Fla. Dist. Ct. App. 2013) (quoting Argonaut Ins. Co. v. Md. Cas. Co., 372 So. 2d 960, 963 (Fla. Dist. Ct. App. 1979)); United Servs. Auto. Ass'n v. State Farm Fire & Cas. Co., 110 P.3d 570, 573 (Okla. Civ. App. 2004).

268. 236 S.E.2d 818 (S.C. 1977).

269. *Id.* at 820.

270. *See, e.g.*, Trinity Universal Ins. Co. v. Emps. Mut. Cas. Co., 592 F.3d 687, 695 (5th Cir. 2010) (applying Texas law); Danaher Corp. v. Travelers Indem. Co., 414 F. Supp. 3d 446, 452 (S.D.N.Y. 2019) (discussing New York law); Zurich Am. Ins. Co. v. Ins. Co. of N. Am., 392 F. Supp. 3d 992, 997 (E.D. Mo. 2019) (applying Missouri law); Cont'l W. Ins. Co. v. Colony Ins. Co., 69 F. Supp. 3d 1075, 1085–86 (D. Colo. 2014) (applying Colorado law); Nucor Corp. v. Emps. Ins. of Wausau, 296 P.3d 74, 83–85 (Ariz. Ct. App. 2012); Cal. Cap. Ins. Co. v. Emps. Comp. Ins. Co., 305 Cal. Rptr. 3d 686, 690–91 (Ct. App. 2023) (quoting Fireman's Fund Ins. Co. v. Md. Cas. Co., 77 Cal. Rptr. 2d 296, 303–04 (Ct. App. 1998)); Nat'l Cas. Co. v. Great Sw. Fire Ins. Co., 833 P.2d 741, 748 (Colo. 1992);

majority position sounds in equity. Because each insurer potentially covering the lawsuit has a duty to defend the insured, each should share in defense costs. Allowing a concurrent primary insurer to avoid contributing to its insured's defense only encourages the breach of the insurer's duty to defend, inasmuch as the carrier can thereby reduce its expenses.[271]

What then of the situation in which one or both concurrent primary insurers owe a duty to pay defense expenses rather than a duty to defend? Do the equitable principles that courts commonly enforce in the duty to defend context apply in this instance? There is little related authority. *Travelers Indemnity Co. v. Insurance Co. of North America*[272] is a rare case that is arguably on-point.

Three corporations known collectively as Leisure Technology were sued in three cases: the *Finkelstein* action, the *Southbridge* action, and the *Ocean Hills* action.[273] Travelers, INA, and Generali insured Leisure Technology. Generali issued a primary CGL policy, INA issued a commercial excess policy, and Travelers issued two CGL policies.[274] Leisure Technology tendered its defense in all three cases to all three insurers. Travelers defended all three actions and, together with Generali, settled the *Finkelstein* and *Southbridge* cases.[275] INA did not participate in the defense or settlement of any of the cases.[276] Travelers accordingly sought (1) a declaratory judgment that INA and Generali had a duty to defend Leisure Technology in the *Finkelstein*, *Southbridge*, and *Ocean Hills* actions; and (2) reimbursement of a portion of its defense costs.[277] Only Travelers' claims against INA are relevant here.

The INA policy did not provide for a duty to defend; rather, it obligated INA to reimburse Leisure Technology's defense costs in certain circumstances. INA's policy provided in pertinent part:

> We have neither the right nor the duty to defend a "suit" seeking damages or to investigate or settle any claim or "suit", nor does this policy apply to "loss adjustment expense", except as outlined below, or prejudgment interest

---

Acuity Ins. Co. v. 960 W. Huron Condo. Ass'n, 138 N.E.3d 189, 200 (Ill. App. Ct. 2019); Selective Way Ins. Co. v. Fireman's Fund Ins. Co., 289 A.3d 719, 739–44 (Md. App. Ct. 2023); Ins. Co. of the State of Pa. v. Great N. Ins. Co., 45 N.E.3d 1283, 1287 (Mass. 2016); Cargill, Inc. v. Ace Am. Ins. Co., 784 N.W.2d 341, 354 (Minn. 2010); Certain Underwriters at Lloyd's London & Excess Ins. Co. Ltd. v. Mass. Bonding & Ins. Co., 230 P.3d 103, 112–13 (Or. Ct. App. 2010); Sharon Steel Corp. v. Aetna Cas. & Sur. Co., 931 P.2d 127, 137–38 (Utah 1997).

271. Douglas R. Richmond, *Cutting through the "Virtually Impenetrable Thicket" of "Other Insurance,"* New Appleman Current Critical Issues in Ins. L., Dec. 2007, at 69, 94.

272. 886 F. Supp. 1520 (S.D. Cal. 1995).

273. *Id.* at 1522–23.

274. *Id.*

275. *Id.* at 1523.

276. *Id.*

277. *Id.* at 1523–24.

arising out of any "occurrences" or offense. We shall have the right and opportunity to assume from the insured the defense and control of any claim or "suit", including any appeal from a judgment, seeking payment of damages covered under this policy that we believe likely to exceed the "retained limit". In such event we and the insured shall cooperate fully.

"Loss adjustment expense" will be apportioned between you and us as follows:

a. If the amount of the judgment or settlement exceeds the amount of the "retained limit", all "loss adjustment expense" in connection therewith will be borne by the insured and us in the same proportion as the insured's and our respective obligations for payment of the judgment or settlement;

b. If the amount of the judgment or settlement does not exceed the amount of the "retained limit", or if the claim or "suit" is settled without payment of damages, the amount of the "loss adjustment expense" shall be borne solely by the insured.[278]

Thus, INA became obligated to reimburse a portion of Leisure Technology's defense costs only if a judgment or settlement exceeded the INA policy's retained limit.[279] The *Finkelstein* and *Southridge* settlements exceeded INA's retained limit but were paid by Travelers rather than by Leisure Technology or by INA.[280]

Travelers argued that INA should be required as a matter of equity to reimburse it for the costs of Leisure Technology's defense in the *Finkelstein* and *Southridge* actions because it had discharged the duty of defending their common insured.[281] As between Travelers and INA, only Travelers had a duty to defend Leisure Technology; INA had to reimburse Leisure Technology's defense costs. "Although these two obligations are not the same," the *Travelers Indemnity* court noted, "in this case INA's duty to reimburse [could] be considered a lesser included common obligation."[282]

The court acknowledged that there were significant differences between the duty to defend and the duty to reimburse defense expenses.[283] Nonetheless, under the circumstances, Travelers' settlement payments on Leisure Technology's behalf were "equivalent to payments by the insured for the purposes of the INA policy."[284] The court therefore concluded that INA had to reimburse

278. *Id.* at 1528.
279. *Id.*
280. *Id.*
281. *Id.*
282. *Id.* at 1529.
283. *Id.*
284. *Id.*

Travelers' defense costs in the *Finkelstein* and *Southbridge* actions according to the terms of its policy.[285]

Travelers Indemnity is an unusual decision on equitable contribution because it involved a primary and an excess insurer rather that concurrent primary insurers. At the same time, it would have made no sense to deny Travelers contribution solely on the basis that the INA policy provided for the reimbursement of defense expenses rather than imposing a duty to defend. In the equitable contribution context, a duty to pay defense expenses is the functional equivalent of a duty to defend, and a concurrent insurer that shirks its duty to pay defense expenses should be subject to liability for equitable contribution just as if it owed a duty to defend that it breached. To hold otherwise would be to allow the insurer that agreed to pay defense expenses to avoid an obligation for which it bargained and for which it collected premiums.

The approach advocated here tracks the law of restitution and unjust enrichment.[286] Borrowing from the Restatement (Third) of Restitution and Unjust Enrichment to explain, if *A* renders to a third party performance for which *A* and *B* are jointly and severally liable, *A* is entitled to restitution from *B* to the extent necessary to prevent *B*'s unjust enrichment.[287] *A*'s claim against *B* is described as contribution rather than as indemnity because *A* paid more than its share of a common liability, rather than paying an obligation that was solely *B*'s.[288] Likewise, where Insurer 1 fully funds the defense of an insured for which it is jointly and severally liable with Insurer 2, Insurer 1 is entitled to contribution from Insurer 2 for Insurer 2's share of the defense costs lest Insurer 2 be unjustly enriched.

285. INA's duty to reimburse defense costs in the *Ocean Hills* action was not ripe for adjudication because that litigation was still being waged. *Id.*

286. *See* Restatement (Third) of Restitution and Unjust Enrichment § 1 (Am. L. Inst. 2011) ("A person who is unjustly enriched at the expense of another is subject to liability in restitution."); *id.* § 3 ("A person is not permitted to profit by his own wrong.").

287. *Id.* § 23(1).

288. *Id.* § 23 cmt. a.

CHAPTER 11
Nonexecution Agreements and Consent Judgments

Douglas R. Richmond

I. Introduction

Liability insurers regularly litigate coverage and bad faith claims predicated on judgments that follow agreements between insureds and claimants in which the insurer had no part. These cases frequently are linked to the insurers' duty to defend and, in particular, to their alleged breaches of that duty.

In a common scenario, an insurer declines to defend an insured in a third-party action based on what the insurer believes to be a lack of coverage, which the insured and the plaintiff treat as a breach of the insurer's duty to defend.[1] The insured and the plaintiff then enter into nonexecution agreement under which they agree that the third-party case will go forward but that the plaintiff will limit any recovery to the proceeds of the insured's policy with the insurer. Under the agreement, the insured further assigns any rights under its policy to the plaintiff or agrees that it will pursue a bad faith claim against its insurer

1. As a rule, an insurer must breach its duty to defend or unreasonably refuse to settle a case within policy limits before an insured may stipulate to a judgment and assign its claims against its insurer to a third party. State Farm Mut. Auto Ins. Co. v. Goddard, 484 P.3d 765, 769 (Colo. App. 2021). In some jurisdictions, however, an insured may enter into a consent judgment when an insurer defends under a reservation of rights. *See, e.g.*, Quihuis v. State Farm Mut. Auto. Ins. Co., 334 P.3d 719, 722 (Ariz. 2014) (explaining and differentiating so-called *Damron* and *Morris* agreements); Com. Ins. Co. v. Szafarowicz, 131 N.E.3d 782, 797 (Mass. 2019) (outlining the conditions required for an insured to be able to settle without the insurer's consent where the insurer is defending under a reservation of rights); *see also* Restatement of the L. of Liab. Ins. § 25 (Am. L. Inst. 2019) (stating when an insured may settle without the insurer's consent and without violating the duty to cooperate in a case where the insurer is defending under a reservation of rights).

for the plaintiff's benefit and pay any sums received through a settlement or judgment to the plaintiff. In either scenario, the plaintiff promises to deem its judgment against the insured satisfied out of the recovery, if any, from the insurer in the planned subsequent litigation. The plaintiff and the insured then try the third-party action to the court. The defense lawyer for the insured (who is often selected and compensated by the plaintiff's lawyer) mounts either a weak defense or no defense at all. In extreme cases, the plaintiff and insured may effectively stage a sham trial by agreeing that the defense lawyer will not make an opening statement, not object to the plaintiff's evidence, not present a defense, and not deliver a closing argument—all unbeknownst to the court.[2] At the conclusion of the one-sided trial (however structured), the plaintiff asks the court to award damages in excess of the insurer's policy limits, which the court, having heard no contrary evidence, obediently does. Thereafter, (1) either the plaintiff as the insured's assignee or the insured sues the insurer for breach of contract and bad faith; or (2) the plaintiff as a judgment creditor files an equitable garnishment action against the insurer and the insured to collect the judgment and the insured crossclaims against the insurer for breach of contract and bad faith.[3]

Alternatively, but analogously, the insured may simply consent to a judgment in excess of policy limits with the plaintiff in exchange for the plaintiff's promise to limit collection of the judgment solely to insurance policy proceeds, coupled with the insured's assignment of its rights against the insurer to the plaintiff or the insured's agreement to pursue a bad faith claim against the insurer for the plaintiff's benefit. After obtaining approval of the judgment in a reasonableness hearing before the court handling the third-party action against the insured,[4] the plaintiff sues the insured and the insurer in an equitable garnishment action to collect the judgment, and the insured crossclaims against the insurer for bad faith and breach of contract. Any recovery goes to the plaintiff to satisfy the consent judgment. As in the first scenario, the insured

2. These manipulated proceedings potentially constitute a fraud on the court. *See* Douglas R. Richmond, *Critical Contours of Fraud on the Court*, 37 Rev. Litig. 1, 3–4 (2018) (describing the type of fraud that constitutes fraud on the court). In addition to providing a basis to set aside the judgment obtained through the fraud, participating in a scheme that qualifies as fraud on the court potentially exposes the lawyers for both parties to sanctions and professional discipline. *See* Model Rules of Pro. Conduct r. 8.4(c) (Am. Bar Ass'n 2023) (prohibiting conduct involving dishonesty, fraud, deceit or misrepresentation); *id.* r. 8.4(d) (prohibiting conduct that is prejudicial to the administration of justice).

3. *See generally* King's Cove Marina, LLC v. Lambert Com. Constr. LLC, 958 N.W.2d 310, 321 (Minn. 2021) ("In the garnishment proceeding, the insurer may challenge not only the scope of coverage under the insurance policy, but also the validity and reasonableness of the settlement.").

4. As explained in Part II, for a consent judgment to be enforceable against an insurer, the judgment must be reasonable in amount and in the method by which it was obtained.

typically is represented on its crossclaim by a lawyer chosen by the plaintiff's lawyer.

In yet another variation, the insured and the plaintiff enter into a consent judgment in excess of the insured's policy limits, along with a nonexecution agreement in which (1) the plaintiff promises to limit collection of the judgment to any insurance proceeds; and (2) the insured assigns its insured's rights against its insurers to the plaintiff. The parties then convene a hearing in the court in which the case is pending to establish that the consent judgment is reasonable. Again, the plaintiff's arguments and presentation of evidence dominates the hearing. Then, with the ostensibly reasonable consent judgment and the insured's assignment of its rights in hand, the plaintiff sues the insurer for breach of contract and bad faith, with the amount of the consent judgment being the presumptive measure of damages.[5]

The judgments entered in these proceedings generally are described as "consent judgments" even though they may be entered following a hearing or trial. The nonexecution agreements that animate the consent judgment process go by various names. In Arizona, depending on the situation, they are known as "*Damron* agreements," "*Morris* agreements," or "*Damron/Morris* agreements" based on the Arizona Supreme Court decisions that first recognized them: *Damron v. Sledge*[6] and *United Services Automobile Ass'n v. Morris*.[7] In Colorado, they are now described as *Nunn* agreements.[8] In Minnesota, North Dakota, and South Dakota they are called "*Miller-Shugart* agreements" in a nod to the Minnesota Supreme Court decision in *Miller v. Shugart*.[9] In other states they are known as "*Coblentz* agreements," after a Fifth Circuit decision applying Florida law, *Coblentz v. American Surety Co. of New York*.[10] One

5. *See generally* Garza v. Perry, 523 P.3d 822, 830 (Wash. Ct. App. 2023) ("A covenant judgment creates a presumptive amount of damages not because it forms a contract with the insured, but because a tortfeasor should not be able to benefit from its wrongdoing.").

6. 460 P.2d 997 (Ariz. 1969) (involving the denial of a defense).

7. 741 P.2d 246 (Ariz. 1987) (involving a defense under a reservation of rights).

8. Auto-Owners Ins. Co. v. Bolt Factory Lofts Owners Ass'n, Inc., 487 P.3d 276, 282 (Colo. 2021) (discussing Nunn v. Mid-Century Ins. Co., 244 P.3d 116, 119–20 (Colo. 2010)).

9. 316 N.W.2d 729 (Minn. 1982); *see, e.g.*, King's Cove Marina, LLC v. Lambert Com. Constr. LLC, 958 N.W.2d 310, 313 n.1 (Minn. 2021); Wangler v. Lerol, 670 N.W.2d. 830, 838 (N.D. 2003); W. Agric. Ins. Co. v. Arbab-Azzein, 940 N.W.2d 865, 867 n.2 (S.D. 2020). Minnesota courts also recognize a similar type of agreement known as a *Drake–Ryan* agreement. A *Drake–Ryan* agreement, named after Minnesota Supreme Court's decision in *Drake v. Ryan*, 514 N.W.2d 785 (Minn. 1994), permits a primary insurer to settle with a plaintiff in exchange for a complete release of any claims against an insured defendant, but also preserves the plaintiff's right to pursue a claim against an excess insurer up to the limits of the excess insurer's policy. Am. Fam. Mut. Ins. Co. v. Donaldson, 820 F.3d 374, 376 n.2 (8th Cir. 2016).

10. 416 F.2d 1059, 1062–63 (5th Cir. 1969); *see, e.g.*, Perera v. U.S. Fid. & Guar. Co., 35 So. 3d 893, 900 (Fla. 2010) (describing "*Coblentz* agreements").

Florida variation is labeled a "*Cunningham* agreement."[11] In Missouri, they are described as "537.065 agreements," in reference to the Missouri statute that allows their entry in certain cases.[12] Alaska courts use the term "covenant settlement agreement,"[13] while Washington courts refer to "covenant judgments."[14] Courts and lawyers in other jurisdictions may describe them in yet other ways.

As for the effectiveness of nonexecution agreements and the enforceability of consent judgments, it usually is true that a person or entity not a party to a settlement agreement—which is what nonexecution agreements are often said to be—is not bound by its terms.[15] Where, however, an insurer breaches its duty to defend, the consent judgment establishes the insured's liability, and the insurer cannot re-litigate issues that either were or could have been litigated in the underlying action in a later declaratory judgment, equitable garnishment, or bad faith action.[16] In short, the insurer cannot re-litigate the insured's liability to the plaintiff,[17] with the exception of a case where a conflict of interest or some action or decision by the insured prevented the insurer from controlling or managing the insured's defense.[18] In any event, the insurer remains entitled to litigate coverage for the judgment and to dispute its alleged bad faith.[19] The nonexecution agreement between the plaintiff and the insured cannot create

11. In a *Cunningham* agreement, the parties agree that they will try the bad faith action against the tortfeasor's insurance company before trying the underlying negligence claim. If no bad faith is found, the plaintiff's claims are settled for the policy limits, and the insured avoids an excess judgment. *See* Kropilak v. 21st Century Ins. Co., 806 F.3d 1062, 1068 (11th Cir. 2015).

12. *See* Mo. Rev. Stat. § 537.065 (2021).

13. Great Divide Ins. Co. v. Carpenter, 79 P.3d 599, 609 (Alaska 2003).

14. Garza v. Perry, 523 P.3d 822, 830 (Wash. Ct. App. 2023).

15. Ahern v. Odyssey Re (London) Ltd., 788 So. 2d 369, 371–72 (Fla. Dist. Ct. App. 2001); Calypso Asset Mgmt., LLC v. 180 Indus., LLC, 171 N.E.3d 790, 806 (Ohio Ct. App. 2021) (quoting State *ex rel.* Dillard Dep't Stores v. Ryan, 910 N.E.2d 438, 443 (Ohio 2009)).

16. Colo. Cas. Ins. Co. v. Safety Control Co., 288 P.3d 764, 770 (Ariz. Ct. App. 2012) (quoting State Farm. Mut. Auto. Ins. Co. v. Paynter, 593 P.2d 948, 950 (Ariz. Ct. App. 1979)); *In re* Est. of Arroyo v. Infinity Indem. Ins. Co., 211 So. 3d 240, 246 (Fla. Dist. Ct. App. 2017); Draggin' Y Cattle Co. v. Junkermier, Clark, Campanella, Stevens, P.C., 439 P.3d 935, 942 (Mont. 2019).

17. *In re Est. of Arroyo*, 211 So. 3d at 246.

18. *Colo. Cas.*, 288 P.3d at 770 n.2; Cox v. Steck, 992 S.W.2d 221, 224 (Mo. Ct. App. 1999); 1 Allan D. Windt, Insurance Claims and Disputes § 6:22, at 6-262 (6th ed. 2013 & Supp. 2023).

19. Hudson Specialty Ins. Co. v. Brash Tygr, LLC, 769 F.3d 586, 593–94 (8th Cir. 2014) (applying Missouri law); Andrew v. Century Sur. Co., 134 F. Supp. 3d 1249, 1263 (D. Nev. 2015) (predicting Nevada law); Nelson v. Am. Home Assur. Co., 824 F. Supp. 2d 909, 914 (D. Minn. 2011) (applying Minnesota law), *aff'd*, 702 F.3d 1038 (8th Cir. 2012); Great Divide Ins. Co. v. Carpenter, 79 P.3d 599, 609 (Alaska 2003); Quihuis v. State Farm Mut. Auto. Ins. Co., 334 P.3d 719, 722, 725–30 (Ariz. 2014); Fokken v. Steichen, 744 N.W.2d 34, 40 (Neb. 2008); Forsman v. Blues, Brews & Bar-B-Ques, Inc., 903 N.W.2d 524, 529 (N.D. 2017); Kobbeman v. Oleson, 574 N.W.2d 633, 636 (S.D. 1998); Clark v. Sputniks, LLC, 368 S.W.3d 431, 438–39 (Tenn. 2012).

coverage,[20] and, while the consent judgment establishes the insured's liability to the plaintiff, it does not create coverage either.[21] Coverage is determined by the terms of the insurance policy.[22] The insured's liability to the plaintiff and coverage for the consent judgment are separate issues.[23] The insured or plaintiff must prove the existence of coverage to collect the consent judgment from the insurer.[24] The insured and plaintiff cannot create coverage by agreement, regardless of whether they do so expressly or do so indirectly by parroting the policy language in the nonexecution agreement or the judgment.[25]

In many respects the consent judgment process is justified. If a carrier denies coverage for a claim or suit and thus refuses to defend the insured, the insured placed in jeopardy as a result should be allowed to protect itself by shifting the risk of loss to the insurer "without first subjecting itself to potential financial ruin."[26] Or, as the California Supreme Court observed, "[w]hen the insurer 'exposes its policyholder to the sharp thrust of personal liability' by breaching its obligations, the insured 'need not indulge in financial masochism.'"[27] If an insured is offered a deal that relieves it of personal liability at a time when its insurance coverage is in doubt, no one can deny that it is generally in the insured's interest to accept the offer, or argue that the insured should not reasonably protect itself.

On the other hand, nonexecution agreements and the related consent judgments are troubling. For one thing, they multiply litigation.[28] They strengthen weak claims, fashion new ones, and inflate or manufacture damages.[29] The courts that first approved consent judgments never intended "to promote the transformation of underlying contract and tort claims into bad faith claims at

20. *See* Fid. Nat'l Title Ins. Co. v. Centerpoint Mech. Lien Claims, LLC, 357 P.3d 170, 177 (Ariz. Ct. App. 2015) (stating that "a *Morris* agreement cannot expand the insured's rights under the insurance contract").

21. Nelson v. Am. Home Assur. Co., 702 F.3d 1038, 1041–42 (8th Cir. 2012) (applying Minnesota law); Mid-Continent Cas. Co. v. Royal Crane, LLC, 169 So. 3d 174, 181–82 (Fla. Dist. Ct. App. 2015).

22. Interlachen Props., LLC v. State Auto Ins. Co., 275 F. Supp. 3d 1094, 1109 (D. Minn. 2017) (citing *Nelson*, 702 F.3d at 1041).

23. S. Guar. Ins. Co. v. Dowse, 605 S.E.2d 27, 29 (Ga. 2004).

24. *Nelson*, 702 F.3d at 1041–42; Forsman v. Blues, Brews and Bar-B-Ques, Inc., 903 N.W.2d 524, 530 (N.D. 2017).

25. *See Nelson*, 702 F.3d at 1042; Shiddell v. Bar Plan Mut., 385 S.W.3d 478, 486 (Mo. Ct. App. 2012).

26. Great Divide Ins. Co. v. Carpenter, 79 P.3d 599, 609 (Alaska 2003).

27. Samson v. Transamerica Ins. Co., 636 P.2d 32, 45 (Cal. 1981) (quoting Critz v. Farmers Ins. Grp., 41 Cal. Rptr. 401, 408 (Ct. App. 1964)).

28. State Farm Fire & Cas. Co. v. Gandy, 925 S.W.2d 696, 711–12 (Tex. 1996).

29. *Id.* at 713–14.

inflated values,"[30] or to allow litigants to extend the insurer's liability "beyond the boundaries contemplated by the contract" in pursuit of injuries that are mostly "fictional,"[31] yet such scenarios abound. Certainly, it is misleading to describe nonexecution agreements as settlement agreements as some courts do because they are intended to prolong litigation, not end it.[32] For another thing, the consent judgment process "encourages collusion between the insured and the plaintiff to raid insurance proceeds."[33]

Nonexecution agreements and consent judgments raise a host of legal issues, but three consistently appear.[34] First, a consent judgment must be reasonable to be enforceable against an insurer. "Reasonableness" usually concerns the amount of the judgment when examined objectively, but it also includes a procedural aspect. To be reasonable, a nonexecution agreement generally must be tested in, or a consent judgment generally must be derived from, a fully adversarial hearing or trial. A consent judgment is not reasonable merely because a judge approved or entered it.

Second, in addition to the reasonableness requirement, the nonexecution agreement and consent judgment must be entered into in good faith and cannot be fraudulent or collusive if the insurer is to be held liable. "Bad faith," "fraud," and "collusion" as those terms are used here should be broadly construed. These forms of misconduct are related but they are not necessarily synonyms for the same behavior.

Third, though not necessarily tied to an insurer's duty to defend, plaintiffs frequently contend that an insurer's duty of good faith and fair dealing compels the insurer to approve a nonexecution agreement that exposes the insurer to bad faith liability or to approve a consent judgment in excess of the policy's liability limits. Insurers disagree for good reasons.

30. Leflet v. Redwood Fire & Cas. Ins. Co., 247 P.3d 180, 184 (Ariz. Ct. App. 2011).

31. *In re* Tutu Water Wells Contamination Litig., 78 F. Supp. 2d 423, 433 (D.V.I. 1999).

32. *Gandy*, 925 S.W.2d at 712.

33. Strahin v. Sullivan, 647 S.E.2d 765, 773 (W. Va. 2007).

34. For a comprehensive discussion of nonexecution agreements, consent judgments, and the legal issues they raise, see Douglas R. Richmond, *The Consent Judgment Quandary of Insurance Law*, 48 Tort Trial & Ins. Prac. L.J. 537 (2013). For additional perspectives, see Jeffrey N. Labovich & Cody S. Moon, *What Insurers and Their Counsel Should Know About Consent Judgments*, For the Def., May 2015, at 34; Don R. Sampen & Alec M. Barinholtz, *Enforcement of Settlements between Insureds and Claimants*, 35 Ins. Litig. Rep. 409 (2013).

II. The Requirement That Consent Judgments Be Reasonable

A. Overview

A consent judgment must be reasonable to be enforceable against an insurer.[35] This is an objective test.[36] Whether a consent judgment is reasonable is a function of its amount and the procedure by which it was obtained.[37]

The reasonableness requirement recognizes that the consent judgment process "can be abused. The insured who is fortunate enough to be able to make such an agreement has no incentive not to agree to very high damage awards."[38] This risk is especially acute in cases in which insureds have little or no ability to satisfy judgments.[39] In any event, the amount of a consent judgment may have little relationship to the strength of the plaintiff's case against the insured.[40] By imposing a reasonableness requirement, courts are trying to recreate the result that would have occurred had the case been resolved at arm's-length by interested parties.[41] As a New Jersey court recognized:

---

35. Home Fed. Sav. Bank v. Ticor Title Ins. Co., 695 F.3d 725, 736 (7th Cir. 2012) (applying Indiana law); Corn Plus Coop. v. Cont'l Cas. Co., 516 F.3d 674, 680 (8th Cir. 2008) (applying Minnesota law); Cont'l Cas. Co. v. Hempel, 4 F. App'x 703, 716 (10th Cir. 2001) (interpreting New Mexico law); Bristol W. Ins. Co. v. Whitt, 406 F. Supp. 2d 771, 784–85 (W.D. Mich. 2005) (applying Michigan law); Conn. Indem. Co. v. Perrotti, 390 F. Supp. 2d 158, 170 (D. Conn. 2005) (quoting Black v. Goodwin, Loomis & Britton, Inc., 681 A.2d 293, 302 (Conn. 1996)); Ayers v. C & D Gen. Contractors, 269 F. Supp. 2d 911, 915 (W.D. Ky. 2003) (predicting Kentucky law); Liberty Mut. Ins. Co. v. Wheelwright Trucking Co., 851 So. 2d 466, 475–76 (Ala. 2002) (discussing Georgia and Alabama law); Great Divide Ins. Co. v. Carpenter, 79 P.3d 599, 609 (Alaska 2003); Leflet v. Redwood Fire & Cas. Ins. Co., 247 P.3d 180, 183 (Ariz. Ct. App. 2011); Hamilton v. Md. Cas. Co., 41 P.3d 128, 134 (Cal. 2002); Nunn v. Mid-Century Ins. Co., 244 P.3d 116, 123 (Colo. 2010); U.S. Fire Ins. Co. v. Hayden Bonded Storage Co., 930 So. 2d 686, 690–91 (Fla. Dist. Ct. App. 2006); Esterovich v. City of Kellogg, 80 P.3d 1040, 1042–43 (Idaho 2003); Guillen v. Potomac Ins. Co. of Ill., 785 N.W.2d 1, 14 (Ill. 2003); Red Giant Oil Co. v. Lawlor, 528 N.W.2d 524, 535 (Iowa 1995); Associated Wholesale Grocers, Inc. v. Americold Corp., 934 P.2d 65, 87 (Kan. 1997); Patrons Oxford Ins. Co. v. Harris, 905 A.2d 819, 827 (Me. 2006); Com. Ins. Co. v. Szafarowicz, 131 N.E.3d 782, 797–98 (Mass. 2019); Sherman v. Mo. Pros. Mut.-Physicians Pro. Indem. Ass'n, 599 S.W.3d 207, 218 (Mo. Ct. App. 2020); Tidyman's Mgmt. Servs. Inc. v. Davis (*Tidyman's I*), 330 P.3d 1139, 1153 (Mont. 2014); Passaic Valley Sewerage Comm'rs v. St. Paul Fire & Marine Ins. Co., 21 A.3d 1151,1162 (N.J. 2011) (quoting Griggs v. Bertram, 443 A.2d 163, 172 (N.J. 1982)); Forsman v. Blues, Brews & Bar-B-Ques, Inc., 903 N.W.2d 524, 529 (N.D. 2017) (quoting Medd v. Fonder, 543 N.W.2d 483, 485 (N.D. 1996)); W. Nat'l Mut. Ins. Co. v. TSP, Inc., 904 N.W.2d 52, 56 n.1 (S.D. 2017); Bird v. Best Plumbing Grp., LLC, 287 P.3d 551, 556 (Wash. 2012).

36. Metro. Life Ins. Co. v. Aetna Cas. & Sur. Co., 730 A.2d 51, 55 (Conn. 1999); Tidyman's Mgmt. Servs. Inc. v. Nat'l Union Fire Ins. Co. (*Tidyman's II*), 378 P.3d 1182, 1186 (Mont. 2016).

37. *Hempel*, 4 F. App'x at 718.

38. Great Divide Ins. Co. v. Carpenter, 79 P.3d 599, 609 (Alaska 2003); *see also* State Farm Mut. Auto. Ins. Co. v. Freyer, 312 P.3d 403, 414 (Mont. 2013) ("The insured has little incentive to minimize the settlement amount in negotiating a stipulated judgment.").

39. Associated Wholesale Grocers, Inc. v. Americold Corp., 934 P.2d 65, 86 (Kan. 1997).

40. *See* Steil v. Fla. Physicians' Ins. Reciprocal, 448 So. 2d 589, 592 (Fla. Dist. Ct. App. 1984) (referring to settlement agreements that accompany consent judgments).

41. Himes v. Safeway Ins. Co., 66 P.3d 74, 81 (Ariz. Ct. App. 2003).

> Reasonableness is not just a matter of the extent of the plaintiff's claims, but rather the extent of the defendant's exposure to liability. . . . Reasonableness requires that the insured expend efforts to determine whether the proposed claims were valid and whether the amount proposed [in a nonexecution agreement or consent judgment] was reflective of the injuries claimed.[42]

Accordingly, and as noted earlier, a nonexecution agreement generally must be tested in, or a consent judgment generally must be derived from, a fully adversarial hearing or trial.[43] This is not to say that a reasonableness hearing connected to a consent judgment always requires the parties to prepare for the hearing "as exhaustively and expensively as if they were preparing for trial."[44] It is to say, however, that the insured-defendant must have an incentive to defend itself reasonably and responsibly in the proceeding leading to the consent judgment, as the Texas Supreme Court emphasized in *Great American Insurance Co. v. Hamel*.[45]

In *Hamel*, Great American Insurance Co. (Great American) declined to defend Mitchell Builders, Ins. (Mitchell) in a construction defect lawsuit by two homeowners, Glen and Marsha Hamel. Apparently threatened with ruinous liability in the absence of insurance coverage, Mitchell reached a pretrial settlement agreement with the Hamels that effectively eliminated any possibility of harm to Mitchell from an adverse verdict and removed any incentive for Mitchell to defend the case.[46] Mitchell then abandoned defenses that it had earlier asserted, entered into a number of stipulations to liability, and minimally prepared for trial.[47] In the bench trial that followed, Mitchell called no witnesses and only the Hamels submitted proposed findings of fact and conclusions of law.[48] The trial court entered judgment for the Hamels, adopted their proposed findings without modification, and awarded them $365,089 in damages. Mitchell then assigned its rights against Great American to the Hamels, who sued Great American. The Hamels prevailed in the trial court and in the Texas Court of Appeals but Great American successfully petitioned the Texas Supreme Court for review.

---

42. Pemaquid Underwriting Brokerage, Inc. v. Certain Underwriters at Lloyd's nSpire Re Ltd., 2011 WL 4483112, at *9 (N.J. Super. Ct. App. Div. Sept. 29, 2011) (citation omitted).
43. Great Am. Ins. Co. v. Hamel, 525 S.W.3d 655, 665–68 (Tex. 2017); State Farm Fire & Cas. Co. v. Gandy, 925 S.W.2d 696, 714 (Tex. 1996); *see also* Calich v. Allstate Ins. Co., No. 21500, 2004 WL 626143, at *2 (Ohio Ct. App. Mar. 31, 2004) ("In cases where an excess judgment has not been adjudicated, an agreed judgment between the insured and a third party is unenforceable against an insurer.").
44. Sykes v. Singh, 428 P.3d 1228, 1234 (Wash. Ct. App. 2018).
45. 525 S.W.3d 655 (Tex. 2017).
46. *Id.* at 660.
47. *Id.* at 660, 665.
48. *Id.* at 661.

Great American contended that the judgment against Mitchell was not binding on it because it was rendered without a fully adversarial trial, as the court had held was required some two decades earlier in *State Farm Fire & Casualty Co. v. Gandy*.[49] In short, Great American argued, Mitchell presented "a sham defense" in the underlying case.[50]

The *Hamel* court reasoned that in deciding whether a trial was fully adversarial, a court should not second guess the parties' trial strategies or tactics.[51] Rather, the controlling factor is "whether, at the time of the underlying trial or settlement, the insured bore an actual risk of liability for the damages awarded or agreed upon, or had some other meaningful incentive to ensure that the judgment or settlement accurately reflect[ed] the plaintiff's damages and thus [its] covered liability loss."[52] As the court further explained:

> When the parties reach an agreement before trial or settlement that deprives one of the parties of its incentive to oppose the other, the proceeding is no longer adversarial. Stated another way, proceedings lose their adversarial nature when, by agreement, one party has no stake in the outcome and thus no meaningful incentive to defend itself. . . . We believe adversity turns on the insured defendant's incentive to defend (or lack thereof), and an after-the-fact evaluation of the parties' trial strategies therefore has no place in the analysis.[53]

Here, Mitchell's pretrial settlement agreement removed any stake it might have had in the outcome of the Hamels' case, and therefore eliminated any incentive it had to contest their claims.[54] "This turned the [d]amage [s]uit into a mere formality—a pass-through trial aimed not at obtaining a judgment reflective of the [plaintiffs'] loss, but instead at obtaining a potentially inflated judgment to enforce against Great American."[55] There was no fully adversarial trial and, accordingly, Great American was not bound by the resulting judgment.[56]

In some cases, the insured and the plaintiff may choose to have their case heard by a single arbitrator—typically selected by the plaintiff—rather than having the plaintiff's alleged damages decided by the trial court or approved by the trial court in a reasonableness hearing. If so, any reasonableness inquiry necessarily encompasses the arbitration process and award.[57] Likewise, the

---

49. 925 S.W.2d 696 (Tex. 1996).
50. *Hamel*, 525 S.W.3d at 665.
51. *Id.* at 666.
52. *Id.*
53. *Id.* at 667.
54. *Id.*
55. *Id.*
56. *Id.* at 668.
57. Kehle v. USAA Cas. Ins. Co., No. 17-80447-CIV-MARRA, 2019 WL 1429674, at *3 (S.D. Fla. Mar. 25, 2019) (applying Florida law).

insurer is entitled to inquire into whether the arbitration process and award were tainted by bad faith, fraud, or collusion.[58]

Finally, because the reasonableness of a consent judgment depends not only on its amount but also on how it was obtained, courts' reasonableness determinations overlap with their reviews of those judgments for bad faith, fraud, and collusion.[59] A consent judgment procured through bad faith, fraud, or collusion is necessarily unreasonable.[60]

B. Allocating the Burden of Proof on Reasonableness

As indicated earlier, an insured who is offered a nonexecution agreement has every incentive to agree to any procedure or judgment proposed by the plaintiff to avoid personal liability. Consequently, a court cannot presume that a resulting consent judgment is reasonable.[61] How, then, should the burden of proof on reasonableness be allocated? Most courts hold that the insured or the plaintiff bears the burden of proving that a consent judgment is reasonable.[62] This allocation is correct for at least three reasons. First, it is fairest, since it was the plaintiff and insured who selected the consent judgment process to resolve their dispute.[63] Second, it is preferable from a practical standpoint because the plaintiff has superior access to the facts bearing on reasonableness.[64] Third, it discourages collusion and overreaching.[65]

Allocation of the burden of proof to the insured or plaintiff takes two forms. Under one approach, the insured or plaintiff must prove by a

58. *See id.* (referring to good faith on the insured's and plaintiff's parts).

59. Midwestern Indem. Co. v. Laikin, 119 F. Supp. 2d 831, 843 (S.D. Ind. 2000) (discussing the evidentiary component of the overlap); Fireman's Fund. Ins. Co. v. Imbesi, 826 A.2d 735, 751 (N.J. Super. Ct. App. Div. 2003).

60. *See* Indep. Sch. Dist. No. 197 v. Accident & Cas. Ins. of Winterthur, 525 N.W.2d 600, 607 (Minn. Ct. App. 1995) ("Collusion would make a facially reasonable settlement unreasonable in fact.").

61. Himes v. Safeway Ins. Co., 66 P.3d 74, 80 (Ariz. Ct. App. 2003).

62. *See, e.g.*, Jimenz v. Gov't Emps. Ins. Co., 651 F. App'x 850, 853 (11th Cir. 2016) (applying Florida law); Corn Plus Coop. v. Cont'l Cas. Co., 516 F.3d 674, 681 (8th Cir. 2008) (applying Minnesota law); Ayers v. C & D Gen. Contractors, 269 F. Supp. 2d 911, 916-17 (W.D. Ky. 2003) (predicting Kentucky law); Safeway Ins. Co. v. Guerrero, 106 P.3d 1020, 1024 (Ariz. 2005); Nunn v. Mid-Century Ins. Co., 244 P.3d 116, 123 (Colo. 2010); Black v. Goodwin, Loomis & Britton, Inc., 681 A.2d 293, 302 (Conn. 1996); Chomat v. N. Ins. Co. of N.Y., 919 So. 2d 535, 537 (Fla. Dist. Ct. App. 2006) (quoting Steil v. Fla. Physicians' Ins. Reciprocal, 448 So. 2d 589, 592 (Fla. Dist. Ct. App. 1984)); Guillen v. Potomac Ins. Co. of Ill., 785 N.W.2d 1, 14 (Ill. 2003); Red Giant Oil Co. v. Lawlor, 528 N.W.2d 524, 535 (Iowa 1995); Associated Wholesale Grocers, Inc. v. Americold Corp., 934 P.2d 65, 87 (Kan. 1997); Patrons Oxford Ins. Co. v. Harris, 905 A.2d 819, 827 (Me. 2006); Com. Ins. Co. v. Szafarowicz, 131 N.E.3d 782, 797 (Mass. 2019); Jorgensen v. Knutson, 662 N.W.2d 893, 904 (Minn. 2003); Hamblin v. Garcia, 441 P.3d 1283, 1287 (Wash. Ct. App. 2019).

63. *Guillen*, 785 N.E.2d at 14.

64. *Id.*

65. Pasha v. Rosemount Mem'l Park, Inc., 781 A.2d 1119, 1123 (N.J. Super. Ct. App. Div. 2001).

preponderance of the evidence that the judgment amount is reasonable.[66] The plaintiff's or insured's failure to carry her burden renders the consent judgment invalid.[67] Utilizing the other approach, the insured or plaintiff "has the burden of initially presenting a prima facie case to establish the reasonableness" of the consent judgment.[68] This requires, at a minimum, that the insured or the plaintiff provide the court with sufficient information to independently evaluate reasonableness.[69] The proof required will vary with the case. Assuming that the plaintiff or insured makes her prima facie showing, the burden then shifts to the insurer to prove by a preponderance of the evidence that the judgment is unreasonable.[70]

Not all courts assign the burden of proof to the insured.[71] In Missouri, the insurer has the burden of proving a consent judgment is *un*reasonable.[72] Courts justify this allocation of the burden of proof based on the insurer's "elect[ion] not to participate in the underlying case" and the belief that it "distributes among the parties the risks attendant to settlement."[73] The fly in this intellectual ointment is Missouri law's allowance of an insured to reject a defense under reservation of rights,[74] which means that an insurer that attempts to participate in the underlying case but that is thwarted by the insured still bears the burden of proof on reasonableness. That result is unfair and, as already suggested, deficient as a practical matter.[75]

C. Proving Reasonableness

Once the burden of proof issue is resolved, the focus shifts to the court's determination of the consent judgment's reasonableness. The test for the

66. *Himes*, 66 P.3d at 81; *Red Giant Oil Co.*, 528 N.W.2d at 535; Fisher v. Am. Fam. Mut. Ins. Co., 579 N.W.2d 599, 607 (N.D. 1998) (quoting Medd v. Fonder, 543 N.W.2d 483, 485 (N.D. 1996)).

67. Ayers v. C & D Gen. Contractors, 269 F. Supp. 2d 911, 916 (W.D. Ky. 2003).

68. Associated Wholesale Grocers, Inc. v. Americold Corp., 934 P.2d 65, 87 (Kan. 1997); *see also* Metro. Prop. & Cas. Ins. Co. v. Westport Ins. Corp., 131 F. Supp. 3d 923, 929 (D. Neb. 2015) (applying Nebraska law); *Ayers*, 269 F. Supp. 2d at 916; Nunn v. Mid-Century Ins. Co., 244 P.3d 116, 123 (Colo. 2010); Chomat v. N. Ins. Co. of N.Y., 919 So. 2d 535, 537 (Fla. Dist. Ct. App. 2006) (quoting *Steil*, 448 So. 2d at 592); Fireman's Fund Ins. Co. v. Imbesi, 826 A.2d 735, 750 (N.J. Super. Ct. App. Div. 2003); *Pasha*, 781 A.2d at 1123.

69. *Americold*, 934 P.2d at 87.

70. *Ayers*, 269 F. Supp. 2d at 916; Guillen v. Potomac Ins. Co. of Ill., 785 N.W.2d 1, 14 (Ill. 2003); *Imbesi*, 826 A.2d at 750.

71. *See, e.g.*, Abbey/Land, LLC v. Glacier Constr. Partners, LLC, 433 P.3d 1230, 1240 (Mont. 2019) (citations omitted) ("The insurer bears the initial burden in challenging the stipulated settlement. . . . The insurer 'must set forth specific facts' demonstrating that the settlement amount is unreasonable or the product of collusion and must request a reasonableness hearing.").

72. Gulf Ins. Co. v. Noble Broad., 936 S.W.2d 810, 816 (Mo. 1997).

73. *Id.*

74. Allen v. Bryers, 512 S.W.3d 17, 32 (Mo. 2016).

75. *Guillen*, 785 N.E.2d at 14; Stonecrafters, Inc. v. Wholesale Life Ins. Brokerage, Inc., 915 N.E.2d 51, 61 (Ill. App. Ct. 2009); *Imbesi*, 826 A.2d at 750.

reasonableness of a consent judgment is what a reasonable and prudent person in the insured-defendant's shoes would have paid to settle the plaintiff's claims.[76] The key point here is that reasonableness is judged exclusively from the insured-defendant's perspective.[77] As an Arizona court explained:

> The "reasonably prudent person" . . . means a person who has a stake in the outcome. It means a person who is making decisions as though the money that pays the settlement comes from his or her own pocket. This is not a test of what a reasonably prudent person would settle the case for with someone else's funds. It is what a "reasonably prudent person" would pay from his or her own resources, assuming they are sufficient, "on the merits" of the case. . . . For purposes of determining reasonableness . . . a "reasonably prudent person" is defined as a person who (1) has the ability to pay a reasonable settlement amount from his or her own funds and (2) makes a settlement decision as though the settlement amount came from those personal funds.[78]

Or, as the Eleventh Circuit similarly observed in *Sidman v. Travelers Casualty & Surety*,[79] a reasonable litigant "would not be indifferent to the amount of a judgment entered against it if its own money were on the line."[80]

Whether a consent judgment is reasonable is generally a question of fact,[81] although a court may grant summary judgment on the issue when the evidence is such that no other conclusion is possible.[82] Reasonableness is evaluated at the time of the agreement on which the consent judgment is predicated.[83] Consequently, subsequent changes in the law or later factual developments generally should not affect the reasonableness of a consent judgment.[84]

76. Cont'l Cas. Co. v. Hempel, 4 F. App'x 703, 717 (10th Cir. 2001) (applying New Mexico law); Waddell v. Titan Ins. Co., 88 P.3d 1141, 1146 (Ariz. Ct. App. 2004) (quoting United Servs. Auto. Ass'n v. Morris, 741 P.2d 246, 254 (Ariz. 1987)); *Guillen*, 783 N.E.2d at 14 (quoting Miller v. Shugart, 316 N.W.2d 729, 735 (Minn. 1982)); Metro. Prop. & Cas. Ins. Co. v. Auto-Owners Mut. Ins. Co., 924 N.W.2d 833, 845 (Iowa 2019) (quoting Red Giant Oil Co. v. Lawlor, 528 N.W.2d 524, 535 (Iowa 1995)); Jorgensen v. Knutson, 662 N.W.2d 893, 904 (Minn. 2003) (quoting *Miller*, 316 N.W.2d at 735); Gulf Ins. Co. v. Noble Broad., 936 S.W.2d 810, 816 (Mo. 1997); D.E.M. v. Ellickson, 555 N.W.2d 596, 602 (N.D. 1996) (quoting Sellie v. N.D. Ins. Guar. Ass'n, 494 N.W.2d 151, 159 (N.D. 1992)).

77. *Red Giant Oil Co.*, 528 N.W.2d at 535; *Guillen*, 783 N.E.2d at 14; *Gulf Ins. Co.*, 936 S.W.2d at 816; *D.E.M.*, 555 N.W.2d at 603.

78. Himes v. Safeway Ins. Co., 66 P.3d 74, 82 (Ariz. Ct. App. 2003) (citation and footnote omitted).

79. 841 F.3d 1197 (11th Cir. 2016) (applying Florida law).

80. *Id.* at 1206.

81. *Red Giant Oil Co.*, 528 N.W.2d at 535; King's Cove Marina, LLC v. Lambert Com. Constr. LLC, 958 N.W.2d 310, 321 (Minn. 2021); *D.E.M.*, 555 N.W.2d at 603; Wood v. Milionis Constr., Inc., 492 P.3d 813, 822 (Wash. 2021).

82. *See, e.g.*, Cont'l Cas. Co. v. Hempel, 4 F. App'x 703, 719 (10th Cir. 2001) (affirming summary judgment for the insurer).

83. Corn Plus Coop. v. Cont'l Cas. Co., 516 F.3d 674, 681 (8th Cir. 2008) (applying Minnesota law); *In re*: RFC & ResCap Liquidating Tr. Action, 399 F. Supp. 3d 804, 813 (D. Minn. 2019) (discussing Minnesota law); *D.E.M.*, 555 N.W.2d at 603.

84. *See, e.g.*, *D.E.M.*, 555 N.W.2d at 603 (involving a subsequently published opinion).

The reasonableness of a consent judgment depends on multiple factors.[85] Courts frequently measure reasonableness by applying the so-called *Chaussee* factors, named after the originating Washington case, *Chaussee v. Maryland Casualty Co.*[86] The *Chaussee* factors are (1) the plaintiff's damages; (2) the merits of the plaintiff's liability theories; (3) the merits of the insured's liability defenses; (4) the plaintiff's comparative fault; (5) the risk and expense of continued litigation; (6) the defendant's ability to pay any settlement or judgment; (7) any evidence of bad faith, fraud, or collusion; (8) the extent of the plaintiff's investigation and preparation of the case; and (9) the interests of parties who are not being released.[87] No single factor controls the reasonableness determination and courts consider all cases individually.[88]

Some courts modify the *Chaussee* factors.[89] Other courts take more basic approaches to outlining the reasonableness inquiry.[90] As the Iowa Supreme Court explained in *Red Giant Oil Co. v. Lawlor*,[91] a court trying to determine what a reasonable and prudent person in the insured's place would have paid to settle the case "must consider facts bearing on the liability and damage aspects of the claim as well as the risks of going to trial."[92]

Regardless of the factors courts typically consider, they are not exclusive.[93] The facts of a given case may suggest other factors that a court should analyze.[94] In no case, however, should an estimate or prediction of what the jury could have awarded in the underlying case be the sole determinant of reasonableness.[95]

Courts must apply whatever standard they select in every case in which they are presented with a consent judgment.[96] The dynamics of the consent judgment regime require such rigor.[97] Indeed, the consent judgment regime is

---

85. *Corn Plus Coop.*, 516 F.3d at 681.

86. 803 P.2d 1339 (Wash. Ct. App. 1991).

87. *Id.* at 1343 (quoting Glover v. Tacoma Gen. Hosp., 658 P.2d 1230, 1236 (Wash. 1983), *abrogated by* Crown Controls, Inc. v. Smiley, 756 P.2d 717, 719–22 (Wash. 1988)).

88. Starr Indem. & Liab. Co. v. PC Collections, LLC, 523 P.3d 805, 816 (Wash. Ct. App. 2023).

89. *See, e.g.*, Cont'l Cas. Co. v. Hempel, 4 F. App'x 703, 717 (10th Cir. 2001) (considering the plaintiff's damages, the merits of the plaintiff's liability theories, the merits of the defendant's liability defenses, the defendant's relative fault in comparison to other potentially liable parties, and the likelihood that the plaintiff would win if the case was litigated to conclusion); Himes v. Safeway Ins. Co., 66 P.3d 74, 85 (Ariz. Ct. App. 2003) (declining to consider the defendant's ability to pay).

90. *See, e.g.*, Patrons Oxford Ins. Co. v. Harris, 905 A.2d 819, 827 (Me. 2006) (requiring a court to consider the defendant's potential liability, the plaintiff's damages, and the defendant's potential personal risk in the event of an adverse verdict).

91. 528 N.W.2d 524 (Iowa 1995).

92. *Id.* at 535.

93. *Himes*, 66 P.3d at 85.

94. *See* Associated Wholesale Grocers, Inc. v. Americold Corp., 934 P.2d 65, 87 (Kan. 1997) (indicating that the *Chaussee* factors may be used for "guidance beyond the factors suggested by the facts" of the case).

95. Jorgenson v. Knutson, 662 N.W.2d 893, 904–05 (Minn. 2003).

96. *Himes*, 66 P.3d at 82.

97. *Id.*

so susceptible to abuse that even consent judgments for amounts within policy limits must be reviewed for reasonableness.[98] The fact that a consent judgment is for an amount within policy limits does not alone establish that a reasonable and prudent person in the insured's position would have paid that sum in settling the case on the merits.[99]

As in proving a claim or defense in any trial or hearing, proof of the reasonableness or unreasonableness of a consent judgment may take many forms. Parties may offer testimony from fact and expert witnesses, introduce stipulations, introduce documentary evidence, ask the court to take judicial notice of facts, offer evidence of verdicts or settlements in similar cases from verdict search services or legal publications, and so on. A party seeking approval of a settlement or consent judgment cannot ask the court "to take on faith" that the agreement or judgment is reasonable.[100] This is true even if the nonexecution agreement or consent judgment was negotiated under the ostensible supervision of another judge, as where the deal was struck during a mediation or settlement conference presided over by a judge serving as a neutral.[101] Nor should a judge's approval of a consent judgment preclude the insurer from litigating reasonableness in a subsequent proceeding.[102]

Finally, it is important to understand that the reasonableness of a consent judgment does not require the judgment amount to be the lowest possible figure the parties might have negotiated or that a court could have approved or awarded.[103] The issue when gauging reasonableness is not whether there was a single correct or perfect judgment amount but whether the judgment "is within a reasonable range of potential recoveries."[104]

---

98. Guillen v. Potomac Ins. Co. if Ill., 785 N.E.2d 1, 15 (Ill. 2003).

99. *Id.*

100. Associated Wholesale Grocers, Inc. v. Americold Corp., 934 P.2d 65, 87 (Kan. 1997); *see also Himes*, 66 P.3d at 83 (stating that a trial judge cannot uncritically accept a settlement amount even if it is stipulated to by experienced lawyers acting in good faith).

101. *Americold*, 934 P.2d at 87; Fireman's Fund Ins. Co. v. Imbesi, 826 A.2d 735, 750–51 (N.J. Super. Ct. App. Div. 2003).

102. *See* Cont'l Cas. Co. v. Hempel, 4 F. App'x 703, 718 (10th Cir. 2001) (stating that the mere fact that a judge approved the settlement leading to a consent judgment did not make it reasonable). *But see* Columbia Cas. Co. v. HIAR Holding, L.L.C., 411 S.W.3d 258 (Mo. 2013) ("[A]n insurer that refuses to defend its insured can thereafter relitigate the issue of the reasonableness of the damages the insured has been declared to owe . . . only if the insured is trying to enforce a settlement amount that has not been the subject of a judgment by a trial judge approving its reasonableness. Where the trial court has entered judgment after a hearing on liability and damages . . . the insurer is not entitled to a second hearing on reasonableness in any . . . garnishment or declaratory judgment action based on the policy.").

103. *See* Country Mut. Ins. Co. v. Olsak, 216 N.E.3d 291, 308 (Ill. App. Ct. 2022).

104. *In re*: RFC & ResCap Liquidating Tr. Action, 399 F. Supp. 3d 804, 813 (D. Minn. 2019) (applying Minnesota law).

D. Representative Cases on Reasonableness

In considering the reasonableness of consent judgments, three cases in which the courts reached differing conclusions are especially representative of courts' approaches to the issue: *Metropolitan Property & Casualty Insurance Co. v. Auto-Owners Mutual Insurance Co.*,[105] *Hamblin v. Garcia*,[106] and *Continental Casualty Co. v. Hempel.*[107] In *Metropolitan*, the court found the consent judgment to be reasonable. The *Hamblin* and *Hempel* courts reached the opposite conclusion.

Metropolitan arose out of an accidental shooting.[108] By way of background, Iowa dentist Jay Lala and his wife Lorrie formed Parker House Properties, L.L.C. (Parker House) to hold property. Parker House owned several investment properties, including land in Floyd County, Iowa, with a farmhouse (the Foothill Avenue property). The Lalas—including their sons Nick and Sam—used the Foothill Avenue property for recreational purposes.

In April 2012, Nick, and his teenage friend, Hunter True, went to the Foothill Avenue property to ride dirt bikes and ATVs. Jay was also at the property that day. He left before the teenagers departed. Before leaving, Jay told Nick to lock up the house.

While Nick was locking up, he saw one of the Lalas' rifles lying on a bed in one of the bedrooms. Jay kept the rifle at the farm for hunting and target shooting. As a matter of routine, Jay expected Nick to secure each firearm in a gun case in one of the bedrooms after ensuring it was unloaded. Nick was very well-versed in gun safety. Nevertheless, on this day, he picked up the rifle and accidentally shot and killed True.

The Lalas had a personal insurance policy through Metropolitan Property & Casualty Insurance Co. (Metropolitan) that covered the family. The Metropolitan policy specifically insured the Foothill Avenue property. Parker House separately purchased a policy from Auto-Owners Mutual Insurance Co. (Auto-Owners) that included commercial general liability (CGL) coverage with a $1 million per occurrence liability limit.

In January 2014, Metropolitan settled with True's parents, Michael and Hillary Carpenter, for $900,000 in exchange for a release of all claims against the Lalas, Parker House, Metropolitan, and Auto-Owners. Jay and Parker House also sought coverage under the Auto-Owners policy. Auto-Owners denied coverage on the basis that its policy only covered individuals with respect to the conduct of a business, and any claims arising out of True's death

105. 924 N.W.2d 833 (Iowa 2019).
106. 441 P.3d 1283 (Wash. Ct. App. 2019).
107. 4 F. App'x 703 (10th Cir. 2001).
108. *Metropolitan*, 924 N.W.2d at 837.

were not business-related. Auto-Owners also asserted that the policy only covered Parker House and not the Lalas.

In June 2014, Metropolitan filed a subrogation action against Auto-Owners. Metropolitan later amended its petition to include Parker House as a defendant and to allege indemnity and contribution claims. In February 2017, Parker House offered to confess judgment in the amount of $450,000, assign its rights against Auto-Owners to Metropolitan, and pay $1,000 of the judgment in exchange for Metropolitan agreeing not to execute on the offer to confess judgment.[109] Metropolitan accepted the offer.

The subrogation case was tried to the court. Auto-Owners introduced expert testimony from two veteran trial lawyers, Max Kirk and David Riley. They testified that the settlement was unreasonable because, if True's estate's case had been tried to a jury, Nick probably would have borne most of the fault, with Jay secondarily liable as the gun owner. Neither lawyer believed a jury would assign fault to Parker House on a premises liability theory.[110]

Metropolitan introduced the testimony of former Iowa Supreme Court Justice Marsha Ternus and Ron Pogge, another experienced lawyer. Pogge opined that a jury would have assigned substantial fault to Parker House under a premises liability theory. He also believed that a jury would find that Nick and Jay were agents of Parker House. Ternus testified that the rifle on the bed created a dangerous condition in the home and that Parker House faced significant exposure on a premises liability theory. She agreed that Nick could be considered Parker House's agent.[111]

The trial court entered judgment against Auto-Owners and in favor of Metropolitan for $450,000. The court found that Parker House was insured under the Auto-Owners' policy because it owned the Foothill Avenue property for investment purposes, which was a business purpose under Auto-Owners' policy. The court found that a jury could determine that Nick was also covered under the Auto-Owners policy as either a Parker House employee or as a volunteer worker when he was securing the rifle and locking the house. The court also concluded that a jury could hold Parker House liable on a premises liability theory. Finally, the court found that Parker House's settlement with Metropolitan was reasonable, such that Metropolitan was entitled to contribution from Auto-Owners.[112] Auto-Owners appealed to the Iowa Supreme Court.

The Iowa Supreme Court began its analysis by explaining that in deciding whether a settlement is reasonable, it considers what a reasonably prudent person in the insured's position would have settled for based on the merits

109. *Id.* at 838.
110. *Id.* at 838–39.
111. *Id.* at 839.
112. *Id.*

of the plaintiff's claim.[113] In doing so, the court analyzes facts bearing on the insured's liability and the plaintiff's damages, as well as the risk of going to trial.[114] The insured need not establish its actual liability to the plaintiff; rather, the insured "need only show a potential liability, as supported by the evidence that culminated in a settlement that is reasonable in view of the size of the possible recovery and likelihood that liability would be established."[115]

The *Metropolitan* court observed that an Iowa federal court had outlined the factors a trial court should evaluate in determining the reasonableness of a consent judgment:

> The ultimate issue to be decided is the reasonableness of a settlement which avoids a trial. Reasonableness, therefore, is not determined by conducting the very trial obviated by the settlement. Consequently, the decisionmaker receives not only the customary evidence on liability and damages but also other evidence, such as expert opinion of trial lawyers evaluating the "customary" evidence. This "other evidence" may include verdicts in comparable cases, the likelihood of favorable or unfavorable rulings on legal defenses and evidence issues if the tort action had been tried, and other factors of forensic significance. The evaluation of this kind of proof is best understood and weighed by a trial judge.[116]

Auto-Owners argued that the trial court should have precluded Ternus's expert testimony because it could not have helped the court understand the evidence or determine a fact in issue.[117] Again, Ternus had opined on whether a jury would apportion liability to Parker House for True's death. The *Metropolitan* court made short work of this argument. The court noted that it afforded trial courts wide latitude in receiving expert testimony during bench trials. Here, given the factors used to evaluate reasonableness, the trial court did not abuse its discretion in allowing Ternus's testimony.[118]

The trial court found that Metropolitan's expert's opinions supported the company's theory that Parker House's settlement was reasonable and prudently avoided the prospect of a worse outcome at trial.[119] In concluding that Parker House's settlement with Metropolitan was reasonable, the trial court stated:

> There is no question that the estate of Hunter True would be able to show liability for his death. Neither party to this case believes that he had any fault. Neither party to this case disputed that the $900,000 settlement for his death

113. *Id.* at 845 (quoting Red Giant Oil Co. v. Lawlor, 528 N.W.2d 524, 535 (Iowa 1995)).
114. *Id.* (quoting *Red Giant Oil Co.*, 528 N.W.2d at 535).
115. *Id.*
116. *Id.* (quoting Gen. Cas. Ins. Co. of Wis. v. Penn-Co Constr., Inc., No. C03-2031-MWB, 2005 WL 503927, at *45 (N.D. Iowa Mar. 2, 2005)).
117. *Id.*
118. *Id.*
119. *Id.*

> was reasonable as damages. However, the question of assignment of fault between Parker House and the individual actors is not readily determinable. It is extremely difficult to find whether a jury would have held Parker House wholly accountable under a premises liability theory, the individual actors wholly accountable under a negligence theory, or split accountability between or among them. Parker House's settlement took the guesswork from the case and avoided a worse outcome.[120]

The *Metropolitan* court concluded the trial court correctly applied the law, and that its factual findings concerning the settlement's reasonableness were supported by substantial evidence. The $900,000 settlement in a case of disputed liability was a reasonable sum for the tragic death of a vibrant teenager.[121]

The plaintiff in *Hamblin v. Garcia*,[122] Andrew Hamblin, was badly injured when his car was struck by a drunk driver. The drunk driver, Luis Garcia, was insured by National General Insurance Co (National General). Hamblin offered to settle with National General for its $100,000 policy limits but sued Garcia after National General countered with a meager $21,000 offer. National General appointed defense counsel for Garcia. As Hamblin's medical expenses and lost earnings soared, he increased his settlement demand to $2 million. As a result, Garcia's lawyers found themselves "in a difficult position," so they used a defense attorney Listserv to find a lawyer with no ties to National General to counsel Garcia.[123] They settled on Brent Beecher.

After Beecher stepped in, Hamblin and Garcia reached "a covenant judgment settlement agreement," whereby Garcia stipulated to a $1.5 million judgment and assigned all claims against National General to Hamblin in exchange for Hamblin's promise not to enforce an excess judgment against Garcia's assets other than his rights against his insurers.[124] The settlement agreement also required that any subsequent suit by Hamblin against National General on the assigned bad faith claims include a request for damages to compensate Garcia for emotional distress resulting from National General's alleged bad faith. The agreement further provided that Hamblin had the discretion to settle with National General, but that Garcia would be entitled to 10 percent of any "global settlement" amount if Hamblin settled without Garcia's express consent.[125]

The parties executed their settlement agreement and notified National General of its terms. National General then intervened in the case. A few months

---

120. *Id.* at 846 (quoting the trial court).
121. *Id.*
122. 441 P.3d 1283 (Wash. Ct. App. 2019).
123. *Id.* at 1286.
124. *Id.*
125. *Id.*

later, the court conducted a reasonableness hearing, considered the parties' arguments, and heard testimony. The court determined that the settlement was reasonable and entered judgment against Garcia. National General appealed.

The Washington Court of Appeals explained that under Washington law, a court must consider the nine factors identified in *Chaussee v. Maryland Casualty Co.*[126] to determine if a settlement is reasonable:

> (1) [T]he releasing party's damages; (2) the merits of the releasing party's liability theory; (3) the merits of the released party's defense theory; (4) the released party's relative fault; (5) the risks and expenses of continued litigation; (6) the released party's ability to pay; (7) any evidence of bad faith, collusion, or fraud; (8) the extent of the releasing party's investigation and preparation; and (9) the interests of the parties not being released.[127]

National General complained that the trial court erred by not considering four of the nine *Chaussee* factors, but the trial court expressly stated that it considered all nine factors.[128] The trial court was not required to explain how it applied each factor.[129] Absent a showing that the trial court applied an incorrect standard, an appellate court reviews a trial court's reasonableness determination for substantial evidence—not for a sufficient explanation.[130] Because National General did not show that the trial court applied an incorrect legal standard, the *Hamblin* court held that the trial court did not abuse its discretion in how it applied the *Chaussee* factors.[131] That holding did not, however, end the court's reasonableness inquiry because a covenant judgment settlement agreement that includes a minimum percentage payment to the insured from any global settlement between the insurer and the tort victim obligates a court to consider "the potential impact on the compensation of the victim for the insured's wrongful conduct."[132]

The court thus returned to Hamblin's and Garcia's settlement agreement and the latter's assignment to Hamblin of his bad faith claims against National General. Under the agreement, Hamblin would control any bad faith litigation, but Garcia retained a role in settlement negotiations despite his "total assignment."[133] If Garcia did not consent to Hamblin's global settlement with National General (if any), then Hamblin had to pay him 10 percent of the settlement amount. This effectively guaranteed Garcia 10 percent of the total

126. 803 P.2d 1339 (Wash. Ct. App. 1991).
127. *Hamblin*, 441 P.3d at 1287 (quoting *Chaussee*, 803 P.2d at 1343).
128. *Id.* at 1288.
129. *Id.*
130. *Id.* (quoting Hidalgo v. Barker, 309 P.3d 687, 697 (Wash. Ct. App. 2013)).
131. *Id.*
132. *Id.* at 1290.
133. *Id.*

amount of any global settlement unless he approved a settlement that paid him less.[134]

The trial court had been troubled by the settlement structure as was the *Hamblin* court on appeal. Garcia's guaranteed payment could reduce Hamblin's recovery for his injuries by reallocating 10 percent of any global settlement to Garcia, regardless of the amount of any true emotional distress damages he suffered. As the court explained, under the first *Chaussee* factor, a court must consider the plaintiff's damages when considering reasonableness, but it is inequitable to bless a settlement that intentionally reduces the plaintiff's damages by redistributing them to the insured tortfeasor.[135] Here, the settlement agreement potentially rewarded Garcia for his misconduct at Hamblin's expense. Because the allocation of 10 percent of any global settlement to Garcia undercut the first *Chaussee* factor and was inequitable, the covenant judgment was not reasonable.[136]

In addition to being instructive on reasonableness, *Continental Casualty Co. v. Hempel*[137] highlights the analytical overlap between reasonableness and fraud or collusion. In *Hempel,* Charles Hempel sued Frank Westerfield, the trustee of two trusts created by the will of Hempel's late father, Daniel Mudge. Hempel alleged that Westerfield breached his duties as trustee in connection with the misappropriation of trust assets by a predecessor trustee, Eugene Graham, and by improperly distributing trust assets to the detriment of Ada Mudge, Hempel's late mother and a trust beneficiary.[138] Hempel also sued his two half-sisters, Graham, and the bank that appointed Westerfield trustee.[139] The litigation began in a Texas state court and was later transferred to a New Mexico state court.[140]

Westerfield's alleged misdeeds spanned many years, during which he was variously insured under Continental Casualty Co. (CNA), St. Paul Fire & Marine Insurance Co. (St. Paul), Home Insurance Co. (Home), and Ranger Insurance Co. (Ranger) policies.[141] Home and St. Paul agreed to defend him in Hempel's suit, but CNA denied coverage based mainly on an exclusion in its policy for dishonest, fraudulent, criminal, or malicious conduct.[142] A federal district court ultimately would conclude that CNA breached its duty to defend Westerfield.[143]

134. *Id.*
135. *Id.*
136. *Id.*
137. 4 F. App'x 703 (10th Cir. 2001).
138. *Id.* at 708.
139. *Id.*
140. *Id.* at 707–08.
141. *Id.* at 708.
142. *Id.*
143. *Id.*

Home retained Briggs Cheney to defend Westerfield. After conducting discovery, Cheney concluded that Hempel's claims were meritorious. As Cheney saw it, the central issues in the case were the damages to which Mrs. Mudge's estate was entitled, and which parties should be held responsible for those damages.[144]

The parties consulted with experts on the value of Mrs. Mudge's rights in the trusts. This was not a simple exercise, since the trusts held shares of stock that had split, and there were additional thorny questions involving stock dividends and stock spinoffs. Hempel's lawyer, John McKetta, first consulted accountant Thomas Glass, who valued Mrs. Mudge's interests in the trusts at between $17.6 million and $27.9 million, depending on the method of calculation.[145] McKetta later consulted a second accountant, Thomas Gilmore, who ran several different scenarios. Depending on the scenario, Gilmore calculated the damages as ranging from $3.7 million to $35.9 million.[146] In contrast, the experts Cheney consulted arrived at significantly lower valuations of Mrs. Mudge's interests in the trusts based on the treatment of stock splits under controlling New Mexico statutes. Cheney's lead expert valued the damages at a high of $2.8 million and a low of $443,000.[147]

As the trial date in the case neared, Hempel offered to settle with all defendants for a combined $5.5 million, but the offer was rejected. About one week before trial, Westerfield hired Floyd Wilson as personal coverage counsel. Wilson and McKetta soon began discussing the idea of an uncontested trial.[148] The negotiations between Wilson and McKetta resulted in a settlement agreement whereby Hempel executed a covenant not to execute on a judgment against Westerfield, although he did not release Westerfield from liability.[149] Westerfield assigned to Hempel 90 percent of the proceeds of the bad faith lawsuit that Westerfield agreed to pursue against the non-settling insurers after the entry of judgment in the state court.[150] Cheney did not view the agreement favorably and thus wrote to Westerfield:

> By this settlement, we have tacitly agreed not to defend the action. In fact, it is not necessarily in your best interests [to make this agreement] as it may impact negatively on subsequent actions against non-settling or non-participating . . . insurance carriers. . . .

144. *Id.* at 709.
145. *Id.*
146. *Id.*
147. *Id.*
148. *Id.* at 710.
149. *Id.*
150. *Id.*

> I will not actively defend you in this matter. I am operating at your instructions not to actively defend. . . . To that end, I . . . will not take actions to minimize any judgment which may be entered.[151]

Soon after reaching this agreement, Hempel settled with the bank for $1.15 million, with his half-sisters for a combined $650,000, with Ranger for $1 million, and with St. Paul for $300,000.[152] Hempel's case against Westerfield went to trial days later.

The case was tried to the court. McKetta and Cheney told the court about the parties' settlement and offered the settlement agreement into evidence.[153] Cheney informed the court that he would not attempt to defend Westerfield at trial.[154] The judge stated on the record that, as he understood matters, the whole purpose of the trial was to allow Hempel to obtain a judgment that would enable him to pursue relief from any non-settling insurers.[155]

Once the trial got underway, McKetta called four witnesses, including an expert on trust administration, Hempel and his wife, and Gilmore. Cheney did not cross-examine any of them, he called no witnesses, and he made no opening statement or closing argument.[156] Gilmore presented multiple damage scenarios, although he did not opine as to which one was proper. At the close of the evidence, the judge found a breach of fiduciary duty by Westerfield. The judge then asked McKetta which of Gilmore's damages calculations he considered proper.[157] McKetta picked the highest one.[158] After lowering the interest rate used in that calculation, the court entered a judgment of approximately $26.38 million for Hempel.[159]

CNA thereafter filed a declaratory judgment action in a New Mexico federal court in which it disclaimed any duty to indemnify Westerfield. CNA alleged that the settlement between Westerfield and Hempel was collusive. The district court agreed with CNA that the judgment was collusive and, as a result, there was no coverage for it. The district court thus entered summary judgment for CNA. Hempel appealed that ruling to the Tenth Circuit, which affirmed the district court.[160]

---

151. *Id.* (emphasis omitted).
152. *Id.* at 710–11.
153. *Id.* at 712.
154. *Id.*
155. *Id.*
156. *Id.*
157. *Id.* at 713.
158. *Id.*
159. *Id.* The judge determined the damages to be slightly more than $29.4 million, but he applied an offset for the combined amount of the settlements with the bank, Hempel's half-sisters, Ranger, and St. Paul. *Id.*
160. *Id.* at 724.

The Tenth Circuit began its review by framing the inquiry as what a reasonable person in Westerfield's place would have settled for on the merits of Hempel's claims.[161] In this inquiry, it planned to examine Hempel's damages, the merits of Hempel's claims, the merits of Westerfield's defenses, Westerfield's comparative fault, and the likelihood of Hempel succeeding on his claims.[162] The court stated that determining the reasonableness of the judgment required more than scrutiny of its amount; consideration of the procedure by which the judgment was obtained also was appropriate.[163] The state court judge's approval of the settlement between Hempel and Westerfield did not make it reasonable.[164] The question for the *Hempel* court was whether there had been an independent adjudication of the facts based on an evidentiary showing, and whether the procedure the parties adopted and the trial court followed created the potential for abuse, collusion, or fraud.[165] Applying these principles, the *Hempel* court concluded that the amount of the judgment was unreasonable and that the method by which the judgment was procured was collusive.[166]

The amount of the judgment—approximately $26.38 million—was "wildly out of proportion" to the value of Hempel's claims provided by other sources.[167] For instance, Hempel offered to settle with all defendants for $5.5 million a few months before trial.[168] The expert witness that Cheney hired calculated Hempel's damages at $2.8 million under "a worst case scenario."[169] Other defendants settled for substantially less (most notably the bank, which paid $1.15 million) and there was no evidence that Westerfield should have borne far greater responsibility for Hempel's damages than the other defendants, especially Graham, the predecessor trustee.[170] In summary, there was no factual basis to conclude that a reasonable and prudent person in Westerfield's shoes would have paid $26.38 million to settle Hempel's lawsuit.[171]

Additionally, Westerfield had several substantial defenses that he did not present at the state court trial. He had a strong statute of limitations defense, Cheney had developed a good damages theory based on the treatment within the trusts of stock splits, and it was clear that other defendants bore significant fault for Hempel's losses.[172] Indeed, the state court judge who heard the case

161. *Id.* at 717 (quoting Miller v. Shugart, 316 N.W.2d 729, 735 (Minn. 1982)).
162. *Id.*
163. *Id.* at 718.
164. *Id.*
165. *Id.* (quoting Nat'l Union Fire Ins. Co. v. Lynette C., 33 Cal. Rptr. 2d 496, 497 (Ct. App. 1994)).
166. *Id.*
167. *Id.*
168. *Id.*
169. *Id.*
170. *Id.*
171. *Id.* (quoting Miller v. Shugart, 316 N.W.2d 729, 735 (Minn. 1982)).
172. *Id.* at 719.

testified that he would have considered apportioning liability against other parties had Westerfield asked him to do so.[173] Westerfield's failure to raise any of these defenses supported the district court's conclusion that the settlement was collusive.[174]

Hempel argued that the consent judgment was not collusive because the state court judge was informed of the settlement and the covenant not to execute.[175] This argument failed because there was no evidence that the judge knew about two critical aspects of the parties' arrangement: (1) Westerfield's 10 percent interest in any judgment entered against him; and (2) the fact that the trial was rigged to allow Hempel to obtain the largest judgment possible.[176]

E. The Effect of a Determination That a Consent Judgment Is Unreasonable

If a court finds that the amount of a consent judgment is unreasonable, the question next becomes the insurer's remedy. Recognizing that the choice of remedy may be left to the trial court's discretion,[177] there are three possibilities: (1) dismiss the action against the insurer, leaving the plaintiff with an uncollectible judgment; (2) let the trial court decide what lesser amount is reasonable and, thus, collectible from the insurer; or (3) void the settlement and reinstate for trial the plaintiff's claims against the insured. Cases explicitly addressing this issue are scarce. The Minnesota Supreme Court adopted the third approach in *Alton M. Johnson Co. v. M.A.I. Co.*[178] As the court reasoned:

> Insurance coverage for the claim having been established and the stipulated settlement being unenforceable, it seems fairest to return the parties to the even footing of a trial on the merits of the main action. The fact that such a trial is a possibility, with its attendant delay, expense and risk, may help deter overreaching in the negotiation of a *Miller-Shugart* settlement. At the same time, the harsh overkill of a forfeiture of the main action is avoided.[179]

Some courts have opted for the second approach and entrusted to the trial court the determination of a reasonable amount.[180] As a plain reading of this alternative suggests, in such cases the parties should try the issue of

---

173. *Id.*
174. *Id.*
175. *Id.*
176. *Id.*
177. *See, e.g.*, Abbey/Land, LLC v. Glacier Constr. Partners, LLC, 433 P.3d 1230, 1245–46 (Mont. 2019).
178. 463 N.W.2d 277 (Minn. 1990).
179. *Id.* at 279.
180. Parking Concepts, Inc. v. Tenney, 83 P.3d 19, 25–26 (Ariz. 2004); Associated Wholesale Grocers, Inc. v. Americold Corp., 934 P.3d 65, 87 (Kan. 1997); Patrons Oxford Ins. Co. v. Harris, 905 A.2d 819, 827 (Me. 2006); Gulf Ins. Co. v. Noble Broad., 936 S.W.2d 810, 816 (Mo. 1997); Fisher v. Am. Fam. Mut. Ins. Co., 579 N.W.2d 599, 607 (N.D. 1998).

reasonableness to the court rather than to a jury,[181] although at least one court has held that reasonableness is a jury question.[182] If a court writing on a blank slate was inclined to try reasonableness to a jury, however, it would be better advised to instead try the underlying action on the merits as the *Alton M. Johnson Co.* court instructed. Trying reasonableness to a jury will be as time-consuming as a trial on the merits or nearly so, yet it is unlikely to achieve the fairness of a trial on the merits and it does not go far enough in deterring overreaching in the consent judgment process.

A few courts have taken the first approach and held that an unreasonable consent judgment is absolutely unenforceable against an insurer, thus requiring the dismissal of the case against the insurer.[183] A court is most likely to select the first option and dismiss any action against an insurer where a consent judgment is unreasonable because it was arrived at in bad faith, or because it is fraudulent or collusive.[184] In that situation, the parties' misconduct justifies that result, which will also serve to deter similar misbehavior in other cases and to protect the integrity of the courts.[185]

III. Consent Judgments Obtained through Bad Faith, Fraud, or Collusion

A. Introduction

Apart from disputing a consent judgment based on its amount, insurers often contend that consent judgments should be unenforceable because they were procured through bad faith, fraud or collusion by the insured and the plaintiff.[186] An insurer is not bound by a consent judgment obtained through bad

181. Am. Cas. Co. v. Kemper, No. CV-07-1149-PHX-GMS, 2009 WL 1749388, at *2–3 (D. Ariz. June 18, 2009) (applying federal law); *Gulf Ins. Co.*, 936 S.W.2d at 816.

182. Nunn v. Mid-Century Ins. Co., 244 P.3d 116, 123 (Colo. 2010).

183. *See, e.g.*, St. Paul Travelers v. Payne, 444 F. Supp. 2d 519, 522 (D.S.C. 2006) (applying South Carolina law).

184. *See, e.g.*, Cont'l Cas. Co. v. Hempel, 4 F. App'x 703, 721 (10th Cir. 2001) (applying New Mexico law); Red Giant Oil Co. v. Lawlor, 528 N.W.2d 524, 535 (Iowa 1995); Patrons Oxford Ins. Co. v. Harris, 905 A.2d 819, 829 (Me. 2006); Abbey/Land, LLC v. Glacier Constr. Partners, LLC, 433 P.3d 1230, 1245–46 (Mont. 2019).

185. *Abbey/Land*, 433 P.3d at 1246.

186. *See* Cent. Mut. Ins. Co. v. Tracy's Treasures, Inc., 19 N.E.3d 1100, 1120 (Ill. App. Ct. 2014) (stating that the settlement in the case could be deemed unreasonable if there was evidence of bad faith, fraud, or collusion); Carpenter v. Lovell's Lounge & Grill, LLC, 59 N.E.3d 330, 341 (Ind. Ct. App. 2016) (observing that "the issues of bad faith or collusion are closely related to the issue of reasonableness of settlement amount, and the evidence often overlaps"); Indep. Sch. Dist. No. 197 v. Accident & Cas. Ins. of Winterthur, 525 N.W.2d 600, 607 (Minn. Ct. App. 1995) ("Reasonableness and collusion, however, are not readily separable issues. Collusion would make a facially reasonable settlement unreasonable in fact.").

faith, fraud, or collusion.[187] Although, a key purpose of a reasonableness hearing in a consent judgment case is to prevent the entry of a collusive or fraudulent judgment,[188] reasonableness hearings often fail in this respect.

The problem when scrutinizing consent judgments for evidence of bad faith, fraud, or collusion is identifying prohibited conduct. These are "broad-brush concepts."[189] Certainly, it is not fraudulent, collusive, or an act of bad faith for an insured simply to enter into a nonexecution agreement.[190] An insured's mere assignment of its rights against its insurer to the plaintiff following the insurer's refusal to defend does not equal bad faith, fraud, or collusion.[191] After all, an insured left undefended by its insurer must be allowed to reasonably protect itself against personal liability. Rather, bad faith, fraud, and collusion are characterized by unfairness to the insurer, or by an effort to harm the insurer's interests.[192] Whether a consent judgment is a product of bad faith, fraud, or collusion is a case- and fact-specific inquiry.[193]

B. Understanding Insureds' Bad Faith in Connection with Nonexecution Agreements and Consent Judgments

Bad faith, fraud, and collusion are related forms of misconduct, but they are not necessarily synonyms for the same behavior.[194] "Bad faith" in this context may include "evasion of the spirit of the bargain, lack of diligence and slacking off, willful rendering of imperfect performance, abuse of a power to

---

187. Sidman v. Travelers Cas. & Sur., 841 F.3d 1197, 1203–07 (11th Cir. 2016) (applying Florida law); Andrew v. Century Sur. Co., 134 F. Supp. 3d 1249, 1268–70 (D. Nev. 2015) (predicting Nevada law); Metro. Prop. & Cas. Ins. Co. v. Westport Ins. Corp., 131 F. Supp. 3d 923, 929 (D. Neb. 2015) (applying Nebraska law); DeSantiago v. Pargas, No. 2 CA-CV 2008-0079, 2009 WL 794929, at *3 (Ariz. Ct. App. Mar. 26, 2009); *Red Giant Oil Co.*, 528 N.W.2d at 535; Fletcher v. Anderson, 3 P.3d 558, 568 (Kan. Ct. App. 2000); Patrons Oxford Ins. Co. v. Harris, 905 A.2d 819, 829 (Me. 2006); Johnson v. W. Bend Mut. Ins. Co., No. A17-1957, 2018 WL 6596270, at *9 (Minn. Ct. App. Dec. 17, 2018) *Abbey/Land*, 433 P.3d at 1240; Rummel v. Lexington Ins. Co., 945 P.2d 970, 985 (N.M. 1997); W. Nat'l Mut. Ins. Co. v. TSP, Inc., 904 N.W.2d 52, 56 n.1 (S.D. 2017); Penn-Am. Ins. Co. v. Osborne, 797 S.E.2d 548, 554–57 (W. Va. 2017).

188. *See* Gosney v. Fireman's Fund Ins. Co., 419 P.3d 447, 474 (Wash. Ct. App. 2018) ("The purpose of a reasonableness hearing in this setting is to present a negotiated settlement to a neutral party—typically a judge—to protect the insurer from excess judgments and fraud or collusion between the settling parties.").

189. *Tracy's Treasures*, 19 N.E.3d at 1120.

190. *See, e.g.*, *Andrew*, 134 F. Supp. 3d at 1267 (referring to fraud and collusion); Tilden-Coil Constructors, Inc. v. Landmark Am. Ins. Co., No. C09-1574JLR, 2011 WL 780876, at *6 (W.D. Wash. Feb. 25, 2011) (discussing collusion); Cont'l Cas. Co. v. Westerfield, 961 F. Supp. 1502, 1505 (D.N.M. 1997) (referring to collusion); *Abbey/Land*, 433 P.3d at 1241–42 (discussing collusion and fraud).

191. *Andrew*, 134 F. Supp. 3d at 1267.

192. *Tracy's Treasures*, 19 N.E.3d at 1121 (quoting *Westerfield*, 961 F. Supp. at 1505).

193. *See Andrew*, 134 F. Supp. 3d at 1268 (referring to fraud and collusion); *Abbey/Land*, 433 P.3d at 1242 (discussing collusion).

194. *See* Carlson v. Zellaha, 482 N.W.2d 281, 283 (Neb. 1992) (emphasis added) ("A consent judgment is subject to collateral attack when the facts demonstrate that the judgment or settlement was entered into fraudulently, collusively, *or* in bad faith.").

specify terms, and interference with or failure to cooperate in the other party's performance."[195] Bad faith also may involve "[d]ishonesty of belief or purpose."[196] As the *Jimenez v. Government Employees Insurance Co.*[197] court outlined, bad faith may be established by evidence of a false claim by the insured, the plaintiff's agreement to share any recovery with the insured, or the insured's failure to try to minimize its liability, as where the amount of a consent judgment is dictated by the plaintiff rather than being negotiated.[198] If a court analogizes an insured's bad faith in the consent judgment process to an insurer's bad faith in failing to settle litigation against its insured within policy limits, an insured's bad faith may be characterized by "a state of mind reflecting dishonest purpose, moral obliquity, furtive design, or ill will."[199]

Wolff v. Royal Insurance Co. of America[200] is a representative case. *Wolff* stemmed from an accident at the 1983 South Dakota State Fair in which two workers, Chris Wolff and Kenneth Kempf, were injured while dismantling a stage after a Wayne Newton concert. Newton's performance had been booked by Don Romeo through his business, the Don Romeo Agency, Inc. Romeo had attended the concert and he thus knew about the accident, but he did not notify his insurer, Royal Insurance Co. of America (Royal), because he did not believe that his agency could be liable for Wolff's and Kempf's injuries.[201] In 1984, Wolff and Kempf sued the Romeo Agency and several other defendants in the U.S. District Court in South Dakota in consolidated actions.

All defendants except the Romeo Agency settled. The plaintiffs initially demanded $200,000 from the Romeo Agency, but finally agreed to accept $25,000 if the Romeo Agency could prove that it was uninsured and incapable of satisfying a larger judgment.[202] The Romeo Agency's defense counsel then called Kenneth Schenk, who was the Romeo Agency's insurance agent, to obtain the desired proof. Schenk instead told the lawyer that the Romeo Agency was insured under a Royal policy.[203]

Soon thereafter, the Romeo Agency asked Royal to acknowledge coverage and defend the Wolff and Kempf lawsuits. The Romeo Agency gave Royal eight hours to decide whether to accept the defense based solely on a copy of

195. Restatement (Second) of Contracts § 205 cmt. d (Am. L. Inst. 1981).
196. *Bad Faith*, Black's Law Dictionary (11th ed. 2019).
197. 651 F. App'x 850 (11th Cir. 2016) (applying Florida law).
198. *Id.* at 854.
199. Carpenter v. Lovell's Lounge & Grill, Inc., 59 N.E.3d 330, 340 (Ind. Ct. App. 2016) (quoting Missler v. State Farm Ins. Co., 41 N.E.3d 297, 302 (Ind. Ct. App. 2015) (internal quotation marks omitted)).
200. 472 N.W.2d 233 (S.D. 1991).
201. *Id.* at 234.
202. *Id.*
203. *Id.*

the Kempf complaint.[204] Royal denied coverage based on late notice.[205] The next day, the Romeo Agency settled with Wolff and Kempf by paying $25,000 and stipulating to a $275,000 judgment.[206] The Romeo Agency assigned to Wolff and Kempf its full rights under the Royal policy and, in exchange, Wolff and Kempf agreed not to execute on the $275,000 judgment.

Wolff and Kempf sued Royal to collect the judgment. Royal contended that the judgment was unenforceable because the parties' settlement was the result of bad faith and collusion.[207] The trial court agreed. The trial court concluded that the Romeo Agency's acceptance of Wolff's and Kempf's promise not to execute on the judgment "was a sham" and breached the cooperation clause in the Royal policy.[208] The case ascended to the South Dakota Supreme Court, which applied Nebraska law pursuant to the parties' stipulation.

The South Dakota Supreme Court concluded that the trial court's decision was supported by substantial evidence and therefore was not clearly erroneous. The *Wolff* court listed the following evidence as supporting the trial court's conclusion:

> (1) neither Romeo, nor the attorneys involved, considered that Romeo Agency had a great amount of liability exposure concerning the accident and that . . . Romeo Agency's potential liability was much less than that of [two other defendants]. Yet, Romeo consented to a judgment of $100,000 more than the settlement reached with [those two defendants];
>
> (2) Royal was given less than eight hours to determine coverage;
>
> (3) the details of the ultimate settlement were cemented before the denial of coverage by Royal, but no information concerning the settlement was shared with Royal;
>
> (4) Wolff's complaint was not forwarded to Royal;
>
> (5) no mention of the parties who had settled nor the amounts of the settlement[s] [were] brought to Royal's attention;
>
> (6) the liability exposure was not presented;
>
> (7) while the $25,000 settlement was conditioned upon proof of no insurance, the prior $200,000 offer (which was $75,000 less than the amount of the stipulated judgment) had no such limitation.[209]

204. *Id.*
205. *Id.*
206. *Id.*
207. *Id.* at 235.
208. *Id.*
209. *Id.*

Based on this evidence, the *Wolff* court affirmed the trial court's determination that the judgment "was unreasonable and arrived at in bad faith."[210]

Carpenter v. Lovell's Lounge & Grill, LLC[211] exemplifies both bad faith and collusion in a consent judgment scenario. In *Carpenter*, Jerry Johnson, a regular patron of Lovell's Lounge & Grill (Lovell's), attacked his ex-girlfriend's new beau, Thomas Carpenter, who was a customer in the lounge. Johnson was convicted of battery. Carpenter sued Lovell's on several theories, which clearly alleged that Johnson intentionally attacked him.[212] Lovell's insurer, Cincinnati Specialty Underwriters Insurance Co. (CSU), denied coverage based mainly on the assault and battery exclusion in its policy. Carpenter soon filed an amended complaint with more allegations of negligence by Lovell's.[213] Lovell's sent the amended complaint to CSU, which again denied coverage based on the assault and battery exclusion. Carpenter and Lovell's then entered into a $1.125 million consent judgment, which dubiously asserted that Johnson was Lovell's agent at the time of the attack and recited that:

> 2. Upon entering Lovell's Lounge, [Johnson] negligently came into physical contact with Carpenter, accidently causing him serious bodily injury. The harm was neither intended nor expected from the standpoint of Johnson or Lovell's Lounge.
>
> * * *
>
> 7. The negligent conduct engaged in by Johnson which caused the harm to Carpenter was foreseeable to Lovell's Lounge, however, while foreseeable to Lovell's Lounge, it was neither intended nor expected from the standpoint of Lovell's Lounge or its employees, including Carpenter.[214]

In the subsequent coverage dispute, CSU asserted that the consent judgment had been procured through "fraud, bad faith, or collusion."[215] The trial court found that the consent judgment "was presented in bad faith and procured through collusion," and held that CSU was not bound by the judgment and did not owe coverage for the loss.[216]

Carpenter appealed to the Indiana Court of Appeals, which easily concluded that CSU met its burden to show by clear and convincing evidence that Carpenter obtained the consent judgment in bad faith or collusively.[217] As the court explained:

210. *Id.* at 236.
211. 59 N.E.3d 330 (Ind. Ct. App. 2016).
212. *Id.* at 332.
213. *Id.*
214. *Id.* at 333.
215. *Id.* at 334.
216. *Id.* at 335.
217. *Id.* at 341.

> The Consent Judgment stipulates that Johnson "negligently came into physical contact with Carpenter, accidently causing him serious bodily injury." . . . This is patently unreasonable in light of all the available evidence and the allegations in the verified amended complaint that Johnson "brutally attacked" Carpenter "with numerous punches and kicks." . . . There is no evidence that . . . Johnson accidently punched and kicked Carpenter. Rather, all the evidence indicates that Johnson intentionally punched and kicked Carpenter.
>
> In addition, the Consent Judgment stipulates that Johnson "performed services for and was an agent of Lovell's lounge" and "was within the scope of his agency at the time of the negligent conduct which was the harm to Carpenter." . . . This stipulation is particularly troubling because the amended complaint did not include any allegations regarding an agency relationship. . . . Although Jeremy testified that Johnson occasionally performed repairs for the Lounge in exchange for free beer, their relationship does not remotely appear to be one of principal/agent. There is no evidence that Johnson had an agreement with Lovell's Lounge to perform services or to represent Lovell's Lounge in any respect. In addition, there is absolutely no evidence that he was performing any services for the Lounge at the time of the Incident. We conclude that there is no rational basis from which one could reasonably infer that Johnson was an agent of Lovell's Lounge or that he was acting within the scope of his agency at the time of the Incident.[218]

Adding even more fuel to the fire, evidence of Lovell's and Carpenter's negotiations over the consent judgment revealed that "they were trying to affect coverage by purposely remaking the [i]ncident so that it would not fall under the [p]olicy's assault and battery exclusion."[219]

Because there was clear and convincing evidence that the consent judgment was obtained "through bad faith or collusion," the court concluded that collateral estoppel did not apply and therefore CSU was not bound by the judgment.[220] The *Carpenter* court affirmed the trial court judgment for CSU.

Finally, in *Travelers Indemnity Co. v. Attorney's Title Insurance Fund*,[221] the court found that the insured did not enter into a settlement agreement that accompanied a consent judgment in good faith as Florida law required. Because good faith and bad faith are opposite sides of the same coin, that finding necessarily meant that the insured acted in bad faith.

Travelers arose out of a case in which Travelers' insured, Attorney's Title Insurance Fund (ATIF), was the plaintiff. The defendant, a joint venture known as Section 10, counterclaimed. Travelers agreed to defend ATIF against

---

218. *Id.* at 341–42 (citations to the record and footnote omitted).
219. *Id.* at 342.
220. *Id.*
221. 194 F. Supp. 3d 1224 (M.D. Fla. 2016).

Section 10's counterclaims under a reservation of rights. ATIF and Section 10 nonetheless entered into a *Coblentz* agreement,[222] under which ATIF consented to a judgment in favor of Section 10 that would be collectible only against Travelers. When ATIF sent Section 10 the first draft of their agreement, it left blank the damages section for their planned consent judgment.[223] Section 10 revised the draft to provide for nearly $42.7 million in damages. Section 10 later revised the agreement again to reduce the damages to $42 million, but neither that figure nor the original one was negotiated with ATIF.[224] In fact, ATIF did nothing to minimize its liability. "Instead, having secured a covenant from Section 10 that the judgment would not be enforced against it, ATIF readily agreed to any damages amount that Section 10 presented."[225] Consequently, ATIF was guilty of bad faith and Section 10 could not enforce the $40 million consent judgment against Travelers.[226]

C. Recognizing Fraud and Collusion in Connection with Nonexecution Agreements and Consent Judgments

1. *Introducing the Concepts of Fraud and Collusion*

Like bad faith by an insured, a finding of collusion or fraud involving an insured prevents the enforcement of a consent judgment against an insurer. Fraud and collusion are related concepts and courts often blend or combine them, even though they are separate types of misconduct. For instance, unlike fraud, collusion does not require the misrepresentation of a material fact.[227] Moreover, both fraud and collusion take many different forms depending on the facts.[228] An insurer may challenge a consent judgment based on fraud *or* collusion; the insurer need not allege both forms of misconduct or prove identical elements to prevail on one theory or the other.[229]

---

222. See *supra* notes 10–11 and accompanying text discussing *Coblentz* and *Cunningham* agreements.

223. *Travelers*, 194 F. Supp. 3d at 1237.

224. *Id.* at 1237–38.

225. *Id.* at 1238.

226. *See id.* (stating that the *Coblentz* agreement "was not made in good faith").

227. Span, Inc. v. Associated Int'l Ins. Co., 277 Cal. Rptr. 828, 839 (Ct. App. 1991).

228. *See id.* ("What constitutes collusion will differ with each fact situation.").

229. *See, e.g.*, MacLean Townhomes, LLC v. Charter Oak Fire Ins. Co., No. C06-1093BHS, 2008 WL 2811161, at *5 (W.D. Wash. July 21, 2008) (footnote and record citation omitted) ("Plaintiff also argues that, in order to establish fraud, Defendant must present evidence as to the nine elements of common-law fraud. . . . Plaintiff, however, has failed to cite a Washington State court case applying the nine elements of fraud to an insurance settlement. Contrary to Plaintiff's argument, Washington State courts hold that settlements may be collaterally attacked if they are the result of fraud *or* collusion.").

2. *Defining Fraud and Collusion in Connection with Nonexecution Agreements and Consent Judgments*

Courts variously define fraud. For example, Missouri courts recognize two types of fraud: extrinsic and intrinsic. "Extrinsic fraud refers to the fraudulent procurement of a judgment, not the propriety of the judgment. . . . It must relate to the manner in which the judgment was obtained."[230] In brief, fraud "is extrinsic when it induces a party to default or to consent to a judgment."[231] Fraud is intrinsic "when a party knowingly uses perjured testimony or otherwise fabricates evidence."[232]

Contrary to the restrictive Missouri approach, courts should generously interpret fraud in the consent judgment context. As a Florida court explained:

> The conduct of an insured can hardly be characterized as fraudulent simply because he stipulates to a large settlement . . . to obtain his release from liability. He has little or nothing to lose because he will never be obligated to pay. As a consequence, the settlement of liability and damages may have very little relationship to the strength of the plaintiff's claim. Due to this problem, the ordinary standard of collusion or fraud is inappropriate.[233]

Other courts have similarly adopted broad understandings of fraud.[234]

---

230. Walker v. Walker, 280 S.W.3d 634, 636 (Mo. Ct. App. 2009).

231. Taggart v. Md. Cas. Co., 242 S.W.3d 755, 758 (Mo. Ct. App. 2008).

232. *Id.*

233. Steil v. Fla. Physicians' Ins. Reciprocal, 448 So. 2d 589, 592 (Fla. Dist. Ct. App. 1984); *see also* Water's Edge Homeowners Ass'n v. Water's Edge Assocs., 216 P.3d 1110, 1123 (Wash. Ct. App. 2009) (recognizing that fraud in the consent judgment context does not "invoke the typical standard of proof for fraud, which must be proved by evidence that is clear, cogent, and convincing").

234. *See, e.g.*, Cont'l Cas. Co. v. Hempel, 4 F. App'x 703, 717 (10th Cir. 2001) (quoting Stephen R. Schmidt, *The Bad Faith Setup*, 29 TORT & INS. L.J. 705, 721 (1994)); Carlson v. Zellaha, 482 N.W.2d 281, 283 (Neb. 1992) (quoting BLACK'S LAW DICTIONARY 660 (6th ed. 1990)).

Courts' definitions of collusion also vary.[235] At the outset, it is worth recalling that the consent judgment process is not necessarily collusive.[236] A covenant not to execute does not alone demonstrate collusion.[237] Likewise, an insured's assignment of its rights against its insurers to a plaintiff, without more, does not evidence collusion.[238] Again, the law generally permits insureds whose insurers have declined to defend them to avoid personal liability by making reasonable settlements (at least up to policy limits) that include covenants not to execute and assignments of their rights against their insurers.[239]

Collusion may be found when a transaction or series of transactions—such as a nonexecution agreement coupled with an assignment of the insured's rights against its insurer—is intended to injure the interests of an absent party, such as an insurer.[240] Collusion may further be described as "a lack of opposition between a plaintiff and an insured that would otherwise assure that the settlement is the result of hard bargaining."[241] At bottom, bad faith, fraud, and

---

235. *See, e.g.*, Spence-Parker v. Md. Ins. Grp., 937 F. Supp. 551, 561 (E.D. Va. 1996) (interpreting Virginia law) ("In essence, collusion is simply fraud accomplished by two or more persons. As such, it incorporates, but does not substantively expand the kind of conduct that constitutes actual or constructive fraud."); Span, Inc. v. Associated Int'l Ins. Co., 277 Cal. Rptr. 828, 839–40 (Ct. App. 1991) (listing several definitions of collusion and stating what constitutes collusion will vary with each fact situation); Stark Liquidation Co. v. Florists' Mut. Ins. Co., 243 S.W.3d 385, 400 (Mo. Ct. App. 2007) (citations omitted) ("Collusion is a 'secret concert of action between two or more for the promotion of some fraudulent purpose.' . . . 'Collusion is also defined as an agreement between two or more persons to defraud another under the forms of law, or to accomplish an illegal purpose.'"); *Tidyman's I*, 330 P.3d at 1156 (emphasis added) (explaining that "[t]he term 'collusion' implies the existence of some sort of agreement aimed at defrauding another or otherwise breaking the law," and the then saying that for the settlement agreements in the case to be collusive, the insurer "would have to point to evidence of *an effort towards wrongdoing* between the plaintiffs and [the defendant-insureds]"); McCruter v. Travelers Home & Marine Ins. Co., 168 N.E.3d 1, 17 (Ohio Ct. App. 2021) ("The definition of 'collusion' includes 'where two persons, apparently in a hostile position and having conflicting interests, by arrangement do some act in order to injure a third person or deceive a court.'" (quoting Valley Paint v. Nat'l Union Fire Ins. Co., No. CA2010-08-060, 2011 WL 947036, at *3 (Ohio Ct. App. Mar. 21, 2011))).

236. Ortiz v. Biscanin, 122 P.3d 365, 381 (Kan. Ct. App. 2004); Associated Ins. Serv., Inc. v. Garcia, 307 S.W.3d 58, 68–69 (Ky. 2010); Abbey/Land, LLC v. Glacier Constr. Partners, LLC, 433 P.3d 1230, 1241–42 (Mont. 2019); Kobbeman v. Oleson, 574 N.W.2d 633, 637 (S.D. 1998).

237. Andrew v. Century Sur. Co., 134 F. Supp. 3d 1249, 1267 (D. Nev. 2015) (predicting Nevada law); Com. Ins. Co. v. Szafarowicz, 131 N.E.3d 782, 798 (Mass. 2019); Tilden-Coil Constructors, Inc. v. Landmark Am. Ins. Co., No. C09-1574JLR, 2011 WL 780876, at *6 (W.D. Wash. Feb. 25, 2011) (applying Washington law).

238. *Andrew*, 134 F. Supp. 3d at 1267.

239. Justin A. Harris, Note, *Judicial Approaches to Stipulated Judgments, Assignments of Rights, and Covenants Not to Execute in Insurance Litigation*, 47 Drake L. Rev. 853, 860 (1999).

240. Cent. Mut. Ins. Co. v. Tracy's Treasures, Inc., 19 N.E.3d 1100, 1120 (Ill. App. Ct. 2014) (quoting Cont'l Cas. Co. v. Westerfield, 961 F. Supp. 1502, 1505 (D.N.M. 1997)); *Abbey/Land, LLC*, 433 P.3d at 1244 (quoting *Westerfield*, 961 F. Supp. at 1505).

241. Indep. Sch. Dist. No. 197 v. Accident & Cas. Ins. of Winterthur, 525 N.W.2d 600, 607 (Minn. Ct. App. 1995).

collusion are all characterized by unfairness to the insurer.[242] Collusion plainly exists when the plaintiff and the insured cooperate to manufacture a bad faith claim against the insurer or to inflate the plaintiff's recovery in order to bloat damages flowing from the insurer's alleged breach of duty.[243] An insured's promise to testify falsely to create coverage would be another obvious example of collusion,[244] as well as an act of bad faith.

Courts often interpret collusion as requiring some element of secrecy.[245] For example, Missouri courts define collusion as "a secret concert of action between two or more people for the promotion of a fraudulent purpose."[246] That approach is misguided, however, because while secrecy may evidence collusion,[247] it is not essential to a finding of collusion.[248]

Courts and parties sometimes invoke dictionary definitions of collusion to hold or argue that secrecy is required for a finding of collusion.[249] But that approach is also flawed because not all dictionaries define collusion as requiring secrecy.[250] In fact, dictionaries are imperfect sources of authority when fixing the meaning of words, as courts and scholars have observed when

---

242. *Tracy's Treasures*, 19 N.E.3d at 1120 (quoting *Westerfield*, 961 F. Supp. at 1505).

243. *Tracy's Treasures*, 19 N.E.3d at 1121 (quoting Safeco Ins. Co. of Am. v. Parks, 88 Cal. Rptr. 3d 730, 748 (Ct. App. 2009)); *Abbey/Land, LLC*, 433 P.3d at 1245; *see also* Andrade v. Jennings, 62 Cal. Rptr. 2d 787, 799–802 (Ct. App. 1997) (reasoning that there was substantial evidence that the parties crafted the settlement to injure the insurer and thus that it was collusive, and that the associated judgment was also collusive); J.B. Aguerre, Inc. v. Am. Guar. & Liab. Ins. Co., 68 Cal. Rptr. 2d 837, 843–44 (Ct. App. 1997) (inflating case value based on concocted punitive damage exposure); Span, Inc. v. Associated Int'l Ins. Co., 277 Cal. Rptr. 828, 839–40 (Ct. App. 1991) (noting that "[c]ollusive assistance in the procurement of a judgment not only constitutes a breach of the cooperation clause but also is a breach of the covenant of good faith and fair dealing," and then noting the lack of an adversarial proceeding and the fact that a meritorious case was not defended); Penn-America Ins. Co. v. Osborne, 797 S.E.2d 548, 556 (W. Va. 2017) (discussing the $1 million valuation of the underlying plaintiff's injuries without any evidence regarding the permanency of the injury, the severity of the injury, alleged permanent disability, medical expenses, or the like).

244. *Andrew*, 134 F. Supp. 3d at 1268.

245. *See, e.g.*, Taggart v. Md. Cas. Co., 242 S.W.3d 755, 758 (Mo. Ct. App. 2008) ("Collusion is a secret concert of action between two or more people for the promotion of a fraudulent purpose."); Carlson v. Zellaha, 482 N.W.2d 281, 283 (Neb. 1992) (noting that in an earlier case the court "defined collusion as a secret agreement or secret cooperation for a fraudulent or deceitful purpose, such as a secret agreement between two or more persons to defraud a person of his rights, often by the forms of law").

246. *Taggart*, 242 S.W.3d at 758.

247. *See, e.g.*, Pasha v. Rosemount Mem'l Park, Inc., 781 A.2d 1119, 1124 (N.J. Super. Ct. App. Div. 2001); Penn-Am. Ins. Co. v. Osborne, 797 S.E.2d 548, 556 (W. Va. 2017).

248. Abbey/Land, LLC v. Glacier Constr. Partners, LLC, 433 P.3d 1230, 1244 (Mont. 2019); Fireman's Fund Ins. Co. v. Imbesi, 826 A.2d 735, 758 (N.J. Super. Ct. App. Div. 2003).

249. *See, e.g.*, Gosney v. Fireman's Fund Ins. Co., 419 P.3d 447, 469 (Wash. Ct. App. 2018) (relying in part on the 2002 edition of a Webster's dictionary when instructing the jury on collusion).

250. *Compare* American Heritage Dictionary of the English Language 363 (2009) (stating that collusion is "[a] secret agreement between two or more parties for a fraudulent, illegal, or deceitful purpose"), *with Collusion*, Black's Law Dictionary (11th ed. 2019) (defining collusion as "[a]n agreement to defraud another or to do or obtain something forbidden by law").

interpreting statutes.[251] In addition, it is easy to compare multiple dictionaries to find a preferred definition.

The risk of collusion is low when a judgment is the result of a fully adversarial trial or hearing.[252] In sharp contrast, a trial in which the defendant does not contest the plaintiff's evidence, presents no evidence of its own, and offers no argument, is powerful evidence of collusion.[253] This is certainly true when a court presiding over such a trial basically rubber stamps a judgment presented by the parties.[254]

3. *Representative Fraud and Collusion Cases*

Sidman v. Travelers Casualty & Surety[255] is an interesting collusion case. *Sidman* arose out of litigation between the Culbreath Isles Property Owners Association (Culbreath) and Phyllis Kirkwood over Kirkwood's failure to maintain her lawn and landscaping. When Culbreath sued Kirkwood in a Florida state court to enforce its restrictive covenants, Kirkwood counterclaimed for slander of title, and also demanded her attorneys' fees and costs under a Florida statute. Culbreath tendered Kirkwood's counterclaim to Travelers, which defended Culbreath under a reservation of rights.[256] Kirkwood won summary judgment and then moved to recover her statutory attorneys' fees and costs. Travelers

251. *See, e.g.*, United States v. Costello, 666 F.3d 1040, 1043 (7th Cir. 2012) ("[T]he choice among meanings [of words in statutes] must have a footing more solid than a dictionary—which is a museum of words, an historical catalog rather than a means to decode the work of legislatures." (quoting Frank H. Easterbrook, *Text, History, and Structure in Statutory Interpretation*, 17 Harv. J. L. & Pub. Pol'y 61, 67 (1994))); *see also* Kevin Werbach, Note, *Looking It Up: Dictionaries and Statutory Interpretation*, 107 Harv. L. Rev. 1437, 1445 (1994) ("[I]t makes no sense to declare a unitary meaning that 'the dictionary' assigns to a term. There are a wide variety of dictionaries . . . and all of them usually provide several entries for each word. The selection of a particular dictionary and a particular definition is not obvious and must be defended on some other grounds of suitability."). Even courts that consider dictionaries to be helpful when attempting to define statutory terms recognize that dictionary definitions are not dispositive. *See, e.g.*, Austin v. Medicis, 230 Cal. Rptr. 3d 528, 538 (Ct. App. 2018) (explaining that "while dictionaries may sometimes be helpful, they are not dispositive"); State v. Scovel, 916 N.W.2d 550, 555 (Minn. 2018) (citations omitted) ("[A]s Judge Learned Hand observed, the dictionary is not foolproof or failsafe. . . . It is not unusual to set aside dictionary definitions when context makes clear that dictionary definitions may not fit."); State v. Carlton, 388 P.3d 1093, 1097 (Or. 2017) ("Of course, dictionary definitions are guides for discernment, not blunt instruments.").

252. *See* Hendricks v. Novae Corp. Underwriting, Ltd., 868 F.3d 542, 548 (7th Cir. 2017) (citing State Farm Fire & Cas. Co. v. Gandy, 925 S.W.2d 696, 714 (Tex. 1996)).

253. *See, e.g.*, Brockmann v. Bd of Cnty. Comm'rs of Cnty. of Shawnee, 404 F. App'x 271, 281 (10th Cir. 2010) (applying Kansas law); Span, Inc. v. Associated Int'l Ins. Co., 277 Cal. Rptr. 828, 840 (Ct. App. 1991) (finding that the record of the underlying bench trial raised a genuine issue of material fact regarding collusion where the defense lawyer hired by the insured mounted no defense).

254. *See, e.g.*, *Brockmann*, 404 F. App'x at 281 (involving a judgment presented to the court that was identical to one shared between the parties prior to trial that identified the court's findings, detailed the amounts of liability by category, assigned the final judgment amounts based upon the percentage of each party's fault, and specified the amount to be awarded).

255. 841 F.3d 1197 (11th Cir. 2016).

256. *Id.* at 1199.

declined to defend Culbreath against Kirkwood's attorneys' fees claim and denied coverage for any such award.[257]

Culbreath and Kirkwood began litigating the attorneys' fees issue. Kirkwood's lawyer, Mark Buell of Buell & Elligett (Buell), asserted that his fees were approximately $87,000 and further said that he would ask the court to multiply them. Culbreath fought the attorneys' fees claim.[258] Culbreath and Kirkwood then began discussing settlement, with Culbreath keeping Travelers informed about the negotiations.[259] When Culbreath informed Travelers' lawyer that it was ready to agree to a $295,000 judgment to resolve Kirkwood's attorneys' fees claim, Travelers' lawyer never objected or told Culbreath not to consent to the judgment.[260] Kirkwood and Culbreath then executed a *Coblentz* agreement in which Culbreath (1) agreed to the entry of a $295,000 judgment against it payable to Buell; and (2) assigned to Kirkwood and Buell all proceeds from any claims Culbreath had against Travelers in exchange for Kirkwood's promise not to enforce the judgment against Culbreath.[261] The court approved the settlement and entered the consent judgment without a hearing.[262]

Kirkwood and Culbreath also executed a promissory note that they did not disclose to the court in which Culbreath agreed to pay Kirkwood or Buell $50,000, minus whatever amount they could pry out of Travelers; if they recovered $50,000 or more, Culbreath would owe nothing.[263] After the court entered the consent judgment, Culbreath assigned its rights against Travelers to Kirkwood and Buell.[264]

Kirkwood was incapacitated by a stroke, and her guardian, Orline Sidman, sued Travelers for breach of contract in a Florida state court. Travelers removed the case to federal court and then moved to dismiss based on Sidman's failure to join Buell as an indispensable party given the rights Buell had acquired in the settlement.[265] Buell then assigned its rights to Florida Policyholders, LLC (FP), an entity Buell created.[266] Sidman and FP subsequently filed an amended complaint against Travelers.

Because Travelers previously had been held to have breached its duty to defend and indemnify Culbreath,[267] the district court conducted a bench trial to determine whether Travelers was bound by Culbreath's and Kirkwood's

257. *Id.*
258. *Id.*
259. *Id.*
260. *Id.*
261. *Id.*
262. *Id.*
263. *Id.*
264. *Id.* at 1200.
265. *Id.*
266. *Id.*
267. This determination was made in a prior appeal in the case. *Id.* (citing Culbreath Isles Prop. Owners Ass'n, Inc. v. Travelers Cas. & Sur. Co. of Am., 601 F. App'x 876, 879 (11th Cir. 2015)).

settlement. Travelers offered evidence of Culbreath's attempt to settle a nearly identical attorney's fees claim by homeowners Richard and Nancy Lewis. Like Kirkwood, the Lewises won summary judgment and then sought their fees from Culbreath. Scott Frick, the Lewises' lawyer, testified that during settlement negotiations, Culbreath offered to agree to any attorneys' fees amount the Lewises sought, as long as they agreed not to enforce the judgment against Culbreath.[268] Frick also testified that Culbreath had acknowledged that it had reached a similar agreement with Kirkwood.[269]

The district court determined that the settlement was unreasonable in its amount and had not been negotiated in good faith, and therefore could not be enforced against Travelers.[270] Specifically, the district court found that Culbreath "'acted in bad faith when it offered to 'lie down' and accept a judgment of $295,000 against it as long as recovery of that sum came from Travelers.'"[271] Sidman and FP appealed.

Sidman and FP argued that evaluating the settlement for reasonableness was improper because "Travelers knew about and acquiesced in the settlement."[272] The Eleventh Circuit rejected this argument, explaining that the practical effect of adopting it would be to hold that where an insurer is given notice of a proposed settlement between its insured and a plaintiff and the insurer fails to object, the insurer would be deemed to have waived all objections to the settlement despite underlying fraud or collusion about which it did not know.[273] Florida law did not support that proposition.[274] As the *Sidman* court further explained:

> We acknowledge that allowing insurers to challenge settlement agreements between their insureds and injured parties after having kept quiet during the settlement negotiations may appear inequitable. . . . Indeed, Sidman and FP portray Travelers as lulling Kirkwood and Culbreath into complacency by failing to object in the state court case to the settlement agreement or consent judgment. But even under the legal framework that Sidman and FP advance, Travelers would not be bound by a settlement agreement that was obtained by fraud or collusion. And we . . . reject[ ] a framework that would, in effect, prohibit . . . insurers from challenging settlement agreements as fraudulent or collusive simply because they had knowledge of the settlement terms, even though the fraudulent or collusive nature of the agreement was not apparent from the face of the settlement or even was hidden . . . by the parties. . . .

268. *Id.*
269. *Id.*
270. *Id.*
271. *Id.* (quoting Culbreath Isles Prop. Owners Ass'n, Inc. v. Travelers Cas. & Sur. Co. of Am., 151 F. Supp. 3d 1282, 1292 (M.D. Fla. 2015), *aff'd*, 841 F.3d 1197 (11th Cir. 2016)).
272. *Id.* at 1203.
273. *Id.*
274. *Id.*

> Had Kirkwood and Culbreath negotiated a reasonable settlement agreement in good faith, they would have been entitled to bind Travelers to it. . . . By choosing instead to collude, they forfeited this right.[275]

In short, the relevant inquiry in determining whether to enforce a *Coblentz* agreement against an insurer that breached its duty to defend is whether the agreement "was produced through fraud or collusion, not whether the insurer had notice of the settlement and an opportunity to object to it."[276] Accordingly, an insurer may challenge a *Coblentz* agreement based on fraud or collusion "notwithstanding its prior notice of and opportunity to challenge the agreement."[277]

The *Sidman* court next considered whether the district court erred by concluding that the settlement agreement was unreasonable in amount and had been negotiated in bad faith. To the contrary, the combination of Culbreath's willingness to agree to any fee award so long as it was not responsible for the judgment and the secret promissory note amply supported the district court's finding of bad faith.[278] The Eleventh Circuit was particularly persuaded of the correctness of the district court's decision by Culbreath's willingness "to lie down and accept a judgment of any amount against it so long as it would not be on the hook to satisfy the judgment" and by the secret side agreement.[279] As the court noted, "[a] reasonable party would not be indifferent to the amount of a judgment entered against it were its own money on the line."[280]

The *Sidman* court concluded that the district court's finding of bad faith in the negotiation of the settlement agreement rested on substantial evidence, and that its refusal to award Sidman and FP reasonable attorneys' fees was therefore proper.[281] The *Sidman* court additionally held "that an agreement in which an insured agrees to accept essentially any judgment amount that the injured party seeks in exchange for a promise to not execute against it is collusive" for consent judgment purposes.[282] The Eleventh Circuit accordingly affirmed the district court's judgment.[283]

In *Penn-America Insurance Co. v. Osborne*,[284] the West Virginia Supreme Court blended collusion and fraud in voiding the assignment of a bad faith claim. In doing so, the court unwound the plaintiff's consent judgment scheme.

275. *Id.* at 1204–05.
276. *Id.* at 1205.
277. *Id.*
278. *Id.* at 1205–06.
279. *Id.* at 1206.
280. *Id.*
281. *Id.* at 1207.
282. *Id.* at 1206.
283. *Id.* at 1207.
284. 797 S.E.2d 548 (W. Va. 2017).

Penn-America was rooted in an accident in which Beecher Osborne, a logger employed by H&H Logging Co., injured his leg on land owned by Heartwood Forestland and leased by Allegheny Timber Products. Osborne sued H&H for deliberately exposing him to an unsafe environment, and in the same action sued Heartwood and Allegheny for negligence.[285] H&H tendered the lawsuit to its insurer, Penn-America, which denied coverage based on the employer's liability exclusion in its policy.[286] H&H then hired defense counsel at its own expense. Allegheny and Heartwood tendered the suit to Allegheny's insurer, Liberty Mutual, which accepted coverage and agreed to defend them.[287]

Allegheny and Heartwood later noticed that their contract with H&H required H&H to defend and indemnify them in connection with Osborne's suit, and they twice requested that H&H or Penn-America do so.[288] Unfortunately, H&H never informed Penn-America of their requests, and Allegheny and Heartwood never communicated directly with Penn-America because they assumed that H&H would transmit their requests.[289] Allegheny and Heartwood also filed a motion for leave to file a third-party complaint for declaratory relief against Penn-America for failing to defend them, but they never set the motion for hearing and they never filed a third-party complaint.[290]

Osborne eventually approached Allegheny and Heartwood about settling. The lawyer hired by Liberty Mutual to defend Allegheny and Heartwood negotiated the settlement terms. Unbeknownst to Penn-America, Osborne, Allegheny, and Heartwood struck a settlement agreement in which they stipulated to these facts:

> (1) Penn-America breached its insurance contract by failing to "provide a defense or insurance coverage related to Osborne's claims against Allegheny and Heartwood"; (2) Due to Penn-America's breach, Allegheny and Heartwood suffered damages because they were "compelled to expend funds and other resources in the defense of this action"; (3) "Allegheny and Heartwood have been compelled to mitigate the claims asserted by Osborne by [entering into a pre-trial settlement agreement] with Osborne to preserve and protect the assets of Allegheny and Heartwood"; and (4) Allegheny and Heartwood tried to resolve coverage issues by filing a third-party complaint for declaratory relief against Penn-America.[291]

285. *Id.* at 550.
286. *Id.* at 550 & n.1.
287. *Id.* at 551.
288. *Id.*
289. *Id.*
290. *Id.*
291. *Id.* (footnotes omitted).

Additionally, Allegheny and Heartwood consented to a $1 million judgment in Osborne's favor and assigned to him any claims they might have against Penn-America for failing to defend them.[292] In exchange, Osborne promised not to attempt to execute on the judgment against Allegheny or Heartwood, instead limiting any recovery to Penn-America based on the assigned claims.[293]

Osborne subsequently sued Penn-America and won summary judgment in the trial court. The trial court proceeding was a one-sided affair. For example, the trial court would not permit Penn-America to discover Osborne's medical records so that it might challenge the reasonableness of the $1 million consent judgment.[294] Penn-America then appealed to the West Virginia Supreme Court, where it found a receptive audience.

The *Penn-America* court reversed the trial court and remanded the case to the trial court with directions to dismiss Osborne's claims against Penn-America with prejudice.[295] In the process, the *Penn-America* court recognized that the combination of assignments of claims against insurers and covenants not to execute "entails a great risk of fraud and collusion."[296] In an effort to address this problem, the court had for at least a decade reasoned that "recovery on an assigned insurance bad faith claim may not be made upon an untrue factual basis."[297] As the court explained, that principle certainly applied here:

> Mr. Osborne's recovery on the assigned claims would be based on a falsehood, i.e., that due to Penn-America's breach, Allegheny and Heartwood were without insurance coverage, and the $1,000,000.00 consent judgment was necessary to protect their assets. At all times . . . Allegheny and Heartwood were provided insurance coverage and a defense by Liberty Mutual Insurance. Further, there was no evidence Allegheny and Heartwood asked Penn-America for coverage.
>
> Moreover, we note another falsehood contained in the pre-trial settlement agreement: that Allegheny and Heartwood filed a third-party complaint for declaratory relief on the Penn-America policy. Even though Allegheny and Heartwood filed a motion seeking permission to file a third-party complaint seeking declaratory relief, they never followed through by bringing the motion on for a hearing. Had Allegheny and Heartwood been more diligent in seeking declaratory relief . . . coverage issues could have been determined before liability under Penn-America's policy. Likewise, Mr. Osborne was entitled to seek the same relief. Instead, Allegheny, Heartwood, and Mr. Osborne sought to bind a non-party to pay Mr. Osborne $1,000,000.00 for an injured leg while

292. *Id.*
293. *Id.*
294. *Id.* at 552.
295. *Id.* at 557.
296. *Id.* at 554 (footnote omitted).
297. *Id.* at 555 (referring to Strahin v. Sulivan, 647 S.E.2d 765 (W. Va. 2007)).

it was prohibited from contesting the lawsuit's reasonable value or stipulated facts.[298]

In finding for Penn-America, the court also noted several "symptoms of fraud and collusion" infecting the case.[299] First, Osborne, Allegheny, and Heartwood misrepresented the facts underlying their assignment.[300] Second, Allegheny and Heartwood never negotiated over the value of Osborne's claim, but instead consented to a $1 million judgment with no evidence to support that amount.[301] Third, Osborne's, Allegheny's, and Heartwood's settlement agreement was characterized by concealment because they never told Penn-America about their negotiations.[302] Once Penn-America learned of the consent judgment and assignment, it was effectively prevented from challenging the judgment's reasonableness.[303] As a result, "through secretive means, Allegheny and Heartwood awarded Mr. Osborne a $1,000,000.00 windfall for his injured leg with Penn-America's money."[304] The *Penn-America* court could not—and correctly did not—permit that result to stand.

Fireman's Fund Insurance Co. v. Imbesi[305] is another instructive case. *Imbesi* arose out of litigation by Sally James (a pseudonym) against her former employers, Click Corporation of America (Click) and North American Beverage (North American), and their owner, John Imbesi. James alleged that during the 19 months she worked for Click and North American, Imbesi repeatedly harassed her. Imbesi allegedly coerced and intimidated James into having sex, and he once raped her. Unbeknownst to James, Imbesi had genital herpes, which he transmitted to her. Imbesi admitted that he had sex with James; he claimed that their relationship was consensual and said he did not alert James to his herpes because he did not think he was contagious. Although Imbesi denied all of James's sexual harassment allegations, he had a sorry record, having previously lost another former employee's sexual harassment lawsuit.

James sued Click, North American, and Imbesi in a Pennsylvania federal court, seeking both compensatory and punitive damages. She alleged multiple claims, including sexual harassment, negligent and intentional infliction of emotional distress, assault and battery, negligent supervision, gender-motivated violence in violation of the federal Violence Against Women Act, and unlawful retaliation. When some of those claims were dismissed, James filed a second action in a Pennsylvania state court based on the same facts.

298. *Id.* at 556.
299. *Id.* (quoting Cont'l Cas. Co. v. Westerfield, 961 F. Supp. 1502, 1505 (D.N.M. 1997)).
300. *Id.*
301. *Id.*
302. *Id.*
303. *Id.*
304. *Id.* at 556–57.
305. 826 A.2d 735 (N.J. Super. Ct. App. Div. 2003).

At different times during Imbesi's alleged abuse of James, Click and North American had general liability and excess coverage with American Motorists Insurance (American Motorists) and Harleysville Mutual Insurance (Harleysville), and workers compensation coverage through Harleysville and Lumbermens Mutual (Lumbermens). Harleysville provided coverage for only five of the 19 months. Imbesi had homeowners insurance through Fireman's Fund Insurance Co. (Fireman's Fund).

The parties eventually discussed settlement. American Motorists and Lumbermens participated in the negotiations; Harleysville and Fireman's Fund denied coverage and thus did not.[306] James settled with the defendants, American Motorists, and Lumbermens. The settlement agreement provided that a $4.15 million consent judgment would be entered in the federal case against Click, North American, and Imbesi.[307] Specifically, judgment was to be entered on the New Jersey Law Against Discrimination, negligent transmission of a venereal disease, and negligent infliction of emotional distress claims.[308] No part of the $4.15 million judgment was allocated to James' claim for punitive damages.[309]

As for payment of the $4.15 million, Click, North American, and Imbesi agreed to collectively pay James $550,000 and assigned James their rights against Fireman's Fund and Harleysville.[310] They guaranteed James an additional $150,000 payable within two years if by then she had recovered nothing from Harleysville and Fireman's Fund.[311] In turn, James agreed to reimburse Click, North American, and Imbesi for this "guarantee payment" depending on the amount she recovered from the two insurers.[312] American Motorists and Lumbermens agreed to pay James $200,000 up front, plus a $100,000 guarantee payment on the same terms arranged by the defendants.[313]

Declaratory judgment and bad faith litigation in New Jersey state court followed. The trial court determined at summary judgment that the settlement was unenforceable against Harleysville because it was unreasonable and collusive.[314] James appealed.

The *Imbesi* court affirmed the trial court. The *Imbesi* court's bases for holding that the settlement was unreasonable overlapped with its reasons

306. *Id.* at 741.
307. *Id.* at 742.
308. *Id.*
309. *Id.*
310. *Id.*
311. *Id.*
312. *Id.*
313. *Id.*
314. *Id.* at 748.

for deeming it collusive and the product of bad faith.[315] The court carefully explained its analysis.

First, James offered little or no admissible evidence to support the reasonableness of the $4.15 million judgment. The court rejected her attempt to rely on "the naked allegations of her complaint" as evidence of the merits of her claims.[316] James offered affidavits from two employment lawyers serving as expert witnesses, but their opinions lacked foundation and their testimony was otherwise flawed.[317] The only supposedly comparable verdict she offered to support the judgment amount came from the earlier case against Imbesi, but that verdict was overwhelmingly composed of punitive damages, while the judgment in this case allocated none of the $4.15 million to punitive damages.[318]

Second, Imbesi never disputed James's valuation of the case.[319] In the settlement conference that led to the consent judgment, Imbesi's lawyers never contested James's valuation of her compensatory damages; in fact, they never even mentioned James's alleged injuries or damages.[320] This information supported a finding of collusion and bad faith.[321]

The court found it "reasonable to question why Imbesi failed to challenge James's valuation of her claims, and instead accepted the concept that [she] should receive millions of dollars in compensatory damages."[322] This was especially peculiar since Imbesi always claimed that his relationship with James was consensual. Probing further, the court noted that little discovery was done in the underlying case.[323] The defendants never obtained an independent medical or psychiatric examination of James.[324] At the same time, there was evidence that James was not as badly injured as she alleged, including interrogatory answers in which she admitted to emotional problems before she met Imbesi, and statements from her doctor that her mental condition and quality of life were improving.[325]

The *Imbesi* court's review of the record revealed "that, at all times, the parties were primarily interested in disposing of the case and suing the [nonsettling] carriers."[326] In addition, the weak evidentiary basis for the $4.15

315. *Id.* at 751.
316. *Id.* at 753.
317. *Id.* at 753–54.
318. *Id.* at 754.
319. *Id.* at 755.
320. *Id.*
321. *Id.* (citing Cont'l Cas. Co. v. Hempel, 4 F. App'x 703, 717 (10th Cir. 2001)).
322. *Id.*
323. *Id.* at 755–56.
324. *Id.* at 756.
325. *Id.*
326. *Id.*

million judgment stood "in stark contrast to the sort of detailed examinations of the potential for liability and damages, including extensive, detailed discussions of the underlying facts and expert opinions" in trial court decisions that reviewing courts had required to affirm the reasonableness of settlement agreements in insurance cases.[327]

An examination of the settlement agreement also supported a finding of bad faith and collusion. The first suspicious term was the allocation of the $4.15 million entirely to compensatory damages despite the nature of James's allegations and the presence of her punitive damage claim.[328] This benefited the defendants because punitive damages are generally uninsurable, and it benefited James, who likely could not have recovered punitive damages from Imbesi, whose assets were potentially difficult to reach.[329] The only parties harmed by this allocation were Harleysville and Fireman's Fund, whose policies potentially covered compensatory damages but did not cover punitive damages.[330] Distilled, this term "clearly represent[ed] an inappropriate attempt to squeeze a settlement for both compensatory and punitive damages into a sum for compensatory damages alone, solely for the purpose of obtaining insurance coverage."[331] As such, it was evidence of collusion and bad faith.[332]

A second suspicious term was the disparity in the amounts paid by the parties and the total amount of the settlement.[333] James agreed to accept $750,000 from the defendants and $250,000 from American Motorists, while seeking more than $3 million from Harleysville and Fireman's Fund.[334] Moreover, she agreed to reimburse up to $250,000 (the guarantee payments) if she prevailed against Harleysville and Fireman's Fund.[335]

Next, the court was strongly suspicious of James's agreement to waive her right to proceed against the defendants if she was unable to recover against Harleysville:

> Indeed . . . this aspect of the Settlement provides strong evidence that the $4.15 million settlement was a sham, which did not truly represent James's losses. If it did, why would she be willing to settle for "only" $1 million and risk the possibility of recovering nothing from the Non-Settling Insurers? We conclude that she agreed to accept $1 million from the settling parties because

---

327. *Id.* (first citing Midwestern Indem. Co. v. Laikin, 119 F. Supp. 2d 831, 845–51 (S.D. Ind. 2000); then citing Excelsior Ins. Co. v. Pennsbury Pain Ctr., 975 F Supp. 342, 354–61 (D.N.J. 1996)).
328. *Id.* at 756–57.
329. *Id.* at 757.
330. *Id.*
331. *Id.*
332. *Id.* (citing Cont'l Cas. Co. v. Hempel, 4 F. App'x 703, 717 (10th Cir. 2001)).
333. *Id.*
334. *Id.*
335. *Id.*

> she believed $1 million was reasonable in the circumstances to compensate her for her losses. Any balance recovered over $1 million was essentially serendipitous.[336]

The final suspicious term was the parties' agreement to make Harleysville liable for the lion's share of the judgment even though it insured Click and North American for only five months of James's 19 months in their employ.[337] Had the settlement agreement been reasonably structured, American Motorists and Lumbermens would have contributed far more than the portion allocated to Harleysville since they were on the risk for almost three times as long.[338] Although it was possible—as James argued—that Imbesi harassed James more severely during the five months that Harleysville insured his companies than he did during the other 14 months he abused her, there was still insufficient evidence to support the parties' allocation of the judgment amount.[339]

Based on these factors, the *Imbesi* court found that the settlement was unreasonable, collusive, and made in bad faith.[340] James argued that the court was not positioned to make this determination based on the record before it and that the case should be remanded for further proceedings, but the court disagreed:

> We find the evidence on these issues was so one-sided that reasonable minds could not differ. . . . No reasonable fact-finder could reach a contrary conclusion. We conclude that the $4.15 million settlement and judgment was contrived to optimize the benefits of the settling parties, to the detriment of the holdout carriers, on damages, coverage and liability and was entered into in bad faith without any sound relationship to the realities of the situation. The claimant recovered $1 million in damages, a reasonable sum in compensation. The balance of $3.15 million is not justified by the indisputable facts.[341]

On that final note, the court affirmed summary judgment for Harleysville.

The *Imbesi* court reached the correct result. Among the indicia of bad faith and collusion the court identified, the concerted effort by the parties and the settling insurers to shift responsibility for the majority of the judgment to the non-settling insurers, Harleysville and State Farm, deserves special mention. The *Imbesi* court's dislike of this scheme is shared by other courts.[342] Consent

336. *Id.*
337. *Id.* at 757–58.
338. *Id.* at 758.
339. *Id.*
340. *Id.*
341. *Id.* at 759.
342. *See, e.g.*, Koehnen v. Herald Fire Ins. Co., 89 F.3d 525, 529–30 (8th Cir. 1996) (applying Minnesota law); Burbach v. Armstrong Rigging & Erecting, Inc., 560 N.W.2d 107, 110 (Minn. Ct. App. 1997) (finding that a *Miller-Shugart* agreement was unenforceable in this situation).

judgments are not devices for "shift[ing] the risk of coverage from one insurer to another."[343] When an insured is being defended by an insurer and thus does not require the protection of a consent judgment, a consent judgment that reflects an attempt to shift liability to another insurer that is not participating in the defense has been held to be collusive as a matter of law.[344]

D. Allocating the Burden of Proof

It is the majority rule that the insurer bears the burden of proving bad faith, fraud, or collusion.[345] This rule is logical given that such conduct generally represents an affirmative defense that an insurer must properly raise.[346] Some courts, however, require the insured to prove that a consent judgment is free of fraud or collusion either in carrying its burden of proof on reasonableness,[347] or simply in establishing that the judgment should be enforced against the insurer.[348] These approaches may seem awkward because they require the insured to prove a negative, but they are not. If the plaintiff makes a prima facie showing that a settlement or judgment is reasonable in part because it is free of fraud or collusion, the burden shifts to the insurer to establish that the settlement or judgment was, in fact, fraudulent or collusive.[349] In short, an insurer that challenges a consent judgment on bad faith, fraud, or collusion grounds must always be prepared to shoulder the burden on those defenses.

343. *Burbach*, 560 N.W.2d at 110.

344. *Koehnen*, 89 F.3d at 530.

345. *See, e.g.*, Andrew v. Century Sur. Co., 134 F. Supp. 3d 1249, 1268 (D. Nev. 2015) (predicting Nevada law); Metro. Prop. & Cas. Ins. Co. v. Westport Ins. Corp., 131 F. Supp. 3d 923, 929 (D. Neb. 2015) (applying Nebraska law); Conn. Indem. Co. v. Perrotti, 390 F. Supp. 2d 158, 170 n.4 (D. Conn. 2005) (applying Connecticut law); Nunn v. Mid-Century Ins. Co., 244 P.3d 116, 123 (Colo. 2010) (describing fraud and collusion as affirmative defenses); Carpenter v. Lovell's Lounge & Grill, LLC, 59 N.E.3d 330, 340 (Ind. Ct. App. 2016) (assigning to the insurer the burden of proving bad faith or collusion by clear and convincing evidence); Red Giant Oil Co. v. Lawlor, 528 N.W.2d 524, 535 (Iowa 1995) (referring to fraud and collusion); Ortiz v. Biscanin, 122 P.3d 365, 381–82 (Kan. Ct. App. 2004) (referring to collusion); Gulf Ins. Co. v. Noble Broad., 936 S.W.2d 810, 816 (Mo. 1997) (referring to collusion); Abbey/Land, LLC v. Glacier Constr. Partners, LLC, 433 P.3d 1230, 1242 (Mont. 2019) (referring to fraud and collusion); Wood v. Milionis Constr., Inc., 492 P.3d 813, 822 (Wash. 2021) (explaining that once the settling parties establish that the settlement undergirding the consent judgment is reasonable, the burden shifts to the insurer to prove fraud or collusion).

346. *Nunn*, 244 P.3d at 123; *Red Giant Oil Co.*, 528 N.W.2d at 535.

347. *See, e.g.*, Safeway Ins. Co. v. Guerrero, 106 P.3d 1020, 1024 (Ariz. 2005) (quoting Parking Concepts, Inc. v. Tenney, 83 P.3d 19, 22 (Ariz. 2004)).

348. *See, e.g.*, Gen Cas. Ins. Co. of Wis. v. Penn-Co Constr., Inc., No. C03-2031-MWB, 2005 WL 503927, at *49 (N.D. Iowa Mar. 2, 2005) (applying Minnesota law).

349. *See* Hamblin v. Garcia, 441 P.3d 1283, 1287–88 (Wash. Ct. App. 2019).

E. Badges of Bad Faith, Fraud, or Collusion

In evaluating consent judgments for bad faith, fraud, or collusion, courts should consider the following nonexclusive factors, some of which may overlap. The weight assigned to individual factors may vary by case, and not all factors will be relevant in all cases.

1. Whether the insured has changed her version of events or otherwise appears to have agreed to testify falsely to trigger potential coverage or to assist the plaintiff.[350]
2. Whether the insured or plaintiff misrepresented any facts to the insurer that would have been material to the insurer's duties to defend or indemnify the insured, withheld, or concealed such facts from the insurer, or otherwise misled the insurer.
3. Whether the plaintiff and the insured have stipulated to facts that were never made known to the insurer or that appear to be false or asserted principally or solely for the purpose of creating insurance coverage.
4. Whether the parties in the underlying case agreed to unreasonable damages in light of the value of the case.[351] That determination may include a comparison of awards in similar cases.[352]
5. Whether the claimed damages were legitimately negotiated in a case where their determination was not entrusted to the court.[353]
6. Whether the judgment was obtained through, or tested in, a fully adversarial trial or hearing.[354] The requirement of a fully adversarial trial or hearing applies equally to arbitration proceedings.
7. Whether the insured-defendant declined to consider or assert, agreed not to assert, or abandoned viable defenses to the plaintiff's claims.[355]

---

350. Andrew v. Century Sur. Co., 134 F. Supp. 3d 1249, 1268–69 (D. Nev. 2015).

351. Capitol Specialty Ins. Corp. v. Higgins, 953 F.3d 95, 107–08 (1st Cir. 2020); *Andrew*, 134 F. Supp. 3d at 1269; Country Mut. Ins. Co. v. Olsak, 216 N.E.3d 291, 306 (Ill. App. Ct. 2022); Abbey/Land, LLC v. Glacier Constr. Partners, LLC, 433 P.3d 1230, 1245 (Mont. 2019).

352. *Olsak*, 216 N.E.3d at 306.

353. Travelers Indem. Co. v. Att'ys' Title Ins. Fund, 194 F. Supp. 3d 1224, 1237–38 (M.D. Fla. 2016) (applying Florida law); Rogers Cartage Co. v. Travelers Indem. Co., 403 N.E.3d 504, 524 (Ill. App. Ct. 2018); *Abbey/Land*, 433 P.3d at 1245; Penn-Am. Ins. Co. v. Osborne, 797 S.E.2d 548, 556 (W. Va. 2017).

354. *See, e.g.*, Brockmann v. Bd. of Cnty. Comm'rs of Cnty. of Shawnee, 404 F. App'x 271, 281 (10th Cir. 2010) (finding collusion where parties held a sham trial); Span, Inc. v. Associated Int'l Ins. Co., 277 Cal. Rptr. 828, 840 (Ct. App. 1991) (involving an underlying bench trial that was basically a sham); *Abbey/Land*, 433 P.3d at 1245 (noting that the insured admitted the plaintiff's allegations of liability and damages and asserted no meaningful affirmative defenses).

355. *See Rogers Cartage Co.*, 403 N.E.3d at 524.

8. Whether, rather than litigating their case in court, the insured and plaintiff agreed to arbitrate their case before an arbitrator proposed or selected by plaintiff's counsel.
9. Whether the lawyer for the insured was referred or recommended by the plaintiff or plaintiff's counsel, was selected for the insured by the plaintiff or plaintiff's counsel, regularly collaborates with the plaintiff's lawyer in other cases, or was compensated by the plaintiff or plaintiff's counsel. The use of such surrogate lawyers frequently is damning evidence of bad faith, fraud, and collusion.
10. Whether the insured's defense lawyer typically maintains a plaintiffs' practice and, in particular, whether the lawyer is regularly involved in bad faith litigation against insurers.
11. Whether the plaintiff and the insured have made any agreements that imply continued litigation rather than settlement, or that are designed to affect future litigation involving the insurer.[356] For example, a nonexecution or other agreement that contemplates a less than fully adversarial hearing or trial, which requires the insured to consent to jurisdiction or venue that otherwise would not exist or be proper, or which provides that the agreement will not be offered as evidence in any future litigation strongly suggests bad faith, fraud, or collusion.[357]
12. Whether there is any relationship between the parties that suggests they did not negotiate the settlement or judgment at arm's-length.[358]
13. Whether any agreements between the insured and the plaintiff are kept secret from the insurer or a court, with such secrecy strongly evidencing bad faith, fraud, or collusion,[359] but not being required for a finding of bad faith, collusion, or fraud.
14. Whether the parties informed the insurer of relevant hearing or trial dates in the underlying case.[360]

356. *See, e.g.*, Century Indem. Co. v. Aero-Motive Co. 336 F. Supp. 2d 739, 753–54 (W.D. Mich. 2004) (finding for the insurer where the insureds had a financial incentive to aid the plaintiff's case against the insurer following a consent judgment and were willing to "change or at least shade their prior testimony" to help the plaintiff); Indep. Sch. Dist. No. 197 v. Accident & Cas. Ins. of Winterthur, 525 N.W.2d 600, 607 (Minn. Ct. App. 1995) (finding possible collusion where the corporate insured agreed to finance the plaintiffs' action against its insurers and the plaintiffs hired the insured's national coverage counsel to represent them); *Abbey/Land*, 433 P.3d at 1245 (observing that the defendant "silenced any party that attempted actually to defend it").

357. The use of "for example" to introduce this list is meant to signal that these are not the only terms that may indicate bad faith, fraud, or collusion; that is, the list is not exclusive or exhaustive. *See, e.g.*, Rezin v. McDonough, No. 22-4179, 2023 WL 4851344, at *3 (Vet. App. July 31, 2023) (explaining that the phrase "for example" signals that a following list of items is non-exhaustive).

358. *See, e.g.*, Fid. Nat'l Title Ins. Co. v. Centerpoint Mech. Lien Claims, LLC, 357 P.3d 170, 176 (Ariz. Ct. App. 2015) ("Rather than representing an arm's length settlement between lien claimants and insureds, the purported *Morris* agreement . . . was between the insureds and an entity they controlled.").

359. Penn-Am. Ins. Co. v. Osborne, 797 S.E.2d 548, 556 (W. Va. 2017).

360. Andrew v. Century Sur. Co., 134 F. Supp. 3d 1249, 1269 (D. Nev. 2015).

15. Whether any factual recitations in the judgment, assignment, or nonexecution agreement are false.[361]
16. Whether the insured has a financial interest in the outcome of any litigation against the insurer,[362] such as sharing in any judgment recovered by the plaintiff in a garnishment or bad faith action,[363] or incurring or retaining personal liability (including enhanced liability) if the plaintiff's suit against the insurer is unsuccessful or does not achieve some specified level of success.[364]
17. Whether the settlement or consent judgment is inflated to improperly benefit the plaintiff, such as where the plaintiff is related to the insured.[365]
18. Whether notice to the insurer of the lawsuit against the insured was given in such a fashion as to effectively invite the insurer to deny a defense (e.g., by withholding information from the insurer, misrepresenting facts, knowingly sending notice to the wrong address or office, or deliberately delaying notice).
19. Whether the insured and the plaintiff entered into a nonexecution agreement or consented or stipulated to a judgment before the insured sought a defense from the insurer.
20. Whether the consent judgment is being used as a mechanism to shift risk between insurers.[366]
21. Any other factors that indicate the parties' intention to prejudice the insurer or to harm its interests.[367]

---

361. *Penn-Am. Ins. Co*, 797 S.E.2d at 556.

362. *See, e.g.*, Sidman v. Travelers Cas. & Sur., 841 F.3d 1197, 1199 (11th Cir. 2016) (agreeing to cap the insured's liability at a low level if the plaintiff recovered nothing from the insurer).

363. *See, e.g.*, Cont'l Cas. Co. v. Hempel, 4 F. App'x 703, 719 (10th Cir. 2001) (holding that a consent judgment was fraudulent and collusive where the insured received a 10 percent interest in any judgment the plaintiff recovered from the insurers); Carlson v. Zellaha, 482 N.W.2d 281, 284 (Neb. 1992) (finding that a consent judgment was collusive where the insured was to receive $575 out of the first $4,000 in exchange for consent to the judgment); Pasha v. Rosemount Mem'l Park, Inc., 781 A.2d 1119, 1124 (N.J. Super. Ct. App. Div. 2001) (noting that the insured paid the plaintiff $30,000 but would receive that sum back from the plaintiffs if they succeeded in their case against the insurer).

364. *See, e.g.*, Century Indem. Co. v. Aero-Motive Co. 336 F. Supp. 2d 739, 753 (W.D. Mich. 2004) (involving the insureds' agreement to pay up to $50,000 in addition to $100,000 already paid if the plaintiff did not recover $800,000 from the insurers).

365. William T. Barker & Ronald D. Kent, New Appleman Insurance Bad Faith Litigation Second Edition § 4.04[5][a], at 4-46.4 (2010 & Supp. 2023).

366. *See, e.g.*, Koehnen v. Herald Fire Ins. Co., 89 F.3d 525, 530 (8th Cir. 1996) (explaining that when an insured is being defended by an insurer, a consent judgment that reflects an effort to shift liability to an insurer that is not participating in the defense is collusive as a matter of law); Burbach v. Armstrong Rigging & Erecting, Inc., 560 N.W.2d 107, 110 (Minn. Ct. App. 1997) (asserting that consent judgments are not devices for "shift[ing] the risk of coverage from one insurer to another"); Fireman's Fund Ins. Co. v. Imbesi, 826 A.2d 735, 750–59 (N.J. Super. Ct. App. Div. 2003) (voiding an unreasonable and collusive consent judgment that was intended in part to shift risk between insurers).

367. Rogers Cartage Co. v. Travelers Indem. Co., 403 N.E.3d 504, 524 (Ill. App. Ct. 2018).

F. The Effect of a Finding of Bad Faith, Fraud, or Collusion

A judgment obtained through bad faith, fraud, or collusion is unenforceable against the insurer.[368] Unable to recover from the insurer and with no recourse against the insured by virtue of the parties' nonexecution agreement, the plaintiff can pursue other tortfeasors. Where the nonexecution agreement includes an escape clause that allows the plaintiff to collect the judgment from the insured upon the judgment's invalidation, the plaintiff may also pursue the insured.

If the insured has damages caused by the insurer's breach of its duty to defend that are untainted by the bad faith, fraud, or collusion, such as reasonable defense costs incurred before negotiation of the offending settlement, the insured arguably should be able to recover those costs. There is, however, a strong counterargument that a finding of bad faith, collusion, or fraud should foreclose any recovery by the insured under principles of deterrence, equity, and the protection of the court system. Of course, if the insured assigned its rights to recover against its insurer to the plaintiff as part of their nonexecution agreement, even damages such as reasonable defense costs incurred before the negotiation of the agreement will be erased by a finding of bad faith, fraud, or collusion.[369]

IV. Insurers Owe No Duty to Approve or Participate in Nonexecution Agreements or Consent Judgments

Sometimes, when an insurer defends under a reservation of rights or defends a case in which excess liability is clear, but the plaintiff will not settle for the insurer's policy limits or will not release the insured in exchange for the insurer's payment of its policy limits, the plaintiff will present the insured with a nonexecution agreement leading to a substantial consent judgment. Often, the plaintiff further insists that the insurer sign the nonexecution agreement or approve the consent judgment even though the amount of the judgment

368. Sidman v. Travelers Cas. & Sur., 841 F.3d 1197, 1207 (11th Cir. 2016) (applying Florida law); Andrew v. Century Sur. Co., 134 F. Supp. 3d 1249, 1268–70 (D. Nev. 2015) (predicting Nevada law); Metro. Prop. & Cas. Ins. Co. v. Westport Ins. Corp., 131 F. Supp. 3d 923, 929 (D. Neb. 2015) (applying Nebraska law); DeSantiago v. Pargas, No. 2 CA-CV 2008-0079, 2009 WL 794929, at *3 (Ariz. Ct. App. Mar. 26, 2009); Red Giant Oil Co. v. Lawlor, 528 N.W.2d 524, 535 (Iowa 1995); Fletcher v. Anderson, 3 P.3d 558, 568 (Kan. Ct. App. 2000); Patrons Oxford Ins. Co. v. Harris, 905 A.2d 819, 829 (Me. 2006); Abbey/Land, LLC v. Glacier Constr. Partners, LLC, 433 P.3d 1230, 1246 (Mont. 2019); Rummel v. Lexington Ins. Co., 945 P.2d 970, 985 (N.M. 1997); W. Nat'l Mut. Ins. Co. v. TSP, Inc., 904 N.W.2d 52, 56 n.1 (S.D. 2017); Penn-Am. Ins. Co. v. Osborne, 797 S.E.2d 548, 553, 556–57 (W. Va. 2017).

369. Carlson v. Century Sur. Co., No. C 11-00356 SI, 2012 WL 1029662, at *11 (N.D. Cal. Mar. 26, 2012) (applying California law).

exceeds the insurer's policy limits. Moreover, the nonexecution agreements in these cases frequently include provisions that are intended to place the insurer at a disadvantage in later bad faith or coverage litigation, such as requiring the insurer to agree that in any such litigation it will not (1) dispute jurisdiction or venue; (2) use the nonexecution agreement as a defense to, or in mitigation of, any claim for damages asserted by the plaintiff or the insured; (3) attempt to introduce the nonexecution agreement into evidence or otherwise reveal it to the court or jury; (4) challenge the insured's assignment of its claims to the plaintiff; (5) argue that the amount of the consent judgment is unreasonable; or (6) contend that the nonexecution agreement or consent judgment violates public policy and is thus void or unenforceable.

Consider the scenario outlined in *Columbia Insurance Co. v. Waymer*,[370] a Fourth Circuit case that arose under South Carolina law. There, Mark Tinsley, the lawyer for the injured parties, the Reynoldses, claimed that Columbia Insurance Co. (CIC) had failed to settle his clients' claims against CIC's insured, Christopher Waymer, within its policy limits.[371] Tinsley later "offered CIC a 'final chance' to settle the case" on the following terms:

> [T]he parties would litigate the extent of the Reynoldses' injuries as well as the existence of bad faith on CIC's part. If the jury found CIC liable in bad faith, then CIC would pay whatever the jury found the Reynoldses' damages to be—without any right to appeal that verdict as excessive. If the jury found CIC had not acted in bad faith, then CIC again would owe the $1 million policy limits. Under either option, CIC would have to waive certain defenses regarding the real party in interest and the applicability of any release given by the Reynoldses.[372]

Can an insurance company be required as part of its duties to its insured to agree to a nonexecution agreement or consent judgment as outlined above or to accept the limitations on its right to vindicate its interests as proposed in *Waymer*? If the insurer declines to do either of these things, does it face bad faith liability for unreasonably failing to protect its insured against personal liability? The short and correct answer to both questions is no.[373] There are at least three good reasons for this answer.

370. 860 F. App'x 848 (4th Cir. 2021).

371. *Id.* at 851.

372. *Id.* at 852.

373. *See, e.g.*, *id.* at 854 (affirming the district court's grant of summary judgment to CIC on the related bad faith claim); Kwiatkowski v. Allstate Ins. Co., 717 F. App'x 910, 913 (11th Cir. 2017) (quoting Kropilak v. 21st Century Ins. Co., 806 F.3d 1062, 1068 (11th Cir. 2015)); *Kropilak*, 806 F.3d at 1068 (citing Berges v. Infinity Ins. Co., 896 So. 2d 665, 671 n.1 (Fla. 2004)); Dorroh v. Deerbrook Ins. Co., 223 F. Supp. 3d 1081, 1095 (E.D. Cal. 2016) (stating that the insurer's refusal to stipulate to an excess judgment was not bad faith as a matter of law), *aff'd*, 751 F. App'x 980 (9th Cir. 2018); Pasina v. Cal. Cas. Indem. Exch., No. 2:08-cv-01199-RCJ-RJJ, 2009 WL 10693522, at *7 (D. Nev. Nov. 4, 2009) (applying Nevada law); *Berges*, 896 So. 2d at 671 n.1 (rejecting such a claim as

First, as a matter of contract law, an insurer has no duty to agree to any of these terms or to take the demanded steps under standard insurance policy language.[374] An insurer cannot be liable for bad faith for failing to engage in some activity or perform some action that its policy does not require.[375]

Second, when it comes to settlement, insurers have no duty to pay more than their applicable policy limits.[376] Yet, paying more than its limits is what the sort of terms discussed here effectively require of an insurer. Any argument by a claimant that an offer to settle within policy limits coupled with a consent judgment in excess of policy limits or some other term that exposes an insurer to extracontractual liability is, in fact, an offer to settle within policy limits, is at best disingenuous.[377]

Third, an insurer's duty of good faith and fair dealing cannot be stretched to compel acceptance of the sort of terms described here because the duty of good faith and fair dealing "cannot be used to create rights and duties not otherwise provided for in the contract, change the contract, or insert new terms in the contract."[378] Furthermore, an insurer's duty of good faith and fair dealing does not oblige the insurer to "place the insured's interests above its own interests,"[379] "ignore its own interests in defense of the insured,"[380] or "actively . . . submerge its own interests."[381] In a state such as Missouri, which defines third-party bad faith as the insurer's intentional disregard of the insured's financial interests in the hope of escaping the responsibility imposed on it by its policy,[382] an insurer's refusal to accept terms that potentially expose it to extracontractual liability cannot constitute bad faith because the insurer is not intentionally disregarding the insured's financial interests in the hope of avoiding its policy obligations. Rather, the insurer is refusing to accept liability for

meritless); Allstate Ins. Co. v. Miller, 212 P.3d 318, 330–31 (Nev. 2009) (stating that the insurer "had no duty to accept a stipulated excess judgment").

374. Robert H. Jerry, II & Douglas R. Richmond, Understanding Insurance Law 742–43 (6th ed. 2018).

375. Manu v. GEICO Cas. Co., 798 S.E.2d 598, 606 (Va. 2017).

376. Am. Physicians Assur. Corp. v. Schmidt, 187 S.W.3d 313, 318 (Ky. 2006); *Miller*, 212 P.3d at 331; Am. Physicians Ins. Exch. v. Garcia, 876 S.W.2d 842, 849 (Tex. 1994); *see also* Restatement of the Law Liab. Ins. § 24 cmt. h (Am. L. Inst. 2019) (stating that the insurer's duty to make reasonable settlement decisions does not obligate it to make or accept settlement offers in excess of its policy limits).

377. *Kropilak*, 806 F.3d at 1068.

378. Jerry & Richmond, *supra* note 374, at 743; *see also* Bernacchi v. First Chi. Ins. Co., 52 F.4th 324, 330 (7th Cir. 2022) ("[T]he covenant cannot be used to 'add terms in order to reach a result more equitable to one of the parties.'" (quoting Mid-West Energy Consultants, Inc. v. Covenant Home, Inc., 815 N.E.2d 911, 916 (Ill. App. Ct. 2004))); Guldseth v. Fam. Med. Assocs. LLC, 45 F.4th 526, 537–38 (1st Cir. 2022) (stating that the covenant of good faith and fair dealing "cannot create rights and duties that are not already present in the existing contractual relationship").

379. Kim v. Allstate Ins. Co., 223 P.3d 1180, 1192 (Wash. Ct. App. 2009).

380. UMIA Ins., Inc. v. Saltz, 515 P.3d 406, 416 (Utah 2022).

381. Kosierowski v. Allstate Ins. Co., 51 F. Supp. 2d 583, 588 (E.D. Pa. 1999).

382. Scottsdale Ins. Co. v. Addison Ins. Co., 448 S.W.3d 818, 828 (Mo. 2014) (quoting Zumwalt v. Utils. Ins. Co., 228 S.W.2d 750, 756 (Mo. 1950)).

which it never bargained—it remains willing to honor the terms of its policy, as by defending the insured, indemnifying the insured up to the liability limits of its policy, or both.

In *Waymer*, the Fourth Circuit evaluated CIC's conduct in line with South Carolina's *Tyger River* doctrine,[383] which holds that "an insurance company must 'sacrifice its interests in favor of' those of the insured when a conflict of interest as to settlement arises."[384] Even under that seemingly demanding standard, however, CIC had no duty to accept a settlement offer that would channel bad faith litigation.[385] CIC's duty to sacrifice its own interests to protect Waymer under the *Tyger River* doctrine did not require CIC to subvert its interests to his, but merely distilled to the established requirement that it settle the Reynoldses' claim "if that was the reasonable thing to do."[386] But settling on Tinsley's terms was not a reasonable course of action. In fact, the terms that Tinsley proposed, which would have subjected CIC to bad faith litigation with at least one hand tied behind its back, provided CIC with an objectively reasonable basis for *refusing* the offer.[387] CIC therefore defeated Waymer's bad faith claim.[388]

Markuson v. State Farm Mutual Insurance Co.[389] is a recent case where the court rejected a bad faith claim predicated on the insurer's refusal to accept settlement offers that involved consent judgments. *Markuson* arose out of a wreck in which Benjamin Markuson's car was struck by a car driven by Eric Saterbo and owned by his father, Stephen Saterbo. Markuson was injured in the accident and sued the Saterbos. The Saterbos were insured under a State Farm policy with liability limits of $300,000. State Farm hired defense counsel

---

383. *See* Tyger River Pine Co. v. Md. Cas. Co., 170 S.E. 346, 348 (S.C. 1933) ("If, in the effort to do this, [the insurer's] own interests conflicted with those of respondent, it was bound, under its contract of indemnity, and in good faith, *to sacrifice its interests in favor of those of the respondent.*").

384. Columbia Ins. Co. v. Waymer, 860 F. App'x 848, 852 (4th Cir. 2021) (quoting Columbia Ins. Co. v. Reynolds, 438 F. Supp. 3d 614, 620 (D.S.C. 2020)).

385. *Id.*

386. *Tyger River*, 170 S.E. at 349; *see Waymer*, 860 F. App'x at 852 (quoting the district court using similar language). The Missouri Supreme Court has also described an insurer's duty of good faith and fair dealing as requiring it to sacrifice its own interests when weighing a policy limits settlement in a case of probable excess liability based on *Tyger River*. Zumwalt v. Utils. Ins. Co., 228 S.W.2d 750, 756 (Mo. 1950) (quoting *Tyger River*, 170 S.E. at 348). But this means only "that the insurer cannot elevate its own interests over the insured's; to the extent the insurer might be tempted to do so, it must 'sacrifice' its own interests so that they are back in balance with the insured's." Jerry & Richmond, *supra* note 374, at 734 n.284. Missouri caselaw after *Zumwalt* clarifies that this interpretation of the "sacrifice" requirement is correct. *See, e.g.*, Landie v. Century Indem. Co., 390 S.W.2d 558, 563 (Mo. Ct. App. 1965) ("[W]here the [insurance] company in good faith believes there is a valid defense to the claim, even though the defense proves unsuccessful and results in a judgment against the insured above the policy limits, the company is not liable, because of such honest mistake, beyond the limits of its policy.").

387. *Waymer*, 860 F. App'x at 855.

388. *Id.* (affirming summary judgment for CIC).

389. __ So. 3d __, 2023 WL 5986322 (Fla. Dist. Ct. App. Sept. 15, 2023).

for the Saterbos and authorized the lawyers to offer Markuson the policy limits to settle. Markuson declined the offer.

Instead, Markuson extended two settlement proposals to the Saterbos with similar terms. Markuson's proposals would have required State Farm to (1) pay the $300,000 policy limits to Markuson; (2) authorize the Saterbos to enter into a $1.9 million consent judgment that would not be recorded or enforced against the Saterbos; and (3) authorize the Saterbos to assign to Markuson their rights in any claims against their insurance agent.[390] In return, Markuson would release his claims against the Saterbos and file a satisfaction of the consent judgment. The proposals did not include a release of State Farm from any bad faith liability.[391] Markuson also made a third proposal in which he simply requested $1.5 million to settle.[392] State Farm rejected all three offers and Markuson's case against the Saterbos went to trial. Markuson won a verdict of just under $3.1 million.

Markuson and the Saterbos thereafter sued State Farm, among others. The Saterbos and Markuson asserted bad faith claims against State Farm based on State Farm's refusal to settle the underlying case. State Farm moved for summary judgment on these counts, asserting that it did not act in bad faith because Markuson's settlement offers included consent judgments above the policy limits and, under the Eleventh Circuit's decision in *Kropilak v. 21st Century Ins. Co.*,[393] it owed no duty to the Saterbos to enter into such consent judgments.[394] State Farm did not seek summary judgment on any bad faith claims that rested on other theories.[395]

The trial court entered partial summary judgment for State Farm. The trial court held that under *Kropilak*, State Farm had no duty to enter into a consent judgment that was in excess of the policy limits as a matter of law.[396] The trial court found that all of Markuson's settlement proposals exposed State Farm to extracontractual liability with no promise that State Farm would be released by entering into the proposed consent judgments. The trial court thus determined that State Farm did not act in bad faith when it did not agree to or negotiate with respect to any of the proposals. Markuson and the Saterbos appealed.

Just as the trial court's decision largely rested on the Eleventh Circuit's decision in *Kropilak*, so did the *Markuson* court's decision. In *Kropilak*, the

390. *Id.* at *1.
391. *Id.*
392. *Id.* n.2.
393. 806 F.3d 1062 (11th Cir. 2015).
394. *Markuson*, 2023 WL 5986322, at *1.
395. The plaintiffs also alleged that that "State Farm (1) failed to exercise good faith in the investigation, evaluation, and negotiation of [Markuson's] claim; (2) failed to handle the claim honestly and with due regard for their insured[s]; and (3) failed to communicate with and advise the insureds." *Id.*
396. *Id.* at *2.

Eleventh Circuit reviewed an order granting summary judgment in favor of the insurer on the insured's claim that it acted in bad faith.[397] Ultimately, the *Kropilak* court held that "an insurer owes no duty under Florida law to enter into a so-called *Cunningham* agreement and likewise owes no duty to its insured to enter into a consent judgment in excess of the limits of its policy."[398] In following *Kropliak*, the *Markuson* outlined the essential aspects of *Cunningham* agreements.

> The holding that "an insurer owes no duty to its insured to enter into a so-called *Cunningham* agreement" relies upon the Florida Supreme Court's holding in *Cunningham v. Standard Guaranty Insurance Co*. . . . In *Cunningham*, the parties "entered into an agreement to try the bad-faith action before trying the underlying negligence claim. The parties further stipulated that if no bad faith was found, the Cunninghams' claims would be settled for the policy limits, and [the insured] would not be exposed to an excess judgment." . . . Ordinarily, to commence a bad faith action against a liability insurer, a party must first "obtain a judgment against the insured in excess of the policy limits." . . . However, the parties' stipulation voluntarily eliminated this procedural prerequisite. Thus, "[t]he stipulation was the functional equivalent of an excess judgment."[399]

In *Markuson*, the plaintiffs' bad faith claims principally turned on State Farm's refusal to enter into a *Cunningham*-type agreement; that is, they contended that State Farm had a duty to authorize the Saterbos to consent to a judgment more than five times the policy limits (thereby expediting planned bad faith litigation) without obtaining a release of State Farm in return. But under Florida law, an insurer has no duty to enter into a *Cunningham* agreement or an equivalent agreement, such as a consent judgment, because these arrangements are the functional equivalent of an excess judgment.[400] Of course, under Florida law, as under the law of other states, an insurer's obligation to negotiate and settle claims on its insured's behalf is bounded by the insurance policy's terms; an insurer has no duty to pay a claim in excess of a policy's liability limits.[401]

The rule announced in *Kropilak* and followed in *Markuson* does not, however, eliminate other theories of bad faith alleged in the same case.[402] Thus, while the trial court correctly held that State Farm had no duty to enter into

---

397. *Id.* (citing Kropilak v. 21st Century Ins. Co., 806 F.3d 1062, 1063–64 (11th Cir. 2015)).
398. *Kropilak*, 806 F.3d at 1070.
399. *Markuson*, 2023 WL 5986322, at *2 (citations omitted).
400. *Id.* (quoting Perera v. U.S. Fid. & Guar. Co., 35 So. 3d 893, 899 (Fla. 2010)).
401. *Id.* (first citing Bethel v. Sec. Nat'l Ins. Co., 949 So. 2d 219, 222 (Fla. Dist. Ct. App. 2006); then citing Mid-Continent Cas. Co. v. Basdeo, 742 F. Supp. 2d 1293, 1336 (S.D. Fla. 2010); and then citing Fla. Stat. § 624.155(4)(a) (2023)).
402. *Id.*

a *Cunningham*-type agreement, and that State Farm's rejection of Markuson's three settlement proposals could not support bad faith liability, it erred by awarding State Farm summary judgment to the extent the plaintiffs alleged unrelated bad faith claims.[403] The *Markuson* court therefore reversed the trial court in part and remanded the case for further proceedings.

V. Conclusion

The nonexecution agreement and consent judgment process is controversial. In many respects it is justified and in other ways it is very troubling. There is merit to both sides of the debate. The many problems with the process, however, call for clear rules for enforcing consent judgments. Three of these rules are simple. First, the consent judgment must be objectively reasonable. Second, the nonexecution agreement and consent judgment must be objectively entered into in good faith and cannot be fraudulent or collusive. Third, insurers cannot be required to participate in or approve nonexecution agreements or consent judgments. Assuming courts thoughtfully apply and rigorously enforce these rules, both insureds and insurers should receive the fair treatment and protection they deserve.

403. *Id.*

Table of Cases